'The Virtuoso Tribe of Arts and Sciences'

Edited by D. G. C. Allan and John L. Abbott

The Virtuoso

STUDIES IN THE EIGHTEENTH-CENTURY

Tribe of

WORK AND MEMBERSHIP

Arts & Sciences

OF THE LONDON SOCIETY OF ARTS

THE UNIVERSITY OF GEORGIA PRESS   *Athens and London*

© 1992 by the University of Georgia Press
Athens, Georgia 30602
All rights reserved
Set in 10/13 Sabon
The paper in this book meets the guidelines for permanence
and durability of the Committee on Production Guidelines
for Book Longevity of the Council on Library Resources.

Printed in the United States of America

96   95   94   93   92   5   4   3   2   1

Library of Congress Cataloging in Publication Data
The Virtuoso tribe of arts and sciences: studies
in the eighteenth-century work and membership
of the London Society of Arts / edited by
D. G. C. Allan and John L. Abbott.
p. cm.
Includes bibliographical references and index.
ISBN 0-8203-1326-2 (alk. paper)
1. Royal Society of Arts (Great Britain)
I. Allan, D. G. C. II. Abbott, John Lawrence.
T26.G7V57 1992   062'.1—dc20

90-11318
CIP

British Library Cataloging in Publication Data available

Some time after I came to London, I met with Mr. Mayne from Scotland, who reminded me that he had got me admitted a member of the Society for the Encouragement of Arts and Sciences in the year 1760.
—*Boswell's London Journal, 1762-63*, 1 December 1762

Some Noble Patriotic Men began
To carry on a Meritorious Plan
Soon as the Public their Proceedings knew
They gain'd Esteem, and great their Number Grew.
—George Cockings, *Arts, Manufactures and Commerce:
A Poem*, 1766

It was confirmed by Sir William Scott, who mentioned that Johnson had told him, that he had several times tried to speak in the Society of Arts and Sciences, but 'had found he could not get on.' From Mr. William Gerrard Hamilton I have heard, that Johnson, . . . acknowledged that he rose in that Society to deliver a speech which he had prepared; 'but (said he,) all my flowers of oratory forsook me.'
—*Boswell's Life of Johnson*, Thursday, 18 April 1771

We are become members of the Society for the Encouragement of the Arts, and have assisted at some of their deliberations, which were conducted with equal spirit and sagacity. My uncle is extremely fond of the Institution, which will certainly be productive of great advantages to the public, if from its democratical form, it does not degenerate into cabal and corruption.
—Tobias Smollett, *Humphry Clinker*, 1771

We do not hesitate to conclude that future ages will consider the founding of this Society as one of the most remarkable epochs in the history of the Arts.
—*Encyclopedia Britannica*, 3rd ed. (1797), vol. 17

CONTENTS

viii   Contents

ILLUSTRATIONS

EDITORS' ACKNOWLEDGEMENTS

Our first thanks go to the Royal Society for the Encouragement of Arts, Manufactures and Commerce for permission to quote from their manuscripts and printed records, and to reprint the studies that have already appeared in their *Journal*. We specifically thank successive chairmen and members of the Society's Library Committee and History Study and Collections Panels, notably, Professor Philip Bagwell, Sir Brian Batsford, Sir Adam Butler, Mr. Timothy Cantell, Mr. James Harrison, and Dame Margaret Weston, and successive editors of the *RSA Journal*, Mr. John Skidmore, Mr. Ian Watt and Mrs. Sarah Curtis, for encouragement to proceed with this work. We also wish to thank Professors Richard Schwartz and John Vance for their helpful comments and suggestions. Acknowledgements to other collections used and to scholars consulted by ourselves and the other contributors are given in the notes. Institutions that have kindly permitted the reproduction of works of art as illustrations are named in the appropriate captions.

Certain of D. G. C. Allan's comments on the changes in the policies and finances of the Society in the eighteenth century are taken from his 1979 University of London Ph.D. thesis, 'The Society for the Encouragement of Arts, Manufactures and Commerce; Organisation, Membership and Objectives in the First Three Decades'.

GENERAL INTRODUCTION

The foundation and support of 'Oeconomical Societies', as of artistic and scientific academies, hospitals, universities, botanical gardens and other public, civic and royal amenities, were features of the international culture of the Enlightenment. At Philadelphia and at St. Petersburg, in German princely states and in the free city of Hamburg, in Dutch and Swiss towns, and in French and even Spanish provinces, organisations were set up to stimulate industry and agriculture by means of monetary grants, honorific awards and the diffusion of knowledge.[1] Though Italy and France could claim the lead in scientific and artistic foundations, it was to the British Isles, first to Dublin and after 1754 to London, that nations looked for models of these new institutions. 'The Society for the Encouragement of Arts, Manufactures and Commerce, instituted in London. Anno MDCCLIV',[2] was admired in the eighteenth century by British and foreign observers, who were struck by the coincidence of its existence and the growth in wealth and power of the nation that had fostered it.[3]

The increase in membership during the Society's first decade impressed both contemporaries and subsequent historians. At the beginning of 1755 there were seventeen subscribing members, and by 1764 there were over two thousand. In 1758 James Theobald began for the Antiquarian Society a chronological register 'of the present age' which had as its opening contribution 'An Account of the Rise and Progress of the Society of London for the encouragement of Arts, Manufactures and Commerce'.[4] In the same year Tobias Smollett published his often-quoted eulogy of the Society in his *History of England*, concluding with the extravagant claim: 'In a word, the society is so numerous, the contributions so considerable, the plan so judiciously laid, and executed with such discretion and spirit, as to promise much more effectual and extensive advantage to the public than ever accrued from all the boasted academies of Christendom'.[5]

Theobald's narrative was expanded and published in 1763 by Thomas

Mortimer, who alleged that the Society was equal to any in Europe 'both with respect to the utility of its designs and the numbers of its members'. Mortimer concluded with the statement 'that this respectable body at present consists of between two and three thousand members'.[6]

The consistently increasing scope of the Society's premiums followed naturally from its expanding membership and financial resources. The first premiums list (1754) offered four awards, the second (1755) twelve, the third (1756) twenty-two and the fourth (1757) sixty-three. In 1758 more than one hundred awards were offered, and the lists were expanded each year throughout the decade, with a spectacular increase in 1762. In the first four years the premiums were listed more or less in the order in which they had occurred to the Society. In 1754 the offer of a premium for the discovery of cobalt deposits came first, followed by the premium offers for madder cultivation and drawings by boys and girls. In 1755 the offers for madder came first, followed by cobalt, drawings, buff leather, tinning, and American silk cultivation. The same order was maintained in 1756, except that offers for paper-making, saltpetre, carpet manufacture, crucibles, and dyeing came between drawings and American silk and replaced buff leather and tinning. In 1757 the premiums offered were given numbers: 1 to 4 were concerned with saltpetre, 5 to 7 with American silk, 8 to 16 with drawings, 17 with cobalt, 18 with borax, 20 with verdigris, 21 with bismuth, 23 with varnish, 24 to 26 with sculpture, 27 to 28 with carpets, 29 to 30 with dyeing, 31 with paper-making, 32 to 40 with planting oaks and elms, 41 to 48 with madder, 49 to 50 with soils and manures, 51 to 52 with crop pests and sheep disease, 53 with sweetening oil, 54 with improving grain colours, 55 to 57 with colonial produce, 59 to 61 with planting firs, 62 with preserving the hulls of ships, and 63 to 65 with planting pines. Finally in 1758 the practice was begun of dividing up the lists into broad subject classifications, which expressed the Society's basic concerns with agriculture, arts, chemistry, colonies, manufactures and mechanics.

The first decade of the Society's history was one of self-congratulation and success. Its progress echoed the mood of the nation, triumphant at current victories in the Seven Years' War and imbued with a view of history which saw the latter part of the reign of George II and the beginnings of the reign of George III as the glorious culmination of centuries of struggle, economic no less than military, against foreign despotism and false religion. That abuses abounded in the nation was readily admitted, but Englishmen could, it was felt, be praised for their generous response to the many public-spirited schemes to reform them. Such a scheme was the Society of Arts, which, as Charles Powell told Shipley in 1754, was 'a Design' which 'no truly benevolent or public spirited Briton can hesitate' to support. 'It will', he continued, 'not only unite in one common Bond all real Patriots, or as I should then call them the Patrons of the Nation, but will in time, I hope utterly extirpate all Party distinctions, the Bar of Society and Civil Government'.[7]

The second decade began with the Society's membership, revenue and premium expenditure at a high level, and with optimistic plans being made for a building costing 'ten to twelve thousands pounds'.[8] Within a year the Society's income and the financial value of its awards began to fall, and although its capital assets were carefully husbanded and it received certain donations and legacies, the remainder of the decade was characterized by a steady erosion of its financial resources. In this way the Society reflected the condition of the country as a whole, which suffered from an economic depression during these years. It also echoed the bitter party strife at Westminster, which prevailed until Lord North came to power in 1770.

In 1771 Dossie held up the example of the Society's President, Lord Romney, whose devotion to the public welfare stood out 'at a period when the dissipation of pleasures, and amusements or the sole engagements of self interest, ambition or party spirit, have taken the place of nearly all regard for more solid, liberal or generous concerns'.[9] The Duke of Northumberland was another peer who, unlike the Marquess of Rockingham, was prepared to mix with 'the virtuoso tribe of Arts and Sciences'.[10] The Duke's presence with Lord Romney at the foundation-laying ceremony at the Adelphi in 1772 must have been considered a social triumph by other members.[11] The House itself, which was completed in 1774, may be regarded as another symbol of the continued self-confidence of the institution.

During the Society's second decade, Arthur Young and other agriculturalists called constantly for the publication of the Society's transactions.[12] They recognized the value of the transactions to the farmer, for the Society devoted much thought and energy to experiments with ploughs, seed drills and new grass and root crops during these years. The whole range of the Society's work was in fact brought before the public, in the first two volumes of Robert Dossie's *Memoirs of Agriculture and Other Oeconomical Arts* (1768, 1771), and in William Bailey's *The Advancement of Arts, Manufactures and Commerce* (1771). Both books were circulated abroad, and the Society maintained its overseas reputation during the decade, as the recruitment of numerous distinguished European corresponding members demonstrates.

The Society's third decade was marked by two attempts to solve the

double problem of falling membership and falling income. The first took
place in 1778 and proved unsuccessful. The second began in 1782 and was
coincidental with, if not the cause of, a solution. Thus for the greater part
of the decade we can, with the gift of hindsight, see that the future of
the institution was in jeopardy. Yet not until 1783 was the possibility of
making the Society dependent on a royal or parliamentary grant given
serious consideration, or Arthur Young's long wished-for annual publication commenced. Before that the members and officers had carried on
their affairs without any awareness of the need for a radical change. A
sense of past achievement, carefully chronicled in the 1778 *Register of Premiums and Bounties*, fostered this optimistic view. The *Register* tabulated
a grand total of £23,551 18s. 2d. in money and £2,461 6s. 0d. in medals and
other emblems of honour distributed since 1754 and also alleged that the
Society's rewards were not 'in any degree equal to the national advantages
obtained by them'.[13] Young shared this belief. 'It is probable', he wrote in
1783, 'that the kingdom has benefitted a thousand pounds for every guinea
these men have expended'. Yet as he pointed out in the same passage, the
Society 'was not very fashionable. People of no account in life have been
its active supporters', whereas 'the men of great property . . . have been
more inclined to give them their ridicule than assistance'.[14]

For although the Presidency of the Society continued to include such
great noblemen as the Duke of Northumberland and had added to its
numbers in 1782 General Eliott, the national hero, it certainly included
as two of its most active members the veteran Edward Hooper, a mild-
mannered Commissioner of the Customs, and Joshua Steele, writer on
speech melody and plantation-owner, both of whom knew great men but
can hardly be considered great themselves. The new Committee Chairmen
were mostly minor figures, and those who possessed reputations, such as
Joseph Hodskinson, the engineer and land surveyor, and Valentine Green,
the mezzotint engraver, were most certainly not men of 'great property'.
Committed to a belief in the worthwhile nature of their great voluntary
endeavour, most of these men seemed to have been taken by surprise when
they found that their enthusiasm was unshared by the nation at large. Ab-
sorbed in technical questions regarding the merits of particular awards or
the niceties of debate at the Society's meetings, the active members did not
contemplate a radical change until the size of the Society's membership
had shrunk to much less than that of the supposedly more exclusive Royal
and Antiquarian societies.[15]

One reason for this attitude may have been that once a person was
committed to the operation of the Society's 'Plan', its wide-ranging and

nonspecialized activities seemed to be connected naturally one with the other, whereas to the public at large its exact terms of reference must have been far from clear. For though much time was spent on agricultural matters, the other divisions of the Society's enormously wide field of interest were not neglected. The promotion of the resources of the North American colonies was brought to an end by the military conflict and subsequent loss of political control in the area; that revolution must have done much to disillusion those who in the 1760s had seen the Society as a great transatlantic institution. By 1783, however, attention had turned to the economic products of the residual empire, and the objects of the Society of Arts became well known in the West Indies. Chemical, mechanical and manufacturing topics continued to invite attention, as did the fine arts, or, as they were then called, 'polite arts'.

Indeed it was in the latter sphere that the Society gained the greatest prestige as the patron of James Barry's widely acclaimed portrayal of 'The Progress of Human Knowledge and Culture', which was exhibited to the public for the first time in 1783. From that year onwards visitors to the Great Room, or purchasers of Barry's descriptive *Account* or his various sets of engravings of the pictures, could see the Society's 'Patriotic and truely noble purposes' expressed in iconographical terms. They could also read each year the volumes of the *Transactions*, which clearly set out the current policies and work of the Society. Coincidental with the conclusion of peace with France, America and Spain and the renewed national optimism which that engendered, these two events marked the year 1783 as a turning point in the history of the Society of Arts. It would soon enter the nineteenth century, as today it approaches the twenty-first, conscious then as now of its place in British history. Indeed, accurately assessing the Society's place in history, a pursuit that the present volume of essays means to join, has itself a long history worth a brief review.

While the eighteenth-century membership celebrated the Society's accomplishments, early and mid-nineteenth-century writers doubted the value of its influence on the economic development of the country.[16] The institution flourished in changing forms, in the years after 1851, and inevitably its domestic chroniclers gave the most favourable interpretations to its eighteenth-century exertions. The first attempt at a documentary history of the Society of Arts was published by Samuel Taylor Davenport, the Society's financial officer, in 1868. It illustrated, said an admirer, 'the magnitude of the influence which, during the preceding century, the Society had exercised upon the arts and manufactures of the country'.[17] Davenport died in 1876, and in the same year Henry Benjamin Wheatley joined the

staff of the Society. Wheatley was a considerable scholar, and his edition of
Pepys's diary was for many years the most useful one available. He was able
to assess the general significance of the Society's history in a manner that
could not have been expected from Davenport. He had a wide knowledge
of seventeenth-century English history, which he derived partly from his
experience as Clerk to the Royal Society. Unfortunately he never published
a book on the Society of Arts, but he did write a series of articles in the
journal *Engineering* in 1891, which would be quoted on many occasions by
historians of the Society in the next century.[18] Wheatley also contributed
several unsigned articles to the Society's *Journal* and compiled a book of
manuscript notes that provided the foundation of the first official history
of the Society, written by his senior colleague Sir Henry Trueman Wood,
which was published under the title *History of the Royal Society of Arts*
in 1913.

Trueman Wood's book is well written and carefully related to the historical knowledge available at the time. It was not, however, reviewed in
any of the important historical journals. Although English historians were
at this period following the German path of intense and detailed scholar-
ship, the work of an eighteenth-century society for the encouragement of
arts, manufactures and commerce did not fall easily into any of the special-
isms that were then being developed. It was not, of course, part of political,
legal or ecclesiastical history. Art history was not then practised as an academic discipline, and those who wrote it naturally concentrated on the
more obvious landmark of the foundation of the Royal Academy of Arts
in 1768. The early economic historians could not have fitted the Society of
Arts into their pattern of feudalism, followed by mercantilism, followed
by laissez-faire. The addition of the prefix *Royal* to the Society of Arts'
name in 1908 meant that Trueman Wood, whose history closed with the
year 1880, was writing under a misleading title. The uninitiated had frequently confused the Society with its scientific senior; now the assumption
that Charles II's Royal Society was the same as that in the Adelphi became
more likely.

In 1951 a scholar cited Trueman Wood's book as his authority for the
history of both the Royal Society and the Royal Society of Arts.[19] In the
three chronologically relevant volumes of the Oxford history of England,
the Society was mentioned in *The Whig Supremacy* as significant in art
history, in *The Reign of George III* as evidence of economic growth, and
in the *Age of Reform, 1815-70* as important in the development of English
education. In the standard bibliography of English history for the eighteenth century, it appeared in connection with afforestation.[20] All were

permissible interpretations of the Society's work but bewildered the students who wished to understand its total scope. They were not assisted by indexes, which sometimes used the modern title 'The Royal Society of Arts' (1908) and sometimes the contemporary one, 'The Society for the encouragement of Arts, Manufactures and Commerce'. Not that contemporaries were consistent; 'The Premium Society' and 'The Society of Arts and Sciences' or the S.P.A.C. were frequent variations of our Society's name in the eighteenth century. Today the abbreviated form RSA is generally employed.[21]

Although a contributor to the *Economic History Review* in 1955 stated that the significance of the foundation of the Society was a 'commonplace in textbooks in economic history', few actually said what the Society did.[22] T. S. Ashton pointed out that the Society's awards were 'small bait' compared with the profits received from private enterprise but said nothing of the Society's work in agriculture or industrial chemistry.[23] W. Bowden's *Industrial Society in England towards the End of the Eighteenth Century* gave a fuller account of the Society's work based on contemporary printed sources.[24] Somewhat later N. J. Smelser endeavoured to fit the Society into his application of theory to social change in the industrial revolution, dismissing 'many of the criticisms of the Society's effectiveness, as well as the belligerent assertions of its practical value'.[25] He saw the Society as an agency for the preliminary stage of structural change, offering general encouragement for general ideas. Although Dr. Smelser's book was published in 1959, it contains no reference to D. Hudson and K. W. Luckhurst's bicentenary history, *The Royal Society of Arts, 1754-1954*, or of K. W. Luckhurst's 1957 Ph.D. thesis, 'Some Aspects of the History of the Society of Arts, London, 1754-1952', which provided references to contemporary manuscript sources. In his thesis Luckhurst described in some detail what he called the 'practical aspects' of the Society's work, extending and modifying the chapters from his and Hudson's book entitled 'Pioneering in Agriculture', 'The Production of Timber and Other Raw Materials', 'The Society and the Industrial Revolution', 'The Textile and Allied Industries' and 'The Encouragement of Commerce'.[26] Yet specialist writers soon began to question some of Luckhurst's assumptions and place others in a more general perspective. D. C. Coleman, writing in 1959, concluded that the Society's premiums had 'very little' effect on the development of the English paper industry.[27] In the same year R. E. Schofield pointed out the very close relationship between the Society of Arts and the Lunar Society of Birmingham and asserted that although 'the importance of the Society's immediate efforts at improving manufactures is hard to determine, the indirect influence of its inspiration was enormous'.[28] Since then, scholars have opened up many rich seams of the Society's early history.

The essays reprinted in this book, with one exception, first appeared in the *Journal of the Royal Society for the Encouragement of Arts, Manufactures and Commerce*. They shed new light on the Society's eighteenth-century origins and contributions during that century to Britain and the world. They illustrate four principal features of the Society during its founding century: 'Notable Members' describes the remarkable personnel the Society drew on in its formative years; 'Useful Arts Promoted' shows the way the Society helped define eighteenth-century cosmopolitanism, equally at home in pragmatic and aesthetic terrains; 'Overseas Interests' illuminates the Society's intersection with North America, both in peace and war, as well as with European nations; and 'Domestic Matters' depicts the institutional settlements that enabled the eighteenth-century Society to persist into the nineteenth century and beyond. These essays are the products of British, American and European scholars, all of whom had access to the archives of the RSA, a unique collection that sheds light on a range of eighteenth-century concerns. As a consequence, chosen texts, while engaging in the speculation that enlivens historical discourse, are consistently rooted in archival evidence. Taken in combination with the sectional commentaries as well as other supporting matter, these essays will, it is hoped, inform readers about a society characterized by the Marquess of Rockingham[29] as that 'Virtuoso Tribe of Arts and Sciences' which did so much to guide creativity in Georgian times.

CHRONOLOGY

HISTORY OF THE SOCIETY

1753
William Shipley publishes his *Proposals*.

1754
First meeting of the Society held at Rawthmell's
Coffee House, Covent Garden; Lords Folkestone
and Romney, Dr. Hales, Henry Baker, Nicholas
Crisp, Shipley and five others present. Premiums
offered for the discovery of cobalt, for the
cultivation of madder and for drawings by boys
and girls.

1755
Constitution, or 'Plan', drawn up by Baker.
Officers elected for the first time; Viscount
Folkestone elected President. First premiums
awarded.

1756
Thomas Hollis, Benjamin Franklin and Samuel
Johnson elected members.

1756
Outbreak of Seven
Years' War.

1757
Robert Dodsley appointed Printer and Stationer
to the Society.

1758
First medals awarded. Society's premiums
divided into classes: Agriculture, Chemistry,
Colonies and Trade, Manufactures, Mechanics,
and Polite Arts. Patents for invention declared
'contrary to the institution of the Society'.

HISTORY OF THE SOCIETY

GENERAL EVENTS

1759
Society moves into premises designed for it by
William Chambers in Denmark Court (Strand).
The Repository for the display of machines and
models of machines opened. Premiums offered
for engraved gems, wood engraving and surveys
of counties.

1760
First exhibition of the works of living artists.

1760
Accession of George III.

1761
Lord Romney elected President. A scheme to
improve the London fish supply undertaken.

1762
Caleb Whitefoord and Francesco Algarotti
elected members.

1763
Award made to Charles Carter for his work on
behalf of the Society in Virginia.

1763
Peace of Paris.

1764
Hargreaves's spinning
jenny invented.

1765
Peak expenditure on premiums reached.

1768
Royal Academy
founded.

1769
Arthur Young elected a member.

1769
Arkwright's spinning
machine patented.
Wedgwood established
at Etruria.

1770
Samuel More elected Secretary.

1771
Thomas Bentley elected a member.

1772
Award to Abraham Staghold for his gun harpoon.
Valentine Green elected a member.

1774
The Society moves to the Adelphi. Andrei
Samborskii elected a member.

HISTORY OF THE SOCIETY

1775
Adam Smith elected a member.

1776
Samuel More inspects Watt's steam engine.

1777
James Barry begins his paintings for the
Great Room.

1778
Register of Premiums published.

1782
Richard Arkwright and Jedediah Strutt elected
members.

1783
First volume of the *Transactions of the Society of
Arts* published.

1785
Caleb Whitefoord elected Chairman of the Committee of Polite Arts and attempts to obtain the services of the Prince of Wales as Patron of the Society.

1787
Establishment of annual ceremony for
presentation of awards.

1789
Duke of Cumberland elected a member.
Addresses of congratulation to the King and
Queen upon the King's recovery.

1791
William Pitt elected a member.

1793
Gold medal awarded to William Bligh for
transporting the breadfruit tree.

1794
Duke of Norfolk elected President.

GENERAL EVENTS

1775
Outbreak of American
Revolution.

1776
Watt's steam engine in
use. *Wealth of Nations*
published.

1778
War with France.

1783
Peace of Versailles.

1787
Cartwright's power
loom used in factories.

1788
George III's first attack
of madness.

1789
Outbreak of French
Revolution.

1793
Board of Agriculture
founded. French Revolu-
tionary War begins.

HISTORY OF THE SOCIETY	GENERAL EVENTS
1796 Premiums offered for a mechanical method of cleaning chimneys.	
	1798 Nelson's victory at the Nile.
1799 Death of Samuel More.	*1799* Royal Institution founded.

'The Virtuoso Tribe of Arts and Sciences'

Part 1

NOTABLE MEMBERS

The Royal Society for the Encouragement of Arts, Manufacturers and Commerce (the RSA), now approaching the two hundred fiftieth anniversary of its foundation with a worldwide membership of fifteen thousand fellows, enjoys a rich history, one best defined by reviewing the activities of those who endowed it through formal membership or through less formal association. Sir Ambrose Fleming and Guglielmo Marconi presented papers at the Society on developments in radio and telegraphy in 1919 and 1924; in 1944 Sir Howard Florey delivered the Peter LeNeve Foster Lecture on the discovery and use of penicillin with Sir Alexander Fleming in the chair. The Society's nineteenth-century membership included such figures as Charles Dickens and Karl Marx, not to mention those who helped link the institution with one of the century's greatest public schemes—the Great Exhibition of 1851. No understanding of the Society's history is complete, however, without an examination of its eighteenth-century membership, of those who served as its founding fathers and set it on a course that remains in force today.

The small assemblage of "Noblemen, Clergy, Gentlemen, & Merchants" who met at Rawthmell's Coffee House, Henrietta Street, on 22 March 1754, hardly anticipated they were establishing an institution that would continue to serve a nation and the world to the end of the twentieth century and beyond. The vigorous and eclectic membership they soon attracted to the Society's ranks augured well, however, for its future. Early members included distinguished noblemen, among them John, 4th Earl of Sandwich; Antony, 4th Earl of Shaftesbury; Philip, 4th Earl of Chesterfield; and George, 1st Baron Anson. Others included Ralph Allen, improver of the Post Office and friend of Pope and Fielding; Sir Joseph Banks, explorer and scientist; Thomas Chippendale, furniture-maker; Robert and James Dodsley, booksellers; Robert Dossie, agriculturalist; Sir John Fielding, magistrate; Benjamin Franklin, statesman and inventor; Thomas Grignion, clockmaker; Stephen Hales, physiologist, botanist, and inventor. The list could go on; any selection omits significant names. Those interested in the arts included Charles Burney, musicologist; David Garrick, actor; Oliver

Goldsmith and Laurence Sterne, authors; and William Hogarth, artist and engraver.

While no single member can claim to embody the spirit of the early Society, the intersection of Samuel Johnson with the young institution seems appropriate and possibly inevitable. Arguably, in no figure so much as in Johnson does one see a literary canon whose diversity matched the varied interests of a Society dedicated not simply to artistic concerns but to practical ones as well. Curiously, while Johnson's membership was known to Boswell and others, it was never systematically explored until the publication of John L. Abbott's essay 'Dr. Johnson and the Society' (chapter 1). In this, Abbott examines the contributions of one of the Society's most notable members, which were considerably more extensive than previously thought. These contributions have the added value of clarifying what Johnson's best biographer has termed his 'obscure middle years'. In chapter 2, D. G. C. Allan and John L. Abbott further illuminate Johnson's relationship with the Society, this time with reference to another important member, Jonas Hanway, and a general Society effort to deal with the intractable problem of prostitution. In this episode, one sees a paradigm of the Society in action—strong personalities in democratic committee structures looking for pragmatic solutions to a pressing social issue.

Other members of the early Society deserve assessment, and some, William Shipley and Stephen Hales among them, have received monographic treatment. In chapter 3, John L. Abbott argues that Thomas Hollis clearly qualifies as one of the Society's notable members. Although the 'strenuous Whig' was accused in his day of atheism, republicanism, and igniting the American Revolution, Hollis can best be seen as one of the steadiest contributors to the Society's welfare in its early years. To follow Hollis is to see the Society itself in action; both were engaged in the seemingly trivial world of minor technology (a search for a better rattrap), as well as in the solidly pragmatic (a search for a better way to extinguish fires) and the essentially artistic (Hollis and the Society encouraged the work of artists, including the young Mary Moser as well as Joseph Nollekens, who later achieved fame as a sculptor).

In J. V. G. Mallet's portrait of Nicholas Crisp (chapter 4), we move from the ranks of the truly great in Johnson and the clearly significant in Hollis to a figure as much defined by his times as he can be said to have altered the landscape for future generations. In Crisp's wide range of interests, including jewellery, porcelain-making, chemistry, dye-making, and technological processes in general, we find one of the best personal manifestations of the Society's wider concerns. Crisp's life suggests, too, that both personal and institutional quests often ended in frustration and failure. Josiah Wedgwood remained 'haunted' by Crisp's sad example, one that shows that the Society's early years were not always characterized by success and stability.

There was always cause for optimism, however, in a Society that subscribed no less than the larger age to the possibility of progress, of perfecting life on earth through the exercise of reason. In much the same milieu in which Crisp suffered disappointment, Caleb Whitefoord, as D. G. C. Allan reveals in chapter 5, seemed blessed at every turn, hardly more so than in his network of associations and friendships that endowed him and the Society he obviously cherished. With this support Whitefoord helped shape one of the Society's principal missions through his chairmanship of the Committee of Polite Arts. Through Whitefoord's good offices a Society properly concerned with developing worlds of commerce and technology never lost sight of important aesthetic goals. The Society observed at first hand what the *European Magazine* said of Whitefoord at his death—that he was one of the '*necessary* links of the great chain that binds Society together'. The eighteenth-century membership collectively and the notable members individually surveyed in this section helped forge the links that bound the young Society of Arts together; they form the initial part of the ligature that joins the Society's present with its past.

1

DR. JOHNSON AND THE SOCIETY

John L. Abbott

H. B. Wheatley in his essay 'The Society of Arts' writes: 'As the condition of England in the middle of the seventeenth century brought about the foundation of the Royal Society and the popular and widely-spread interest in the investigation of science, so the condition of the country in the middle of the eighteenth century brought about the formation of the Society of Arts for the encouragement of the applications of science for the general good. As Dryden, Waller, Evelyn, and the literary coterie of the Restoration period largely supported the Royal Society, so the circle that surrounded Dr. Johnson took a lively interest in the success of the Society of Arts.'[1]

The Johnson Circle was well represented at the Society, and an examination of the Society's records testifies to the participation of such figures as David Garrick, Oliver Goldsmith, Sir Joshua Reynolds, Topham Beauclerk, Henry Thrale, the brewer of Southwark, as well as those of the Age of Johnson, though certainly not of the Circle, like John Wilkes. Various writers have commented, though briefly, about Johnson's connections with the Society. The anonymous author of 'Dr. Johnson and His Friends at the Society of Arts' (undoubtedly H. B. Wheatley) records in some detail Johnson's participation in Society affairs and more fully the activities of Johnson's friends, particularly those literary personages who seemed to be no less enthusiastic in their support of the Society than their more me-

Originally appeared in *Jrl. RSA*, 115 (Apr.-May, 1967), 395-400, 486-91.

Dr. Johnson in his later years; from a portrait by James Barry, undated. Courtesy of the Trustees of the National Portrait Gallery.

chanically inclined colleagues.[2] Sir Henry Trueman Wood in *History of the Royal Society of Arts* notes Johnson's membership of the Society and states: 'He took a great deal of interest in the Society, attended its meetings, and took part in its deliberations, though by his own account he was no orator.'[3] Hudson and Luckhurst in their study, *The Royal Society of Arts, 1754-1954*, refer frequently to Johnson and comment: 'The Society naturally treasures its association with the great man of the age, whose neat "Sam: Johnson" stands in the signature-book beside the promise to pay £2 2s. a year.'[4]

Not surprisingly there are a number of references in *Boswell's Life of Johnson* to Johnson's participation in the Society. Boswell writes, for instance, that Sir William Scott mentioned that Johnson told him that several times he had attempted to speak in the Society of Arts and Sciences but 'had found he could not get on'.[5] 'From Mr. William Gerrard Hamilton', Boswell records, 'I have heard, that Johnson, when observing to him that it was prudent for a man who had not been accustomed to speak in publick, to begin his speech in as simple a manner as possible, acknowledged that he rose in that society to deliver a speech which he had prepared: "but (said he), all my flowers of oratory forsook me".'[6] Dr. Andrew Kippis in his article on John Gilbert Cooper in the *Biographia Britannica*, however, gives another, more triumphant, view of Johnson's oratorical abilities before the Society. He writes that the Great Room of the Society 'was for several years the place where many persons chose to try, or to display, their oratorical abilities. Dr. Goldsmith, I remember, made an attempt at a speech, but was obliged to sit down in confusion. I once heard Dr. Johnson speak there, upon a subject relative to mechanics, with a propriety, perspicuity, and energy which excited general admiration.'[7]

Dr. Johnson's signature in the Society's signature book joins those of such illustrious figures of the period as Thomas Chippendale, Samuel Richardson, Edward Gibbon and William Hogarth. The Society's Manuscript Subscription Book reveals that Samuel Johnson, A.M., of Temple Lane was proposed for membership by Mr. Stuart and elected on 1st December 1756, his annual dues being £2 2s.[8] Johnson's dues payments ran from 3rd March 1757 to 3rd March 1763, but after making payments on 3rd March 1757 and 30th November 1758 he failed to render again until his double payment on 25th March 1760. Why he fell into arrears is not clear, but the reason given for his double payment is that he wished to cast his vote for Robert Dossie, who was proposed for membership in the Society by Edward Nourse and elected on 2nd April 1760.[9] Johnson may well have been at the Society on that date to cast his vote, though he might also have done it by proxy. Dossie served on a number of Society committees, showed a great interest in various Society schemes, and introduced seven new members before the year was out.[10] Johnson's admiration for Dossie is evident not only from his haste to pay up his dues in order to be able to cast his vote for him but from Boswell's testimony: 'Johnson', he writes, 'was well acquainted with Mr. Dossie, author of a treatise on Agriculture,[11] and said of him, "Sir, of the objects which the Society of Arts have chiefly in view, the chymical effects of bodies operating upon other bodies, he knows more than almost any man".'[12]

There is in the *Life* another example of Johnson's interest in a candidate for membership of the Society, this time concerning a person who was less successful in gaining Johnson's support than Dossie had been. Boswell comments: 'On this occasion he mentioned a circumstance, as characteristick of the Scotch. "One of that nation, (said he,) who had been a candidate, against whom I voted, came up to me with a civil salutation. Now, Sir, this is their way. An Englishman would have stomached it, and been sulky, and never have taken further notice of you; but a Scotchman, Sir, though you vote nineteen times against him, will accost you with equal complaisance after each time, and the twentieth time, Sir, he will get your vote."'[13]

Boswell also mentions briefly Dr. Johnson's relationship with another prominent member of the Society, Thomas Hollis, whose name permeates Society records during the years of Johnson's membership. Johnson and Hollis served on Society committees together and must have met from time to time at the Society. It would be difficult to find a member who served the Society with more loyalty and vigour than Hollis, though the comments on him in the *Life* are none too laudatory. Boswell writes, for instance: 'One of the company mentioned Mr. Thomas Hollis, the strenuous Whig, who used to send over Europe presents of democratical books, with their boards stamped with daggers and caps of liberty. Mrs. Carter said, "He was a bad man. He used to talk uncharitably." JOHNSON: "Poh! poh! Madam; who is the worse for being talked of uncharitably? Besides, he was a dull poor creature as ever lived, and I believe he would not have done harm to a man whom he knew to be of very opposite principles to his own." ' [14]

Hollis was aware of Johnson's literary abilities and approached him with writing assignments on several occasions: 'I remember once at the Society of Arts, when an advertisement was to be drawn up,' Johnson continues his commentary on Hollis, 'he pointed me out as the man who could do it best. This, you will observe, was kindness to me. I however slipt away, and escaped it.' [15] If Johnson managed to slip away from Hollis this time, however, he did accede to another Hollis request—that he compose an introduction to the *Proceedings of the Committee Appointed to Manage the Contributions . . . for Cloathing French Prisoners of War.* [16]

Dr. Johnson's connection with a major undertaking in 1760, the artists' exhibition, which was given the Society's support and held on their premises, has been noted briefly by Hudson and Luckhurst, who write: 'With the help of Dr. Johnson, the artists composed a letter to the Society, which, with a short memorandum of their proposals, was dispatched on February 26, 1760.' [17] Johnson also wrote the preface for the artists' catalogue for the 1762 exhibition in Spring Gardens, a piece which exhibits characteristic Johnsonian vigour and felicity of expression. [18]

Various writers, then, have noted Johnson's connections with the Society of Arts, and when taken together their comments give some idea of his participation in the Society during the years he held membership. A more tangible record exists, though, which reveals more fully the scope of Johnson's Society activities. The archives, specifically the Minutes of the Society, the Minutes of Committees, and a single volume of Miscellaneous Committee Minutes 1760-78, contain a number of references to Johnson. Such information, largely unknown to Johnsonians, is of considerable value in that it sheds at least some light upon Johnson's 'obscure middle years'—that time of his life about which so little is known.[19] Boswell was apparently unaware of the extent of Johnson's connection with the Society as described in its records, though he himself was proposed for membership by Mr. Main and elected on 30th April 1759. His own connection with the Society, or rather lack of it, is not without interest.

In the *London Journal* for 1st December 1762 Boswell writes that Mr. Mayne ('Main' in Society records), who proposed him for Society membership, reminded him that he was now three years in arrears in his dues and that full payment would be needed for his reinstatement. Attempting to live in London on £200 a year at this time, Boswell viewed the prospect of paying up with no small sense of alarm. Rather triumphantly, though, he devised a scheme to extricate himself from this impending financial disaster and records it with some relish in his journal. He writes: 'I went and called on Mr. Box, the collector (admirably named); found him a very civil man; told him that I had been in Scotland almost ever since my admission to the Society, and that I was now uncertain how long I might stay in London. If therefore it was possible to have my name struck off the list so that I should never be considered as having been a member, and might afterwards when sure of settling in London be admitted a member of that elegant, useful, and noble Society, it would make me very happy. I treated him with so much complaisance and put the argument so home to him that he agreed to my proposal; and I left him with a cheerful heart at the thoughts of having six guineas to spend which I had given up for lost.'[20] Boswell never did pay any dues to the Society, but it is interesting to speculate that had circumstances been somewhat different the meeting of Boswell and Johnson might well have taken place on the Society's premises.

The Minutes of the Society confirm the Manuscript Subscription records—that Johnson was proposed by Mr. Stuart and elected on 1st December 1756.[21] They reveal in addition, however, the fact that he was proposed at a meeting held on 24th November 1756 and that his address at the time was Gough Square, Fleet Street, and not Temple Lane, as the Manuscript Subscription Book states. A 'Mr. Johnson' who attended a general meeting of the Society held at the Strand on 2nd March 1757 was undoubtedly Samuel, as he was the only Johnson to be a member at the time.[22] On 1st February 1758 a 'Mr. Johnson' proposed Dr. James Grainger, of Bond's Court, Walbrook, for membership.[23] Again, the reference is undoubtedly to Samuel, for the reason just given. Dr. Grainger receives frequent mention in the *Life*, of course, but never in this particular context.

On 17th May 1758 the Society in a general meeting discussed various

plans for establishing a charity house for the reception of repenting prostitutes. Plans submitted were signed with such mottoes as, 'There is more
Joy in Heaven over one Sinner that repenteth than over Ninety and nine
just Persons that need no Repentance', 'No complaining—no begging in
the Streets' and 'Evils may be more easily prevented than cured'.[24] It was
ordered that the several plans be referred to the consideration of a committee which included 'Mr. Sam: Johnson' and some fifty others, including
David Garrick, Thomas Hollis, and John Wilkes.[25] Some relevant Society records for this particular committee are lacking, but as no trace of
it appears in subsequent volumes, it appears that efforts to establish such
a charity house failed. Johnson may well have attended meetings of the
above committee, though there is no way of knowing. Even this single reference to his appointment is useful, revealing as it does an aspect of his
Society activities which at the same time complements what we already
know about his attitude towards life's unfortunates. For those so inclined,
moreover, the presence of Samuel Johnson and John Wilkes on the same
committee can give rise to speculations of various kinds.

There are no references to Johnson in Society records for the rest of
1758 and all of 1759, the period in which he fell behind in his dues. From
1760 on Samuel Johnson's name appears with increasing frequency in the
Society's records until it disappears altogether in 1762. The Minutes of the
Society for 18th June 1760, for instance, show that 'Mr. S. Johnson' was
added to the committee responsible for making the Society's large room
more commodious,[26] and his activities on this committee are revealed in
a single reference to him in the Miscellaneous Committee Minutes. At a
meeting held in the Strand on 5th July 1760 with Sir Thomas Robinson
presiding, 'Mr. S. Johnson' and twelve others resolved such matters as that
the 'Benches be 32 Inches instead of 31 so as to carry the five first Benches
to the Pillars'.[27]

After this period (July 1760) one must exercise caution in examining
the Society's records, for three more Johnsons joined the Society, and it is
not always clear just which of them is referred to. Robert Johnson, Esq.,
of Cavenham Hall, Suffolk, proposed by Thomas Hollis, was elected on
20th August 1760; Mr. James Johnson of Crosby Square, proposed by
Mr. Crisp, was elected 5th November 1760; and William Johnson, Esq.,
of Number 10 Crown Office Row, Temple, proposed by Mr. Stephenson,
was elected on 10th December 1760.[28] Their terms of membership coincide
with Johnson's, and some confusion does result. Fortunately, though, the
Society's Secretary took some pains to distinguish Samuel from the other
Johnsons. On 19th November 1760, for instance, in a meeting held in the

Strand, Mr. Hooper, a Vice President, drew lots to decide the priorities of chairmen for the several committees, and for the Committee of Correspondence the name of 'S. Johnson' is drawn third (behind Mr. Locke and Mr. Hanway) in the fourth draw.[29] There are no subsequent references, however, to Johnson's connections with this committee, and this appears to be the only time that he is even mentioned in a possible administrative capacity in the Society.

In several places in the records, however, a 'Johnson' is referred to without any identifying Christian name or initial. On 6th May 1761, for example, a committee on 'Certificates of Candidates for History and Landscape and Paintings' met in the Strand with Thomas Brand in the chair and a 'Mr. Johnson' in attendance.[30] On 18th June 1761 a 'Mr. Johnson' with Dr. Fordyce, Mr. Dossie and others attended a committee which was involved with an 'Experiment on the Cudbear dye compared with Archile prepared for dying'. This committee witnessed a series of experiments and adjourned until seven o'clock that evening, though the 'Mr. Johnson' did not appear at the evening meeting.[31] On 11th February 1762, however, Samuel Johnson definitely returns, attending a committee entitled in the Society's records 'On Claims for Diminishing Friction of a Saw Mill'. 'Mr. S. Johnson' and thirty-one others conclude that the model proposed is not sufficiently original or workable to receive a premium.[32] Confusion returns next month, for on 23rd March 1762 a 'Mr. Johnson' attended a committee bearing the title 'On Machine for Polishing Marble',[33] and the confusion persists in the reference to a 'Mr. Johnson' who was present at a committee, 'On Drawings', which met on 11th June 1762.[34]

Should one conclude from the above evidence that only those Johnsons so identified by a Christian name or initial were Samuel Johnson? It would seem perhaps that one might be less in error to assume that all the Johnsons referred to during this period were Samuel Johnson than to assume they were not. The Society's Secretary evidently followed no pattern in his references to Samuel Johnson, listing him at various times as 'Mr. Johnson' (the identification is positive when no other Johnson held membership), 'S.' and 'Sam:' Johnson. It might be argued, moreover, that those Johnsons who joined the Society after Samuel Johnson did would be in greater need of specific identification. Certainly the nature of the committees on which 'Mr. Johnson' served offer no clue, since Samuel Johnson confined himself to no particular area of activities. Society records may offer slight support for the above argument. On 3rd March 1761 a 'Rev. Mr. Johnson' is listed as attending a committee held 'In Consideration of the Annual Elections and a Committee on Trade and Colonies . . .'[35] Here it would appear that the Secretary had attempted to distinguish the 'Rev. Mr. Johnson' from the Johnson he most likely would have been confused with—Samuel Johnson, whose Society activities at this time were at a peak. Such evidence, though, will hardly convince the sceptical, myself included, and Thomas Hollis's diary, now at Harvard's Houghton Library, suggests quite clearly, for instance, that the Johnson referred to at the meetings on 6th May 1761 and 18th June 1761 was Robert Johnson, Esq., of Cavenham Hall, Suffolk. Hollis dined with him frequently during this time, and the two probably attended Society meetings after dining. Unfortunately the identification of the four 'Johnsons' is forever obscured, though one is forced to conclude, somewhat sadly, that they probably weren't Samuel Johnson.[36]

Dr. Johnson's service on two other Society committees is certain from an examination of the records. The Minutes of the Society for 25th November 1761 read in part: 'A Letter signed by a Member was read concerning a Method which he apprehended he had discovered of preserving Water sweet and wholesome; and expressing his Desire of presenting it, through Means of the Society, to the public; if on the further necessary Tryals it shall be found so considerably useful. Resolved, That the above mentioned Letter be refered to the Consideration of a Committee.'[37] The proposal interested the Society considerably, for a committee including 'Mr. Johnson', Benjamin Franklin and thirty-three others was formed.[38] The Miscellaneous Committee Minutes for 27th November 1761 reveal that a committee 'On Preserving Water Sweet' met, with 'Mr. S. Johnson' (confirming the identification of the 'Mr. Johnson' above) and twenty-nine others in attendance.[39] At this meeting Joseph Gardiner, a member, declared himself the author of the letter and of the process to preserve water by mixing it with common clay. Various experiments involving 'New River Water', 'Thames Water', and 'Rain Water' were ordered. The committee met again on 21st December 1761, but Johnson did not attend.[40] He did appear, though, at a meeting held on 11th January 1762, this time listed as 'Mr. S. Johnson'.[41] The committee 'On Preserving Water Sweet' met a number of times after this date, but Johnson ceased to attend its meetings. His absence is not surprising, however. The Gardiner process was having mixed results at best, and interest in it was obviously weakening. On 5th October 1762 only Samuel More and Gardiner himself appeared at a committee meeting.[42]

To encourage excellence in various fields the Society offered premiums or rewards, often cash; sometimes an appropriate medal. The following announcement by the Society appeared in 1761: 'A Gold Medal will be given for the best Treatise on the Arts of Peace, containing an Historical Account of the progressive Improvements of Agriculture, Manufactures and Commerce, in that Part of *Great-Britain* called *England,* with the Effects of those Improvements on the Morals and Manners of the People, and pointing out the most practicable Means for their future Advancement.'[43] The announcement concluded with instructions to would-be contestants as to how they should submit their entries for judging.

The Minutes of the Society for 16th December 1761 record that 'The Treatise on the Arts of Peace was referred to the consideration of a Committee', which included 'Mr. S. Johnson', Benjamin Franklin, Thomas Hollis, and some seventeen others.[44] The size of the committee is again an indication of the Society's interest in the project. At first it would appear from the records that only one entry had been submitted, and that promptly rejected. The Miscellaneous Committee Minutes for 22nd December 1761 read: 'The Treatise on the Arts of Peace which had been referred to the committee by the Society Dec. 16th was read. Resolved, it is the Opinion of this Committee that the above Treatise has not sufficient Merit to intitle the Author to the Medal offered by the Society.'[45] Johnson did not attend this meeting, though it is possible that he had given his opinion on the treatise at some point in the proceedings.

There were two entries, though. The Minutes of the Society for 23rd December 1761 reveal that a second entry was submitted and temporarily overlooked: 'The Secretary acquainted the Society, That he had committed an Error in telling them, That there was but one Claimant of the Premium for a Treatise on the Arts of Peace; that he had received a Bundle of Papers bearing a different Title, and his not having Time to examine them were the Occasion of this Mistake.'[46] This second entry was referred to the same committee which met with 'Mr. S. Johnson' in attendance on 26th January 1762. The committee minutes read: 'Proceeded to read the Treatise on the Arts of Peace and having read as far as the 12th page inclusive during which the Author having given no Authorities for facts that he has laid down and some of the numbers and sums of Money quoted, being contrary to probability and inconsistent in themselves, the Committee are of the Opinion that, so far, it has no merit.' But it was not rejected out of hand as the previous entry was. The Minutes conclude: 'Read to Page 16th inclusive in which the Committee having discovered no inconsistencies are of Opinion to proceed in the farther reading thereof.'[47] Without Johnson the committee met on 2nd February 1762, when they 'Proceeded to read the Treatise on the Arts of Peace. Resolved, it is the Opinion of this Committee that the Treatise is not deserving of the Reward offered, and that therefore it be returned to the Author.' That was the apparent end of the second treatise submitted to the Society of Arts. In the archives, however, there is an anonymously written 'Dissertation' on much the same subject as above, and it appears to be one of the two entries submitted in this particular contest. Thomas Hollis states in his diary, moreover, that Dr. Johnson refused to write such a composition and that Dr. John Hawkesworth, a contemporary writer of some eminence at this time, actually did write a dissertation.[48]

Dr. Johnson's name appears thrice more in the Society's records, each time as the proposer of a would-be member. 'Mr. S. Johnson' proposed Mr. Richard Bathurst, M.B., of Gray's Inn, on 6th January 1762,[49] 'Mr. Sam Johnson' proposed John Bell, Esq., of Hart Street, Bloomsbury, on 3rd February 1762,[50] and 'Mr. S. Johnson' proposed Mr. Edmund Allen, Printer, Bolt Court, Fleet Street, on 31st March 1762.[51] All were subsequently elected and all appear in the *Life*, though not in this particular connection.

A brief summary of the references to Johnson's Society activities over a period of several years gives a clear picture of the extent of his contacts in this connection. There are, for instance, some *twenty-five* specific references to Samuel Johnson in the Society's records—more if the 'Mr. Johnson' referred to in several places was indeed Samuel Johnson (and, as we have seen, there is some support for this view). Johnson *definitely* served on *five* Society committees and possibly four others as well, and he proposed four men for membership. Finally, there are a number of references to Johnson's connection outside of the archives, in writers like Boswell and Dr. Kippis, all of whom testify to the fact that for several years at least Johnson displayed considerable interest in the Society's affairs.

Dr. Johnson's connection with the Society of Arts really didn't cease, though, with the last reference to him in its records, for the painter James Barry placed Johnson in the fifth picture of his magnificent series of paintings which to this day graces the walls of the Society's Great Room. Barry's six paintings present in a sweeping panorama the development of civilization from primitive to modern times, and the fifth painting is a highly idealized view of a distribution of the Society's premiums, which he has represented as taking place in front of Somerset House, with St. Paul's in the background. Taking their places of honour in this picture are the illustrious figures who contributed so much to the Society in its early days— Lord Folkestone, the Society's first President; Lord Romney, the second; William Shipley, the Society's founder, who sits in the left-hand corner with 'the Plan of the Institution' in his hand; and Arthur Young the agriculturist, who is shown just above Shipley. Near the centre of the picture

Mrs. Elizabeth Montagu appears, and farther to the right stands Dr. Johnson, between the Duchesses of Rutland and Devonshire, whom he is trying to persuade to follow Mrs. Montagu's illustrious example of womanhood.

Barry's tribute to Dr. Johnson, which forever links him to the Society, is not only pictorial but verbal, and one feels sure that those who came to know Johnson through the Society of Arts as well as elsewhere shared the painter's sentiments. Barry writes:

> My admiration of the genius and abilities of this great master of morality, Dr. Johnson, cannot be more than it is; but my estimation of his literary abilities is next to nothing, when compared with my reverence for his consistent, manly and well-spent life; so long a writer, in such a town as London, and through many vicissitudes, without ever being betrayed into a single meanness, that at this day he might be ashamed to avow. Above all that extraordinary stretch of virtue that induced him to be so singularly active in assisting and bringing forward all his competitors of worth and ability, particularly at that period of their reputation, when it was easy for him to have crushed them, if he had been so inclined. In the history of the arts, we find but a few examples of the practice of this apparently very difficult virtue . . .[52]

Society and other records reveal, then, that for several years Dr. Johnson gave some measure of his physical and intellectual energies to the Society of Arts, and these records show not only Johnson's connections with this illustrious body but serve at the same time as an index to the interests, activities, and associations of a man whose name marks the age during which the Society came into being.

2

'COMPASSION AND HORROR IN EVERY HUMANE MIND': SAMUEL JOHNSON, THE SOCIETY OF ARTS, AND EIGHTEENTH-CENTURY PROSTITUTION

D. G. C. Allan and John L. Abbott

Eighteenth-century London was overrun with prostitutes, a blight that brought strong moral condemnation but also attempts at regeneration, one of which joined the Society of Arts with the century's most famous writer and moralist, Samuel Johnson.[1] At mid-century, Johnson and many other Society members attempted to resolve a problem surveyed in a variety of sources: direct commentary by observers of the contemporary scene; artistic depictions; fictional testimony; and autobiographical revelations. From the century's beginning to its end these commentators provided vivid portraits of prostitution.

Writing early in the century in *Some Considerations Upon Street-Walkers . . . In Two Letters to a Member of Parliament,* Daniel Defoe wrote:

> With what Impatience and Indignation have I walked from *Charing-Cross* to *Ludgate,* when being in full Speed upon important Business, I have every

Originally appeared in *Jnl. RSA*, 136 (Sept.-Oct., 1988), 749-54, 827-32.

now and then been put to the Halt; sometimes by the full Encounter of an audacious Harlot, whose impudent Leer shewed she only stopp'd my Passage in order to draw my Observation on her; at other times, by Twitches on the Sleeve, lewd and ogling Salutations . . .

In *Satan's Harvest Home* (1749) an observer of the London scene exclaimed:

When a person unacquainted with the *Town,* passes at Night thro' any of our principal streets, he is apt to wonder, whence that vast Body of *Courtezans,* which stands ready, on small Purchase, to obey the Laws of Nature, and gratify the Lust of every drunken Rake-hell, can take its Rise. *Where the Devil* do all these *B——hes come from?* being a common *Fleet-street Phrase,* and in the Mouth of every Stranger . . .

At century's end (1791) a foreign visitor, M. D'Archenholz, in *A Picture of England: Containing A Description of the Laws, and Manners of England* provided one of the fullest illuminations of prostitution. 'London is said to contain fifty thousand prostitutes, without reckoning kept-mistresses,' D'Archenholz argues, and adds that 'in the parish of Maryle-bone only, which is the largest and best peopled in the capital, thirty thousand ladies of pleasure reside, of whom seventeen hundred are reckoned to be house-keepers.' Streetwalkers, however visible, were only an obvious fraction of the total prostitute population; illicit commerce was often conducted in less public contexts. 'House-keepers', or matrons, provided numerous prostitutes with lodging, board, clothing and protection not available in the streets. Prostitutes were to be found, too, in fashionable quarters in St. James's 'where a great number are kept for people of fashion', D'Archenholz notes, and he observed, too, that London provided 'a species of houses called *bagnios,* the sole intention of which is to procure pleasure. These are magnificent buildings, and the furniture contained in them is not unworthy of the palace of a prince.' Upon the death of his father and coming into a substantial inheritance, a country youth headed to such a gaudy interior. Treating it as a hotel and not a temporary accommodation (though this was much against custom), he proceeded to run up a bill of twelve hundred guineas in eleven days, a sum fortunately reduced at a later date by a court of justice.[2]

The reality of street prostitution imposed itself, however, on those with no access to or interest in such corrupt private interiors. Eighteenth-century London was geographically compact, making confrontation with prostitutes almost inevitable. 'They accost the passengers, and offer to accompany them,' D'Archenholz writes. 'They even surround them in crowds, stop and overwhelm them with caresses and entreaties.' Such populations included married women and very young girls. D'Archenholz comments that he 'beheld with surprize, mingled with terror, girls from eight to nine years old make a proffer of their charms: and such is the corruption of the human heart, that even they have their lovers.' Age itself was no barrier. D'Archenholz adds that 'towards midnight, when the young women have disappeared, and the streets become deserted, then the old wretches of fifty or sixty years of age, descend from their garrets, and attack the intoxicated passengers, who are often prevailed upon to satisfy their passions in the open street, with these female monsters.'[3]

Not surprisingly, an age that valued realism incorporated such scenes in a variety of texts. Few struck the popular imagination with greater force than Hogarth, who brilliantly depicted the world D'Archenholz observed in *A Harlot's Progress* and *A Rake's Progress*. In the various plates of the former, one witnesses Mary or Moll Hackabout's arrival in London, where she is greeted by a notorious bawd, probably a Mother Needham, keeper of an infamous brothel favoured by the aristocracy. Through her, Moll enjoys a temporary rise in a world of glitter and finery that serves only as a prelude to degradation, disease, incarceration and finally death at the age of twenty-three in Bridewell Prison. Moll's decline is mirrored in the sexual fall of Tom Rakewell, who abandons a responsible bourgeois life for the stews, only to end mad in Bethlehem Hospital. However hyperbolic Hogarth's etchings may seem, the commentary of D'Archenholz and others suggests they might be closer to photograph than caricature.[4]

Prostitutes and prostitution help define the novels and essays of the century. Defoe's *Roxana* (1724) is punctuated with references to whoring. In *Clarissa* (1748-9) we witness the protracted struggle of Richardson's heroine caught in a terrible sexual undertow as a consequence of filial disobedience that places her in the hands of a bawd named Mrs. Sinclair. John Hawkesworth promulgated Richardsonian morality in his popular *Adventurer* essays (1752-4), several of which are devoted to the story of a prostitute named Nancy and her father Agamus. Having abandoned Nancy in infancy to a parish nurse, Agamus contented himself 'with strolling from one prostitute to another, of whom I have seen many generations perish.'[5] One evening, he picked up a particularly fresh girl; only in recognizing marks on her body that proved her to be his daughter did Agamus avoid compounding illegal intercourse with even greater moral violation, incest itself. While Hawkesworth provides a detailed narrative of how both male and female were drawn into the web of prostitution, his series concludes with pedestrian moral observations making Nancy largely responsible for

William Hogarth, *A Harlot's Progress* (1732), plate 1. By permission of the British Library.

her own fate. Here he shows himself to be less than sensitive to the conditions that trapped so many young women of the century, though more so than a far more famous writer.

While close observers of the scene, like D'Archenholz, and imaginative artists, like Defoe, Hogarth, Richardson and Hawkesworth, provide vivid illuminations of eighteenth-century prostitution, perhaps no text serves so well to describe this world as *Boswell's London Journal, 1762-63*. It delivers with astonishing frankness and clarity a portrait of mid-century prostitution. The journal is punctuated, in fact, by Boswell's connections with London prostitutes: the earliest occurs on 25 November 1762 (ten days after the journal begins); the last takes place on 1 August 1763 (the journal closes three days later). Between these dates and at fairly regular intervals Boswell met a variety of prostitutes. On Thursday 25 November 1762 he reflected that he 'had now been some time in town without female sport'. Although he picked up a girl in the Strand, 'with intention to enjoy her in armour', she had none. Boswell wisely avoided further intercourse. Such illicit commerce was constantly on his mind, even while listening to a sermon on Sunday 28 November 1762 entitled 'By what means shall a

young man learn to order his ways'. While Boswell's journal entires involving prostitution are usually short, one for Tuesday 14 December provides
a survey of some length. He writes:

> It is very curious to think that I have now been in London several weeks
> without ever enjoying the delightful sex, although I am surrounded with
> numbers of free-hearted ladies of all kinds: from the splendid Madam at fifty
> guineas a night, down to the civil nymph with white-thread stockings who
> tramps along the Strand and will resign her engaging person to your honour
> for a pint of wine and a shilling.[6]

Although some might note the conscious literary quality of this entry, its
historical content is more useful as Boswell examines mid-century prostitution, especially its cost and availability. In noting the cost of a 'splendid Madam', one might recall Boswell's own allowance of £200 a year
and Johnson's view that life could be sustained in the capital on some
£30 annually. Boswell, however, underestimated the worth of particular favourites. D'Archenholz refers to the celebrated Kitty Fisher, a great
beauty of twenty-five, fully conscious of her merit. 'She demanded a hundred guineas a night, for the use of her charms,' he records, 'and she was
never without her votaries, to whom the offering did not seem too exor-
bitant. Among them was the late Duke of York, a brother to the king.'
On one occasion, however, he left less—a fifty-pound note. 'This present
so much offended Miss Fisher,' D'Archenholz writes, 'that she declared
that her doors should ever be shut against him in future; and to shew, by
the most convincing proofs, how much she despised his present, she clapt
the bank-note between two slices of bread and butter and eat it for her
breakfast.'[7]

Boswell, of course, had no such illustrious liaisons; his connections with
London prostitutes were of a far lesser order. Without exception, it seems,
they were short, brutal affairs (invariably outdoors), taken often on the
spur of the moment. On Thursday 31 March 1763 he writes:

> At night I strolled into the Park and took the first whore I met, whom I with-
> out many words copulated with free from danger, being safely sheathed. She
> was ugly and lean and her breath smelled of spirits. I never asked her name.
> When it was done, she slunk off. I had a low opinion of this gross practice
> and resolved to do it no more.

Such resolves were frequently broken—on Saturday 9 April 1763 'with a
strong, plump, good-humoured girl called Nancy Baker'; on Wednesday
13 April 1763 'with a monstrous big whore in the Strand'; on Tuesday

10 May 1763 with 'a jolly young damsel' taken on Westminster Bridge. 'The whim of doing it there with the Thames rolling below us amused me much', Boswell comments.[8]

While Boswell left a vividly documented record of numerous illicit sexual connections in his journal, it contained repeated castigation of such conduct. Like the century as a whole, he could not condone prostitution, even in the privacy of his journal. There were, however, two significant exceptions: Bernard Mandeville's *A Modest Defence of Publick Stews* (1724) and John Cleland's *Fanny Hill* (1748-9). In his *Defence*, Mandeville continues an argument first presented in his famed *The Fable of the Bees* (1714) where he claimed that private vices can produce socially desirable results. Regarding prostitution, Mandeville insists that civil authorities should permit (and control) what cannot be eradicated. Public stews, he argues, will concentrate a social evil that is otherwise widely dispersed through the city; such houses can be regulated, bringing order to a traffic that often leads to social disruption. Other tangible benefits will result: disease can be controlled; valuable time could be saved (the search for prostitutes was economically costly); children of such unions, spared infanticide, could be properly reared; marriage would be strengthened (a consequence of man's greater sense of reality about women); the debauchery of modest women would cease.[9] John Cleland, in offering a romantic inversion of Hogarth's moralistic harlot's progress in *Fanny Hill*, indirectly confirms Mandeville's view that prostitution needs regulation more than eradication. Fanny moves through an idealized sexual world defined by mutual enjoyment of prostitute and customer, one virtually immune from the traditional scourges of the trade—pregnancy and disease. Cleland sanitizes Hogarth's gloomy interiors and renders them cosmetically exciting.

If in Mandeville and Cleland one sees philosophic and novelistic aberrants defining prostitution that most would reject, a rarer text confirms that in practice, if not in preachment, many supported their views. How else to account for *Harris's List of Covent-Garden Ladies: Or Man of Pleasure's Kalender,* which appeared in various versions late in the century? In these guides one sees something of Mandeville's regulated world of prostitution—Harris directed readers to private dwellings, to settings between the ranker street commerce and the opulent interiors favoured by the privileged. In tone, though, the guides seem more indebted to Cleland: the numerous vignettes of ladies of pleasure are reminiscent of *Fanny Hill*'s fervent prose, which at once disguises and heightens sexual activity through euphemism and elegant periphrasis.[10]

In such figures and in Defoe, Hogarth, D'Archenholz, Richardson,

Hawkesworth, Boswell, Mandeville and Cleland, one gains a wide perspective of how the century as a whole viewed prostitution. Samuel Johnson provides a unique commentary on the subject, both in his literary canon and in his personal efforts to alleviate this grave social problem. Not surprisingly, Boswell's *Life* provides extensive coverage of Johnson's ideas about prostitution, not to mention his thoughts on the proper relationship between the sexes generally. Given Boswell's activities in London at the time of their meeting on 16 May 1763, it is not unexpected that such subject matter occurs with some frequency in his biography. Shortly before and immediately after his meeting with Johnson in Tom Davies' bookshop, Boswell had connections with prostitutes; on Tuesday 7 May 1763 with a young girl called Alice Gibbs whom he took rashly without protection.[11]

On Friday 5 April 1776 (appropriately Good Friday) Boswell and Johnson conversed about the licensed stews at Rome, which Johnson strongly censured. 'So then, Sir, you would allow no irregular intercourse whatever between the sexes?' Boswell asked. Johnson's reply was unequivocal: 'To be sure I would not, Sir. I would punish it much more than is done, and so restrain it. In all countries there has been fornication, as in all countries there has been theft; but there may be more or less of one, as well as the other, in proportion to the force of law.' Johnson continued, demolishing the claim that stews contributed to public order: 'It is very absurd to argue, as has often been done,' he asserted, 'that prostitutes are necessary to prevent the violent effects of appetite from violating the decent order of life; nay, should be permitted, in order to preserve the chastity of our wives and daughters. Depend upon it, Sir, severe laws, steadily enforced, would be sufficient against those evils, and would promote marriage.'[12]

In spite of such strong declarations, Johnson's connections with prostitutes have excited curiosity about his motives, possibly even his conduct, when dealing with them. Even Boswell's *Life,* which consistently presents Johnson as a moral monolith, contains potentially suggestive material. Writing 'with all possible respect and delicacy', he notes that Johnson's conduct

> after he came to London, and had associated with Savage and others, was not so strictly virtuous, in one respect, as when he was a younger man. It is well known, that his amorous inclinations were uncommonly strong and impetuous. He once owned to many of his friends, that he used to take women of the town to taverns, and hear them relate their history. In short, it must not be concealed, that, like many other good and pious men, among whom we may place the Apostle Paul upon his own authority, Johnson was not free from propensities which were ever 'warring against the law of his mind'— and that in his combats with them, he was sometimes overcome.[13]

'Respect and delicacy' aside, Boswell's innuendo concerning Johnson's moral lapses seems unmistakable—he speaks with the frankness modern students of Johnson would insist upon when biography, not hagiography, is at issue. While as late as 1939 W. C. B. Watkins argued that to mistake Johnson's motive in such conversations would be 'absurd', a decade later Katherine Balderston, in her celebrated study of 'Johnson's Vile Melancholy', fearlessly linked Johnson and Mrs. Thrale in a real or imagined sexual relationship involving a 'secret', a padlock, and bondage and disciplinary practices. More recently, Dr. Bernard Meyer, in his study of the fascination various writers and other historical figures have had for fallen women, flatly refuses to accept Watkins' and similar apologies for Johnson's behaviour. 'These opinions were apparently dictated less by earnest pursuit of biographical truth,' he declares, 'than by the wishful thinking that is the common handmaiden of hero worship; there is abundant evidence that throughout his life Johnson was caught in the snares of tormenting sexual conflicts in which his consorting with streetwalkers undoubtedly offered him some promise of scopophilic and vicarious erotic gratification.'[14]

Thus it is that a great figure can be framed—initially by a close friend; much later by a man of science. One questions whether either engages in 'an earnest pursuit of truth' so much as in a definition of character based less on evidence and more on supposition and manipulation of language. Boswell's source, called 'well known', surely fails contemporary biographical standards for specificity; his idea that Johnson's 'amorous inclinations' may have been excessive is referred to a norm that has not yet been established. Some would argue that Dr. Meyer's assessment is even worse in yoking speculation with dubious scientific support. 'Scopophilic and vicarious erotic gratification'? 'Consorting'? 'Snares'? Is Johnson's relationship with prostitutes to be defined by a vocabulary that is a curious mixture of the scientific and Victorian? Perhaps this would disturb some less than the implied irony of Meyer's argument: what is the essential difference between Johnson's receiving erotic gratification from conversing with prostitutes and that by scholars or psychologists who assess the same subject—indeed, of any who read such material? A possible circle of guilt quickly spreads. The point of this study, however, is not to deny what is universally recognized to be true about Johnson's life or anyone's—that character and personality are rich composites defined by a host of sources; it is to show that Johnson's relationship with prostitutes had a factual base whose clarification is a necessary first step to profitable speculation.[15] Consider the following.

While George Steevens confirms that Johnson conversed with prostitutes, he suggests that he carried 'these unfortunate creatures into a tavern, for the sake of striving to awaken in them a proper sense of their condition'. Steevens addresses, too, the somewhat unusual confrontation of the abandoned with the moralist that stimulated questions in Johnson's time no less than our own. 'His younger friends now and then affected to tax him with less chaste intentions', Steevens records. 'But he would answer—"No Sir; we never proceeded to the *Opus Magnum*. On the contrary, I have rather been disconcerted and shocked by the replies of these giddy wenches, than flattered or diverted by their tricks." '[16] The facts of a subject's life, at least those still recoverable, do not always fit the more imaginative speculations of biographer or reader; in Johnson's case they sometimes deflate such speculation.

Johnson's marriage to a much older woman has excited a good deal of commentary, and the circumstances of Tetty's burial, not in London, but in Bromley, Kent, seemed to offer some evidence of a troubled union that had ended in separation. Neither Boswell nor Sir John Hawkins, Johnson's biographers who knew him best, could provide an answer, though evidence was available. Tetty actually died in London; she was buried in Bromley by Johnson's close friend, John Hawkesworth, who had just interred his father at the same site. Tetty's death and burial in Bromley defines a friendship, then, and not Johnson's marriage. Similarly, the source of Johnson's 'vile melancholy' may originate less in the psychological terrain Katherine Balderston attempted to define and more in the pedestrian materials identified by Professor James Gray. He suggests that the curious letter in French that Johnson wrote to Mrs. Thrale refers to rather mundane details concerning the Thrale household at Streatham rather than the interiors of a tormented mind. These included the desperate illness of Mrs. Thrale's mother as well as her concern for her children. A simple, striking fact potentially reduces the erotic to the ordinary: Streatham, including Johnson's room, was undergoing extensive renovation. A letter that seems to point to a desire for discipline (even 'bondage') might rather refer to the turmoil of interior decoration. Many would agree that the latter is capable of exciting the passions.[17]

Such material will never convince the sceptical, but facts provide focus while speculation leads to diffusion. In Johnson's case sufficient facts remain to provide a fairly clear view of his relationships with eighteenth-century prostitutes. These suggest that in his literary canon (in works acknowledged and anonymous), in his private life and in public forums he reacted to this social problem with sympathy and a pragmatic desire to see it alleviated.

While Boswell and Steevens suggest that Johnson conversed with prostitutes simply to hear their stories, William Cook recounts a particularly vivid encounter between Johnson and a woman that speaks powerfully to his sympathy for such unfortunates. Coming up Fleet Street at about two o'clock in the morning, Johnson was arrested by the cries of a person in distress. He discovered 'an unhappy female, almost naked, and perishing on a truss of straw'. She told her sad story of being turned out by an inhuman landlord. Failing to find a carriage for her, Johnson 'kneeled down by her side, raised her in his arms, wrapped his great coat about her, placed her on his back, and in this carried her home to his house'. Although she suffered from an apparent venereal complaint, rather than turning her out, Johnson 'kept her in his house for above thirteen weeks, where she was regularly attended by a physician, who recovered her'. Not content with her physical health alone, Johnson established her in a milliner's shop 'where she was living some years ago in very considerable repute'.[18]

While there is no proof that this woman was a prostitute, she found herself in the milieu of hopelessness and abandonment that defined their condition, one that Johnson illuminated in *Ramblers* 170 and 171. Boswell, citing Malone, suggested that the source of these papers originated in Johnson's conversation with a prostitute 'under a tree in the King's Bench Walk in the Temple'.[19] Although this could be their specific genesis, Johnson's heroine Misella defines the sad paradigm of a generation of young women enticed to London and soon destroyed by it. The power of these papers lies not in the originality of the narrative or in Johnson's ability to suggest the contours of prostitutes' lives; rather it stems from Johnson's condemnation of those who so willingly abuse them. Misella's words in *Rambler* 170 clearly embody Johnson's deeply felt sentiments:

> I know not why it should afford subject of exultation to overpower on any terms the resolution, or surprise the caution of a girl; but of all the boasters that deck themselves in the spoils of innocence and beauty, they surely have the least pretensions to triumph who submit to owe their success to some casual influence. They neither employ the graces of fancy, nor the force of understanding, in their attempts; they cannot please their vanity with the art of their approaches, the delicacy of their adulations, the elegance of their address, or the efficacy of their eloquence; nor applaud themselves as possessed of any qualities by which affection is attracted. They surmount no obstacles, they defeat no rivals, but attack only those who cannot resist, and are often content to possess the body without any solicitude to gain the heart.[20]

Johnson's prose is heightened when compared with other utterances concerning prostitution—Mandeville's pragmatism, Cleland's romantic endorsement, Hawkesworth's muddled good intentions and Boswell's frank journal entries. He makes not the prostitute but her abuser the object of scathing assessment, 'reptiles whom their own servants would have despised,' Misella argues, 'had they not been their servants, and with whom beggary would have disdained intercourse, had she not been allured by hopes of relief.' For those persuaded by arguments that Johnson suffered lapses with prostitutes or derived some erotic gratification in conversing with them, such words are a strong corrective. So, too, is his moving conclusion to *Rambler* 171, where he writes:

> If those who pass their days in plenty and security could visit for an hour the dismal receptacles to which the prostitute retires from her nocturnal excursions, and see the wretches that lie crowded together, mad with intemperance, ghastly with famine, nauseous with filth, and noisome with disease; it would not be easy for any degree of abhorrence to harden them against compassion, or to repress the desire which they must immediately feel to rescue such numbers of human beings from a state so dreadful.[21]

Several years later Johnson worked 'to rescue such numbers of human beings from a state so dreadful' in an effort that involved an anonymous use of his literary powers and public participation with concerned members of the Society of Arts.

While Johnson's association with the Society of Arts has been documented in previous essays in the *Journal of the Royal Society of Arts*, a brief summary here can suggest its dimensions.[22] There are some twenty-five references to Samuel Johnson in the Society's archives, even more if the 'Mr. Johnson' referred to at times is the writer and not another figure of the same name. Such references span a period from his election on 1 December 1756 to 31 March 1762, when he proposed Mr. Edmund Allen, Printer, Bolt Court, Fleet Street, for membership. During his tenure at the Society, Johnson definitely served on five committees and possibly four others as well. Johnson joined Jonas Hanway, Saunders Welch and a number of other prominent members in 1758 in specific address to an issue he had reviewed with so much passion in *Ramblers* 170 and 171—prostitution.

In attending meetings of the Society of Arts, Johnson, Welch and other members were brought face to face with the evidence of prostitution; for in the years 1756-9 the Society had its headquarters in John Fielding's house on the north side of the Strand not far from Covent Garden, and many of its most active members resided or lodged in the area.[23] Covent Garden was notorious for its numerous *bagnios,* which were mostly of a disreputable character. The one kept by Betty Careless and her successor 'Mother' Douglas was especially well known. Hogarth portrayed Mother

Douglas in his 'March to Finchley' and in the execution scene of 'Industry and Idleness'. She is said to have retired with an ample fortune and become an ardent church-goer. The Strand itself was frequented by streetwalkers. Jonas Hanway, who lodged immediately opposite the Society's premises, wrote that 'We need but step out of doors, to see what situation we are in at present. The number of prostitutes is so great . . . that we should doubt whether every female we meet is not an harlot', and a correspondent of the *London Chronicle* in 1758 believed that 'the whole street from Ludgate to Charing Cross is one continuous brothel'.[24]

Since Tudor times and earlier the magistrates of London had attempted to prevent prostitution by punishment. The City Bridewell was a place where, as Dekker put it, 'the bawd, the rogue, the whore' received 'hard hands, or laced correction'. This institution and its companion in Westminster still flourished in the middle of the eighteenth century. In Plate 4 of his *Harlot's Progress,* Hogarth shows his heroine in the Westminster Bridewell 'reduced to the wretched alternative of beating hemp or receiving the correction of a severe task master'. Yet legal restraints, as Hogarth well knew, could be evaded or long postponed by bribery and influence. In spite of the exertions of reforming justices such as Saunders Welch and the Fieldings, the law provided no answer to the question. Nor were the exhortations and admonitions of the clergy, some of whom, like the Society's founding member and Vice President, Dr. Stephen Hales, still imposed public penance for fornication, effective in limiting promiscuity. The Societies for the Reformation of Manners, once active in promoting the prosecution of brothel keepers, seem to have fallen into decline in the 1740s. Perhaps then the answer lay in providing some refuge for the prostitutes themselves?[25]

'Exposed and deserted children', often the offspring of unfortunate women of the streets, could be granted refuge in the Foundling Hospital, Thomas Coram's addition to the growing number of London hospitals which were such a feature of the period. Opened in Hatton Garden in 1741, it was moved four years later to Lamb's Conduit Fields, where impressive buildings were erected for its use. In due course a fine chapel was built, and the court room was ornamented with paintings by Hogarth, who, like Bishop Maddox, Jonas Hanway and many other Governors, also became members of the Society of Arts. To them the hospital must have seemed a tangible example of the success which could attend a scheme of public philanthropy designed to mitigate a problem no less acute than that of prostitution.[26]

Because Johnson had addressed the problem in his writings and in personal conversations with prostitutes, he agreed with those who felt the Society of Arts had a role to play. These included his adversary over the question of tea-drinking, Jonas Hanway. First alerted to the problem of London prostitution by Robert Dingley, his partner in the Russia Trade, soon after his return from St. Petersburg in 1750, Hanway gave an enthusiastic welcome to Dingley's *Proposals for Establishing a Public Place of Reception for Penitent Prostitutes*, when they were published early in 1758. In a pamphlet of his own he set forth sound mercantilist arguments in favour of Dingley's plan:

> *First,* if you can stop the progress of those diseases, which are so fatal to the human species, you will save a number of subjects to the State. *Next,* if you can *check* libertinism, you will not only prevent great *misery,* but also great *confusion* among the lower classes of the people: and *lastly,* in proportion as you lessen the number of *prostitutes,* it may be presumed that the number of *marriages* will increase, as well as the number of souls saved.[27]

On 22 March 1758 Hanway, with copies of his pamphlet by his side, rose at a Society of Arts meeting to propose 'the giving a Premium for the best proposal or Plan for the Establishment of a Charity House or Charity Houses for the Reception and Employment of Girls whose poverty expose them to the Danger of becoming Prostitutes; also of such Common Prostitutes as are inclined to forsake their Evil Course of Life, and become Virtuous and useful Members of the Community'.[28] Could such a premium be considered suitable for a Society 'instituted . . . for the encouragement of arts, manufactures and commerce'?

The consistently increasing scope of the Society's premiums in its early years followed naturally from its expanding membership and financial resources. Suggestions for premium subjects were constantly received from members and other interested persons. The Society's objects as set forth in its title, 'the encouragement of arts, manufactures and commerce', seemed capable of the widest possible interpretation, and the adoption or otherwise of a particular suggestion would depend largely on the special interests of influential members. Thus Henry Baker actively promoted the proposals to reward the discovery of cobalt in England and Wales and the cultivation of silk in North America, but would give no support to his friend Arderon's suggestion that the Society should give premiums for musical composition. 'Music,' he would tell Arderon in 1764, 'is certainly a most delightful Science, but does not come properly under the Plan of the Society of Arts, etc. which points chiefly at the Procuring or Improvement of the Necessaries of Life . . . Commerce, or such Subjects as can either gain Money or save it to the Nation.' Similarly in 1756 Robert Dodsley's suggestion that the Society should add 'the encouragement of Letters' to its title was found unacceptable by his fellow members. Jonas Hanway's idea of assisting repentant prostitutes, however, would have seemed consistent with the intention of rewarding 'Productions, Inventions or Improvements, as shall tend to the employment of the Poor' proclaimed in both William Shipley's first premium notice and in Henry Baker's 'Plan'.[29]

Bourchier Cleeve, who in 1751 had almost succeeded in obtaining parliamentary support for a scheme whereby county funds should be started for the maintenance of workhouses, was one of a number of members of the Society who proposed that it should take up the question of workhouse management in the years 1756-8. Having served as an Overseer of the Poor, Cleeve reported to the Society that 'he found the poor people very Insolent and Idle . . . Children from their Cradles are whipped to be Thieves, the Consequences of which is shocking in Thought'.[30]

William Bailey laid special emphasis on the spinning of flax and hemp. 'Nothing,' he told the Society in 1757, 'can be of greater consequence to our Poor, and to the Trading people in general, or more worthy the attention of this Honourable Society.' Unless encouraged to spin these commodities, 'a multitude of Men, Women and children . . . would be excessively miserable, and become burdens to their respective parishes'. The Society's premium for spinning by workhouse inmates stated its belief that 'good Order and Regulation in *Workhouses* must greatly conduce to amend the Morals of the Poor, to incite Industry and promote our Manufactures', and the preamble to its 1758 book of *Rules and Orders* suggested that 'the readiest way perhaps of reforming Habits of Vice, is to remove those of Idleness, itself the greatest political Vice'. Although the fundamental purpose of the Society was the increase of national riches and the improvement of arts, it was prepared to invoke the cause of public morality. Thus the transformation of prostitutes into 'worthy members of the community' was by no means an unlikely object for it to pursue, and Hanway's proposal received no hostile comments at the meeting of 22 March 1758.[31]

The formal record of the occasion is provided in the surviving minutes. Lord Romney was in the chair, but we do not know how many other members attended, since by that date the meetings had become so crowded that the Secretary, George Box, had given up recording attendances.[32] The proceedings began with the reading of the previous week's minutes and the election of the ten members proposed on that occasion. These included John Wilkes, who had been proposed by his brother Israel, and J. M. Marchetti, Thomas Hollis' nominee. After the election came various items of business—advertisements for premiums on chemical, manufacturing and agricultural subjects were approved and reports from the Secretary and a Committee Chairman received. A letter on verdigris was read and the form of the reply to be sent to its author determined, followed by Hanway's proposal, which was referred, as was customary, to an ad hoc committee, with Henry Baker, Peter Wyche, Charles and Robert Dingley, Thomas Hollis, Edward Hooper and Hanway himself amongst the twenty-one members named. Next another member proposed a premium for 'the Discovery of a cheap composition for marking sheep', and this was also referred to the committee appointed to consider Hanway's proposal. Finally, it was recorded that 'Mr. Hanway presented to the several Members of the Society present, a Pamphlet of which he is the Author, Entitled a Proposal for the Relief and Employment of Friendless Girls and repenting Prostitutes, for which Thanks were returned him'; candidates for election to membership were proposed, and the Society 'Adjourned to Wednesday 29 March at 6 p.m. precisely'.[33]

Though no minutes of its deliberations survive for the committee appointed on the 22nd, we can be certain that it met and approved both Hanway's proposed premium, for which it was clearly well briefed, and the one proposed for sheep marking. The text of the former, as reported at the Society's meeting held on the 29th and finally approved on 5 April was as follows:

> The miserable Condition of *common Prostitutes*, and the Ruin they spread around, must raise Compassion and Horror in every humane mind: in order therefore to put some Stop to that Torrent of Distemper, Vice and Villainy, which sweeps away Multitudes of both Sexes, the *Society's Medal* in Gold will be given, as an honorary Reward, for *a Plan*, which shall be judged best calculated, for the effectual Establishment of a *Charity House,* or Charity Houses, to receive and employ such common Prostitutes as are desirous to forsake their evil Courses, and are inclinable to put themselves into a Way of Life, which, by a Mixture of Piety and useful Industry, will in a few Years render them worthy Members of the Community. All Plans are to be sent to the Society on or before the Third *Wednesday* in *May* next. Each Writer is desired to mark his Plan with some Sentence or Verse, etc. . . . .[34]

A week later the Society published the notice in the *Daily Advertiser* and the *Public Advertiser* and included it in its printed list of premiums for 1758.[35] Nine plans were delivered to the Society on 17 May, six marked with mottoes, two by initials and one under the name of its author, Charles Palmer.

The minutes list them as:

No. 1. Signed Charles Palmer.
   2. With this Motto: There is more Joy in Heaven over one Sinner that
      repenteth than over Ninety and nine just Persons that need no Repen-
      tence.
   3. Signed J.
   4. Signed A. M.
   5. With this Motto: No complaining, no begging in the Streets.
   6. [With this Motto]: Nihil Humani a me Alienum puto.
   7. [With this Motto]: A Well Wisher to the Charity.
   8. [With this Motto]: Pro Patria.
   9. [With this Motto]: Evils may be more easily prevented than cured.[36]

The plans were referred to a giant committee of fifty-one members,
amongst whom were all the interested members already named as well as
William Bailey, Bourchier Cleeve, John Fielding, David Garrick, Samuel
Johnson, Saunders Welch and Israel and John Wilkes. Fortunately rough
unbound minutes have survived for this committee, recording both the
names of those attending and the substance of its deliberations for meetings
held on 23 and 30 May and 6 June.

At its first meeting, when Peter Wyche, one of the Dingley brothers and
both the Wilkeses were present, the minutes tell us:

Mr. Hanway's Letter read.
Mr. Palmer's Letter read, but in the opinion of the Committee is not a Plan.
Mr. Fielding's Plan read.
Plan signed J. read.
No. 5 not read.
  " 6 Referred to a further Consideration.
  " 2 Referred to a further Consideration.
Adjourned to this Day 7 night at 6.[37]

It may be presumed that Hanway's letter was a recommendation for his
friend Robert Dingley's proposals, and that Fielding's plan was the same
as his printed *Plan for a preservatory and reformatory for the benefit of
deserted girls and penitent prostitutes*. No. 6 was the plan submitted to the
Society under the motto 'Nihil Humani, etc.' and no. 2 the one designated
by the quotation 'There is more Joy, etc.'

At the committee's next meeting, held on 30 May, Peter Wyche took the
chair, and twenty other members attended, amongst whom were Bailey,
Garrick, Johnson, Hanway, Welch and Israel Wilkes. Plans nos. 5, 7, 8,
and 9 were read, and it was agreed that permission should be obtained to
give consideration to the one by Welch, which he had sent to the Society
on or before 24 May.[38] Welch's proposal, though submitted late, deserves

Saunders Welch;
lithograph by Abraham
Wivell after Sir Joshua
Reynolds. Courtesy of
the Trustees of the
British Museum.

special mention. Arguably, he brought the strongest credentials of all the committee members to bear on the troublesome problem of prostitution. He was High Constable of Holborn during Henry Fielding's magistracy and served as his chief assistant. In recommending Welch to the Lord Chancellor as Justice of the Peace, Fielding described him 'as one of the best officers who was ever concerned in the execution of justice'. Welch was appointed to this post in April 1755. While members of the committee certainly knew about his legal qualifications, they might not have known that he and Johnson were close friends. Boswell, in fact, in the *Life*, defines in considerable detail their friendship, part of which was generated by Johnson's keen interest in Welch's judicial activities. 'Johnson who had an eager and unceasing curiosity to know human life in all its variety, told me', Boswell writes, 'that he attended Mr. Welch in his office for a whole winter, to hear the examinations of the culprits; but that he found an almost uniform tenor of misfortune, wretchedness, and profligacy.'

What the committee certainly did not know was that Johnson actively assisted Welch in the same plan that he had submitted to the Society committee on which he and Johnson sat. It remained a secret until an eminent twentieth-century Johnson scholar, E. L. McAdam, Jr., declared: 'In this pamphlet, I believe, Johnson assisted, though there is no external evidence available'. Although McAdam noted Welch's dedication of his proposal to

'Viscount Folkestone, president, and to the vice presidents and members of the Society for Encouraging Arts and Manufactures', he had no knowledge of Johnson's participation in the very committee that received the proposal, not to mention his larger involvement in Society activities. Here indeed is the external evidence that one can use to claim at least portions of Welch's pamphlet for the already varied Johnsonian canon.[39]

There are, of course, many unanswered questions concerning Johnson's connection with Welch's proposal. Did he suggest that Welch submit it in the first place, knowing that he could speak with real authority about the world of 'wretchedness and profligacy' in which prostitutes so often found themselves? Did Welch himself initiate the project, turning then to Johnson for advice and even direct contribution? Quantifying the exact assistance Johnson gave is probably impossible, though McAdam's claim that Johnson's involvement is seen at the beginning and at the end of Welch's pamphlet seems reasonable. Few Johnsonians would be opposed to adding to that vast miscellany called the Johnsonian canon the following lines from Welch's conclusion; they would agree with McAdam that here one sees 'the grand style, wholly different in its rhythm and incisiveness from anything previously written by Welch':

> Thus have I endeavoured to model an institution, which by a due mixture of mildness and severity may redress an enormity which has long infested our streets, and disgraced our government; which has brought to the *grave* multitudes of the young by disease, and of the old by sorrow. I have laid down rules of an hospital, in which penitence may be sheltered, and corruption be reclaimed; where honest industry may be inculcated by instruction, or inforced by chastisement: where those who were once educated in the knowledge of religion, may gradually revive the principles which had been almost extinguished by intercourse with bad example, and by successive vicissitudes of riots and distress: and the light of instruction may be imparted to those, whose minds have been hitherto clouded with ignorance, whom poverty has resigned to guilt without a check, and whose intellectual powers have served them to no other purpose than those of fraud, and rapine, treachery and seduction.[40]

Permission to consider Welch's plan was granted by the Society on 31 May, and on 6 June the committee held its final and decisive meeting. On this occasion twenty-three members attended, including those whom we have already named as attending on the 30th. Chief among these, of course, were Johnson and Welch himself. The meeting began with the reading of Welch's plan which, with nos. 8 and 9, were referred for further consideration. After this a decision seems to have been reached to take a vote on all the entries, including Charles Palmer's originally disqualified proposal and nos. 2, 4 and 6, one of which may have been entered by John Fielding and read at the first meeting of the committee. Presumably all the unread plans were read before the vote, since in its final recommendation the committee talks of 'having read through the ten Plans referred to their consideration'. The minutes of the vote specify the numbers of 'hands' raised on behalf of the various entries:

No. 1. Charles Palmer	None
2. 'There is more Joy etc.'	Ditto
3. signed J.	Ditto
4. " A. M.	Ditto
5. 'No Complaining'	Ditto
6. 'Nihil Humani etc.'	2 Hands
7. 'A Well Wisher etc.'	None
8. 'Pro Patria.'	Ditto
9. 'Evils may be etc.'	Ditto
10. Saunders Welch	9 Hands[41]

Welch being clearly the winner, it was agreed to recommend that he be given the premium, and the Chairman, Peter Wyche, reported this to the Society's meeting held on the following day. The Society minutes say that the members 'deliberated thereon' and 'determined that none of the Ten Plans have sufficient Merit to entitle them to the Premium'.[42]

It seems likely that Hanway and his friends were behind this over-turning of the committee's decision, since he and they would surely have wished the medal to go to whichever of the candidates approached most nearly to the spirit of Robert Dingley's proposals. It is well known that Hanway objected to certain details of Saunders Welch's plan and that he found John Fielding an annoying competitor in his philanthropic projects. Hanway would have certainly been jealous of a medal going to either of them, though he would co-operate with them in public. He probably re-garded his idea of a Society of Arts medal to further the cause of reforming prostitutes as just one part of his campaign to secure the foundation of the Magdalen Hospital, but his activity on its behalf did not lead to an abatement of his interest in the general work of the Society. Similarly John Fielding proceeded with the foundation of the Female Orphan Asylum, be-came a governor of the Magdalen Hospital and at the same time continued to be a supporter of the Society of Arts. Welch, who became a governor of both the Hospital and the Asylum, also maintained his membership of the Society. He paid his 1757 dues on 29 June 1758 but then, like Johnson, fell into arrears until March 1760, when they both cleared their indebtedness to the Society probably in order to vote for Robert Dossie as a candidate for the Secretaryship.[43]

One might speculate, too, that Johnson himself contributed directly to Welch's defeat, that Hanway knew that the 'truly good Man and very able Writer' identified in the *London Chronicle* for 17 May 1757 as the author of the scathing attack on his essay on tea in the *Literary Magazine* was none other than Johnson himself. Given the small intellectual community both inhabited and the obvious stylistic power of some of the passages in Welch's proposals, it would not take too refined a literary sensibility to see the Rambler's pen at work. If true, Hanway would not have backed a proposal linked to Johnson and his friend. Did Johnson himself suspect this was the case? If so, perhaps it partially inspired his parody of Hanway as 'Dick Wormwood' in *Idler* 83 for 17 November 1759 and a later stinging comment to Boswell: 'Jonas, (said he,) acquired some reputation by travelling abroad, but lost it all by travelling at home'.[44]

There is little room for speculation, given the facts available in the Society's archives and elsewhere, that Johnson's relationships with prostitutes were based on any motive other than defining ways to improve their wretched lot. In this he and Hanway were in complete agreement, the one calling attention to 'a state so dreadful', the other asking for 'compassion and horror in every humane mind'. Whatever their personal differences, they and other Society members approached the problem of prostitution in a pragmatic spirit coloured far more by benevolence than censure, one that has characterized most subsequent attempts to ameliorate this intractable social problem. That in itself was a beginning.

3

THOMAS HOLLIS AND THE SOCIETY, 1756-1774

John L. Abbott

Derek Hudson and Kenneth W. Luckhurst in their history of the Society comment that the list of famous names connected with the Society in its early years 'is so extensive that it might almost seem easier to compile a list of the eminent men of the mid–eighteenth century who were *not* members.'[1] That this is not an exaggerated claim can be seen in the Society's Manuscript Subscription Book, whose pages contain the names of such distinguished figures as Sir Joseph Banks, Dr. Charles Burney, Benjamin Franklin, David Garrick, Oliver Goldsmith, William Hogarth and Samuel Johnson and his illustrious biographer James Boswell, whose only real connection with the Society was in avoiding the payment of his dues.

The Society flourished in its early years not only because of the contributions of these celebrated men but also by the work of a number of members who are better known to specialists in the period. Such a man was Thomas Hollis, who became active in the Society a few years after its founding in 1754 and left its ranks in 1770, a few years before it moved to its present quarters in Adelphi. His contributions to the Society during this time, particularly during the late 1750s and early 1760s, were enormous, and one cannot read long in the Society's records without encountering

Originally appeared in *Jnl. RSA*, 119 (Sept., Oct., Nov., 1971), 711-15, 803-7, 874-78.

his name. These contributions have yet to be described and evaluated, and it is the purpose of this article to do so—not only through the use of the Society's archives but also through Hollis's unpublished *Diary*, which provides a unique source of information about the Society's early years and one active member's participation in it.[2]

Thomas Hollis was born on 14th April 1720 in London, lived as a child in the house of the Scotts of Wolverhampton, his maternal grandparents, and was later educated at Newport, Shropshire and St. Albans. He studied in Amsterdam in 1732 with a view to learning Dutch and French in order to pursue a commercial career, a goal he abandoned when he inherited a large fortune from his father's estate and that of his great uncle, another Thomas Hollis, the benefactor of Harvard College. Mr. and Mrs. John Hollister, his guardians, then modified his education, and he attended the class of Dr. John Ward, professor of Rhetoric at Gresham College, who was a major influence on young Hollis, as were the dissenting ministers of Pinner's Hall. In February of 1738/39 Hollis moved to Number 6, New Square, Lincoln's Inn, where he lived in chambers until 1748.[3] A dim figure to-day, Hollis once generated considerable controversy, especially for his political views, which some found dangerous and radical. The Johnson Circle found cause to speak of Hollis, and Boswell preserves in the *Life of Johnson* a scarcely flattering portrait of the man.

> One of the company mentioned Mr. Thomas Hollis, the strenuous Whig, who used to send over Europe presents of democratical books, with their boards stamped with daggers and caps of liberty. Mrs. Carter said, 'He was a bad man. He used to talk uncharitably.' JOHNSON. 'Poh! poh! Madam; who is the worse for being talked of uncharitably? Besides, he was a dull poor creature as ever lived, and I believe he would not have done harm to a man whom he knew to be of very opposite principles to his own.
>
> 'I remember once at the Society of Arts, when an advertisement was to be drawn up, he pointed me out as the man who could do it best. This, you will observe, was kindness to me. I however slipt away, and escaped it.'
>
> Mrs. Carter having said of the same person, 'I doubt he was an Atheist.' JOHNSON. 'I don't know that. He might perhaps have become one, if he had had time to ripen, (smiling). He might have exuberated into an Atheist.'[4]

Boswell's account does little to enhance Hollis's memory, and in a single entry he is charged with radical political views, a lack of charity in his talk, dullness, and possible atheistic tendencies. It is not a flattering picture, and an even worse one appears in an exchange between the Reverend Baptist-Noel Turner and Johnson which John Nichols preserves in his *Illustrations of Literary History*. Turner comments:

Thomas Hollis, 'drawn by F. Uwins and engraved by Charles Warren from an original bust in the possession of Dr. Disney'; frontispiece to the Society's *Transactions*, Vol. 23, 1805. Courtesy of the RSA.

This Mr. Hollis, it may be proper to say, was a bigotted Whig, or Republican; one who misspent an ample fortune in paving the way for sedition and revolt in this and the neighboring kingdoms, by dispersing democratical works, and sometimes highly ornamented with daggers, caps of liberty, &c. His favourite author was Milton, though I fear he respected the rebel rather than the bard. . . . This Hollis, indeed, might be said even to have laid the first train of combustibles for the American explosion; he having long ago sent a present of some elegant book or books, to Harvard-college, in New Cambridge, accompanied by the following curious document: 'People of Massachusetts! when your country shall be cultivated, adorned like this country, and ye shall become elegant, refined in civil life, then—if not before—"ware your liberties!"'[5]

According to the Society's Manuscript Subscription Book, Thomas Hollis, Esq., of Bedford Street, Covent Garden, was elected on 17th March 1756 (on the proposal of Mr. Major) and became a perpetual subscriber in 1759, entitling him to attend the Society for the rest of his life. Society records give a full picture of Hollis's varied activities during his first years of membership, and by the middle of 1759 his *Diary* provides a valuable supplement.

Thomas Hollis attended his first meeting of the Society on 5th January 1757. He did not appear again until 23rd February, but thereafter his attendance became more regular. Society Minutes reveal his participation at meetings on 2nd, 9th, and 16th March, and the 23rd, when he proposed Matthew Duane, Esq., Lincoln's Inn, and Mr. Benjamin Ralph, Secretary's Office, Bank, for membership. These were the first of many men Hollis proposed for membership in the Society, and one of his important contributions during his association was in adding new supporters to the Society's ranks. On 30th March 1757 Hollis received his first committee appointment—one established to consider two letters describing processes for making saltpetre.[6] This was to be the beginning of committee service whose range and variety was equalled by few members during this period.

Hollis attended another Society meeting on 6th April 1757 and joined a committee on the 20th to evaluate a scheme Mr. Hooper proposed to award 'Premiums to Parishes (having Work-houses) for spinning Flax and Hemp by their Poor; and also a premium for the most practical, concise and best Scheme and Directions for the Management of a Parish Workhouse, and the Employment of the poor.' Also on the 20th Hollis proposed his dear friend and eventual heir, Thomas Brand, Esq., of Craven Street, Strand, a man who was to make important contributions as chairman of the committee on 'Polite Arts'.[7]

Hollis attended Society meetings on 27th April, on 4th and 18th May and on the 25th was appointed to a committee to consider a proposal to give a 'Premium for Inventing a Composition for enamelling Stone to be as free from Flaws or Blisters as copper or any other Metal enamelled is capable to be'. Society Minutes thereafter reveal his attendance on 1st June, 6th July, 7th and 21st September, and on 2nd November he joined a committee 'to provide the different Subjects for the various Premiums to be drawn for' and reported for in on 9th November. Hollis appeared five more times at the Society during 1757, on 16th, 23rd, and 30th November and 7th December, and on the 14th, when he was appointed to a committee 'to revise the Rules and Orders of the Society'.[8] In his first year of active membership in the Society Hollis had already displayed considerable vigour, and this was only a sample of the greater involvement to come.

Hollis received a wide variety of committee assignments in 1758 and evidently was interested in most aspects of the Society's extensive activities. On 4th January 1758 he joined a committee 'to determine the several Premiums for Drawings'; on 11th January committees 'to consider of proper Subjects for Premiums for the year ensuing' and 'what Manner Experiments are to be made on the Composition for securing Ships Bottoms from Worms and other external Injuries'; on 1st February Hollis and a large group were chosen 'to make Inquiry for a proper Place for the Reception of the Society', and on the same day he was asked to serve on a committee of correspondence. On 8th March 1758 Hollis and other Society members formed a committee to evaluate a proposal made by Dr. Tucker, who wished the Society to award an 'Honorary or Lucrative Premium to the person who shall compose the most useful History on the Arts, of the Peaceful Industry and Civil and Commercial Improvements within that part of Great Britain called England.' A week later, on 15th March, Hollis became a member of a committee to determine the premiums for various models made of clay, wax, and brown wax.[9]

Though the Society from the beginning was chiefly concerned with arts, manufactures and commerce, sometimes its activities had social and humanitarian overtones. This can be seen when on 22nd March 1758 Mr. Hanway proposed 'the giving a Premium for the best proposal or Plan for the Establishment of a Charity House or Charity Houses for the Reception and Employment of Girls whose poverty expose them to the Danger of becoming Prostitutes; also of such Common Prostitutes as are inclined to forsake their Evil Course of Life, and become Virtuous and useful Members of the Community.' A large and illustrious committee undertook the exploration of this issue, and besides Hollis its membership included John Wilkes, Samuel Johnson, David Garrick, Dr. Ramsay, Dr. Manningham, Thomas Brand and Hanway himself. Society Minutes show that by 17th May 1758 plans had been submitted with such mottoes as 'There is more Joy in Heaven over one Sinner that repenteth than over Ninety and nine just Persons that need no Repentence'; 'No complaining, no begging in the Streets'; 'Evils may be more easily prevented than cured'.[10]

More often, however, service on Society committees involved practical projects, and on 10th May 1758 Hollis accepted appointment to a committee to study a proposal by Sir George Savile to give a premium 'for producing the best Model in Wood of a Ship of certain Dimensions and which will soonest pass thro' an equal Space of Water'. Later in the month, on 31st May, Hollis received his most important assignment to date—on a committee to audit the treasurer's accounts. Then, as now, the finances

of an institution were of importance, and the fact that Hollis not only received this assignment but reported for it on 19th July suggests that he was
held in some esteem by his Society colleagues.[11]

Sir Henry Trueman Wood in his *History of the Royal Society of Arts*
states that 'The work done by the Society in encouraging the art of die-
sinking during the latter part of the eighteenth century deserves special
note' and shows that the improved character of British medals was related
to the Society's encouragement of this art form. In addition, citing Edward
Hawkins's *Medallic Illustrations of the History of Great Britain and Ireland* (1885), Wood says that various medals rewarded by the Society 'were
produced under the direction of Thomas Hollis, the republican writer, and
that he presented copies of the Goree medal [celebrating Admiral Keppel's
victory over the French in his capture of a small island of that name on
the west coast of Africa] to Pitt, Keppel, and Akenside'.[12] Thomas Hollis
was indeed active in the production of medals at this time. Society Minutes for 7th June 1758, for instance, show that Hollis took membership on
a committee to see that 'new Dies and new Puncheons be cut for a new
Medal, according to the Designs of Mr. Stuart, the value in Gold not to
be less than five nor to exceed Eight Guineas'. Some months later Society
Minutes for 18th October 1758 read: 'Mr. Thomas Hollis reported from
the Committee appointed to carry the Designs for the Medal into Execution, to whom was referred the consideration of appointing a proper
Subject for the Medallion, That they are of Opinion, That the said Subject
be as follows, viz: Liberty with her Attributes, on the Face, and the Barons
obtaining Magna Charta at Runing Med, on the Reverse.'[13]

Professor Robbins in her study of Hollis discusses how he disseminated
books, coins, medals and pictures 'illustrative of the history and principles
of liberty' and comments as well that Hollis 'regarded his taste for the arts
as something to be curbed in his disposition'.[14] In this particular instance,
however, his fervent support for liberty and his artistic impulses found a
common home in the proposed medal.

Although work on the production of a new medal occupied Hollis during the year, he did accept other assignments: on 2nd August he was appointed to another committee to attend to Society finances; on 1st November he joined Benjamin Franklin and others to inspect and try several hand
mills delivered to the Society; on 8th November he accepted appointments
to committees involved with premiums and ordinary business; and on 6th
December he and other Society members formed a committee 'to consider
of giving a Premium for encouraging the Growth of Cinnamon in Suma-

tra'.[15] In all, 1758 was a busy and productive year for Hollis, and the range and importance of his committee assignments suggest that his worth to the Society had been recognized.

Society Minutes record that on 10th January 1759 Mr. Shipley acquainted the Society that 'upwards of 60 Drawings were delivered in for the Premiums offered'.[16] Hollis, Joshua Reynolds and a number of other members were chosen to evaluate them, and to trace the deliberations of this committee on 'Drawings' is to see the seriousness with which the Society conducted itself in this particular area. One sees as well that Hollis played an important rôle since he took the chair in committee meetings held on 16th, 22nd, 27th and 30th January, 3rd and 8th February and reported for the committee on 14th February.[17]

Minutes for 30th January and 8th February reveal that one of the committee's concerns was to ensure the authenticity of work submitted, and precautions were taken to prevent tracing or other plagiarism. On 30th January, for instance, 'Mr. Brand acquainted the committee, That Mr. Cipriani [Gresse's Master] had assured him, that the Drawing produced by Gresse was fairly & intirely his own Performance, and That he thought him a very diligent Youth. His Grace the Duke of Richmond acquainted the Committee the above Gresse was drawing from his Grace's Collection & was very diligent.' On 8th February Hollis himself 'acquainted the Committee, That the several Candidates had in order to give Proof of their Abilities drawn before Mr. Long Mr. Brand & himself, pursuant to the Resolution of the last Meeting and the Specimens of the Candidates were produced to the committee.'

On 14th February Hollis reported the committee's decisions to the Society with the following comment: 'The Chairman of the above Committee having recommended to the Consideration of the Society the Extraordinary merit of Miss Mary Moser who gained the first Premium in class 63, a Silver Medal was order'd to be presented to her as a further Reward for such her Extraordinary Merit; and that the Inscriptions on the Reverse of the said Medal be, round The Wreath TO MARY MOSER and within the Wreath FOR A FLOWER PIECE MDCCIX.' This particular picture now rests at the Society, and one might accept as did Hollis and the committee in 1759 that it is a piece of 'extraordinary merit'.[18]

By following Hollis's service to the Society in 1759 one gains not only an insight into its interest in encouraging the arts but into a variety of other schemes it promoted as well. On 4th April 1759, for example, Hollis was asked to join a committee 'to examine the several Blocks of Ships delivered in the Society for the Premium offered for that Article'; on 9th May he became a member of a committee to examine 'A Proposal of Mr. Wyche's relating to the Preservation of Foreign foods'; and on 20th June he became a member of a committee 'to consider a parcel of Flax or Yarn dyed green' which had to conclude on 4th July with Hollis in attendance 'That the same is not worthy of any Premium the Colour thereof being bad & easily discharged'.[19] Happily such failures were often offset by successes.

On 19th December 1759 Hollis was asked with other Society members to investigate 'A very curious Lock made by Mr. Edward Gascoigne' and on the 24th 'Mr. Gascoigne having taken the said Lock to Pieces before the said committee and likewise given a Particular Description thereof, and he having acquainted them that it is intirely his own Invention [the committee] are of Opinion that the said Mr. Gascoigne be rewarded with a Bounty of Ten Guineas for his Ingenuity in making the said Lock.'[20] Though Society records give a full account of Gascoigne's successful lock, the Hollis *Diary* provides further information which is of some value.

Hollis writes on 24th December: 'At a Committee of the Soc. for promot. arts & comm. to assist Gascoigne, a very ingenious Locksmith, towards obtaining a small portion of the £200 allowed by the Society to be distributed among ingenious Mechanics etc. etc.' This entry is innocuous enough, but it does reveal what the committee minutes do not—the information that Hollis went to the meeting not so much as a neutral observer of the lock but as a partisan bent on supporting Gascoigne and his ingenious mechanism. The Hollis *Diary* in this case confirms what one naturally suspects—that work went on behind the scenes and that however impartial the Society's committee system appeared, it did not operate in a political vacuum.

Hollis's contributions to the Society during 1760 were great, and his name is found throughout Society records. Once again he displayed an interest in many areas of Society activities, though a great portion of his energies was devoted to 'Polite Arts'. If 1760 was for Hollis a period of intense activity in Society affairs, it was also the time when the beginnings of his disaffection with the institution are first seen, and one may, with reference to his *Diary,* make some assessment why he left the Society's ranks a few years hence.

On 2nd January 1760 'A Motion was made by Mr. Fitzherbert, That a Committee be appointed to consider what Officers are proper and necessary for the Society and of the Stipends fitting for them.' A large committee was named which included Hollis as well as the president and vice presidents of the Society. It met on 12th and 19th January and on 2nd February, each time with Hollis in attendance, and prepared an extensive report proposing among other things 'That there ought to be a Secretary and an Assistant Secretary to the Society: The propriety and even necessity of this Additional Officer they apprehend arises from the great increase of Business both in Quantity and Quality.'[21] One might assume by his appointment and attendance at committee meetings that Hollis made some contribution, but his *Diary,* rather than formal Society records, reveals its true significance.

On 12th January 1760, the date of the first meeting of the 'Officers' committee, Hollis writes in his *Diary* 'Within the morning. Dined at a tavern with Mr. Brand. In the evening at the Committee for promot. arts and comm. "To consider what offices are proper and necessary for the Society, & of the stipends fitting for them." Suggested a scheme of such offices, which had the honor to be unanimously approved of; & which I am not without hopes will fully answer the purposes of this ingenious & most noble Society.' On 2nd February 1760 he writes again in his *Diary*: 'In the evening at a Committee of the Society for promot. arts and Commerce "To consider what offices are proper and necessary for the Society, and of the stipends fitting for them". The proceedings of the Committee compleated, effectively on the scheme thrown out by me jan. 12; and in general good temper of the Members of it, and the Report ordered to be made on Wednesday next.' Hollis does not indulge in self-praise, even within the private confines of his *Diary,* but one may detect a note of satisfaction in his entry for 6th February 1760, when writing in reference to the above he says that 'the same was confirmed, in a very full assembly, and after an ample & noble exemplification of them'.

In one instance a *Diary* entry reveals the tensions of Society meetings not seen in the more discreet minutes. On 27th February 1760 Hollis attended the Society and 'proposed the appointing a day for the annual dinner as usual, which was intended to have been dropped by the President [Lord Folkestone] and some of his friends, without taking notice of it in the Society. Carried the proposition unanimously, but sorely against the Presidents inclination.' Hollis does not use emotional language, and if he reports that Lord Folkestone was 'sorely' tried by his proposal, this must have been the case. Perhaps he had second thoughts about his successful gambit, for his entry on 11th March 1760 concerning the dinner is restrained: 'Dined at the St. Albans Tavern at the annual dinner of the Society for promot. arts and commerce', he writes, 'in consequence of a motion made by me feb. 27, in the Society to that end.'

It is doubtful whether Lord Folkestone could have held Hollis's minor parliamentary triumph against him for long, for at this time he was obviously a respected member of the Society. Indeed, on the day of his dinner-vote victory he joined Dr. Manningham, Mr. Ramsay, Thomas Brand, Captain Blake, Israel Wilkes and others on a committee to consider the request from Mr. Francis Hayman, chairman of the Committee of Artists, to use the Society's room for their exhibition. On 5th March 1760 Hollis was appointed to a committee to 'form a proper Method of Ballotting for the new Secretary consistent with the Rules and Orders of the Society'; on 17th March he joined a committee charged with giving 'Directions for placing the Tables and Benches in the most commodious Manner for the Members to come up to the Ballotting Glass and return from Thence'; and on 30th April Hollis along with Benjamin Franklin, John Ellis, Thomas Brand, Dr. Manningham and Joshua Steele formed a committee to consider a letter by Mr. Wyche 'relating to Improvements in Agriculture'.[22]

Committee assignments were settled on 12th November 1760, and Hollis is listed in committees of 'Correspondence' and 'Premiums'. On 19th November the minutes indicate that 'Mr. Hollis desired Leave to decline being Chairman of "Polite Arts," ' though his good friend, Thomas Brand, accepted the post, and it is clear that he and Hollis in their vigorous conduct of this committee's affairs acted as co-chairmen.[23] The Hollis *Diary* again provides a valuable supplement to Society records concerning the work of this committee, as well as Hollis's other Society activities.

Hollis writes in his *Diary* for 23rd May 1760: 'Dr. Templeman with me in the morning to settle the Premiums for polite arts, which are proposed to be given this Year by the Society for P.A.C. for publication', another entry which shows that Society business took place outside as well as within its walls. The fabric of Hollis's life during 1760 was, in fact, dominated by his relationship with the Society, as a *Diary* entry for 13th June suggests: 'In the morning Dr Templeman with me on Society affairs. . . . In the evening at a Committee of the Society for promoting arts and commerce. Walked afterwards a turn on Constitution hill with Capt. Blake.' On this particular day, then, Hollis was involved from morning to night either with Society affairs or with its members.

If Hollis passed pleasant hours at the Society of Arts, at least one meeting of 'Polite Arts' disturbed him deeply—so much so that he writes about it at great length in his *Diary*. This entry suggests, moreover, that committee meetings were not always the decorous affairs reported in the minutes but could be somewhat acrimonious occasions. Hollis writes for 20th December 1760:

In the evening at a Committee of the Soc. P.A.C. on polite arts, to reconsider the Drawings given in for the Premium for Landskapes, in consequence of some things thrown out by me in the Society on Wednesday last to shew that the Committee had, probably, adjudged the first premium wrong. This Committee unwilling to begin or take another ballot on the drawings the names of the Candidates being then all known, & drew up a Resolution to that end for the Report to the Society. Mr. Kirby, an ingenious artist (tho' little known to me,) at the Committee, and his behaviour there ill-humoured & petulant to me, his Son having gained the first premium in the Landskapes, though I apprehend he was really intituled only to the second, or rather the third; but I disreguarded & despised it wholly having the testimony of my own Mind for the integrity & disinterestedness of, my proceedure in this affair.

A further *Diary* entry, on 31st December 1760, reveals that Hollis was somewhat resigned to his defeat: 'At a meeting of the Society for promoting arts & Commerce', he writes: 'The Society confirmed the premium on the Landskapes. Said nothing on the occasion, nor anyone else. Glad the affair ended in this manner *upon the whole,* as the method of deciding on premiums for drawing is now settled so as to prevent a like inconvenience in the future.'

Hollis suffered a second disappointment during 1760 when he became involved in William Bailey's unsuccessful attempt to gain the post of Registrar of the Society. That Hollis became involved at all in this election seems somewhat strange in light of Professor Robbins's comments about his distrust of the political life of his time. She writes: 'Hollis not only did not stand for Parliament; he never cast a vote in his life. The whole political system upset and disgusted him. He wept when he saw in March 1768 the "dirty bankrupt" Blehr parading before Borough electors soliciting votes. His letters are full of horror at court influence and heavy bribery.' Whatever his political views were, Hollis was politically active in the Society during 1760 and found, perhaps to his discomfort, that even in a model parliamentary democracy like the Society of Arts majority rule can seem a stern tyrant indeed.[24]

Hollis comments at some length in his *Diary* about the assistance he gave William Bailey in his attempt to secure the post of Registrar, and for all that he apparently disdained the crass realities of the political process, for a time Hollis found himself acting something like a modern campaign manager. On 30th September 1760 he wrote in his *Diary:* 'Mr. Bailey with me in the evening to desire my Vote for Register of the Society for P.A.C. now becoming vacant by the intended Resignation of Mr. Shipley, & for

which place he thinks to offer himself a Candidate. Assured him of my regard for him & disposition to serve him, believing him to be an ingenious
& worthy man, and fit for that place; but said I could not give him an
absolute promise of my Vote till I knew all the Candidates.' Hollis's comments are interesting since they show clearly that candidates campaigned
for Society offices, and Bailey probably approached Hollis not simply for
his vote but because he had a certain amount of influence among Society
members. In subsequent *Diary* entries it becomes clear that Hollis was
more than a passive supporter of Bailey's cause.

On 13th November 1760 he comments: 'Sent for the ingenious but unfortunate & indigent Mr William Bailey, now a Candidate for the place of
register at the Society for promoting arts and commerce; gave him some
information & advice which I hope may be useful to him, and desired him
to accept of five guineas to enable him to go through the expenses of can-
vassing more easily.' A few days later, on 16th November Hollis writes:
'In the evening Mr. Bailey with me for three hours, to consult with me
in reguard to his canvess for Register of the Society for promot. arts &
comm.' From such entries it is clear that if Hollis avoided the heat of direct
political battle he was willing to give aid behind the scenes. His efforts,
however, were futile, and he was once again overruled by the majority. He
records Bailey's defeat in a *Diary* entry for 4th December 1760: 'At the
Society for promot. arts & commerce to vote for a Register in the place
of Mr. Shipley who had resigned. Voted for the ingenious Mr. Bailey, who
however lost the Election, Mr. Tuckwell being chosen.'

In 1760, then, Hollis enjoyed some political success within Society
circles and suffered reverses as well. Although a pragmatist might concentrate on the former, it is possible Hollis was unable to avoid fixing on the
latter, and the seeds of the discontent that ultimately caused his separation
from the Society might have been sown at this time.

Whatever disappointment Thomas Hollis experienced from the rebuffs
over the landscape premium and Bailey's defeat, he continued to serve
the Society with vigour throughout 1761, concentrating again on 'Polite
Arts', which elected him chairman.[25] In his *Diary* for 18th November he
writes, however: 'At the Soc. P.A.C. Had the honor of being chosen there
Chairman of the Committee of Polite Arts. Excused myself from accepting of that Chair, as last year, pursuant to the Resolution which I have
long since taken, of not accepting any distinct honors.' Hollis and Brand
continued to work closely on the committee, and it settled numerous premiums on painting, drawing, sculpture, and other objects of art. The Hollis
Diary provides a fairly full record of the activities of this committee. On

27th March 1761 he records: 'At a Committee of the S.P.A.C. Established the Premiums for Marble Statues, Marble Basso rilievo's, & for Dies for Medals. Produced several Medals belonging to my own Cabinet to the Committee, & spoke to them & the Subject of Medals, nationally considered, with honesty & warmth.' Hollis evidently enjoyed sharing his knowledge with others and apparently did not hesitate to offer his opinions as well. On 18th May 1761 he writes in his *Diary:* 'Mr. Fitzherbert breakfasted with me. Much conversation with him relating to the dies & medals which are shortly to be made for his Majesty; and concerning the propriety of a premium being proposed at the Soc. p.a.c. for the die of a Guinea. Totally against this last proposition, & assigned my reasons.'

In supporting Bailey's quest for the post of Registrar Hollis showed an ability to judge character; two *Diary* entries in July 1761 reveal his artistic judgement as well, as he came to the aid of Joseph Nollekens, a pupil of William Shipley's and one of the outstanding sculptors of the period. On 17th July he writes: 'At Mr. Nollekens to view a model of a basso relievo, which he designs to execute for a Premium given out by the Society for promoting arts & commerce.' On 24th July he adds: 'At Mr. Nollekens to assist him what little matter I may be able about his intended Basso relievo for the Premium of the Soc. promot. arts & comm.' Again it appears that committee business was conducted behind the scenes, though in retrospect one can hardly fault Hollis for whatever assistance he gave to this fine artist.

As in previous years Hollis's Society activities were not confined to 'Polite Arts', and one is impressed by the range of his assignments. Along with other members he turned his attention to matters great and small. On 15th January, for instance, he joined a committee at which 'Mr Kitchin's Letter concerning a Machine for taking Rats alive was read. Mr Kitchin was called in, and shewed his Machine. Resolved, That it is the Opinion of this Committee, That Mr Kitchin's Machine is upon an old principle and of no peculiar merit'. A few days later, on 21st January, Hollis had rapidly ascended the chain of being and turned from a consideration of a better rattrap to a committee charged with drawing up an address to the King. On 4th March 1761 he was appointed to a committee 'to consider in what Manner to make the great Room more convenient, and to contain more Members than at present'; on 1st July he became a member of a committee to evaluate 'Mr. Jackson's Patent and Specification for making Isinglass'; and on 25th November Hollis and a distinguished group of men, including Captain Blake, Nicholas Crisp, Dr. Maty, Samuel Johnson, Robert Dossie, Benjamin Franklin and Thomas Brand were appointed to investigate a process 'to keep water sweet and wholesome'.[26]

Although *Diary* references to other aspects of Society activities at this time besides 'Polite Arts' are infrequent and brief, some are of interest. On 3rd March 1761 Hollis writes in his *Diary,* concerning the annual election: '[It was] well made, although a President & four New Vice presidents were to be chosen', a comment which suggests that even within the civilized, parliamentary confines of the Society an orderly election was not to be taken for granted. Another entry, for 21st May 1761, reveals that Hollis witnessed one of the Society's more celebrated trials—that of Ambrose Godfrey's ingenious process to extinguish fires. Hollis writes: 'At the building lately fired by order of the S.P.A.C. to trye Mr Godfrey's method of extinguishing fires, to view it.'[27]

No scheme attracted more attention during 1761, however, than Captain John Blake's to provide inland areas with fresh fish. Once again the Hollis *Diary* provides information not available in Society records and shows clearly his opposition to Blake's idea. On 4th November he comments: 'At the Society for promoting arts & Commerce, at which a proposition was made by Dr. Manningham, & seconded by Mr. V. President Eckersal [*sic*], for allowing the Sum of £2000 towards carrying into execution a scheme (offered by Capt. Blake) for better supplying the town with fish by land carriage or otherwise. The proposition carried with a high hand; yet voted against it heartily; not because the Idea of encouraging the Fishery for supplying the town more effectively with fish is not a right one but because the scheme *as tendered* was crude & big with great novelties & inconvenience to the Society.' A week later, on 11th November 1761, Hollis records that 'The strange proposition of Dr. Manningham's of this day sev'night was confirmed', but, he adds, 'held up my hand, with some *few* other persons against it, as before'. Hollis was again outvoted, and perhaps this event contributed further to his disaffection with the Society. While he apparently envisaged some of the difficulties the fish scheme presented, his attitude evinced a conservatism somewhat inconsistent with the Society's enthusiastic early years.[28]

Hollis remained active in the Society during 1762 and continued to give generously of his time, not only to 'Polite Arts', which prospered under his leadership and Thomas Brand's, but in other areas as well. On 17th March, for example, he was appointed to a committee to purchase books, and on 5th May he joined a committee to look into the problem of giving Dr. Templeman 'a proper Person to assist him in carrying on the Affairs of the Society with greater Dispatch'. The day before its consideration by the Society William Shipley consulted Hollis about his important scheme for a Repository of Arts. Hollis writes for 11th May 1762: 'Mr Shipley with me for an hour to communicate a scheme which he intends to lay before the Society for promoting arts & commerce & believes an excellent one, but which appears to me to be big with inconveniences.' On 26th May 1762 he and others formed a committee to look into repairs to the Great Room, and on 21st July he signed a petition along with a number of Society members concerned about the safety of their meeting place 'to remove the Meetings of the Society to some other place for one Month'. On 15th December he and a committee were named to consider 'A Letter from Mr Shipley . . . containing a Proposal for improving the Fishery of this Kingdom.'[29]

While there are many references to the Society in the *Diary* during 1762, most are brief, though they show that the Society still figured prominently in Hollis's life and he is careful to record his attendance. On 10th March 1762 he comments: 'At the Soc. promot. arts & comm. Staid till near 12.' On 17th March he writes: 'At a morning Committee of polite arts to determine on models in clay. Dined at Townsends with Mr. Brand and Mr. Lloyd. At the Soc. promot. arts & commerce.'

Hollis's participation in Society affairs is noticeably reduced in 1763, though references to his activities are still frequent in Society records and his *Diary*. Society Minutes show that on 19th January 1763 Hollis was appointed once again to the Exhibition committee; on 1st March he received one vote for Vice President; and on 30th November he joined a committee to consider a motion made 'that Certificates be given by the Society with the Pecuniary Premiums and Bounties to such Candidates as shall be thought Deserving.'[30]

From a *Diary* entry written on 28th February 1763 it appears that Hollis's advice was still solicited. He writes: 'Mr. Shirley Chairman of the Committee of trade, & Mr. John White of Newgate street, hatter, with me there by appointment, from 5 to 7 to consider of the best method of establishing premiums for English straw & chip hats, for fullest employment of the Poor.' On 13th August a *Diary* entry indicates another service Hollis performed for the Society: 'Busy the whole morning in preparing a number of the publications of the Soc. promot. arts & comm. for dispersion about the Country', an activity he was similarly engaged in according to an entry for 19th August. On 22nd November he states in his *Diary* that he was with 'Dr. Templeman, on affairs relating to the Society for promoting arts & commerce' and finally, on 29th December he reports he 'Delivered a small box containing eight of the publications of the Society for promoting arts & commerce' to a party in Switzerland.

References to Hollis in Society records apparently cease in 1764, though his *Diary* shows he was still concerned with its affairs. On 10th January

1764 he writes: 'At Mrs. Stranges, by invitation, to see a drawing of her eldest daughter's, a pretty one, which she proposes to put into the Society for promot. arts & comm. for a premium.'[31] Later in the year on 28th November he records in his *Diary:* 'Sir William Dalrymple with me to seek information relating to Persons skilled in metallurgy in this Town & likewise in the likelyest methods of exciting emulation & increasing knowledge in Ores, and the several processes relating to them, with a view to the County of Cornwall in particular, by premiums to be constituted by the Society for promot. arts & Commerce. Gave him the information I was able to give, readily.'

Again in 1765 there are no apparent references to Hollis in the Society's records, though one *Diary* entry for 22nd March shows that he had not lost touch completely. He writes: 'With Dr. Templeman to desire him pursuance of Mr. Valltravers request to me in his last letter, to cause that learned & excellent Gentleman Frederic Samuel Schmidt of Berne in Switzerland to be elected honorary Member of the Society for promoting arts & commerce, which he promised. Subscribed in the Society's book ten Guineas toward the Building that is intended to be erected for the use of that Society.'

Hollis's separation from the Society evidently was absolute during 1766, 1767, and 1768, but before he left London in 1770 to retire to his property in the country he returned once again. He did not participate to any great extent, and his final visits seem more a farewell to an institution to which he had devoted so much time for over half a decade. An entry in his *Diary* for 19th December 1769 is particularly interesting:

> At a Committee of the Society for promoting arts and commerce in the Strand; on a reference to it to consider, whether it will be proper for the Society [to] continue where they are or to remove elsewhere. Urged strenuously the fitness of the Society's possessing a House of their own point of conveniency, profit and decorum. The whole Committee came into that opinion; but as the matter is of great importance, the further consideration of it was deferred till friday Jan. 11. This is the first time, that I have been at the Society [or] any of its Committees of many years. But our disgusts should end; the agony of my own private studies and plan, thank God, is passed; I have always wished well to this useful Society under all its irregularities; and the present, appeared to me to be a great occasion, in relation to it.

On 11th January 1770 Hollis writes again in his *Diary* about his return to the Society: 'At a weekly meeting of the Society in the Strand; after an absence of many years from those meetings. Lord Romney was in the

Chair. Was very kindly received by his Lordship and the Members most of whom were of my antient acquaintance.' On 12th January he refers once again to the discussion about finding new quarters for the Society: 'At a Committee of the S.P.A.C. on the matter before agitated dec. 29, the fitness of seeking out obtaining a permanent dwelling house for the Society. Supported my former opinion, which was much controverted, & will, probably, as expected, be soon finally disagreed to in the Society.'

Hollis reports in his *Diary* that he attended a Society meeting on 17th January and in two subsequent references mentions the heated election for the post of Secretary. On 23rd January he writes: 'At the Society in the Strand to give my ballot for a new Secretary.' Of the three candidates, Samuel More, John Stewart, and Timothy Brecknock, Hollis gave his vote to More, finding him 'the least enestimable' of the group—not a particularly happy reflection on the political state of affairs at the time but understandable, perhaps, to a twentieth century reader.[32] Hollis's reaction to the outcome of the election which he reports in his *Diary* for 24th January is brief and impassive: 'At a weekly meeting of the Society in the Strand. It seems Mr. Moore [*sic*] was elected on the ballot by a great Majority, and he took his place in the Society as Secretary, accordingly at this meeting.'

The last *Diary* reference to the Society is found in an entry for 3rd April 1770, when Hollis writes: 'At S. for P.A.C. in the Strand. Stayed there from 7 to 10½. The Scots are very intriguing in that Society. Helped prevent some Mischief of theirs.' Just who the intriguing Scots were and what mischief Hollis prevented is, unfortunately, impossible to answer. Committee Minutes show that Hollis attended meetings of 'Chemistry' on 14th April, 'Agriculture' on 23rd April, and, rather appropriately, his final appearance at the Society was at 'Polite Arts' on 15th June 1770.[33]

Hollis bequeathed a small legacy to the Society on his death in 1774, and information about it is found in the Society's *Miscellaneous Transactions*. On 2nd March 1774 there is the comment: 'The following Letter from Thomas Brand Hollis Esq[r] addressed to the R[t]. Hono[ble] Lord Romney with a Bank Note value one hundred Pounds inclosed having been received Thanks were order'd to Mr. Brand Hollis for this early Notice and payment of the Legacy and the Bank Note therein inclosed was delivered to the Collector.'

The letter itself reads:

My Lord,
 I have the honour to acquaint your Lordships, that the late Thomas Hollis Esqr member of the Society of Arts & Commerce over which your Lordship

so emminently presides, to testify his regard and esteem, has in his will left the following devise. I give to the Noble Society instituted for promoting Arts and Commerce in the Strand London one hundred pounds which I have taken the liberty to inclose to your Lordship.

This letter was signed by Thomas Brand Hollis, 1st March 1774, Pall Mall.

Thomas Hollis did indeed 'testify his regard and esteem' for the Society of Arts, and in no way more clearly than in his generous expenditure of time and energy in its meetings and in the work of its various committees, especially 'Polite Arts'. Though eschewing the formal prerogatives of power, Hollis was nevertheless a powerful and influential member of the Society during its early formative years, and his *Diary* and Society records reflect this fact. One can, after examining these resources, hardly exaggerate the importance of his contributions, and in noting their range and variety one can risk an assertion which could be made about few Society members—that without Hollis the development of the Society in the late 1750s and early 1760s would not have been the same. Hollis was for a time so central to the Society that to trace his work there is to see the institution itself in operation. In her brilliant study of Hollis, Professor Robbins suggests that this self-effacing man may have provided some of the intellectual combustibles for the American Revolution. If this claim is too large for some to accept, they might agree with a less dramatic conclusion that Thomas Hollis was in part responsible for the quieter revolution in the eighteenth century called the Society of Arts.

NICHOLAS CRISP, FOUNDING MEMBER
OF THE SOCIETY OF ARTS

J. V. G. Mallet

The earliest historian of the Society of Arts tells us that when William Shipley moved to London in 1753 to found the Society, 'the only persons that he was acquainted with at this time in London, who were capable of forwarding his design were, Mr. Henry Baker, Mr. Messiter and Mr. Crispe'.[1] All these men were among the eleven who attended the first meeting of the Society at Rawthmell's Coffee House on 22nd March 1754, when men of science like Baker and professional men like the surgeon Messiter linked themselves under the patronage of the nobility to promote the arts, manufactures and commerce of their country. Many of the earliest members of the Society have their memorials in print; but because the life of Nicholas Crisp, jeweller and would-be porcelain-maker, ended in failure, posterity has by and large rewarded him with neglect. In this paper, the writer hopes to show that Crisp deserved somewhat better of his countrymen, not least because of the services he rendered to the Society of Arts.

Nicholas Crisp was born about 1704, second son of 'Thomas Crispe of Witham in the County of Essex Draper and Ffreeman and Citizen of London', who died when Nicholas was about four. The late Aubrey Toppin has speculated that Nicholas may have been named after the seventeenth-

Originally appeared in *Jnl. RSA*, 120 (Dec., 1972), 28-32; 121 (Jan.-Feb., 1973), 92-96, 170-74.

century loyalist Sir Nicholas Crisp, who invented a system for making bricks, but the relationship between the two men seems never to have been established.[2] Under his father's will Nicholas was to inherit property consisting of the 'Three Mariners with the Outhouses', two cottages, 'and alsoe all that newly erected Tenement with the yard &c.' in the occupation of 'Emanuel Bayley, Weaver or his Assignees'.[3] Nicholas was also to have £300.

By the eighteenth century the choice of a City Company was often little indication of the trade a man was to pursue. Whatever his father's real profession had been, Nicholas was on 3rd July 1719 bound apprentice for seven years to John Michael Harnigh of Forster Lane, Jeweller, whose City Company was not the Goldsmiths' but the Haberdashers'. For some reason Crisp did not become free until 5th May 1732, when the records of the Haberdashers' Company show him as 'Nicholas Crispe of Bucklersbury, Jeweller, freed by John Michael Harnigh of Gould Street, Jeweller'. Crisp joined the Livery the same day. Nothing seems known about his master, though Sir Ambrose Heal has recorded a jeweller called Michael Harnick as being at Warwick Lane in 1753.

Almost at once, on 9th June 1732, Crisp himself took an apprentice, Thomas Flavell, son of a Clerkenwell blacksmith. On 7th May 1736, he took another, Thomas Knight, the son of a Basingstoke innkeeper. Both apprenticeships were for the usual period of seven years, and on each occasion Crisp's address is given as Bucklersbury and his profession as 'Jeweller'. When Flavell was freed on 3rd September 1742 by 'Nicholas Crisp, Bow Churchyard, Jeweller' he was described as of 'Wood Street, Jeweller'. He is probably the Thomas Flavill, Jeweller, recorded by Heal as being at Carey Lane in 1753. Knight was not freed until 2nd May 1764, when he was described as of 'Nevills Court, Fetter Lane, Merchant'.[4] Two further apprentices of Crisp's, John Bacon and Edward Crisp, will be mentioned later.

The Land-Tax Registers preserved in the Guildhall Library show that Crisp was established in his new premises at Bow Churchyard, Cheapside, in 1740. From the same source it appears that in 1754 he took two other premises adjoining one another and ten doors away from his original house, which argues for expansion or change in the nature of his business. Both before and after his move to Bow Churchyard, he was known as a jeweller, and he was still listed as such in *Mortimer's Director* of 1763.[5] But since he is not known to have registered a mark at the Goldsmiths' Hall, his work is likely to remain unrecognized. Indeed he may have been more a retailer than a maker of jewellery; he certainly traded in precious stones. The writer has not, however, found the evidence that presumably underlies the statement made in the various editions of Britten and Baillie, that Crisp was a watchmaker from 1754 to 1759.[6]

In 1736 Crisp was married in St. Mildred's, Poultry. The entry in the church register reads:

> October First.
> Nicholas Crisp of St. Bennet Sherehog London Batchelor, & Mary Whitaker of St. John Hackney in com. Middlesex Spinster.[7]

The register says nothing about Mary Whitaker's parents, so it would be hard to find out whether the marriage brought Crisp any appreciable increase in wealth.

Crisp's business interests were not confined to jewellery, for in 1741 he and his elder brother Thomas, who was a diamond-cutter, speculated together on a ship bound for the East Indies,[8] and by the 1760s, as we shall see, the Crisps were heavily involved in this type of investment.

Around 1751 Crisp seems, like several other jewellers and silversmiths of his day, to have become interested in the new and risky trade of making procelain, a material which was in direct competition with gold and silver for many uses. In partnership with a Lambeth potter called John Sanders he took a licence to mine soaprock on Lord Falmouth's estate in Cornwall for a ten-year period, dating from 24th June 1751.[9] Cornish soaprock was already in use at this date as an ingredient of the soft-paste porcelain made at Benjamin Lund's porcelain factory in Bristol, soon to be bought out by the Worcester factory, who continued to use this ingredient. It has recently come to light that Crisp actually took delivery of 29 tons 12 hundredweight of Cornish soaprock, paying £28 3s. 6d. for it on 14th November 1752.[10]

The John Sanders who shared Crisp's soaprock concession was presumably a maker of tin-glazed earthenwares (delftwares) and clearly had an interest in new methods, for the *Public Advertiser* for 8th February 1754 carried an announcement concerning the Dublin Delftware manufacturer, John Delamain: 'We hear that Mr. Delamain the inventor of the kiln for burning white glazed earthenware with pitcoal instead of wood, has lodged a model of his kiln with the ingenious Mr. Sanders, potter of Vauxhall, etc.'[11] By about 1761 John Sanders is known to have taken into partnership over his pottery business in Glasshouse Street, Vauxhall (then reckoned part of the Parish of Lambeth), a certain Henry Richards.[12] But since we hear nothing of Crisp in connection with delftware, and nothing of Richards in connection with soaprock or porcelain, John Sanders may have kept the two ventures financially separate.

Some researches by the late Aubrey Toppin suggest that the porcelain venture may have been conducted at premises in Nine Elms, near the boundaries of Battersea and Vauxhall, then rated in the Parish of Battersea. Toppin found in the Battersea Rate Books the single entry 'Saunders and Crisp for Territthouse', and other entries for 'Saunders & Co.'[13] The Volume of the Battersea Rate-Books for 1752-8 has at some time been rebound, with many pages missing and others in the wrong order and, worse still, the page numbers have mostly been trimmed off by the binders. This is serious, because only at the beginning of each quarter does a date appear. Toppin seems to have been only partly aware of this problem, and the dates he gives for various entries must therefore be treated with reserve. At the bottom of each page of entries, there is a total sum, and since the total from each page was added up at the end of the entries for every quarter, one often has warning when a page is out of place. Thus Toppin's entry 'Saunders & Crisp for Territt [or as seems more likely, Turret] house' is almost certainly out of sequence, and should probably be dated in the second or third quarter of 1752 rather than in the first quarter of 1754. Whatever the low-rated Turret or Territt house may have been, it appears to have given way to a more valuable 'Mill and 2 houses' soon after Saunders & Co moved in. It is of course impossible to tell whether Crisp retained an interest in this Nine Elms site during the whole or part of the period between the fourth quarter of 1752 and the third quarter of 1757, when the properties were rated to Saunders and Co. Thereafter comes a gap until the second quarter of 1760, when a more reliably bound volume shows the properties that interest us under the name of Sanders' new partner: 'Hen^y. Richards & Comp^y'. The last mention of Richards is for the last two quarters of 1766.

All we can deduce from this is that if the Nine Elms Site was taken by Crisp and Sanders in 1752, the year when Crisp and Sanders are known to have taken delivery of Cornish soaprock, then there is a strong probability that this is the place where they attempted to make porcelain. We can only guess how long they may have persisted, for it is possible that if the porcelain proved unrewarding, Sanders (later in partnership with Richards) might have found other uses for the site. The extra premises taken by Crisp at Bow Churchyard half-way through 1754 could even have been used as showrooms for the porcelain: it might be more than coincidence that these rooms were given up at about the same time as Richards & Co gave up the Nine Elms site. Speculation apart, it is worth bearing in mind the facts about the Nine Elms site (which locals probably thought of as lying in Vauxhall) when considering what we can learn of Crisp's porcelain venture from the careers of John Bolton and John Bacon.

John Bolton was an experienced potter who declared in the course of a lawsuit that he had been employed by Crisp and Sanders at their China factory at Vauxhall but had been induced to leave and set up a 'Porcelain Manufactory' at Kentish Town at Whitsuntide in 1755.[14]

Shortly after Bolton's departure, John Bacon, later famous as a sculptor, was apprenticed to Nicholas Crisp on 7th June 1755.[15] Bacon's earliest biography states that Crisp had 'a Manufactory of china at Lambeth, which Mr. Bacon sometimes attended'.[16] Later biographers progressively embroidered on the theme of what exactly Bacon did at the factory. The Reverend Richard Cecil says in his obituary of the artist that Bacon was employed in 'painting on porcelain' and in 'forming shepherds, shepherdesses and suchlike ornamental pieces'. In eighteenth-century English, 'ornamental pieces' is as likely to have meant painted decoration as modelled figures. Cecil continues: 'Yet for a self-taught artist to perform even works like these with taste, and in less than two years form (as he did) all the models for the manufactory, was to give indications of no ordinary powers'. The use of the phrase 'in less than two years' could be taken to mean that less than two years after Bacon was apprenticed, and long before he took his freedom, his master gave up the attempt to make porcelain. It is also worth remembering that in an eighteenth-century context the 'models' for the factory are as likely to have been the master moulds for such things as spouts and handles as for ceramic figures.

Crisp's porcelain has never been identified. Because John Bacon later became a sculptor it has usually been assumed that he modelled figures for Crisp, though the evidence for this is rather suspect. Because Crisp had premises near St. Mary le Bow in the City, confusion has even arisen between his factory and the quite distinct Bow porcelain factory near Stratford, Essex. One group of porcelain, however, has recently been brought into question as possibly from Crisp's Vauxhall factory, and that is the so-called 'A-Marked' class of porcelains. The thought has even crossed the present writer's mind that the letter 'A', found either incised or painted in underglaze blue beneath some of these wares, might stand for 'Arts', testifying to Crisp's connection with the Society of Arts. But the Society would not have liked to be associated with an individual manufacturer in this way, and Crisp would surely not have risked giving such a cause for offence. Other possible makers of the 'A-Marked' wares cannot yet be eliminated, and all that can at present be said is that these porcelains are quite possibly of Crisp's making.[17]

While he was pursuing his careers as jeweller and porcelain-maker, and in the year he helped found the Society of Arts, Nicholas Crisp's name appeared at the head of six others as co-author of a book entitled *A Refu-*

*tation of Sir Crisp Gascoyne's Address to the Liverymen of London by a
Clear State of the Case of Elizabeth Canning. . . .*[18] The book was pub-
lished in 1754 by J. Payne, who was also one of its authors, and we can feel
confident that this is no confusion with some other Nicholas Crisp, for the
Minutes of the Society of Arts show that in the following year 'Mr. Crisp
presented to the Society from the Editor, Mr. Payne, a Book in 8vo Neatly
Bound in blue Morocco, gilt and letter'd, intitled Sculptura or the Art of
Chalcography, by John Evelyn Esq'.[19]

Elizabeth Canning, to whose case Crisp and his co-authors devoted so
much time, was a poor servant girl who claimed to have been first robbed
and then dragged to a brothel, where she alleged that she was intimidated
until such time as she should herself become a prostitute.

After a jury declared Elizabeth Canning guilty of perjury and condemned her to transportation, Crisp, Payne and the others rushed out their
pamphlet. The verdict was not reversed, but at the request of Elizabeth
Canning's supporters she was sent to New England rather than to some
harsher clime. *The Dictionary of National Biography* classifies this otherwise obscure woman as 'malefactor' *tout court*; yet doubts linger as to
whether justice really was done her. Nor is it easy to guess how Nicholas
Crisp first became involved in this Hogarthian case, though having once
taken Canning's part, he and his fellow-authors clearly felt their own
reputations needed defending against Gascoyne's innuendos that they had
encouraged Elizabeth Canning to perjure herself.

Philanthropist or not, Crisp was evidently a church-goer. He may have
begun life as a nonconformist, for several of the men he proposed for membership of the Society of Arts were dissenters,[20] and he himself was 'for a
great number of years' a member of a dissenting congregation meeting at
Bury Street.[21] There is also, apparently, evidence that he was a Method-
ist.[22] But from 1753 until his departure from London, his name crops up in
the Vestry Book of St. Mary le Bow, the beautiful Wren church in whose
precincts he lived.[23] He attended a vestry meeting, for instance, on 29th
November 1758, when George Dance the elder and William Chambers reported on a survey they had made of the church; and on 17th April 1761,
it was 'Resolved that the Churchwardens and Mr. Nicholas Crisp be and
they are hereby impowered to settle with Messrs. Dance and Chambers
their demands relating to the Survey of the late Repairs'. As Clerk of the
City Works the ageing Dance had a stranglehold on architectural jobs in
the City; but it may have been due to Crisp that the up-and-coming Chambers was called in also, for since 1757 Chambers had been a member of the
Society of Arts, whose rooms he soon afterwards remodelled.[24]

CRISP AND THE SOCIETY

We can gain some idea of the atmosphere at the early meetings of the Society of Arts from a letter written by Henry Baker on 20th November 1755:

> new Members are coming in daily, and before the Winter is over their Number will be doubled. And the disinterested application every one exerts to promote the Public Good is much beyond what I ever saw among any other set of People: for we often sit from 6 till 10 or 11 o'clock at Night, we go on with the utmost Harmony, and the Greatest and the Meanest are equally industrious in the same Design, all Rank and Distance is laid aside, and everyone is listened to with due Attention.[25]

Nicholas Crisp, jeweller of Bow Churchyard, found himself in the company of the social and intellectual elite of his country; and the Society's minutes show that he also was 'listened to with due Attention'.

In the Society's earliest year or two there was a real danger that it might snuff out during the summer months, when the gentry were on their country estates. A small nucleus of business and professional men tended the guttering flame at such times, and even among these Crisp was a model for steady attendance at meetings. D. G. C. Allan has shown that Crisp attended nine out of the first fifteen meetings of the Society,[26] while the Minute Books show that he missed only six out of forty meetings in 1756, and eight the following year.

The men Crisp proposed for membership of the Society were, like him, of a middle-class standing, and included an apothecary, a cheesemonger, a seed merchant, an attorney and a dissenting divine.[27] They also included John Howard (1726?-1790), who was later to make a major contribution to prison reform, Michael Henry Spang, a sculptor of merit, and both the younger John Ellicott (1706-1772), perhaps the most distinguished watchmaker of his day, and Edward Ellicott, his son and successor.[28] Whether or not Crisp himself was concerned in the watch trade, friendship between the Crisp family and the Ellicotts seems to have been of long standing, for when Crisp's father made his last will in 1708, he left 'my ffriend John Ellicott of London' (presumably the elder John Ellicott) two guineas to buy a ring.[29]

Committee Minutes were not kept by the Society until 1758, but the Minutes of the General Meetings show that before then Crisp was in demand for the most diverse Committees. Thus in 1755 he and four others were concerned over some ores sent by Dr. Russell of Truro. In 1756 he was on the Accounts Committee and on Committees concerned with premiums for crucibles and for paper suitable for engravers; he reported from the Committee appointed to agree terms with Mr. Fielding for the lease of rooms; he was on the Committee to decide the bill of fare for the Society's dinner. Buff-leather, grapes, dates, cochineal, assaying-furnaces—seemingly nothing was beyond his scope. Crisp seems to have thrived in the atmosphere of inspired amateurism of those early days, and even found himself, along with Henry Cheere, the sculptor, and William Hogarth, the painter, earnestly concerned to foster silk-worms in Georgia.[30]

From 1757 onwards, as the Society expanded, the functions of different Committees were classified, yet Crisp was not easy to pigeon-hole. The Committee of Chemistry seems especially to have kindled his interest, and in 1762 he was one of the two specially elected chairmen of it. But he also on one occasion took the Chair at a Committee of Agriculture, as well as chairing several miscellaneous committees. He sometimes attended committees on Colonies and Trade, Mechanics and Manufactures, or Polite Arts, while his business experience made him in demand for auditing the Society's accounts. Most of the topics on which he lavished his time form part of the general history of the Society, and we need here consider only those to which he made some particular contribution.

Crisp's skill in assaying continued to be respected even when the Society had many eminent men of science among its membership. He was on the Committee set up in September 1756 to consider Henry Baker's proposal that an assaying furnace should be installed on the Society's premises,[31] and in November he reported back to the Society that their kitchens were suitable for 'erecting Assaying Furnaces'.[32] The proposal alarmed members on grounds of potential expense and of the danger of fire. In January Crisp reported to the Society once more from the Committee, and a well-reasoned report on the subject in his handwriting seems to have been delivered on this occasion.[33] 'The name Furnace', he wrote, 'seems to have something very formidable in its sound; but by those your Committee proposed, is meant no more, than a small Smiths Forge, with Bellows; a small Wind Furnace common in the Houses of all Workers in Metals; a small Reverbatory Furnace to calcine, or Test in, of five or six Inches Diameter, and a Sand Heat'.[34] His arguments as to the cheapness, safety and usefulness of this equipment carried the day; and furnaces were soon afterwards erected.

It was probably Crisp's own experiences as a worker in metal that prompted him to propose, in February 1756, that a premium be offered for making Borax.[35] The proposal was rather unusually referred back to him alone, rather than to a Committee. The wording he suggested for offering this premium emphasizes the use of Borax in 'Vitrifications', in the 'fusion of Ores' and in Soldering.[36] Crisp's proposal for a premium for Borax was adopted, and his continued interest in the subject is shown by his attendance at the Chemistry Committees which discussed substitutes for Borax in March and May, 1764.[37]

In November 1758 Crisp proposed that premiums be offered for 'the best Model of a Wind and Water Mill; also a Premium for the best model of a Tide Water Mill'.[38] This he followed up with a proposal for giving a premium to encourage the erecting of saw-mills.[39] Premiums for these subjects were in due course offered by the Society. Apart from mills Crisp showed little interest in mechanical subjects, and if he really was a watchmaker rather than a maker of watch-cases, he seems to have taken no leading part when time-pieces were under discussion.[40]

Nor is there greater evidence of Crisp's activity over a proposed premium for porcelain, though, as we have seen, he was or had been concerned in this manufacture. On 2nd February 1757 'A Motion was made by Mr. Cleeve to give a Premium for making in England the best piece of Porcelain in Imitation of the Dresden'. According to the Society's Minutes, discussion of Bourchier Cleeve's motion was postponed till the following meeting, when it was again postponed, 'Mr. Cleeve not being present'. On 16th February, although Cleeve was present, it was 'Ordered that Mr. Cleeve's Motion for giving a Premium for making the best piece of Porcelain in Imitation of that made in Dresden be postponed'.[41] Then no more is heard of the proposal. The existing porcelain factories in England and in France all made soft-paste, unless Crisp's was the exception, and that this perfectly sensible suggestion for awarding a premium to the maker of a British hard-paste was killed by postponement is curious; Crisp himself was present at all three meetings, yet his views on the matter were not recorded. Probably he was only too content to let the matter drop, for eighteenth-century porcelain-makers tended to be secretive about their formulae.

Crisp's interests in ceramics, metal-working and chemistry were all engaged by the proposal, first mooted in April 1755, that premiums be offered for making crucibles and retorts from native British clays.[42] His principal contribution was a memorandum dated 25th February 1756, prepared in collaboration with Dr. Clark, in which the different types of crucible are listed.[43] Crisp seems also to have taken an interest in the crucibles and retorts submitted for premiums from time to time, by such claimants as Mr. John Christian Erffurt of Turk's Row, Chelsea, who in 1757 had his turned by Mr. White of Fulham,[44] or Mr. Joan Sefforth and Mr. Richards in 1759.[45]

Enamels must have interested Crisp in his capacity as porcelain-maker as well as jeweller. He took the Chair at a Committee in 1760 when the white enamel made by a Mr. Narbell (Nerbell or Nebell) was discussed and attended when this inventor demonstrated how he made his enamel out of calcined tin and lead, calcined flints, potash and small quantities of cerus and calcined talc.[46] Narbell's enamel was on this occasion found inferior to the Venetian white as a ground for enamel miniaturists to paint on, though a small bonus was recommended. A similar verdict awaited one of the samples of crimson-coloured enamel submitted for trial early in 1765 to the enamel miniaturists Moser and Meyer, and to some other men, including Dr. Morris and Crisp.[47] It was probably Crisp's chemical knowledge that made his views valuable on this occasion, but it is possible he may have had some artistic skills as well.

Unfortunately two sketches he made for the Society's first medal in April 1756 have not survived with the letter they accompanied. The award of medals as honorary premiums had been part of Shipley's original proposals of 1753, but the idea had lapsed and was only revived when Henry Baker, at the suggestion of his correspondent William Arderon, proposed it in April 1756, himself producing a sketch.[48] Crisp was one of the Committee appointed to consider the idea, along with Baker, Hogarth, Cheere, Highmore and others. At the following meeting Crisp's suggestions for the design of the medal were read.[49] Although part of this letter has already been quoted in this series as illustrating satisfaction with the Whig administration of George II,[50] further passages seem worth attention here for the light they throw on Crisp's view of the Society, indeed on his whole cast of mind and his visual imagination:

> In a medall given for the encouragement of Arts the first Figure that presents it self is that of Minerva, the mistress or Goddess of Arts, the peculiar patroness of Athens, the City where they rose to the greatest perfection.
>
> This it perhaps will be said is common, undoubtedly it is, but it is common because beautifull and proper. Beautiful as the masculine strength is tempered with the female softness, and the plumes of the Casque, and the flowings of her robe, may be variously and gracefully disposed: proper as this emblem includes the ideas, of encouraging, protecting, and carrying to perfection all the Arts. if she is represented as receiving into her Arms a young boy [the word 'girl' was first written, but crossed out], this will strongly picture the great design of this Society, to encourage the ingenuity

and industry of young persons of Genius. if her shield bears the Arms of England, or the cross of St. George, and on the banks of the river on which she sitts, rises a view of St. Pauls Cupola, this will picture her as the British, not the Athenian Minerva, and point out the seat of the Society, and if at the mouth of the same river a ship enters, this will be a proper emblem of commerce, which it is also our express design to promote.

Thus far the figure and what may be easily connected with it will be simple and expressive of two of the designs of this Society, to encourage Arts and Commerce.

The other title and design of the Society, to Encourage Manufactures is not so easily represented. But as the two principall machines in the World, the Water-Mill and the Wind-Mill, which tho common are most wonderful inventions, have by the ingenuity of our own Countrymen, been adapted to various purposes of our manufactures, and without them they could not possibly subsist, or at all vye with foreigners. would not the representation of these two principall machines on the back ground, make an agreeable picture, without embarrassing the principall figure, and be expressive of the ingenuity of our countrymen in curious application of these wonderfull machines, to almost the various purposes of our manufactures?

Astonishingly, George Michael Moser, who was asked to chase a design for the medal, managed to squeeze most of this (though with modifications) onto the medal. For the reverse Crisp proposed an equally complicated allegory with King George flanked by figures of 'Freedom and Property', continuing disarmingly: 'It will be said perhaps that these designs are not simple enough. I allow simplicity to be a beauty, so is comprehensiveness.' As to the execution of the model, Crisp argued that it should be chased on copper, 'as the art of chasing is carryed to as great a heighth as it can well be among us, tho the introduction of the trifling French Watch-cases among us seems to bid fair for its destruction.'

Moser, who chased the prototype medal, was noted as the best chaser in England until the waning of the rococo taste for elaborately chased metalwork, and the introduction of flatter watch-cases, forced him to become an enameller. In any event, the die-cutter, Yeo, said that the gold-value of a medal of the size designed by Moser would be 15 guineas, which the Society thought too much, and the elaborate allegory that Crisp had helped concoct was replaced by a comparatively austere and classical design thought up by Stuart. Not disheartened, Crisp continued to attend those meetings of the Committee of Polite Arts when the design of medals was discussed.[51]

At the very first meeting of the Society, on 22nd March 1754, the offer of premiums for madder and cobalt was considered. For each of these Crisp himself at length gained a premium.

Madder roots were used to produce a red dye which was usually imported to Britain, though the British climate was not unsuitable to its growth. On 14th December 1757, the Committee on Madder decided that of the samples submitted those 'in the basket marked N°C. 1' were the best produced of two years' growth, and awarded a £20 premium. It was found that Crisp was the grower of the prize-winning roots. He can hardly have grown them at Bow Churchyard, the address he gave when sending in the roots,[52] but as we shall see in the final part of this paper, he had kept a foothold at Witham, Essex. His continued link with that county is suggested by the way he reported in 1756 'on an extraordinary production of Corn in Essex'.[53] Crisp did not attempt to repeat his triumph, but soon afterwards 'A Motion was made by Mr. Crisp, that a Committee be appointed to consider the best method of promoting the further Growth of Madder'. He was himself chosen a member of this Committee.[54]

Crisp's interest in cobalt, and in its derivatives, zaffer and smalt, was more serious. The Society's advertisements of the premiums are wont to speak of 'Zaffer being used in painting of China and Earthenware and Smalt a principal ingredient of Powder Blue'. Even if Crisp did not use cobalt-blue on his porcelain, his partner, John Sanders, would have used it on his delftware pottery. Cobalt was also used in the form of 'powder-blue' for whitening linen.[55]

In April and May 1755, Crisp three times showed the Society results of the experiments he had made on cobalt ores from Pengreep, near Truro, which had been submitted for a premium by the mine's owner, Francis Beauchamp. Crisp seems to have had no difficulty in producing blue glass from this ore at a time when Dr. Lewis and Dr. Morris failed.[56] On 14th May he handed in to the Society a paper on his experiments.[57] Beauchamp eventually received a premium.

In October 1756, when Josiah Peat sent samples of supposed cobalt from Wirksworth in Derbyshire, Crisp's opinion was again sought, and after making experiments, he reported that 'the same has not the least Appearance of cobalt in it'.[58]

Crisp must also have learnt much about cobalt as one of the Committee set up in 1758 to judge the essays on cobalt received in response to the advertisement of a gold medal for the best treatise on searching for cobalt, trying it, and making zaffer and smalt from it. In November 1759 the Committee awarded the medal to 'John Gottlob Lohmann, Dr. of Physic and Director of Mines to the King of Prussia'.[59]

Then, in January 1764, a premium was claimed anonymously (as had now become the rule) for the discovery of a native source of zaffer and smalt. Samples were sent for trial to chemists, enamel miniaturists (Moser and Meyer), to Dr. Wall of the Worcester porcelain factory, and to Stephen Williams, a linen draper.[60] At a meeting of the Chemistry Committee on 11th February an unsigned letter from the candidate was read. This still survives, and it would have been surprising if no one had recognized that it is in Crisp's handwriting. In it he shows his familiarity with the principal authors on the subject and says that 'the Mine has been worked some time at a considerable expence; that they are now at work on the Vein; that a considerable quantity is raised and now in Town; and that preparations are made for carrying on the Manufactures of Smalt and Zaffer'.[61]

The Committee recommended that a premium of £50 be awarded, and that a premium should be offered for 'a Manufactory of Zaffre and Smalt'.[62]

At this time Crisp's financial affairs were in the gravest disarray; even his reputation for honesty could have been called in question. Remembering this, one can guess from the discreet Minutes of the meeting held on 13th February that the announcement of his name as the successful candidate for the cobalt premium may have caused an unpleasant scene. 'A Motion was made, that, whenever any Member of this Society shall accept of a Premium or Bounty, he shall no longer be deemed a Member, unless re-elected: candidates for honorary Premiums and Medals excepted.' This was not carried, but the next item in the Minutes reads: 'A Motion was made that any Person who for the future shall be guilty of Hissing or Clapping during the Meeting of this Society, shall for that Evening be expelled the Room'.[63] This motion was not carried either, but tempers seem to have been running high, and it can hardly be accident that the Minutes of this meeting avoid mentioning Crisp's controversial name.

In the calmer atmosphere of the Chemistry Committee's meeting held on 21st April, however, 'Mr. Crisp attending produced several Letters he had received concerning the Mine in Scotland from whence the Cobalt was taken, and giving an account that there is a Considerable Quantity of the like Cobalt in the Same Mine and apparently sufficient for Establishing a Manufactory'. It was accordingly resolved that Crisp be paid his £50 premium.[64]

That Crisp, at the height of his financial worries, should have discovered a cobalt mine in Scotland is a singular and hitherto unsuspected fact. His award and the controversy arising from it were apparently the reasons why, in May of that year, members of the Society were finally debarred from winning its premiums.[65]

'CRISP—POOR CRISP'

At the time when Nicholas Crisp was helping to found the Society of Arts he had every outward appearance of prosperity. But in the early 1760s his business affairs went wrong, and he eventually left London to start a new life in Devon. Two principal factors, the one interacting on the other, seem to have brought about his downfall: his involvement in the affairs of a fellow jeweller, Andrew Hunter of Great Russell Street; and his share in managing the fortune of John Andrews, of Queen Square, Middlesex, who had earlier headed the East India Company's settlement in 'Bandarmalankor' (Bandarulanka).

The jeweller, Hunter, went bankrupt on 13th April 1762, and Nicholas Crisp was appointed one of the assignees of his estate, undertaking to manage Hunter's affairs on behalf of the creditors, of whom Crisp himself appears to have been one. In his capacity as assignee Crisp received upwards of £2,000 out of Hunter's estate, but Hunter's creditors, finding Crisp 'to grow remiss in his said trust and that he was not inclined to take any step towards making a dividend',[66] got the Clerk of the Commissioners in Bankruptcy to make him advertise in the *London Gazette* that a dividend of Hunter's estate was to be made on 31st October 1763.[67] Crisp attended this meeting, which was held at the Guildhall, and produced his accounts, from which it appeared that a balance of over £1,500 from Hunter's estate remained in his hands. Several of the creditors afterwards applied to Crisp for payment of their shares of the dividend, but were 'under various Pretences put off and Diverted by the said Nicholas Crisp from the payment thereof and in some short time afterwards the said Nicholas Crisp absolutely obsconded and turned out insolvent and unable to pay the said Dividend of four Shillings in the pound'.[68]

In consequence of Crisp's failure to produce the money due to Hunter's creditors, or perhaps of the bad publicity attending this failure, Nicholas and his partners, his elder brother, Thomas, and his nephew and former apprentice, Edward Crisp, were all bankrupted on 17th November 1763.[69] For some reason the creditor who initiated bankruptcy proceedings was Crisp's friend, the clockmaker John Ellicott.

Why Nicholas Crisp was unable to pay back what he owed to Hunter's creditors becomes clearer in the light of his involvement with John

Andrews. Ever since March 1746, Andrews had run an account with Thomas and Nicholas Crisp.[70] At first this was a simple banking arrangement whereby Andrews paid relatively small sums into an account, and the Crisps, during Andrews' absence in India, paid small sums to 'Mr. Andrews senior'.

Meanwhile, out in India John Andrews became friendly with a certain Thomas Saunders, Governor of the East India Company's Settlement in Madras. In 1754 Saunders, deciding for his health's sake to retire, agreed to transact some business for Andrews in England, though how far the former undertook responsibility was later disputed between the two. Andrews now began to send very considerable sums of money home, sometimes in the form of jewels, which makes sense of his choice of Thomas Crisp, a diamond-cutter, and Nicholas Crisp, a jeweller, as his 'attornies or agents'. Andrews' account with the Crisps shows that the first such large payment, for £2,166 13s. 4d., reached them on 10th July 1757. By the time the Crisps were bankrupted in November 1763, by their own computation they had £18,212 17s. 11d. of Andrews' money in capital and interest. According to the Crisps' own story Andrews directed Saunders and themselves to invest this money 'in such a way as not to be attended with any hazard or risque', and the Crisps had answered that they had invested or would invest 'on Government or other good Security' on his behalf.[71] No effective control was exercised by Thomas Saunders, and the Crisps interpreted the instructions in a very loose spirit, investing only £675 in East India Company stock and £600 in the Blackfriars Bridge project. The remainder they invested in the cargoes of various ships,[72] or as Andrews less charitably interpreted their actions, applied 'to their own Private Advantage'.[73]

Whatever the business ethics of the day may have been in such cases, this situation was found alarming by a friend whom Andrews sent to look into his affairs in anticipation of his return to England in the spring of 1762. Thomas and Nicholas Crisp offered as security the title deeds of their estates at Witham and Great Totham in Essex, a quantity of jewels, the bills of sale of shares in some East India Company ships, invoices of goods in Russia, and two bonds on a certain George Mandeville.[74] The Crisps computed that the value of this security was greater than their debt to Andrews, and the latter does seem to have been temporarily soothed to the extent that he entrusted Nicholas Crisp with a diamond ring for sale as late as October 1763, on the eve of the Crisps' bankruptcy.[75] But in soothing Andrews it looks as if Nicholas Crisp overtaxed his resources to a point where he was unable to satisfy the demands of Hunter's creditors. After the bankruptcy all funds in Crisp's hands were presumably seized, including £95 banked with him by a Congregation of Protestant dissenters which met in Bury Street and of which he had for many years been a member.[76]

The late Aubrey Toppin, who consulted some but not all of the legal documents here cited, suggested that the Crisps could not produce the money because it had been swallowed up in the Vauxhall porcelain venture discussed above. Toppin was probably influenced by his mistaken belief that the Saunders who was connected with Andrews was identical with the Sanders who was a partner in the porcelain factory with Nicholas Crisp. But it now appears that Thomas Saunders of Madras and later of Norfolk Street, Westminster, was an entirely different person from John Sanders, the Vauxhall potter, and was probably not even related to him.[77] The Cornish soaprock concession had been let to other men on 1st January 1760, more than a year before it would ordinarily have expired, so it looks as if by then Crisp and Sanders had no further use for the material. The porcelain venture does not seem to have been a financial success, but it can scarcely have been more than a contributory factor to Crisp's troubles. Some of the 'considerable expence' attending the cobalt mine in Scotland may have fallen upon Crisp. There is also a story that Crisp kept his own coach, which suggests a style of living rather extravagant for a man of his station.[78]

It is not yet known how well Crisp succeeded in extricating himself from his financial troubles. Toppin drew gloomy conclusions from the fact that when John Bacon took his freedom on 4th July 1764 Crisp was described in the records of the Haberdashers' Company as 'Traveller'.[79] Yet the last-named document still describes him as 'of Bow Churchyard,' and his name continued to appear in the Land Tax Registers there up to 1766, after which someone called Charles Hurst took on from him all three of his houses.[80]

On the other hand he never again, after March 1764, paid his two guineas subscription to the Society of Arts, though his name continued to appear in the printed lists of members up to 1774, the year of his death. In 1762 he had been listed merely as 'Crisp, Mr. Nicholas', but in the lists for 1770, 1772 and 1774 he was described as 'Crisp, Mr. Nicholas, Merchant, Indeo, Devon'.[81] He had never, like Shipley and Baker, been voted a perpetual member for his services, but it was presumably kindness on the part of his friends in the Society, rather than a mere oversight, that kept his name from being deleted from the lists of members after he had ceased to pay.

Indio (or Indeo), Crisp's new address, lies near Bovey Tracey, some

fourteen miles from Exeter, and the idea has recently been canvassed that
his removal to Devon must be connected with an announcement in December 1764 'that a few gentlemen of fortune have undertaken to set up a
new manufactory of china at Exeter'.[82] Though this still seems likely, it
is clear from the Minutes of the Chemistry Committee of the Society of
Arts that Crisp himself was still in London at the time of this announcement. On 22nd December 1764, for instance, when the sweetening of sea
water was under discussion by the Committee for Chemistry, it was recorded that 'Mr. Crisp having been so obliging as to offer to get a proper
quantity of Sea Water, Resolved that Mr. Crisp be desired to get thirty Gallons'.[83] Again, on 10th January 1765 Crisp brought the Committee 'foure
Pennyweight of lead' produced from Litharge which had been used in
an experiment. In the same month he was active over the scarlet enamel
colour.

After the beginning of 1766 Crisp's attendance at Committees became
more spasmodic and eventually ceased altogether. The last signs of his attendance that the present writer has discovered are for 25th January 1766,
when he attended the Committee for Chemistry; 22nd December 1766,
when he attended a Committee for Agriculture; 6th January 1767, when
he attended the Committee for Chemistry; and 13th January 1767, when
he attended both the Committee for Manufactures and the Committee for
Colonies. On 14th March 1767, however, when a premium for the manufacture of porcelain was discussed by the Committee for Chemistry, he
was not present. By this time Crisp was probably at Bovey Tracey, himself
reattempting that very manufacture.

Stonewares of Staffordshire type had been made at Bovey Tracey since
about 1750, though apparently with only moderate success. Good pipe-
clay, an ingredient used both in stonewares and in soft-paste porcelain, was
to be had locally, and there was an abundant supply of lignite for fuel.[84] In
late May or early June 1775, Josiah Wedgwood visited Bovey Tracey:

> To see a pot work which had been many years carried on at that place,
> & under so many apparent advantages, that it would be a matter of surprise
> to those who have not considered the difficulty of removing a manufacture,
> that it was not in a more flourishing and improved state than we saw it. A
> Mr. Crisp from London endeavored to make a kind of porcelain here, but
> did little more than make some experiments, and those unsuccessful ones.
> They afterwards made white stone ware, glazed with Salts, & had a fireman,
> and I believe some other workmen, from our country, but it was still a losing
> concern to them.[85]

Crisp had died the year before Wedgwood's visit and was buried at Bovey Tracey church.[86] His will has apparently not survived the bombing of Exeter in the second world war, but that it was written and proved at all suggests that Crisp did not die destitute.[87] Yet his misfortunes must have been felt by his family, and there is perhaps a hint of something of the kind in the obituary of one of his daughters which appeared in the *Gentleman's Magazine* for 1788:

> At Honiton, Devon, after having been afflicted some months with a lin-gering illness, Miss Anne Crisp, youngest daughter of the late Mr. Nich. C. jeweller, of Bow Churchyard, London, and first cousin of Miss S. C. who died Sept. 2; a young lady of an amiable disposition, who had borne many of the trying vicissitudes of life with Christian meekness and fortitude, and whose death is greatly lamented by all her relations and friends.[88]

The Miss Sarah Crisp alluded to died at Stoke Newington and is described in the *Gentleman's Magazine* as '3d and youngest daught. of the late Mr. Tho.C. of Witham, Co. Essex, who, with her eldest sister, have for several years kept a young Ladies' boarding-school of considerable repute in that place.'[89]

Finally, the *Gentleman's Magazine* recorded in 1794 the death of Crisp's wife:

> Very much regretted, at the Rev. N. Delahay Symonds's (the house of her son in-law, in Castle-green, Taunton), in the 82nd year of her age, Mrs. Crisp, relict of the late Nicholas C. esq. of Bow Church-yard, Lond.[90]

Clearly the family preferred Nicholas to be remembered for his days at Bow Churchyard rather than for his second career at Bovey Tracey.

For Nicholas Crisp himself I have found no obituary, though a passage from one of Wedgwood's letters might serve for an epitaph. Wedgwood was writing on 6th August 1775 to Bentley, his partner, describing some recent ceramic experiments of his own:

> but I have had too much experience of the delicacy, & unaccountable un-certainty of these fine bodies to be very sanguine in my expectations—And Crisp—Poor Crisp haunts my imagination continually—Ever pursuing—just upon the point of overtaking—but never in possession of his favorite object: There are many good lessons in that poor Man's life, labours & catastrophe if we schemers could profit by example; but that wisdom, alass, is denied us.[91]

That is how Crisp appeared to a thrusting and successful Staffordshire potter, and perhaps the contrast between the two men is instructive. Josiah

Wedgwood was born and bred to the single trade of the potter, and though he shared Crisp's scientific curiosity and could on occasion act in a generous and public-spirited manner, his main energies were directed single-mindedly towards the production and sale of pottery. Wedgwood did not, like Crisp, spend time experimenting on ores and clays unless he thought they might be capable of use in pottery; the paper which secured his election to the Royal Society was devoted to a pyrometer for measuring the temperature of kilns; his promotion of the Trent and Mersey Canal scheme was motivated by interest in the transport of pottery and the raw materials that went into its making; even Wedgwood's snobbery was harnessed for the purpose of marketing pottery.

Crisp does not seem to have integrated his many interests in the same way. Jewellery; porcelain-making; chemistry; the defence of a servant-girl against supposed maladministration of justice; trade with Russia and the East; the growing of madder roots; plans to exploit a cobalt mine in Scotland; perhaps also watchmaking: it is an odd mixture, and must have led to much dissipation of energy. Yet Crisp evidently passed, until the time of his financial collapse, as a competent and trustworthy business-man, a man to whom a congregation of dissenters would entrust a fund, or who would be chosen to play a leading part in auditing the accounts of the Society of Arts.

We can only guess how many of Crisp's troubles were due to defects of his own character, how many to sheer bad luck. The diversity of his enthusiasms may have led to private loss; yet if he himself failed to benefit from this diversity, the records of the Society of Arts make it plain that his countrymen did not.[92]

5

CALEB WHITEFOORD, FRS, FSA, 1734-1810: COMMITTEE CHAIRMAN AND VICE PRESIDENT OF THE SOCIETY

D. G. C. Allan

The commemoration of the bicentenary of the American War of Independence focused attention on Caleb Whitefoord, a member of the Society who combined the trade of a wine merchant with the profession of a political journalist, served his country in a major diplomatic enterprise, and was the enthusiastic patron of some of the most distinguished artists of the British School.

Caleb Whitefoord was the son of Colonel Charles Whitefoord, whose honourable conduct during the '45 had earned him the respect alike of Whigs and Jacobites. In old age, as the young Wilkie noted, Caleb proudly displayed a sword in his study to remind the world that he was a 'Whitefoord of that ilk'. He had, however, been intended for the ministry of the Scottish Church and had subsequently come to London—where an apparently successful apprenticeship and partnership in the Portuguese wine trade, supplemented by a substantial inheritance, gave him leisure to enjoy the play, dine at the clubs, become a connoisseur of prints and paintings, and to write numerous articles for the *Public Advertiser*.

Originally appeared in *Jnl. RSA,* 127 (Apr.-May, 1979), 306-9, 371-75.

Whose talents to fit any station were fit,
Yet happy if Woodfall confessed him a wit.[1]

His friend Garrick's verdict, so often quoted, reflected the popular view that he wasted his energy in political journalism. Yet to a young Scotsman in the London society of the 1760s who wished to preserve his good name, ability in that field was a valuable asset. 'What first engaged me in political controversy', he wrote, 'was a desire of undeceiving the public . . . that most places of trust and profit in England were engrossed by Scotchmen. This assertion, false and absurd as it was, had been frequently repeated by the *North Britain* and *Monitor*, and . . . every John Bull in the Kingdom believed it as firmly as his creed.' Whitefoord earned the gratitude of the government by exposing the absurdity of Wilkes and the 'pseudo-patriots' and on one occasion amused the whole town by advertising for 'a new Grievance'. He was not, however, partisan, and he claimed that 'whenever any change of ministry happened and the party writers on both sides began the work of serious abuse, I have always endeavoured to make such changes a matter of *laughter*'.[2]

Whitefoord remained the firm friend of Lord Bute after that minister had become the target for public obloquy, and his known loyalty to Dr. Franklin, in spite of the rift with the American colonies, led to his being chosen by Lord Shelburne to go to Paris in 1782 and open peace negotiations. His best-remembered literary success was an anthology of 'Cross Readings' from the newspapers. These absurdly contrasted quotations— 'The sword of state was carried before Sir John Fielding and committed to Newgate' is my own favourite—amused such diverse critics as Smollett, Johnson, Goldsmith, and Horace Walpole.[3]

Whitefoord's enthusiasm for the arts led him into a lifelong association with Sir Joshua Reynolds and the affairs of the Royal Academy, and in old age he played an important part in the establishment of the British Institution. His large collection of pictures was exceptional for a man of moderate fortune, illustrating, it was said, 'the Triumph of Taste over Riches'. He was supposed to have the habit of touching up his old masters—but we have only the word of an enemy for this story. There is, however, no doubt that he practised as an amateur artist. He completed a portrait of Benjamin Franklin which was 'acknowledged to bear a strong and striking likeness'. His own portrait of Franklin has not survived, but the Royal Society still treasures one by Joseph Wright which Caleb commissioned at the time of the peace negotiations and subsequently presented to that Society. The

Society of Arts similarly benefited from Caleb's interest in portraiture. It was thanks to his friendship with the artist that Richard Cosway presented his *William Shipley* and *Peter Templeman,* and thus the Society secured portraits of its Founder and one of its most celebrated Secretaries. James Barry, the Irish history painter who decorated the Society of Arts' meeting room in the Adelphi with six great canvases depicting the 'Progress of Human Culture and Knowledge' and whose manic temperament needed all the friendship it could get, was given enthusiastic support by Caleb Whitefoord, both on the triumphant day in 1799 when he received the Society's Gold Medal and two hundred guineas 'with every designation and tribute of respect' and in his last sad years of poverty when an annuity was raised on his behalf.[4]

Whitefoord's association with the Society of Arts began in 1762 when he was elected a member on the proposal of Dr. Benjamin Franklin, who was his next-door neighbour in Craven Street, off the Strand. He does not appear to have been active in the Society until the late 1770s, when he began a period of involvement which lasted until his death in 1810.

His attendances at the Society's Committees seem to begin in the session of 1778-9 when he was present at meetings of the Committees of Correspondence and Papers, Miscellaneous Matters, and Polite Arts. From then until early in 1784 only two attendances are recorded, one in February 1780 and the other in February 1782 and both at the Committee of Correspondence and Papers. The latter part of this period of nonattendance coincided with his thirteen months' stay in Paris, and even after his return to London in April 1783 he was much occupied with business connected with his diplomatic mission. In February 1784, however, we find him present at the Committee of Accounts and Polite Arts and in March and April again at the Polite Arts Committee. The year 1785 sees him present at all these committees as well as those of Correspondence and Papers and Colonies and Trade. The last mentioned Committee has a special significance because Caleb was one of its two chairmen, having been originally elected for the sessions 1778-9 and 1779-80 and, after some unsuccessful candidatures for other committee chairmanships, being re-elected for 1783-4 and 1784-5.[5]

In his first period as a chairman of the Colonies and Trade Committee he had attended none of the five meetings which this near-moribund body had held. He was also absent from the Committee's two meetings for the session 1783-4, and his only recorded service as chairman was for the solitary meeting held in 1784-5. It is hardly surprising that he did not seek re-election for the succeeding session but contested instead the more congenial, if more onerous, chairmanship of the Committee of Polite Arts. He was duly elected and began a period of active service to this Committee which lasted until the end of the century.[6]

Before considering Caleb's services as chairman of the Polite Arts Committee mention must be made of an important episode in his relations with the Society which had taken place in 1785. This was his attempt to secure the appointment of the Prince of Wales as Patron of the Society. The story of the Prince's favourable response and of the curious failure of the Society to follow up its overtures has been often told. Part of Caleb's letter describing the incident is also familiar, having been printed in the Society's Bicentenary History. The opening and unpublished section of the letter, however, is interesting as evidence of the desire felt by so many members of the Society at that time for some sort of official recognition of their institution. The full text is as follows:

> Craven Street
> 14 December 1785
>
> Sir,
>
> Happening to be present at a General meeting of the Society about three weeks ago, I was very forcibly struck with some Observations, which fell from Mr. Green, Chairman of the Committee of Polite Arts. No Member I believe is more zealous and active in the Service of the Society, or has its real Interests more at heart than the worthy Chairman; for which reason Sir, his Observations are allways listened to by me, with all due Attention. I remember Sir, he was lamenting (as many of us have often done) that the Society's Finances were in so low a state; and that we were prevented by our Poverty, from giving so much Encouragement to Genius and Merit, as We could wish to do: He also mentioned as a matter deeply to be regretted, that the Society was totally deprived of *Royal Patronage*—He observed, that Foreigners who came to the Society's Room, generally asked if the Institution was honoured with the Patronage of his Majesty? No—Of the Prince of Wales, or any of the Princes?—No—Nor of Parliament?—No, was still the Answer; and Foreigners therefore went away under Impressions rather disadvantageous to the Society. Such was the Scope of the Observations which fell from the worthy Chairman; I do not pretend to the precise words, but only to give the general Idea.
>
> After I went home that evening, I turned this matter in my Thoughts, and the day following I called on Mr. Green, and told him, I had been thinking on what he had said the night before in the Society, concerning the want of Royal Patronage. That perhaps there wou'd be an *impropriety* in our making any Application to the King; as his Majesty was allready Patron of the Royal Society, the Royal Academy, etc. But it struck me, that there could

be *no* Impropriety, in our making such a Request of the Prince of Wales. I said, from what I had heard of the gracious and benevolent Disposition of his Royal Highness, there was good Reason to suppose that he would be happy to give every Encouragement and Support to an Institution, whose Labours were solely directed to public Utility, and national Advantage: And I was convinced in my own Mind, that if any Person in the Confidence of the Prince were to state to him in a proper manner, the various advantages and improvements in the polite Arts, in Manufactures, in Commerce, and in Agriculture, which have been the Result of the Encouragement given by this Society, that his Royal Highness would clearly see, that the Institution was highly deserving of his Patronage.

Impressed with this Idea, I soon afterwards applied to a Gentleman, who sometimes has the Honour of being admitted to the Prince's presence; and I requested of him, that he would seize the earliest Opportunity of setting in a just and fair Light, the Society's Merits; and of soliciting his Royal Highness's Patronage.

The Gentleman most readily and cheerfully undertook the Commission; and I am happy to be able to inform the Society that he has succeeded in the main Object of it. I was last night favoured with a Letter from him, in which He tells me, that after a proper Introduction of the Subject, he had asked, *if* his Royal Highness should be applied to, whether he would choose to confer on the Society, the Honour of becoming its Patron? The Prince was graciously pleased to answer in the *affirmative,* and added, 'that it would all-ways give him Pleasure, to patronize whatever appeared so much calculated to promote the Public Good'.

The above gracious answer of the Prince, I intended to have communicated this Evening to the Society, *viva voce;* but as I am prevented from attending the meeting, by a violent Cold and hoarseness, I have to request that you Sir will officially lay this matter before the Society; that they may consider of, and determine upon the properest method of applying to his Royal High-ness, either by Deputation from the Presidency, Memorial or Petition, or such other mode, as they in their Wisdom shall think fit.

I beg youll believe me to be, with great Respect

Sir

Your most obedient
humble servant
Caleb Whitefoord

Mr. Samuel More,
Secretary of the Society, for the Encouragement
of Arts, &c.[7]

This letter was considered by the Society on the same day that it was written, and the Minutes record the passing of two motions:

that thanks be returned to Mr. Whitefoord for this fresh instance of his attention to the Interests and welfare of the Society. Agreed to. . . . that the
letter from Mr. Whitefoord be referred to the President and Vice Presidents
of the Society and that they be requested to promote the object of the letter
in such manner as to them shall seem most proper and effectual, and that
they be also desired to meet for the above purpose as soon as convenient.
Agreed to.

They also record that another

letter from Mr. Whitefoord was read acquainting the Society that on his having applied to Mr. Cosway to request the loan of the portrait of Mr. Shipley
in order that a plate might be engraved from it, Mr. Cosway had told him
that the Society were welcome not only to the use of the portrait in order to
make an engraving but that the picture itself was much at their service if the
Society would do him the honour to accept it.

Caleb was evidently exerting himself to the full in order to be of service
to the Society. We can imagine his disappointment when a week later a
faction in the membership, possibly jealous of his growing influence and
worried by rumours of the Prince of Wales's marriage to Mrs. Fitzherbert,
rejected 'A motion . . . that an Engraving be made from the original portrait
of Mr Shipley presented by Mr. Cosway', and passed 'A motion . . . that
the further consideration of that part of the minutes relative to applying to
His Royal Highness the Prince of Wales be post-poned'.[8]

Caleb expressed his hurt feelings over the Shipley portrait in a MS
memorandum which has survived amongst his papers. In it he describes
how he had first seen the portrait in Cosway's studio some years before
and had remembered this when the Society began looking for a source
for an engraved frontispiece showing the Society's Founder for Volume 4
of the *Transactions*. He had attended a meeting and 'rose up (in order
to save the Society Expense and Trouble) and told them, that an Artist,
a particular friend of mine, (Mr. Cosway) had got an original Portrait of
Mr. Shipley which I would undertake to procure. I was answered, that the
Society only wanted the loan of it in order to make an Engraving'.

Caleb then visited Cosway and

observed to him that this was a good Opportunity for doing a very liberal
thing viz. to give the Portrait at once, to the Society as a Present, with a
handsome Message . . . Mr. Cosway admitted that it was the best use that
could be made of it, and added you may send a handsome Message to the
Society along with it. Accordingly as soon as I received the Portrait, I wrote
a letter to the Secretary in which I introduced a Message from Mr. Cosway

in the handsomest terms I could . . . Consequently Mr. Cosway received the
thanks of the Society. But no notice whatever was taken of *me:* probably
because from motives of Delicacy, I did not attend the Report . . . I was
somewhat hurt and disappointed at this seeming Neglect . . . I also met with
another Disappointment in this Business; for the Society did not after all
make an Engraving from the Portrait I had provided.

However all this did not prevent me from doing my utmost for the Society's Advantage, whenever any Business occurr'd wherein I could be useful.[9]

Of the twelve members of the Society of Arts who were elected as
chairmen of the Committee of Polite Arts during the eighteenth century,
only one, Matthew Duane, Whitefoord's immediate predecessor, exceeded
Caleb Whitefoord in length of service. Until 1786 Caleb served as 'second chairman' with his friend Valentine Green, the mezzotint engraver,
as the senior officer. Then Green moved to another Committee and was
succeeded by Caleb, who remained 'first chairman' until his elevation to
the Vice Presidency in 1800. During the period of Caleb's chairmanship
the Polite Arts Committee continued its work of examining candidates for
premiums for the various classes of painting, drawing, sculpture and engraving. County maps and artists' materials as well as domestic matters
such as the negotiations with James Barry and the arrangement of the Society's pictures also continued to come before the Committee. The minutes
show that Caleb was involved in all these matters and that, in particular, he took an active part in assessing Thomas Kirk's historical drawing
The Judgement of Paris (1786), Turner's landscape drawing (1793) and the
various drawings submitted by Stephen Francis Rigaud (1794, 1799), John
James Masquerier (1794, 1795, 1796, 1799), Robert Smirke (1797) and
William Francis Englehart (1797); to name but a few of the better known
prize-winners. He authorized consultations with Reynolds, West, Copley,
and Peters over Miss Emma Jane Greenland's use of wax colours in 1786
and with Cosway over Mr. George Blackman's oil colour cakes in 1794.[10]

In 1797 any resentment which might have lingered in Caleb's mind over
the treatment he had received from the Society when he had obtained for
it the portrait of Shipley by Cosway would have been brought to an end
by the Society's extremely gracious response to a further successful nego-
tiation of a gift from the artist. Caleb obtained from Cosway a portrait of
Dr. Peter Templeman, an early Secretary of the Society, and sent it to the
Society with 'a public letter' praising Cosway's generosity. As a precaution
against another rebuff, he also wrote to his friend Valentine Green, as the
minutes of the Committee of Polite Arts for 6th February 1797 show:

Caleb Whitefoord;
artist unknown.
Courtesy of the RSA.

Resumed the Consideration of the Portrait of Dr. Templeman. Read a
Letter from Mr. Whitefoord to Val. Green, Esq. on the Subject, in which
Mr. Whitefoord says that from all Circumstances he is clearly of the Opin-
ion that the Society owes the Possession of the Portraits of Mr. Shipley and
Dr. Templeman to Him, as it was through his Means they were obtained, that
in saying this he does not mean to detract from the Merit of Mr. Cosway; but
Mr. Cosway was not a Member of the Society, and Mr. Whitefoord thinks he
had no Idea of giving the Pictures to the Society unless at his or some other
zealous Member's Request; that he obtained the Portrait of Mr. Shipley for a
Plate to be engraven for a Frontispiece to One of the Volumes of Transactions
but managed it so as to get the property of it.

That some years Afterwards finding the Portrait of Dr. Templeman he got
the promise of that to form a Companion to Mr. Shipley. That in his public Letter He has joined Mr. Cosway's Name with his own, He hopes and
wishes they may not be separated in any Mark of favour or approbation
which the Committee may recommend to the Society.

Resolved to recommend to the Society to return Thanks to Caleb Whitefoord, Esq. for the Zeal shewn by Him for the Interest of the Society by
which the Portrait of their Founder Mr. Shipley was obtained for their
use, and also for the present of the Portrait of Dr. Templeman procured
by him from R. Cosway, Esq. R.A. to be a Companion to the Portrait of
Mr. Shipley.[11]

By 1800 Caleb Whitefoord had come to be regarded as one of the most important members of the Society of Arts, and it can have come as no surprise when, on the 22nd March of that year, he was elected a Vice President of the Society. The Society's *Rules and Orders* provided for sixteen Vice Presidents, and Caleb was elected in succession to Francis Stephens, who had resigned on 29th January. An example of Caleb's prestige in the Society at this time is his taking the chair at a Society meeting on 19th March, which was before his actual election as a Vice President. He had earned the Society's gratitude through his long years of service as a Committee Chairman and by a steady adherence to his determination made after the rebuff of 1785 to do his 'utmost for the Society's Advantage, whenever any Business occurr'd wherein I could be useful'. As with his chairmanship of the Polite Arts Committee, Caleb was conscientious in fulfilling his obligations as a Vice President to preside at Society meetings over the years. The Society of Arts had become a part of his life. In 1801, for example, he wrote to his wife: 'Today I dine and pass the Evening with our friend D'Israeli and tomorrow I am to be in the President's Chair at the Society'. It is interesting that he does not bother to specify which Society he means.[12]

The Society's appreciation of Caleb's services was shown by the unprecedented 'motion' passed when the news of his death was communicated by the Secretary. In previous instances the reporting of the death of a Vice President had been followed simply by an announcement of a decision to elect a successor to the office. On this occasion two members rose and moved 'That the Society have learned with the deepest regret the lamented death of their late Vice-President Caleb Whitefoord, Esq. who for a period of nearly half a Century as a Member of this Society, with equal honour to himself and benefit to the public, zealously promoted the objects of Science and usefulness'. This complimentary motion was carried without dissent.[13]

For some thirty years Caleb lived in Craven Street and then moved to No. 2 James Street, Adelphi, where his friend Isaac Disraeli, whom he proposed for membership of the Society of Arts, also had an apartment. At James Street, wrote J. T. Smith, Caleb created a picture gallery in an octagonal room with an upper light which 'was considered by Mr. Christie of so excellent a shape for the exhibition of pictures that he adopted it when he fitted up his great room in King Street'. After four years he moved again, probably because of his growing family—he had married in 1800—to a large house in Argyll Street, near Oxford Street, and there he stayed until his death in 1810. Argyll Street is within easy walking distance of Mortimer Street, where his friend Joseph Nollekens, the sculptor, lived. Smith says that 'at this time Caleb was so constant a guardian of Nollekens's knocker, that no one ventured to cope with his wit on that sculptor's threshold; for like Goldsmith's goose, he stoutly kept up his right to the pond's side . . . Advanced on the journey of life as Nollekens was, little did this "Cross-reader" imagine that the road he was treading was straiter for him, and that an earlier period was fixed for his own departure.'[14]

Smith wrote after his own disappointment as the expected heir to Nollekens' fortune, and there is little reason to believe his suggestion that Caleb, who since 1790 had been in receipt of an income from the government, was playing the part of Corvino to Nollekens' Volpone. Similarly his account of Nollekens' meanness is contradicted by the sculptor's legacies to Caleb Whitefoord's widow and five children. Smith's description of Caleb's appearance, however, is of great interest. 'Caleb Whitefoord', he wrote in his *Book for a Rainy Day*, 'was what is usually called a slight built man and much addicted when in conversation to shrug up his shoulders. He had a thin face, with little eyes. His dress, upon which he bestowed great attention, was in some instances singular, particularly in his hat and wig.' In the *Life of Nollekens* he describes him 'as the last gentleman who wore the true Garrick cut'.[15]

It was this characteristic of retaining an eighteenth-century style of dress into the nineteenth century which Wilkie caught so well in his *Letter of Introduction*. Wilkie had come down from Scotland at the age of nineteen bearing a letter of introduction to Caleb from Sir George Sandilands. The seventy-year-old Vice President of the Society of Arts, who had once been intimate with Sir Joshua Reynolds and was the friend of Cosway, West and Barry, was caught slightly off balance by the aspiring painter's youthful air and gave him the famous 'dubious look' which Wilkie was to record for the delight of posterity. The painting, and Wilkie's preliminary sketch, are of interest for the hints they give of the appearance of the interior of Caleb's House in Argyll Street. Since Wilkie was working from memory four years after Caleb's death and is known to have used his own possessions as props in his compositions, we cannot be sure of his accuracy. Yet the ambience of taste and connoisseurship is undoubtedly correct. What is certain is that the house contained not only a hundred or more oil paintings; 'chiefly Italian pictures and choice specimens of Sir Joshua Reynolds', but a large collection of drawings, medals and prints by the 'great Italian masters . . . and the English masters . . . the most complete perhaps in England . . . proofs of Mr. West, Mr. Cosway, etc. etc.', as the enthusiastic auctioneer maintained.[16]

At his death the *European Magazine* aptly described Caleb Whitefoord as one of those men of 'easy, good natured, social disposition, that . . .

have always seemed *necessary* links of the great chain that binds Society together . . . With a very considerable portion of *real humour* and *ready wit* he was liberal in his ideas, unassuming in his manners, and in his classical and literary attainments highly respectable'. His one weakness, as the obituary tactfully pointed out, was a failure to apply himself to any one work of creative endeavour. Yet as his surviving manuscripts show, he preferred to work behind the scenes, and his historical significance lies not merely in his famous flurry into international diplomacy but in his long years of voluntary work, both institutionally and personally, in promoting the arts and letters of his country.[17]

Part 2

USEFUL ARTS PROMOTED

The Society's commitment to support a range of human endeavours was clear from the title it chose to define its several missions, as well as from the six principal committees it developed early in its history, through which it conducted much of its business: Agriculture, Chemistry, Polite Arts, Manufactures, Mechanics, and Colonies and Trade. The Society quickly recognized that while the world became necessarily more specialized, the Society must look to ways to address seemingly different subjects, to fund and support a variety of activities under a common roof with common administrative and financial assistance. The minutes of the Society's first meeting show the intent of the founders to endow both pragmatic and artistic goals. Members sought ways to encourage the discovery of the mineral cobalt, because of its value both as a colouring agent for glass and as a washing substance, and the cultivation of the madder plant as a source for a dye essential to the textile industry. At the same time they proposed a premium for youths under the age of sixteen who produced 'the best Pieces of Drawing, and Show themselves most capable, when properly examined.' The essays in this section reveal how the Society supported the 'useful arts', a category given a variety of definitions, from the essentially aesthetic to the clearly pragmatic.

In chapter 6, D. G. C. Allan clarifies the Society's early interest in beaux-arts; it intended not simply to encourage depictions of beauty but to make London a strong artistic rival to Paris. The Society viewed art as aesthetic capital that would enrich the nation in tangible ways. The Society's early years were particularly blessed by those who could speak persuasively for the arts. To cite the membership of Reynolds, Hogarth, Benjamin West or Allan Ramsay is to indicate only the most recognizable figures who served the arts. Others made essential contributions, among them the engraver Giovanni Cipriani, and Sir Henry Cheere himself, who worked with Hogarth and others to stimulate artistic activity. While the London artistic community consistently sought patrons other than the Society, the young institution gave both its major and lesser practitioners vital support.

In chapter 7, Gertrud Seidmann observes that even a minor artistic speciality like gem engraving received Society encouragement. In supporting the work of such figures as Nathaniel Marchant and Edward Burch, the Society saw that gem engraving flourished on native grounds, making available to a local community (Samuel Johnson among them) an art form hitherto available chiefly on the Continent. Leo J. De Freitas's commentary on wood engraving (chapter 8) complements the essay on gem engraving, though wood engraving was joined less to aesthetic considerations and more to the requirements of commerce, particularly those of printing. There were, in fact, few better illustrations of what the Society meant by the 'useful arts', and it was through its encouragement that wood engraving became linked to the revolution in print that characterized the later eighteenth century.

In chapter 9, J. B. Harley demonstrates how the 'useful arts' in the context of cartography take on special meaning. Arguably, there is no art more useful than determining where one is. In encouraging map-making through open competition and insisting that surveyors use modern techniques of surface measurement, the Society helped fix reliable maps of the nation. Harley's essay characterizes the collection as a whole: with careful use of the Society's archives and other collateral material, he defines but does not exaggerate the institution's contributions to a particular subject.

Perhaps in no context so much as in whaling were the useful and aesthetic combined: whale oil fuelled a preindustrial economy, primarily in domestic lighting; whalebone was the eighteenth-century plastic, finding incorporation in a variety of items, including ladies' corsets, umbrellas, and furniture; and the whale's fluids provided cosmetic and medicinal materials. In chapter 10, Walter M. Stern provides a full review of the Society's extensive involvement in the improvement of whaling, one that involved definitions of the 'useful arts' now seen to be vicious and short-sighted.

In chapter 11, John Sunderland explores the terrain of art history in the context of Samuel Johnson's *Idler* no. 45 and the Society's prize for history painting. Both, he shows, deviated from accepted academic thinking on the genre. Here one sees a special definition of the 'useful arts', one that argues essentially in an aesthetic context that Britain is sufficiently endowed culturally to provide its own matter for artistic representation. This essay echoes, then, the first in this section, and both serve as part of the special definition of the 'useful arts' that the Society used to find ways of accommodating and encouraging the seemingly disparate worlds of arts, manufactures and commerce.

ARTISTS AND THE SOCIETY

IN THE EIGHTEENTH CENTURY

D. G. C. *Allan*

William Shipley, the Northampton drawing master, philanthropist and amateur scientist, nurtured the idea of founding in England what his friend Henry Baker called 'a Society to give Premiums in the Manner of that in Ireland'.[1] The Dublin Society for Promoting Husbandry and other useful arts offered premiums to young painters, and this aspect of its work was clearly in Shipley's mind when he wrote, in his 1753 *Scheme* for an English Society, of giving premiums for 'those Arts and Sciences which are at a low ebb amongst us; as Poetry, Painting, Tapestry, Architecture, etc.' Yet although there is some evidence to link Shipley with the St. Martin's Lane artistic coterie, it is significant that he turned to no London artist to assist him in the foundation of the Society. When his friends in Northampton encouraged him to proceed with his scheme in London, he looked to Henry Baker, FRS, the microscopist, and to Dr. Stephen Hales, FRS, divine and eminent naturalist, for encouragement. These men together with two other Fellows of the Royal Society, two Peers of the Realm, a surgeon, a linen draper, a pottery manufacturer and a gentleman whose profession was not stated formed the group of ten who met Shipley at Rawthmell's Coffee House, Covent Garden, to found the Society of Arts on 22nd March 1754.[2]

Originally appeared in *Jnl. RSA*, 132 (Feb., Mar., Apr., May, 1984), 204-5, 271-76, 339-41, 401-6.

It was certainly not a Society of Artists, and its chief publicist, Henry Baker, wrote to his Cornish correspondent William Borlase in August:

> that some Noblemen and Gentlemen of Fortune, at the head of whom are Lord Romney, Lord Folkestone, Lord Shaftesbury, the Bishop of Worcester, Dr. Hales &c are forming a Society to encourage Industry, by giving Rewards for the Discovery of useful things, and for the Improvement of Arts and Manufactures: And as *Cobalt* may probably be found in your Country, you'l be so good to put the Papers into Such Hands as you think most likely to seek after it.

Borlase replied saying that he had dispersed the papers relating to cobalt. He then went on to make a remark of striking relevance to our subject:

> I congratulate you Sir, and my other friends in London upon the plan for rewarding Industry and Discovery being patronised by Gents. so able . . . there is no question but it will be attended with improvement in Arts here in England as well as elsewhere, and I hope may in time further an Academy for all the Arts of Designing equal to any in Europe especially if it shall be so happy as to meet with the Sanction of Authority and the countenance of the Royal Family—you know very well that Louis the 14th was the Soul and Spirit of all those Improvements in France, which make it the present Envy of the World.[3]

How did this idea come into Borlase's mind?

A partial answer may be found by returning to that first meeting of Shipley, Baker and their friends at Rawthmell's Coffee House. The minutes record as the first item of business after the formation of the Society the proposal 'to consider, whether a Reward should not be given for the finding of Cobalt in this Kingdom', then 'to consider whether a Reward should not be given for the Cultivation of Madder in this Kingdom', and thirdly, after these two quasi scientific topics, that:

> It was likewise proposed, to consider of giving Rewards for the Encouragement of Boys and Girls in the Art of Drawing, and it being the opinion of all present that the Art of Drawing is absolutely necessary in many Employments, Trades and Manufactures, and that the Encouragement thereof may prove of great Utility to the Public, it was resolved to bestow Premiums on a certain number of Boys and Girls under the Age of Sixteen, who shall produce the best Pieces of Drawing, and Show themselves most capable, when properly examined.[4]

The premium offers for drawings developed into an elaborate system of classified competitions for various sorts of excellence in what were called 'the polite arts'. We shall consider the growth and relative decline of the system in relation to other aspects of the Society's work, but first it is important to examine the concept of an 'Academy for all the Arts of Designing equal to any in Europe' receiving Royal Patronage, which occurred to Borlase when he saw the list of the Society's first drawing premiums. It had been in the minds of several persons in the 1740s and early 1750s. Dr. Samuel Madden, the originator and supplementer of the Dublin Society's premiums, tried to establish a premium fund in England at some point before the death of Frederick, Prince of Wales. He had, as he told Shipley in 1757, sought the patronage of his 'dear and ever honoured Master the late Prince of Wales, but I am sorry to say', Madden continued, 'though the Prince approved it and my zeal, he told me his finances would not bear such a Burden, which was fitter for his Royal Father's Encouragement (or words to that Effect) than his, and so it is dropped neglected.'[5] Unlike his son and grandson, George II had little general interest in the arts, so Shipley received no Royal support when he established his Society in 1754. By that time, Frederick, Prince of Wales, was dead, but the Princess Dowager maintained her late husband's 'second court' at Leicester House, and her Clerk of the Closet, Dr. Stephen Hales, did give assistance to Shipley in his scheme.[6]

The idea of a national academy of arts, supported by a 'Royal Foundation', had been put forward in 1749 by the architect John Gwynn, who belonged to the late Prince's circle, to which Shipley was also linked. Gwynn shared Shipley's belief in the value of drawing instruction for all classes. 'There is scarce any Mechanic, let his Employment be ever so simple', he wrote, 'who may not receive advantage' from it. He pointed out that although the Royal Society was older, he believed, and superior to the French Academy of Sciences, and the Académie Française itself, he thought, had become degenerate, yet France had in her Academy of Painting and Sculpture an institution which gave her 'Glory and Advantage'. Were such an academy 'imitated and improved upon', London, Gwynn believed, would become 'a Seat of Arts, as it is now of Commerce, inferior to none in the Universe'.[7] The Society of the Dilettanti under the leadership of Sir Francis Dashwood—later to become an active supporter of Shipley's Society—was also putting forward a scheme for a public academy at this time. The Dilettanti's project was probably the one which gave rise to a proposed meeting of the St. Martin's Lane artists called in October 1753 to elect twenty-four 'professors' for a public academy for the improvement of painting, sculpture, and architecture. Those who proposed the 1753 meeting came forward two years later with a printed plan and draft charter for a Royal Academy which one of their number, Henry Cheere, the sculptor, laid before the Society of Arts. This 1755 plan contained arguments based on economic interest and national self-esteem which must have appealed to Shipley and the five other foundation members when they heard them read out at a meeting of the Society held on 19th February. Cheere believed: 'the whole Secret lies in this: when Princes for their Grandeur . . . have had Recourse to painting, the Encouragement given to the Professor, gave Spirit to the Art, and others thought it worth their while to Distinguish themselves, in hope of receiving the like Reward'. Royal patronage so described was eminently desirable, as Shipley and his friends knew very well. Yet more immediately available were subventions from the Nobility. Had not Lords Romney and Folkestone guaranteed the Society's initial premiums, and were not the Dilettanti prepared to spend monies on an Academy? The plan concluded:

> A Charter for such a Royal Academy has been prepared by which the said Committee of Artists are to be Impowered to receive Contributions towards a Fund for defraying the Charge of the same. A Plan has also been prepared, for Oeconomising, and directing the whole, which it is hoped is not liable to any Material Exceptions; And all that is wanting to carry it into Execution is the Benevolence of the Public.
>
> As then the Undertaking is of a Public Nature, as the Expence to the Public will be Inconsiderable in Comparison to the Advantages to be Expected from it, as a distinguished Set of Noblemen and Gentlemen long ago Convinced of the Necessity of such a Plan Set apart a Sum of Money to be Applied to a Similar Use when Opportunity should Offer; as pecuniary Rewards have been Offered by another Society of Noblemen, and Gentlemen, to Stimulate and Encourage young Beginners, and as no Foundation, how Narrow in its Views and purposes soever has ever yet wanted patrons and Benefactors, it would become criminal even to suppose a possibility, That such a One as this would be suffered to Perish in the Birth for want of Assistance Only.[8]

A formal record of the Society's reaction to Cheere's proposals is contained in the minutes. They note quite simply: 'Mr. Cheere brought a plan for the founding of an Academy for Painting, Sculpture, etc. which was read out and the Copy presented to the Society for which thanks were ordered to those Gentlemen who had formed it, and a correspondence was desired with the said Gentlemen.'[9]

The 'correspondence' would not take place until 1760, when the artists, though still not yet organized as an Academy, felt confident enough to plan a major exhibition of their works and approached the Society, in

Johnson's eloquent phrase, for 'that Countenance Novelty must always need'.[10] By then the Society could count on a considerable revenue from subscriptions and was administering an elaborate system of premiums for the 'polite arts'.

MEMBERS AND PREMIUMS IN THE FIRST DECADE, 1755-64

By 1764 the membership of the Society of Arts reflected a wide spectrum of ranks and occupations in which artists occupied a small but brilliant section. Out of a total of some 2,136 members, there were 213 with titles; 66 clergymen; 48 with naval or military designations; 898 'Esquires' of whom 5 said they were 'Merchants', 80 'Gentlemen'; 99 medical men; and 812 entitled 'Mister' with or without an additional occupational description. In this latter group 378 admitted to a trade or craft, and of these 46 used designations associated with the 'Polite Arts'. There were, for instance, 14 'Engravers' and 10 'Painters', small numbers when compared with 88 merchants, but capable of comparison with the 15 'Linen Drapers', 14 'Mercers', 12 'Booksellers', 10 'Brokers', and 10 'Haberdashers' and certainly exceeding the solitary 'Paper Manufacturer', 'Perfumer', 'Plumber', 'Organ Builder', 'Vinegar Merchant' and numerous other occupations restricted to one representative in the lists.

There were certain curious variations in the styles adopted by the artist members. Robert Edge Pine and Richard Cosway, for instance, called themselves 'Artist', whereas Francis Cotes and Benjamin West used the style 'Painter', which David Martin, unlike J. H. Mortimer, qualified as 'History Painter'. Thomas Hudson called himself 'Portrait Painter', and Thomas Payne 'Landscape Painter'. George James called himself 'Limner', but James Scouler preferred 'Miniature Painter'. Nicholas Read was described as 'Statuary', and John Devall, Jnr., as 'Mason'. William Woollett was simply 'Engraver', but William Pether was 'Painter and Mezzotint Engraver'. Then we can augment this roll call of outstanding talent and increase the total of artist members by adding to it the names of fourteen known artists who preferred to give no occupational designation in the Society's Subscription Book. For example, Cipriani, William Hoare, Reynolds, Shipley and six others were all plain 'Misters' to which Reynolds added 'FRS' and Shipley 'Gentleman'. John Astley, Allan Ramsay, John Shackleton and Christian Zincke were all 'Esquires', Ramsay and Shackleton being no doubt justified in claiming the higher status by virtue of their royal appointments, and Astley and Zincke because of their private wealth.[11] Then most superior of all and of especial interest to our story of the Society's artist members was Sir Henry Cheere, Knt.[12]

The minutes of the meeting of the Society held on 19th February 1755 not only record, as has already been mentioned, that 'Mr. Cheere brought a plan for the founding of an Academy' but that 'the following Gentlemen being paid Subscribers signed the Book, viz. Mr. Nettleton, Mr. Cheere and Mr. Dalton'. From this we can see that the first two artists apart from Shipley to join the Society were Cheere and Dalton, who used the circumstances of their election to canvass support for their proposed academy. The constitution of the Society under which candidates for membership had to be proposed by existing members had not yet come into force, but both Cheere and Dalton would have been well known to those present.[13] Their names had been included amongst the 'five of the most eminent Masters in drawing' who were 'desired to assist in determining the Merit of the Drawings made by Boys and Girls . . . claiming the Premiums to be given by the Society',[14] and on 15th January 1755 they had attended a meeting of the Society to perform this function.

The next artist to be elected a member was Hogarth. He joined on 31st December 1755 on Cheere's proposal and on 21st January 1756 acted as one of the judges of the premium drawings in company with both Cheere and Dalton. In later years as the total membership grew, a distinction developed between the active and general membership, and as we shall see, committee chairmen and committee members would make up the former group. To assess the contribution of the artist members to the work of the Society we shall need to see which of them can be counted as coming within this category. But before this, when speaking of the early years we can certainly include both Cheere and Hogarth amongst the active élite. For not only did they act as judges for the prize-winning drawings, they were also nominated to serve on *ad hoc* committees covering other aspects of the Society's interests.

Thus we can see that practising artists were first brought into the membership of the Society through participation in its work of encouraging drawing and that, like William Borlase, they at once connected this with the idea of a public academy of arts. Although this academy took more than a decade to materialize and was to be entirely separate from the Society, the artist members were prepared to play an active part in the Society's general work in these early years.

On 4th February 1756 both Hogarth and Cheere were nominated to the committee appointed to make arrangements for the Society to rent accommodation in John Fielding's house in the Strand, and in April to committees on medals and buff leather. At the end of the year they were included in the committee appointed to consider encouraging the production of silk cocoons in Georgia and other possible subjects for premiums. Both Cheere and Hogarth, in company with Reynolds and Joshua Kirby, who had now joined the Society on 'Athenian' Stuart's proposal, were appointed as judges for the premium drawings on 26th January and on 2nd February 1757 as members of a committee to regulate the future method of judging. We find Cheere and Hogarth attending a Society meeting on 9th February and Hogarth and Reynolds being nominated to a committee on verdigris on the 16th. It has been suggested that it was this sort of non-artistic aspect of the Society's work which caused Reynolds to give up his membership in 1764, though the dispute over the exhibitions seems a more likely cause.[15]

Kirby seems to have confined his committee work to artistic subjects and was still active in 1760, when Thomas Hollis recorded his 'ill humour and petulant' behaviour at a meeting 'to reconsider the drawings given in for the Premium for Landscapes'. Kirby was annoyed because the award already voted to his son was being brought into question. He continued, however, as a member of the Society until 1765, when, like Reynolds, he probably resigned because of his association with the rival exhibiting society of artists. Hogarth, who had stopped paying his subscription in 1758, turned against the Society on the ground that he had no real belief in the value of its drawing premiums. He thought these raised false expectations of future employment amongst the young artists who won them and could not be of assistance to English manufactures, which, in his view, needed no improvement.[16] Perhaps he fell out with Allan Ramsay, who had emerged since his election as the most active artist member of the Society. By 1761 Ramsay's appearances at the Society were so frequent that Horace Walpole thought them worthy of record.[17]

Committee service and in particular committee chairmanship provide convenient indexes of a member's contribution to the work of the Society. Provision for the appointment of a committee was first made on 24th April 1754, at the Society's third meeting after its foundation. In November of the same year the fourth Wednesday in the month was set aside for committee meetings. The Society's 'Plan', which was approved on 19th February 1755, mentions only an annually appointed committee of accounts, but it is evident that the Society felt itself constitutionally empowered to appoint *ad hoc* committees, since twenty-two such bodies were appointed during the period down to 23rd February 1757. Then at a meeting held on 2nd March 1757 a motion proposing the annual appointment of eight standing committees with the titles 'Correspondence', 'Rules, Orders and Ordinary Business', 'Colonies and Trade', 'Minerals and Chymical Subjects', 'Mechanics and Manufactures', 'Agriculture', 'Arts and Literature' and 'Accounts' was carried unanimously. Standing committees more or less according to this pattern were to be used by the Society, together with *ad hoc* committees, down to the middle of the nineteenth century, but it was not until 1760 that their precise form took shape.[18]

The regulations relating to the *composition* of the Society's committees had also taken time to evolve. The earliest mention of the appointment of an *ad hoc* committee occurs in the Society's minutes for 10th December 1755, when five members were named as a committee to investigate British ores. The next reference comes a week later when seven persons were appointed to determine Shipley's invigilation fees, and the important rider added that 'any other member of the Society' would be regarded as belonging to the committee should he 'be pleased to attend'. The same regulation applied to the Society's first annual standing committee, that of Accounts, and the 1758 *Rules and Orders* laid down the rule which was to prevail until the nineteenth century: 'Notwithstanding particular gentlemen are named for each committee every Member that shall please to attend is of every Committee'.[19] The *ad hoc* committees were named at the time of their appointment, which might be at any of the Wednesday meetings throughout the year. The use which the Society made of them increased rapidly up to 1760 and then declined, probably as a result of the growing importance of the standing committees. Their sizes ranged from single figures to twenty or more, and in special cases, the total would exceed fifty. Certain names occur again and again in those listed, with the foundation members and present and future active vice presidents and chairmen serving with regularity over the years. We have already noted that Cheere, Hogarth and Reynolds did their stint; Allan Ramsay was also frequently appointed to committees. A giant 'Committee of Premiums' with sixty-nine members was first named in 1760 and then reappointed in 1761. The only artists included were Ramsay and Robert Edge Pine. In 1762 it was divided up into six separate committees (see table 1).

No regulations were laid down for the choosing of the chairmen of the various committees until 1758, when the first *Rules and Orders* confirmed what had probably been the practice until that year: 'When any particular Business is referred to a Committee, on the first Meeting of such Committee they are to elect a Chairman from amongst themselves.' Then in 1760 came the decision to hold annual elections for two chairmen for each

Table 1.

Committees in 1762		Named members
Committee of Polite & Liberal Arts	28	(including Ramsay, Devis, Reynolds and Shackleton)
Committee of Agriculture	21	(no artists)
Committee of Manufactures	21	(")
Committee of Mechanics	26	(")
Committee of Chemistry, Dyeing & Mineralogy	25	(")
Committee of British Colonies & Trade	25	(")[20]

one of the various standing committees. In the first two of these elections there was no restriction on the sort of member who might be elected as a committee chairman, but thereafter it was resolved that 'The chairmen of several Committees of Premiums shall be chosen from among the members who do not profess the Arts, Manufactures or Branches of Trade, which are the peculiar objects of these Committees'. The minutes of the Society do not indicate the reason for this limitation, but it is perhaps significant that Allan Ramsay, who had been put forward unsuccessfully as a candidate for chairman of the Committee of Correspondence and Papers in November 1760 and had previously taken the chair at two meetings of the Polite Arts Committee, where he was a regular attender, excused himself from being chosen chairman of the latter only a week before the regulation excluding professionals was carried.[21]

Although Ramsay continued as a subscribing member of the Society for the rest of the decade, he did not again attend the committee. It would be wrong to assume, however, that this body was without professional advice. A group of artist members was prepared to serve under a lay chairman in the years 1762, 1763 and 1764, and very few meetings were held without one or more artist members being present.[22] The extent of their activity can be seen from the number of their attendances:

1762	Attendances
William Bellers, landscape painter	16
William Shipley, the founder	15
Robert Edge Pine, history painter and premium winner	14
James Basire, engraver to the Society of Antiquaries	6
Arthur Devis, painter of conversation pieces	6
John Finlayson, engraver, and Secretary to the Free Society	4

1762   *Attendances*

Nicholas Anderson, engraver, proposed as a member
  by Shipley   4
Richard Cosway, premium winner and Shipley's
  ex-pupil   4
John Boydell, engraver   2
Henry Millington, described as 'Artist' in the
  Subscription Book   2
  (and some better known figures who each attended
  on one occasion only, e.g. Cheere, Anthony
  Highmore, Thomas Hudson, J. H. Mortimer and
  William Pether, as well as the architects, Chambers
  and Mylne.)

1763   *Attendances*
John Finlayson   21
Shipley and Bellers   18 each
Gaetano Manini, exhibitor of history painting at the
  Society of Artists and the Free Society   14
James Basire   10
R. E. Pine   7
Arthur Devis   5
Pether   4
Boydell   3
William Pars, premium winner and ex-pupil of Shipley   2
  (Mortimer again came to one meeting, as did
  Alexander Bannerman the engraver, who like
  Manini and Pars had not been present the
  previous year.)

1764   *Attendances*
Bellers   15
Finlayson   11
Shipley   9
Basire   7
Pine   7
Boydell   6
Manini   5
Bannerman   4
Devis   4
Mylne, architect   4
John Donaldson, miniature painter   4
Francis Cotes, ex-pupil of Shipley and early premium
  winner   3

1764   *Attendances*

Thomas Keyse, future premium winner   2

   (These three, Donaldson, Cotes and Keyes, had
   not attended in the previous years. Mortimer again
   attended once, as did Cheere, who had not been
   present in 1763.)

It appears from this record of attendances that although the more prominent and established artists were ceasing to play a part in the Society's affairs, a considerable interest in its work was still being taken by a body of competent professionals. The first point may well have been connected with the rise of the exhibiting societies. This story has often been told. Briefly what happened was that the London artists who had advocated the erection of a public academy in 1753 and 1755, and most of whom became members of the Society, held an exhibition under the Society's aegis in 1760; the suggestion having been first made by Pine in 1759. In 1761 their ranks were split over the method of managing the exhibition, and as a result two exhibitions were held, one in the Society's rooms and the other in Spring Gardens, under the auspices of a newly established 'Society of Artists of Great Britain'. In 1762 the artists who exhibited in the Society's Rooms also formed themselves into a Society and in 1763 took the title 'The Free Society of Artists'. After some internal divisions within its own ranks, the Free Society again exhibited at the Society's Rooms in 1764, but in 1765 had to look elsewhere as a resolution to allow an exhibition was defeated at a meeting of the Society.[23] It is not surprising therefore to find that in the years 1762-4 artists such as Bellers, Basire, Finlayson and Devis, who were all members of the Free Society, should be active in the affairs of the Society of Arts, whereas Hayman, Ramsay and Reynolds, who were leading members of the Society of Artists of Great Britain, should be conspicuously absent from the meetings of its committee of Polite Arts. Pine, though not a member of the Free Society, exhibited at its exhibitions down to 1764 and benefited greatly from the Society of Arts as a winner of its premiums. Before commenting on the rather scandalous fact that until 1764 members were allowed to compete for the Society's pecuniary rewards, a word should be said about the premium system and its growth in the Society's first decade.

The Society's first premiums list (1754) offered four awards, the second (1755) twelve, the third (1756) twenty-two and the fourth (1757) sixty-three. In 1758 more than one hundred awards were offered, and the lists were expanded each year until 1764, when a total of 364 was reached. In

Table 2.

| Year | Premiums Offered | | Place of the 'Polite Arts' in relation to other categories |
	Total	Polite Arts	
1758	122	22	Equal second with Chemistry (Agriculture first with 33)
1759	152	40	First
1760	165	43	First
1761	197	61	First
1762	303	86	Second (Agriculture first with 87)
1763	375	107	Second (Colonies first with 112)
1764	380	106	Second (Colonies first with 123)

| Year | Premiums and Bounties Awarded | | Place of the 'Polite Arts' in relation to other categories |
	Total	Polite Arts	
1758	51	39	First
1759	91	66	First
1760	76	62	First
1761	101	76	First
1762	71	44	First
1763	124	74	First
1764	147	99	First

the first four years the premiums were listed more or less in the order in which they had occurred to the Society. Then in 1758 the practice was begun of dividing up the lists into broad subject classifications, similar to those used for the standing premium committees.

The progress of the 'Polite Arts' category was then spectacular[24] (see table 2).

The printed list of premiums issued in 1758 offered awards to young persons according to a schedule ranging from Life figures to copying prints, for drawings of 'the Human Figure', 'Statues', 'Casts', 'Landscapes', and 'Beasts, Birds, Fruits or Flowers'. Some of these were confined to students in 'The Academy for Painting, etc. in *St. Martin's Lane*' (where Cheere, Hogarth and Ramsay exercised authority), others were for candidates who had studied in the Duke of Richmond's gallery (Wilton, its Keeper, was a member of the Society, as was the Duke himself) and yet others were restricted to young ladies and gentlemen.

In the same list, there were also offers of premiums for drawings of designs for weavers, calico-printers, cabinetmakers and coachmakers and for manufacturers of iron, brass, china, earthenware, or 'any other Mechanic Trade that requires Taste'. All these were for young people. There was also a prize for a copper medal, open to candidates a little older, but still under twenty-five. During the next few years the list was extended by the addition of engraving, mezzotinting, etching, gem-engraving, cameo-cutting and modelling, bronze-casting, mechanical drawing, and architectural and furniture designs. Some premiums were awarded under these various heads, but on the whole, writes Trueman Wood, 'the response was hardly satisfactory as the number of entries in the purely artistic classes was far more numerous'.[25]

In 1759 the Society began to offer the exceptionally large prizes of 100, 50 and 20 guineas for paintings in oil colours of subjects from British or Irish history containing not less than three human figures as large as life. This competition was open to artists of all ages, and we find Pine carrying off the first prize at the age of 30 in 1760 and repeating his success in 1763, when there was the well-known dispute over who should be placed second: George Romney or John Hamilton Mortimer.[26]

These premiums for history painting resulted from a concern to point moral lessons from the past and even to make comments on the political present. 'Republican' Hollis was an important influence, and Samuel Johnson himself was occupied with the matter.[27] In this way lay members of the Society were prepared to depart from the view that the polite arts premiums were intended only to assist manufactures.[28]

Shipley would not have disapproved of this modification of his scheme, since in 1762 he proposed that the Society should sponsor a Repository of Arts where 'Original pictures' would be on permanent exhibition for artists to copy. He also was shrewd enough to see that an interest in the 'polite arts' increased the popularity of the Society and encouraged the recruitment of new members. 'Had we not patronised these very entertaining and extensive subjects . . . this Society had not now existed' was his retrospective comment on this period, when 'twenty to thirty new members were balloted for in an evening'.[29] Such popularity, however, was destined to be checked in the Society's second decade.

THE SECOND DECADE, 1765-74

The growth in the Society's membership which had given so much satisfaction to William Shipley in the Society's first decade came to an end at the beginning of the second. The number of subscribing members claimed by the Society in its printed lists fell from 2,485 in 1764 to 1,891 in 1770, and by 1774 only 1,506 were being claimed. The actual number of members paying their subscriptions was only 584 in 1774, compared with 1,376 in 1770. Many members fell into arrears with their subscriptions. The Society's Collector calculated the number of members in arrears as 1,119 in 1774. This not only presented a major financial problem but suggested a decline in the members' enthusiasm for the objects of the Society. More significant as an indication of its waning popularity was a fall in the number of new members elected each year from 1765 until 1769 and the continuing high numbers of resignations during the same period.[30]

Resignation took the form of the discontented members 'declining' to pay their subscription, this fact being noted in the Subscription Book, with, to the historian's loss, no record of the reasons for their displeasure. We can speculate that they might have been annoyed at the expenditure in the fairly recent past of so much of the Society's income on Blake's fish scheme and disappointed at the faulty structure of their new building in Denmark Court and their being forced 'to carry on their business in a tavern'.[31] An outstanding abuse, only recently remedied, was that members had been granted monetary awards, with artists, such as Robert Edge Pine, William Pars, John Finlayson and John Mortimer, all benefiting in this suspicious manner. Pine, elected in 1758, won the 100 guineas premium for history painting in 1760 and 1763. Pars, elected in 1762, received the third premium of 20 guineas for an oil painting of a history piece in 1764. Finlayson, also elected in 1762, received the first premium (15 guineas) for painting in enamel in 1764. Mortimer, who had won awards each year from 1759 to 1764, joined the Society on 8th February 1764. He was in consequence a member of the Society during the period when his claim for the premium for history painting was under consideration. He was voted the first prize of 100 guineas by the Committee of Polite Arts on 24th April 1764. The 'Rule and Order' making members ineligible for pecuniary awards was passed on 2nd May 1764.[32] It must have taken a while for the membership at large to realize that this reform had been adopted, and there were still certainly grounds for discontent regarding the administration of the Society's awards.

In 1768 many members would have been shocked at the discovery of a long-standing fraud which had been perpetrated by one of their fellows, a certain Dr. John Stephens, who had pocketed the agricultural premiums he had claimed on behalf of non-existent planters. In the same year the press published what the Society called 'false, scandalous, malicious and injurious' articles about the adjudication of the polite art premiums. The villain in this case was Jared Leigh, amateur artist and formerly active member of the Committee of Polite Arts, who had recently resigned from the Society but still tampered with its affairs. Richard Wright, the marine artist and premium winner, told the Committee that 'the Artists in general imagined that Mr. Leigh could do what he would in the Society and that several of them had been thereby deterred from becoming Candidates and that Mr. Wright himself would not have put in for a Premium this Year in Sea Pieces but because he had heard that Mr. Leigh had left the Society.'[33]

The artist group of members reflected the general decline of the Society. In the years 1765 to 1774, 23 artists resigned, including Arthur Devis, John Donaldson, Richard Cosway, James Basire and Francis Vivares, and only ten appear to have been elected. The new recruits were generally men of the second rank in regard to talent, though Ozias Humphry, former pupil of Shipley, who was elected in 1767, achieved remarkable success as a miniature painter. Future activists in the Society's affairs were Valentine Green, the mezzotint engraver, elected in 1772, and Samuel Hieronymus Grimm, 'Landscape Painter', who joined the Society in the succeeding year. Until 1768 the work of the Polite Arts Committee continued to be assisted by a sizeable group of active artist members, and we find the same names as were listed in the minutes for the first decade with Shipley, Basire and Bellers remaining especially active. Shipley retired to Maidstone after his marriage in November 1767, and in May 1768, following the committee's inquiries into the Jared Leigh scandal a veritable 'Flight of the artists' began. In 1769 out of 20 meetings held by the committee only one appears to have been attended by an artist, and in 1770 the figure was 2 out of 13. In 1771 no artist appears to have attended, and in 1772 again a solitary attendance was recorded. The position improved in the last two years of the decade with two veterans, Boydell and Pine, turning up for a meeting each, the first in 1773 and the second in 1774, and four new names, making up a total of 25 meetings attended by artists out of 29 meetings held in these two years. Listed in order of numbers of attendances, the four new active artists in 1773 and 1774 were Valentine Green with 23 attendances and Hieronymus Grimm with 14 attendances; then came Philip Buckley, designated 'Painter', and the better-known David Martin, an exhibitor like

Table 3.

	Premiums offered		Place of the 'Polite Arts' in relation to the other categories
Year	Total	Polite Arts	
1765	310	93	Second
1766	186	41	Third
1767	140	19	Second
1768	155	37	Second
1769	176	28	Second
1770	178	29	Second
1771	182	25	Second
1772	219	28	Second
1773	260	35	Second
1774	296	34	Third

Green and Grimm at the Incorporated Society's exhibitions. Both attended once in 1773. Clearly Green and Grimm had emerged as the leading artists in the Society.[34]

As with the size of the membership, upon which the Society's income inevitably depended, the financial value both of the premiums offered and of the premiums and bounties given showed an absolute decline between 1765 and 1774 in spite of a relative recovery towards the end of the period. The same was true of the *numbers* of premiums offered, which fell from 310 in 1765 to 140 in 1767, and then rose in small amounts until the figure of 296 was reached at the end of the decade. The 'polite arts' premiums reflected the general pattern, though their recovery towards the end was not so marked (see table 3). The number of premiums and bounties actually awarded by the Society declined from 149 in 1765 to 23 in 1768 and remained under 30 until 1771, when the total given was 37. In 1772 there were 46 awards, but the total was reduced to 45 in 1775 and to 29 in 1774. The polite arts awards were generally the most numerous, being ahead of all the other categories in every year except in 1767 and 1769, when they were in second place to agriculture, and in 1771, when they were equalled by the agricultural awards as the most numerous of the categories. Their overall decline, however, indicates a growing lack of response to the Society's efforts in this field, which was particularly noticeable in the years 1768 and 1769, when, as we have seen, a public scandal hovered over the work of the Committee of Polite Arts (see table 4).

Table 4.

| Year | Awards Made | | Place of the 'Polite Arts' in relation to the other categories |
	Total	Polite Arts	
1765	149	92	First
1766	118	55	First
1767	58	17	Second
1768	23	10	First
1769	28	10	Second
1770	24	17	First
1771	37	14	First (with Agriculture)
1772	46	20	First
1773	45	23	First
1774	29	16	First

In the subject range of the polite arts premiums, various sorts of drawing, chiefly for juveniles, continued to be encouraged, and at the end of the decade we still find prizes being offered for patterns for silk weavers and calico printers and for models of furniture and ornaments. With the Royal Academy now established and the Incorporated Society still confident of the success of its annual exhibitions, it might have appeared that the Society of Arts had little to offer the mature artist. Yet at the end of the decade a plan was put forward to associate the leading members of the profession with its ideals and objectives. This was the scheme initiated by Valentine Green in 1774 to adorn the newly built meeting room in the Adelphi with historical scenes painted by Barry, Cipriani, Dance, Angelica Kauffman, Mortimer, Reynolds, West and Wright and allegorical subjects 'relative to the Institution and views of the Society' by Romney and Penny. As is well known, Barry alone performed the task, and it was his 'very signal exertion in the line of the polite arts' which did much to revive the Society's national reputation after the erosion of its finances and membership had caused such a dangerous situation in the late 1770s.[35]

MEMBERS AND PREMIUMS IN THE YEARS AFTER 1775

The total of paying members of the Society fell from 515 in 1775 to 311 in 1782, the lowest recorded figure since 1758. Some recovery took

place after 1784, and although there was no return to the intensive recruitment of the 1760s, the century ended with the Society having at least 625
contributing members. The members in arrears totalled 1,181 in 1776, and
it was hoped that some at least could be persuaded to renew their contributions. With this object a circular letter was sent out in March 1778
saying that two years' contributions would be sufficient to cancel all previous obligations. A few responded to this offer in an encouraging manner.
Others felt that the Society was sufficiently well established to be able to
do without their assistance or wrote to say that they had already communicated with the Collector. Most, like Sir Henry Cheere and Hieronymus
Grimm, ignored the request, and the Society was forced to give up printing
their names in the membership lists. The recruitment of new artist members, however, did not seem to reflect the general pattern. In the years 1775
to 1784 at least 14 new artists were elected as compared with 9 in the previous decade. But from 1785 until the end of the century, when the general
membership was increasing, only ten artists appear to have joined.[36]

The first recruit in 1775 was the French engraver François Godefroy,
who was said to have joined simply to have his name in the list of members and who gave up subscribing after only one year. David Adamson,
'Painter', of Oxford Street, also elected in 1775, was by contrast a most
loyal member and paid his two guineas regularly throughout the period.
In 1776 Richard Collins was the only recruit, and no artists at all seem to
have been elected in 1777. In 1778, however, there were four: Francis Bartolozzi and William Byrne the engravers, John Greenwood the painter and
John Bacon the sculptor, all of whom were proposed by Valentine Green.
Bacon always thought well of the Society, being grateful for the initial encouragement he had received as a result of its premiums. He occasionally
attended the Committee of Polite Arts in the years 1778 to 1794, as did
the veteran sculptor John Hayward. John Downman, ARA, also attended
in the 1780s, as did John Hall, 'Historical Engraver to his Majesty'; both
were elected on Green's proposal, the first in 1782 and the other in 1787.
John Johnson is an example of a sculptor who paid his subscription to the
Society on a regular basis from 1787 to 1812. He can be contrasted with
Richard Westmacott the elder, who paid only two subscriptions; one in
1788 and another in 1789. Although Benjamin West, the President of the
Royal Academy, rejoined the Society on Alderman Boydell's proposal in
1794, only three more artists seem to have been elected between then and
the end of the century. John Bingley, 'Statuary', joined in 1795, and Arthur
William Devis in 1796. James Barry was elected on 16th January 1799,
which was not long before his expulsion from the Academy. This turbulent
genius had become increasingly identified with the Society of Arts since

Valentine Green;
mezzotint from the
portrait by L. F. Abbott,
1788. Courtesy of the
RSA.

the first exhibition of his great works for the Meeting Room in 1783. That
he aimed his darts as frequently at his 'friends' in the Adelphi as he did at
those in Somerset House goes without saying. Yet the Society as a whole
had gained much from the lustre of his name and preferred to offer him
canonization, as an alternative to the martyrdom he sought either at its
hands or at the Academy's. The decline in the recruitment of artist members, in spite of Valentine Green's intentions to the contrary, can surely be
explained by a justifiable fear of coming near the special preserve of that
troubled genius.[37]

Not only was Valentine Green the most active artist member in this
period, but he also ranked amongst the active élite of the total membership as a committee chairman. In 1775 he was elected chairman of the
Committee of Correspondence and Papers, and although he gave up this
office in 1780, he continued to attend the Committee's meetings with great
regularity. In 1787 he again agreed to serve as chairman and was re-elected
each year until 1798. He was interested in the publication of the Society's
Transactions, Volume 1 of which appeared in 1783, and he seems to have
clashed with the agriculturalist Arthur Young, who played a leading rôle
in initiating the publication: 'I was the first to propose that annual publication . . . and Valentine Green, the engraver, had the impudence to assert
it originated with him', wrote Young in his autobiography.[38]

The Committee's minutes shed no light on Green's work in regard to
Volume 1, but they definitely confirm his interest in the succeeding an-

nual issues. As late as 1798, when lack of funds had obliged him to resign his membership, he still felt concerned enough to write to Samuel More, giving his professional advice on the engraved portraits used as frontispieces.[39] Green also had a long record of attendance at the Committee of Miscellaneous Matters, and he was concerned with the declining membership roll when it came under consideration of the Committee in 1782. Before that there had been his scheme for decorating the Great Room, which ultimately led to the initiation of Barry's cycle in 1777 and gained Green an honorary Gold Medal for his 'repeated services' to the Society. In 1785 he deplored the lack of royal patronage for the Society, and this led directly to the well-known approach to the Prince of Wales by Green's friend and fellow committee chairman, Caleb Whitefoord. Twelve years later Green made another abortive attempt to anticipate the Society's future by proposing the establishment of a governing council. When Green faced financial ruin at the end of the century as a result of the collapse of his print venture, Whitefoord came to his rescue and amongst many substantial kindnesses bought and gave back to him his gold medal. Had he had more knowledge of industry and commerce Green might well have succeeded as salaried secretary of the Society in 1799. Eventually thanks to his popularity in the world of art he secured the Keepership of the newly founded British Institution.[40]

In 1780, as we have mentioned, Green had declined to serve as chairman of the Correspondence Committee although he was actually elected to the office. This was because the members of the Society seemed to be prepared to overlook the 1761 regulation barring specialist chairmen and had also chosen him to preside at the Committee of Polite Arts, where he was, of course, already a regular attender. He remained chairman of the Polite Arts Committee until 1786, when he reverted to his former office. It was while holding the chairmanship of the Polite Arts Committee that he approached the Council of the Royal Academy with the idea that they should be the judges of a new annual premium to be offered by the Society 'For the best Historical Painting in Oil, being an Original Composition of five or more human figures, the principal figure not less than twenty six inches high. Painted by a Student of the Royal Academy, and submitted to public view in their Exhibition of 1784'.[41] After taking trouble to draft the terms of the award and to elicit the prior approval of the Academy, Green had the chagrin to find his proposal rejected by his own Committee at a meeting with himself in the chair. The minutes dated 5th December 1783 record that consideration being given to a

letter from Valentine Green, Esq. on a premium to be given by the Society
and determined by the Royal Academy for a painting to be done by a student
of that Academy,
Resolved it is the opinion of the Committee that this is not a proper Object
of the further attention of the Society.

Yet the minutes show that Green continued to preside at the Committee
later in the year and in 1784, when the judging of premium entries for
county maps, paintings on enamel and historical drawings took place. He
remained a regular attender at the Committee even after he gave up the
chairmanship and was even present at two meetings in 1797. The main
function of the Committee was of course the judging of premiums belonging to the category of Polite Arts.

For assessing the premium entries the Committee had long since ceased
to employ the assistance of professional 'Judges' and now relied exclusively on the professional skill of such artist members as were willing to
attend and the connoisseurship of lay members such as Caleb Whitefoord.
Only when the Committee was asked by the Society to consider technical questions regarding paint substances did it call in professional advice
from outside. Thus in 1794 Thomas Stothard was asked to give his opinion on George Blackman's 'oil-colour cakes', and in 1798 Richard Westall
and Thomas Daniell assisted the Committee in determining the merit of
Timothy Sheldrake's 'manner of painting believed by him to be similar
to that practised in the Venetian School'.[42] Blackman and Sheldrake both
received bounties from the Society. 'Bounties' were the name the Society
gave for the occasional awards it made for discoveries which were not
covered by its offer of 'Premiums'.

Let us see what had become of this system of awards after 1775. A
peak of 342 premium offers was reached in 1776, which was the highest
for twelve years, but after that the number fell until 1782, when 170 offers
were made. There was an increase to 175 in 1783, a further fall to 167 in
1784, and then a long upward swing from 1785 until 1791, when a total of
244 was reached. For the rest of the century the average was 246. In terms
of premiums offered the polite arts offers were in second place from 1778
until 1792, after which they fell below 'chemistry' as well as 'agriculture'.
In the last three years of the century they were also below the offers made
in the class of 'colonies and trade'. Their absolute decline over the whole
period can be seen by comparing the figures for 1775 and 1799 (see table 5).

In 1780 the total of awards made fell below 30 and was below that figure
until 1789, which was a freak year with a total of 65. Then from 1790 until

Table 5.

| Category | Premiums Offered | |
	1775	1799
Agriculture	197	140
Chemistry	19	40
Colonies and Trade	61	25
Manufactures	11	10
Mechanics	8	14
Polite Arts	37	21

the end of the century the annual average was 29. The polite arts were the pre-eminent category amongst the rewards made until 1788 when they fell to second place behind 'agriculture'. In 1789 they fell below 'mechanics' as well. In 1791 they regained their position as the second most numerous category and in 1797 and 1798 were once again at the top of the table. The last year of the century saw them again overtaken by 'agriculture', but the difference was only that between 8 and 7. The figures for 1775 and 1799 are shown in table 6.

Certain changes took place in the character of the polite arts premiums in the last quarter of the century. The offers for designs for calico printers were stopped in 1778, and this marked the virtual abandonment of the Society's direct concern with making the arts serve manufactures, though this objective was still proclaimed.[43] There was also an end to the premiums for history and landscape painting after 1780, in spite of a public suggestion by James Barry for 'one good premium every second . . . or third year', which he made in his 1783 *Account* of his paintings in the Meeting Room and of Valentine Green's proposal of 1784 which we have already noted.[44] The premiums for drawing, modelling and engraving continued to be offered, and the emphasis was on rewarding young artists, both amateurs and professionals.

Notwithstanding the contraction in the numbers and scope of the premiums, the calibre of the successful candidates remained high. Thus there were the awards made in 1779 to John Downman for an historical painting and to Richard Samuel for an historical drawing. Downman, as we have seen, became a member of the Society, and Samuel served as assistant secretary. Then there were William Martin's landscape paintings, which received a premium in 1780, and the young Thomas Lawrence's drawing of Raphael's *Transfiguration*, which gained an award in 1784. These were matched in the next decades by awards for drawings by Turner (1793), William Westall (1798) and Stephen Francis Rigaud (1799). In 1800 John Sell Cotman received an award for his 'drawing of the mill near Dorking'. Several engravers, sculptors and architects also stand out from the lists. Awards for engraving were received by Bewick (1775), William Coleman (1775, 1776, 1777), Isaac Taylor (1791), Charlton R. Nesbitt (1798), and for sculpture by John Bacon (1776, 1777, 1778), Thomas Englehart (1777), Charles Hotwell (1787), J. C. Lochée (1775, 1776, 1790), Charles Rossi (1794). In the class of architectural drawings, which from 1781 onwards was encouraged by the means of John Stock's endowment, there was the award made to Robert Smirke in 1797.[45]

The Society's attitude to the polite arts towards the end of the century was well set out by Samuel More in the address he gave at the time of the 1797 distribution of awards in the Meeting Room. More began by invoking the tremendous efforts made in the Society's early years:

> To promote in this Country a Just and true Taste for Drawing Painting, Sculpture, Architecture Engraving and whatever is usually styled The Polite and Liberal Arts was the first Object that attracted the Society's Attention and was justly for many Years a most favoured one; By a Register of the Rewards bestowed by this Society from its Institution it is apparent what great Sums have been bestowed under this Class, and that many of Those Artists who now make conspicuous figures in this Country gained their first Renown and were stimulated to those Exertions to which they owe their present Fame by the Rewards which they obtained here.

Table 6.

Category	Awards Made	
	1775	*1799*
Agriculture	4	8
Chemistry	4	1
Colonies and Trade	2	1
Manufactures	4	1
Mechanics	5	6
Miscellaneous	—	1
Polite Arts	16	7

As an immediately visible example of this last point he referred to

> the three Statues of Mars, Venus, and Narcissus which form Part of the
> Ornaments of this Room [and] stand conspicuous Proofs of the Advantages
> resulting from the . . . Rewards so deservedly in his Younger Days adjudged
> to Mr. John Bacon whose Works they are and who so richly merited the
> repeated Honours of the Society bestowed upon him, And which he still
> mentions as the Principal Inducement to apply himself . . . to the Study of
> his Profession.

He then went on to remind his audience of the Society's pioneer work for
exhibitions, to mention Hayman's letter of 1760 as 'an historical Anecdote
not generally known but which the Archives of the Society demonstratively
Prove' and to point out what he claimed were its consequences:

> After such Exhibitions had been made during several Years The various
> Branches of the Polite Arts were arrived at such a State as obtained Them
> the Patronage and Favour of Majesty and the Royal Academy was instituted.
> How they have flourished under that Patronage the Public can judge from
> the annual Exhibitions made at Somerset House.

Skating over the less complimentary fact that the Society's exhibitions
had been continued by the Free Society and not the Incorporated Society,
More was sowing the seeds of the legend that the Society had been a sort
of founder of the Royal Academy. Having thus flattered his audience, he
concluded by setting forth the Society's current policy in regard to the
polite arts:

> But the Arts having thus gained a high Degree of Support and protection
> elsewhere It has not been thought necessary for this Society to continue
> offering many of the Premiums that formerly stood on their Books under
> this Head, and the Rewards now offered by them are chiefly confined to the
> Encouragement of such Young Beginners as may hereafter intend to become
> Professors in the several Branches of the Polite Arts, or to Those in such
> higher Spheres of Life as may at a distant Period take upon them the Patron-
> age of future Artists, and Who, having given Proofs of Taste and Abilities,
> will be justly allowed as best able to determine on the Merits of others.[46]

This interest in pupils and patrons became firmly established in the next
century and went hand in hand with an ever-increasing pride in the Society's original association with the great names of the British School. Henry
Cole, who certainly did not neglect the industrial side of the Society's
work, thought it nonetheless appropriate that fine art exhibitions should
be held in the Society's House, and that prominent artists such as Thomas
Webster, J. C. Horsley, Charles Eastlake, and Daniel Maclise should join
the membership in 1847.[47] Horsley and Eastlake, like William Ross who

was also a member and Mulready whose work was the subject of the
1848 exhibition, had received juvenile awards from the Society, as had
Landseer, Frith and Millais. These names would be intoned over the years
in company with those of such early prize-winning prodigies as Cosway,
Mary Moser, Mortimer, Nollekens and Romney. The signature book containing the autographs of former members such as Cheere, Hogarth and
Reynolds became a treasured relic, and the backdrop to all the Society's
meetings, however much concerned with science and technology, were the
great works of Barry, fluctuating in public esteem but a constant reminder
that the Society had indeed been a Society of *Arts*.[48]

APPENDIX I. Checklist of Artist Members of the Society, 1754-1800,
with Dates of Election

Dates, titles and designations are taken from the MS Subscription Books, 1754-62, 1764-72,
1773-92, 1793-1802.
Subscribing Members

Adamson, Mr. David, *Painter,* 26 April 1775
Anderson, Mr. Nicholas, *Engraver,* 29 March 1758
Ashby, Mr. Harry, *Engraver,* 1 March 1780
Astley, John, 23 April 1760
Bacon, John, Esq., RA, *Artist,* 13 May 1778
Bannerman, Mr. Alexander, *Engraver,* 2 Nov. 1763
Baron, Mr. Bernard, *Engraver,* 3 June 1761
Barraud, Mr. Philip, *Engraver,* 20 Oct. 1762
Barrett, Mr. George, *Landscape Painter,* 28 March 1764
Barry, Jas., Esq., RA, 16 Jan. 1799
Bartolozzi, Francis, Esq., RA, 27 Feb. 1778
Basire, Mr. James, *jun., Engraver,* 29 Nov. 1758
Beastel, Mr. Leander, *Painter,* 5 Nov. 1760
Bellers, Mr. William, *Artist,* 15 Nov. 1758
Bickham, Mr. George, *Engraver,* 1 Sept. 1762
Bingley, Mr. John, *Statuary,* 7 Jan. 1795
Boulton, Mr. Samuel, *Herald Painter,* 13 Jan. 1762
Boydell, Mr. John, *Engraver,* 30 April 1760
Brookshaw, Mr. George, *Artist,* 19 Feb. 1783
Browne, Mr. John, *Engraver,* 8 Feb. 1764
Buckley, Mr. Philip, *Painter,* 2 Feb. 1772
Burch, Mr. Edward, *Seal Engraver,* 10 Feb. 1762
Byrne, Mr. William, *Engraver,* 25 Feb. 1778
Carpentiers, Mr. Adriaen, 30 April 1760
Cheere, Henry, Esq., 19 Feb. 1755
Cipriani, Mr. Giovanni, 7 Feb. 1759

Clee, Mr. Robert, *Engraver,* 14 Dec. 1763
Collet, Mr. John, 5 March 1760
Collins, Mr. Richard, *Portrait Painter,* 1 May 1776
Collivoe, Mr. Isaac, *Painter,* 26 April 1762
Cosway, Mr. Richard, *Artist,* 7 April 1762
Cotes, Mr. Francis, *Painter,* 9 April 1760
Cozens, Mr. Alexander, 23 April 1760
Dalton, Mr. Richard, 5 Feb. 1755
Devall, Mr. John, *jun., Mason,* 6 May 1761
Devis, Mr. Arthur, *Artist,* 13 May 1761
Devis, Arthur Wm., Esq., 21 Dec. 1796
Dixon, Mr. Joseph, *Mason,* 5 Nov. 1760
Donaldson, Mr. John, *Portrait Painter,* 29 Feb. 1764
Downman, John, Esq., ARA, 13 Nov. 1782
Drake, Mr. Nathan, *Colourman,* 16 Feb. 1763
Du Bourg, Mr. Richard, *Artist,* 27 Nov. 1782
Finlayson, Mr. John, *Miniature Painter,* 1 Sept. 1762
Finney, Mr. Samuel, 30 April 1760
Frye, Mr. Thomas, *Artist,* 14 May 1760
Gardnor, Mr. John, *Writing Master,* 10 June 1761
Godefroy, Mr. François, *Engraver,* 15 March 1775
Gossett, Mr. Isaac, *Artist,* 19 Jan. 1763
Green, Mr. Valentine, *Engraver,* 25 Nov. 1772
Greenwood, Mr. John, *Painter,* 25 Feb. 1778
Grimm, Mr. Hieronymus, *Landscape Painter,* 24 Nov. 1773
Grosse, Francis, Esq., 8 Feb. 1758
Hall, Mr. John, *Portrait Painter,* 18 Sept. 1762
Hall, John, Esq., *Historical Engraver to His Majesty,* 25 April 1787
Hamilton, Mr. William, 14 May 1760
Handasyde, Mr. Charles, 9 April 1760
Hayman, Mr. Francis, 13 April 1757
Hayward, Mr. Richard, *Statuary,* 23 Nov. 1757
Heuart, Mr. Charles, *Painter,* 11 May 1763
Hewson, Mr. Stephen, *Portrait Painter,* 23 Feb. 1791
Hickey, Thomas, Esq., 9 Dec. 1772
Highmore, Mr. Anthony, 2 April 1755
Hincks, Mr. William, *Miniature Painter,* 3 March 1784
Hoare, Mr. William, 10 Dec. 1760
Hogarth, William, Esq., 31 Dec. 1755
Hone, Nathaniel, Esq., 14 Feb. 1759
Hoppner, Mr. John, *Artist,* 23 Nov. 1791
Hudson, Mr. Thomas, *Portrait Painter,* 2 Dec. 1761
Humphry, Mr. Ozias, *Miniature Painter,* 17 Feb. 1768

James, Mr. Geo., *Limner*, 25 Nov. 1761

Jefferys, Mr. Thomas, 5 Dec. 1759

Jelf, Mr. William, *Mason*, 2 Sept. 1761

Johnson, John, *Jun.*, Esq., 28 March 1787

Johnstone, Mr. John, *Seal Engraver*, 30 May 1764

Kettle, Mr. Tilly, *Portrait Painter*, 26 Dec. 1764

Keyse, Mr. Thomas, *Flower Painter*, 20 Oct. 1762

Kirby, Mr. Joshua, 17 Nov. 1756

Leigh, Mr. Jared, 5 Nov. 1760

McArdel, Mr. James, 9 June 1756

Major, Mr. Thomas, *Engraver*, 11 Feb. 1756

Manini, Mr. Gaeton, *Artist*, 4 March 1761

Martin, Mr. David, *History Painter*, 15 Feb. 1764

Mathias, Mr. Gabriel, 5 May 1756

Meyer, Mr. Jeremiah, 7 March 1759

Millington, Mr. Henry, *Artist*, 1 July 1761

Mortimer, Mr. John, *Painter*, 8 Feb. 1764

Moser, Mr. Geo., *Engraver*, 30 April 1760

Mynde, Mr. James, *Engraver*, 27 May 1761

Newton, Francis, Esq., 21 Nov. 1770

Noireterre, Mlle de, *Artist*, 22 Nov. 1786

Pars, Mr. William, *Portrait Painter*, 10 Nov. 1762

Parsons, Mr. Francis, *Portrait Painter*, 15 Feb. 1764

Payne, Mr. Thomas, *Landscape Painter*, 20 Oct. 1762

Penny, Mr. Edward, *History Painter*, 20 Feb. 1765

Pether, Mr. William, *Painter and Mezzotint Engraver*, 15 Sept. 1762

Philpot, Mr. Browne, *Herald Painter*, 13 Jan. 1762

Pincot, Mr. Daniel, *Portrait Painter*, 14 Jan. 1767

Pine, Mr. Robert Edge, *Artist*, 4 Jan. 1758

Pingo, Mr. Thomas, *Engraver*, 30 April 1760

Ramsay, Allan, Esq., 14 Dec. 1757

Read, Mr. Nicholas, *Statuary*, 9 March 1763

Reynolds, Sir Joshua, 1 Sept. 1756

Roper, Mr. Richard, *Portrait Painter*, 18 April 1764

Roubiliac, Mr. Fras. Lewis, 7 May 1760

Russell, John, 8 April 1789

Sandby, Mr. Paul, 29 April 1761

Sandby, Mr. Thos., RA, 9 April 1760

Scouler, Mr. James, *Miniature Painter*, 11 Nov. 1761

Shackleton, John, Esq., 8 March 1758

Sherlock, Mr. William, 19 March 1760

Shipley, Mr. William, 5 Feb. 1755

Smith, Mr. Joachim, 29 March 1758

Spang, Mr. Michael Henry, 6 May 1761
Stephen, Mr. Thomas, *Mason,* 2 Nov. 1757
Stewart, Mr. Charles, *Painter,* 15 Nov. 1763
Stewart, Mr. George, *Painter,* 15 Feb. 1764
Strange, Mr. Robert, 30 Jan. 1760
Sulivan, Mr. Luke, *Miniature Painter,* 9 Jan. 1765
Taylor, Mr. Joseph, *Stone Seal Engraver,* 20 April 1763
Tyler, Mr. William, 28 Feb. 1759
Vandyke, Mr. Philip, *Portrait Painter,* 10 Nov. 1762
Vivarez, Mr. Francis, *Engraver,* 5 Aug. 1761
Walsh, Mr. John, *Statuary,* 20 Oct. 1762
Watson, Mr. Thomas, *Engraver,* 22 March 1780
West, Mr. Benjamin, *Painter: President of the Royal Academy,* 28 Nov. 1764
    and 27 March 1794
Westmacott, Mr. Richard, 9 April 1788
Williams, Mr. John, *Portrait Painter,* 1 Sept. 1762
Wilthen, Mr. Luke, *Artist,* 7 Jan. 1784
Wilton, Mr. Joseph, 16 Feb. 1757
Woollet, Mr. William, *Engraver,* 14 April 1762
Zincke, Christian, Esq., 26 Nov. 1760

Corresponding Members
Jenkins, Mr. Thomas, FSA, *Painter* (Rome), 2 Dec. 1761
Paderni, Mr. Camillus, *Keeper of his Sicilian Majesty's Museum,* 2 Jan. 1771
Rosa, Josh., *Professor of Painting* (Dresden), 11 March 1772

	Artists												Total meetings attended by artists	Total meetings
	Green	Grimm	Boydell	Bacon	Shipley	Hayward	Hall	Hincks	Downman	Hewson	Devis	Barry		
1775	9	11											13	14
1776	9	11											11	11
1777	8	5											9	9
1778	8		1	1									8	12
1779	4			2									5	11
1780	5												5	6
1781	7				1								7	9
1782	7				1								8	10
1783	6					2							6	6
1784	11												11	11
1785	9						3	1					9	9
1786	8								2				8	10
1787	6			2			1		1				8	12
1788	3						1						4	14
1789	1					1							1	5
1790	2												2	5
1791										1			1	4
1792													—	9
1793	1												1	6
1794	1			1									2	7
1795													—	5
1796											1		1	7
1797	2												2	8
1798													—	10
1799												3	3	7

7

'A VERY ANCIENT, USEFUL

AND CURIOUS ART': THE SOCIETY

AND THE REVIVAL OF GEM-ENGRAVING

IN EIGHTEENTH-CENTURY ENGLAND

Gertrud Seidmann

Although premiums for Drawing were among the very first to be offered by the newly founded Society, it was not until 1758—no doubt the result of proliferating ideas as well as increased membership—that special attention was paid to 'Premiums for Improving the Arts'. An early addition to this category, considered on a proposal by Thomas Brand, a chairman of the Society's still embryonic Committee of the Polite Arts, was a premium for 'a Human Figure which shall be best engraven in Entaglio on a Cornelian'.[1]

That gem-engraving should have such a high priority may seem surprising, but there were good reasons for it, not only in the general climate of taste but also in the special circumstances of the Society. An interest in engraved gems, one facet of the prevailing interest in antiquities, was certainly widespread among the cultivated classes in England by the middle of the eighteenth century. Grand Tourists, whether of a scholarly bent or

Originally appeared in *Jnl. RSA*, 132 (Nov., Dec., 1984), 811-13, 64-66; 133 (Jan., 1985), 150-53.

simply following the dictates of fashion, had been returning from Rome for some decades with ancient stones—or gems that passed as such—in their pockets or on their fingers. More portable and far less costly than the coveted marbles, like these they were usually obtained through such intermediaries as the busy resident English, Scottish and Irish artist-antiquary-cicerone-dealers.[2] Some of these 'ancient' gems so greatly treasured are now considered to be products of the Renaissance; others were modern copies and imitations, intended to deceive; but there was also a genuine demand from collectors for copies of famous stones or motifs, which could be commissioned from contemporary craftsmen, several of whom had set up flourishing family workshops, especially in Rome, such as the Costanzi, the Pazzaglia and the Pichler.[3] They were able to make use of ancient models, even without access to the originals in prestigious collections, through more or less faithful engravings in scholarly publications; but their practice was transformed with the appearance of the first commercially produced and cheaply sold collections of *casts* from engraved gems. These appear to have originated in 1739, with the establishment in Rome of a workshop by Christian Dehn, who had learnt the craft in the service of the savant-collector Philipp von Stosch.

He was followed by many others, and not only in Rome; for the largest collection of such casts was eventually produced in London, by the Scot James Tassie.[4] The most durable of these were in the form of negative casts, or *impressions,* from intaglio sealstones, in sulphur (usually coloured red) or in white plaster, and therefore appearing as tiny bas-reliefs or cameos (impressions from cameos were positive casts, also in cameo form); *pastes,* which could be produced from the same moulds, were glass imitations of intaglios and cameos, which could be equally sharp, and if made in coloured glass, or in colourless underlaid with a sliver of stone, could pass as imitation gems. Before long, gem-engravers were able to have such models in their thousands at hand to help them to reproduce and vary favourite motifs, including those newly created by contemporary artists with higher aspirations, whose works were equally diffused in this way. Most popular among these were miniature copies of the ancient works of sculpture which were then the most widely admired works of art.[5] When the Society therefore embarked on the encouragement of the art of gem-engraving in England, it may have hoped to establish an equally flourishing centre at home; for though not unknown, it was sparsely practised.

The technique of working on stone, mostly hard-stone quartzes, transmitted since Antiquity—chiefly by means of minute wheels and drills set in a lathe and charged with diamond or corundum powder in an oily medium—was used by eighteenth-century seal-cutters, occasionally commissioned to use colourful stones in preference to silver or steel for armorial signets; there was a tenuous tradition, too, of engraving portrait heads of rulers or 'illustrious men' on stone.[6] One gifted English seal-cutter, Thomas Bateman Wray (1715-79), living in provincial Salisbury, but employed and no doubt guided by metropolitan jewellers and noble patrons, successfully raised himself to practise the higher art of gem-engraving and produced ancient subjects, such as a highly accomplished *Cicero* signed with his own name in Greek letters;[7] but there was no plethora of competitors or followers. Even the accomplished German engraver Lorenz Natter (1705-63), who had tried to settle in London, found there was insufficient interest in his art, despite his publication in London, in English and French, of *A Treatise on the Ancient Method of Engraving on Precious Stones* (1754) and his contacts with some of the most ardent collectors of the day.[8] One of his faithful patrons, though, was Thomas Hollis, the influential member of the Society and its Committee for the Polite Arts, who commissioned Natter to engrave his own portrait, a head of his friend, travelling companion and eventual heir, Thomas Brand, and an important cameo with a political 'message'.

Hollis's interest in engraved gems had probably been awakened on his foreign travels; in Rome he had made friends with the antiquarian Abbate Rodolfo Venuti, an associate of Stosch's, who published a famous stone by Agathangelos, later copied by Natter. In Venice he had associated with Consul Joseph Smith, whose famous gem collection was later bought by King George III. His own collection of ancient stones was by no means negligible, and examples from it were considered worthy of inclusion in cabinets of impressions.[9] Hollis, we know, was adept at backing out of the limelight; and we shall not go far wrong in associating him with the proposal put to the Society by his *alter ego* Brand, whose own knowledge of virtu and antiquities was considered 'particularly chaste and correct'.

There was another good reason, though, for the Society's interest, for gem-engraving could be seen to combine with its lofty aspirations to an art practised by the ancients the very practical advantage of a craft ancillary to the jewellery trade. Intaglios set in rings and fobs were used for sealing—an indispensable practice before the introduction of postage stamps in 1840—cameos were considered especially suitable for ladies' bracelets, and portrait cameos for rings and medallions; jewellers such as Nicholas Crisp and Isaac L'Advocaat were among the Society's early members.

Thomas Brand's proposal was duly 'referred to the consideration of the Committee of Premiums', and at its session on 10th March 1759, a sec-

A gem-engraver in
his studio, c. 1800.
Courtesy of the RSA.

tion of it, the nucleus of the later Committee of Polite Arts, agreeing that
a premium should be offered for 'engraving on a Cornelian', drew up an
advertisement, stating not only the conditions for the competition but also
its grounds for setting it up:

> As the art of engraving on Gems is a very antient, useful and curious art,
> that has always been esteemed yet it is but little practiced in this Nation; it
> is proposed to give for a Naked Human Figure which shall be best engraven
> in Intaglio on an Oval Red Cornelian, executed the best with Regard to
> the Drawing Depth and Freedom of Engraving and excellence of Polish by
> Persons under the Age of 26 after a Model or Impression appointed by the
> Society; to be delivered sealed up on or before the last Wednesday in January
> 1760, 10 Guineas. And that which gains the Premium is to be left with them
> one month and three Impressions from it to become their Property.[10]

This was not quite enough: on 30th May, the Society's meeting ordered
an *ad hoc* committee of twenty-three named members (of which the first

two were Brand and Hollis) 'and any other Members of the Society who will please to attend' to 'consider of a proper Subject for the Engraving in Intaglio': but on the appointed day, 'but few Gentlemen attending', no decision was reached. Neither Brand nor Hollis was present, but one notes the attendance of Nicholas Crisp, not originally named, and that of 'Mr. Duane'. Matthew Duane of Lincoln's Inn, a member recruited by Hollis, was himself an ardent collector of gems.[11] The Society was not content to let the matter drag on: the Committee was sharply ordered to meet again, and on 4th July, meeting for the first time in 'the Society's new Appartments' in the Strand, determined on a subject. The Advertisement had spoken of 'a Naked Figure . . . after a Model or Impression': they courageously decided against an impression, that is, copying a cast from a known gem, and chose 'the Meliager [sic] in the Duke of Richmond's collection',[12] i.e., a sculptural model in the shape of the plaster cast from this ancient statue, then one of the seven most admired antiquities in the world,[13] in the Duke's collection which was open to artists for study and which was a rich source of models for many of the Society's competitions. The Duke also owned casts of the Apollo Belvedere, the Apollo Medici, the Antinous Capitolinus, the Dying Gladiator, the Dancing Faun, the Head of Alexander and Michelangelo's Bacchus—every one of which was to be set, at one time or another, as a premium subject for gem-engraving.

Six months later, on 30th January 1760, the Society could at last be informed that three sealed boxes containing intaglios had been delivered: on 7th February, a committee including Thomas Hollis, with Thomas Brand in the Chair, proceeded to the opening of the boxes and considered the entries. One intaglio of the *Meleager* was found to be engraved on a white chalcedony instead of a red cornelian and disqualified; the second attracted no votes at all, the third seven from the nine members present, and was declared the winner. Its engraver was named as Thomas Smith, Jr., aged 19, residing in Salusbury Court, Fleet Street. Called before the Committee, he produced the preliminary drawing and said he had 'finished the whole in 9 or 10 days polishing and all'.[14] After pocketing his ten guineas, he disappears from the annals of the Society. Neither his *Meleager* nor the other two gems are now traceable, and the three impressions of each which were to be left with the Society have disappeared; but we may possibly discern traces of two of them later, in James Tassie's cast collection: he reproduced one *Meleager* after a chalcedony original, and another his cataloguer, Rudolf Erich Raspe, describes as 'a work without taste'.[15] Thomas Smith figures in later trade directories as a seal engraver; he did not exhibit.

In its first invitation to competitors for a premium in gem-engraving, the Society had stated that it was 'but little practiced in this Nation' and had set an unusually high age for entrants: twenty-six; thus tacitly suggesting that fully trained seal-engravers, conversant with the technique of engraving on stone, and in possession of the necessary tools, ought to try their hand.[16] They may have been disappointed with the result, which bore out their original opinion; but, nothing daunted, they set a second competition, even adding a new premium for cameo-engraving. The subjects set for November 1760 were the *Meleager* again, but now for a cameo on an onyx, and for intaglio, the *Apollo Medici,* of course again from the Duke of Richmond's cast. The age limit for intaglio was reduced to 24—perhaps in consequence of the youthful prize-winner of the previous year—while that for cameo was set at 30. An interesting addition, though, was a premium of 15 guineas for 'the greatest number of casts in glass commonly called Pastes, the most varied compounded and perfected both in colours and subjects . . . not less than 20': an encouragement to manufacture, hand in hand with art. Tucked away in an earlier section of the printed premium lists, there was yet another related subject: a premium was offered for the 'purifying' of onyxes and cornelians.[17] By the second half of the eighteenth century, much thought and labour were indeed applied to the production of fine colours in hard-stones by artificial means, for the quartzes supplied, principally by the German mining industry, could not vie in beauty with the glowing cornelians from Middle Eastern sources and the brilliant contrasts in banded onyxes from India and Arabia used by the ancients.[18]

It seems, though, that no entries were received for engraved gems or for pastes in 1760—perhaps the time had been too short.[19] At the end of the year, the same subjects were set again, for November 1761, the premiums even increased by adding second prizes for intaglio and cameo, so that there were five classes in all. Yet only a single candidate presented himself; but because of the excellence of his work, the committee agreed to award him the first prize for his intaglio of the *Apollo Medici* in full.[20] The candidate was found to be Nathaniel Marchant. On 8th January 1762, he 'attended and gave satisfaction'. It is the earliest mention so far discovered of an artist who was to achieve not only local but European fame.

Nathaniel Marchant, then 22 years of age, came from an ancient Sussex family.[21] It was not until he won his third premium from the Society, in 1764, that his address was recorded in the Minutes: he is to be found residing with Edward Burch, who also won a prize that year. This evidence indicates that Marchant was the apprentice or pupil of Burch, who was nine years older and already an established seal-cutter—or, as was noted

Nathaniel Marchant;
attributed to Hugh
Douglas Hamilton.
Courtesy of the
Trustees of Sir John
Soane's Museum.

later in Rome, 'scolar to Birch'.[22] By 1765, his apprenticeship was evidently over, for he left Burch's house to lodge 'at Mr. March's hosier without Temple Bar'; and over the following years we can monitor his progress as he moved closer to London's artists' quarter around Covent Garden and joined Burch as an exhibitor with the recently founded Society of Artists, so closely linked to the Society of Arts, exhibiting in its rooms, with many of its members early prize-winners.[23] During the 1760s, the records of the two societies reveal something of their lives, their work and their amicable relationship.

Marchant's first premium, as we have seen, was gained in 1761; the following year he won another first prize for intaglio, for a *Head of Homer in the British Museum*. His master Burch won a first prize for a cameo of the *Apollo Medici,* and there were two other winners, in the six classes now offered. The offer for pastes, too, was at last taken up, and won by Samuel More, later the mainstay and Secretary of the Society who, though only 20 were asked for, lavishly produced '100 various casts'. He had, of course, 'been bred a chymist'.[24] He won twice, followed by two others, but the market for the manufacture of these pretty glass paste imitation gems was scooped by the able and industrious James Tassie, who eventually offered more than 15,000 models for sale.[25] Tassie did not settle in London until 1766. No premium then being offered for gem reproductions, he nevertheless produced a number of portrait heads in a composition of his own invention 'resembling antique onyx' to the Society, which awarded him a well-deserved bounty of ten guineas.[26]

Prizes for gem-engraving continued to be offered annually meanwhile until 1766, then once more in 1768. But whereas they had started with intaglios, cameos, showy objects for ladies' jewels, gradually came to take precedence over seals in the antique taste, for their husbands' collections— a characteristic sign of changing tastes.[27]

Overall, among the prize-winners, Marchant comes first, with four first prizes, all for intaglio, the remaining two subjects being the *Dancing Faun* and a head of the *Apollo Belvedere*. Robert Staples, member of a family of working jewellers, also won four, but all second prizes. Next came Burch, with three, two of them for cameo. Nehemia Spicer also gained three, but each of them reduced in value, for cameo. Lewis Pingo, later Chief Engraver to the Mint, a member of the family of engravers and medallists, won two, John Frewin and Thomas Smith (the first prize-winner), one each.[28] Among them, only Burch and Marchant were to make their names as gem-engravers. But there was another candidate, later to become as celebrated, whose name does not figure in the lists of prize-winners, although he was twice chosen for works entered anonymously.

William Brown, the Committee for Polite Arts decided, 'being excluded by Minutes of the Society dated 14th July, 1762', could not be entitled to a premium, for, 'having used disingenuous methods to impose on the Society', he was 'deemed incapable of obtaining any premium for the future'. Brown, then aged fourteen, had blotted his copybook by cheating at drawing.[29] As it turned out, this disgrace did him no harm. He set up an exceedingly flourishing workshop with his brother Charles; about half their estimated output—no less than two hundred gems—was bought up or commissioned by Catherine the Great.[30]

Edward Burch and Nathaniel Marchant were meanwhile exhibiting with the Society of Artists—neither joined the Free Society—showing, among other work, their prize-winning gems. Edward Burch was in fact at one stage a 'Director', or member of the Committee; but in November 1769 he refused renomination, suggesting Marchant instead.[31] Dissension, as we know, was rife among the artists, but Burch had, in any case, chosen to throw in his lot with the latest comer. Two months earlier, aged almost 40, he had enrolled as a student at the Royal Academy.[32]

For a decade, from 1759 to 1768, while Grand Tourists and their bear-leaders, antiquaries and artists returned from Rome with engraved gems on their fingers or *dactyliothecae* of impressions among their luggage, the Society did its best to encourage an English School of gem-engravers. From the single task set for a premium of ten guineas in 1759, four years later the offers had risen to eight: first and second prizes each, for four different subjects in cameo and intaglio, the total sum of money available being ninety guineas (£98.10s.). In fact, only 45 guineas were paid out, for, as in other years, competitors were few.[33] Over the ten years, altogether forty-two premiums were offered in gem-engraving: eighteen were gained, by seven different artists (and one, as we have seen, remained unrewarded).[34] Despite the increasing diffusion of the taste for engraved gems among the cultured and the travelled, their interest was primarily directed towards ancient gems. Modern artists, the evidence goes to show, were not as yet able to earn their living in England by this art alone. Even the busy Wray, and the widely travelled Natter, patronized by royalty and nobility, were unable to subsist by the engraving of gemstones in the antique taste alone,[35] and only Natter calls himself 'Engraver in Gems' in Mortimer's 1763 London Directory of the 'Masters and Professors of the Polite and Liberal Arts and Sciences'. Humbler members of the profession made it clear that they were seal-engravers (though Edward Burch and Thomas Smith, Jr., both proclaim themselves 'Engraver in Stone', for steel and silver were still fashionable).[36]

It was with the humbler craft of armorial seal-engraving—or even the cutting of simple initials—that those aspiring to emulate the ancients and the 'artists of the Cincequento' earned the bulk of their living. The ambitious and hard-working Nathaniel Marchant was only able to show, when he began to exhibit with the Society of Artists in 1765, the two subjects for which he had received premiums in 1763 and at the beginning of that very year—a *Homer* and a *Dancing Faun*—and rarely more than two or three in any one year. Yet compared with the exhibits of his far more prolific former master, Edward Burch, his subjects are more consistently classical—a *Minerva,* a *Hygieia,* an *Atalanta*—and sculptural models are implied or mentioned: 'the *Apollo Belvedere*', 'from an antique bust of Sappho', 'from the Dying Gladiator, in the Duke of Richmond's gallery'. Burch, meanwhile, intermingles casts from his *Antinous* and *Head of Neptune* with a cameo of *St. George,* a 'Portrait of a lady', a *Head of Shakespeare* and one of Inigo Jones, finishing up, in fine style, with 'A frame of casts, in sulphur, from gems: viz., a sacrifice, three emblematical pieces, two portraits, and a Venus'.[37] He was clearly happy to prove his versatility and his skill in translating all manner of images into sealstones or cameos, which seemed to assure him of a brilliant future.

At this moment, when he had entered the recently founded Royal Academy as a student, though aged already thirty-nine and sufficiently well established to have a pupil of his own, Edward Burch could already take pride in a remarkable career. Of humble origin, he started his working life 'in a laborious pursuit, where the muscular powers alone were essential', as his obituary politely periphrases it (he is reputed to have been a Thames waterman), but his talent for drawing enabled him to become an artist.[38] Self-taught as a seal-engraver, as he repeatedly stresses, he was later assiduous in attending the St. Martin's Lane Academy, where he was greatly inspired by the anatomy lectures of Dr. William Hunter, and the academy in the Duke of Richmond's Gallery.[39] He was a prolific and brilliant gem-cutter, selecting exquisite stones, and although following the fashion for antique models, pioneered, as we have seen, by the Society, he was equally ready to cut portraits of 'illustrious men', or of contemporaries, and prided himself particularly on his figure studies from the living model, 'the position taken from Nature'. Indeed in his *Reposing Hercules,* an 'anatomical figure', he delineated 'every external muscle which is required for a figure six feet high'—a veritable *tour de force,* and one that may strike another eye as misguided in this medium and on this tiny scale. It was a credo he was to affirm, a quarter of a century later and all the more firmly and even stridently, in pointed contrast to the smooth, rounded forms and the shallow cutting (reminiscent of classicizing gems of the age of Augustus) favoured, with equally brilliant success, by his former pupil, Nathaniel Marchant.

But for the present, Burch enjoyed a remarkable renown. The list of his patrons extended from the Prince of Wales and the Duke of York to noble collectors and fellow artists.[40] His rise in the Royal Academy was spectacular: after his enrolment as a student in the autumn of 1769, he left the Society of Artists to exhibit at the Royal Academy in 1770. It was only their second exhibition; one year later he was an ARA, and in the following year elected a full Academician: in the first list of elected members he appears in the place of Francis Cotes (ob. 1770), one of the nominated foundation members. Cipriani, Zucchi, Reynolds, Dr. Burney and Dr. Johnson all owned stones by him.[41]

Of Nathaniel Marchant, too, we get occasional glimpses during this decade of the 1760s, as he won further premiums—all for intaglios after ancient sculptures—until 1765, when, aged 26, he evidently ceased to be under Burch's tutelage, moved away, and at the same time began to exhibit himself.[42] Relations between the two men seem to have been amicable. In 1768 Marchant wrote, in his easy flowing hand, in both their names to the Society of Artists that in their opinion 'the word Sculptor is more applicable to our profession than Engraver', a point underlined by their both occasionally showing the wax models which were the preliminaries to their engravings, a technique evidently employed by both.[43] Their request was granted, and Burch was elected an RA as 'sculptor'; but the scribe evidently came from a more favoured background than his former master, who, even in his maturity, was much castigated for his foul language by his fellow-academician John Russell.[44] By the end of the decade Marchant had, in successive moves from 'without Temple Bar', come to live in the centre of London's artists' quarter, in Bedford Street, Covent Garden, and he was also evidently on happy, sociable terms with many of them. 'Mr. Mortimer' provided him with a drawing for his *Head of Niobe;* with Mortimer, Gandon, 'Evan Lloyd the Parson' (a poet and great frequenter of artistic company) and others he was encountered at the Devil Tavern by Thomas Jones.[45] From later documents and reminiscences it is clear that these were the years during which he made friends with Romney, with Ozias Humphry, probably with Nollekens and many others with whom he is seen to be on terms of long-standing intimacy in years to come; and certainly with Joseph Farington, like the others an early prize-winner of the Society and exhibitor with the Society of Artists, through the pages of whose diary, a quarter of a century later, we get such a lively picture of Marchant at the peak of his success.[46]

It may have been loyalty to these friends in the Society of Artists which kept Marchant back from joining Burch in his application to the Royal Academy. He may also have felt sufficiently confident, and been kept sufficiently busy, to consider his future assured; for among the list of his patrons which he later published, there were many early Members of the Society who may have got to know of him through his successes there. They included the jeweller Isaac L'Advocaat, who later functioned as his banker. Among the cognoscenti in the Committee of Polite Arts was Hollis's nominee, the lawyer Matthew Duane. At his sale, where '50 various ancient gems' were sold for 15 shillings, a *Bacchus and Ariadne* by Marchant fetched 23 guineas—by far the highest price but one, a Greek gem from a famous collection. (A 'fine gem' by Burch fetched three guineas.) Duane was a friend of Louis Dutens, who travelled abroad with the Duke of Northumberland's younger son, Lord Algernon Percy. Two of Marchant's gems, now in the Northumberland Collection, were commissioned by Lord Algernon.[47] The most important of the Society's members to patronize Marchant, though, was George, 4th Duke of Marlborough, a fanatical glyptophile. Marchant's *Hercules leading Alcestis to Admetus* was described by the cataloguer of the Duke's collection as his masterpiece.[48]

Such patronage enabled Marchant to fulfil his ambition to study the ancient sculptures, the models of his art, which the Society of Arts had so insistently placed before him in the form of casts, at the source. In the year of Burch's election as a Royal Academician, Marchant set out for Rome.[49]

There he was to remain for sixteen years, acquiring fame and a sizeable competence, before returning home, to the society not only of his artist friends but also of the connoisseurs and the nobility who had taken him up. Official recognition and public appointments were disappointingly slow to follow, but he had before him the spectacle of Burch, a long-standing Academician indeed (while Marchant was kept waiting as an ARA for many years), now virtually destitute, supported by the Academy through a sinecure as Librarian. Though Burch was clearly jealous and there were tensions, it is agreeable to record that Marchant invited him to dine the day before his long delayed election as Royal Academician.[50]

Not long before, an exasperating but entertaining chapter in the history of the Society of Arts had brought Marchant back into its orbit. On the instigation of Barry, the Society began, in 1801, to consider commissioning a new medal; but the choice of design proved difficult: 24 competition entries were, one and all, 'laid aside'. Eventually Mr. Papworth's design of a Britannia with Mercury and Minerva, with the head of the President, the Duke of Norfolk, on the reverse 'boldly relieved', seemed—almost—suitable. At this stage Mr. Nathaniel Marchant, the eminent artist, Engraver at the Royal Mint and the Stamp Office, was called in to cut the die. After some reminders, he produced his models—three years later. The bald resolutions of Society meetings now fairly hum with implied strife: on the very day the Committee is told to confer with Marchant 'with a view to speedy completion', the Society's full meeting decides to ask him 'to suspend proceedings'—and deliberations are to start again 'ab initio'! Exit Marchant. A Medal, designed by Flaxman, the dies sunk by Pidgeon, was delivered in November 1806.[51] In 1808, Marchant exhibited 'a model in wax of the Duke of Norfolk, intended to be engraved on a steel die'.[52]

Marchant died in 1816, in his grand apartment in Somerset House. His lengthy epitaph praises his 'talents . . . which have rendered him celebrated throughout Europe and do honour to his native Country'—talents which were nurtured by the astute connoisseurship of the members of the Society of Arts.

THE SOCIETY AND WOOD ENGRAVING

IN THE EIGHTEENTH CENTURY

Leo J. De Freitas

In 1759 when the Society of Arts offered its first premium for en-graving on wood, it was responding to William Shipley's original desire that his premium society should encourage 'the revival and advancement of those Arts and Sciences which are at a low ebb amongst us'.[1] In the mid–eighteenth century printing from the wood block was generally con-sidered to be in a state of decline.[2] Its days of eminence were believed past, and it was thought to have now fallen from the high estate of Art into the hands of hacks. The cause of this condition was identified as the combined influences of poor draughtsmanship and indifferent craftsmanship, and to many all that could be seen in the contemporary wood-block print was a debased product made all the more unremarkable and contemptible when it was compared with the exceptionally fine work of talented native line engravers.[3]

Despite the significant quantity of bad work, however, for those dis-cerning enough there were examples of more than mere competent con-temporary work in evidence to argue that the medium still possessed a potential, and that it languished in a degenerate state simply for the want of the correct encouragement and application. Given the self-assumed re-sponsibility of the Society to encourage useful invention and innovation, it

Originally appeared in *Jnl. RSA*, 133 (July, Aug., Sept., 1985), 569-71, 662-64, 732-33.

is not surprising that the medium should have at some point attracted the attention of the members. Indeed, with a potential as a relatively inexpensive process of reproduction awaiting exploitation, it almost defined itself as worthy of their concern.

The Society's archives show that once the decision to offer an award for 'Wood Engraving' was taken in 1759 no time at all was lost in drafting and advertising the premium.[4] Although the archives are quite precise on dates of meetings and resolutions then made, they are—perhaps in the spirit of collective responsibility—less helpful in the identification of individuals' specific contributions to proceedings. Consequently we do not know who first introduced the wood-engraving premium for debate. We do, however, have the names of the thirteen members of the Committee of the Polite Arts that drafted the first premium, and three in particular attract our attention as potentially more interested in the fortunes of the process than any of the others. Thomas Major (1720-99), the engraver, together with his friend Robert Edge Pine (1730-88), the painter, were the only professional artists represented on the committee.[5] For a number of reasons it is unlikely that they actually introduced the premium even if they influenced the form it was to take.[6]

A more probable agent was the energetic polymath and dynamic founder-member of the Society, Henry Baker, FRS (1698-1774). The Society's archives show that not only did Baker have specific interests in publishing, printing and related trades but that he was also particularly well informed in these areas.[7] It is likely therefore that Baker would have been singularly aware of the commercial value of a cheap illustrative process and aware too of the potential resting in the wood-block process. Further, in the light of his wide range of interests, his professional impartiality in the issue, and his relentless concern with so much that might be considered 'improving' in the arts and sciences, one may judge that Baker enjoyed the knowledge and broader perspectives necessary to see beyond the poor performances of much contemporary wood-block imagery, to the possibility of better work, and be convinced of the value of encouraging its 'revival and advancement' through the Society's premiums.

The first premium offer reads as follows: 'For an engraving in wood in the manner of Albrecht Dürer or Titian which shall be performed with the best regard to the drawing knowledge of the lights and shades and freedom of cutting by youths under the age of 19 after drawings approved by the Society—6 guineas'.[8] Given that weaknesses in both drawing and craft skills were considered responsible for the condition of the wood-block process, it is not surprising to see the Society exercising a patriarchal concern over the choice of original drawing to be copied; if the 'foundation' was secure it was more likely that the venture would be a success.[9] Significantly, candidates were encouraged to emulate the work of master painters from the past who had also designed for the wood block.[10] Possibly it was argued that with no acceptable examples from the medium itself at hand, contemporary wood-block prints being so despised, the work of esteemed masters and the disciplined exercises of the studio were the most expeditious ways of setting the sights of the candidates and establishing the standards the Society wished to achieve.

Studying and drawing from the works (or copies) of established masters is the training which both Thomas Major and Robert Pine would undoubtedly have shared as professionals. As their experience would have been called upon during the debate on the first premium, it seems likely that they influenced the choice of models. The specific exemplars cited for guidance in this first premium were dropped in those that followed in 1760[11] and 1762,[12] but the tradition of the fine arts and the ethos of the studio nonetheless constantly influenced the form of the awards through the condition that prints were to contain 'figure studies'.

There were no candidates for either the first (1759) or second (1760) premiums despite the extension of the age limit from nineteen to twenty-one and the doubling of the prize money to be won, from six to twelve guineas. Disappointed perhaps with this lack of response, the Society let two years pass before once more offering a premium for 'the best Engraving on Wood'.[13]

On the evening of 11th November 1763 the Committee for Polite Arts recorded that premium winners had been successfully balloted for.[14] From the *Register of the Premiums and Bounties given by the Society*[15] the winners are identified as Simon Watts and James Deacon;[16] Watts took the first premium and Deacon the second.

As earlier, the premium had required the candidates to submit work containing 'figure studies', and both men cut facsimiles of Luca Cambiaso's (1527-85) drawings in which the figure dominated.[17] Watts's *Assumption of the Virgin* is demonstrably more accomplished than Deacon's *Combat with Lions*, exhibiting a 'freedom of cutting' that most assuredly met with the examiners' high approval, but both prints are soundly in the tradition of the wood cut, being severely linear, and hardly demonstrate 'drawing knowledge of the lights and shades'. As copies of an artist's drawings or sketches, these prints—later to be used in Charles Rogers' *A Collection of Prints in Imitation of Drawings* (1778)—are adjuncts to the fine arts, serving in the subordinate rôle of 'handmaid to the arts'. Here the wood-block print is demonstrating its potential as a relatively cheap process of reproduction for the dissemination of unique works of art. The prints, especially Watts's, are competent exercises in the medium, but they are constrained by the very exemplars upon which they are based. They are imitations of drawings owing all to the original pen and ink line and demonstrating little of the intrinsic qualities of the wood block.

Having eventually found acceptable candidates for its premium, the Society's interest in the process appears to have waned for a while; ten years were to elapse before 'Engraving on Wood' once again drew the attention of the members. This lapse of time coincides with the steadily weakening financial position of the Society during the second decade of its existence,[18] but although the wood-engraving premium may have been one of the casualties of these stringent times, disappointment at the poor response to the earlier premiums must have contributed to the Society's decision temporarily to suspend the award. In the following decade a very different approach to the encouragement of wood engraving emerges in the Society's premiums; an approach signifying a shift from the dominance of the fine art ethos to the practical requirements of commerce.

THE REQUIREMENTS OF COMMERCE, 1774-8

Significant changes mark the renewed interest in 'wood engraving' shown by the Society in 1774:

For the best engraving on wood or type metal[19] for illustrating works in Arts or Sciences or for decorating books and capable of being worked off with letter press—Twenty guineas.
   Specimens of the Engraving united with the letter press to be produced on or before the first Tuesday in February 1775.
   Note: The representations of Animals, Plants or Machines or proper designs for head or tail pieces or chapters for the decoration of books are the subjects desired to be produced in claim of this premium.[20]

This premium offer differed substantially from the offers of 1759, 1760 and 1762. The Society now unambiguously became engaged with the utilitarian and commercial potentials of the process. It is not the wood-block print per se, perhaps to be framed or tipped-in to an album or book, but a technical means of cheaply illustrating works from the printing press that is now being encouraged. The practical conditions imposed on the candidates must be seen as an attempt by the committee to underwrite its intention of promoting a useful and viable commercial process.[21]

These and other changes in the premium are of some moment. Here the commonly recognized potential of the wood block as a relatively cheap form of printing illustrations is seized upon in a most direct and willing manner: candidates are encouraged to submit illustrations of a didactic and informative kind; told to demonstrate, by printing their work in conjunction with type, the particular advantage of the wood-block processes in the publishing of books; and further, untrammelled by examples from the past and the conventions of other processes or media, left alone to work in a style and with techniques of their own. An effective combination of stipulation, guidance and freedom permeates the premium—in contrast to the prescriptive conditions of earlier ones—and argues for a particularly well-informed group behind it.

As with the earlier premiums the archives do not identify the deviser or devisers of the new premium. A comparative analysis, however, of the members who made up the committees of 1759 and 1774 show important differences in social and economic status between them, reflected perhaps in the new emphasis of the wood-engraving premium.

It is known that the years 1765-74 witnessed an increase in the number of merchants, manufacturers, tradesmen and craftsmen who served on the Society's various committees as chairmen.[22] They displaced, to a degree, the more privileged or wealthier members who had held these posts before. This shift in balance from chairmen able to enjoy some sort of leisured life to those engaged in the pragmatic pursuits of medicine, trade and manufacture is reflected in the overall composition of the committees here under consideration.

An engraver, a painter and a toyman are the only identifiable representatives of the professional and commercial membership on the 1759 committee. On the larger committee of 1774, however, a builder, an engineer, a draughtsman, a linen draper and a surgeon, besides a landscape painter, an engraver, a toyman and at least one printer, can be found.[23] The businesslike character of the re-drafted premium surely stems from the practical experience of these men.

The premium was not won outright by any one candidate but shared between three of the four men who had submitted work. Two prizes of seven guineas each were awarded to a London engraver, William Coleman, and a provincial engraver, Thomas Bewick of Newcastle-upon-Tyne.[24] The remaining six guineas was awarded to Thomas Hodgson, a printer and engraver then at work in the metropolis.[25] Some idea of the flush of personal pride a successful candidate could feel on receiving the Society's acclaim can be enjoyed through the relevant passage in the famous engraver's autobiography:

this [premium] I received shortly after I was out of my apprenticeship & it was left to my choice whether I would have it in a Gold medal or in Money— £7. 7s.—I preferred the latter, and I never in my life felt greater pleasure than in that of presenting it to my Mother—On this occasion among the several congratulations of kind neighbours—those from Mr. Gregson, my old School Master stood preeminent—he flew from Ovingham, where the news first arrived—over to Eltingham to congratulate my father and mother, upon the occasion and the feelings and overflowings of his heart can be better imagined than described.[26]

Coleman and Bewick both clearly deserved their awards. Not only did their entries satisfy the practical conditions of the premium, but their exemplary demonstrations of new techniques in engraving on wood showed them to have broken with the wood-*cutting* codes of the past and embarked on a different road uncluttered by the conventions and limitations of the older technique. In this they were modern young men suggesting a future rather than representing the past.

Already at this early stage in his eventful career Bewick's characteristic style and technique are clearly apparent in *The Hound and the Huntsman,* and if Coleman's *George I* is unavoidably more restrained and less engaging than Bewick's work, it, too, clearly demonstrates an engraving skill that comfortably integrates the image with the text. In comparison, Hodgson's *Palestrina Presenting His Work on Music to the Pope* is largely in the tradition of the wood cut.[27]

In the work of these engravers, then, the Society must have felt that its support of the premium was well justified. If anything further remained to be desired from these candidates, it would have been that one of them had submitted some kind of technical or scientific illustration.[28] Nonetheless, the possible connection between fine engraving on wood and the commercial requirements of the printing press had been demonstrated. The little illustrations sat confidently with the texts, and the blocks from which they had been printed had been locked up—an integral part of the whole printing process—with the types and successfully printed from. The proofs in the committee members' hands must have given much satisfaction.

This success led the committee to continue the offer of an award for the 'best Engraving on Wood' until the end of the decade. Little further headway was made, however, and at a meeting in March 1778 the Committee resolved to discontinue the premium.[29] In 1798 an unsolicited wood-engraved print appears to have revived the Society's interest, and a new phase in its sponsorship of the process began with a series of premiums that was to extend well into the following century.[30]

Wood engraving as a commercial process might be said to have been

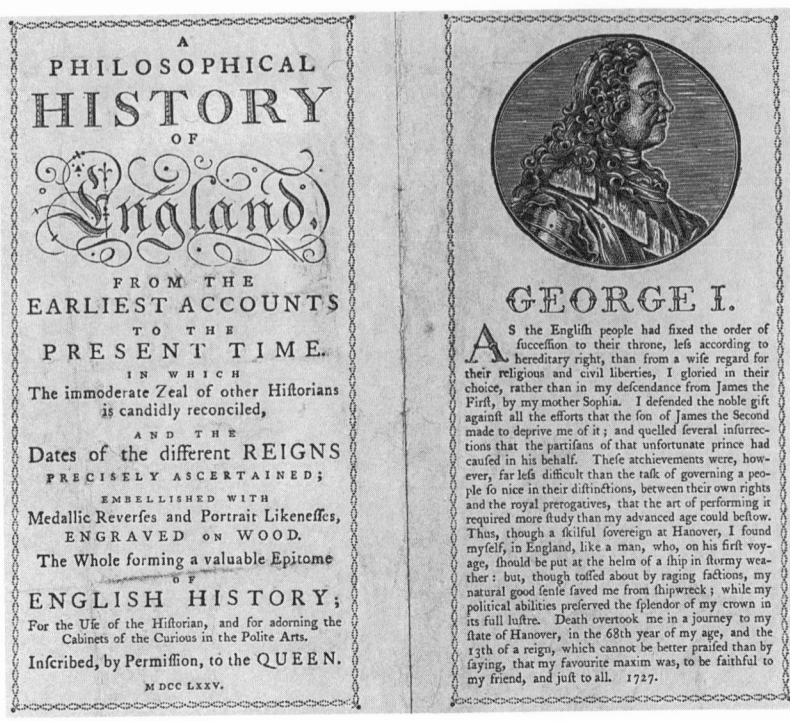

William Coleman, *King George I* with letterpress; premium-winning wood engraving, 1775. Courtesy of the RSA.

primed in the eighteenth century and in the early nineteenth to have developed into the established commercial craft that came to dominate popular illustration in books and magazines. So the issues and objectives to be confronted in the new century were different from those of fifty years earlier, and the Society's premiums were to take on a different, but perhaps no less important, rôle.

ARTS OR COMMERCE ?

The Society's policies regarding the encouragement of wood engraving in the eighteenth century were informed, and divided, by the demands of the fine arts and commerce. Indeed, whether the Society should encourage the process through the example of past masters or whether it should promote the commercial potential through direct association with the worlds of printing and publishing seems to have been a dilemma. To support the arts interpretation might mean the avoidance of the wider utilitarian exploitation of the process, but to encourage the commercial application might be narrowly to deny the prestigious and valid fine art tradition in printing from the wood block.

The particular historical reputation of the wood-block print together with its contemporary status ensured that such confusion or uncertainty was not limited to the members of the Society alone. The eminence of those artists who had designed for the wood block in the past gave to the process a renown that even the most unsympathetic of critics found impossible to deny.[31] At the same time, however, the ephemeral ends to which the mid-eighteenth-century wood block were largely put—illustrating such printing and publishing marginalia as bill-heads, pamphlets, chapbooks and broadsheets—seemed to demonstrate that its employment was now limited to the mundane and unexceptional needs of commerce and trade.[32]

The Society's first premiums were so conditioned that candidates were persuaded to emulate the past as represented by the tradition of the great masters, with the almost inevitable result that their work became simply slavish imitations. If this was the sole intention of the premium, then to have encouraged wood-block prints along the path so triumphantly dominated in the eighteenth century by line engraving seems, in retrospect, an error of judgement.

In the light of the carefully reworded 1774 premium we may assume that the Society did not consider its first encounters with the process an unqualified success. Therefore the Society had a different and more definite idea of the objectives of the premium: the aim was to encourage the improvement of the wood-block process as a reproductive means with the object of securing a cheap and viable illustrative process for the dissemination of knowledge. In this explicit emphasis the experience of men of trade and technical knowledge can be seen successfully influencing the direction the Society was now taking with regard to engraving on wood. There was little doubt in the minds of the committee men of 1774 that what was being pursued was the encouragement of a useful process of reproduction with good commercial potential.

Within the limits the Society set itself in the 1770s, some measure of success can be claimed for the premiums for engraving on wood. Had the members, however, been interested in making more direct use of the fruits of their patronage, perhaps the development and application of the process would have been more dynamically promoted.[33]

With this speculation in mind, one may ask, what was the real significance of the Society in the history of wood engraving in the eighteenth century? To begin with, it recognized the potential and practical value of the process at a time when the wood block was all but condemned to permanent discredit, and by so recognizing it the Society in some measure restored importance and status to the process. Again, by drafting and redrafting the premiums the Society resolutely engaged with the problems of how best to encourage and apply the process. It enjoyed most success when insisting on the practical relationship between the wood block and the printing and publishing trades, and as such its work presaged the remarkably effective partnership between commercial engraving on wood and the popular press that was to follow in the Victorian period. And finally, as can be seen from Thomas Bewick's pride at winning the Society's honours himself, and the satisfaction he gained from the success some of his apprentices enjoyed with later premiums, the social and psychological importance of the Society's acclaim must not be underestimated.[34] To self-respecting, independent craftsmen the Society of Arts' awards meant a great deal, and to Bewick, as to others, the esteem to be earned from winning a premium cannot be discounted in the confidence they sought and the success they enjoyed as commercial engravers on wood.

THE SOCIETY AND THE SURVEYS

OF ENGLISH COUNTIES, 1759-1809

J. B. Harley

The prizes offered by the Society of Arts to map-makers engaged on new county surveys were the outcome of one of its minor activities during the first half century of its life. From 1759, when awards for county maps were first approved, to 1809, when the last award was made, the Society gave recognition in money and medals to surveys of eleven English counties and in addition of Cardiganshire and of North Wales. The circumstances and effects of these incentives have not hitherto been discussed in detail, although the value of the Society's initiative in stimulating county cartographers has been recognized. The present study, using the materials in the Society Archives, discusses the origin of premiums for maps, traces the response to them, and attempts to assess their significance to English cartography.

The steps by which maps were brought to the notice of the Society were taken by two men, William Borlase (1695-1772) and Henry Baker (1698-1774). During the early 1750s William Borlase, Vicar of Ludgvan near Penzance, was diligently compiling materials on the antiquities and natural history of Cornwall. That the countryside lacked a good coverage of topographical maps must have been constantly impressed upon him as

Originally appeared in *Jnl. RSA*, 111 (Dec., 1963), 43-46; 112 (Jan., Mar., June, 1964), 119-24, 269-75, 538-43.

field observations led him into the recesses of his native county. Perhaps (after missing a turning through an inaccurate small-scale map), he sympathized with the correspondent of the *Gentleman's Magazine* who had tartly referred to 'Moll's little erroneous trifles' when writing in 1748 of the lack of correct maps in north-west England. One outcome of such experiences with maps was that in at least three letters to his friend Henry Baker (which are preserved in the John Rylands library) he put down his views on the subject. Baker was also a naturalist, an antiquarian and Fellow of the Royal Society, and as an original member of the newly formed Society of Arts, one whom Borlase hoped might be in a key position to further the cause of cartography.[1] The first of these letters (in effect the opening chapter in the Society's promotion of cartography) makes some interesting comments on the low ebb of county map-making in mid-eighteenth-century England and includes a plea for a national survey organization well in advance of the foundation of the Ordnance Survey in 1791:

> I would [Borlase wrote in September 1755] submit to you as a friend, whether the state of British Geography be not very low, and at present wholly destitute of any public encouragement. Our Maps of England and its counties are extremely defective. We have but one good county map that I know, and the head lands of all our shores are at this time disputed and even where Halley himself made his observations. So that another Survey was undertaken about 14 years since, and a very good apparatus of instruments appointed, and put into proper hands as was then imagined. But the event did not answer the expectation and as this actual survey under the inspection of more than one Skilful Surveyor may be dispaired of till the Government interposes and attempts what would be so much for the honour as well as Commerce of this Island, 'tis to be wished that some people of weight would, when a proper opportunity offers, hint the necessity of such a Survey; and, as what your Society appears to relish is likely to be soon generally approved, if among your premiums for Drawings some reward were offered for the best plan measurement and actual Survey of city or District, it might move the attention of the public towards Geography, and in time, perhaps, incline the Administration to take this matter into their hands (as I am informed it does in some foreign Countries) and employ proper persons every year from actual surveys to make accurate Maps of Districts, till the whole Island is regularly surveyed.

A second letter (of January 1756) repeated the argument for 'a general Geographical Survey'.[2]

As a result of this correspondence Baker sent a memorandum to the Society of Arts in February 1756 on the 'Utility of bestowing a Premium for the best map or Plan of any District, County or City in this Kingdom, or any of the Coasts thereof, made from an actual Measurement and Survey', and quoted Borlase's letter in full. Some action was determined upon because in December 1756 Borlase again wrote to Baker thanking the Society 'for the kind notice they take of my hint as to the defects of present charts and maps'. He resumed his indictment of British cartography: 'That branch of knowledge (though our pamphlet Shops are full of boasted Surveys) when it is examined accurately will be found . . . excessive low, oppressed as it is with errors arising (not to mention the ill capacity of common Map-makers) from hasty observations without a variety of good instruments.' That such arguments were soundly based must partly account for their eventual success with the Society. But the climate of opinion also favoured cartographic improvement; apparently even in the provinces there was an awareness that Louis XV in commissioning Cassini de Thury to map the whole of France upon a trigonometrical framework had given the lead to Europe.[3] England was lagging, and Baker's proposals of 1756 were thus the more acceptable.

Thereafter, however, the Society dallied in offering its patronage. December 1758 saw the desirability of premiums for county surveys still being debated, by this time in the Committee of Polite Arts, under whose surveillance maps had been placed. Not until March 1759 was a series of Premiums for original county surveys finally approved in principle.[4]

A suitable wording for an advertisement was sought, but this occasioned further discussion, which throws more light upon the precise aims of the Society in accepting Baker's proposals. It was recognized, for example, that good maps had many practical applications: 'A Complete Knowledge of the Situations, Bearings, Levels and other Topographical Circumstances of this Kingdom, being of great use in planning any scheme for the Improvement of Highways, making Rivers Navigable and providing other means for the Ease and Advancement of the National Commerce'. Moreover, the same text reveals the hope of the Society not merely to stimulate an unrelated succession of maps of individual counties, but 'to give proper surveyors such Encouragement as may induce them to make accurate Surveys of two or three Counties towards completing the whole'. The plea of Borlase and others for a national survey could be answered, it was felt, by putting together a fairly uniform series of county maps. Although in 1768 Robert Dossie still wrote of the county surveys 'furnishing materials for a complete map of England', the idea had been abandoned in practice. A revised advertisement drafted and published in 1759 made reference only to maps of single counties. Three main conditions were attached to this first offer: the Society intended to give a premium not exceeding £100 for 'an Accurate Actual Survey of any county'; there was to be no time limit for payment of the premium after the map had been submitted, so that the Society 'may be better able to procure Satisfactory Proof of the Merit of such performance'; and an additional gratuity was offered for 'an exact and accurate Level of the Rivers in any County Surveyed that are capable of being made navigable'.[5]

Publication of the offered award was not the end of the matter, for some members still felt dissatisfied with its conditions. In November 1759 the Committee of Polite Arts advised that the advertisement was still ambiguous and did not fully explain the intention of the Society. It hoped to formulate more precise standards in the new county maps. A further draft of an advertisement reveals concern with surveying methods. The premium was to be more specifically for a trigonometrical survey, and the instruments to be used were named: 'The Horizontal Distances of all places in the Map to be taken with the Theodolite or plain Table and the roads to be measured with a Perambulator and noted down in Figures.' A minute of March 1760 explained that 'The intention of the Words Theodolite or Plain Table . . . was to guard against taking the Angles by the Circumferentor or such like uncertain Instruments; but that if the surveys of any Counties taken by the Candidates be done Trigonometrically by a new invented Instrument of known use and certainty, that such Surveys shall be entitled to the premium according to their merit.'[6]

Evidently the committee had received expert advice. Perhaps they had been warned by Thomas Jefferys the cartographer, an early member of the Society, that professional surveyors were liable to be conservative in the use of improved instruments. Although more accurate theodolites were available by 1750, some county surveys were still based on road traverse and angled with the circumferentor or surveying compass, versions of which had been in use since Elizabethan times, but which were capable of an error even of several degrees. As was made clear to the Society in a letter dated October 1760 (which reinforced Borlase's arguments), new and exact instruments would be essential in the surveys they envisaged.[7]

Two final recommendations were made by the Committee in this formative stage of the awards. First, the one-inch-to-one-mile scale was selected. Although the popularity of this scale had been firmly established through John Ogilby's road surveys (first published in 1675) and although it had already been employed in a number of county maps, the choice helped to standardize its use in the second half of the eighteenth century and to sever the links with the older surveys, which, still in the tradition of Saxton and

Speed, were constructed on scales of less than one inch to one mile. Secondly, an attempt was made to quicken the leisurely pace characteristic of county surveys, where the making of a map could be spread out over five years or more. Candidates for the Society's premiums were to be allowed one or, at most, two years to complete and deliver their surveys.[8]

After the first offer in 1759, it was not until 1762 that the Society next advertised a premium for county maps. Then, only one of the interim conditions discussed above, that insisting on the one-inch scale, was incorporated. Perhaps (and with some justification) the members decided that any surveyor worthy of the award should know all about triangulation and theodolites. The premium was renewed annually, with only slight modification, until 1766. More than just encouragement had been offered to county surveyors; an attempt was launched to promote new standards. What was the response which the Society received?

THE RESPONSE TO THE AWARDS, 1759-66

Only a few candidates responded to the Society's offer of a premium of £100 for a county survey, first made in 1759, renewed in 1762, and granted annually until 1766. There were three applicants in 1759, four in 1760, and from 1761 to 1765 (excepting 1763) one in each year. Moreover, only two map-makers, Benjamin Donn and Peter Perez Burdett, received the £100 prize for their surveys of Devonshire and Derbyshire. The present article describes first the events leading to these two premiums and, secondly, outlines the background to the unsuccessful applications.

Benjamin Donn, 'teacher of mathematics and natural philosophy on the Newtonian principles in his home town of Bideford, quickly answered the Society's advertisement. In the autumn of 1759 he informed them that he would begin to survey Devon immediately upon receipt of the instruments from London. By next spring survey was under way, a quick start being possible because the Society's scheme for county surveys was, Donn implies, 'not essentially different from what I had drawn up for myself'.[9]

Printed proposals for the map accompanied his letter, forming a blueprint fairly typical of the new surveys of the period: landscape features to be depicted were enumerated; reference was made to the 'new and rational method' of surveying 'by the Assistance of a curious set of Instruments'; roads, 'at least the High Roads', were to be actually measured; and particular care taken with the latitude and longitude of harbours, capes and headlands, for on these 'the Safety of Ships, and consequently the Lives of Sailors' depended. Subscribers were to pay one and a half guineas for the map in sheets, 'pasted on Canvas with Rollers Two Guineas', and with colouring, five shillings extra. To accelerate survey Donn had employed several assistants. Even so, the field survey was not completed until September 1763. Hindrance by weather and the winter season, traversing the countryside on horse or on foot, experimenting with new instruments, planning within a limited budget and operating as a part-time or amateur surveyor—all these factors retarded the pace of the work. But the Society of Arts (Donn may have reflected) with its stipulation of only two years for the whole undertaking was insensitive to the needs of the practical surveyor. He had found it necessary to obtain an extension until April 1764, but by this date had to report to the Society that Thomas Jefferys the engraver 'found it impossible to be done within the Time'. A further extension enabled the map to be published on 1st January 1765.[10]

Donn's worries were not, however, ended. His eligibility for the premium was queried by Vice President Mr. William Fitzherbert, who, suspecting that Jefferys the engraver was part-owner of the map, apparently tried to invalidate the claim. Donn wrote sharply to Fitzherbert and the Society: his map 'was not an Engraver's Job, but an accurate Survey at the expense of nearly £2,000 . . . the largest work ever done of the kind at private expense'.[11] The explanation was accepted and the prize money voted to Donn in November 1765.

The survey of Derbyshire, for which Burdett was awarded £100, shares a background similar to that of the Devon survey. Its author was an amateur surveyor who, while living in Derby, was also an artist and engraver, and one of the friends of the painter Joseph Wright. Burdett's proposals are similar to those for the survey of Devon. Again, although assistants, including Joseph Whyman, were employed, it took from 1762 to 1767 to complete the map. Finally, like Donn, Burdett contracted out the engraving to a professional London cartographer, in this case Thomas Kitchin.[12]

The Derbyshire award also shows the Society developing procedures of assessing county surveys. Publication day was 17th April 1767. On 5th June Burdett was summoned to answer questions on the map. He told members of the Committee of Polite Arts how 'his Survey was drawn on the Plate upon a scale of one Inch to a Mile, but in Printing off from the Plate on Paper there is a small contraction'. He had, however, 'scarcely omitted a Farm House detached from a town or village' and 'the Bearings and distances are exactly laid down'. The surveyor's testimony furnished only part evidence, for Mr. Fitzherbert had also made judicious inquiries in the county. His report was favourable: 'Mr. Burdett has been everywhere in the County and has been employed in the Work five Years.[13] The premium was granted.

Thus two amateur cartographers secured the first premiums in the Society's efforts to encourage topographical survey. Yet the nine unsuccessful applicants included three professional cartographers and three estate surveyors, but only one amateur—apart from the two candidates who cannot be identified.[14] Why were the more experienced map-makers unsuccessful?

John Rocque was first of the professional county map-makers to apply for the premium. In July 1759 he informed the Society that he was surveying Berkshire, Oxfordshire and Buckinghamshire. The first six sheets of the map were sent as a specimen to enable them 'to judge of the great care I take to give the public satisfaction'. The enterprise had involved him in great expense, but some reward from the Society would allow him to finish not only 'the said three Counties but also to Undertake the County of Kent'. Several Society meetings considered his letter, but he was deemed ineligible; his map of Berkshire was not a response to the Society advertisement, for although published in 1761, its survey stretched back a decade.[15] The surveys of Buckinghamshire, Oxfordshire and Kent did not materialize under his hand, for John Rocque died in 1762.

Isaac Taylor of Ross-on-Wye was also an experienced map-maker. As the author of one-inch maps of Herefordshire (1754) and Hampshire (1759), of two town plans, as well as numerous estate maps, he may have felt some confidence in his application. His proposals to the Society in 1761 were for a survey of Dorset, for which he was accepted as candidate in 1762. The map was published in 1765 and submitted to the Society for adjudication at the same time as Donn's Devon. It was rejected, but the minutes throw no light on the grounds for the decision, stating only that consideration of the map was adjourned. Richard Gough, however, suggests that its place-names were too inaccurately rendered to merit a premium, and related how an offer of correction from the Dorsetshire county historian Hutchins had been refused by its author.[16] But Isaac Taylor was undeterred by lack of recognition: before his death in 1788 surveys of Worcestershire (1772) and Gloucestershire (1779) were added to his other county maps.

More puzzling than either of these cases was the failure of Thomas Jefferys to obtain a premium. His experience as a London map publisher and engraver, his professional status as Geographer to the King and his contribution to county cartography all seemed to fit him for an award. After the introduction of the premiums and before his death in 1771 he was associated—sometimes as publisher employing surveyors and sometimes as engraver—with at least ten county maps. Based on trigonometrical survey and plane-table work, at the one-inch scale or larger, these were fair specimens of the cartography the Society was encouraging. Moreover, if Gough's information was correct, Jefferys had deliberately undertaken these surveys 'in consequence of a premium of £100 offered by the Society of Arts'.[17]

Jefferys decided to claim his reward on the surveys of two counties in 1765. He was tersely informed that as a member of the Society he could not 'be candidate for that Article, and that the advertisement requires . . . the person . . . who intend[s] to make out such survey shall give notice thereof'. In 1769 he again submitted, this time his survey of Oxfordshire. It was ordered on this occasion that his letter 'be laid aside as he did not pay his arrears at the Time he declined [i.e., left the Society] nor since; and that the map be returned to him'.[18] Jefferys, who died two years later, did not receive a premium. Why did the Society interpret its regulations so strictly in his case? Had there been a clash of personalities behind the scenes which counted for more than the merits of the maps?

The remaining four unsuccessful applicants were lesser cartographers. The one amateur, Dr. Charles Mason, was Woodwardian Professor of Geology at Trinity College, Cambridge. In 1759 his map of Cambridgeshire was 'almost finished having been the work of many years'. His candidature was accepted, but only the trigonometrical framework of the survey was completed before his death. For some years his widow tried unsuccessfully to have the map finished with the help of Elstobb and Turpin, two Cambridge surveyors. Stephen McDougall, a Glasgow estate surveyor, was more cavalier in his approach to the Society. In 1760 he cautioned them by letter that the premium was 'too little for a man to execute the survey,' but that the right financial support (300 half-guinea subscriptions in advance) would tempt him southwards, preferably to survey Somerset, 'as I could get readily from here by sea'. He was not engaged. Isaac Thompson, the Newcastle-upon-Tyne printer, publisher and estate surveyor, less presumptuously offered a survey of Northumberland in 1760. Again there is no evidence that it was started, and a few years later Andrew Armstrong was busy with his map of the same county. Likewise Charles Wilkinson, a Nottingham surveyor and schoolmaster, did not produce the survey of Nottinghamshire he proposed to the Society in 1764. Thomas Jefferys had also commissioned an unsuccessful survey of that county, and finally, by 1776 it was mapped by John Chapman.[19] These were signs of a growing competition to share in the new mapping of England, which was to react on the Society's policy towards county maps.

THE CHANGES OF POLICY, 1767-1801

Between 1767 and 1801 the Society of Arts followed two policies towards county cartography. First, from 1767 to 1786, the regular premiums of £100 for county surveys were discontinued and replaced by occasional 'honorary' awards or bounties.[20] Secondly, from 1787 to 1801, prizes of either fifty pounds or a gold medal were offered annually for an accurate county map. The last year for any award to be advertised was 1801.

The first phase represented a change of policy explained by Robert Dossie as arising from 'Too great a multiplicity of applications', and the desire to avoid 'Appropriating too great a part of their funds to one object'. But, 'the example is set [he argued] and the utility displayed, by the maps already obtained . . . and this alone may possibly procure the rest to be performed, by the aid of private subscriptions, and the encouragement of the gentlemen in the respective counties'.[21] Not every member of the Society shared this opinion. A proposal in 1771 sought to reintroduce the awards and to renew the £100 premium, but the recommendation was not accepted. The Society did not, however, turn its back on the county maps entirely, for as Dossie observed, 'an offer from any person well recommended, to make a map of one of the remaining counties, would meet with attention'.

This rather vague promise maintained only tenuous links between the Society and county cartography; although quite a number of new surveys were undertaken from 1767 to 1786, unabated by the withdrawal of the premiums, only six map-makers inquired if the Society would support their projects. Two were unsuccessful,[22] but four—Andrew Armstrong, John Prior, William Day and Joseph Hodskinson—received bounties for surveys of Northumberland (1769), Leicestershire (1779), Somerset (1782) and Suffolk (1783). The circumstances of the awards add several details to our knowledge of these cartographers and reveal the methods employed by the Society of Arts to assess the quality of surveys.

In 1768, Armstrong, describing himself as 'Lieut. on half pay from the 32nd Regt.', informed the Society that their advertisements had induced him to map Northumberland, but that he had been unaware of the withdrawal of the premiums. The survey—taken with the assistance of his son Mostyn John Armstrong—was already at the engraver's, and if the Society would give him 'the encouragement the former Undertakers of such Maps . . . have received', it would be completed with the 'Utmost Expedition'. A second letter affords more details of the making of the map. The whole survey had lasted three years, but the survey of the boundary with Durham and Cumberland, located 'on Mountainous and Barren hills', had alone taken a full summer. In the interior of the county Armstrong 'had waited on most of [the gentry] or their Stewards for information'—implying one method of compiling topographical data. On the other hand, he had surveyed in the field 'Valuable Antiquities', such as the Roman Wall, and marked the battle sites in a county 'formerly the scene of action when the Two nations were at wars', which suggest on his part a professional interest in military history. Further proof of the originality of his survey was provided by a statement of the costs incurred in its making, a unique fragment of cartographical history.[23]

For a month the map was hung in the Society's Great Room for the inspection of members, whose satisfaction was expressed in the bounty of fifty guineas given to Armstrong. Perhaps encouraged by this success, he surveyed in Scotland during the early 1770s and then returned southwards to survey Lincolnshire (1779), the map being unsuccessfully submitted to the Society, and Rutland (1780). By 1782, however, his cartographic career was declining, and a last contact with the Society was an attempt (again without success) to sell to the institution the copper-plates of his Northumberland map for £20.[24]

John Prior, a clergyman and a schoolmaster, unlike Armstrong, was not a field surveyor. His Leicestershire prospectus shows that the survey was the work of Joseph Whyman, although 'under the direction' of Prior. The map was more carefully assessed by the Society than that of Armstrong's. The Earl of Huntingdon in a letter to Lord Romney vouched its accuracy; in addition, Joseph Hodskinson, a London surveyor and a member of the Society, had 'examined some of the Principal Angles given in this survey and [found them] planned with Accuracy'. In the fashion of Burdett's Derbyshire and Armstrong's Durham, Prior included a triangulation diagram on his map, 'to show the principal Stations in this survey, from whence all other places are projected', thus facilitating the testing of its accuracy. He was awarded twenty guineas and a silver medal, after an attempt to award him a gold medal had been frustrated.[25]

The next map to be considered by the Society was that of Somerset by William Day, a local surveyor of Blagdon in the same county. Procedures for its assessment were also thorough. Members of the Society who were natives of Somerset were summoned to the next meeting of the committee. Three witnesses appeared and testified that the survey was 'well and properly laid down'. After 'being fully informed of the truth of the bearings, distances of places etc.', twenty guineas and a silver medal were voted to Day, while Charles Harcourt Masters, his assistant (trained by Day in the art of surveying) received the 'great silver Pallet with a suitable inscription'. The latter's reward stemmed from Day's recommendation: writing to the Society he explained that he had placed his name upon the map for being 'so honest and industrious during the survey'.[26]

Suffolk, by Joseph Hodskinson, was the last survey to be rewarded before regular premiums were reintroduced, and also the first undertaken entirely by professional London map-makers—the first five awards had gone to little-known, virtually amateur, county surveyors. Hodskinson, whose office was in Arundel Street, Strand, had been associated with three of Jefferys' county surveys. Suffolk he surveyed himself, while William Faden, successor to Jefferys as Geographer to the King, engraved and published the map. The Society as usual sought the opinion of referees familiar with the county, and the agriculturalist Arthur Young reported from Bradfield Hall on the merits of the map. A severe chill—the symptoms of which he described at length—had prevented him from making a more thorough scrutiny, but the survey was 'very correct in all the places that I have yet particularly examined. . . . We esteem it here a very valuable acquisition. Some slight errors I have heard mentioned, but they are few and such as are unavoidable in such a work. Our former survey by Kirby was a miserable one.'[27] In 1784 the Society's gold medal went to Hodskinson.

This award marked the beginning of the new policy: in 1787 the Society restored the regular premiums which were offered annually till 1801. Listing the maps already in its possession, it offered the gold medal or fifty pounds to the surveyor who would produce an accurate survey of any county in England and Wales. It also required each candidate to submit 'Certificates of Accuracy' with their maps. But there was no rapid increase in the number of applications; in this next period only six map-makers applied to the Society, two unsuccessfully, four successfully. Two awards went to William Faden for maps of Hampshire (1791) and Sussex (1795); one (a gold medal) went to William Yates, the Liverpool surveyor and customs' officer, for his Lancashire (1787); the last (fifty guineas) to Richard Davis, an Oxfordshire farmer, enclosure commissioner and agricultural writer for his Oxfordshire (1797).[28]

For Davis and Yates, county surveying was (in the now established trend of prize-winners) only a part-time occupation. Particular interest therefore attaches to the success of William Faden, a professional London cartographer. Two causes were contributory: first there was his influential position in the English map-making trade at the close of the eighteenth century, and secondly his successful relationship with the Society. His cartographical rôle was that of organizer rather than practical surveyor: the resources of his engraving shop and publishing house were contracted out to the surveyor in a small way of business; as regular bidder at the auction rooms he concentrated the copper-plates of many county surveys in his own hands to publish new, but often ill-revised, editions; but in other cases, if a county lacked a modern survey, he would, like Jefferys, commission a map. Hampshire, surveyed by Thomas Milne from 1788 to 1790, but published by Faden, was undertaken in this way. An award to Faden resulted after the Society had 'Examined . . . some of the Field Work by which the survey was made', and learnt that the magistrates in the various districts of the county approved of the map. Faden, his eye to profit, selected the 'pecuniary reward' rather than the gold medal.[29]

The other Faden award associated him with the completion of the map of Sussex by Thomas Yeakell and William Gardner. The first four sheets (at two inches to one mile) had been published from 1778 to 1783 before its authors, estate surveyors in the employ of the Duke of Richmond, had entered the service of the Board of Ordnance. In 1791 Gardner and Thomas Gream, a land surveyor with an office in Villiers Street, Strand, issued a prospectus to finish the map at one inch to one mile, but Faden appears to have bought them out, and he published the new map in 1795. Submitting to the Society in 1796, Faden received a gold medal as 'a Token of their approbation'. Relationships between Society and cartographer were obviously friendly. This is confirmed by the fact that in 1794 the Society had sent Faden a list of its county maps, and, finding 'many articles . . . wanting', he presented complimentary copies of eleven surveys, while from the copper-plates of several out-of-print surveys he promised to send maps at the first opportunity.[30]

But not even this liberality gained Faden a third award from the Society. His Norfolk (1797), surveyed by Thomas Donald and Thomas Milne (and which had involved him in public controversy with Mostyn John Armstrong), was rejected on grounds of not conforming to the time limit of the advertisement. But the most interesting item in the minutes of this committee was a request to Faden: he had to obtain 'Information from the Gentleman who has surveyed the County of Norfolk under the Direction of the House of Commons, and also from the Post Master General as may supply . . . corroborating evidence in favour of the Improvement by this Map'. The reference to the House of Commons survey was to the presence of Board of Ordnance Surveyors who had been mapping in Norfolk in the 1790s (although not in connection with the triangulation for Ordnance Survey maps, which did not begin in this county till 1813), and that to the

Post Master General concerned his survey of roads undertaken by John Cary.[31] In the 1790s more powerful, official patrons of cartography were emerging. The Society's awareness of these developments probably contributed to its final withdrawal from this aspect of its work in the following decade.

THE SOCIETY'S PLACE IN CARTOGRAPHICAL HISTORY

In 1802 the Society of Arts discontinued the premiums for county maps. The reasons for the decision were not stated, but they were apparently no secret to the map-publishing trade of the day: the engraver Samuel John Neele had been 'informed that the Society have lately suspended the offer of premiums for English Maps in Consequence of the Trigonometrical Survey of England ordered by [the] Government'. The Society's action had quickly followed the publication of the first Ordnance Survey map in 1801.[32]

Candidates continued to apply for the awards, however, and such applications were not dismissed out of hand by the Society. For example, in 1806 James Sherriff, a south Staffordshire surveyor, described a map of Warwickshire, begun in 1799, as a response to the premiums, and was assured that in the event of his survey being published and submitted with 'proper Certificates', it would be considered. William Larkin, a drawing of whose map of West Meath lay at the workshop of the engraver Neele, received a similar promise.[33] Thus, in practice, the Society continued to make awards until 1809.

Apart from fifty guineas given in 1803 to Richard Horwood for his Map of London, three more prizes were given for county maps. Of these, the award to John Evans of forty-five guineas for a map of North Wales (1795) was a muddled episode; but the gold medal to John Cary for a map of Cardiganshire (1803), and the fifteen guineas to Robert Baugh for a map of Shropshire (1808), complete the awards launched in the eighteenth century without further incident.[34] In all, the Society had rewarded thirteen county surveys from 1759 to 1809, disbursing £460 in cash, and giving four gold medals, three silver medals and one silver palette. What was the influence of this patronage upon the cartography of the period?

It is clear that the second half of the eighteenth century saw notable improvements in county map-making. England was virtually remapped with greater accuracy and in more detail than in nearly two centuries following the pioneer surveys of Christopher Saxton in the 1570s. In 1750, topographical maps were inadequate. In 1800, the traveller through England could have purchased vastly improved surveys; every English county, almost without exception, had been mapped at the one-inch scale or larger. As the Society's interest in map-making was coeval with these improved surveys, its influence must be carefully rated. To Sir Henry Trueman Wood, the publication of the new county maps could 'without much doubt be traced to the offer by the Society of a prize of £100'; while according to Edward Lynam, the Society 'had an influence on English county maps as great and as fruitful as that of the Royal Society upon geodesy and methods of surveying'.[35] The truth of these assertions may perhaps be accepted in broad outline, but, on the other hand, they clearly need qualification in the light both of the Society's objectives and of other influences effecting cartographical improvement. The question arises, would the new county maps have come into existence without the Society's awards?

The Society had only partial success in the fulfilment of its stated objectives. Its early attempt to make the cartographers finish their surveys more expeditiously did not succeed. For example, William Day took more than seven years to survey Somerset without detriment to his prize. The idea of building the surveys into a national map was also a failure, for a map of England based on the new one-inch-to-one-mile maps did not materialize in the eighteenth century. This realization of the inherent difficulties of integrating diverse county maps may, however, have helped to demonstrate the need for the Board of Ordnance surveys at public expense. It was left to Charles Smith and John Cary to use the late eighteenth-century surveys extensively in the production of their vastly improved *New English Atlases*, which, published in the first decade of the nineteenth century, provide a more uniform, although smaller scale, national map coverage.[36]

In standardizing the format and improving the quality of county maps, the Society experienced greater success. Although there were earlier county maps on the one-inch-to-one-mile scale and it had been employed in military survey and for road books, during the period of the awards the scale became almost standard for original surveys. Simultaneously, greater accuracy was widely achieved by the general adoption of trigonometrical survey, and the whole scope of the topographical survey was enlarged to give more detailed treatment of both natural and man-made features. The Society's careful assessment of the maps submitted for awards must also have furthered the application of new standards of accuracy. The practice of appointing referees for maps, of examining field note books, of demanding certificates of accuracy, and of checking the triangulation of surveys, cannot have passed unnoticed in the surveying profession. But the Society had

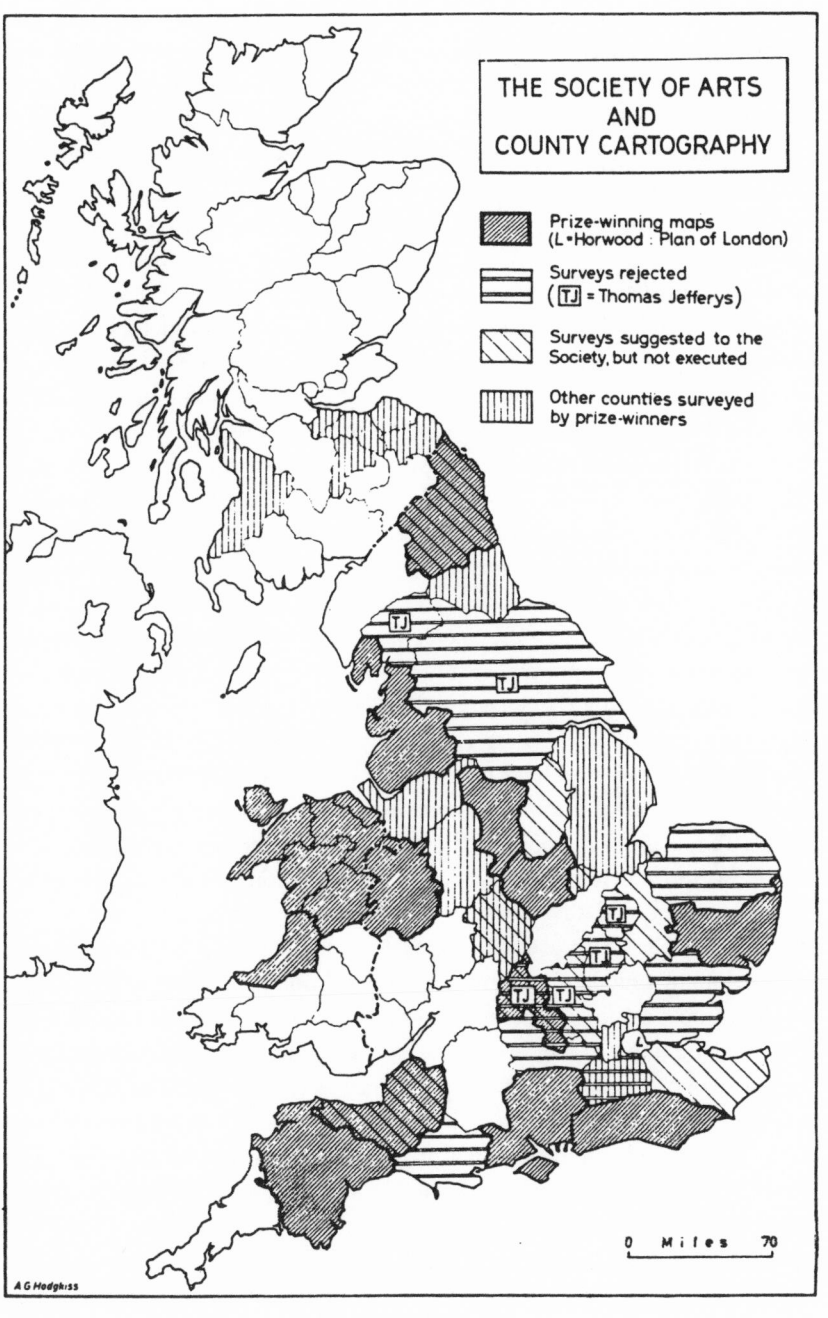

THE SOCIETY OF ARTS
AND
COUNTY CARTOGRAPHY

Prize-winning maps
(L = Horwood : Plan of London)

Surveys rejected
(TJ = Thomas Jefferys)

Surveys suggested to the
Society, but not executed

Other counties surveyed
by prize-winners

TJ

TJ

TJ

TJ

TJ TJ

0   Miles   70

not the powers either to regulate the map-publishing trade or to curb the faulty practices of individual surveyors. Thus, although the Board of Ordnance surveyors severely censured the county maps of the Society's period, one feels that Richard Gough fairly lays the blame on the cartographers, not the Society, wishing 'that the abilities of some were more answerable to the encouragement afforded to them'.[37]

The fact that prizes went to only thirteen county surveys would seem to underestimate the extent of the Society's influence on the mapping of England and Wales. Many county map-makers had links, if only indirect, with the Society. There were, first, the unsuccessful and ineligible candidates (especially Jefferys) who had mapped in aggregate a large area of England partly in response to the awards. Secondly, some prize-winners such as Burdett, Armstrong and Yates were apparently encouraged by their rewards to undertake other surveys; these maps, of comparable accuracy, suggest the extension of the Society's influence into other counties. Thirdly, even the unsuccessful schemes proposed to the Society contributed something to the idea of cartographical improvement.

The number of amateurs who applied for awards reveals the degree to which a knowledge of the Society's offer awakened interest in provincial, as well as metropolitan, cartographers of the period, notwithstanding changes of policy by the Society and the withdrawal of regular premiums from 1767 to 1786 and after 1801. To part-time surveyors in particular the proposals may well have opened new cartographical vistas: they could make a local contribution to an improved national map; and, in return, the Society's recognition would, in the words of William Yates, introduce their maps 'to more general knowledge in the Kingdom'. At its lowest value such prestige could advance sales. But to some surveyors, the cash prizes, particularly the £100 premium, may have been a strong inducement. In this company one may perhaps place the schoolmaster Donn, 'obliged to spend almost all [his] time in procuring the common necessaries of life', Burdett, the improvident artist, or Armstrong, half soldier, half surveyor, rather than professional cartographers such as Jefferys or Faden, for whom county maps formed only a small part of total enterprises.[38]

This financial rôle of the awards must not, however, be over-stressed. The total of £460 paid by the Society was inadequate to finance a single county map, and the costs of survey quoted by several surveyors emphasize that any premium would only defray a modest proportion of their expenses. Armstrong's Northumberland was relatively cheaply produced at a cost of £516; Donn's Devon cost nearly £2,000; and Day's Somerset cost more than 'a thousand Guineas exclusive my great time and labour'. These

surveyors were not necessarily guilty of exaggeration, because independent
sources confirm the high costs of eighteenth-century county map-making:
Yeakell and Gardner calculated that £2,400 would be needed over six
years for the surveying, drawing and engraving of their map of Sussex,
and a comparable scale of costs was later established for the production of
Irish county maps.[39]

Thus, the Society did not act as capitalist to the new wave of surveys,
which were financed primarily by the subscriptions of the county gentry. It
may be noted that of the maps rewarded by the Society, Burdett's Derbyshire alone was dedicated to the Society, in preference to prominent members of the nobility. The securing of such subscribers became an important
preliminary task; it was said of Donn that he would travel 30 miles for
20 subscribers, or 50 miles for 30 subscribers. Most maps had upwards of
200 subscribers: Prior had 275 for his Leicestershire, Chapman and André
240 for their Essex, and Yates declared he would not publish Lancashire
until 800 copies were subscribed for (although the names of only 252 landowners were engraved on the map). The Evans map of North Wales had
fared better, for 280 subscribers had bought 658 copies of the map between
them.[40] These subscriptions, from the gentry, clergy and farmers resident
in the counties, gave local support to the surveys which the Society encouraged on a national level. The names of the gentry engraved on some
maps, and the prominence with which their houses and parks are depicted,
reflect the interest of this social class in the new surveys.

Clearly other formative influences were also active in the new cartography, but they are outside the scope of this paper. For example, the activities
of professional cartographers such as Jefferys, Kitchin, Cary and Faden;
the developments in military surveying; advances in the theory of surveying
and in the craft of instrument-making; the growth of estate surveying; the
general background of a period of economic improvement—all these factors must be evaluated alongside the Society's contribution of the second
half of the eighteenth century. The Society was partner in a field in which
eventually the initiative was taken by the government from both professional and amateur map-makers. But, meanwhile, it helped to co-ordinate
and cross-fertilize the efforts of these two groups, and to disseminate some
of the new ideas of county survey. The remapping of England would probably have occurred without the Society's intervention, but the institution
hastened and directed the process. In the three or four decades prior to the
foundation of the Ordnance Survey, it was the only independent national
body to devote serious attention to this facet of England's improvement.

10

THE SOCIETY AND THE IMPROVEMENT
OF WHALING

Walter M. Stern

Some writers believe that whale fishing began at the end of the ninth century.[1] Kings of England, in their capacity as dukes of Guyenne, taxed whaling in 1197; by this time, Basques and Bayonnais appear to have pursued whales, chiefly in the Bay of Biscay, originally employing spears and arrows. Once a cord was attached to the spear or arrow, the principle of the harpoon as a mechanism for catching whales had been established. Whales were hunted because they intruded into the herring fishery, tearing the nets; only subsequently did they become appreciated for their flesh, which could be eaten, and their tongues, which were regarded as a delicacy. Not being aggressive animals, whales retreated to less accessible waters, especially to the coasts of Iceland and Norway and the North Cape. Pursuit took hunters to Newfoundland and the Greenland ice.[2]

By the late sixteenth century the whaling fleet, recruited from a number of countries, consisted of 50 to 60 vessels. Spitzbergen was the principal base. Some of the ships were English, having been lured to the area by the search for the North East or North West passage to Cathay; they found the sea around Greenland 'full of whales and other sea monsters'. Trade along the North East passage was the prerogative of the Muscovy Company, which on its reincorporation in 1576-7 received a monopoly of

Originally appeared in *Jnl. RSA*, 128 (Sept., Oct., Nov., 1980), 689-90, 772-76, 856-64.

killing whales for 20 years. Others engaged in fishing for cod, however, encountered whales around Newfoundland.[3] By this time, they had learnt about train oil, as the oil extracted from whales is called; it first figures in the Muscovy Company's accounts in 1604-6. By the early seventeenth century, the English dominated the whale fishery, successfully competing with other nations, above all with the Dutch. In 1618 the Dutch for the first time drove the English from the whaling grounds; they, and the Danes, continued to harass the English, whose primacy declined from 1626 onwards, owing partly to Dutch superiority, partly to rivalry among themselves. For a hundred years, English whaling activity languished.[4]

The Dutch organized whale fishing (the Lesser Fishery) with the same meticulous care which they had brought to the Great Fishery (of herrings in the North Sea), not allowing whaling personnel to take service in foreign ships, prohibiting the export of whaling ships or implements and the sale of catches in markets other than Dutch and confining whaling ships to port in times of war.[5] Only Dutch subjects could use whalers fitted out in Holland; processing of whales was established at points close to the fishing grounds. Dutch ships caught more whales than they could transport; so carrier ships were employed to take the surplus produce home. Though whales became scarcer and more difficult to locate in the second half of the seventeenth century, rationalization of fishing methods and monopolization of the trade left the Dutch in command.[6]

The loss of the trade spurred both Scottish and English interests into setting up companies devoted solely to whaling. A Scottish Greenland Company, established in 1622, made a false start and did not survive long;[7] Sir William Scawen started its English counterpart over 70 years later, in 1693-4, with a capital of £40,000, authorized in 1696 to be increased to £82,000; the incorporating Act gave it a monopoly of importing free from duty for 14 years all products derived from whales caught by its ships. It used up all its capital and failed. Elking lists the weaknesses from which it suffered: lack of experienced British commanders while skilled foreign harpooners were employed in, but not given command of, ships; captains remunerated by fixed salary, instead of a commission on catches; poor and inexpert processing of produce so that it fetched low prices; inadequate care of equipment and cost control.[8]

Some people in Britain were convinced that a more capable effort would succeed. One such was Sir John Eyles, Bart., Sub-Governor of the famous or notorious South Sea Company. Once its bubble had burst, the Company needed a new and less sensational hunting ground than the London stock market. Eyles regarded the South Sea Company as an ideal instrument for the revival of English whale fishing, but he had to persuade his fellow directors. He therefore asked Henry Elking for an expert appreciation of the technicalities of the trade, showing the profits made by the Dutch in the Greenland whale fishery between 1675 and 1721 (150 million guilders, equivalent to £14 million), and enumerating all the advantages over the Dutch which could accrue to the English in this activity. Elking's *A View of the Greenland Trade and Whale Fishing* was laid before the South Sea Company's Court of Directors in 1722; two years later the Company fitted out its first whalers, supported by an Act of Parliament which exempted from import duty for seven years all whaling produce, provided the whales had been caught in Greenland waters by British ships manned by a crew of whom at least one-third was British. No British fishermen had experience of whaling; so the Company engaged experts from Holstein. Table 1 shows the number of ships sent out from 1726 to 1732. By the latter year, the South Sea Company had lost more than £175,000, over £22,000 for each year of operation; it despaired of making the whale fishery pay.[9]

British whale fishing revived in the second half of the eighteenth century, as the result partly of government bounties, partly of technical improvements. Other nations took equal advantage of these opportunities. Over the last two centuries, whale fishing has become a particularly repugnant trade, from which every nation tries to snatch the largest possible share to the exclusion of others. Whales are shy and inoffensive creatures, defenceless against the weapons of modern technique. It is not proposed here to horrify and depress readers by a description of the long drawn-out agony of the whale, its body pierced by a harpoon, trying to escape its pursuers, who maim it with further harpoons until it slowly bleeds to death; there can be few crueller ways of destroying a living creature. Suffice it to say that nations for commercial reasons kill whales in excessive numbers by particularly revolting methods, thereby threatening to exterminate the species. Attempts to limit the slaughter by legislation have proved futile, because it takes place on the high sea where no country has power over what another country does; the quarry, remaining outside territorial waters, is not the property of any one nation, and legislators are more concerned to secure what they consider a fair share to their own nationals than to preserve whales, let alone mitigate the cruelty of killing methods. While the Society of Arts originally helped to perfect these methods, the humanitarian aspect of its activities, which K. W. Luckhurst mentions in more modern times, justifies the hope that it would now be ranged on the side of the whales rather than on that of their killers.[10]

A Society devoted to the encouragement of the arts, manufactures and

Table 1. Whaling Ships Sent Out by the
South Sea Company and Their Catch

Year	Ships	Whales Caught	Ships Lost
1726	24	16½*	—
1727	25	22½*	2
1728	23	18	—
1729	23	27½*	1
1730	22	12	—
1731	22	14	1
1732	21	24½*	—

*Half a whale results from two ships of different
nationality striking, and therefore having to divide,
a whale.

commerce in the middle of the eighteenth century had reason to take an
interest in whaling. At two stages in the chain of events which led from
the pursuit of the whale to the utilization of its produce, the possibilities
of technical improvement appeared promising: one, clearly indicated by
the early history of the trade, to secure larger and more certain catches to
each ship; the other, to make material gained from whales more widely
available and acceptable to users. The whale yielded a number of products
for which, in the state of technique of the eighteenth century, there were
no substitutes. Whalebone, a horny substance embedded in the animal's
upper jaws, had very great commercial value, when separated, rubbed
clean by scrubbing, soaking in a warm soda solution, washing in warm
water, drying in the open and polishing with a brush and hair cloth. It
sold at £700 a ton in the early eighteenth century. The fashion trade of
Paris coveted it for ladies' corsets, umbrellas, parasols and ornamental
head dresses; it imparted strength, elasticity and flexibility to the backs
and seats of chairs and sofas and could also be used to reinforce their
stuffing and that of mattresses, cushions and settees; it served as a material for trunks and portmanteaux, ram and fishing rods, shafts, springs
and wheels of carriages; even hygrometers were made of whalebone.[11]
A diseased sperm whale secreted from its intestines a light inflammable
fatty substance named ambergris, opaque in lustre, ashy in colour, with
marbled variegations, and developing a pleasant odour, when heated. To
manufacturers of perfume, ambergris was worth more than its weight in
gold. Whale meat constituted food for humans and animals; it could be

salted down and preserved; if too old for consumption, it would still serve as manure. The tail of the whale boiled down into glue; the jaw bones served as ribs in the construction of arches, gateway posts and sheds. Any whalebone unfit for more refined use could be ground into bonemeal.[12]

THE EDULCORATION OF TRAIN OIL

Whatever the luxury uses of whale produce, the most important raw material to an economy innocent of mineral oil was the train oil gained from the whale. Among a great variety of uses, that of illuminant took pride of place; it was the only chief and effective source of lighting for both public and private places, as the Society of Arts acknowledged when it ordered on 14th May 1760 'That the Great Room be for the future lighted with Oil instead of Candles'. The candles which it replaced had themselves been a mixture of spermaceti oil, a superior form of whale oil, and beeswax. Furthermore, soft soap was made of the oil of any whales not caught in the ice; leather and coarse woollen cloth had to be treated with oil during manufacture; coarse paints and varnishes were made of oil. Lubrication required oil, and combined with tar it was used in ship work and the manufacture of cordage. Tinks, the ultimate refuse of the extraction process, made prussian blue and ammonia, while spermaceti oil went into unguents and ointments. When gas lighting spread in the early nineteenth century, oil conversion into gas became a widely used process.[13]

Whalers obtained oil from the blubber, a layer of fat twelve to eighteen inches thick in a fully grown large whale; in the young animal, it was the colour of hog's lard, turning reddish as the whale aged. Blubber could be rendered into train oil in the proportion of four to three. Depending on the type of whale, an animal yielded from 10 to 80 tons of oil, the average being nearer the top than the bottom limit. But this was only the ordinary oil—thick, viscid and evil-smelling. From the head of a particular species, the sperm whale, could be filtered a neutral, odourless and nearly tasteless fatty substance—white, brittle and soft to the touch. This rendered down into spermaceti oil, much preferred for both lighting and lubricating purposes, owing to the characteristics described. Ordinary users looked upon the colour of whale oil as a standard of value: pale oil (honey-coloured or reddish-brown) commanded the highest price, followed by brown oil, whereas black oil, the residue of processing, remained viscid and opaque and could be used only for inferior purposes. More discriminating users had a detailed classification of which colour was only the outward indicator: spermaceti oil came uppermost, followed by the blubber oil of the

sperm whale; third was the oil extracted by first boiling the blubber of
fin whales, whereas the second boiling resulted in oil of the fourth class;
what could be coaxed from meat and blubber remaining in a closed boiler
yielded the fifth class, with the bones, scraps and sperm meat finally being
reduced to the lowest type of oil.[14]

In Elking's day, the extraction of the oil was done on the whalers; only
the Dutch had shore stations near to the whaling grounds. Subsequently
the other nations established them. The processing involved cutting the
blubber out of the whale, which had to be done by severing the dead animal's tail, raising the whale a few inches above the water, belly upward,
dividing the blubber into oblong slips and flaying each slip off separately
by pulling upward, first from the belly and under-jaw, subsequently turning the whale on its side to remove the lip and expose the whalebone (its
removal was a technique of its own), and eventually removing the blubber
from all other parts. The blubber was then divided into manageable pieces,
all extraneous substances, such as skin and remnants of muscle, being removed, and boiled in copper boilers over a wood fire. The finer oil could
be drained off after one boiling, the second quality of oil resulted from a
further boiling; eventually the boiler had to be closed to build up steam
pressure, which expelled from the boiler the less abundant and more viscid
oil yielded by what was left of blubber, whale meat and bones.[15]

The sickening smell of the common train oil made it extremely unpleasant to use; it was foetid, and when burnt in lamps, gave off an odour
normally associated with organic matter in a state of putrefaction. Robert
Dossie and other scientists associated with the Society of Arts, when they
turned their attention to the oil, described it as 'vicious' train oil; one is
tempted to treat the term as a corruption of viscid, but it clearly denotes
their reaction to the stink. Indeed, wool combers could not use train oil at
all and were reduced to a coarse form of olive oil, known to the trade as
Gallipoli oil (from the area whence it was imported), which was far more
expensive. Candles equally were made of imported oil; the substitution
of train oil in these uses would have saved money and foreign currency.
These were the considerations which led Dr. Peter Shaw to suggest to the
Society of Arts the offer of a premium for what came to be known as the
edulcoration—that is, the sweetening and purification—of train oil.[16]

There were precedents for edulcoration. The *Gentleman's Magazine* for
1756 gave an account of a ventilator contrived by Dr. Stephen Hales which
had been designed to remove the smell from 'ill-tasted milk' and stinking
water. Oil was not mentioned among the liquids to be so purified, but the
description included a method of separating oil from water. In view of

Dr. Hales's close links with the Society, it is not surprising that the latter welcomed Dr. Shaw's proposal. Accordingly, it offered a premium in 1757 and continued to do so up to 1760. Along with train oil, it also specified seal oil. The Society did not require to be informed of the method of edulcoration, but stipulated that processed oil should be suitable for the use of clothiers and soap boilers and able to serve as a substitute for olive oil in uses other than food. The first response came at the end of 1759, when the Society received a small parcel of train oil edulcorated, without any indication of the method employed, and a description of a method of edulcorating train oil, unaccompanied by samples. It was not obvious whether the two dispatches emanated from the same source; they were referred to the Committee of Premiums which does not appear to have taken any further steps in the matter, except to recommend the continuation of the premium offer. A more serious submission occurred a year later, at the end of 1760. Mr. Household of Whittlesea in the Isle of Ely was no stranger to the Society of Arts, with which he corresponded regarding planks of oak suitable for ships' bottoms, and on the subject of catching rats. Obviously a many-sided man of ingenious disposition, he submitted samples of train oil, one in its original state, the other edulcorated. The Committee of Chemistry had to investigate them in a hurry, as one of the containers leaked. The Committee concluded, and the Society endorsed the finding, that Mr. Household's sample 'did not come up to the Idea of the Society in their Advertisement'. Robert Dossie, describing the Committee of Chemistry's investigation, used less restrained language. He found it difficult to decide which smelt worse, the original or the edulcorated oil, as the latter had added 'an empyreumatic smell to the putrid factor, which was very little diminished'. Moreover, the oil had darkened in processing and looked opaque—both indications of low quality. The failure to produce a serviceable oil did not surprise Dossie. He knew that it would need a long series of experiments, involving filtration through sand and other substances, washing with water and ventilating with air, to achieve the purpose. This would be too expensive a procedure for £10 to constitute adequate compensation. He therefore suggested, and the Society agreed, that the premium be discontinued.[17]

Contrary to what the abolition of the premium might suggest, edulcoration of train oil occupied most of the Committee of Chemistry's time during the year 1761. It is impossible to determine from its minutes how much time; though the impression is gained that some of its meetings lasted much longer than others, the number of hours spent in any meeting cannot be deduced from the minutes. Sometimes a meeting dealt with two or three subjects, possibly not at equal length, but in the absence of evidence regarding time spent on each, one-half or one-third of the meeting has been attributed to train oil. If two separate meetings were held on the same day, usually under different chairmen, they have been counted as two; if a meeting was adjourned for a meal or for a chemical reaction to take effect, it has been treated as one. If insufficient members assembled to constitute a quorum, no account has been taken of the meeting, as no business was transacted. That leaves the puzzling meeting of 27th November 1761, which is described as devoted to edulcorating train oil, with twenty members present, but with no record of what happened. Subject to all these reservations, of 45 meetings which the Committee of Chemistry held between 28th April 1761 and 2nd January 1762, 30 (excluding the one without minutes) were fully, 6 to the extent of one-half and 2 to the extent of one-third devoted to the edulcoration of train oil.

Subsequent events make it obvious that, when Dossie reflected on the inadequacy of the premium, he had not only decided to attempt a solution of the problem himself, but had already embarked on the long course of experiments he saw as requisite to succeed. That he should not have disclosed this to the Society at this stage is natural; had he failed, it would have been unpleasant and unnecessary to publicize defeat. Until convinced that he had discovered a satisfactory method of edulcorating train oil, he had every reason to keep his experiments to himself. How he dealt with the situation by anonymously submitting his proposals in a letter signed A.B., offering to reveal the method of edulcoration in return for £100, and continuing to chair the Committee of Chemistry until he officially identified himself as the proposer on 15th June has been described by Trueman Wood and Gibbs and need not here be recapitulated. Gibbs accepts that the other members of the Committee of Chemistry remained unaware of the identity of A.B. until 7th August (that date is an error) and attributes the anonymity to Dossie's modesty. Close examination of the Committee's minutes raises the suspicion that anonymity amounted to no more than courteous fiction. Gibbs mentions that Dossie had adopted the signature of A.B. on earlier occasions; this must have been known to other members. The processes to which the Committee had to subject the train oil during experiments were complicated and lengthy; many of them took place in the laboratory of Dr. Fordyce, one of the members, with sometimes only two other members of the Committee present, of whom Dossie was one. Without running instructions from the author of the method to guide them, it is unlikely that the experimenters could have acted appropriately throughout the long series of trials.[18]

In his anonymous proposal, Dossie outlined three alternative processes, the first to edulcorate train oil to a moderate degree, almost without any expense, the second to a great degree, without applying heat, the third to the greatest degree of purity, as was required for instance in woollen manufacture, employing heat. The importance of the distinction rested not only on the expense but also on the availability of heating equipment which would make processes Nos. 1 and 3 more complicated for users to operate. The Committee of Chemistry decided to pursue all three processes, one after the other, using one gallon of the most stinking train oil for each. It was a self-sacrificial resolution: experiments on such material during summer months must have put a severe strain on the olfactory organs of the participants. The Committee devoted its first five meetings exclusively to process No. 1, while the other processes were included in the next five meetings. Four of the latter five took place in Dr. Fordyce's laboratory; only to formulate its report on process No. 1 did the Committee return for its tenth meeting to the Society's premises. The cheapness of process No. 1 resulted from the use of ingredients of the most common kind: water, powdered lime, powdered chalk and common salt. The report, conveyed by Dossie himself to the Society's main meeting on behalf of the Committee of Chemistry, was favourable: A.B. had complied with the conditions on which the Society had agreed to reimburse his expenses of £100. The Committee estimated the expenses of the process at 2s. per ton, whereas Gallipoli oil, hitherto used for purposes for which the train oil could not be substituted, cost £15 per ton more than train oil. Moreover, purified oil burnt better in lamps than the original article. The Society unanimously voted Dossie his £100, and a vote of thanks to him was passed with equal unanimity. Dossie was invited to write up his method for publication. But a motion suggesting that additional expenses incurred in endeavours to improve the process further merited the award of another £50 met with dissent; the resolution was referred back, pending further experiments, the issue remaining undecided.[19]

Meanwhile, from the sixth meeting onwards, the Committee had set in train experiments on Dossie's process No. 2. These proved much harder to complete than the trials of process No. 1, but as they dispensed with the application of heat and therefore had the widest potential scope, the Committee took the greatest trouble with them. They required seventeen meetings in all, stretching from 25th May to 1st September. The additional ingredient needed for processes Nos. 2 and 3 was pearl ash, but process No. 2 depended on continual and prolonged stirring of the mixture. Several times the Committee ordered the Register to stir the mixture three times a day on every day until the Committee reconvened, and he some-times had to specify exactly at what times of day the stirring had been done. In addition, the Committee introduced a complication by adding cod oil and seal oil to the train oil on trial. Seal oil was soon dismissed from the experiments, but the Committee was anxious to compare the effect of the process on the best and on the worst Newfoundland cod oil. On 11th July, in Dossie's absence, the Committee for the first time for-mulated findings on train oil; they were unfavourable. It had not greatly improved in smell; the colour had turned worse in the first stage of the process and improved little in the second; it remained turbid throughout the process. On 14th July, with Dossie still absent, the Committee concen-trated on the worst Newfoundland oil, which it found improved in smell, though otherwise very little changed. On the following day, with Dossie returned to the fold, the Committee found the worst Newfoundland oil after treatment nearly as good as the best Newfoundland oil before treat-ment. By 3rd August, the Committee was in a position to compare both Newfoundland cod oils after treatment: both were considerably improved in smell and colour, but the originally worst oil still smelt considerably worse than the best. It was not until 7th August that Dossie reminded the Committee that all the claims made under the pseudonym of A.B. related to train oil only and that therefore experiments made with cod oil did not bear on his proposals at all; the Committee then decided to discontinue testing any oils other than train oil.[20] It found train oil edulcorated by pro-cess No. 2 much improved in smell and colour, not only compared to its original state but even compared to spermaceti oil; it smelt sweeter and cast a clearer and better light in a lamp. As regarded cost, the expenses of edulcorating a ton of train oil by process No. 2 were computed at 17s. 6d., though large-scale purchase of ingredients might reduce them slightly. The Committee concluded by repeating its recommendation for an award of another £50 to Dossie in reimbursement of his expenses. The full meeting of the Society considered the report on 2nd September but did not accord it the enthusiastic reception which Dossie's process No. 1 had enjoyed. A division was demanded, and though both resolutions were carried, that embodying the substantial findings passed by 53 votes to 34, that suggest-ing the additional reimbursement by 44 to 42 only. It is not apparent that the sum was ever paid.[21]

Dossie's third process occupied the Committee of Chemistry only at three meetings, those of 25th May, 3rd and 5th June, all in Dr. Fordyce's laboratory, with Dossie in the chair. Though the minutes describe the method of purification which could be reinforced by additionally subjecting the mixture to process No. 2, no conclusions appear to have been reached; nothing was reported by the Committee to the main body of the Society. This did not prevent Dossie from including process No. 3 in the published description of his methods. He claimed that it worked better the more vicious the oil, not only removing the bad smell but also changing the colour from brown to light amber. Oil treated by this process would neither putrefy again nor leave foul residue, when burnt in a lamp. Its fluidity would make it go further in woollen manufacture, and it could be more easily scoured out of the wool. If manufacturers required a thicker oil, this could be achieved by an admixture of tallow or fat. There is no evidence that these findings were endorsed by the Society of Arts, except insofar as it had countenanced Dossie's *verbatim* report on his methods.[22]

That, however, was by no means the end of the edulcoration of oil or of the labours of the Committee of Chemistry. Even before conclusions had been reached on Dossie's process No. 2, another member of that Committee, Dr. Jenty, had engaged in experiments on oil purification which he submitted to the Society on 26th August; they were of course referred to the Committee of Chemistry. Unlike Dossie, Jenty did not undertake in advance to demonstrate his experiments to the Committee or reveal his methods, but proposed to be judged by the specimens of oil which he had produced. The Committee, with Dossie in the chair, refused to make any report unless given more information. Having pondered the Committee's attitude for six weeks, Jenty became more forthcoming and proclaimed his readiness to disclose the process if the Society so desired. The Committee then gave its opinion: the vicious train oil was improved in colour and smell by Jenty's treatment, but the improvement in smell was small; whereas the cod oil had been considerably improved in both respects. Jenty had submitted specimens of further oils, but the Committee did not pronounce upon them until it received a direct instruction from the Society's meeting. It thereupon decided that Jenty had considerably improved the colour of rape oil, but not at all its smell, that his linseed oil had been improved in colour, but smelt more offensively after than before treatment, and that an oil described by Jenty as compound oil No. 1, intended for woollen manufacture, was less offensive in smell than Gallipoli oil. Compound oil No. 2 should have served the same purpose, but being adjudged considerably more foetid than No. 1, received no further consideration. Compound oil No. 1 was sent to a wool comber and spinner and to a hosier for their opinions as to its value in their manufacturing processes; moreover, a little later a Mr. James Maynard from Honiton, occupation not stated, applied for three gallons of it to make proper experiments. This was the last time Dr. Jenty's oils received mention.[23]

Both Dossie and Jenty had submitted their proposals in summer, when the stink of train oil must have been at its most offensive. The third member of the Committee of Chemistry to engage in edulcorating experiments was more considerate; not until 21st October 1761 did Dr. Michael Morris acquaint the Society with the fact that he also wished two methods to be tested. He had been in the chair of the Committee of Chemistry for some of the Dossie and Jenty proceedings; he now vacated it when informing the Committee that his methods consisted of mixing the oil with either cold or warm water. The Committee decided to perform experiments simultaneously on a large and on a small scale. A barrel churn was procured so that the mixture of oil and water could be turned over for a period and then left to settle for some time; these processes were repeated several times, with more water added—washing the oil with water, as the Committee called it. By 12th November, the Committee could discern no difference in the small-scale experiment, whether the water used by way of admixture had been warm or cold; the oil had coagulated, and some of the water remained in the mixture. The large-scale experiment produced oil free from all turbidness, but not at all improved in colour and only slightly in smell. That, however, was a provisional verdict based on three washings only. Oil washed four times was pronounced on 16th November to be improved a little over oil washed three times, though it had grown so turbid that nothing could be said about its colour. As regards small-scale tests, there was still no difference between the use of warm and cold water, but a great improvement in smell. By 21st November, some of the oil had been washed seven times, with consequent improvement in smell over oil washed only four times; it had also improved in colour, but remained turbid. Large-scale experiments had led to better smell and colour than small-scale. This was the last occasion on which Dr. Morris attended the Committee; he was subsequently revealed to have gone to Portugal. Not that this prevented the indefatigable Committee from pursuing its labours; it tried the oil again by 4th December, but found it only a little further improved in smell and colour; a motion recording more substantial improvement was lost. On 11th December, Morris' edulcorated oil was used in a lamp where it burnt only slightly sweeter, but no clearer, than the original oil and lasted nearly as long.

The Committee finally formulated these findings for a report to the Society's main body, but added that the process led to a loss of approximately a quarter of the oil and that the method was too laborious and wasteful, and the degree of improvement too small, for practical purposes. This report was rendered on 2nd January 1762. The Society, in fairness to Dr. Morris, held it over until June in the hope of his return from Portugal.

Eventually, it received and endorsed the report, apart from admitting any improvement in smell.

Not everybody agreed with this negative appreciation. The *Gentleman's Magazine* for 1762 carried an unsigned letter to the editor. It described the process of washing oil with water by means of a barrel churn, not mentioning Dr. Morris by name, but attributing the method to 'a very ingenuous [*sic*] gentleman', who started by using every one of Dossie's ingredients singly, eliminating the others, to isolate its effects. The letter deplored the timing of the experiment: oil in November was too thick for water to act upon it with the same efficacy as in July. The writer claimed, nevertheless, that the experiment had succeeded beyond expectation and that the oil had been brought to so great a degree of sweetness that many doubted whether it could be the oil on which the experiment had been performed. The letter constituted a valiant attempt to vindicate the achievement of Dr. Morris, who was unable, owing to his absence from the country, to speak for himself. Nothing in the letter, however, refuted the finding of the Committee of Chemistry bearing on the labour and waste involved in the process; though no answer to the letter was published, Morris' method was never adopted in practice. Dossie's process remained the one and only successful method of edulcorating train oil; it was published at the time in the *Annual Register* and the *Gentleman's Magazine* and republished, with only the terminology updated, in the *Transactions of the Society of Arts* in 1802.[24]

Publication did not apparently make Dossie's edulcoration process as widely known as the Society had hoped; the *Transactions* in 1802, recording that different members had lately inquired about it, republished it in its original form. On this occasion Dossie added to the description of his processes the chemical reasoning which had guided him. The smell of the oil proceeded partly from the great heat employed in extracting it from blubber, partly from the putrefaction of the gelatinous fluids and bile formed in the whale's blubber and liver. To remove the first cause, Dossie could only suggest a method which dispensed with heat; hence the importance attached to his process No. 2. Most of his comment concentrated on the smell caused by putrefaction, part of which was rancid and peculiar to oil, the other part emanating from all putrefying matter. He was therefore concerned to rid the oil of gelatinous fluid and bile. He discussed a number of substances efficacious for this purpose, dimissing most of them as unsuitable on account of either their chemical properties or their cost. Lixiviate salt emerged as the most effective agent, but the coagulation of the oil, though removing the putrid scent, left behind a strong and bitter empyreumatic smell which needed to be dispersed by the addition of common salt resolving the coagulum. Lixiviate salt was expensive; Dossie recommended the addition of small quantities of lime and chalk to cheapen the process. Water was required for the action of the salts and the separation, but could do little by itself. Where no human consumption was involved, calcined earth and ochrous earth of iron could be applied to advantage, but their properties poisoned food. It was therefore a question of incurring heavy expense (process No. 2) by using much lixiviate salt and employing no heat, or economizing by the application of heat, using lime, chalk and sea salt (process No. 1) and, in non-comestible uses, lead and red ochre.[25]

THE INCREASE IN THE CATCH

If bound for an Antarctic expedition, whalers reckoned to be away from Britain for three years, whereas the Arctic journey was completed in one summer: they set out by the middle of April, passed through the ice to the fishing grounds by the end of May at the latest, and had two months of catching before starting the return journey. For economical operation, ships had to be of a tonnage between 250 and 400, substantially built to withstand the impact of the ice, with large spaces between decks to store and process blubber. They carried seven boats, each of which was manned for the actual operations by a harpooner, whose business was the management of the harpoons, a boat-steerer responsible for the boat's movements, a line manager attending to the running out and coiling in of lines, and a number of oarsmen. Whales, once sighted, were usually pursued by a pack of four boats. A whale spends on the surface only two minutes for every five to fifteen minutes under water; it can travel half a mile while submerged, leaving an eddy or wake which traces its course. The harpoon has to strike its body because it cannot penetrate its head. The operation is dangerous: tails and fins deliver blows which can sink a boat, and the pull on the line wound round a bollard can cause friction sufficient to set the boat on fire.[26]

British governments were aware of the value of the whale fishery to the country; whale products had to be imported from abroad if British ships could not obtain them. But the need for public revenue tempted governments to burden whale products with duties, all the more as, like imports, they were brought in ships, hence easily detectable. Early government policy alternated between the aims of encouraging and taxing the trade. In an *Act for the Encouragement of the Greenland and Eastland Trades* . . . , liberty was given 'to all persons to trade into and from Greenland and there to take whales . . . and to import all sorts of oil, blubber and fins'; if caught by and imported in English ships, these were free from duty, whereas colonial and plantation ships paid a duty, foreign ships a much higher one. English ships were defined as vessels victualled in and starting the voyage from England; to give special encouragement, the requirement that three-quarters of the crew had to be English was reduced to one-half for ten years. The Act was renewed for another four years in 1689.[27] The legislation aimed at having whalebone and fins, as well as oil, brought to Britain for processing. British and foreign sailors, however, smuggled much whalebone into the country in short lengths, cut ready for use; in this form, though not exempt from duties, it could easily be concealed in a mixed cargo. Forfeiture of cut whalebone thus smuggled was ordered by an Act of 1697-8.[28] William III needed revenue to wage war: another law in the same year imposed a 3d. per pound weight duty on all whale fins imported by the Greenland Company, doubling that rate for ships not belonging to that Company. As these duties did not deter smugglers, penalties of £30 on anybody found in possession of, and £50 on the master of a ship concerned with, such irregularly imported cut whalebone were added.[29]

By the beginning of the eighteenth century there was, however, no longer any Greenland Company with a monopoly to be protected: the trade was thrown open to all British subjects as though they were members of that Company; foreigners employed on British whaling ships were granted protection from impressment.[30] This did not suffice to revive whaling; in 1723, all whale fins, oil and blubber were relieved of import duty, provided the whales had been caught in the Greenland seas by British ships. Only one-third of their crews needed to be British, showing how far whaling skill at this time had to be recruited abroad. The exemption was extended to the Davis Straits two years later, and these provisions were indefinitely continued in 1732.[31] Yet the trade languished. The preamble of an *Act for the further Encouragement of the Whale Fishery carried on by his Majesty's British Subjects,* passed in 1733, sadly recited that 'Acts previously passed to encourage whale fishing have been by many years experience found insufficient to regain this beneficial trade, which is at present in great danger of being entirely lost'. It therefore provided for a bounty of 20s. per ton to be paid to every British ship of 200 or more tons on completion of a voyage to Greenland or Davis Straits waters. That bounty was to continue for 73 years.[32] This exertion on the government's part proved unavailing. In 1740 the bounty was increased to 30s., in 1750 to 40s.; at last the trade responded by a tenfold expansion within the decade.[33] Figures for

Table 2. Greenland Whaling Trade of English (not Scottish) Ships

	Bounty		Ships p.a.	
Years	s per ton	£ paid	No.	tonnage
1734-1739	20	1,085	4.5	1,329
1740-1749	30	1,260	3.7	1,203
1750-1759	40	27,175	43.3	13,812
1760-1769	40	20,327	35.3	10,919
1770-1776	40	36,046	65.2	19,652
1777-1781	30	25,096	58.3	16,775
1782-1786	40	57,490	94.2	28,756
1787-1791	30	n.a.	167.0	48,283
1792-1794	25	n.a.	78.3	22,255
1795-1806	20	n.a.	71.8	20,901

From Jenkins, *History of the Whale Fisheries*, p. 306.

the Greenland part of the trade only (and excluding Scottish participation) are available from 1734 onwards and have been embodied in Table 2. From 1750 there are comprehensive statistics for Greenland and Davis Straits whaling up to 1788, separating English and Scottish activities, which form the subject of Table 3. The tables suggest that number and tonnage of ships employed in the trade varied directly with the rate of bounty offered: as soon as it reached 40s. a ton, whaling was undertaken on a substantial scale, accounting for the upswings from 1750 to 1756 and from 1762 to 1775 (though in the latter Scotland merely remained on an even keel), the downswing in-between being caused by the Seven Years' War, whereas the experiment of reducing the bounty to 30s. in 1777, as well as the American War of Independence, promptly curtailed operations. The government disbursed what were by eighteenth-century standards substantial sums by way of bounties, but had reason to be pleased with the success of its policy. A progressive reduction in bounty to 20s. in 1782 and to nothing in 1785 had been planned. Instead, it had to be restored to the 40s. level in 1782 to fuel a new upswing. When it was progressively reduced from 1787 onwards, activities halved, but the trade was now too firmly established to fade away, as it had done on earlier occasions.[34]

The success of the trade cannot, however, be measured purely by the number or tonnage of ships setting out on whaling expeditions (or even

Table 3. British Greenland and Davis Straits Whale Fisheries, 1750-1788

	England					Scotland				
	Ships		Bounties			Ships		Bounties		
Year	No.	Tonnage	£	s	d	No.	Tonnage	£	s	d
1750	19	6,264	10,507	3	3	1	333	666	0	0
1751	23	7,360	16,530	19	10	6	1,933	3,866	2	11
1752	30	9,871	17,231	9	5	10	3,137	6,274	2	11
1753	35	11,814	27,693	0	11	14	4,294	8,567	13	4
1754	52	17,235	31,328	6	9	15	4,680	9,361	5	0
1755	66	21,293	45,634	18	8	16	4,964	9,929	5	0
1756	67	21,328	42,103	1	0	16	4,964	9,315	5	0
1757	55	17,221	34,450	0	0	15	4,530	8,567	13	4
1758	52	15,399	27,006	6	1	15	4,499	8,271	13	4
1759	34	10,337	19,273	18	1	15	4,479	8,959	13	4
1760	40	12,082	20,540	5	6	14	4,238	8,477	13	4
1761	31	9,789	19,247	15	8	14	4,238	8,477	13	4
1762	28	8,877	13,358	6	9	14	4,238	8,045	13	4
1763	30	9,416	18,465	15	9	10	3,109	5,649	0	0
1764	32	10,261	19,463	16	1	10	3,140	6,281	0	0
1765	33	10,099	18,748	17	9	8	2,559	5,119	0	0
1766	35	10,015	19,947	2	5	9	2,797	5,595	0	0
1767	39	12,284	24,537	9	2	9	2,797	5,595	0	0
1768	41	12,802	24,026	18	1	9	2,797	5,595	0	0
1769	44	13,471	24,935	12	11	9	2,797	5,595	0	0
1770	50	14,775	29,240	18	11	9	2,797	5,595	0	0
1771	50	14,700	27,891	7	6	9	2,797	5,595	0	0
1772	50	15,378	29,089	12	11	9	2,797	5,595	0	0
1773	55	16,712	31,231	13	9	10	3,016	6,033	0	0
1774	65	19,770	37,863	2	6	9	2,773	5,547	0	0
1775	96	29,131	54,978	13	10	9	2,773	4,503	0	0
1776	91	27,047	52,028	3	1	7	2,251	4,503	0	0
1777	77	21,917	30,942	5	3	7	2,251	2,880	15	0
1778	71	20,291	29,280	8	4	5	1,587	1,923	15	0
1779	59	16,907	25,294	16	1	3	957	1,435	15	0
1780	52	14,900	21,584	12	4	4	1,282	1,923	15	0
1781	34	9,859	14,379	12	4	5	1,459	2,189	5	0
1782	38	11,122	21,156	2	2	6	1,764	2,190	0	0
1783	47	14,268	27,017	12	6	4	1,095	2,190	0	0
1784	89	27,224	53,162	2	1	7	2,047	4,094	10	0

Table 3. continued

| | England | | | | | Scotland | | | | |
| | Ships | | Bounties | | | Ships | | Bounties | | |
Year	No.	Tonnage	£	s	d	No.	Tonnage	£	s	d
1785	136	41,741	84,122	6	2	13	3,865	7,729	16	0
1786	162	49,426	101,996	9	6	23	6,997	13,993	19	4
1787	219	64,280	95,038	17	1	31	9,057	13,454	19	6
1788	222	63,399	93,768	0	9	31	8,910	13,230	3	6
TOTAL	2,449	740,065	1,335,098	1	2	430	130,998	242,837	19	2

From Macpherson, *Annals of Commerce*, quoted by Scoresby, *The Whale Fishery*, p. 119. (The figures should be treated with suspicion; some are very repetitive, others very round, and jumps from one year to another can be very large. But the general trend is likely to be correct.)

returning from whaling expeditions, which by no means amounted to the same); it depended at least as much on what cargo each whaler brought home. Hand harpooning was a chancy and haphazard method of killing and catching whales (here again, killing was not equivalent to catching; whales often proved irrecoverable). A mechanically propelled harpoon could hit whales at a much greater distance, thus reducing the danger which arose from the whaling boat having to come close; if the harpoon

Table 4. British Ships Departing for the Whale Fishery in 1788

Numbers from Ports of Departure						Average Tonnage	
London	91	Leith	6	Exeter	2	Under 300	129
Hull	36	Ipswich	5	Whitehaven	2	300-350	97
Liverpool	21	Dunbar	5	Stockton	2	350-400	16
Whitby	20	Aberdeen	4	Greenock	2	400-500	11
Newcastle	20	Bo'ness	4	Scarborough	1	565	1
Yarmouth	8	Glasgow	4	Grangemouth	1	987	1
Sunderland	8	Montrose	3	Queensferry	1		—
Lynn	6	Dundee	3				255

From Scoresby, *The Whale Fishery*, p. 86.

had greater penetrating power, it was more likely to remain attached to the struggling whale and secure it for the whalers. Around 1730, a swivel gun had been designed to propel harpoons, but it proved difficult and dangerous to employ; it fell into disuse because harpooners refused to operate it. A somewhat shadowy body, the Anti-Gallican Society, established in London around 1750, took an interest in whaling, because it disliked French technical superiority and used every opportunity to boost British achievements likely to substitute home products for imports from France. During the decade for which its existence is documented, it presented in 1753 a medal to a Captain John Mead for having caught the greatest number of whales in the season last past.[35]

This presentation foreshadowed the activities of the Society of Arts, which on three occasions, in 1775, 1777 and 1782, engaged in discussions to what extent, and in what form, premiums might further the increase in the catch of British whalers. It decided to assist progress on two lines: a better harpoon and an improved propelling mechanism. The premiums offered, showing period of offer, claims made and accepted are most easily presented in tabular form (Table 5).[36] Premiums proved unproductive of much ingenuity; for three of them—taking the greatest number of whales (no less than three) by the gun harpoon and two crossbow methods of firing harpoons—no claims were made at all, and in more than half of the 31 years during which premiums were offered, no claims reached the Society. This relates merely to the quantitative aspect of invention, however; the qualitative side is more important. The burden of testing and adjudicating on submissions fell to the Committee of Mechanics which worked at least as hard as had its chemistry counterpart on the edulcoration of train oil. The Committee attended field trials before the more satisfactory models could be handed over to one or more whaling captains for testing in actual operations. Table 6 shows the field trials undertaken by the Committee in various locations—12 or perhaps 11, as a trial on 3rd February 1776 at Greenland Dock was planned, but no minutes exist to indicate whether it took place.[37]

A harpoon is an arrow-shaped dart, two or three feet long, made of iron and attached to a wooden handle used for throwing or striking. In the course of the eighteenth century, it had been modified by the addition of barbs in the reverse direction, preventing the whale from shaking out the harpoon which had struck it. Harpoons became blunted by use and had to be resharpened before re-use, and their shanks were liable to break.[38] The first inventor of a new model was no newcomer to the Society's awards. Abraham Staghold, a blacksmith, had earned a bounty from the Society

Table 5. Premiums Offered, Claims Made and Accepted, in Respect of Increasing the Catch of Whalers

Premium Periods	I 1773-1779		II 1775-1797 1799-1805		III 1775-1781		IV 1782-1791		V 1782-1789 1791-1793		VI 1786-1789		VII 1786-1787	
	m	a	m	a	m	a	m	a	m	a	m	a	m	a
Claims m[ade] and a[ccepted] 1775	1	1	1	1	—	—	—	—	—	—	—	—	—	—
1776	—	—	1	1	—	—	—	—	—	—	—	—	—	—
1777	1	1	4	4	—	—	—	—	—	—	—	—	—	—
1778	1	1	3	3	—	—	—	—	—	—	—	—	—	—
1779	1	1	1	1	—	—	—	—	—	—	—	—	—	—
1780	—	—	—	—	—	—	—	—	—	—	—	—	—	—
1781	—	—	—	—	—	—	—	—	—	—	—	—	—	—
1782	—	—	—	—	—	—	—	—	—	—	—	—	—	—
1783	—	—	1	1	—	—	—	—	—	—	—	—	—	—
1784	—	—	2	2	—	—	—	0	—	—	—	—	—	—
1785	—	—	—	—	—	—	1	—	—	—	—	—	—	—
1786	—	—	—	—	—	—	—	—	—	—	—	—	—	—
1787	—	—	10	0	—	—	—	—	—	—	—	—	—	—
1788	—	—	2	2	—	—	—	—	—	—	—	—	—	—
1789	—	—	8	6	—	—	—	—	1	1	—	—	—	—
1790	—	—	12	9	—	—	—	—	—	—	—	—	—	—
1791	—	—	12	12	—	—	—	—	—	—	—	—	—	—
1792	—	—	—	—	—	—	—	—	1	1	—	—	—	—
1793	—	—	—	—	—	—	—	—	—	—	—	—	—	—
→1800	—	—	1	1	—	—	—	—	—	—	—	—	—	—

I most satisfactory account of the use of gun harpoons in taking whales
II taking whales by the gun harpoon
III taking the greatest number of whales (no less than three) by the gun harpoon
IV construction of gun harpoons
V construction of harpoon guns
VI taking whales by crossbow
VII construction of crossbows

Table 6. Field Trials of Whaling Equipment by the Committee
of Mechanics

Mr. Barnard's Yard	Greenland Dock	Kennington Common	Adelphi Wharf
16 Jan. 1772	25 Feb. 1772	16 Nov. 1775	26 May 1786
	?3 Feb. 1776	8 May 1777	
	1 Feb. 1777	31 May 1777	
	17 May 1777		
	5 Mar. 1778		
	3 May 1792		
	9 May 1793		

in 1770 for a jack for house and ship building purposes.[39] A very full description of the harpoon which he submitted to the Society in 1771-2 has come down to us; it illustrates and records in detail the improvements embodied in it, especially the ring to which the line is attached and the way in which the line is coiled to prevent tangling.[40] First trials were not encouraging, showing the usual weaknesses: the harpoon first bent, later was lost because the ring holding the line broke. The harpoon was not deflected, however, and struck with great force, hence it was worth persevering with. In the presence of two whaling captains, six more firings took place, in which the harpoon again kept direction, but travelled either too far or not far enough. The captains were impressed: it improved the chances of securing a whale from one in twenty at a distance of four fathom to better than one in five at a distance of 15 fathom. They carried six swivel guns and 24 of Staghold's harpoons on their next whaling expedition and rendered very substantial reports, testifying to the increase of their success rate; they could fire from a much greater distance than before, though still suffering from breakages of harpoons and lines. The Society's meeting held an inquisitorial discussion on the degree of merit inherent in Staghold's harpoon, in the course of which the bounty awarded was reduced from £50 to £30.[41]

Only at this stage did the Society offer the first premium, not for an invention, but for the best account of the satisfactory use of the gun harpoon. Several practising whale captains considered it even more useful in the ice-free waters of Davis Straits than in the Greenland ice, because the whale stayed on the surface for a shorter period and became aware of approaching boats much earlier; also, harpoons would not be broken through impact on the ice. Captains experimenting with the gun harpoon in Davis Straits believed a man could be sure of his whale in smooth water at a distance of 12 fathom.[42]

Staghold had had the field to himself until the Society's publicity attracted other inventors. The first, unnamed, knew nothing about whaling, had never as much as seen a gun harpoon, let alone tried those he had invented; the Committee made short shrift of him. The next two constructors, Brignell and Gibson, had designed new guns as well as new harpoons. The latter still broke, so specimens of three types—Staghold's, Brignell's and Gibson's—were made of the best and toughest iron obtainable. A fourth inventor, Simcock, submitted a harpoon of his own construction to be tested at the same time. The trials took place at Greenland Dock, but the minutes do not indicate that the Committee was impressed. Nor did a correspondent identified only by the initials H.I.—he may have been a Mr. Brooksbank whose harpoon was preserved in the repository—satisfy the Committee that his method of striking whales constituted an improvement.[43]

For a time, new designs concentrated on the rings which fastened the line to the harpoons. Made of metal, they often broke during firing. It occurred to Staghold to construct them of multiple strands of copper or iron wire. In five test firings, only one ring broke completely; iron wire rings proved so successful that Staghold was recommended for a bounty. Another 24 trials showed wire rings to be pulled out of shape by the impact of the harpoon on the target; unless restored to roundness, they were liable to break at the next firing. The Committee drafted an advertisement for a premium for wire rings on the basis of this experience; there is no evidence whether it was offered.[44]

In 1782 the Duke of Northumberland submitted a hand harpoon constructed by Nathaniel Bayles from Newcastle which, instead of a point, ended in a triangle, with all its three edges designed to enter the whale. This, combined with unusually strong barbs, led the inventor to claim that his harpoon would secure the whale in all circumstances. Several whaling captains, consulted by the Committee, gave their opinion that such a harpoon would be very useful against a whale rising in a hole in the ice, but was too heavy for normal use; it weighed 7¼ lb. as against the 4½ to 5 lb. of an ordinary harpoon, thus would reduce the number of harpoons a vessel could carry on a voyage. The captains were prepared to incur costs of £1. 1s. per harpoon for purposes of limited trials; Bayles would not supply at less than £5. 5s. In the circumstances, his invention went no further, though he presented his model to the Society.[45] Jarman's gun harpoon reached the Society at much the same time as Bayles' hand harpoon. He was asked to report on any practical trial his harpoon had undergone and in due course produced certificates from two whalers of hitting and taking two whales at a distance of 10 fathom, using Jarman's harpoon, but one harpoon had been much bent, even partly broken by the impact. In the circumstances, the Committee did not pursue this construction further.

The next set of ideas concerned barbs. Three barbs, fastened to the harpoon by spring-loaded sliding rings which projected them outward on firing and drew them back on striking the whale, were rejected by the Committee: springs were notoriously defective in cold climates; it would be difficult to fix the barbs within the rings, and sea water would probably put the joints out of order.[46] The next four inventors fared little better. Walcott submitted a harpoon with cross-fangs movable on hinges at right angles to the barbs, designed to expand and hold the whale more securely while it attempted to shake off the harpoon; the model was carefully preserved and the inventor thanked for presenting it. Greenstreet mounted two barbs on the stem and two parallel, but movable, barbs a little behind them, designed to turn at right angle to the fixed barbs; the stem also had a stubb rising up a spiral groove. At a trial, the model failed to work. Fawell constructed a hand harpoon 7 ft. long, 20 lb. in weight, made entirely of iron, with a lance attached to it lengthwise, a box 5 ft. from the end containing a pulley with a rope wound around it, fastened to the bottom of the lance; two more lances could be added and pulled by the same rope. The lances were designed to embed further in the wounded whale as it struggled to free itself. This monstrous contraption was passed to several whaling captains to try out; no report on it ever came back. Logan gave his harpoon a hollow stem and fixed it to a rope by a noose slipped far enough over the stem to stop half an inch behind the harpoon's centre of gravity when firing took place. Ten test shots elicited that, though lighter than the Society's harpoons, it was carried less far than the latter and had no advantages.[47]

This succession of failures might have suggested that innovation had reached its useful limits as regards harpoons, but there was light at the end of the tunnel. Lieutenant George Bell, of the Royal Artillery, an ingenious man, had in his day submitted other inventions to the Society, including a new method of extinguishing fires and a manner of breaking mooring chains under water. Both his gun and his harpoon were shortened, and he coiled his rope in a different manner. A serving naval officer not well endowed with finance, he was unwilling to produce trial equipment at his own expense. How the cost problem was overcome is not on record, but three experienced whaling captains watching eight trial shots at Greenland Dock were most enthusiastic: the harpoon was the most satisfactory yet tried by the Society, having been fired eight times with the same line attached to it without sustaining injury and keeping good direction throughout. Bell was awarded a bounty of 20 guineas for his harpoon, its shank encircled by two hollow half-cylinders from breech to head, the outer circumference fitting the calibre of the gun. This brought the Society's search for a more suitable harpoon to a triumphant conclusion.[48]

Swivel guns had not been used for firing harpoons since the 1730s. If the jack for which Staghold had received a bounty from the Society in 1770 had been 'a contrivance consisting of a roller, winch . . . or iron wheel with cogs'—one of the meanings attributed to the word by the *New English Dictionary* of 1901—he may have used it to modify the gun which he borrowed from Mr. Barnard, a member of the Committee of Mechanics, to try his harpoons. Malyn saw nothing new or remarkable in the gun, describing it as 'a wrought-iron swivel gun with a lock fixed to it'. Not until 1775 did a whitesmith come up with a new invention: Richard Gibson, of Whitby, presented to the Society a harpoon and a gun, described as 'a masterly piece of work, the addition and manner of fixing the lock ingenious'; he was recommended for a bounty of 30 guineas. When one of the whaling captains suggested to the Committee of Mechanics guns lighter than those hitherto used, the Committee referred him to Gibson in the belief that he would find the latter's wrought-iron gun satisfactory. A proper ram rod was made for Gibson's gun, and the model in the Society's possession was subsequently repaired.[49]

A gun constructed by somebody called Bignell was tested at the same time as Gibson's, but as it receives no further mention, it cannot have been thought to be of any consequence. A Mr. Simcock early in 1777 commended a machine he had designed for heaving the lead at sea; it was a kind of mortar, adjusted by a square, a spirit level and two screw sights, but in spite of all this, the adjustment remained uncertain. When tried, it required more powder than existing guns to project the harpoon and imparted excessive violence to it. Simcock was given a consolation prize of ten guineas, but the Committee found his contraption useless. The premium offered by the Society indicated the fault of existing guns: they were too hard to handle, hence harpooners did not like them. A more manageable gun was required.[50]

It took the best part of a decade for that challenge to find a response. The Society had such doubts about the potential improvement of harpoon guns that it suggested launching harpoons by crossbow—a stillborn endeavour this turned out to be. Eventually a gunsmith called Moore from East Smithfield rose to the opportunity with a gun tested in whaling by several people in the trade, who certified that it was an improvement on anything known before. Moore covered lock and trigger of his gun against damage by pieces of iron sliding in grooves; these covers were automatically withdrawn at the moment of firing and subsequently replaced. He also prevented the cock from being put out of action and pulled the trigger by means of a ring at the breech. He was awarded a silver medal, his construction being recommended for publication. When the Montrose New Whale Fishing Company, acting through Sir John Sinclair, applied to the Society for two harpoon guns to be used by its ships in the Davis Straits, it was referred to Moore for the best equipment which could be obtained.[51]

George Bell sent alongside his improved harpoons a shortened gun which had sights—he called them disparts—fixed on it to enable more accurate aiming. The gun had two locks, reducing the risk of missing fire. The whole outfit, including harpoons and a gun made of brass, could be produced for £7. The bounty awarded to Bell covered gun as well as harpoons; he achieved the greatest improvement of whaling equipment sponsored by the Society.[52]

To a reviewer of the efforts made in order to put the British whaling industry on its feet, it is clear that the Society of Arts could not influence the number of ships engaged in whaling; this was a function of government policy determined by duties on the one hand, bounties on the other. When it came to rendering each trip of a ship more productive, however, the Society's endeavours were successful in two respects: the Society made train oil more acceptable in a range of uses and enabled each ship to hit a larger number of whales, with enhanced chances of recovering one.

11

SAMUEL JOHNSON

AND HISTORY PAINTING

John Sunderland

There are a number of well-known stories and anecdotes which connect Samuel Johnson with the life of artists and the visual arts, but none suggest that he considered himself a great authority on the subject.[1] In the last year of his life, 1784, he claimed that he was able to run up the entire staircase at Somerset House to the Great Room at the top where the Royal Academy exhibition was held.[2] It is quite a climb even though the steps are shallow. But it seems he ran up the stairs not in excited anticipation at the prospect of viewing the pictures, but to prove his state of health.

We know that he helped the Society of Artists in the very early 1760s to produce letters and statements of their aims.[3] On 19th January 1760 this newly formed Society 'Resolved. That Mr Johnson may have the form of a letter drawn up by this Society to correct in order to be sent to the Society for the Encouragement of Arts, &c. to sollicite the Use of their Room for the Exhibition.' The artists had turned to him because of his celebrated command of the English language and his ability to express their thoughts in an elegant and dignified way. But he wrote to Baretti in 1761 in a vein which suggests he did not have much admiration for the paintings in the exhibition of that year. 'The Exhibition', he wrote, 'has filled the heads of the artists and lovers of art. Surely life, if it be not long, is tedious, since

Originally appeared in *Jnl. RSA*, 134 (Nov., 1986), 834-41.

we are forced to call in the aid of so many trifles to rid us of our time—of that time which can never return.[4]

Joshua Reynolds, apparently, did not always deal with Johnson in a kindly way, despite the mutual respect which existed between them. Boswell records that in 1775 he went with Reynolds and Johnson to the house of Richard Owen Cambridge in Twickenham. Whilst Johnson went to look at the books on the shelves, Reynolds said, 'He runs to the books as I do to the pictures: but I have the advantage. I can see much more of the pictures than he can see of the books.'[5]

But however that may be, I am concerned in this article with a very brief moment in time when Samuel Johnson, the Society of Arts and English history painting in general came together in quite a significant juxtaposition of circumstance and intent. I am not a Johnson scholar and am very much indebted to Robert Folkenflik, who pointed out to me Johnson's essay in the *Idler*, no. 45, published on 24th February 1759, in which Johnson's involvement in the question of history painting becomes clear.

In 1758 the Society for the Encouragement of Arts, Manufactures and Commerce decided to give a premium or prize for History Painting. At a meeting on 29th November in this year the Society, according to the minutes, 'Order'd that it be referred to the same Committee [the Committee of Premiums] to consider of giving a Premium for the Improvement of History Painting in this Country.' This committee met on 19th January 1759 and again on 2nd February under the heading of the 'Polite and Liberal Arts' to discuss this. These two meetings drew up the proposals that were put before the Society as a whole on 28th February. At this meeting of the Society a quite significant change was made to one of the proposals put forward by the two preceding committee meetings. Johnson's interest in history painting and the circumstances surrounding this change in the committee's proposals are what I am basically concerned with. There is no evidence or reason to suppose that Johnson himself had anything to do with the change. It is clear, however, from Johnson's essay in the *Idler*, no. 45, in the issue of Payne's *Universal Chronicle* for 17th-24th February 1759, and this date of publication, that Johnson was aware of the proposals of the committee and had his own ideas about the question under discussion.

In the committee meeting of 2nd February it was decided that six historical subjects should be proposed for the premium and that the Society as a whole should choose one to be the subject for the competition. The six subjects chosen at this meeting were, according to the Minutes for 2nd February,

Boadicea telling her Distresses to Cassibelan and Paulinus in the presence of her two Daughters.

Queen Eleanora sucking the Poison out of King Edward's wound after he was shot with a Poisoned Arrow.

Regulus taking leave of his Friends when he departed for Carthage.

The Death of Socrates.

The Death of Epaminondas.

The Birth of Commerce as described by Mr Glover in his Poem called London.[6]

The amendment came at the Society Meeting of 28th February when, under Resolution 9, 'The Society disagreed to the Second Resolution [the proposal of six subjects]; and Resolved that the Candidates shall chuse their Subjects out of the English History only.'[7] The first resolution was agreed, that 100 guineas Premium should be given 'for the best Original Piece of History painting containing not less than three human Figures as big as Life, and that 50 Guineas be given for the Second best Piece of the like Kind'. The regulation leaving the choice of subject matter to the artist 'out of the English History' came into force for the first premium and remained substantially unchanged in succeeding years. Small changes in the rubric occurred. In 1761 'British' history was substituted for 'English'[8] and in 1763 this gave way in turn to 'British or Irish'.[9]

In the absence of any evidence, we can only speculate as to why the Society amended the proposals of the Committee with regard to the choice of subjects. The six subjects initially suggested included three from English or British national history—Boadicea, Queen Eleanora and the Birth of Commerce—and three from classical history—Regulus, Socrates and Epaminondas. It is likely that the Society opted to encourage depictions of national history, as its overall concern was to stimulate national endeavour. In any case, this choice of national history relates to the whole question of what was then considered to come under the heading of 'History' painting within the structured academic hierarchy of the genres of painting. This is a complicated issue which I shall touch on briefly later. It is interesting that although the Society was concerned with national endeavour the competition was open to foreign artists painting in England as well as British painters. The fourth resolution of the Society Meeting of 28th February stated that the whole of each picture had to be painted in England, that the age of the candidates was to be unlimited and that the subject of any nation could be a candidate, provided the picture was painted in England.[10] Indeed, in the first three years of the competition, prizes were won by the Italian artist, Andrea Casali.[11]

Although Samuel Johnson had no official rôle in the Society's deliberations in these matters, he was obviously aware of what was going on.
In the *Idler*, no. 45, he discusses portraiture and history painting, preferring the former but allowing the latter a due place in the visual arts. His
essay was published between the Committee meetings of 19th January and
2nd February and the Society meeting of 28th February. He refers to 'the
reward now offered for an historical picture', which shows that he must
have heard of the discussion from someone on the Committee. Perhaps the
most likely contact was Joshua Reynolds, who attended the meeting on
2nd February. Johnson referred to the reward or prize before it was officially advertised or officially sanctioned by the Society as a whole. Either
he believed an advertisement was about to appear, possibly in one of the
newspapers, or he could have simply been doing a 'puff' for the Society
and the Premium. Johnson was a member of the Society of Arts, having
been elected in December 1756, and although he allowed his subscription
dues to lapse for a time he remained a member of the Society for some
years, making a number of contributions to the proceedings.[12]

His *Idler* essay starts with a defence of portraiture. 'Genius', he writes,
'is chiefly exerted in historical pictures, and the art of the painter of portraits is often lost in the obscurity of his subject. But it is in painting as
in life; what is greatest is not always best. I should grieve to see Reynolds
transfer to heroes and to goddesses, to empty splendour and to airy fiction, that art which is now employed in diffusing friendship, in reviving
tenderness, in quickening the affections of the absent, and continuing the
presence of the dead.'[13] But after this splendid defence of portraiture, and
perhaps with some of Reynolds's own ideas running in his mind, he continues, 'Yet in a nation great and opulent there is room, and ought to
be patronage, for an art like that of painting through all its diversities;
and it is to be wished, that the reward now offered for an historical picture, may excite an honest emulation, and give beginning to an English
School.' These sentences show that Johnson was aware of the current debates about history painting and other genrès of art. The *Idler* essay appeared ten years before Reynolds's *Discourses* started, but the academic
view of the primacy of history painting in the hierarchy of genres was
already long established and accepted. The basic ideas of Renaissance and
French seventeenth-century art theory were reinforced and confirmed in
the early years of the eighteenth century in England by the writings of
Shaftesbury and Jonathan Richardson.[14] In fact, Johnson's defence of portraiture goes against the academic thinking of the time but illustrates his
independence of mind, common sense and humanity in a way that is typical
of his thinking.

Johnson then goes on to discuss the types and subjects of historical painting that could be attempted for the premium. Interestingly, most of the subjects he discusses are different from those proposed by the Committee of the Society of Arts, but they have the same kind of mix between classical subjects and national history. He considers the Death of Hercules, Achilles and the Trojan Prince, the Discovery of Ulysses by his Nurse, the Death of Epaminondas and finally, and most interesting of all, the Dissolution of Parliament by Oliver Cromwell. He chooses this last subject as the most satisfactory and dramatic one for the painter, which is a most unusual and original choice at a time when painters hardly illustrated the Cromwellian period at all.[15]

Johnson's discussion of the suitability of the subjects he mentions for depiction in painting shows that he was aware of the current academic debates of the time and the traditions of art theory: He writes of the difficulty of equating what may be a dramatic moment in a poem or a work of literature with what a visual artist can express in a painting which depicts only one moment in time. For example, Johnson argues that it is difficult to depict the Death of Hercules because of the problem of the successive actions involved in the story. The subject of Achilles and the Trojan Prince is problematic, he claims, because the dialogue is important and language cannot be painted. The Discovery of Ulysses by his Nurse is promising, but as it would only include two figures, the composition, according to Johnson, 'will want variety'. Johnson is in these arguments touching on the large subject of *ut pictura poesis,* as in painting, so in poetry, which had taxed academic theorists for centuries, and he puts his own views on the subject without actually mentioning the Latin quotation from Horace's *Ars Poetica,* but in a brief and informed way.[16]

Johnson's eventual choice of Cromwell Dissolving the Long Parliament, although highly original in 1759, was a prophetic one. Benjamin West exhibited the subject at the Royal Academy in 1783, choosing exactly the moment which Johnson describes in his essay.[17] 'The point of time may be chosen', Johnson writes, 'when Cromwell, looking round the pandaemonium with contempt, ordered the bauble to be taken away; and Harrison laid hands on the Speaker to drag him from the chair.' Johnson was attracted to this event, probably suggested to him by Edmund Ludlow's *Memoirs,* by its combination of high drama and historical significance, but it was a subject untried by artists and from a then relatively unfashionable historical period. It was perhaps partly the puritanical religious zeal of Cromwell which made him on the whole an unsympathetic character to the tolerant and latitudinarian climate of opinion in the middle years of the eighteenth century. David Hume, the philosopher and historian, gives

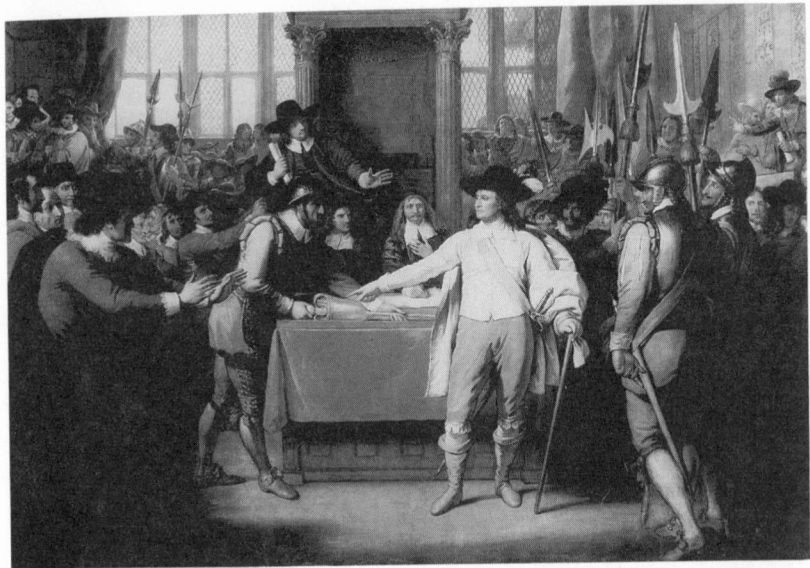

Benjamin West, *Cromwell Dissolving the Long Parliament*, 1782; oil on canvas, 152.4 x 213.4 cm. Collection of The Montclair Art Museum, Montclair, New Jersey.

some idea of the view of Johnson's contemporaries about Cromwell when he describes him as something of a paradox. Hume writes that Cromwell was 'a mixture of so much absurdity with so much penetration . . . tempering such violent ambition and such enraged fanaticism with so much regard to justice and humanity'.[18]

Cromwellian subjects illustrated in painting gradually increase in English and French art in the early part of the nineteenth century, probably reaching a peak in England following the historical writings of Thomas Carlyle and continuing in such popular 'costume pieces' as William Frederick Yeames's '*And when did you last see your father?*' painted in 1878.[19] The story of the illustration of Cromwellian subjects in the Romantic period can only be briefly mentioned here,[20] but the interesting point is that Johnson should have chosen the subject as suitable for painting as early as 1759, at least 50 years before any popular vogue for Cromwell and the Civil War period started.

Although Benjamin West exhibited *Cromwell Dissolving the Long Parliament* at the Royal Academy more than 20 years after Johnson's *Idler* essay, there may be more than a coincidental connection. First, West chooses the exact moment to depict which Johnson selected, suggesting

Benjamin West, *The Death of Epaminondas*; oil on canvas, 222.2 x 179.4 cm. Courtesy of the Royal Collection, Kensington Palace; copyright reserved to Her Majesty Queen Elizabeth II.

that the painter may have read Johnson's essay, or at least have heard about it. We know that West met Dr. Johnson. He was introduced to him by Dr. William Markham, the headmaster of Westminster School.[21] West also painted a rare subject, the *Death of Epaminondas*, for George III in 1773. Johnson discussed this subject in his essay, putting it second only to the Cromwell as suitable for depiction. Epaminondas was also on the list of subjects drawn up by the Committee of the Society of Arts on 2nd February 1759. Indeed, it is the only subject which both the Committee and Johnson mentioned and included in their separate list of choices. West's *Death of Epaminondas*[22] was, in itself, a pair or pendant to his painting of the *Death of the Chevalier Bayard*,[23] also painted for the King, in 1772. These two paintings, in their turn, were conceived of as connected with West's famous painting of the *Death of General Wolfe*.[24] West painted the original *Death of Wolfe* for Earl Grosvenor, and it was exhibited at the Royal Academy in 1771, where George III admired it and commissioned West to paint a replica, which now hangs at Kensington Palace. The three paintings, of Wolfe, Epaminondas and Bayard, were conceived by West as history paintings on the theme of the death of a famous general or commander in battle: first chronologically a classical hero, the Theban Epaminondas, next a late medieval hero, the Frenchman Bayard, who died in 1551, and lastly a modern hero, Wolfe, who died as recently, as far as West's contemporaries were concerned, as 1759.

The conventional academic argument about History painting at the time, as expressed by Reynolds in particular, was that this highest branch of painting should depict the grandeur of man's endeavours and sufferings, in order to educate and excite the spectator towards serious thoughts and noble virtue. But the academic view was that the events chosen should be taken from a time far in the past, from Biblical events, or from classical mythology and history. Such events would present heroic human endeavour in its most pure and generalized form, unsullied by any fashions of the day and not connected with contemporary, or near contemporary, events, which, however heroic they may have been, did not have behind them the dignifying processes of distance in time, myth, legend and universal human appeal. West's *Death of Wolfe* was a clear and documented case of the artist claiming that modern history could be just as heroic as ancient history, just as worthy of inclusion in a so-called 'History' painting. When critics complained that West's *Death of Wolfe* was too modern in subject, and that the figures were not clothed in classical timeless draperies to remove them from the particular peculiarities of a modern period of time, West replied 'the event intended to be commemorated took place on the 13th of September, 1759, in a region of the world [North America] unknown to the Greeks and Romans, and at a period of time when no such nations, nor heroes in their costumes existed'.[25] This debate about the suitability, or lack of suitability, of recent historical events depicted in modern dress was an important one at the time of West's painting, at the beginning of the 1770s. I have only sketched out here the briefest idea of the argument.

But it is clearly important in relation to the choice of subject matter made by the Committee of the Society of Arts and by Johnson.

It is especially interesting that Johnson should choose a relatively modern subject, Oliver Cromwell, as early as 1759, thus up to a point foreshadowing the debate surrounding West's *Death of Wolfe* by a decade. But I think some qualification should be made here. There was a distinction, at least in academic thinking, in the second half of the eighteenth century, between conventional History painting, that is, subjects taken from the Bible, Ancient History and Classical Mythology, and the much more recent practice of depicting national history, mainly seen as events from Saxon and medieval times stretching up to the seventeenth century. This national history, which the Society of Arts eventually decided as the subject for a major Premium, was seen as in some ways distinct from the more generalized and ideal History painting which Reynolds advocated. It was seen, I think, at least by the academics, as a lower genre, emulating the grander History painting, deriving inspiration from it and influenced by it in style and conception, but, judged in absolute terms, a lower form of art. But this distinction was to a certain extent turned on its head by the Society of Arts. The Society chose the subject of national history for its major Premium in painting, open to all artists working in England. But it also offered Premiums in certain years, of a lower value and for more restricted and junior entry, for Greek or Roman classical history.[26] The fact that Greek or Roman subjects were chosen for less important premiums does not necessarily mean that the Society thought this subject matter was less important than the national history. But it does seem significant, in the context of the academic thinking of the time, that the Society should have deliberately chosen to ask for a subject 'out of the English History only' for its main Premium in the fine or 'polite' arts.

Painting of modern history certainly became more popular with the public, and an increasingly large public was coming to art through exhibitions and through the spread of reproductive engravings after paintings during the course of the 1760s and onwards. An instructive example is the comparison between John Singleton Copley's *Death of Major Peirson*, exhibited in 1783,[27] and James Barry's history paintings which decorate the Society of Arts and which were completed at almost the same time. Barry's cycle, the *Progress of Human Culture*, though it has very original and individual characteristics, largely follows the academic conventions of Grand Style History painting, whilst Copley's *Death of Major Peirson* shows a contemporary heroic event which took place in the Channel Islands in 1781, with Major Peirson dying in battle whilst French troops were successfully expelled from the town of St. Helier. Copley took great trouble to paint accurate modern costumes and uniforms and to accurately portray the architecture of the town. The success of the painting depends on its particular and topical appeal, not on generalized and idealized events, including symbols and allegories from the familiar vocabulary of traditional myths and legends. It is true that Barry in his cycle also depicts contemporary people and events, and his iconography is in fact much more individual and modern than the compositions may initially suggest, but his whole conception is still within the traditional framework of the Grand Style. Copley's *Death of Major Peirson* was exhibited on its own, as was Barry's work in the Society, but Copley's picture was immensely popular with a much wider public, and his financial rewards, through the exhibition of the painting and engravings after it, were much greater than those that Barry achieved through the public exhibition of the mural paintings in the Society.

Returning to the Premiums offered for history painting by the Society of Arts, it is likely that there was a wider public for the depiction of national history than for Grand Style academic 'History'. The publication in the course of the eighteenth century of substantial books on English history had catered for and increased interest in the national past. Rapin's *History of England* . . . was published, initially in French (1724-36), but was soon translated into English (1725-31).[28] David Hume's *History of England,* the first volume of which was published in 1754, probably soon became more widely read than Rapin. At the same time the basic political stability of England under the Hanoverian Succession, the rising economic success of England and the expanding trading Empire all helped to instil in the English an interest and pride in their national past. At the beginning of the nineteenth century the artist Henry Fuseli also pointed to the national interest in factual rather than ideological matters. He complained that the English had no taste for what he called 'Poetical' painting, by which he meant imaginative subject painting, including aspects of Grand Style History, but said that they preferred 'matter of fact', suggesting that there was a taste for factual national history.[29]

Among the early prize-winners for the History Painting Premium which the Society of Arts offered was Robert Edge Pine, who was a member of the Society's Committee which met on 2nd February 1759, or at least one assumes he was the 'Mr Pine' mentioned in the Minutes. In 1760 his *The Surrender of Calais to Edward III* won the first premium, and the second prize in the same year went to Andrea Casali for his *Assassination of Edward the Martyr*. John Hamilton Mortimer won the first premium in

The Surrender of Calais to Edward III; engraving by F. Aliamet after Robert Edge Pine. Courtesy of the Courtauld Institute of Art.

1764 with his *St. Paul Preaching to the Ancient Britons*.[30] Although these are all subjects from English medieval or pre-medieval history, none of them are the same as those listed by the Committee of the Society of Arts. If we look at this list again, we find that Boadicea was an extremely rare subject in art in the eighteenth century. In 1783 Conrad Martin Metz exhibited *Queen Boadicea Preparing to Engage the Romans* at the Royal Academy, and in 1787 the same artist exhibited, also at the Royal Academy, *Boadicea* with, in parenthesis, 'Cowper's Poems' given as the source.[31] Another subject the Committee chose for consideration, *Queen Eleanora Sucking the Poison out of King Edward's Wound after He was Shot with a Poisoned Arrow,* was depicted later by both Angelica Kauffmann and by William Blake.[32]

As to the other non-English subjects chosen by the Committee, *Regulus Taking Leave of his Friends when He Departed for Carthage* was a relatively well-known classical story but does not appear to have been painted all that often. But again it is interesting that Benjamin West painted the subject, choosing it for an important occasion in his career. His *Departure of Regulus from Rome* was exhibited at the first exhibition of the Royal Academy in 1769, and indeed George III instructed West to exhibit it at the Royal Academy.[33] It was the first painting by West to enter the Royal Collection, thus starting the long and fruitful period of patronage which West received from the King. Its neoclassical style was not only suitable to the classical subject matter. It also demonstrated that West was in the vanguard of developments in the new serious and 'noble' style of painting that was being advocated on the continent of Europe in the 1750s and 1760s. The *Death of Socrates*, also on the Committee's list, was a subject which found more favour in France, the most famous example being Jacques-Louis David's painting of 1787.[34] The fullest development of the neoclassical style, appropriate to such subjects as Regulus and Socrates, did take place in France during and after the 1789 Revolution. But Benjamin West was one of the artists who made significant contributions to the early stages of this serious and sober manner of treating such subjects. I have already discussed the *Death of Epaminondas* and the link between West and the choice of both the Committee of the Society and Samuel Johnson in his *Idler* essay.

I have no knowledge at present of any depictions of the *Birth of Commerce* as described by Mr. Glover in his *Poem called London*, although Barry's own depiction in the Society of *Commerce, or the Triumph of the Thames* may well have some kind of connection, though I have been unable to find any evidence for this. Barry does not mention Glover's poem in his published account of the series of paintings he executed for the Great Room of the Society.[35]

The deliberations of the Society of Arts on the question of historical subjects, together with Samuel Johnson's own discussion in the *Idler* essay, throw interesting light on a whole complex of issues concerning 'History' painting, and I have tried to focus on some of them, albeit briefly. Both the Society and Johnson took an independent stance, interesting for the way in which they, with their different ideas, both deviated from and accepted current academic thinking. The Society's choice of the national history as a subject for a major Premium boosted this genre, perhaps at the expense of the more traditional Grand Style History. Johnson also chose an event from national history. Significantly, both the Society and Johnson considered subjects from classical history and national history in the same argument and therefore on the same level of importance. Above all, they were clearly concerned more with the relevance and dramatic possibilities of the subject matter for a contemporary public than with the niceties of academic debate.

Part 3

OVERSEAS INTERESTS

The Society's early years were shaped by the history of Britain, particularly as it was being defined by changes in its North American empire as well as by its ties with Europe. Given the pragmatic spirit that endowed the Society from the start, it inevitably concerned itself with the nation's overseas empire. In its committees on Agriculture and on Colonies and Trade, the Society actively participated in the formation of the larger empire, if only on a modest scale. In chapter 12, Robert Leroy Hilldrup provides a detailed view of the economic links that developed between Great Britain and colonial Virginia, links the Society helped formulate as it worked to define the new discipline of agricultural economics. He shows that while the latter was defined by raw materials—tobacco, hemp, saltpetre and wines, to name a few—the campaign to promote Virginia's prosperity had other ends in mind, among them freeing Great Britain from dependence on imports from nonnative sources—hemp and rhubarb from Russia, for example. Strong economic ties between the motherland and colonies could not exist, however, in a political vacuum: in the home government's disallowal of Virginia's Two Penny Act of 1758, one sees a clear anticipation of the troubles that lay ahead, as the colonies moved to rebellion, revolution and separation.

In chapter 13, D. G. C. Allan provides an original view of the war in the context of the Society that during 'six bewildering years' saw its local and transatlantic membership divided by rival definitions of loyalty, patriotism and treason. Nowhere is this schism seen more clearly than in Benjamin Franklin's separation from the Society and, more painfully, from his son who remained loyal to the Crown. Such fissures profoundly affected the Society's membership, though fortunately they did not frustrate its essential missions.

In his review of the Society's eighteenth-century associations with Germany (chapter 14), Hans-Joachim Braun provides clear evidence of a larger European mission that also defined it. The interest German inventors and others took in the London Society and the various German societies that paralleled it on the Continent confirms W. H. G. Armytage's notion of a 'Common market of Science' in the eighteenth century that in tempering strong nationalism anticipated larger federations now taking shape. George Truett Hollis's sketch of Count Francesco Algarotti (chapter 15), the Enlightenment polymath, suggests that a common humanistic culture also existed, stimulated by the Society itself. Few figures of the time could claim greater knowledge of painting, architecture and opera than Algarotti, and he saw in the Society a membership aggressively committed to the arts, particularly in Thomas Hollis, who proposed him for membership. He dedicated his *Saggio sopra la pittura* to the Society, a work circulated in four languages that permanently links one of Europe's greatest aestheticians with an institution that consistently endowed the arts during its early history.

In chapter 16, A. G. Cross shows that the Society's influence extended to Russia, a fact demonstrated in the visit of Ivan Sudakov, a serf studying agriculture, husbandry and the art of distilling in Britain. Sudakov's diary provides a unique account of the Society's eighteenth-century history, giving details of scenes and meetings with no parallel in the period. In this section the Society's history is illuminated at the outset by news from colonial Virginia and ultimately by material in the Lenin State Library in Moscow, clear proof of the range of its eighteenth-century overseas influence and activities.

12

A CAMPAIGN TO PROMOTE THE

PROSPERITY OF COLONIAL VIRGINIA

Robert Leroy Hilldrup

Alarmed by the declining prosperity of the colony, the General Assembly of Virginia established a committee in 1759 for the purpose of encouraging economic diversification. In a limited sense, this committee was a progenitor of the Virginia Department of Conservation and Development. It also encouraged the establishment of some industries and engaged in some promotional work such as is associated to-day with the activities of a chamber of commerce.

This committee consisted of nineteen prominent political leaders. Their duties were to raise and administer a bounty fund and to correspond with 'all such persons as they shall judge may give them any useful insight or intelligence in any art or manufacture'. The Assembly itself appropriated one thousand pounds to be used for bounties and stipulated that no one bounty should exceed twenty pounds. It required the committee to keep a journal of their proceedings and to publish in the *Virginia Gazette* lists of bounties offered and an account of any useful discoveries or inventions made.[1]

Charles Carter, a Burgess from King George County who had promoted diversification substantially in the management of his own plantations and

Originally appeared in *The Virginia Magazine of History and Biography*, 67 (1959). Reprinted in *Jnl. RSA*, 108 (Nov., Dec., 1960), 940-41, 53-56; 109 (Jan., 1961), 117-22.

other business affairs, sponsored this law.[2] A leader in the Assembly, he became chairman of the committee of nineteen named in the Act and conducted most of the correspondence with the Society of Arts of London. It is with the activity of this committee with the Society that the present study is chiefly concerned.

When the Society was notified by a letter from Lieutenant Governor Francis Fauquier of the formation of the Virginia Committee, it promptly sought to correspond with it.[3] The letter of invitation was written on 1st July 1760, and Fauquier communicated its contents to Charles Carter, who read it to six members of the committee meeting in the Capitol at Williamsburg on 8th October 1760. Those present besides Carter were John Blair, Peyton Randolph, Edmund Pendleton, Benjamin Harrison, Lewis Burwell and William Digges. They accepted the invitation with evident pleasure and directed Carter to make an appropriate reply. Thus began a correspondence between Carter and Peter Wyche, Chairman of the Committee of Agriculture of the Society of Arts, which lasted several years.

Charles Carter (1707-64) was a son of Robert ('King') Carter and a brother of both Robert Carter of Nomini Hall and Landon Carter of Sabine Hall.[4] After some training in Latin and other subjects at school in England, Charles had returned to Virginia before he was 17 and plunged into planting and other business in the colony, including the mining of copper near the present boundary of Fairfax and Loudoun counties.

When his father died in 1732, Charles inherited many plantations. He moved first from Urbanna to Stanstead, above Falmouth, and then, later, to Cleve, near Dogue, in King George County, which was henceforth his residence.[5] In his will he stated that he had begun a new method of agriculture at Cleve and desired that the plan be carried out in accordance with the directions set forth in *A new system of Virginia Husbandry, or the Little farm improved wherein the business of making Tobo., farming, improving lands and making Wine, are largely treated of and earnestly recommended,* which he had written, he declared, for the benefit of his children. Moreover, the will reveals that Carter was engaged extensively in raising wheat, milling flour, and the baking of ships' biscuits.[6]

Little seems to be known of the life of Peter Wyche. He was elected a Fellow of the Royal Society in 1745, and he may have been descended from his seventeenth-century namesake, who was also a Fellow of that Society. Wyche became a member of the Society of Arts in 1755 and worked actively on its behalf until his death eight years later. He was chairman and an originator of the Committee of Agriculture, and in his obituary by 'A brother member of the Society of Arts' in the *Museum Rusticum,* it was

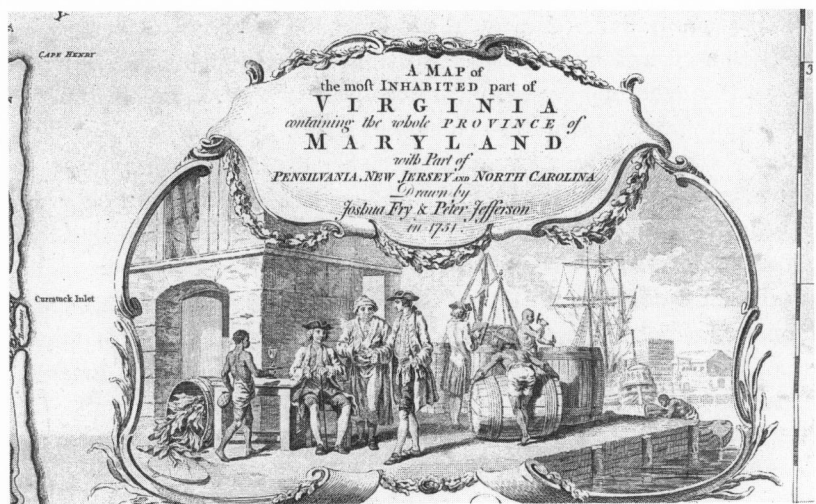

A mid-eighteenth-century wharfside scene in Virginia (from Fry and Jefferson's 'Map of the Most Inhabited Part of Virginia', 1751). Courtesy of the Trustees of the British Museum.

stated that 'to him alone is entirely owing the correspondence which the society carries on with our American Colonies.'[7]

In his first letter to Wyche, Carter set forth the necessity for Virginia to get away from its unhealthy economic dependence upon tobacco.[8] In support of his position, he declared that most of the inhabitants were engaged in tobacco raising and were exporting nearly 60,000 hogsheads of tobacco a year, each hogshead weighing upon an average of 900 lb. If this trend continued, he felt that the supply of tobacco would soon exceed its consumption and the consequence to the colony would be inevitable ruin. Besides, consumption might quickly decline because tobacco was a luxury, subject like other luxuries to the fickleness of fashion. Then, too, it was harmful to the health. 'Indeed', he warned, 'if the common Consumers were sensible of the great Proportion of poysonous Quality contained in this Narcotick Plant, they would be induced to lay it aside, to preserve their Healths & save their Money.' Moreover, the high duties on tobacco had already 'given rise to so many Frauds' that honest traders could not sell it at a profit at prevailing low prices, and hence the planters could not obtain enough money from its sale to supply themselves with necessary manufactured goods from Great Britain.

Carter then directed his attention to definite ways for diversifying the economy of Virginia which would be mutually beneficial to the colony and the empire. He proposed the production of iron, tar, pitch, turpentine, hemp, flax, masts and other wood products, saltpetre, fisheries and wines. In advocating these products he declared that the colonies could soon supply Britain with iron equivalent in quality to the best Swedish. Tar, pitch and turpentine could be had in abundance, and the production of white tar should be encouraged immediately because it was far superior to ordinary tar in the manufacture of cordage. Hemp was 'extremely natural' to the soil and climate of Virginia and could be raised in ample supply for the entire empire if the British Government would restrain the importation of Russian hemp. Flax also grew well in the colony, and with proper encouragement 'sufficient Quantities fit for sail cloth might be annually exported'. An ample supply of mast yards and all other useful timbers of the fir were already being produced in the northern colonies.

If the methods used in the East Indies, France and Prussia were adopted, Carter claimed, Virginia could also produce large quantities of saltpetre. It had 'in all the back Parts various Places where the Brute Creatures are wont to lick the Salt'. From such a saltlick Carter declared he had made good saltpetre and used it successfully in curing bacon. Moreover, he had found that all the soils on which tobacco grew abundantly were 'charged with Nitre'. Using the Virginia saltpetre, sulphur and charcoal, he had made 'a strong Pistol Powder', as strong as any he had ever imported from Britain.

As for ordinary salt, he believed great beds of it were to be found along the rivers above the fall line, much strong salt water was in the bay and ocean, and on the seaboard side of the Eastern Shore it was said that the sedge of the marshes was covered with salt in the summer, which the common people cut and beat off for the use of their families. It was a pity, he continued, that an exclusive patent for making salt in America had been granted to Andrew Read. Read still had not begun a salt work in Virginia, and his monopoly on salt-making should be revoked. Likewise, Carter urged that the British should abolish their monopoly of supplying salt to the southern colonies. By using Lisbon salt, the foundation could be laid for 'a most glorious herring Fishery', without interfering with the British fishery. Carter was not alone in his desire for the coarse salt of Lisbon; North Carolinians also found that the British salt monopoly interfered with the development of their fisheries.[9]

Fish were to be had in abundance, he declared. From December to April vast schools of herring came out of the sea into the inlets of the Carolinas and into Chesapeake Bay and its estuaries to spawn. But the salt obtainable from Great Britain was either too weak or too small to preserve them.

Many trials had proved that they could not be cured properly unless the salt was of a grain of the size of 'english Pease which as it dissolves is continually strengthening the Pickle and keeps the Fish cool'. Carter suspected that the schools of herring which touched the coast of Virginia were performing a circuit around the Atlantic and that they arrived on the coast of England in June.

Besides the herring, Virginia had many other fish, such as 'Corbits, Drums, Bonettas, Rocks, Shads of various Sorts, and old Wives'. The 'old Wives' were so fat in the month of September, Carter said, 'that by pressing them, without Prejudice to the Fish, a Gallon of Oil has been made out of a Hundred'. Quantities of sturgeons were in the rivers from March to the middle of September. From them, Great Britain might be supplied with a 'delicious Food and Caviary', if persons skilled in curing such fish could be prevailed upon to come into the colony.

In his discussion on the propagation of grapes, Carter confessed he had never heard of the 'Zant and Cephalonia' until he had seen a letter from Wyche (probably the one written to Fauquier). Nor could he say anything about the value of other grapes of the Mediterranean, since he was 'very little acquainted' with their wines. Instead, he would choose to cultivate the varieties of France, Spain, Portugal, Madeira, Faval, Teneriffe and the Canary Islands.

Virginia's interest in grapes was an old one. Lord De La Warr had brought Frenchmen to the colony to dress vines as early as 1610; and Sir Edwin Sandys had exuberantly reported to the officials in London in 1619 that the Frenchmen in Virginia thought vines would grow even better there than in France.[10]

Turning to sericulture, Carter declared that he had often found, in Virginia, moths similar to the Bombyx and had attempted to produce silk from them by hatching their eggs and feeding them on mulberry leaves, but that he had failed to raise any. During the next season he intended to try feeding them on leaves of the apple and other trees.

In this sort of experimentation Carter was hardly the pioneer. Like the attempts to produce wine, the experiment with silk production had been carried on over many years with only minor success. Captain John Smith witnessed the first attempt. On 2nd August 1619, the first General Assembly had enacted a law requiring every man to plant and maintain in growth each year at least six mulberry trees,[11] and Sir Edwin Sandys had informed the London Company in 1620 that some indigenous silk worms had been found in the native mulberry trees of Virginia.[12] Yet in Carter's century a naturalist found the people still ignorant of the art of silk-making.[13]

During the spring of 1762 Charles Carter sent to the Society of Arts a 'taste' of his winter grape and white Lisbon grape wines, a keg of sturgeon, and a root of what was called in Virginia 'Turkey Rhubarb'. Moreover, he promised to send them the seeds of vetch and timothy grass.[14]

He desired that the 'Turkey Rhubarb' be examined to ascertain its medicinal qualities. Carter did not say so, but it would seem that Virginians called the plant by this name because of its resemblance to the original 'Turkey Rhubarb', the medicinal rhubarb from China, which in the fourteenth century had reached Europe through the ports of Aleppo and Smyrna. In Carter's day Russia had a monopoly of supplying it to the Western world. Among Virginians, rhubarb was a popular stomachic.

Wyche sent Carter in 1763 'a few seed of the very best Russia or Turkey Rhubarb that ever was sent to England'. A Mr. Baker (no doubt Henry Baker) had given them to Wyche for Carter, who was enjoined to grow good plants from them and save their seed, for Baker never expected to be able to get any more. Doubtless Russia was maintaining its monopoly by prohibiting the exportation of the seed. At the same time, Wyche urged the Virginians to raise more bees, for wax was in great demand in England.[15]

The vetch seed Carter promised to send to Wyche was also called 'Luping' seed. This plant was the same, according to Carter, as the vetch described in the writings of Dr. John Mitchell. Dr. Mitchell had collected and published much botanical data on Virginia between 1721 and 1746, and he continued his scientific publications after he went to England in 1746. He was still living at the time of the Carter-Wyche correspondence, for he did not die until 1768. It is thought by some authorities that he was a native of Virginia.[16]

The timothy grass of which Carter promised seed was, he declared, the grass named after its first cultivator. Undoubtedly this is a reference to Timothy Hanson, who is believed to have brought the seed of this grass from Europe to Maryland about 1720.[17] Carter enthusiastically recommended it, for it vegetated in winter like wheat, afforded a rich hay in June and was 'very agreeable to all sorts of Cattle'.

In the same letter Carter also informed the Society that he had received its shipment of olives and had divided them among the members of his committee with the request that each should try to raise olive trees.[18] It seems that an experiment in the raising of olives was already in progress in Virginia, for during the next year Carter sent to the Society a sample from the colony which it pronounced to be 'much less than the Lucca olives' in quality.[19]

In response to a request of Wyche's, Carter described more fully in

1762 the white tar he had mentioned in an earlier letter to the Society.[20]
It was, he wrote, 'an accidental discovery'. He had decided to call it a
white tar because there were already in the colony two darker kinds—
common or black tar, made from scorched knots of pine, and green tar,
made from trees barked at a proper season ten feet above the ground with
a list of bark left on the north side. These trees were in a few months en-
riched with resinous matter, which was refined and was fairly satisfactory.
The black tar, in contrast, was entirely useless in cordage, because it was
'impregnated with fiery particles'.

Turning his attention to other medicinal plants he had not previously
mentioned, Carter then wrote about the sweet gum, American-ipecac or
Indian physic, 'Black gound Tree', and 'our Jallup'.

He thought that gum extracted from the sweet gum tree appeared to be
the balsam of Tolu.[21] Carter thus compared the extract of the sweet gum to
a fragrant reddish-brown semi-solid or solid balsam obtained from a South
American tree. The South American variety is still used as a stomachic, a
stimulating expectorant, an antiseptic and a flavouring for cough syrups.
Carter wrote that the sweet gum balsam resembled the South American
kind in being vastly beneficial in all catarrhs and fluxes. Sweet gum wood,
he pointed out incidentally, was valuable for all 'inside work'—by which
he presumably meant interior woodwork and furniture.

In regard to the American-ipecac, he wrote, 'We have also a species
of the Ipeacuacana growing wild in our woods which when cultivated
were equally strong and Efficatious as that used in Britain.' Literally *ipeca-
cuanha* means a small, roadside emetic plant. The variety Carter mentioned
is evidently a herbacious perennial that belongs to the native species of
the rose family. It is still commonly known as American-ipecac or Indian
physic.[22]

In describing the qualities of the 'Black gound Tree', Carter declared:

> there is likewise in our Mountains Trees whose bark and leaves resemble
> much the Quinquina or Jesuits bark. It bears a Cone and was discovered by
> the Indians under the name of the Black gound [gowned] Tree by which I
> suppose they mean the Romish Missionaries and commonly take it for fevers
> and agues; and in obstinate Quarterns, when the Jesuits bark has failed, a
> cure has been performed by giving it in the same Manner.

In Carter's description of the medicinal uses of this tree, 'Quarterns'
is evidently a reference to quartan malarial fever, in which the parox-
ysms occur approximately every seventy-two hours. It is not as virulent as the malign tertian fevers, which are sometimes called aestivo-

autumnal (or black-water) fever.[23] Carter's 'Black gound Tree' bears no resemblance to the marsh elder, which is often called in the United States the 'Jesuit Bark'.[24]

Carter also mentioned a 'tree' that was 'called by the upper inhabitants allspice'. Presumably this was the wild allspice which grows in the woods of Virginia, though it is an aromatic shrub or bush rather than a tree. Carter claimed for it no commercial or medicinal value.

Carter's 'Jallup' was probably the root of pokeweed, for William Byrd II wrote in 1708, 'there is a Paper of a Root which I think very like Jalop, we call the plant here Poke'. After examining Byrd's sample, his correspondent, Sir Hans Sloane, had informed him they were not the same.[25] Originally the term 'jalup' was used solely to designate the purgative tuberous root of a Mexican plant or the powder made from it. Dr. Wyndham B. Blanton has found that jalup was a favourite medicine among eighteenth-century Virginians.[26]

Concerning 'Pot Ash', Carter wrote:

> I must also add that the Refuse or Trash from our Tobacco Crops & the succers that grow after the Crop is housed, would properly managed, afford a considerable quanty of the best Pot Ash, of which I convinced Mr. Thomas Stevens some time ago, & on his application the sum of £100 was voted by the General Assembly to Erect a Furnace & process a quantity of Tobacco Ashes in order to his making a publick Experiment, which by some difference with the Ministry he was prevented [from] carrying on, & for which he by Letter made an Apology and last Summer came in Person to Excuse himself, and as he was under such difficulties & the great quantity of trash Tobacco saved, made use of before his Return for Manure, no steps are taken according to his Method; and we have at this time [c. 1760] only one Work for making Pearl Ashes that I know off: It gives me great concern that anything should happen to prevent so beneficial a Work; whether his imprudent Resentment may not exasperate the Ministry so much against him as to lose this Advantage to Great Britain and this Colony, Time can only show.[27]

Carter's reference to Stevens' experience may be regarded as evidence of the strict, retarding control exercised by the home government over the development of manufacturing in Virginia.

In the quoted passage from Carter's letter, Carter wrote about 'Pot Ash' and 'Pearl Ashes'. Pearl ashes were refined from potash. Usually pearl ashes were made from wood ashes, except the ashes of pine or chestnut, by leaching the ashes and boiling the resulting lye into a brown salt, which was impure potassium carbonate, or ordinary potash. The brown substance was then remelted and refined to make pearl ashes, a white substance. A cord of wood yielded from three to five pounds of pearl ashes.[28]

Seemingly, pearl ashes were produced for the export trade only in small quantities, despite the efforts of Carter. Only seven casks were exported from the upper District of James River between 25th October 1765, and 25th October 1766, while none had been shipped from that district in the two previous years.[29]

When the home government disallowed Virginia's Two Penny Act of 1758, Carter indignantly protested to the Society that the Act had been necessary.

> We hope [he continued] as we shall use every Measure in our Power to promote Arts & Manufacturers in this Infant Colony, that we may rise in Reputation, and shortly convince your Board that we the least Deserve the Reflections cast on us by the Right Reverd. the Lord Bishop of London, and restore us to our Ancient Constitution; which at present we are deprived of by the most unjust Charges exhibited against us by the cruel Misrepresentation of some avaricious Clergymen who to Enrich themselves would have involved our Country in Ruin. I can with great Truth affirm, We stand in point of Loyalty in Rank with the most dutiful Subjects, and poor as we are, have exerted ourselves during the Course of this ruinous War [the French and Indian] beyond our Abilities, which we hope will soon be made appear by our Agent Edwd. Montague Esqr. I have sent Mr. Wyche two Pamphlets in answer to the Charge of the Clergy, & hope from a serious consideration of them, their *false* clamour will fall to the Ground.[30]

The two pamphlets Charles Carter sent probably were Landon Carter's *A Letter to the Right Reverend Father in God, the Lord Bishop of London* (1759) and Richard Bland's *A Letter to the Clergy of Virginia . . .* (1760). The Bishop of London was Thomas Sherlock. Having accepted the Reverend John Camm's statements on behalf of the Virginia clergy as to conditions in Virginia, Sherlock had charged the General Assembly of Virginia with virtual treason and intentional disloyalty to the King. As a result, Lieutenant Governor Fauquier had been instructed by the home government not to consent to any Bill passed by the General Assembly that would expire in less than two years. By making laws of short duration the General Assembly had prevented them from being vetoed by the Privy Council.[31]

The Society of Arts encouraged the colony to diversify its economy. In 1761 Wyche informed Carter that the membership of the Society was composed of not less than 2000 of the nobility and gentry, whose actual subscription amounted to 4,000 guineas to be given for the advancement and encouragement of all things that 'promote the Grandeur and Welfare of England'.[32] It was especially interested in encouraging in Virginia the production of wines, hemp, fisheries and fish oil, saltpetre and potash.

Interest was also shown in Carter's white tar and in foreign grapes, roots, plants or herbs that would vegetate in England, as turnips did, for the first four months of the year, thus furnishing additional green feed for the livestock.

Concerning wines, Carter's winter grape wine aroused the most speculation among members of the Society, none of whom had ever heard of such a variety. Some thought it was a sweet wine. Others were of the opinion that it must be of the Rhenish sort. Wyche believed a good market could be found in England, if it were of the latter kind, for German wines were in vogue there.

He reminded Carter that the French used their inferior grapes for making brandy and wondered if it would not be wise for Virginia to pursue the same policy. More money could be kept in the colony, he pointed out, if the Virginians would use a native brandy as a substitute for rum and arrack. Surely the slaves could be supplied more cheaply with an inferior native brandy than with foreign rum.

Wyche did not want Carter to conclude from his correspondence that he was 'an advocate for spiritous Liquors'. They should be used only in cases of necessity. 'The Abuse of them', he declared, 'is much to be Condemned and Not to be tolerated in any Kingdom whatever'.

Wyche promised to send to Virginia at the proper season cuttings of the Burgundy, Champagne, Claret and Spanish grapes. He had already shipped to Alexander Garden, of South Carolina, the famous botanist (not the minister of that name), slips of the Zant and Tokay grapes.[33] Wyche had been advised that they had arrived safely and in a vegetating condition. Furthermore, he had spoken to a Mr. Forrester for some of the Zant grapes from Piedmont, for he had found it was high treason to obtain cuttings from Zant itself. These cuttings he would send as soon as convenient. Mr. Frye, a gentleman from Antigua, had informed him that the grapes of Antigua were better than those of Spain and that cuttings could be obtained from that island without difficulty. Wyche therefore suggested that Carter might order them directly, thus saving time.

In 1762 Carter wrote that he had 1,800 vines in his vineyard but doubted if he would make more than one hogshead of wine because of the severity of the summer drought.[34] Like his contemporaries, he did not know that certain parasites in eastern North America were destroying the roots of the European grape vines.[35]

Wyche discussed, moreover, methods of clearing wine. The lees in wine could be precipitated by pouring brandy in it, by cooling it either in a cellar or with salt, or by throwing wood shavings and sawdust into the cask, which was the method used by the French in clearing Burgundy so that it could be sold for old wine within a few months, if mixed with a wine of superior age.[36]

Despite all these efforts, Virginians exported to Great Britain in the fiscal year 1768 only 13 tons and 135 gallons of wine, certainly not a very impressive quantity. In the same year, Virginians imported 396,580 gallons of rum from overseas and an additional 78,264 gallons from other North American colonies.[37]

As for hemp, the Society of Arts allotted £700 to be bestowed on those who cultivated it in America. Wyche thought all the hemp the Colonies could produce would be used in New England, where shipbuilding was 'very great'. Even though none was directly shipped to England, the whole empire would benefit, he reasoned, because an increase in the supply anywhere in the empire would help to free the British navy from its dependence upon Russian hemp. It was computed, he stated, that Britain was paying Russia £740,000 annually for hemp and other naval stores. Therefore the Society had also granted £500 to encourage the growth of hemp in the United Kingdom. No Englishman could approve of the British fleet's being under the control of a Russian monarch, he said. The English had already seen too much of that condition during the conflict in progress— the French and Indian War.[38] Despite Wyche's prediction that America would produce no hemp for exportation, Virginia did later export some hemp to Great Britain—212 tons in 1768, for instance.[39]

Wyche presumed that the hemp in America, like that in England, had originally come from Russia. He described the English variety as growing to a height of six feet, adding that the Society intended to try to improve it by obtaining seeds of a species that grew to twelve feet in Lombardy.

In Wyche's opinion, the export of herring and other fish taken along the coast of Virginia might be made the basis for a profitable trade with the West Indies. Besides, the oil of such fish should be of great usefulness in Virginia if a process could be devised of 'edulcorating' it. Carter would be sent an authentic account of an experiment the Society was conducting along these lines, if it made a useful discovery. Perhaps fish oil would become highly important to staple manufacturers and a useful illuminating fuel for the lamps of Virginia.

The fishing industry of Virginia did not become an immediate success. In the fiscal year 1768 only 54 kegs and 465 barrels of fish (pickled) were exported, all to the British and foreign West Indies. No mention was made of fish oil.[40]

Concerning saltpetre, Wyche declared that a premium of £200 had been

advertised to encourage its manufacture. A saltpetre plant erected in Chelsea at considerable cost was not furnishing a sufficient quantity. Besides,
its price was too high. Britain's main supply of the commodity was still
being imported at an excessively high rate from Bengal by the East India
Company, which was under a contract with the British Government to
keep the latter supplied. In Wyche's opinion, the company desired to get
rid of its contract, and the Government wanted to obtain its saltpetre at
less cost.[41]

In 1762 Carter sent Wyche a sample of saltpetre made in Virginia by an
illiterate, poverty-stricken old man named Jeremiah Brown, who had been
developing his process for ten years, whenever he could spare the time
from the daily labour required to maintain his large family. Because of his
poverty, Brown had used only two or three pots and a few dishes. Yet he
had extracted small crystal shoots of saltpetre, 'the Size of Tobacco Pipe
stems', from the sources available in Virginia. Carter claimed the sources
were the litter from 'any Houses used for Tobacco, Horses & Cattle. . . .
All north sides of Hills & old worn out lands covered with Bushes'. A
small quantity of this saltpetre made all sorts of fish 'as red as salmon'. It
also burned well, according to Carter, who urged the Society to set Brown
up in business by giving him needed financial support.

William Lewis, the distinguished chemist, and Samuel More, who was
to become Secretary of the Society in 1770, tested the Virginia saltpetre
and reported their findings to the Society. Lewis conducted nine experiments and came to the conclusion 'That greatest part of the Virginia salt
is perfect nitre, or composed of nitrous acid and vegetable alcali; That it
contains also a considerable quantity of a salt, composed of the same acid
and some other basis, in part earthy, but not calcarous: and that great part
of this heterogene salt, but not the whole, becomes nitre on being supplied
with a vegetable alcaline basis'.[42]

Lewis' descriptive expression, 'composed of nitrous acid and vegetable
alcali', would be expressed in modern chemical terminology as potassium
nitrate (KNO_3), which is the original saltpetre used in gunpowder. By experimentation he found that it exploded well when mixed with charcoal in
the proportions of ten to three and in other proportions also. He eliminated
the possibility of the compound being the 'mineral alcali'—that is, sodium
nitrate ($NaNO_3$)—by burning it. It did not 'yield a yellow flame'. By adding a filtered solution of chalk to pure *aqua fortis* (nitric acid) and mixing
them with a filtered solution of Virginia nitre, he determined that the Virginia salt contained no 'vitriolated tartar', for the whole mixture remained
limpid, without the least cloudiness. By adding vitriol (sulphuric acid) to

a filtered solution of the nitre, he tested for a 'calcarious' or calcium base. Had calcium been present it would have combined with the vitriol and precipitated as a salt. Instead, the solution became only slightly cloudy, which Lewis attributed to the extraneous substance in the saltpetre. Lewis also detected evidence of such a substance as a residue after the burning or exploding of the saltpetre. Because of an insufficient supply he did not attempt to determine the percentage of pure nitre in the mixture.[43]

More's experiments consisted mainly of comparing the Virginia salt-petre with the common saltpetre of England. He found it was equal to the English saltpetre in quality and that the gunpowder he made with it in the proportions of 18 of nitre, 3 of powdered charcoal and 3 of sulphur was as good as gunpowder he made when English nitrate was substituted. Neither, however, was as good as manufactured gunpowder, a fact which More attributed to the superiority of mixing in the factory rather than any inferiority in the saltpetre.[44]

The Society of Arts shared with the Virginia Committee the information it obtained when it revived the use of 'the obsolete Chemical Fluid of Mr. Ambrose Godfrey for the speedy extinction of fires either in Houses or on Board of Ships by Suffocation & Explosion'. An experiment in this method of fire-fighting was carried on successfully in the presence of some of the royal family and a huge crowd in Marylebone Fields on 21st May 1761. The Society ordered a pamphlet to be prepared on the subject for distribution and promised to send a copy to Carter.[45]

After seeing a published list of the bounties offered by the Society, Charles Dick, a Virginian, sought to claim a premium by submitting a record which showed that he had shipped a total of 133 casks and 10 hogsheads of pearl ash from Fredericksburg to England via named vessels between 1757 and 1761 inclusive. He stated that he had manufactured it at a great expense and with difficulty.[46] He thought potash could be made in large quantities, but the method was not generally known in Virginia. Proper equipment was not always available, and the planters were often not interested in saving and selling their wood ashes. Dick then described a process of manufacture which he could use if he could only obtain a cop-per ladle and an iron rod a little longer than the depth of the iron pot, and flattened at one end in the manner of a broad chisel for scraping frequently the bottom of the pot when the lye began to thicken.

Dick felt that some real progress was being made in the production of hemp and the manufacture of cordage. He took a dim view of the progress in wine-making, but believed that profitable vineyards could be cultivated upon the mountainsides and limestone lands of Virginia. Silk was raised only by a few people as a curiosity. Sturgeons abounded, but a good receipt for pickling them was needed; also a market. The planters had no raisin grapes or olive trees with which to experiment. Scammony and opium poppies should also be sent for a trial. He claimed that abundant cobalt deposits existed in the back country of Virginia but that they were too far from means of navigation for the ore to be brought to market.[47]

Certainly the correspondence between the Society and the Virginia Committee helped to promote economic diversification in Virginia, even though none of the projects discussed ever developed into a major crop or dominant industry of the colony. Hemp and cordage became important. Significant experiments were undertaken in the making of pearl ash and saltpetre. A greater knowledge was obtained about grapes and their culture. It was realized more fully that the development of the fisheries depended upon a better quality of salt, better methods of pickling, an improved process for refining the fish oil, and a good market. Improvements in the manufacture of tar were worth seeking. The medicinal qualities of herbs needed further investigation. It became more apparent that the silk industry and certain other proposed undertakings would fail.

In 1763 the Society awarded a gold medal to Carter 'for care and industry to promote in Virginia the purposes of this Society in the British colonies'.[48] Such recognition had its disadvantages, however. In June of the same year, after Governor Fauquier and Colonel Thornton had been appointed to the Virginia Committee to fill vacancies, a letter was read from Wyche in which Charles Carter 'was the Heroe'. This caused so much jealousy in the Committee, according to Charles' letter to his brother, Landon, that 'they did not take any notice of the Honour done them by the society and all my endeavours were little regarded. Colo. Thornton and Colo. Tayloe can inform you that I shalt for the Future give them very little trouble and carry on the whole correspondence myself. They did not vouchsafe to give me any instructions'.[49]

Indirectly, the correspondence may have kept the attention of the planters more constantly focused upon the need for economic diversification along lines that were more readily available. Many planters, including George Washington and Robert Carter of Nomini Hall, turned to wheat, corn, peas and beans, and livestock as their chief money crops after the French and Indian War. In 1768 Virginia exported overseas over 500,000 bushels of corn, nearly 45,000 bushels of peas and beans, nearly 15,000 barrels of bread and flour, more than 130,000 bushels of wheat, approximately 7,200 barrels of beef, pork and hams, 13,255 bushels of oats, and 2,700 pounds of indigo. Lumbering and wood products were also important, with overseas exports in 1768 being in excess of 105,000 hoops, at least 15,000 feet of oars, more than 615,000 feet of plank and scantling (not including over 52,000 feet of timber pine), and 23,333 barrels of pitch, tar and turpentine. The iron industry was also on the march, with an exportation of 585 tons of iron bars and 854 tons of pig iron. Only about 42,000 hogsheads of tobacco were exported, well below the nearly 60,000 hogsheads Carter estimated as having been exported annually eight years earlier.[50] But, despite progress in diversification, Virginia's exportation of tobacco exceeded 60,000 hogsheads in the early 1770s: 65,208 hogsheads were exported in the fiscal year between 25th October 1771 and 25th October 1772, and 69,587 hogsheads were shipped in the following fiscal year.[51] Tobacco alone represented over 75 per cent of the total value of goods exported from Virginia and Maryland in 1775.[52]

13

'THE PRESENT UNHAPPY DISPUTES':
THE SOCIETY AND THE LOSS OF THE
AMERICAN COLONIES, 1774-1783

D. G. C. Allan

In the year the United States of America was born, the Society came of age. Yet although its methods of operation had long been settled and an influential and distinguished membership recruited, the Society of Arts was still concerned during the period 1775 to 1783 with major questions of domestic organization and policy. So while in America the contending armies fought over vast distances and the various colonial communities experienced the ordeals of mob violence, martial law, siege and counter-siege, and were divided between a majority who prayed for the success of the continental congress and a minority, by no means insubstantial, who still blessed His Majesty, other and less bloodthirsty questions required the attention of the members of the Society in London. During these years the move to the House in the Adelphi was completed and James Barry's paintings for the Great Room brought to a stage when the artist would allow them to be exhibited to the public. The machines in the new repository were catalogued, the first cumulative *Register* of awards was published and plans were laid for the annual publication of a volume of *Transactions*. The Society's income and membership, which had been de-

Originally appeared in *Jnl. RSA*, 130 (Jan., Feb., Mar., 1982), 97-101, 156-61, 223-27.

creasing since 1765, continued to fall until 1782, when an upwards swing began which was to last until the next war period. The routine activities remained the same. On 19th April 1775, the day of the battle of Lexington, the Society discussed a proposal to limit the speaking time of some of its more loquacious members and referred a model of a pump and a letter on tinning copper (with samples) to the appropriate committees. On 13th March 1776, when preparations were under way for the evacuation of Boston, the Society met to renew its agricultural and mechanical premiums and received Robert Laurie's examples of coloured mezzotint printing. On 8th October 1777, the day after the disaster of Saratoga, the Society began its 1777 to 1778 session in the customary manner, and in the same way the session for 1781 to 1782 was commenced soon after Cornwallis's surrender at Yorktown. Such examples could be multiplied, and they are not in themselves remarkable.[1] They should nonetheless be kept in mind when the effects of the American conflict on the Society of Arts are considered. The Society continued to exist, although its membership was divided and its colonial premiums almost totally eliminated.

Since its earliest days the Society had been interested in North America. At its third meeting a proposal was made for 'extending the premiums to raw silk produced in our plantations'. The proposal was implemented in the premium list issued on 5th April 1755, and this was the first of a special category of premiums to be offered 'For the advantage of the *British* Colonies and Trade' which was to appear in the annual list for many years. When standing committees were established by the Society in 1757, there was one set up 'For Colonies and Trade', and one of its most active chairmen in the Society's formative years was John Pownall, Secretary of His Majesty's Commissioners for Trade and Plantations. Fifteen of these Commissioners were also members of the Society. The professed objects of the Society in regard to the Colonies were therefore closely linked to official British policy. It believed that 'Nothing can more effectively promote the Commercial Interest of Great Britain and its Colonies . . . than giving Encouragement to the Growth, Culture and Production in the said Colonies of such Commodities as are of either necessary consumption in Great Britain or are essential to its Manufactures, many of which . . . are now Imported at a great disadvantage from foreign Countries'.[2] Thus the Society's premiums were designed to help the British textile industry by reducing its dependence on foreign raw materials, like silk, and to supplement the native supply of bleaching materials, cordage and oils. The creation of a colonial wine industry was also intended to assist in the economic struggle with rival European powers.

In order to carry on this work the Society undertook the annual expenditure of a considerable proportion of its financial resources and built up an extensive network of American correspondence and membership. The political storms which had hovered over the continent since the Stamp Act agitations and which burst into final catastrophe in the late 1770s were bound to have their effect sooner or later on the Society of Arts.

The number of awards offered in the class of Colonies and Trade reached their peak in 1764 with a total of 123, which was more than in any other premium category. The number actually awarded was greatest in 1766, when 11 awards representing a total value of £674 11s. and one gold medal were granted. Thereafter the Colonial awards declined each year until 1779, when they ceased entirely, and were not resumed until twenty years had elapsed.[3] An acceptance of the traditional view of the Colonies as a source of economic strength for the mother country was modified by an earnest desire to be on friendly and familiar terms with the colonists, who deserved to be cherished as fellow subjects of the King, and, in the eyes of some members, as fellow and equal 'citizens of the world'. Shipley expressed such a tender interpretation of mercantilist doctrine when he wrote to Franklin on behalf of the Society in 1756:

> Their Desire is to make Great Britain and her Colonies mutually dear and serviceable to each other: They know their Interests are the same, and are perfectly convinced, that giving Premiums in America, may, in many Cases, be more Advantageous to the Mother Country than the same Sums bestowed at Home. They detest all narrow minded partiality and unreasonable Jealousies, and hope the Mother Country will always protect and Cherish her Colonies with a Maternal Care and Affection; which as far as in them lies, they shall always endeavour to promote.[4]

Politically the early members of the Society believed that the colonists had the same rights of freedom as were possessed by all Englishmen, and that there was the same need to root out corruption and abuses in America as in the mother country.

Franklin's plans for colonial reform were mentioned by Shipley to Dr. Samuel Madden in 1757. Madden commented: 'I am rejoiced at Mr. Franklin's coming over with so good a Plan which to the shame of Governments has been overlooked such a number of years. If our Colonies be not properly modelled and protected nothing but Ruin and disgrace can follow'.[5] Thomas Hollis once sent a manifesto accompanying one of his many gifts to Harvard: 'People of Massachusetts! when your country shall be cultivated, adorned like this country, and ye shall become elegant, re-

Benjamin Franklin,
c. 1779; portrait bust by
J. J. Caffieri presented
to the Society in 1791.
Courtesy of the RSA.

fined in civil life, then—if not before—"ware your liberties!" '[6] Franklin
and other American correspondents of the Society frequently expressed
their approval of its work for both the Colonies and the mother country in
these early years. In 1758 Robert Pringle testified his 'Zeal, Good Wishes
and Very Very Hearty Inclinations for the Success and Continuance of so
Generous, Laudable and Beneficial an Undertaking so Conducive to the
Good, Welfare and Prosperity of our Nation', and in the following year
Alexander Garden described the Society's scheme for a botanic garden in
South Carolina as 'truly noble'. Edward Antill of New Jersey told the Society in 1769: 'I have A Real Affection for my mother Country [and] . . . I
read with pleasure, nay with Transport, the proposals of this most grand
and Beneficient Society. I see with great Satisfaction the Arts, Agriculture,
and Commerce rising and improving from every quarter, and a foundation
laid for Surprising effects . . . and for great increase of wealth and power

to the Nation which I pray God to Establish for Ever'. In 1770 Benjamin Gale, who had been awarded a Gold Medal by the Society, spoke in appreciation of its 'pleasure in the Prosperity of the Colonies, which if properly Encouraged will add a Certain Lusture to the Throne, Afford Commerce to the Merchants, and Employment to the Manufactures of Great Brittain'. He was writing to Franklin, who was at that time in London and in close association with the Society's headquarters.[7] Franklin's involvement in the work of the Society during his years in London is well known, and the evolution of his political sentiments has been vividly described by J. P. Greene.[8] His 'Alienation' from the Society's policy towards the Colonies has received less attention. When news of the 'Boston Massacre' of 5th March 1770 caused him to explode in rage against what he called 'the arbitrary power of a corrupt Parliament, that does not like us, and conceives itself to have an Interest in keeping us down'—he was still careful to express his loyalty to the King 'who' he believed, 'has the best Disposition towards us'—he took a critical look at the whole economic relationship between the mother country and the Colonies.[9] In some intemperate marginalia written on to his copy of Dean Tucker's *Letter from a Merchant* he expressed his complete disgust at the system of premiums and bounties so beloved of the Society of Arts and mercantilist parliamentarians. Tucker, who had done much to assist in the establishment of the Society, pointed out the many economic benefits which the American colonies received from the mother country:

> Parliament *now gives you a Bounty of £8 per Ton for exporting your Hemp from North America;* but will allow me nothing for growing it here in England; nay, will tax me very severely for fetching it from any other country; though it be an Article most essentially necessary for all the Purposes of Shipping and Navigation. Moreover in respect to the Culture of Raw Silk, you have an immense Parliamentary Premium for that Purpose; and you receive farther Encouragements from our Society for Arts and Sciences, which is continually adding fresh Rewards:—but I can receive no Encouragement either from the one, or from the other, to bear my Expenses at first setting out:—though most undeniably the white Mulberry-Trees can thrive as well on my Grounds as they can in Switzerland, Brandenburgh, Denmark, or Sweden, where vast Quantities are now raising. Take another instance: Why shall I not be permitted to buy Pitch, Tar, and Turpentine,—without which I cannot put my Ships to Sea,—and Indigo, so useful in many Manufactures;—why shall not I be permitted to purchase these Articles wherever I can, the best in their kind and on the best Terms?—No, I shall not; for though they are all raw Materials, which therefore ought to have been im-

ported Duty free, yet I am restrained by an heavy Duty, almost equal to a Prohibition, from purchasing them anywhere, but from you:—Whereas you on the contrary, are paid a Bounty for selling these very Articles, at the only Market, in which you could sell them to advantage, viz. the English.

Franklin noted his answer in the margin:

Did ever any North American bring his Hemp to England for this Bounty? We have yet not enough for our own Consumption. We begin to make our own Cordage. You want to suppress that Manufacture and would do it by getting the raw Material from us: You want to be supply'd with Hemp for your Manufactures, and Russia demands Money. These were the Motives for giving what you pleased to call a *Bounty* to us. We thank you for your Bounties. We love you and therefore must be oblig'd to you for being good to yourselves. You do not encourage raising Hemp in England, because you know it impoverishes the richest Grounds; your Land Owners are all against it. What you call Bounties given by Parliament and the Society are nothing more than Inducements offered us, to induce us to leave Employments that are more profitable and engage in such as would be less so without your Bounty; to quit a Business profitable to ourselves and engage in one that shall be profitable to you; this is the true Spirit of all your Bounties. Your Duties on foreign Articles are from the same Motives. Pitch, Tar and Turpentine used to cost you £5 a Barrel when you had them from Foreigners, who us'd you ill into the Bargain, thinking you could not do without them. You gave a bounty of 5s. a Barrel to the Colonies, and they have brought you such Plenty as to reduce the Price to 10s. a Barrel. Take back your Bounties when you please, since you upbraid us with them. Buy your Indigo Pitch, Silk, and Tobacco where you please, and let us buy our Manufactures where we please. I fancy we shall be Gainers. I am sick of these *forged Obligations*.[10]

It is perhaps significant that the only committees of the Society attended by Franklin in the years 1767 to 1773 were those of Agriculture and Mechanics, and that he does not appear to have attended at any committee after 18th March 1773. Two years later, having endured the ordeal of his exposure before the Lords of the Council in Whitehall and expressed his scorn for the government's policy in his *Rules for Reducing a Great Empire to a small one* and similar political squibs, he left for America, cherishing his stays at the Shipley family home, Twyford in Hampshire.[11] The American crisis was by this time reaching its acute stage. Members of the Society read in their newspapers and magazines a bewildering series of assertions and counter-assertions. General Gage's proclamation of June 1775 described how 'The authors of the present unnatural revolt, never daring to trust their cause or their actions to the judgment of an impartial public, or even

Twyford House, Hampshire, in the mid-eighteenth century; reproduced courtesy of the RSA from an unpublished photograph of a painting now lost. The house was inherited by the Reverend Jonathan Shipley, Dean of Winchester and later Bishop of St. Asaph, who was William Shipley's elder brother. In 1771 Benjamin Franklin wrote the first part of his autobiography while staying at Twyford House.

to the dispassionate reflection of their followers, have uniformly placed their chief confidence in the suppression of truth, and while indefatigable and shameless pains have been taken to obstruct every appeal to the real interest of the people of America, the grossest forgeries, calumnies, and absurdities that ever insulted human understanding, have been imposed upon their credulity.' Also published in London was the *Declaration by the Representatives of the United Colonies of North America, now met in General Congress at Philadelphia, setting forth the Causes and Necessity of their taking up Arms*. This set out to justify the rebellious actions referred to by General Gage as the final resort of an injured people:

> We for ten years incessantly and ineffectually besieged the throne as supplicants; we reasoned, we remonstrated with Parliament in the most mild and decent language; but Administration, sensible that we should regard these oppressive measures as freemen ought to do, sent over fleets and armies to enforce them . . . We have pursued every temperate, every respectful measure; we have even proceeded to break off our commercial intercourse with our fellow subjects as the last peaceable admonition, that our attachment to no nation upon earth should supplant our attachment to liberty. This, we flattered ourselves, was the ultimate step of the controversy: but subsequent events have shewn, how vain was this hope of finding moderation in our enemies!

The Congress's Declaration appeared in July, and in August British subjects were placed in no doubt as to their legal responsibilities by a Royal Proclamation employing the time-honoured phraseology of Tudor and Stuart times. It showed:

> That, whereas many subjects in divers parts of the American colonies have at length proceeded to open and avowed Rebellion; and whereas there is reason to apprehend that such rebellion hath been much promoted by the traiterous correspondence, counsels, and comfort, of divers wicked and desperate persons within this realm; to the end, therefore, that none may through ignorance neglect or violate their duty, it is declared, that not only all officers, civil and military, are obliged to exert their utmost endeavours to suppress such Rebellion, and bring the Traitors to justice, but that every subject within the Realm, and the dominions thereunto belonging, are bound by law to be aiding and assisting in the suppression of the same, and in disclosing all traiterous conspiracies and attempts against the King, his Crown, and dignity.

The *Gentleman's Magazine*,[12] which had printed all these documents, continued its regular reporting of 'the Proceedings of the American Colonists' in 1776, though in April of that year they were momentarily replaced by the trial of the Duchess of Kingston for bigamy: 'the importance of the above trial', noted the Editor, 'and our desire to gratify our readers with the substance of it at once, has obliged us to postpone the Account of American Affairs, and the rather as our late advices from thence are not to be relied upon.' The issue for August contained a splendid miscellany of topics well suited to readers in the Adelphi: there were items entitled 'Enquiry as to the Power of Fire-engines', the 'Odious Practice of blowing Meat', a 'Description of Chepstow Castle, Monmouthshire', the 'Character of Pope Clement XI', the 'Noble Plan of the late John Bradley Blake' and 'A wonderful Experience for the Head acke [*sic*]'. There was also printed, however, the full text of the 'Declaration of American Independency', only omitting the words 'King' and 'Tyrant'. Its rolling peroration must have sent a chill through the hearts of the virtuosi:

> That these United colonies are, and of right ought to be, *free and independent states,* and that they are absolved from all allegiance to the British crown, and that all political connection between them and the state of Great Britain, is, and ought to be, totally dissolved; and that, as free and independent states, they have full power to levy war, conclude peace, contract alliances, establish commerce, and to do all other acts and things which independent states may of right do. And for the support of this declaration, with a firm reliance on the protection of Divine Providence, we mutually pledge to each other our lives, our fortunes, and our sacred honour.[13]

Now began six bewildering years for the Society's members. Most immediately concerned were those who were themselves American.

THE AMERICAN MEMBERSHIP

Under the Society's constitution, or 'Plan' as it was called, adopted in February 1755, provision was made for the election of 'Foreigners, or Persons that do not usually reside in Great Britain' as corresponding members who were excused from making a financial contribution to the Society.[14] The first to be elected in this manner was Archdeacon Pococke of Dublin, who was chosen on 5th March, and the second was Dr. Alexander Garden of South Carolina, elected later in the same month. In the ten years following, 118 more corresponding members were elected, of whom 45 came from North America. The total for the next decade was 109, with 23 from North America. No Americans were elected in 1776, one only in 1777 and none at all in the years down to 1787.[15]

The term 'corresponding' was the expression of a hope rather than the imposition of a condition, and only some dozen of these American members actually wrote to the Society. Their correspondence was, with one exception, confined to the years before 1770.[16] The Society's chief object seems to have been to build up a list of influential persons who would further the Society's objects in the Colonies, and some pride was taken as numbers grew and distinction increased. Until at least 1777 the Society published annual lists of its members. The list for that year included, in spite of the war then in progress, the names of 53 American corresponding members and of at least seven American subscribing members, amongst whom was 'P. Franklin, Benjamin, LL.D, FRS'. Franklin had been elected a corresponding member in 1756 and had sent as a donation the sum of twenty guineas, which entitled him to the status of a 'Perpetual' subscribing member, indicated in the lists by a capital 'P' before his name. Writers on the Society's history have often referred to his membership but have largely neglected the other American members.[17] With the help of modern transatlantic scholars it has been possible to identify all the subscribing members listed in 1777 and 42 of the corresponding members. This gives a total of 49, from which we must subtract 10 who appear to have died before 1774 and to which we must add one (Jabez Maude Fisher) who was elected after the list was published. Of these remaining 40 we can say that 25 were more or less loyal to the Crown, 14 inclined to the revolutionary side and one, Nicholas Waln, a Philadelphian Quaker, declined for conscience' sake to take part in the conflict.[18]

Let us first of all examine the revolutionaries, since they challenged the existing order, though some would have argued it was the supposedly 'arbitrary' acts of the British Crown and Parliament which were disturbing the *status quo*. Looking at them from North to South, in Massachusetts we have James Bowdoin, a wealthy merchant who had scientific interests, and had collaborated with Franklin on some electrical experiments. He opposed the measures of Governor Hutchinson and became president of the revolutionary constituent convention in his province.[19] Bowdoin was both a corresponding member and a subscribing member of the Society, having paid a life subscription at the time of his election. In consequence his name, like Franklin's, still appeared in the Society's list in 1783, and, as Founder-President of the American Academy of Arts and Sciences, he used the curious designatory letters of 'F. Soc. Arts, Man. and Com. *Lond.*'[20]

In Connecticut there was Dr. Benjamin Gale, whose enthusiasm for the Society when he received a gold medal in 1770 was noted earlier in this study. Gale mounted a press campaign in favour of the American cause and described the mother country in 1775 as a 'Kingdom of Tyrants and Asses'. Sir James Jay, the eminent physician of New York, first of all supported the revolutionary cause and then changed to support the Crown. Less extreme initially was Philip Livingston of New York. A wealthy merchant and landowner, he feared the consequences of a breach with Britain, but decided in the end to use his vast wealth in support of the Continental Congress and to append his signature to the Declaration of Independence. Also from New York was Philip Schuyler, a prosperous country gentleman who lived in a commodious and comfortable farmhouse near Saratoga. He had been a supply officer in the colonial forces during the Seven Years' War, and in June 1775 he accepted the rank of Major General in command of the revolutionary army sent to attempt the conquest of Canada.[21]

Another American Major General drawn from the Society's ranks was William Alexander, the titular Earl of Stirling, who had paid a life subscription at his election in 1760 and been awarded the Society's gold medal in 1767 for planting 2,100 vines in New Jersey. After serving briefly in the French and Indian War, he had journeyed to England in 1756 and remained there for five years, during most of which he was engaged in a fruitless attempt to secure recognition of his claim to the lapsed Earldom of Stirling. Upon his return to America, he had developed a considerable estate at Baskingridge, Somerset County, New Jersey, which soon became his permanent residence. He was appointed a member of the Governor's Council and assumed a leading rôle in the political, economic and social life of New Jersey. With the outbreak of the Revolution, he cast his considerable prestige and ability on the side of independence and won distinction as Major General in the Continental Army.[22]

From Philadelphia came Drs. Benjamin Rush and John Morgan. Both were eminent in the scientific and medical world, and both were appointed to high-ranking positions in the medical services of the revolutionary army. Rush had been particularly active in fomenting opposition to the home government and had associated with such activists as Thomas Jefferson, John Adams and Thomas Paine. Like Philip Livingston, already mentioned, he signed the Declaration of Independence. The Virginians, Theodore Bland, Arthur Lee and James Madison, also supported the revolutionary cause. Bland, who had retired from a prosperous medical practice to become a planter, was one of the twenty-four Virginian gentlemen who removed the arms from the Governor's palace in Williamsburg on 24th June 1774. He subsequently had a distinguished career as a cavalry officer in the revolutionary army. Lee was, like Bland, a Doctor of Medicine, and had obtained some eminence in the world of science. He had been elected a Fellow of the Royal Society in 1766, and, in the same year, had joined the Society of Arts with Franklin as one of his proposers. He served the revolutionary cause in important diplomatic missions and felt so strongly against Great Britain that he took the unusual step of resigning from the Royal Society, earning a well-known rebuke from Sir Joseph Banks, who pointed out the great difference between political associations and scientific societies whose interests 'belong . . . to the community of man and mind'.[23] Another physician, Dr. Corbyn Griffin, served on the revolutionary committee of safety for York County. A clergyman, the Reverend James Madison of William and Mary College, was elected a subscribing member of the Society of Arts in 1775 when in England for the purpose of receiving ordination. On his return to Williamsburg he became an active champion of the American cause, 'even', it was said, 'going so far as to speak of Heaven as a republic rather than a kingdom'. He allowed his subscription to the Society to lapse, as did Samuel Farley, a 'Son of Liberty' from Georgia, who was elected in February 1776 and paid only one year's dues.[24]

The farthest south of the corresponding members were those from South Carolina, where, in 1775, of the seven listed, one was dead, two were in England and three were more or less loyal to the Crown.[25] The most celebrated was Dr. Alexander Garden, the botanist, of Charleston, South Carolina. He had been the first American to be elected into the Society and was a friend of the Society's founder, William Shipley. In the spring of 1774 he was forced, though ill of a putrid fever, to sign the articles supporting the Continental Association. Feeling too weak and sick to read them, he signed, but with the reservation that if they contained anything inimical to his allegiance to the King, he would renounce them. When he was recovered he read the terms of the Association and remarked that though he did not consider them 'entirely rebellious', he doubted if he would have signed them had he been well. The mere fact that he had signed the Articles protected him from the outrages committed against other loyalists, but during the years 1776 to 1780 he made repeated plans to leave for England. When war came to Charleston in 1781 he attended the wounded on both sides, and in 1782, with his property confiscated by the rebels, he finally reached the safety of the mother country.[26] Aaron Loocock, a merchant-planter, who had written to the Society in 1775 about cultivating madder in South Carolina, also sailed from Charleston to England. His loyalty was more doubtful than Garden's, and he returned as soon as peace was signed.[27] Thomas Smith, a wealthy retired merchant and landowner, took no active part in the conflict but was considered to be in sympathy with the Crown.[28]

John Rutherford, of North Carolina, was another corresponding member of the Society whose property was confiscated because of his loyalty to the Crown. The Lieutenant Governor, George Mercer, who had been elected a subscribing member of the Society in 1769, was away from the province during the troubles. Also fortunately absent from the revolutionary scene was George William Fairfax of Belvoir, Virginia. A member of the Council of the Colony, he had gone to England in 1773 to take up an inheritance, and had not returned for fear of the coming revolution. The rebels confiscated part of his property, but he was able to live in some comfort at Bath for the rest of his life. During the war he showed much kindness to American prisoners carried to England.

Gilbert Barclay, a Scottish merchant living in Philadelphia, had been elected a corresponding member in 1773. He had loyalist sympathies and retired to Scotland on account of the revolution.[29] Two other loyal Philadelphians who belonged to the Society when the Revolution broke out were the Reverend Dr. William Smith, a 'soft and polite' clergyman said to be a potential Bishop of America, and James Allen, a member of Chief Justice Allen's stalwartly loyal family. Smith survived the conflict, but Allen was taken ill in 1776 and died the following year. 'At present in England' was Hugh Ferguson, another Philadelphian with a Scottish name, when he was elected to the Society on 6th December 1775. This date suggests he had loyalist sympathies, or some other good reason for not wanting to be in the rebel capital. Two years later the Society elected Jabez Maude Fisher, when Philadelphia was again under Royal control. In 1779 Fisher fled to New York on account of his loyalty and ultimately found safety in England. He was the last American corresponding member to be elected for a decade.

In New Jersey, a gentleman called Michael Kearney stood out as a loyalist. The Governor, William Franklin, was also a corresponding member. William was the son of Benjamin Franklin and in spite of his father's views stood firmly on the side of the Government, and endured a painful imprisonment at the hands of the revolutionaries. His devotion to duty was commemorated in Benjamin West's picture of the *Reception of the American Loyalists by Great Britain in the Year 1783*, where his portrait appears at the head of the refugees. The description of the painting cites that 'having his Majesty's commission of Governor of New Jersey, [he] preserved his fidelity and loyalty to his Sovereign from the commencement to the conclusion of the contest, notwithstanding powerful incitements to the contrary'. The rift between father and son was ultimately healed, despite the elder Franklin's complaints to his friends about William's conduct, and it was certainly to the family's advantage to have close relations occupying positions of importance on both sides in the conflict.[30]

Another loyalist member who suffered imprisonment for his beliefs was Major Philip Skene of Wood Creek, New York. A landowner and surveyor of royal woods, he had seen active service in Flanders, the West Indies and Canada. When endeavouring to raise a regiment for the King in June 1775, he fell into the hands of agents of the Congress and was held a prisoner until the end of 1776, when he was exchanged for James Lovell, a Massachusetts Whig. It was said that even when jailed at Hartford, Connecticut, he would still harangue the people from the prison window, calling on them to cease their rebellion.[31]

Possibly also a loyalist was a New York corresponding member called simply 'Captain' Paterson in the Society's lists. He may be the John Paterson of New York who signed a loyal address to the King in 1779. The Royal Governor of New York, General William Tryon, who fought for his province several times in the field, had been a subscribing member of the Society since 1760 and paid his dues throughout the conflict. John Antill of New York, who was elected a subscribing member of the Society in 1774 and whose father, Edward Antill, had received a premium from the Society for planting vines in New Jersey, fought for the Crown as a Major in the loyal New Jersey volunteers.

Connecticut produced four loyalist members of the Society, three of whom, Peter and Joseph Harrison and Jared Ingersoll, held offices in the revenue service, which made them obnoxious to the popular party. Peter

Reception of the American Loyalists by Great Britain in the Year 1783; engraving by H. Moses after the painting by Benjamin West. Courtesy of the RSA.

Harrison is remembered as the greatest American architect of the colonial period; he died of shock at the news of the battle of Lexington. Joseph Harrison was roughly handled by a mob and had his property damaged and confiscated. He found safety in England in 1777. Jared Ingersoll, who had endeavoured to carry out the unpopular duties of Stamp-distributor in 1765, having seen himself hanged in effigy and being forced to cry 'Liberty and Property' three times, had accepted the position of Judge of Vice Admiralty at Philadelphia in 1770, which he lost at the time of the Revolution. In 1777 he was still known for his 'formal toryism'; he died in 1781 having apparently escaped imprisonment. The fourth of the Society's Connecticut loyalists was Elihu Hall, an eminent lawyer from Wallingford county, who was probably related to Colonel Phineas Lyman, a corresponding member who had died in 1775 and whose name does not appear in the 1777 list. Lyman had enjoined the strictest loyalty on his family before he died, and Elihu Hall preferred to flee to England rather than live under revolutionary rule.[32]

Three corresponding members took ship for Halifax, Nova Scotia, when the Boston loyalists were evacuated by the Royal Navy in 1776. They were Peter Oliver, George Erving and Silvester Gardiner. Oliver had held the office of Chief Justice of Massachusetts since 1756 and would not countenance rebellion. He was imprisoned and banished by the revolutionaries. Erving was a merchant who supported Governor Hutchinson and had his property confiscated as a result. Silvester Gardiner was a wealthy and public-spirited physician, who showed his support for the Royal cause by giving hospitality to the Governor, to General Gage and other government officials. He believed, he told a correspondent in 1776, that the existing riches of the colonies were 'owing almost solely to the protection and patronage of the Parent State'; the colonies had been 'nourished in their infancy, and supported in their more adult age, with all the attention of an affectionate parent'. Britain had been ever solicitous of the Americans' interests, and the result was that the colonists in the 1760s had been 'in full possession and enjoyment of all the peace and all the security which the best government in the world can give'. In short, he concluded, 'I don't believe there ever was a people in any age or part of the World that enjoyed so much liberty as the people of America did under the mild indulgent Government (God bless it) of England'.[33] How 'mildly and indulgently' this government was now behaving in the face of provocation, justified or unjustified, was also a matter of keen debate in the imperial capital.

THE HOME MEMBERSHIP

Although Lord Romney, the President of the Society, spoke and wrote in support of Chatham's plan to conciliate the colonies once Britain was at war, he was active in his rôle as Colonel of the West Kent Militia.[34] His son and heir, the Honourable Charles Marsham, who was a Vice President, also fluctuated in his attitudes, as did Earl Percy. Of the remaining ten Vice Presidents four were definitely opposed to the Government's American policy, four supported it and two are not known to have expressed political opinions. The pro-Americans consisted of the Duke of Richmond, a leading opposition politician; Sir George Savile, an influential independent M.P.; William, Earl of Radnor, who, though claiming to be a 'steady supporter of the Crown', voted for Chatham's conciliation Bill in 1775, also spoke twice against the bill to restrain American trade, and, in 1776, petitioned against the continuation of the war; and Joshua Steele, whose sympathy with the colonial cause will be discussed below. On the Government side there were the Duke of Northumberland, the Earl Harcourt, Sir Charles Whitworth and Owen Salusbury Brereton. The attitudes of the two remaining Vice Presidents, Keane Fitzgerald and

Edward Hooper, who with Brereton and Steele were by far the most active in the Society's affairs, cannot be established, though it is possible that as a Chief Commissioner of the Customs Hooper felt a sense of loyalty to the administration.

Next to the active Vice Presidents, the members who had most influence in the Society's affairs were the chairmen of the nine standing committees. Two chairmen for each committee were elected annually, and interested members sometimes sought re-election for a series of years. During the period 1775 to 1783 five persons held office as chairmen of the Committee of Colonies and Trade, and five chairmen of other committees occasionally presided in the absence of the titular holder of the office. These were the ten members who would have had most concern with the developments in America. There is evidence to show that four of these committee chairmen expressed views on the conflict. They were John Lind, the lawyer and political writer; Joshua Steele, the expert on the melody of speech; Caleb Whitefoord, the wine merchant and connoisseur, and Alexander Small, the army surgeon and agricultural expert. Let us look at each in turn.

The most explicit supporter of the Government side was John Lind, who was actually engaged by the Ministry to write in favour of its cause. His *Remarks on the Principal Acts of the Thirteenth Parliament of Great Britain* (1775) elicited the praise of the Whig Dr. Parr, who called it 'the ablest book I ever read in defence of the American War'. In 1776 Lind published *An Answer to the Declaration of the American Congress* and *Three Letters to Dr. Price*, in which he exposed the sinister intentions of the 'patricides'.[35] The continued presence of his name in the lists of the chairmen of the committee for Colonies and Trade suggests the existence of a loyalist group within the Society. For although Lind did not once attend the meetings of the committee to which he had been assigned, he was nonetheless elected a chairman for three successive sessions, from 1775 to 1778.

Representing the other point of view was Joshua Steele, who had published a pamphlet sympathizing with American grievances in the 1760s and wrote anonymously to Benjamin Franklin in October 1778, as 'a friend that loves, esteems and knows you, as a Man, a Philosopher and a Patriot, but who while his country is under the sway of Ignorance and Malevolence, dares not put his name to a mere philosophic letter: lest by miscarriage and misconstruction it should be voted into a treasonable correspondence'.[36] The subject of Steele's letter to Franklin will be considered below, but first we must consider the other committee chairmen.

Caleb Whitefoord, the wine merchant, was also a friend of Franklin's, having been his neighbour in Craven Street and having been proposed by him as a member of the Society. No letters between them are extant for the war period, though they were to meet again in Paris in 1782 during the peace negotiations, when Whitefoord stood up stoutly for the interests of his own country. Some indications of his *sympathy,* as distinct from support, for the American cause are given in a letter he wrote many years later to the American Philosophical Society:

> Your venerated President, the late Dr. Benjamin Franklin, had for many years honoured me with his Friendship; and perhaps that Intimacy, which was the Pride and the Happiness of my Life, may have in some Degree recommended me to your notice . . . I have long been a sincere Well-wisher to America, and no-one lamented more the unhappy Quarrel between the Colonies and the Parent State: And having lent a helping hand to stop the Horrors of War, and to negociate a Peace between the two Countries, I have the satisfaction to think, that I have not lived in vain.[37]

The fourth chairman associated with the Society's Committee for Colonies and Trade whose views on the conflict can be deduced from his correspondence was Alexander Small. He had known Franklin in the pre-war period and resumed the correspondence with him after the Peace. Small's expressions of sympathy for the American loyalists and his stalwart patriotism received a rebuke from Franklin in 1789:

> I find by your letters that every man has patience enough to bear calmly and coolly the injuries done other people: you have perfectly forgiven the Royalists, and you seem to wonder that we should still retain any resentment against them for their joining with the savages to burn our houses, and murder and scalp our friends, our wives and our children. I forget who it was said, 'we are commanded to forgive our enemies, but we are no where commanded to forgive our friends;' certain it is however, that atrocious injuries done to us by our friends are naturally more deeply resented than the same done by enemies. They have left us to live under the government of their King in England and Nova Scotia. We do not miss them, nor wish their return; nor do we envy them their present happiness. The accounts you give me of the great prospects you have respecting your manufactures, agriculture and commerce, are pleasing to me, for I still love England and wish it prosperity.[38]

Among the seventeen other committee chairmen who held office in the war period but who did not preside at the Committee of Colonies were Valentine Green, the artist, and Arthur Young, the writer on agriculture. Green held the position of mezzotint engraver to the King and was an Associate of the Royal Academy. It seems unlikely that he shared his friend

Barry's fanatical sympathy with the American cause. Young made his only public comment on the revolution in the preface to his *Tour in Ireland*, published in 1780, a copy of which he presented to the Society. He blamed what he called 'that baleful monopolizing spirit of commerce that wished to govern great nations, on the maxims of the counter'. It has been suggested that his attitude derived from the influence of Adam Smith, who had joined the Society in 1775.[39] This did, however, prevent Young from supporting patriotic subscriptions to assist the war effort. Green and Young were perhaps the most influential members of the Society at this time, but their chief concern was to extend the Society's work in the direction of their special interests—respectively the fine arts and agriculture; Colonial matters would have no special appeal for them.

Samuel More, the Society's Secretary since 1770, would probably have been sympathetic to the American cause, though his official position required circumspection. He had been elected without his knowledge and possibly on the proposal of Franklin, as a member of the American Philosophical Society in 1774. In 1786 when the troubles were over, the American Society sent out magnificent engraved diplomas to its members at home and abroad. More acknowledged his with enthusiasm, and three years later he wrote to Franklin making kind inquiries about his health and referring to 'the fire of liberty' which was spreading itself over France. The American sage, having experienced one revolution, was far from sanguine at the prospects of another.[40]

Nothing can be said of the views of the Assistant Secretaries, George Box and Richard Samuel, or of Alexander Mabyn Bailey, the Register. But Bailey's rival and ultimate successor, George Cockings, had made his attitude clear in 1766. Cockings warned his fellow Americans in his doggerel poem, 'Arts, Manufactures and Commerce' to be 'Obedient Children' and deserve the love of the Mother Country:

> May FILIAL DUTY all their Actions guide:
> May they more tractable, more placid grow,
> Be wise betimes, and their true Int'rest know;
> Nor in her Bosom fix, by Tumults rude,
> The poignant Stings of black INGRATITUDE...
> So may the Colonists in Love and Peace,
> With Britain live, and civil Discord cease;
> Oh! never may arrive that fatal Day,
> When She shall cease her soft maternal Sway!
> Tis thought a dread Attempt by bravest Men,
> To rouze the dormant LION from his Den![41]

Amongst the general subscribing membership of the Society, which at the opening of the conflict was nominally over one and a half thousand— though two-thirds of this total were in arrears with their subscriptions— there must have been the same division of opinion. The government itself was represented by Lord North, the Prime Minister, the Earl of Dartmouth, Lord Privy Seal, Viscount Weymouth and the Earl of Hillsborough, successive Secretaries of State, the Earl of Sandwich, first Lord of the Admiralty, Viscount Barrington, Secretary at War, and by the Duke of Montagu, Viscounts Bateman and Beauchamp and Lord John Murray, all loyal noblemen. The opposition had an equally impressive group of peers amongst the membership. The Duke of Grafton, the Duke of Portland, the Marquess of Rockingham, the Earl of Darlington, Earl Spencer, Earl Verney and Viscount Palmerston were all to be found in the lists of the Society. The Duke of Chandos, also a member, is an example of an eminent nobleman who varied in his opinions on the American conflict.

Prominent ex-members whose opposing views on the American question were notorious and whose association with the Society was made permanent by Barry in 1778 were Edmund Burke and Samuel Johnson. With them in the same painting Barry placed Mrs. Montagu, the senior lady member, who had commented in 1774, 'America is our child, and a very perverse one'.[42] Barry himself had published an aquatint in 1776 called *The Phoenix; or, The Resurrection of Freedom*, which showed Algernon Sidney, John Locke and other Whig heroes mourning the death of liberty in Britain, and across the waters in America the three graces dancing before the temple of Liberty. In his paintings for the Society's meeting room he signalled his support for the American cause by portraying Pitt the Elder as Pericles in the *Olympic Victors* and giving the personified figure of the Continent of America in the *Triumph of the Thames* an expression of anger. To his account of *The Distribution of Premiums in the Society of Arts* he appended a footnote containing a quotation from a French periodical, which contrasted the beneficial ideals of the Society's members with the evil work of their fellow countrymen who 'forged iron fetters for America, and thunderbolts to set the world ablaze'.[43]

Yet twenty-eight of the members at this time held military or naval rank, and though some of these had retired from active service by 1775— Admirals Hawke, Knowles and Pocock and General Oglethorpe are examples—there were those whose duty it was to fight for King and country. Such were Admiral Lord Howe, who commanded the North American station from 1775 till 1778; Colonel Archibald Campbell, who, having been captured by the rebels in Boston at the start of the conflict, was subsequently exchanged and took command of the successful expedition for the reconquest of Georgia in 1778; and most illustrious of all, Major General George Eliott, the hero of Gibraltar, elected a Vice President on 4th December 1782. Yet the peacemakers were also represented. The Secretary of the Peace Commission, Caleb Whitefoord, was, as we have seen, a member, and so also was the Chief Commissioner, Richard Oswald.

The dichotomy in the attitude of the Society is well illustrated in the circumstances surrounding the publication and distribution of the cumulative *Register of Premiums and Bounties* in 1778. The 'Observations on the rewards bestowed in the class of colonies and trade', which were placed at the conclusion of the third section of the *Register*, contained a re-assertion of the Society's belief in the value of the navigation system:

> The Society, influenced by the tenor and spirit of sundry acts of parliament, subsisting for more than a century past, and being of opinion, that to encourage in the British Colonies the culture and produce of such commodities as we must otherwise import from foreign nations, would be more advantageous to the navigation and commerce of this kingdom, than if the like things could be raised within the island of Great-Britain, have liberally extended their premiums and bounties for sundry articles suited to the climates and circumstances of the North-American provinces.

The observations concluded, however, with an implied criticism of the war—though whether the colonists or the Administration were to blame was left unstated: 'The success [of the Society's premiums] bore a most favourable aspect when their further correspondence with North-America was interrupted by the present unhappy disputes.'[44]

The preparation and publication of the *Register* was largely the work of the Society's Committee of Correspondence and Papers, with Joshua Steele in the chair. His anonymous letter to Franklin, which we have already partially quoted, accompanied a copy of the *Register*. Steele explained that it was 'not sent to you by the Society at large, but by your Friends and Men of Honour, who know you are entitled thereto as a perpetual Member and who do not see any particular clause in the Capture, Prohibitory, or, as I may say, in the Amputation Act, that should restrain them from giving you these Philosophical Rights.'

Yet Steele had presided at the meeting of the Committee on 7th March 1778 which passed the following resolutions:

> Resolved that a Copy of the Register of Rewards, be handsomely bound
> in Turkey Leather of English Manufacture to be presented to
> The King, by the President.

> Resolved that it be inscribed to His Majesty in the following words
> To The King
> This Register of Rewards bestowed by the Society for the
> encouragement of Arts, Manufactures and Commerce, together with short
> observations on their Effects is, with all Duty and Humility, inscribed
> by his Majesty's
> most faithful and
> loyal Subjects
> The President
> Vice-Presidents
> and Members.[45]

Veneration for the person of the monarch as distinct from approval or disapproval of the activities of his ministers was to become an established policy for institutions such as the Society of Arts, and it served the Society well on this occasion.

We have already noted the effect of the conflict on the premiums awarded by the Society in the class of colonies and trade. The last award made to the Continental colonies, as opposed to the West Indies and the Mosquito Shore, was for the import of indigo from East Florida in 1774. No North Americans seem to have claimed any of the Society's awards between 1773 and the Canadian hemp campaign of the early 1800s. The Society's Committee of Colonies and Trade became nearly moribund during the course of the conflict. It dutifully recommended the renewal of the Society's American premiums down to 1777, when it proposed to omit the word 'American' from the offers for cotton, annatto and indigo. Instead of the announcement in the premium list reading, for example, 'For the best specimen of Indigo, made in His Majesty's Dominions in America or the West Indies . . . the Gold Medal', they proposed the wording 'made in his Majesty's dominions in the West Indies'. This suggestion was disallowed by the Society. By 1780, however, it had concurred in the Committee's desire to cease offering American premiums. Thus the 1779 list was the last to offer medals for American wines and vineyards. The colonial section of the list was still headed 'Premiums offered for the Advantage of the British American Colonies', and this remained the case until 1783, when the phrase 'Premiums offered for the advantage of the British Colonies' was adopted.[46]

The recognition of the loss of America did not mean an end of the Society's mercantilist attitude to the Colonies, and ambitious schemes for the economic development of the Empire were undertaken in the early nineteenth century. In the newly independent American states public premiums continued to be offered for nationally valuable produce, and it is a fitting epilogue to this story to recall that the first American to be elected as a Corresponding Member of the Society in the post-revolutionary period was Alexander Hamilton.[47]

APPENDIX. Americans Named in the Society's List of Members, 1st August 1777

I. Corresponding Members
*Allen, James, Esq., of Philadelphia
*Barclay, Gilbert, Esq., of Philadelphia
†Barrel, Mr. Nathaniel, of Portsmouth, New Hampshire
 Bestley, Mr. Isaac, of New York
‡Bland, Dr. Theodore, of Causam, Virginia
‡Bowdoin, Hon. James, of Roxbury, Massachusetts Bay
 Burd, Samuel, MD, of New York
 Carey, Mr. Samuel, of Boston, New England
 Condey, Rev. Jeremiah, MA, of Boston, New England
†Dalrymple, Col., of Fort Johnson, North Carolina
†De St. Pierre, M. Louis du Menil, of New Bourdeaux, South Carolina
*Erving, Mr. George, of Boston, New England
*Fairfax, George William, Esq., of Belvoir, Virginia
†Fauquier, Francis, Esq., FRS, of Virginia
*Ferguson, Hugh, Esq., of Philadelphia
*Franklin, William, Esq., of the Jerseys
‡Gale, Mr. Benjamin, of Killingworth, Connecticut
*Garden, Alexander, MD, of South Carolina
‡Gardiner, Silvester, MD, of Boston, New England
†Griffin, Dr. Corbyn, of Norfolk County, Virginia
*Hall, Mr. Elihu, of Wallingford, Connecticut
 Hammond, John, Esq., of Maryland
*Harrison, Joseph, Esq., of New Haven, Connecticut
*Harrison, Peter, Esq., of New Haven, Connecticut
†Heron, Benjamin, Esq., of Cape Fear, South Carolina
*Ingersal, Jared, Esq., of New Haven, Connecticut
 Irwin, Thomas, Esq., of Boston, New England
*Jay, Sir James, Knt., of New York
*Kearny, Capt. Michael, of Monmouth, New Jersey
 Lawson, Alexander, Esq., of Maryland
‡Lee, Arthur, MD, of Williamsburg, Virginia
 Lee, Thomas, of Boston, New England
‡Livingston, Philip, Esq., of New York
*Loocock, Mr. Aaron, of Charles Town, South Carolina

Mascarene, John, Esq., of Boston, New England
Miller, Joseph, Esq., of Boston, New England
‡Morgan, John, MD, FRS, of Philadelphia
*Oliver, Hon. Peter, of Middleborough, Massachusetts Bay
*Paterson, Capt., of New York
†Pollock, Cullen, Esq., of Edenton, North Carolina
†Quincy, Mr. Edmund, of Boston, New England
Rogers, John, Esq., of Boston, New England
‡Rush, Dr. Benjamin, of Philadelphia
*Rutherford, John, Esq., of Cape Fear, North Carolina
‡Schuyler, Philip, Esq., of Albany, New York
†Shirley, Mr. Thomas, of Charles Town, South Carolina
*Skene, Major Philip, of Wood Creek, New York
†Smith, Benjamin, Esq., of South Carolina
*Smith, Thomas, Esq., of South Carolina
*Smith, Rev. Dr. William, of Philadelphia, North America
†Tennet, John Van Brugh, MD, of New York
°Waln, Nicholas, Esq., of Philadelphia
*Woodmason, Mr. Charles, of South Carolina

II. Subscribing Members
‡Farley, Samuel, Esq., of Georgia
‡Franklin, Benjamin, LLD, FRS
‡Madison, Mr. James, of Williamsburg, Virginia
*Mercer, George, Esq., of North Carolina
*Robinson, John, Esq., of Boston, New England
‡Stirling, William Alexander, Earl of
*Tryon, Colonel William

*Loyalist.
†Dead or likely to be dead before the revolution.
‡Revolutionary.
°Neutral.

Note: The styles and addresses of the members are those given in the 1777 list.

14

SOME NOTES ON THE GERMANIC ASSOCIATIONS OF THE SOCIETY IN THE EIGHTEENTH CENTURY

Hans-Joachim Braun

The reasons which made German inventors of the eighteenth century apply to the Society of Arts were manifold. A great number of them knew about the Society's Premium lists which circulated in Germany and were often reprinted in German journals. As in England, people in Germany became more and more interested in problems of agriculture, manufacture and commerce. In contrast to England, however, these activities in Germany were mainly the result of efforts made by the State and not so much an enterprise of the citizens themselves. There were exceptions, of course, such as the work of the Patriotic Society of Hamburg. This Society was closely modelled on the Society of Arts, and private initiative played the dominant rôle in its foundation and remained decisive during the whole time of its existence.[1]

Reading the reports of German travellers who went to England during the eighteenth and the beginning of the nineteenth centuries, one finds much praise for English life and institutions, praise which was often so lavish that historians speak of an 'Anglomania'.[2] Sophie von La Roche, who visited England in 1786, expressed her enthusiasm for the 'Volun-

Originally appeared in *Jnl. RSA*, 119 (June, July, 1971), 476-79, 558-62.

tary Society for the Improvement of Agriculture and the Arts'. She was delighted with its repository as well as with its efforts for afforestation in England and showed a keen interest in the Society's system of offering premiums. 'Noble land', she wrote, 'where the virtue of humanity is recommended and extolled.'[3]

Normally the traveller's reports quickly pass over the darker sides of the Industrial Revolution and devote most space to praise of the English constitution, democracy, liberalism or philanthropy. Compared with Germany, England had a considerable attraction for scientists and scholars interested in political, economic and social problems. In almost all books on England, the following differences between the two countries were stressed:

1. England possessed a great number of able manufacturers, businessmen and tradesmen. This was mainly due to the fact that in England only the eldest son inherited the title and the estate. The other sons could go into industry and commerce, where they were often quite successful, mainly because of their good education.
2. Inventors praised English patent laws, which gave them the opportunity of drawing profit from their inventions. In Germany, patent laws did not come into existence until 1877.
3. There was a recurrent complaint about guilds in Germany. Whilst in England they had lost their influence by the eighteenth century, they were still an important factor in German industry, often restricting the activity of able artisans.[4]

Quite a few German inventors wanted merely to obtain a particular premium. Others thought that the Society might be interested in an invention they had made, even if a premium had not been offered for it. Another category—if one tries to classify them—did not mention any financial reward at all. This does not mean, of course, that these inventors were completely averse to the idea of being rewarded or that they were more diffident than the others. A reward was certainly an attraction, but in some cases the ideal of free communication of knowledge was the prevailing factor. In these cases, tangible reward played quite a minor rôle.

In a recent article W. H. G. Armytage, a historian of education, talks about 'the Common Market of Science' in the eighteenth century.[5] In that century, liberal interchange of knowledge was indeed a reality. Scientists and scholars of every rank and denomination regarded themselves as living in a 'community of mind', a 'republic of scholars',[6] so to speak, in which national interest played a subsidiary part.

The Society of Arts had quite a considerable number of German correspondents. I shall confine myself to mentioning only a few, who actually had a bearing on industry in England. It seems to me that in this context dye-stuffs (especially cobalt), crucibles, and paper made from vegetable material were of particular importance. An article on paper-making was contributed to this series by Professor Coleman in 1959, so I can confine myself to a few sentences on this topic.[7]

To start with dye-stuffs: from its foundation, the Society of Arts was concerned with madder. At its second meeting in 1754, it offered a premium of £30 'for raising and curing no less than 20 lb. of madder'.[8] Of particular interest was the method of dyeing cotton Turkey red, a process which was probably first practised in India and afterwards used by Greek dyers in Turkey.[9] Already in 1693, an Augsburg dyer, Jeremias Neuhofer, had applied this method successfully, and by the mid–eighteenth century it was known throughout Germany. This accounts for the fact that letters of several German dyers can be found in the Society's archives. Johann Heinrich Scharff from Göttingen, a town which had a famous university and close connections with England, owned several dye-houses and had a good reputation in Germany.[10] In November 1758, Scharff wrote to the Society of Arts telling it that the Haarlem Society had offered a premium of two hundred ducats for cotton of a Turkey red colour, which was of quality equal to the material imported from Turkey, Arabia and East India.[11] The Haarlem Society, however, had deferred its decision about the award of the prize to March 1759. So, in the meantime, Scharff turned to the Society of Arts, hoping to receive a financial reward from it. The Society, however, was only interested in dyeing Turkey red in England and so did not give a reward to Scharff. In June 1760, a premium of £50 was offered 'for dying Cotton Yarn of the same red Colour, as that which is dyed in Turkey, and which like the Turkey will keep its Colour after many repeated washings'.[12] In 1761 and 1764, two English dyers received £50 and £100 respectively for dyeing Turkey red, but this process did not spread far in England afterwards.

Another problem was that of dyeing silk Turkey red. Dyeing silk proved to be more complicated, and French dyers especially tried to find a method which would make this possible. The Frenchman Macquer was one of the first to succeed in this, and a description of the process was published in 1768. Macquer immersed the silk first in a diluted mordant and then in cochineal. He thus separated two processes which were usually done together and so succeeded in dyeing silk a fast red. The theory of dyeing commonly held in the early eighteenth century was mechanical, insofar as it was assumed that particles of the dye entered the pores of the dyed material. The retention of the dye was explained as due chiefly to the action of cold in contracting or closing the pores of the fabric, thereby imprisoning the colouring matter in the texture of the material.

Macquer was not satisfied with this theory and thought that some chemical process was involved, an idea which was later taken up by Berthollet, who contributed to a theory of chemical affinity. A. Wolf in his authoritative *History of Science, Technology and Philosophy in the 18th Century* names Macquer as the first to succeed in dying silk Turkey red.[13] It seems, however, likely that the German Baron Beust had already achieved this a few years earlier. In 1762 he wrote to the Society of Arts, addressing it as the 'Society of Arts and Sciences', that neither in England nor in Europe had there been found a method of dyeing silk a purple colour. 'However of late', he continued, 'it is happily discovered a way to dye this colour in silk, that it not only will stand Proof against the air and sun, but even if it is put in lemon, Wine, or Vinegar, it will not lose the last from its real beauty; it is to be done at a trifling expense, without Cochenille or Indigo, and the materials required are plentifully to be had in this kingdom.'[14]

It was not until 1765 that the Society invited the Baron to show his method of dyeing silk purple before the Committee of Chemistry. In the Minutes we read that the experiments were 'deemed . . . worthy the further consideration of the Society having stood the trials with Lemon Juice and Vinegar as proposed by the Baron's letter without any material alteration'. It was resolved 'that the Baron's Crimson Dye is worthy the further attention of the Society'.[15]

On 14th December 1765, a motion was made and agreed to that the Committee of Chemistry should ask the Baron if he was 'willing to discover his Secrets in Dying and upon what Terms, and the committee was given full power to negotiate with the Baron'.[16] The Baron, however, refused to disclose his secrets, giving the reason that they would thereby come to the knowledge of other countries. After this, the Society was of course no longer interested in the Baron's method of dyeing silk, as its aim was to spread knowledge of the process over the country.

The Baron's refusal is not difficult to understand: the Seven Years' War, which ended in 1763, must have been fresh in his mind, and the feelings especially of the German nobility towards France were not very warm. He probably knew quite well that various efforts had been made in France to dye silk a fast red. The application of his method in this country would have led to similar developments in France, to the disadvantage of Prussia.

The Baron, however, could not prevent Macquer's finding the process by himself and spreading the information all over France.

In the Society of Arts' endeavours for cobalt, a German scholar, Johann Gottlieb Lehmann from Berlin, had quite an important share. In 1754, a premium of £30 was offered for the best quantity of cobalt (not less than 20 lb.) produced in England. Cobalt ore was required for the production of its silicates zaffer and smalt, which impart a beautiful blue colour to glass. In 1753, a total of over 200,000 lb. of smalt was imported into England, so that the Society had a strong motive for its interest in the discovery of cobalt mines in Britain.[17]

As English scientists had neglected cobalt so far, the Society decided to apply to German scientists as well, the first time it addressed itself to a foreign country. In Germany, cobalt mining had a long tradition, especially in Saxony. Already in the first part of the seventeenth century there were a number of cobalt works in the area.

In the Royal Society's *Philosophical Transactions* for 1726 we find an explicit commentary on cobalt and the associated minerals by J. H. Linck, a German naturalist of Leipzig, who was a busy correspondent of several learned societies. He gives a detailed description of the mineral cobalt and comments on the uses of zaffer and smalt.[18]

After giving a premium of £30 to Francis Beauchamp of Pengreep, who had found cobalt on his estate, the Society of Arts in May 1756 offered 'a gold Medal worth 20 Guineas as a reward to the author of the best Natural History of Cobalt'.[19] There were only five entries, and the winner was Dr. Johann Gottlieb Lehmann. Lehmann was Doctor of Medicine and Prussian Councillor of the Mines in Berlin. In 1761, he was appointed Professor of Chemistry at the University of St. Petersburg, and four years later, in 1765, he travelled through the provinces of Russia busy with mineralogical studies.

In his letter to the Society, Lehmann wrote that he had been concerned with cobalt for more than three years and that he possessed a collection of more than 300 cobalt pieces.[20] In this he was quite typical of an age in which collecting and collections were very popular indeed. Almost everything was collected and classified. One of the most famous examples in this context is Linnaeus.

Lehmann asserted in his letter that his main intent in writing to the Society was to be useful to it, not to receive a prize. The remark can be taken at its face value. Though he certainly did not reject the gold medal given to him, there is no reason for doubting the sincerity of his words and his feeling of belonging to an international body of scientists.

Cobalt mining in Cornwall was, however, not as successful as the Society might have wished. One of the greatest difficulties was to recognize the metal, which was always closely connected with other minerals. In spite of these difficulties there are hints that cobalt mining was carried on in Cornwall at the end of the eighteenth century.[21]

Another matter which concerned the Committee of Chemistry was the supply of crucibles. Until the middle of the eighteenth century, they were imported from abroad, mainly from Germany. The Society, however, tried to introduce their manufacture into England, and from the 'Observations on the effects of Rewards bestowed in the Class of Chemistry, Dyeing and Mineralogy', which the Society published in the first Volume of its *Transactions,* we learn that in Chelsea crucibles were not only made for use at home, but that considerable quantities were exported as well.[22] The Society was interested in enlarging the manufacture of crucibles, and from 1757 onwards offered premiums for producing them of British materials equal in fineness to those previously imported.

Already in 1756, the Society had received a letter from Johann Christian Erffurt, a German chemist, who lived in Chelsea.[23] This letter contained a certificate 'signed by six different persons on the goodness of crucibles made by John Christian Erffurt of Chelsea'. It was certified that these six persons had tried Erffurt's crucibles and had found that they were 'in every respect according to the use of each of [them]' and that they believed 'that none had been made heretofore in England so good as these'.

Not Erffurt, however, but Johann Seiffert received the first premium given to a German artisan for making crucibles. In 1759, he obtained £30 after numerous trials of his products and those of other manufacturers.[24] Three years later, in 1762, another German artisan, Jacob Lieberich, applied to the Society, with the information that he had established a manufactory for the making of crucibles in Masham Street, Westminster, 'which had cost him some paine and Great Expence'.[25] He submitted half a dozen crucibles to the Society for trial and offered to produce a quantity sufficient to supply all England. The trials showed that the quality of his crucibles was quite satisfactory, and Lieberich was given a bounty of 20 guineas. In 1766, he received another bounty of £50.[26] On the whole, one can say that German manufacturers of crucibles played an important part in establishing this manufacture in England.

Only a few words need be said about paper-making. During the eighteenth century, there was throughout Europe a shortage of linen rags for the production of paper. So inventors were forced to think of other materials which could be used. As early as 1716 a book was published under the title *Essays for the Month of December 1716, to be continued Monthly, by the Society of Gentlemen. For the benefit of the People in England.* In this it was proposed to produce paper from raw hemp, and a description of the process was given. In Germany, it was chiefly two scholars, J. C. Schäffer and J. Claproth, who were busy trying to find new materials for paper-making.

Schäffer, for instance, made experiments with nettles, straw, wood, moss, wasps' nests and other things. It was easy to supply him with straw or wood; the wasps' nests were inevitably more difficult to obtain, and Schäffer was often mocked about this. In 1768 he was awarded a silver medal by the Society of Arts, after having—in 1766—communicated his method of making paper without rags.[27] Schäffer says in his letter that Mr. Cole, a member of the Society of Arts, had visited him in Ratisbon, where Schäffer lived, and that Cole had suggested that he should enter into correspondence with the Society.[28]

Another German scholar, J. Claproth, Professor of Law at the University of Göttingen, was the inventor of a method 'to make old printed paper new again by entirely defacing and abluting the block print'. Claproth sent a manuscript in which he described the process to the Society of Arts, but the Society does not seem to have been very interested in it.[29] Mathias Koops, probably a German from Hamburg, however, who possessed a paper manufactory at Mill Bank, made use of Schäffer's as well as of Claproth's method. In 1800 and 1801, he was granted patents for re-making used paper and for producing paper from vegetable material. Hunter, a historian of paper-making, holds that Koops was responsible for the growth of the paper industry as it is to-day.[30]

RELATIONS WITH GERMAN SOCIETIES

In the eighteenth century, the Society of Arts had connections with almost all major economic societies in Europe, as its archives prove. If one examines these links, there appears to be a relationship of giving and taking, from which both sides could profit. On the whole, however, the Society of Arts was the giver, the distributor of knowledge, and in most cases, foreign societies first turned to the Society in London for information. One instance in which the Society of Arts took the initiative was concerned with winter-growing forage plants. It entered into a correspondence with major societies on the matter and tried to find a crop which would be green and nutritious in the latter half of the winter. The proposal was even made to collect winter-growing forage plants from northern regions such as North Russia and Lapland, because it was supposed that the plants might stand the less frigid temperatures in England.[31]

The Society of Arts' inquiry about winter-growing plants aroused quite a good response; among other forage plants timothy and gorse especially were recommended.[32] Of special interest were comparative trials with drill husbandry and broadcasting, and the Society tried to learn as much as possible about the outcome of these trials in other countries. One of the members of the Economic Society of Berne in Switzerland, Schmidt von Rossau, wrote to the Society of Arts on the subject of winter pabulum for cattle.[33] Schmidt von Rossau was not a farmer, but a scholar, whose main fields of interest were history, theology and the religion of Ancient Egypt. He had written numerous treatises on these subjects, and in 1762 he became Professor of Ancient History at the University of Basle. Apart from historical and theological problems, he was concerned with agriculture, a combination which, in the eighteenth century, was not as strange as it may seem to us to-day. At the beginning of 1764, Schmidt left Switzerland and accepted an offer made to him by the Margrave Karl Friedrich of Baden-Durlach, of whom I shall treat later. Schmidt was well aware of innovations in agriculture, and he was a busy correspondent of the Society of Arts.

If one compares the years of foundation of the societies in Britain and Germany, one finds that the first German society was instituted in 1763 in Thuringia. This society, however, was only of minor importance. The first economic society in Britain was the 'Society of Improvers in the Knowledge of Agriculture' founded in Edinburgh in 1723; but again it does not seem to have been very active, to judge by its proceedings, parts of which were published under the title *Select Transactions*.

More important was the 'Dublin Society for Improving Husbandry, Manufactures, and other useful Arts' founded in 1731, a body with which a few well-known German scientists had close links: J. L. Hildebrandt received a gold medal for his treatise on work-houses in 1765,[34] and prominent in the field of mineralogy were N. G. Leske, Professor at Leipzig and owner of the famous cabinet of mineralogy, and K. L. (afterwards Sir Charles) Giesecke, who in 1813 was appointed Professor of Mineralogy to the Dublin Society and who played an important part in the progress of mineralogical research in Ireland. Giesecke made extensive tours in Greenland, where he collected minerals and made charts.

Though economic societies in Germany came into being later than in Britain, there were already plans for establishing them at the beginning of the eighteenth century. In 1701, the philosopher Leibniz wrote on the occasion of the foundation of the Berlin Academy that 'one should aim at utility. Not only the arts and sciences are important but also the improvement of land and people, agriculture, manufacture and commerce'.[35] As to their purpose, the German Academies of that time can be compared with the Royal Society of London for the Improving of Natural Knowledge. Their interest was to a large extent theoretical and 'academic', but they often tried to derive practical use from their work as well. The German scientist von Rohr, however, accused the academies of dealing only with matters which gave pleasure to the scientists, and of neglecting those of practical benefit to the country.

The situation altered with the foundation and growing activity of the German Economic Societies. The most important of these, the Society at Leipzig, had relatively close connections with the Society of Arts. The Leipzig Society was founded in 1764 and was quite successful in the propagation of new agricultural methods, various sorts of crops and grasses, as well as model farms and schools. Like most of the other societies, the Leipzig Society was mainly concerned with agriculture, though it had a committee of manufactures and committees of mineralogy, chemistry and mechanics also.

Hans Hubrig, a German historian, divided the Economic Societies into 'Patriotic Societies', mainly concerned with manufacture and commerce and essentially mercantilist in their aims, and 'Economic Societies', mainly concerned with agriculture.[36] In the activities of the latter, he maintained, a physiocratic concept was often prevalent. As to Patriotic Societies, it must be made quite clear that in this context patriotism is not to be equated with nationalism. The kind of patriotism meant here was directed inwards rather than outwards. Its first aim was the promotion of the countries' welfares.

Now this classification of Hubrig's is, as he has to admit himself, rather debatable, as all clear-cut classifications of historical phenomena are, but if we provisionally accept this distinction, the Leipzig Society has to be regarded as an Economic Society. Quite a large part of its members were noblemen, who co-operated with craftsmen, tradesmen and owners of manufactories. As these noblemen had no intention of reforming the old feudal system, the societies' work was not as effective as it would have been if reforms had taken place.

In September 1766, D. G. Tachselt, Secretary to the Leipzig Society, tried to establish a connection between Leipzig and the Society of Arts. In his letter, he spoke of the 'patriotic aims which both societies have in common', admired the 'sublime patriotism' of the Society in London and asked it to send its reports to Leipzig, which the Society of Arts undertook to do.[37] The Leipzig Society took up the idea of the Society of Arts' repository and established a similar one, which contained mainly implements used in agriculture. In this repository, we find among other things a model of Thomas Perren's 'Machine for Spinning, Doubling, and Twisting, as well as a model of Hales's ventilator'.[38] Seyfert, who was the Leipzig Society's correspondent in London, procured various sorts of seeds, especially timothy grass and burnet, which were grown in the area around Lübeck with considerable success.

A rather interesting figure in the Leipzig Society was Siegmund Leberecht Hadelich, who was also a correspondent of the Society of Arts. Hadelich was Mayor of Erfurt in Thuringia and Professor of Philosophy and Economic Science at the University. Like Schäffer and Claproth, Hadelich was interested in the problem of substitutes for rags, which were commonly used in the manufacture of paper. Because of the lack of wood in the region around Erfurt, this city had to import wood from foreign countries for a considerable sum of money. As a remedy against this, Hadelich made experiments with other burnable materials such as sulphur, vitriol and bituminous earth. He used flax for producing canvas, cables, and threads and became quite well known for his 'German cotton', a substitute for normal cotton.[39]

Hadelich tried to interest the Leipzig Society in this new kind of cotton, but the Society was slow in taking up his suggestions and was probably rather doubtful about their value. So, in July 1766, he wrote to the Society of Arts, informing it of a new kind of cotton wool of which he sent a specimen. He offered to communicate to the society the whole process of manufacturing this cotton, in return for a premium or an annual retainer.[40] Hadelich was well informed about the activities of the Society of Arts and its endeavours to obtain cotton from the American colonies. His letter was read to the Committee of Manufactures on 14th October 1766, and it was resolved 'to desire him to send an account of the tree from whence the cotton is got, or to send a specimen of the tree itself, and to send any other instruction he thinks proper'.[41]

In his reply, Hadelich gave a description of the cotton, which the Committee of Manufactures found to be not 'of a staple to be manufactured here to advantage'.[42] It was decided to inform Hadelich that his cotton as well as other matters he had mentioned in his letter were not worthy of any future attention by the Society.[43]

On 15th December 1766, Hadelich wrote another letter to London in which he complained about the slow reception of inventions in Germany and offered his 'German cotton' again.[44] Hadelich is an example of an inventor turning to a foreign country because his inventions were neglected in his own. 'All regions in Germany', he wrote, 'complain about lack of money and food. But can one be astonished about this if every year 1,137,800 Taler are, to the greatest disadvantage of the population, spent on cotton wool from other countries, whilst nature has provided large quantities of cotton in Germany itself.'[45] He went on to complain about the money which had to be paid for French, English and Dutch cotton.

Hadelich's attitude in this matter is self-contradictory. On the one hand he urged an increase in the German domestic production of cotton to save the money which must otherwise be spent on importing it, and on the other he offered his 'German cotton' to England, a country which already exported large quantities of ordinary cotton to Germany. Hadelich asked the Society of Arts for a quick reply and said that he would try to sell his new cotton in Holland if he did not soon get satisfaction from London. It is quite apparent that his motives were self-seeking. He was also disappointed and irritated by the neglect of his inventions in Germany. These personal feelings, however, are only to be found in comparatively few of the letters sent to the Society of Arts by foreign correspondents.

Of common interest to both the Society of Arts and the Leipzig Society were the endeavours for the promotion of bee-keeping and 'quilting in the loom'. The Society of Arts began offering premiums for quilting in 1761 and was quite successful in propagating this new kind of weaving. The Leipzig Society was informed about the Society of Arts' activities and its success in this field and tried to establish quilting in Saxony. In its *Transactions* the question was asked 'if there was a skilful craftsman, who was able to manufacture this kind of cotton of which a description was given'.[46] This advertisement did not remain unanswered. Two owners of manufactories offered to apply the method of quilting. One of them said that once in 1741 he had produced cotton by quilting, but as this product had attracted only few customers, he had had to give it up.[47] Now the situation had changed, however, and with the encouragement of the Leipzig Society, which realized that by 1760 quite a lot of money had to be spent on imported goods manufactured by this method, this weaver took up quilting again. Here is an instance of the Society of Arts' influencing a German Society and thereby having an effect on a special branch of industry in Germany.

Another German Society to be considered here is the 'Society for Improving Agriculture' founded at Celle in Lower Saxony in 1764. This Society had particularly close links with England and was very interested in the Society of Arts' work. The initiative for its foundation came from George III, King of England and Elector of Hanover. As is well known, George III was very interested in agricultural matters himself and was to be found quite often in the fields, having discussions with farmers.

Though Hanover did not take part in the Seven Years' War (1756-63), it suffered from the far-reaching economic consequences of the conflict and needed to improve its agriculture. So the Privy Councillor von Behr, who lived in London, having the function of a Hanoverian Minister, received the King's order to contact Jobst Anton von Hinüber, who was known as an experienced farmer and had travelled in England for a long time, thereby gaining a good knowledge of English husbandry. Von Hinüber owned a model farm near Hanover, where he practised new farming methods he had observed during his stay in England. It was through his extensive collection of books and pamphlets on agriculture that Albrecht Thaer, the 'German Arthur Young', as he was called, came into contact with English innovations in husbandry.

In 1764, the Society of Celle was established, with Rules and Orders modelled on those of the Society of Arts. Though there are only two letters preserved in the Society of Arts' archives written by von Hinüber on behalf of the Celle Society (one dating from 1761[48] and the other from the following year[49]), the Transactions of the Society of Celle prove that it was well acquainted with the work of the London Society and with English agriculture as a whole. In his first letter to the Society of Arts, von Hinüber mentioned that he had 'seen through the Channel of Newspapers that that little Insect called weevil is in England no less than here [in Germany], a destroyer of the Granaries, and that the only true method of purifying the Granaries of these noxious animals is unknown'.[50]

German newspapers of that time had rather an important share in distributing knowledge of English agriculture, and by the end of the eighteenth century quite a considerable number of these papers were in existence. As to the problem of weevils, von Hinüber recommended the work of Dinglinger, a writer on agricultural problems, who had received a reward of 25 ducats from the Patriotic Society of Hamburg. Dinglinger's method, however, was not considered very effective by the Society of Arts' Committee of Agriculture. In the Minutes of this Committee, we read that on 30th January 1769, 'Mr. Hinüber's letter relating to a granary for corn was read and postponed to further consideration'.

To judge by the Minutes, there seems never to have been any further discussion on this topic. This is not surprising, as the method proposed by Dinglinger was rather elementary, and though it was awarded a prize at

Hamburg, it seems doubtful if it was really effective. It merely consisted in 'promoting the free passage of the air upon the floor and through the corn. The Weevil cannot bear a thorough air'. Von Hinüber, however, asserts that in spite of the simplicity of the method, he was a witness of the usefulness of this expedient, having tried it with success.

As English horse-hoes and ploughs were superior to the German ones, Hinüber's friend, Albrecht Thaer, who had a large share in spreading agricultural innovations in Germany, tried to find an artisan able to reconstruct English agricultural implements. In this he succeeded, and so Small's Rotherham plough and Ducket's trenching plough—the latter had been awarded a bounty by the Society of Arts in 1769—were remodelled by an able artisan and soon became popular in Germany. As Small's plough was very suitable for ploughing on marshy land, the Celle Society ordered a considerable number of them to be manufactured at the Einsiedel iron works in Saxony and to be given to farmers in the marshes of North Germany.[51]

English ploughs were propagated also by the Society at Karlsruhe. Its president was the Margrave Karl Friedrich, a follower of physiocratic principles. The Margrave tried to apply these principles to his country but failed because Baden-Durlach did not lend itself to these methods, being a land of small farms and not big estates, which were demanded by the physiocrats. Apart from this failure, the Margrave was very active in economic matters. Already at the age of 15, in 1743, he had travelled through Europe, visiting Switzerland, France, Belgium, Holland and England. His travels had very little in common with the well-known 'Grand Tour' of the Princes and well-to-do young people of the eighteenth century. Already during his early journeys, the Margrave was interested in agricultural and industrial innovations. He attracted well-known scientists and inventors to his court at Karlsruhe and was a member of various Economic Societies. In 1765, he founded the 'Society of useful Sciences for the Advancement of the Common Good'.

Samuel Schmidt von Rossau and J. J. Reinhardt, two correspondents of the Society of Arts, played a decisive rôle in Karlsruhe. In his correspondence with the Society of Arts, Schmidt asked for fruit trees to be sent to Karlsruhe, where a tree nursery was being established. Unfortunately, the trees sent did not arrive there, as Schmidt mentioned in three letters to the Society of Arts. There were trees from England in the tree nursery at Karlsruhe, however, as can be learned from a letter which Reinhardt, a friend of Schmidt's, wrote to the Leipzig Intelligence Paper in 1765.[52] Reinhardt was among other things concerned with schools of industry, and he established several of them in the area of Baden-Durlach, using English schools of industry as models.

In the manuscript transactions of the Karlsruhe Society, we find numerous discussions among members of English innovations in general and the Society of Arts in particular. The Premium List of the Society of Arts of 21st April 1762 was discussed extensively, and agricultural matters figure especially.[53]

The last society I shall deal with is the Patriotic Society established at Hamburg in 1765. This body was modelled on both the Society of Arts and the 'Société royale d'agriculture de la généralité de Paris', founded in 1761. The founder of the Hamburg Society, Pauli, wrote to the Society of Arts that 'he always considered this body as the wise and enlightened mother to a weak child, who is in need of a good education'.[54] He asked the Society of Arts to send its publications to Hamburg and proposed to issue a journal, to which inventors and philanthropists of all parts of Europe could contribute.

Pauli had a good example in William Shipley and mentioned him in a small book published in 1765 under the title *An Encouragement to all true patriots of Hamburg to establish a Patriotic Society for the Encouragement of Arts, Manufactures and Commerce similar to the Societies in London and Paris.*[55] Pauli, who was well aware of Shipley's Northampton fuel scheme, took the initiative to erect various storehouses for wood, peat and coal. In summer, when these materials were cheap, Pauli filled the storehouses with fuel, and in winter he sold it to the poor at the same price. On the model of Shipley's drawing school, Pauli founded a school in 1767. This drawing school started with the instruction of sixteen young craftsmen in design for industrial purposes. The number of pupils increased quickly, and the school enlarged its curriculum by adding physics, chemistry, mechanics and other subjects.

The premiums offered by the Society at Hamburg were often for the same objects as those of the Society of Arts. The Hamburg Society was in possession of the Society of Arts' Premium Lists and studied them at its meetings. Yet it would certainly be wrong to assume that the Patriotic Society offered premiums for certain inventions for the sole reason that the Society of Arts had done so before. One has to take into account that the economic conditions of the two countries were different, and so it might be necessary to promote quite different matters. It seems likely, however, that the Patriotic Society adopted certain ideas for premiums where these seemed to be of use to Hamburg as well. Unfortunately, the Minutes of the

Hamburg Society were destroyed by fire, and so this conjecture cannot be substantiated.

Among the premiums offered by both the Society of Arts and the Patriotic Society were those for dying Turkey red, sal amoniac, for madder, flax, hemp, timber, bleaching and saw mills. A link between the Society of Arts and the Patriotic Society of Hamburg was established by the Count von Berchthold, who, by his contemporaries, was called 'the German Howard'. Berchthold had travelled through Europe for thirteen years and through Asia and Africa for four years, always trying to relieve the most pressing social needs or distributing the means of alleviating distress among the people. During his journeys, his favourite places of call were the Economic Societies, where he could be sure that his ideas would receive well-deserved publicity. He visited the Society of Arts as well as the Patriotic Society, presenting to them his writings and models of various life-saving apparatuses. To the Society of Arts, he gave a 'Model of a Boat and Apparatus for assisting Persons in Danger of Drowning by the breaking of Ice'.[56] This boat had been invented by Thomas Ritzler of Hamburg, and its use was encouraged by the Patriotic Society.[57]

Berchthold succeeded in establishing a public repository near Vienna, where all the important life-saving devices could be collected. Such philanthropical interests were, with other motives, an essential influence behind the Economic Societies of the eighteenth Century.

Berchthold's eulogy of the founder of the London Society of Arts was quoted by D. G. C. Allan in his *William Shipley*. This tribute from a German Count to an English artist may serve as a fitting conclusion to these notes: 'Thrice happy the country which can boast . . . a Shipley'.[58]

APPENDIX. German Corresponding Members of the Society of Arts in the Eighteenth Century *

Albert Karl Ludwig Graf Gaisberg, Baden
Johann Bernoulli, Berlin
Hans Moritz Graf von Brühl, London
Johann Sebastian Clais, Baden
Detlev Karl Graf von Einsiedel, Wolkenburg
Johann Reinhold Forster, Göttingen
Joseph Gärtner, Tübingen
Karl Graf von Heithausen, Silesia
Johann Gottlieb Lehmann, Berlin
Jobst Anton von Hinüber, Marienwerder

Ludwig Alexander Friedrich Graf von Itzenplitz
Johann Franz von Lichtenstein, Frankfurt
Margrave Karl Friedrich von Baden-Durlach
Hofrat Medicus, Mannheim
F. H. Niemann, Hanover
Friedrich Wilhelm Graf von Reden
Johann Jacob Reinhardt, Baden
Heinrich Rigal, Mannheim
Joseph Rosa, Dresden
Johann Seiferth, Göttingen
Johann Peter Ernst von Scheffler, Danzig
Friedrich Samuel Schmidt von Rossau, Karlsruhe
Peter Siegmund Friedrich Stegmann, Berlin
Baron von Stosch, Berlin
M. Treuer, Baden
Georg Friedrich Wehrs, Hanover
Jeremias Woldyke, Jena
Nathaniel Matthäus Wolff
Johann Zorn, Kempten

*List of Corresponding Members of the Society of Arts, London, 1762 ff.

15

COUNT FRANCESCO ALGAROTTI
AND THE SOCIETY

George Truett Hollis

At the Society's meeting at Devil Tavern, Temple Bar, on 22nd December 1762, the name of 'Francis Count Algarotti' was proposed as a Corresponding Member by Vice President Edward Hooper, Esq., who was presiding.[1] Francesco Algarotti (1712-64) was noted as one of the most gifted and versatile figures of the Enlightenment. A friend of Voltaire and the geometrician Maupertuis, the Venetian-born Algarotti was Chamberlain to Frederick the Great, who gave him the title of count in 1740 soon after he had joined the new king's court in Berlin. Algarotti was a poet as well as a prolific writer on a wide range of subjects, from Newton's theories of optics to the reform of opera.[2] From 1742 to 1747 he served as adviser to Augustus III, King of Poland and Elector of Saxony, on the selection of Italian paintings for the picture gallery in Dresden. In 1749 Algarotti left Frederick's court again to return to Italy because of ill health. Continuing to write essays and to maintain a large correspondence, he finally settled in Pisa, where he shared a villa with a painter friend, Mauro Tesi.

Algarotti's proposed membership in the Society was 'balloted for' at the next meeting on 29th December 1762, and he was elected a Corresponding Member.[3] Later in the same meeting the Minutes record:

Originally appeared in *Jnl. RSA*, 124 (Aug., Sept., Oct., 1975), 605-8, 668-71, 728-30.

An Extract of a Letter from Wm. Taylor Howe Esq. to Thomas Hollis Esq. dated Pisa Nov:r 21:st 1762 was read, giving an account that the celebrated Count Algarotti was going to publish at Lucca *an Essay on Painting*, which he dedicates to *The Society instituted at London for promoting Arts Manufactures and Commerce;* on Account of the Protection and Encouragement which that Noble Society now gives to that Art. The Dedication to the Society was inclosed in the Letter by the Count's Order. Likewise was inclosed *an Epistle* in Blank Verse *upon the benefits of Commerce*, which the Count presents to the Society and hopes they will accept in respect to the Subject, as being the principle cause and characteristics of Great Britain's Superiority over other Nations.

Mr. Lockman being desired to translate the above-mentioned Dedication by Count Algarotti was pleased to give his consent.[4]

The timing of Algarotti's election followed immediately by the announcement of the dedication to the Society of a tract on painting in Italian to be published in Italy by one not previously connected in any way with the Society seems curious.[5] It prompts several questions. Why did Edward Hooper and not Thomas Hollis, who was the obvious link to the Italian essayist, sponsor Algarotti? What circumstances or who prompted the dedication of the *Essay on Painting* to the Society?

The Society member most interested and active in the committee on 'Polite Arts' was Thomas Hollis.[6] He undoubtedly persuaded Hooper to present Algarotti's name for membership since he himself would have to present the dedication to the Society sent to him by William Taylor Howe.[7] Hollis had been in correspondence with Howe, a young Englishman travelling in Italy.[8] Howe was not a member of the Society, but through Howe as intermediary, Thomas Hollis arranged for the dedication of a new and enlarged edition of Algarotti's important essay on the reform of opera (*Saggio sopra l'opera in musica*) to William Pitt and the dedication of a new edition of his essay on painting (*Saggio sopra la pittura*) to the Society. These dedications were commissioned as compliments and support for the ideals of an individual and an institution in which Thomas Hollis fervently believed.[9] As was his practice, he sought to keep his part in these commissions anonymous.

In his letter to Howe in Pisa, dated 'Pall Mall, dec. 28, 1762' (the day before the Society's meeting at which Algarotti was elected a Corresponding Member and his dedication to the Society presented), Hollis reports to his intermediary in Italy on the progress of the dedication to William Pitt and concludes:

On Friday, or this day sixnight, you shall hear from me again, concerning the remaining part of your Commission.

My compliments being presented, respectfully to the Count [Algarotti], & affectionately to Yourself, I bid you heartily farewell,

Thomas Hollis [10]

His next letter to Howe exactly one month later commences with a summary of events regarding Algarotti and the Society. The letter is quoted in its entirety since it deals with 'the remaining part of your Commission', i.e., the dedication of Algarotti's *Saggio sopra la pittura* to the Society.

Pall Mall, jan. 28, 1763

Dear Sir,

The translation was read in the Society wednesday the 19th, and universally applauded; and the thanks of the Society were unanimously voted to Count Algarotti, to be communicated to him, with his election as a corresponding member, by letter by the Secretary. At the ensuing meeting, that letter was read, according to rule, and approved; [11] and I have the honor to inclose it to You.

My Commissions are now ended. Both of them were delicate, the first especially. They have been conducted in the best manner I could imagine and with the greatest dispatch; and if the Count & You should be satisfied with the proceedings, I shall rejoice. 'L'Epistola in versi sopra il Commercio' is much commended by our ablest judges, for the elegance of its composition & of the extensiveness & beneficence of its views; and all agree, that the 'Saggio sopra la pittura' is likely to prove a master and most *useful* performance.

For me, a plain man, as You well know, little judge of learning or its refinements, who aim[s] only at probity and benevolence, I can but present my unfeigned respects to this accomplished and renowned Gentleman, with deepest thanks for his favors.

Now and ever I am and shall be

Dear Sir,

Your affectionate friend
and most obedient servant
T. Hollis [12]

Thus Thomas Hollis had accomplished what he set out to do: to honour a national political leader and the Society by connecting their names with the works of a well-known writer whose publications were likely to have a wide circulation. He could be well pleased with his double coup. It had taken quite some time to arrange matters properly for the dedication to the Society. Algarotti signed the dedication 'Bologna 17 Marzo 1762'. His name was not proposed to the Society until 22nd December 1762, and the dedication was not presented until 29th December, after his election. The transaction had, indeed, been 'delicate'.[13]

The dedication itself is a paean to the English nation and a solicitation for patronage of a national school of painting by the Society. It contains a précis of the essay, as well. In no other dedication does Algarotti express such personal interest, perhaps because he himself was an artist and perhaps also because of his admiration for English society and institutions. The dedication to this important aesthetic and didactic tract reads:

To the Society instituted in London for promoting arts manufactures commerce

Francesco Algarotti

When Rome had extended her empire into Asia, Africa, and almost over all Europe, she saw her citizens arrived at the summit of military glory. In their pretensions to science, however, the Romans gave place to the Greeks, whom they revered as their masters in the School of Arts.

England hath established her dominion by settling as numerous and more distant colonies; while conquest hath displayed the ensigns of her power and extended her commerce throughout the whole world. Equally respectable in arts and arms, the English nation claims the superiority also in the world of Science; particularly with regard to the cultivation of those arts, which contribute most to the strength and splendour of a state. These are Agriculture and Architecture; one the sovereign mistress of the polite arts, the other a nursing mother to all. Painting, indeed, hath but recently engaged the attention of the English so far as to inspire them with a design of contending with the Italians, for those honours of which the latter have long boasted an exclusive possession. The design is, nevertheless, become formidable, in being promoted by a Society, among whom superiority in place is only the tribute due to superior merit; a Society, instituted by a free people, and composed of the choicest public spirits of their age and country, who, while they generously encourage the best artists, excite emulation in others, by exhibiting the works of all to public view; therein appealing, even from their own judgment, to that of a learned, ingenious and sensible nation.

Under so distinguished a patronage, it is hardly possible this elegant art should not soon flourish in London, as it hath done in the milder climates of Parma, Venice and Rome.

In the mean time, that I may not be wanting, in my best endeavours, to restore painting to its former splendour in my own country, I have attempted, in this Essay, to investigate its first principles; and to point out those studies, which are requisite to form a compleat painter, all which the ancient masters, therefore, actually cultivated. What benefit may hence result to my countrymen, I presume not to determine: I am not conscious, however, of doing anything with which I ought to reproach myself, altho', incapable of

exciting their zeal, I should awaken so noble a spirit in the breasts of foreigners, or should even furnish them with the means of disputing with us, the
prize in view. Motives of universal philanthropy ought, doubtless to prevail
over partial and local attachments to particular men of countries.

Permit me also to add, that, if our Italian painters are soon to be excelled
by the English, in the practice of their profession, it behoves us, at least, to
shew that we are not inferior to any people in the world, in the knowledge
of its theory: so that even our rivals may willingly be instructed by us in the
art, which hath been the delight and study of every polished and ingenious
nation, in all climates and in all ages.

Bologna, March 17, 1762 [14]

Algarotti thus pays tribute to the Society for its encouragement of the
arts, particularly through the Exhibition of Paintings at the Society in the
spring of 1761.

Count Francesco Algarotti responded from Pisa on 28th February 1763
to the Society's letter informing him of his election as Corresponding
Member and thanking him for the dedication to the Society of his forthcoming book on painting.[15] Society activist Thomas Hollis had forwarded
the Society's letter to Algarotti through his intermediary William Taylor
Howe, then travelling in Italy. Algarotti graciously accepts the honor of
'Corrispondente' as a compliment to all Italy and states that he will soon
send 'la mia operetta', the *Saggio sopra la pittura*, then being published in
Livorno.

The book, however, was several months in arriving from Italy. In the
meantime Algarotti had been informed by Howe of Hollis's rôle in the
commissions for the dedications of the new editions of the *Saggio sopra
l'opera in musica* to William Pitt and the *Saggio sopra la pittura* to the
Society. On 2nd February 1763 Algarotti dedicated his new book, *Saggio
sopra l'Accademia di Franchia che è in Roma*, to Hollis, 'the only Dedication and this against his consent and knowledge'.[16] Still smarting at being
publicly recognized, Hollis writes to Howe on 10th May 1763:

> I do acknowledge that I might & *ought* to have wrote [*sic*] to You earlier
> concerning the dedication. I did not however, certainly, see that matter in the
> same light when I wrote my last two letters as I do now; was much hurried
> then & before; and did apprehend, tho' injudiciously, I should have been
> in time to have prevented the publication of it. That prevention I sought for
> reasons heretofore given,[17] and I was sincere in them, and for this further
> reason, That the Count ascribed more merit, much higher merit to me, in
> the Dedication, as a member of the Society, the noble Society for promoting
> arts & commerce, than fell to my share; arising from his too partial opinion

of me, & his not having been sufficiently apprized of the real State of the Society and its members, many of which members had rendered the same service to the Society that I had done, full out, and several of them much greater.[18]

Finally, the parcels containing Algarotti's three essays on painting, opera and the French Academy in Rome, published in Livorno, arrived in London in July. Thomas Hollis set about dispersing them. His diary entry for 20th July 1763 reads, in part: 'Buisy [sic] all the morning farther in preparing the parcells from Count Algarotti. . . . With Dr. Templeman [Secretary of the Society] to deliver him two parcells from Count Algarotti, one for the Society, & one for himself.'[19] To Howe, in whose boxes the parcels had been shipped, Hollis writes a full report on 2nd August and, incidentally, identifies Edward Hooper, Esq., one of the Society's Vice Presidents and sponsor of Algarotti. The lengthy letter is quoted in large part because of the light it sheds on the dissemination of Algarotti's tracts in England and the activities of Society members. The books arrived in two separate shipments; the first on the ship *Beverly,* the second on the *Groignard.*[20]

On the Groignard's coming out of Quarantain I immediately procured the parcel containing the Copies of the *Essay on the Opera in music,* and dispersed those copies according to the directions which had been given to me, and my best judgment. Soon after, I put into the Post with my own hand, a letter which Dr. Templeman had written to Count Algarotti on occasion of the copy of the Essay that he had been pleased to bestow on the Soc. for prot. arts & comm. The two copies left to my disposal I presented, one to the British Museum, the other to Dr. Akinside [physician to the Queen and poet]; and forwarded a letter of thanks from the Trustees of the British Museum to Count Algarotti for their copy not long after.

Your boxes were opened at the Custom house, from a general order in such cases, nor was that circumstance avoidable, and all the things were taken out, & the books weighed, and a duty of £3..6.. set on them, and a curious fan-mount declared to be prohibited merchandise, and, by strictness of law, to be burned. But on giving in a petition to the Commissioners, that the whole was the property of a studious, excellent English gentleman, tho' unfortunately an invalid, on his return from Italy; the boxes were ordered to be delivered *free of duty or restriction of any kind,* & they were afterwards disposed of in the manner related in my letter of July 22. This unusual, polite, & well-understood behaviour was principally owing to a very accomplished Gentleman & leading Commissioner, Edward Hooper, Esq., who knew the exception to a general rule, & to seperate [sic], distinguish the Baggage, trifles of a gentleman, from the goods, entries of a Trader. . . .

From Dr. Templeman I shall forward a letter to Count Algarotti, as it comes to hand, having had the regular sanction of the Society, in the course of a week or Fortnight.

The seven copies of the *Essay on the French Academy* which were left to my disposal, have been distributed as follows. To the British Museum; together with a copy of the *Essay on painting,* begged to that end of Dr. Templeman. The Bodleian & Radclif libraries, Oxford. The University library, Cambridge. The public library of the University of Glasgow. The Advocate library, at Edingburg, and The public library of the University of Dublin.

. . . *The Essay on painting* must figure eminently everywhere; but here, to the majority of our Artists, who are untravelled & struggle under greater inconveniences in many respects than those of most Countries that are civilized, it will guide & form them exceedingly; nor can our most finished Gentlemen peruse it without instruction & delight.[21]

In writing directly to Algarotti on 9th August, Hollis reports again on the distribution of the essays and describes them as 'master-productions, ALLOWED, of ability, elegance and beneficence'.[22] He encloses the letter from Dr. Templeman as promised.

The *Saggio sopra la pittura* is probably Algarotti's most important and most original essay.[23] In it he combines the various requirements for the education of a good painter and critic with discussions on the essence of painting. The originality of the work, however, consists in the clear exposition of the aesthetic problem. He affirms for painting the principle of ideal imitation that is 'more philosophical, more instructive, and more beautiful than the real'.

Within a month of the arrival of Algarotti's essays in London, an English edition of the *Saggio sopra la pittura* was advertised. Thomas Hollis took note. In his diary entry for 9th August he records: 'At Lockyer Davis's to desire him to cause the *Essay on painting* of Count Algarotti, now translating for publication by his order to be well translated.'[24] To William Taylor Howe, then at Spa, he writes on 13th September: 'Soon after the Treatises had been presented to the Society an advertisement for the publication of a translation of the *Essay on painting* appeared in the public papers. On inquiry, I found, that Lockyer Davis, a bookseller of eminence in Holbourn was the author of that advertisement & the intended publisher of that work.'[25]

Others were interested in Algarotti's essay dedicated to the Society. From Switzerland Rodolph de Valtravers, a Corresponding Member of the Society, writes to Dr. Templeman on 5th October 1763:

Count Algarotti's Essay on painting is not yet come to my knowledge but hope to get it soon from Prof. [Abbé Johann J.] Winkelmann at Rome. A Society erected for the Encouragement of that as well as other liberal arts, deserves the Homage of that learned & ingenuous Nobleman, & will find many a useful Hint and observation, to distinguish the several Degrees of Perfection in that noble Art.[26]

The critical reception of *An Essay on Painting* (London, 1764) was very favourable. *The Monthly Review,* after remarking on the difficulty of the task, praises the work and its author highly.

It would, indeed, be something strange if that philosophic spirit, which hath of late years diffused itself into almost every branch of science, as well moral as physical, should not exert some influence in favour of the polite arts. The Essay before us is, in fact, a proof that it really has: the noble and ingenious Author having treated his subject with the same philosophical spirit and precision, that he might have used in solving a metaphysical problem.[27]

As to the English translation, the reviewer deemed it 'very unworthy of the original'.[28] The name of the translator is not given. Perhaps the same 'Mr. Lockman' who translated the dedication for the Society also translated the Italian text for the publisher as well.[29]

In 1769 the *Saggio sopra la pittura* in its final version of 1763 with the dedication to the Society was translated into French along with the essay on the French Academy in Rome.[30] The same year it appeared in German, accompanied by Algarotti's essays on architecture and on opera.[31] Thus its dissemination in four languages also carried the name of the Society and one of its activities, the support of the visual arts through an annual exhibition and premiums, to a wider audience, linked with the name of one of its more illustrious Corresponding Members.

Algarotti's rôle as 'Corrispondente' was severely handicapped by his debilitating illness, phthisis. In his last letter to the Society, dated Bologna, 6th September 1763, Algarotti explains his not answering the Society's letter of June because of his illness for three months. He credits his recovery, in large part, to the approval shown by the Society and the English nation to his works and to the manner in which that has been signified 'by one Englishman [Howe] and one Society member [Hollis]'.[32]

On 24th June 1764 Algarotti died at Pisa, aged fifty-two. On receiving the news, Thomas Hollis writes to a friend that he is 'in great affliction' over the death of the Count whom he had planned 'to have employed on a treatise for the service of the public, on a subject he had desired of me.'[33]

On 14th November 1764 Hollis received a parcel from Italy containing three sets of a new edition of Algarotti's complete works which the Count had forwarded in April before his death. One set was a present to William Pitt, another to Thomas Hollis, and the third set a present to the Society, a final tribute to the 'illustre Accademia' from the 'late accomplished and beneficent Algarotti'.[34]

Francesco Algarotti's death at Pisa on 24th June 1764 ended a brief but significant association with the Society as a Corresponding Member in Italy. The dedication to the Society of his important *Saggio sopra la pittura* (Livorno, 1763; English translation, London, 1764, with title of *An essay on painting written in Italian by Count Algarotti F.R.S., F.S.A.*) proved a worthy contribution and certainly gave cause for high expectations.

One member of the Society who had plans in mind for the employment of Algarotti's considerable talents was Thomas Hollis, Esq. The editor and compiler of the *Memoirs of Thomas Hollis* describes the relationship of the two in the following terms:

> Count Francesco Algarotti was a learned, polite, and accomplished noble-man, chamberlain to the king of Prussia, a friend and correspondent of Mr. Hollis, whom the count highly esteemed, and became (upon Mr. Hollis's recommendation, it is believed) fellow of the . . . society for promoting arts and commerce. Mr. Hollis, on his part, was not behind the count in esteem and affection, stiling him one of the most accomplished and benefi-cent gentlemen in Europe.[35]

In writing to a friend concerning Algarotti's death, Hollis indicates not only his grief but also his aborted plans for the commission of a new work.

> I am in great affliction at present on the news just received of the death of count Algarotti, which happened lately at Pisa, with whom I have been united for some time in an intire friendship, and whose great abilities, knowl-edge of the world, and good mind, I was just going to have employed on a treatise for the service of the public, on a subject he had desired of me, to which he of all others, it is probable, was most equal.[36]

Several questions come to mind immediately. How was it that Algarotti had desired a 'subject' from Thomas Hollis? What was the subject of this 'treatise for the service of the public' which Hollis envisioned for the cele-brated Italian count's 'great abilities, knowledge of the world, and good mind'? What would be so challenging that only Algarotti 'of all others, it is probable, was most equal'?

The first of these questions can be answered by a letter from Algarotti to 'Tommaso Hollis a Londra', dated 'Pisa 5. novembre 1763'. Algarotti writes:

In consequence of all this [friendship, gifts of books, commissions for two dedications, etc.] I entreat you to command me, to regard me from now on as your minister, commissary and agent in Italy . . . and most happy particularly I would be, if I could ever give you some sign of that profound gratitude and esteem with which I have the honour to sign![37]

As to the second and third questions, one must conjecture a bit since Thomas Hollis did not give a specific title for the 'treatise' he had in mind for Algarotti to write. In this writer's opinion, it was related to 'The Treatise on the Arts of Peace' for which the Society had unsuccessfully offered a prize in 1761.[38] Hollis was on the committee to judge the entries in the contest and took a personal interest in getting two of the best English writers to undertake it.[39] Entries in his diary show the extent of his involvement:

[December] 17 [1761]. . . . At Mr. Payne's [the bookseller] to desire him to engage Mr. [Samuel] Johnson to write a Dissertation on the polite & liberal arts; their use & benefit to civil life & manners, to commerce; the State of them in this Nation; the views of the Society, the noble Society for promoting arts & commerce in respect to them; the success of those views already, & the future expectations from them. Gave him Five Guineas to present to Mr. Johnson for writing the Dissertation & one Guinea for himself. Dined at the Devil tavern alone.

[December] 18 [1761]. . . . At a Committee of polite arts till late.

dec. 21 [1761]. . . . Then Mr. Payne to acquaint me, that Mr. Johnson declines writing the desired Dissertation as not sufficiently informed of the several matters to which it must relate. On considering the matter farther with Mr. Payne, desired him to engage Mr. [John] Hawksworth to write it.

jan. 3 [1762]. . . . Mr. Payne with me for an hour in the morning to read to me the Dissertation written by Mr. Hawksworth, mentioned dec. 21; in which, unhappily, he has not succeeded.[40]

The compiler of Hollis's *Memoirs* concludes his summary of the affair thus:

Mr. Hollis does not say in what respect Mr. Hawkesworth failed. The ingenious authors of the Rambler [Johnson] and Adventurer [Hawkesworth] were certainly, in point of abilities, equal to the task; and yet perhaps there were not two men in the kingdom less likely to answer to Mr. Hollis's ideas of such a performance. But there we leave it.[41]

But did Thomas Hollis 'leave it' there? The relationship cultivated with Algarotti through William Taylor Howe in Pisa and his subsequent actions seem to indicate that he did not abandon the idea of the 'Dissertation on the polite & liberal arts'. After commissioning Algarotti to dedicate the new edition of his *Saggio sopra la pittura* to the Society and securing Algarotti's membership in the Society, Hollis even proposed that Algarotti visit England. In a letter to his intermediary Howe, dated 'Pall Mall, Sept. 13, 1763', Hollis explains:

> The public will be highly obliged to you for the proposed new & very fine edition of the works of so elegant & valuable an Author as Count Algarotti. But might that work not be jointly carried on here in England?
>
> The Count is a Citizen of the World, is not tied, it may be, to any spot, is in highest esteem, I apprehend, amongst our ingenuous & first People; and, by a change of climate & nation for a time, might, it is possible, better his Health, & pass that time in a new & yet not unacceptable manner.[42]

That Algarotti seriously considered the invitation is reflected in Hollis's letter to Howe on 20th December 1763: 'I rejoice exceedingly that Count Algarotti is so well & established & has his thoughts of visiting this Country.[43]

Algarotti became the recipient of additional gifts of books and prints sent to Italy by Hollis. He busied himself in October and November 1763 'preparing books & tracts . . . intended to be sent, with others, to Count Algarotti of Bologna as a present' and writing notes in the books. In January 1764 he sent another 'small parcel of books, which are designed as a further present to Count Algarotti'.[44] In a letter to William Taylor Howe dated 6th March 1764, Hollis reports: 'Count Algarotti has written to me in a very obliging manner concerning the Prints & Bagatelli which you had assigned to him'.[45]

The last gift to Algarotti was sent in May 1764. It arrived after Algarotti's death in June. To his friend Thomas Jenkins,[46] English painter and dealer in antiquaries in Rome, Hollis writes:

> Add this favour to many others, to accept chearfully whatever may come to you from Leghorn that was first intended for Count Algarotti. The contents are books, with a few prints, many of them scarce, many of them curious, many of them singularly bound, and all of them intended for the entertainment and use of that accomplished and beneficent gentleman, and for the honor of Old England. There are many loose notes in the books; read them, if you will, alone; and then burn them immediately. The death of the Count, with whom I became linked in an entire friendship, has afflicted me exceedingly.[47]

Thus were Thomas Hollis's hopes dashed for the realization of a 'treatise for the service of the public' to be written by Algarotti in England, passing his 'time in a new & yet not unacceptable manner', in a task that he 'of all others, it is probable, was most equal': 'a dissertation on the polite & liberal arts'. Certainly Algarotti, the enlightened author of essays on painting, architecture, opera reform, etc., was the ideal choice for such a work. One can readily understand Hollis's statement to Howe in his letter of 6th July 1764: 'Few lament the loss of the late most accomplished, beneficent Count Algarotti, particularly or publicly than I do.'[48]

The loss is the Society's and ours as well. The Society might have had its sought-for 'Treatise on the Arts of Peace', and we might have had a major assessment of the arts in the eighteenth century by a contemporary observer and participant, the ingenious Algarotti.

16

EARLY CONTACTS OF THE SOCIETY
WITH RUSSIA

A. G. Cross

In two articles published in the *Journal of the Royal Society of Arts* in December 1965 and December 1967 Professor J. A. Prescott described the founding of the Russian Free Economic Society in St. Petersburg two hundred years previously and the example and stimulus afforded by the Society of Arts in its organization and activities. He outlined the particular contribution which was made by Count Jacob Johann Sievers (1732-1808), who presented a memorandum to the Empress Catherine II in 1765, drawing attention to the English society, the birth of which he had himself witnessed over a decade earlier while serving in the Russian Embassy in London. After many years in state service Sievers retired and devoted himself to, among other things, the rearing of silk-worms. He contributed a paper on the subject to the *Transactions* of the Society of Arts in 1798 and was elected to Corresponding Membership on the strength of it.[1] Sievers was not, however, the first and certainly not the last Corresponding Member of the Society residing in Russia. The number of such members testifies to the very real scholarly exchange which existed between England and Russia at the end of the eighteenth century and which can be amplified from the records of other learned bodies, such as the Royal Society, the Society of Antiquaries, the Board of Agriculture and many Scottish

Originally appeared in *Jnl. RSA*, 125 (Mar., Apr., May, 1976), 204-7, 256-58, 334-36.

societies. In this article on the Society of Arts' contacts with Russia in the eighteenth century, attention will be focused on the identities and activities of the Society's Corresponding Members in Russia; two remarkable Russians who were elected subscribing members of the Society during their long residence in London; and the account of a meeting of the Society in April 1785 and the description of the Great Room and Repository which are contained in an unpublished Russian manuscript.

The corresponding members included both Russians and Britons in influential positions in Russian service. Of the four Britons elected, three were Scottish and doctors, and two, one a Scot and the other the only Englishman, were recipients of gold medals from the Society. The first to be elected, on 30th April 1755, was James Mounsey (1700?-1773), of Lochmaben in Dumfriesshire, who entered Russian service in 1736 as a *lekar*, or surgeon.[2] After gaining his M.D. at the University of Rheims in 1740, he rapidly gained promotion in Russia and finished his career there in 1762 with the position of *arkhiater*, or head of the Russian Medical Chancery. Although Mounsey was a doctor of undoubted skill and great knowledge, his interests ranged widely and his varied communications to the Royal Society brought him election to that body in March 1749. His contributions were presented to the Royal Society and his election engineered by his friend of long standing, Henry Baker, who was also a founder-member of the Society of Arts. Baker sponsored Mounsey's election to the Society and passed on suggestions which Mounsey made concerning ways of stimulating the sale of British goods abroad. In a letter, dated Moscow, 7th November 1759, Mounsey opined that British craftsmen were too concerned with niceties and intricacies and neglected 'a pleasing variety' which would appeal to foreigners. He further suggested to the Society that 'Proper Consuls, and some young brisk intelligent Lads sent under their Protection, might I think give constant Intelligence how to suit British Manufactures to foreign Markets'.[3] In 1762, shortly after the accession of Catherine the Great, Mounsey returned to Britain, carrying with him a box of seeds of the 'true rhubarb', *Rheum palmatum,* which was to cause great excitement among medical men and learned societies and bring Mounsey his modest measure of immortality. Robert Dossie, beginning his 'Account of the late Introduction of the True or Palmated Rhubarb, into Great Britain' with the remark that 'the importance of Rhubarb, as an article in the *Materia Medica,* is too well known to require any discussion here', noted his own representations to the Society of Arts in 1760 'to pursue the requisite measures of introducing the culture of the true rhubarb' and mentioned the rôle of Mounsey.[4] Dossie's lengthy article was only

James Mounsey; engraving by G. E. Schmidt, St. Petersburg, 1762.
Courtesy of the RSA.

one of a veritable flood of communications on rhubarb to appear in such
publications as the *Philosophical Transactions* of the Royal Society, the
Memoirs of Agriculture and the *Letters and Papers in Agriculture, Plant-
ing, &c* of the Bath Society for the Encouragement of Agriculture, Arts,
Manufactures and Commerce, between 1765 and the end of the century.[5]
In 1763 the Society of Arts had set up a committee to do what Dossie had

asked; in 1769 it awarded Mounsey a gold medal for 'having introduced the seed of the true rhubarb some years before'. The Society distributed some twenty medals, gold and silver, over the next quarter of a century for the successful cultivation of true rhubarb.[6]

The Society's second Corresponding Member in Russia was Dr. John Rogerson (1741-1823), a relation of Mounsey's and persuaded by him to seek his fortune in Russia shortly after completing his M.D. at Edinburgh in 1765. It was possibly Mounsey who suggested Rogerson's name to Henry Baker as a good man to fill the gap left by his own departure from Russia, and Rogerson was elected on 25th June 1766.[7] Rogerson was to remain some fifty years in Russia, achieving a reputation which far eclipsed Mounsey's, due largely to his position as body physician to Catherine from 1776 until her death twenty years later. He enjoyed similar eminence under her successors, Paul I and Alexander I, before retiring finally to Scotland in 1816. Despite the recognition and trust he earned as a physician and the numerous honours he gained from both Russian and British learned societies, Rogerson has left no legacy as a writer or scholar; he was esteemed as a worldly, civilized man, more as a diplomat and courtier than as the contributor of scholarly papers. The Society of Arts might have found a better correspondent but no one better connected or more influential.[8]

The third Scots doctor, Matthew Guthrie (1743-1807), who was elected in 1792, was much more in the Mounsey mould.[9] Guthrie left Scotland for Russia in 1769 and spent the rest of his life there, pursuing a successful career primarily as a physician to the First and Second Corps of Cadets in Petersburg. Unlike Rogerson, to whom honours of an academic nature came unsought, Guthrie initiated correspondence with learned societies and scholars and encouraged election to membership. A fellow-countryman, Sir John Carr, visiting Russia in 1804, described Guthrie as 'a gentleman of the most amiable manners, a philosopher, and well known to the world for his various scientific and literary productions'.[10] Guthrie indeed ranged widely in his interests and writings and published an impressive number of books and articles in journals. He published papers on various scientific topics in the *Transactions* of the Royal Societies of London and of Edinburgh, in the *Memoirs* of the Literary and Philosophical Society of Manchester and in the *Trudy* ('Works') of the Russian Free Economical Society. He was a member of all four bodies. In addition he was a Corresponding Member of the Society of Antiquaries of Scotland, and in the year following his election to the Society of Arts, he became a corresponding member of Sir John Sinclair's Board of Agriculture. Between 1792 and 1794 he sent no fewer than fifty contributions under the pseudonym of 'Arcticus' to *The Bee,* a journal edited in Edinburgh by James Anderson. He brought out a work on Russian antiquities (1795) and edited and supplemented his wife's *Tour through the Taurida, or Crimea* (1802). These titles do not exhaust all that he wrote, and it remains a matter of surprise that, as far as is known, the Society of Arts never received a contribution from him.[11]

The Society did receive and print a contribution from Robert Hynam (1737-1818), Watchmaker to the Court in St. Petersburg, to whom it had awarded a gold medal in 1796. The award was made for Hynam's instrument for gauging the cutters for wheels in clocks and watches on condition that he send the Society the complete instrument together with the calculations he had made for it. Hynam eventually complied and received his medal; his letters, tables and plates were printed in the *Transactions* in 1799, the year in which he was elected a Corresponding Member.[12] Hynam had worked in Russia since 1776 and sired a whole line of Hynams who became imperial clockmakers. Apart from the many superb clocks and watches which he made, Hynam produced the standard Russian weights and measures and from 1811 until his death was the director of the factory of official standard measures in St. Petersburg.[13]

In addition to the four Britons briefly characterized above, the Society elected two Russians to corresponding membership in the eighteenth century. One was Sievers, and he was preceded in 1792 by Count Friedrich von Anhalt, who was at that time President of the Russian Free Economic Society.[14] Anhalt was the first serving President of the Russian Society to be recognized by the Society of Arts, and it seems curious that none of his immediate successors was invited after his death in 1794. The next elections of Russians as Corresponding Members date from 1804, when Aleksandr Aleksandrovich Vitovtov (1770-1840), Secretary of State under Alexander I, and Andrei Fedorovich Deriabin (1770-1820), at the time Head of the Department of Mines in the Urals, were honoured.[15]

RUSSIAN SUBSCRIBING MEMBERS

In addition to the Society's Corresponding Members in Russia, both Russian and British, there were also three Russians who were subscribing members during their residence in London in the eighteenth century. The first was Count Ivan Grigor'evich Chernyshev (1726-97), who arrived in London in November 1768 as Russian Ambassador Extraordinary and returned to Russia the following summer. He was a founder-member of the Free Economic Society of St. Petersburg and became the first member of that society to be elected to membership of its English counterpart. His election took place on 31st May 1769 with Henry Baker once more prominent among the sponsors.[16] Scathingly characterized a decade later as 'Anglois à l'enthousiaste sans savoir pourquoi', Count Chernyshev was charmed by his reception in England and always retained a veneration for all things English and a continuing interest in agriculture and husbandry.[17] Of more immediate significance, however, are the activities of the later Russian subscribing members.

Father Andrei Afanas'evich Samborskii (1732-1815) was elected on 21st March 1774, and Father Iakov Ivanovich Smirnov (1754-1840) on 27th March 1782.[18] The two men had much in common: both were Ukrainians who were initially recruited for service in the Russian church in London as assistants to the chaplain, and both were subsequently ordained and succeeded to the chaplaincy. Samborskii arrived in 1765 and became chaplain in 1769; in 1776 he personally recruited Smirnov, who succeeded him on his return to Russia in 1779. Samborskii saw Smirnov as his protégé and 'worthy successor', and both men were bound by the ties of close friendship and shared interests. These interests went far beyond the theological and pastoral and brought them into contact with the leading figures in English cultural and social life. Both men were convinced Anglophiles and throughout their lives did much to foster and maintain good Anglo-Russian relations. Samborskii lived for fifteen years in England until his return in 1779, and he made one further short visit in 1784; Smirnov arrived as a young man of 21 and, once he became chaplain, never saw his homeland again during the remaining sixty years of his life.

Smirnov not only inherited Samborskii's position as chaplain but also his wide circle of English friends and acquaintances, including many who were prominent members of the Society of Arts. It is not without interest to note that the Russian chapel was situated between 1757 and 1786 in Burlington Gardens on Clifford Street, where the first President of the Society, Lord Folkestone, and one of the first Vice Presidents, Lord Romney, had townhouses. Samborskii's membership was sponsored by Jean Magalhaens and Smirnov's by Thomas Mortimer, but the members for whom they had perhaps the greatest esteem were Arthur Young and John Arbuthnot, two outstanding examples of the 'practical' and 'rational' English farmer. Samborskii was inspired with high ideals of effecting a great agricultural revolution in Russia, along English lines, which would ensure the prosperity of peasant and landowner alike and bring people nearer to God by the contentment gained from a life in tune with nature. As he was to write to Alexander I in 1804, his system had always been one of 'the religion of the Gospels and the religion of the countryside, from which come good morals and industriousness'.[19]

Shortly after his election to the Society, Samborskii conceived the plan of bringing to England a group of young Russians who would study agriculture under Young and Arbuthnot and then return to spread their knowledge and expertise throughout the Russian empire. In a petition which he presented to Catherine the Great in 1775 he outlined the course of study which they would take, on the completion of which 'my colleagues could be admitted, following my example, as members of the Economic Society [as he called the Society of Arts], which includes the most learned men, and become acquainted with their inventions'.[20] The Empress granted his wish, and among the group of six students with whom he returned from Russia in 1776 was Smirnov, one of three students specifically recruited to combine service in the church with their agricultural pursuits. The students studied for a year at Mitcham with Arbuthnot and then went farther afield, singly or in twos and threes, to gain experience with Young in Suffolk, with Robert Bakewell at Dishley Grange in Leicestershire, in Kent, Hertfordshire and elsewhere. Only Smirnov in fact eventually became a member of the Society of Arts, as Samborskii had hoped, but another, Ivan Komov, was elected a corresponding member of the Bath Society in 1780. The students, with the exception of Smirnov, who remained behind as chaplain and whom Young hailed as the ablest of the group, returned to Russia in 1784 to become 'professors of agriculture'. They were appointed as assistants to the Directors of Economy in various regions of the Empire, in Moscow, Kiev and the southern Ukraine, and put their skills to good use. Several of them published articles and books in which they passed on information about English methods and adapted them to Russian conditions. Samborskii himself had returned to Russia in 1779 'carrying from Mr. Younge's house, in Suffolk, ploughs, harrows, and other implements of agriculture' and with hopes of establishing a school of practical agriculture near Petersburg.[21] He was appointed, however, to a series of positions with members of the Imperial family, which frustrated his plans. Only in 1797, in the reign of Paul I, was a school set up along the lines projected by Samborskii, and he was appointed its first director. The experiment was only partially successful, and Samborskii himself occupied his post for less than two years before his appointment as domestic chaplain to one of the Tsar's daughters. Nevertheless, despite the continual disappointments and frustrations which he encountered, he played an important if hitherto unsung rôle in aiding the spread of English agricultural methods and techniques in Russia.

Smirnov remained in England, continuing and widening his predecessor's range of activities. He gained in prestige and standing and in 1811 served as a steward in the Society of Arts. Smirnov's expertise in agricul-

tural matters was widely recognized and was brought to the attention of
Catherine herself in an interesting letter from Baron Grimm in 1795, in
which he passed on the views of his friend, James, the 7th Earl of Findlater.[22] Findlater suggested that Smirnov could play a key rôle in furthering
the progress of agriculture in Russia and might be asked to translate important English works, such as the *Transactions* of the Society of Arts,
the publications of the Bath Society and works by Sir John Sinclair. Two
years previously, in 1793, Smirnov had been elected an honorary member
of Sinclair's newly founded Board of Agriculture, and he acted to a certain
extent as the go-between of the English society and the Russian Free Economic Society. Arthur Young, who makes frequent reference to Smirnov
in his *Autobiography,* notes that in general he was 'greatly employed by
the nobility of that Empire [Russia] in agricultural commissions', in some
of which he sought the help of Young.[23] Smirnov's deep respect for his
English friend is given notable expression in a letter to him in 1802, in
which he also referred to the encouragement given to agriculture by the
new Emperor Alexander I:

> my very worthy Friend and Master, the true original Source of all the ratio-
> nal agricultural Knowledge, now so happily extending through Europe and
> to the end of the World; [to] the Man, who more than any other Indi-
> vidual without Exception, had ventured to point out to Mankind the true
> Foundation of their Comfort, and real Happiness. Here my dear Sir Divine
> Providence is visibly raising, in the Person of His Imperial Majesty, a very
> powerful Instrument to spread about your benevolent Views, to speed the
> Plough. Such example will have unbounded Influence, for in Russia, I believe,
> more than in any Country—*Regis ad exemplum totus componitur Orbis*.[24]

To a greater degree than any of the early Corresponding Members in Russia, Samborskii and Smirnov occupy a distinctive place among the members of the Society of Arts in the eighteenth century and deserve to be
rescued from the general oblivion which has been their fate.[25]

THE VISIT OF A RUSSIAN SERF

At a meeting in April 1785 the Society of Arts had an unusual
if unnoticed visitor. On that occasion Father Iakov Ivanovich Smirnov,
chaplain to the Russian church in London and a member of the Society,
had brought with him a young fellow countryman by the name of Ivan
Sudakov. Sudakov had arrived in England the previous summer in the care
of Father Andrei Samborskii (Smirnov's predecessor both as chaplain and

as a member of the Society) and had come to study all aspects of English agriculture and husbandry, but particularly the art of distilling. In this respect he was not unusual, for a number of young Russians had been in England studying agriculture (if not distilling!) under the supervision of Arthur Young and John Arbuthnot. He was unusual in that he was a serf, valet to the powerful Count Ivan Chernyshev, erstwhile Russian Ambassador in London and himself a member of the Society of Arts in 1769. Sudakov remained in England for a year and then returned to Russia and to the obscurity from which he had briefly appeared. If he had not left his own memorial in the form of meticulously kept diaries of his activities in England, even that episode in his life would have passed without trace. These diaries have never been published and have been merely described in a catalogue of manuscripts held in the Lenin State Library in Moscow.[26] Sudakov himself, as far as I am aware, has featured only in a footnote in a work on the activities in England of a more famous contemporary.

Sudakov was, however, a very talented man who had received through the whim of his master what he described in the dedication of his diaries as 'the education not of a slave but of a true noble'. His intelligence, his powers of observation and his ability as a draughtsman are all revealed in his diaries, which are of great interest, particularly to an English audience, by reason of their detailed descriptions of farms, estates, factories and institutions and the carefully drawn and coloured plans and sketches of buildings, gardens and farm implements. The description of his visit to the Society of Arts and the three accompanying drawings well illustrate these aspects of his work.

He begins by giving the dimensions and arrangement, together with a plan, of the Great Room. It will be noted that he has described the subject matter of five of the six Barry paintings, omitting 'Orpheus'. He then proceeds to the meeting itself.

> At 7 o'clock the President takes his seat, flanked by two secretaries. The secretary on the right-hand side reads out the proposals from members which were unresolved from the last meeting; when they have been read out once, they are repeated with appropriate arguments and with a reading of the rules, before they are put to the vote; members in favour raise their right hand, those against, their left. A debate follows, sometimes with strong expressions and shouting, sometimes with seemliness. When I was there, a member proposed ways of increasing the Society's revenues, for every new member is obliged to propose something new, which in this case was as follows: each member should be allowed to introduce two friends to the meetings of the Society and each visitor should pay one shilling. The pro-

posal that each member should be allowed to bring two friends as visitors was accepted but there was great opposition to the fee of one shilling, for all unanimously asserted that in seeking to raise revenues the noble Society should not overlook the possibility that it would bring more censure and dishonour than profit which would anyway be so small as to be unworthy of consideration.

Although not extensive, Sudakov's account is valuable and possibly unique as a description of a meeting of the Society by a non-member and is enlivened by details which do not find their way into official accounts and minutes. Other entries in his diaries have shown Sudakov to be a generally reliable and accurate observer, although in this specific case there is some confusion as to the actual meeting which he attended and what matters were in fact discussed. Sudakov dates the meeting as 17th April, but in 1785 there was no meeting on that day. The minute books of the Society do, however, record the proceedings of a General Meeting on the 20th April, when a Vice President, James Davison, was in the chair. There is no exact correspondence between the minutes and Sudakov's account, but the discrepancies would seem to arise from Sudakov's fairly rudimentary knowledge of English. Among the propositions discussed was one which had been postponed from the previous meeting and concerned not access to the Society's meetings in general but to a viewing of the Barry paintings. The proposals were: 'Each Person, Members excepted admitted to view the paintings in the Society Great Room are to pay one shilling, descriptive Catalogue gratis. Each member shall be at liberty at the usual hours personally to introduce one Friend to view the Pictures.'[27] The fact that 'no motion was made thereon' would seem to support Sudakov's allusion to the differences of opinion expressed by members.

It is interesting that at the same meeting the officers of the Society were asked to be vigilant to prevent attempts by members and strangers to sketch the Barry paintings or indeed any busts, pictures, casts, etc., in the Society's possession.[28] Sudakov, unaware or undeterred by such admonitions, visited the Repository after the meeting and noted and drew 'a mattock for raising turnips'. It seems likely that this implement was the 'Tool for digging up, and cutting Turneps [sic], by Mr. Winsor,' entered as item 60 in the *Catalogue of the Machines and Tools in the Repositories of the Society,* which was published in 1783.[29] Sudakov's third and final drawing of a chandelier in the Great Room is also valuable, when seen in the context of Wood's remarks in his history of the Society that 'at first the Great Room seems to have been lighted by candles, though I have never been quite able to satisfy myself that the six chandeliers or "branches" brought from the old house, and placed in the corners and middle of the room, were for candles or oil'.[30] Sudakov's description is, however, not conclusive, for he writes of 'a burning wick in the chandelier [which] is surrounded by a glass. In this way the side beams are restricted and make the light very great'. His drawing suggests nonetheless that candles were used.

Part 4

DOMESTIC MATTERS

In defining its various missions, settling its constitution (primarily through an elaborate committee structure) and moving to its permanent home in the Adelphi, the Society did much in its early years to settle those domestic matters that have kept it viable through the centuries. To review these accomplishments, however, it is still best to turn to notable members who did so much to effect them. Among them the contributions of Robert Dodsley, the first printer and stationer to the Society, stand out. In chapter 17, James E. Tierney shows that while Dodsley was not a founding father, he deserves to be remembered as one who helped shape the course of the new Society. Although his formal position attests to his official duties in filling orders for printing, paper and advertising (printing costs were probably the most expensive single item in the Society's budget), Dodsley was much more than a Society functionary. In him, the Society had engaged what in modern terms is known as a public relations expert, one connected as few figures of his time were with a larger world of print, press, journalism and literature generally. Few members endowed the Society more in its formative decades.

D. G. C. Allan's examination of the contest for the Secretaryship in 1769-1770 (chapter 18) reveals that in its first years of existence the Society had achieved national prominence. The Secretaryship could be as hotly contested as a seat in Parliament. This election involved a vigorous exercise of press and advertising, back-room caballing and even attempts to alter the Society's constitution in redefining membership requirements. And all this occurred in the context of the anti-Scots fervor that defined the period. The resolution to this contest, which had its bizarre moments, was surprisingly pacific. Samuel More was easily elected and went on to serve the Society with great distinction.

Whatever the potential of the other candidates to serve the Society, G. E. Mercer, who held the Secretaryship himself from 1961 to 1973, reveals in chapter 19 that More was in a class by himself. More's tenure is admirable not simply for its length (he was associated with the Society for thirty-eight of its first forty-five years) but also for the way he personally embodied its mission. In an institution that encouraged specialization, he could be taken seriously as a chemist; in one that sought to support multiple fields simultaneously, he could speak effectively on mineralogy, mechanics, manufactures and agriculture; and in one that encouraged the arts, he won two premiums for sets of impressions in paste of antique cameos and intaglios. Even these accomplishments fail to suggest his administrative contributions to the Society and his ability to refer its good work to outsiders whose assistance would become crucial to its future success. The death of 'Mr. More of the Adelphi' on 11 October 1799 marks the end of an era. He deserves to stand with a select few who endowed the Society in its early years with sufficient capital to persist to this day.

In concluding a series of essays devoted to domestic matters, D. G. C. Allan provides a portrait of one of the most singular figures ever associated with the Society (chapter 20). In a narrow sense, James Barry helped settle the Society simply through art, in murals that define its interior as the Adam brothers defined its Adelphi exterior. But Barry provides much more. In his series of paintings 'analogous to the views of the Institution', he provided, in Samuel Johnson's words, 'a grasp of mind . . . which you find no where else'. Barry's murals provide an attenuated, Enlightenment version of Nicolas Poussin's *A Dance to the Music of Time*. Here history is not cyclical, but progressive. One moves from primitive and classical times to a world of familiar faces—to William Shipley, Samuel More, Stephen Hales, Samuel Johnson and others. Barry's genius takes one into history and imaginatively out of history in a special evocation of 'The Virtuoso Tribe of Arts and Sciences' that defined the eighteenth-century foundations of the Society for the Encouragement of Arts, Manufactures and Commerce.

17

ROBERT DODSLEY: THE FIRST PRINTER
AND STATIONER TO THE SOCIETY

James E. Tierney

With noticeable pride, Secretary George Box recorded in the three-year-old Society's Minutes on 6th April 1757 that Robert Dodsley 'who has long taken Care of correctly printing whatever has been order'd for the press, was proposed and unanimously appointed Printer and Stationer to this Society'. For historians of the eighteenth-century book trade, the title the Society chose to bestow on Dodsley seems curious indeed, for, by trade, he was neither a printer nor a stationer, but rather a bookseller, what would be comparable to a modern publisher. The curiosity is compounded by the fact that two bona fide printers, Matthew Jenour (1707-86) and the well-known Samuel Richardson (1689-1761), had also been members of the Society during the previous year and a half; in fact, Jenour had been elected at the same meeting as Dodsley.[1] One can only imagine that the Society was led to surmount formal trade distinctions in the naming of Dodsley because not only had he faithfully and 'long taken Care of' its printing needs but he had also been an active committee member over the period; in short, it was fitting.

On the other hand, one cannot overlook Dodsley's stature in contemporary English society, a matter that would have proved an attractive feature for a young organization attempting to establish its national image.

Originally appeared in *Jnl. RSA*, 131 (July, Aug., 1983), 480-83, 563-66.

In 1757, Dodsley was known throughout the country as a distinguished London businessman and author, with influential connections among the learned, the nobility and the government. Although it would be misleading to suggest that the Society's selection was prompted by opportunism, certainly the body stood to gain by its appointment of Dodsley. Such a pleasant secondary gain becomes evident upon a review of Dodsley's accomplishments by 6th April 1757.

At the time of his appointment, Robert Dodsley (1703-64) flourished as London's premier publisher of *belles lettres,* as well as a successful dramatist and poet in his own right. But like other eighteenth-century success stories, his began outside of London in humbler circumstances. He had been born in Mansfield, served briefly there as a weaver's apprentice, and then took to the road, working as a footman in the houses of distinguished families.[2] In these houses his verses began to be noticed by major men of letters. In 1729, Daniel Defoe wrote a Preface for Dodsley's poem *Servitude.* In the early 1730s, Alexander Pope was complimenting his verses and interceding with the theatre manager John Rich for Dodsley's *The Toy-Shop,* a play that scored an immediate and continuing success at Covent Garden in 1735.[3] That year proved pivotal for Dodsley's career, for he parlayed the profits from *The Toy-Shop,* along with a £100 contribution from Pope, into the opening of his bookseller's shop at the Sign of Tully's Head in Pall Mall.

With Pope's patronage, Dodsley's services were soon sought after by writers of the first and second rank. Together with other booksellers, he published Volume 2 of Pope's *Works* in 1735. On his own, he issued the rage of 1737, Richard Glover's *Leonidas;* Samuel Johnson's first major poem, *London* (1738); Christopher Pitt's translation of the *Aeneid* (1740); William Shenstone's *The Schoolmistress* (1742); the first of Edward Young's *Night Thoughts* (1742); and the tenth volume of Jonathan Swift's *Miscellanies* (1745). By the early 1740s, his reputation had begun to attract authors writing in other fields. Henry Baker, one of the founders of the Society, issued his *Microscope Made Easy* (1742) from Tully's Head, as did Richard Pococke his *Description of the East* (1743), and Gilbert West his *Observations on the History and Evidences of the Resurrection* (1746). So did his business prosper that in the first eleven years Dodsley had issued no fewer than one hundred and ninety-nine titles and editions. But even this record would seem paltry when compared with that of the next dozen years.

As he became established, Dodsley began to extend to others the same generous patronage he himself had enjoyed. Besides the first works of some notables already mentioned, Dodsley encouraged or at least saw to the publication of many more. Pleased with the bookseller's handling of his *London,* Samuel Johnson brought him *The Vanity of Human Wishes* and *Irene* in 1749, followed by *Rasselas* in 1759. Boswell tells us that it was Dodsley who suggested to Johnson the idea of a *Dictionary of the English Language,* a work that Dodsley joined other booksellers to publish in 1755. It is no wonder that Johnson later referred to the publisher as 'My patron, Doddy'.[4] Among other fashionable authors for whom Dodsley served as publisher or adviser, or both, ranked Mark Akenside, Edmund Burke, William Collins, Henry Fielding, Thomas Gray, Edward Moore, Samuel Richardson, Joseph Spence, and the Warton brothers, to mention only a handful.

Meanwhile Dodsley's own literary successes brought him further honours in the capital city. By 1741, he had produced four plays, three of which had been acted in London theatres within the same month during the 1737-8 season, making him the most successful playwright of that season.[5] Over the next few years, his poems, plays and prose continued to find eager readers and audiences. His *Triumph of Peace* (1749), with music by Thomas Arne, was acted at Drury Lane; *Economy of Human Life* (1750) was translated into many languages on the Continent; his *Chronicles of the Kings of England* had reached a third edition by 1745; and the general appreciation of his works called for a collected edition of selected pieces under the title *Trifles* in 1745.

Besides the reputation he had earned in the trade by issuing the works of major figures, Dodsley gained a household name for publishing important periodicals and multi-volume collections. By the time of his selection as the Society's Printer, he had published three journals and had shares in at least two thrice-weekly newspapers. He had engaged Mark Akenside to edit his *Museum; or, Literary and Historical Register* (1746-7) and Edward Moore to conduct the *World* (1753-6), both periodicals known for their extensive list of fashionable contributors. With other booksellers, he began the thrice-weekly newspaper the *London Chronicle* on the first day of 1757 and held shares in the influential *London Evening Post.*

One of his special achievements in the literary world was the editing of a twelve-volume collection of early English dramas, entitled *A Select Collection of Old Plays* (1744). By reaching back into the early Renaissance for plays long out of print, Dodsley made available texts from the old English tradition that might have otherwise perished. But probably most talked about in his day was Dodsley's *Collection of Poems by Several Hands,* a six-volume publication begun in 1748 and completed in 1758.[6] A wide

Robert Dodsley; portrait
by Sir Joshua Reynolds.
By permission of the
Governors of Dulwich
Picture Gallery.

sampling of contemporary poetry, the *Collection* proved so representative
of the period's practising poets that it has been regarded by modern literary historians as a reflection of the age's literary taste. Indeed, so broad
was its coverage that when, many years ago, the late Wilmarth Lewis (the
1976 recipient of the Society's Benjamin Franklin medal) founded a society of eighteenth-century scholars at Yale, the society chose to call itself
'Dodsley's Collection'.

This was the Robert Dodsley the Society appointed its first Printer and
Stationer; and one can understand why its vote was unanimous. Dodsley
had reached the zenith of his career and was surrounded by influential
authors, on terms with many of the country's nobility, esteemed by all for
his literary taste and known in the trade for his shrewd business sense and
fair dealing. The young Society could not have put itself in better hands for
reaching the public or dealing with the press.

Proposed by Dr. Richard Manningham during the Society's second
year, Dodsley was elected on 2nd July 1755 and, from the start, made
his enthusiasm for the body's work and success quite evident. Early on,
although Society or Committee Minutes do not record the occasion, he
seems to have served as a kind of policy consultant (possibly on the Committee on Correspondence), for the first matter linked with his name in
the Minutes of the following autumn involves an organizational matter

only incidentally concerned with printing. Charles Powell (1712-96), an original member and a philanthropist of South Wales, had proposed the formation of county organizations with the same objectives as those of the London society. Vice President Charles Whitworth, although praising Powell's suggestion, believed that such bodies, if set up, ought to be branches of the national society, not separate entities, as Powell had proposed. It was during the ensuing debate that Dodsley's rôle surfaced.[7] In a letter to the Society read at its 1st October meeting, Dodsley offered his opinion regarding the value of airing Powell's proposal in the public press. Addressed probably to William Shipley, the current Secretary, the letter is quoted in part:

> Dear Sir
> I send you enclos'd M.[r] Powel's Letter, and also M.[r] Whitworth's. I must own, tho I think M.[r] Powel's a very sensible Letter, that I cannot see any good reason why it should be printed by the Society; nay I do not perceive how it can come with propriety from us, unless it had contain'd some new Proposals relative to y[e] Objects of our Society; or some hints towards any Improvements in Arts Manufactures or Comerce, w[ch] it was proper to lay before the Public in hopes of further information. But as it contains nothing of this sort, I do not see what end we propose to answer by printing it.[8]

Apparently Dodsley's recommendation on Society policy was not so much honoured as his professional advice on printing, for the next month Powell's letter appeared in the *Gentleman's Magazine*, though in a somewhat altered state.[9]

A letter of the following spring finds Dodsley proposing a new name for the Society.[10] In his conclusion to the letter, written on 17th March 1756 and addressed to the President of the Society, Lord Folkestone, Dodsley suggests that his fellow members consider the name 'The British Society; for the Encouragement of Letters, Arts, and Manufactures'. Quite clearly, Dodsley, as a literary man, had hoped to induce the organization to include the fostering of the art of Letters in its mission, whereas it had previously focused on the polite arts; that is, those conducive to industry. He claims that many members share his view that the Society's 'basis and foundation' ought to be extended to cover the 'Encouragement of Letters'. He does not suggest offering premiums to authors for writing on given subjects, which he acknowledges 'might perhaps tend only to set many scribblers at work', but rather the awarding, *post factum*, of some honour to any of 'true Genius' who produce some 'extraordinary Work, in literature'.

Although his fellow members apparently rejected both his proposed title and the expansion of the Society's concerns, the suggestions emerge significant in themselves, for they imply that the Society was still struggling to find an appropriate name for itself, as well as to define the parameters of its mission.[11] In fact, even as late as December of that year, Dodsley seems to have found it worthwhile to propose still another title, although by this time he had temporarily accommodated himself to the more practical designs of the Society.

Dec.[r] 14th 1756

Gentlemen:

As the fixing a Name to our Society has been thought a matter of some consequence, and seems not yet perhaps to have been happily hit upon, the writer of this begs leave, with great deference to the Society, to propose One to their consideration. He thinks that in chusing a Name three things should principally be regarded, viz: that it be well-sounding, significant, and unaffected. The Name propos'd is indeed a Word, but it is so easy in its pronunciation that it would soon be familiar to the ear; and if its meaning is very obvious, and if no harshness [or] impropriety be found in its composition, he apprehends its being new should rather be a recommendation than an objection to it. He humbly proposes therefore that it should be consider'd, whether we may not take the Name of

The Philopatrian Society of London
for the Encouragement of
Arts, Manufactures and Commerce.

This Name he apprehends most happily includes the very Motive and bond of our Association, namely the Love of our Country; and as every man either is or ought to be a Lover of his Country, and as most men wish at least to be thought so, he is of opinion that so honourable and engaging a Name may include many to associate with us in these good designs, which he hopes will always continue to give propriety to such an Appellation. He is

Gentlemen
with great respect
A Member & Wellwisher to the Society[12]

The Society had not heard the last of Dodsley's plea on behalf of Letters; in this matter, he proved undaunted. On 21st June 1757, he is writing again on the subject.[13] This time he takes a most unusual, but equally unsuccessful, tack. Signing himself 'Honestus' and claiming to be a well-wisher though not a member of the Society, he attempts to affect the persona of the disinterested but intelligent observer so frequently assumed by correspondents of contemporary journals and magazines. After a lengthy, discussive introduction, 'Honestus' finally reveals his purpose: to encourage the Society to promote the 'Knowledge of our own Language in its several

Branches of Reading, Speaking & writing it, with Elegance and propriety'. The author adds in postscript that he would appreciate a response, 'directed for B. Z. at M.ʳ Lindsays Orange Merchant on Ludgate Hill'. One wonders why this whimsically pseudonymous letter—never mentioned in the Minutes—was ever preserved in the Guard Books; only materials considered at meetings or regarded as of some special consequence were normally reserved there. One can only imagine that Secretary George Box recognized Dodsley's hand and regarded the letter as one more statement in the continuing debate at the heart of the Society's business, possibly one he himself favoured.

Ultimately Dodsley's persistence won. Not too long after this letter— namely, on 8th March 1758—Dodsley himself was appointed to a committee to consider a premium for composing 'the most useful History of the Arts, of the Peaceful Industry and Civil and Commercial Improvements within that part of Great Britain called England'.[14] The story of the development of this prize, as well as its outcome, has been told elsewhere.[15] Here it seems necessary only to remark that Dodsley would ultimately be deprived of assisting the committee in its work; his frequent, unwelcome visitor, the gout, would see to that. But his pain must have been eased in his later years by the realization that his campaign for Letters had finally been victorious, if only on a limited scale.

Two other Dodsley letters, although not directed to the Society nor primarily concerned with its business, deserve mention here. From 1755 until 1758, Dodsley had continually revised his tragedy *Cleone*, hoping with each revision to gain David Garrick's approval for its performance at Drury Lane. Garrick, however, rejected each revision, causing Dodsley regular disappointment and sometimes even throwing their friendship into jeopardy. The Society figures in one of these flare-ups, in the autumn of 1757. In a letter, Dodsley challenged Garrick to perform *Cleone* at Drury Lane, promising that he would offer the profits of the third night to the 'Society for the Encouragement of Arts, Manufactures and Commerce'.[16] (As their payment, playwrights received the gate receipts of every third night of a play's performance, less production costs.) Of course Garrick did not accept the challenge, and during the falling-out that ensued, several of their mutual friends attempted to intercede. To one of these, Dr. Thomas Gataker, the King's surgeon, Dodsley repeated his benevolent gesture on the Society's behalf in a letter written on 4th November 1757.[17] Although nothing ever came of the proposal, the fact that Dodsley had designated the Society as the beneficiary of a play over which he had laboured for three years and on which he was ready to stake his career reveals how central to his thoughts lay the welfare of the organization.[18]

Although Dodsley was at the height of his career when elected to the Society, the year 1755 marked the beginning of his bout with the illness that would plague him until his death nine years later. Earlier, the reader might have wondered why the bookseller's participation in the Society's proceedings was so often carried on by letter. The answer is found in the conclusion to his very first letter to the Society: 'I should not have troubled you with this, but that I am not able to attend ye Society to night, being confin'd with ye gout.' For eight months, spanning the end of 1756 and the beginning of 1757, he would be laid up, complaining bitterly of his confinement.[19] Hence, although appointed to many committees, Dodsley found regular attendance impossible.

Nevertheless, when he anticipated some special benefit to the Society from his presence, he made it a point to be on hand. Although he complained to William Shenstone through November and December of 1756 that he had been confined since his summer visit to the Leasowes,[20] the Society's Minutes list him as present at the meeting of 1st December. Of course it was probably no coincidence that a candidate who would become one of the Society's more active members, his friend Samuel Johnson, was scheduled for balloting that evening. And the Minutes make clear that Dodsley did not stay long, possibly only for the election, one of the first regular agenda items.

Yet, despite his absences, his service to the Society in several capacities proved regular and most useful, as both its Minutes and Committee Minutes testify. After his involvement with the Powell proposal, his next committee assignment (4th February 1756) found him joined with Charles Whitworth, William Hogarth, Nicholas Crisp and Joseph Highmore for the purpose of drawing up an advertisement to encourage the manufacture of paper for fine prints. Representing the committee at the Society's meeting of 11th February, Dodsley argued on behalf of a premium for anyone who could produce paper comparable to the French import used for printing from copper plates. The committee's suggestions were eventually supported by the membership, and an advertisement for the premium was ordered at the 7th April meeting.

Dodsley next served on a rather significant committee established at the 1st December 1756 meeting, one charged with drawing up a new plan for the Society. Unfortunately this committee's meetings concurred with the longest of his early confinements with the gout. Nonetheless, he did attempt to contribute to its work, as his letter of 14th December (quoted earlier) demonstrates.

Still another committee, mentioned in the Minutes of 23rd February

1757, for the purpose of considering the best methods of improving several kinds of British paper, shows Dodsley again serving with Hogarth, and now also with Samuel Richardson. On 8th March 1758 he was appointed to the committee that he had been largely responsible for instigating, the committee to consider a premium for the production of a treatise on the 'History of Arts of Peaceful Industry'. The committee's recommendations were ultimately agreed to, advertisements were placed in the newspapers and proposals were scheduled to be submitted over the next three years. But Dodsley's deteriorating condition ultimately deprived him of the opportunity to judge a competition he had worked so hard to effect. During 1758, Dodsley's name appears once more, this time as attending a meeting of the Committee on Ordinary Business on 13th November. He seems to have attended, however, out of personal interest, for the Minutes do not show that he had been appointed to the committee.[21]

On 31st January of the following year Dodsley was appointed to a committee for judging submissions of paper produced from silk. Again he was joined by Richardson, but now also by fellow-bookseller Jacob Tonson. On 7th March this committee seems to have recommended a further advertisement, seeking a method for the discharge of colour from silk rags used for paper-making. Although Dodsley's name is missing from the committee list in October, in April of the next year both Dodsley and his brother James appear on a committee to judge two parcels of silk paper. Possibly this is the same committee on which the Dodsleys served for the purpose of judging three pieces of drugget and two reams of marbled paper, a committee mentioned in the 13th February 1760 Minutes. In both of the latter cases, however, the committee's reports were questioned, further investigation conducted, and additional reports submitted but postponed. The brief insights afforded by the Minutes suggest that questions arose regarding not the quality of the specimens but rather the integrity of the submissions.

Whatever the case, the difficulties Dodsley encountered with the procedures of these last two committees, as well as with the Society's handling of their reports, apparently proved too taxing for his morale and waning health. After July of 1761, although he continued to pay his dues until his death three years later, his name fails to appear in the Society's Minutes.

Dodsley's participation in committee work, however, constituted but one phase of his service to the Society. Tracing his name in the Minutes shows that his official title of Printer and Stationer had not been idly bestowed; he was kept quite busy filling the Society's orders for printing, paper and advertising. In fact, a review of these activities reveals some interesting insights to the Society's operation in the late 1750s, especially as they bear on the young organization's budget. Dodsley's purchases on behalf of the Society are found enumerated in the itemized bills he submitted at its meetings on a semi-annual basis and which the Secretary copied into the Minutes. These bills, together with other allusions in the Minutes, show that the Society, growing in members with each meeting, frequently ordered its membership list reprinted; that since only a portion of its members attended meetings regularly, meetings were ordered to be advertised in the newspapers, especially general meetings; that occasional announcements to members, formal committee summons, balloting lists, and forms to acquaint new members of their election were printed on a regular basis; that numerous premium lists required not only the printing of flyers and covering letters but also advertising, usually in daily, thrice-weekly and monthly publications; that the burgeoning Society found it necessary to alter and therefore reprint its plan and rules; and that the Society's extensive correspondence with well-wishers, projectors, applicants, recipients of awards, etc., demanded a regular supply of stationery. Finally, the Society occasionally sponsored such publications as Johann Gottlieb Lehmann's essay on cobalt, of which the membership at its 28th November 1759 meeting ordered Dodsley to have a thousand copies printed.

It is not surprising, then, that Dodsley's bills amounted to considerable sums; in fact, they probably proved the Society's largest and most consistent expense.[22] Unfortunately, however, although we are told that Dodsley had 'long taken care' of the Society's printing needs, such services are not recorded until after he had been appointed Printer and Stationer. The first bill mentioned in the Minutes, a voucher for £32 15s. 6d., Dodsley presented at the 20th July 1757 meeting; it was ordered to be paid on the spot. A smaller bill of £13 2s. 6d. was submitted and ordered to be paid on 11th January 1758. Approximately six months later, Dodsley presented a bill for £70 17s. 8d. But by this time the Society had established an audit committee to review all budgetary expenditures. Consequently the bill was submitted to the committee for review, and when fully approved, ordered to be paid two weeks later, on 19th July. On 7th February 1759, the Society received Dodsley's bill for £43 12s. 11½d., which also was referred to the audit committee. This bill was considerably delayed in payment; in fact, it was not ordered to be paid until 5th September, a point at which Dodsley was ready to submit still another bill.[23] Most significantly, the committee had reduced the payment by £1 17s. 0d. Two weeks later, Dodsley submitted the largest bill to date, amounting to £90 4s. 6d., and, of course, it was referred to the committee. This series of bills corroborates other evidence of the Society's growth in its first five years; it is clear that not only its membership was spiralling with each year but also its activities and outlays for these activities.

Events occurring within the interim of these two last bills provide the occasion for a last look at Dodsley's active participation in the Society. Apparently the long delay in paying his 7th February bill had also involved some reconsideration of one aspect of the bookseller's service to the Society. Not only had the audit committee reduced his bill, but the Society Minutes for 5th September (when the bill was ordered to be paid) indicate that the membership voted to have all future advertisements placed directly in newspapers and magazines by the Secretary, rather than through Dodsley. Even earlier, however, another curious directive suggests the eroding of Dodsley's total management of the Society's printing needs. On 4th July, the Society had ordered to be printed by Matthew Jenour one thousand covering letters for the new premium list. The latter instance marks the first occasion, at least as mentioned in the Minutes, on which a printer had been employed without Dodsley's mediation.

At first these events might suggest that the growing Society had begun to phase out Dodsley's services, preferring a more direct, perhaps more economical, relationship with the press. A closer look at the facts, however, argues differently. Probably the Society's change of policy in 1759 can be principally explained by an event of April of that year: Dodsley's illness had required his retirement from Pall Mall and his leaving the business to his younger brother James. Incessant attacks of the gout had at last made his active pursuit of business, as well as regular attendance at Society meetings, unmanageable. Although he would, after retirement, continue to advise his brother and even see some of his own publications through the press, he accomplished these matters at a leisurely pace without the daily pressures of operating London's leading publishing house. It is more likely, then, that the Society, by deciding to go elsewhere for some of its printing needs, merely responded to Dodsley's own gradual withdrawal from active life.

On the other hand, although his personal management of the Society's affairs was soon concluded, the Society's link with Tully's Head was by no means finished. During 1759, Dodsley's last year in Pall Mall, apparently he had convinced the Society to employ the services of his successor at Tully's Head. He had set the machinery going within a month of his retirement by procuring his brother's election to the Society in early May.[24] And apparently the path between the Society's quarters and Pall Mall continued well trod, for a bill from the new Master of Tully's Head for

'Stationery Printing etc.', presented in August of 1760, amounted to £72 13s. 9d. The difference, of course, was that James would now be sharing the business. Matthew Jenour, for one, submitted a bill for printing and advertising amounting to £19 2s. 0d. on 3rd December 1760.

Although Robert Dodsley's active service to the Society spanned but five years, these years were charged with excitement and importance; this formative period saw a small group of vital, imaginative patriots merge their dreams and efforts to establish a permanent society that would endow their country with numerous benefits and much praise. Although not one of the founding fathers, Dodsley shared their vision and contributed his mite towards its realization: let us call it, he urged, 'The Philopatrian Society of London, [for the name] most happily includes the very Motive and bond of our Association, namely the Love of our Country . . . So honourable and engaging a Name may include many to associate with us in these good designs.' Fortunately this kind of enthusiasm, as the Society's history has shown, did not depend upon the fixing of a name.

18

THE CONTEST FOR THE SECRETARYSHIP, 1769-1770

D. G. C. Allan

Before the establishment of a governing council the Society's Secretaries, like all its other officers, paid as well as honorary, were elected by a ballot in which the entire membership of the Society was entitled to participate. Although the offices were held for a year at a time only, the Secretaries could count on security of tenure, generally for life, once they had won their first election. The Secretaryship of the Society was vacant on three occasions in the eighteenth century, in 1760, 1769 and 1799. The first and third elections are remembered chiefly because of the intended candidatures of Oliver Goldsmith and Edmund Cartwright.[1] Involved indirectly in the second was another important historical figure, Edmund Burke.

In 1769 both the Society of Arts and the wider world of English politics were occupied by electoral controversies. Though Wilkes and Middlesex predominated in the columns of the London newspapers, readers were also kept informed of the competition for the vacancy caused by the death of Dr. Peter Templeman, and the election held by the Society for his successor was as hotly contested as any for a seat in Parliament. For amongst the candidates for the Society's Secretaryship was a man who was himself well acquainted with political life. This was John Stewart, sometime secret agent for the Earl of Shelburne and at this date attached to the interests

Originally appeared in *Jnl. RSA*, 112 (Aug., Oct., Dec., 1964), 715-19, 865-69, 33-37; 113 (Feb., 1965), 199-202.

of the Marquess of Rockingham and on terms of personal friendship with Edmund Burke.[2]

To win, Stewart would need to overcome three opponents. The most formidable was the ultimately successful Samuel More, an influential member of the Society, who had assisted Dr. Templeman in the management of the Secretarial business, and who was, as his subsequent record revealed, admirably qualified for the office.[3] The others were Timothy Brecknock, a lawyer with some literary reputation,[4] and Lemuel Dole Nelme, a Board of Trade official with a special interest in linguistics.[5] Both were lightweights who would present no problems to the skilful Stewart.

Dr. Peter Templeman died on 23rd September 1769 after an acute bout of the illness which had troubled him for twenty years.[6] Lord Romney, President of the Society, communicated the news to a meeting held on 11th October. George Box, the Assistant Secretary, was at once appointed Acting Secretary, and an extraordinary general meeting was fixed for 14th November, when an election to fill the vacancy would be held. Candidates for the Secretaryship were to submit their 'Petitions or Memorials' in person on or before 25th October, and notices of these resolutions were to be published three times in the newspapers and gazettes. Such procedure was entirely in accordance with the section in the Society's *Rules and Orders* 'Of officers and the manner of their election'.[7] The only unusual feature about the meeting of 11th October was the extremely large number of names proposed for membership of the Society. The majority of the proposers were almost certainly acting in the interests of John Stewart, who had begun to canvass for the vacant Secretaryship within two days of Dr. Templeman's death.[8]

On 24th September, Stewart wrote to Burke informing him that 'Dr. Templeman is at last dead and I stand Candidate for the Office of Secretary to the Society of Arts, Commerce etc.' He reminded Burke that he had approved of his idea of trying for the office 'Two years ago'—which suggests that he had followed the successive illnesses of Dr. Templeman with more than sympathetic interest. The President of the Society, Lord Romney, received a call from Stewart soon after Templeman's death. He showed 'great cordiality', but as Stewart told Burke 'he wished in this affair to go along with the Vice-Presidents'. Two of these, Sir George Savile and the Duke of Richmond, were known to Burke, and Stewart hoped they might be persuaded to support his candidature.[9] Burke responded to Stewart's appeal for assistance (which had been reinforced by his cousin, William Burke) by showing his letter to Sir George Savile, who gave him 'no answer' on the matter, and by writing himself on 9th October to the

Marquess of Rockingham, whom he begged to put 'in mind of Little Stuart [*sic*] in his pursuit of the Secretaryship of the Arts and Commerce'.[10]

Lord Rockingham, though himself a member of the Society, had, as he told Burke on 1st October, 'very few acquaintances among the virtuoso tribe of Arts and Sciences'. He did, however, 'speak to' some members, telling them that he knew 'Mr. Stewart to be a very ingenious man and one I wish well to'. He would be able to say more if Burke would tell him whether Stewart had 'much acquaintance' amongst the membership 'and whether he has ever put himself on that line of study which may render him properly fit for the office'.[11]

Stewart based his claim to be qualified for the Secretaryship on his skill as linguist—for which there is ample evidence[12]—and the opportunities which his travels had given him to observe the arts and manufactures of Europe and the commerce and industry of America and the West Indies.[13] Of the depth of his knowledge in these subjects there can be no certainty. His work on steam engines and his election to the Royal Society, which was described in a charming letter he wrote to Warren Hastings in 1776, show that his interest in scientific matters was strong enough to outlast his association with the Society of Arts.[14] He had joined the Society in 1766 and had served as a chairman of its Committee of Colonies and Trades for the session 1767-8, and had been a regular attender at other Committees. But his attitude to the Secretaryship of the Society was decidedly cynical. He compared it with the Secretaryship to the East India Company's Commission of Supervisors, for which he had competed unsuccessfully, as something like becoming *d'évèque meunier*. 'However, one must take things as they find them', he added philosophically.[15] For a man who had once been granted £1,000 by the Treasury for his services, the salary of £150 a year provided by the Society must have seemed very small indeed. With it, however, went the well-fitted house which had tempted Dr. Templeman from the British Museum, and prospects of security which the East India Company would not have appeared to offer in 1769.[16]

The startling fall in East India stock prices which began in the spring of 1769 was disastrous for a number of influential speculators, amongst whom was Stewart's closest friend, Lauchlin Macleane, M.P., called by Sir Lewis Namier 'one of the most interesting figures in the political underworld of his time'.[17] In spite of his own difficulties Macleane gave full support to Stewart in his candidature, applying to the Society's contest the long experience he had had of disputed elections at East India House. Himself a member of ten months' standing, he proposed eleven new members for election at the meeting of 11th October. Fifteen names were also put forward by Macleane's friend, Laurence Sulivan, the dominant Director of the East India Company, and a member of the Society since 1755.[18] They included Richard Burke, Sr., and Theobald Burke's name was amongst another group of fourteen. Of the total of 76 new members proposed at this meeting, 67 were put forward by persons who were knowingly or unknowingly working for John Stewart. The groups of proposers overlap to bring within this category a most influential group of members of the Society, including six Chairmen of Committees, one of whom was Thomas Stewart, John's brother.[19] Lord Rockingham need not have doubted the extent of Stewart's acquaintance with the members of the Society.

THE QUESTION OF MEMBERS IN ARREARS AND THE CAMPAIGN IN THE NEWSPAPERS

Nothing appeared in the minutes of the Society's Meeting of 11th October 1769 to suggest that exception was taken to the large number of new members proposed by Stewart's supporters. But notice was taken of the fact that some of the candidates were former members who had 'declined' to pay their subscriptions and were considered, therefore, as having formally resigned from the Society. At the conclusion of the meeting a motion was carried referring 'to the Committee appointed to settle the Regulations for the Election of a Secretary, to consider the case of such gentlemen who have been formerly elected Members of the Society who are now or may be proposed to be re-elected Members'. The Committee was to 'meet for the above purpose' on 14th October, which was three days earlier than the day fixed for it to give consideration to the apparently more urgent and certainly more important matter of drawing up the regulations for the election of a Secretary.[20]

When this Committee met on 14th October, the Acting Secretary reported that six former members of the Society had been proposed for re-election at the Society's meeting of 11th October, and that five of these six were on record as having resigned from the Society. The Minutes record no expression of disapproval at this discovery. The next matter to be recorded is a motion that any former member who discharged the arrears of his subscription should 'be considered as a member whether he had declined or not'. That some objection was made to this is clear from a counter-motion 'that this question be not now put'. But it was overridden, and the motion was carried with the confirmatory amendment 'being a Member' added to the words 'whether he had declined'.[21]

John Stewart, who had been present at the Committee meeting on 14th

October, was no doubt satisfied at the passage of this motion. He could now increase the number of his supporters in the Society not only by proposing new members but also by persuading old ones to pay up their arrears. The Society's Subscription Book shows that between 11th and 25th October, 15 members paid up their arrears and that between 25th October and the date of the election of a Secretary a further 27 qualified in this way to vote in the contest. Two years' subscription—four guineas—was owed by a majority of the members in arrears, but three were prepared to pay eight guineas, for four years, one ten guineas for five years, and two twelve guineas for six years.[22] Which, if any, of the candidates benefited from these additional votes is impossible to determine. It seems likely that Stewart was the most persuasive. Eleven of those who paid their arrears appear to have been linked to his circle.[23] His skill as a lobbyist, however, was to recoil disastrously.

The candidates for the Secretaryship canvassed publicly for votes in advertisements which they inserted in the London newspapers. During the week following Dr. Templeman's death on 23rd September 1769, the *Public Advertiser* carried requests for support from More, Brecknock and Stewart. These notices were repeated at intervals during the month of October, and they also appeared in the *Gazetteer*.[24] The partisans of the candidates extended the campaign by writing letters to the editors of those publications or by inserting announcements of their own. John Stewart was subjected to a prolonged attack in which his attempt to pack the membership of the Society was exposed to the public in a savage manner. The *Gazetteer* for 17th October contained the following lampoon on his nationality:

> To the Members of the Society of Arts,
> Gentlemen,
> We, the Mac Johnstones,[25] Mac Stewarts, Mac Phersons, Mac Murrays, and all the rest of the Macs of North Britain, intend giving your Society two guineas a piece, to be immediately balloted members of your Society, that we may chuse for you a new Secretary out of one of ourselves. We can assure you that he is a bonny young North Briton; and if you want a specimen of his abilities, only read the extraordinary North Britain of five sheets, published by him some months ago, wherein he plainly proves that all the sense, learning, and abilities of us, North Britons, is far superior to that of the English; and that the establishment of your Society is a convincing proof of all your ignorance. After this high compliment paid to your understandings by the bonny lad, you can nay do less than chuse us Members and him your Secretary; and if you wonay black-ball us all tomorrow, you will give all

the world a convincing proof that you are all as wise as he has represented you, and after we are elected Members, and have chose you a Secretary, you shall not be troubled with us, or our money, any more, till you want another new Secretary; and consider what an honour it will be to your country, to have a Scotch Secretary to an English Society of Arts, etc. Pray come early tomorrow neight, for the ballot begins at six o'clock.

Next day's issue repeated this notice and also carried a letter from 'A Lover of Fun' which described the enjoyment which could be had from disrupting political meetings and annoying fellow Club-men. The place which afforded the most fun was the Society for the Encouragement of Arts!

A more moderate letter was signed by 'A Member' who declared himself 'divested of national and personal prejudice against the candidate'. His 'warmth' arose 'merely from a sense of the unfairness of the endeavour, by bringing in such a force to dragoon the Society into acceptance of him for their Secretary'. He admitted that 'the election of so many gentlemen, members, would bring into the Society's treasury a large sum of money; but the bad consequences attending the admission of such a member in the interest of one man, would, certainly outbalance that advantage, and be productive, in the end, of aggravated ills, even to the very annihilation of the institution'. He warned the Society that unless it agreed 'to determine by a resolution this day *to postpone the election of any new members till after that of the Secretary,* the present, as well as the future interest of the Society, will inevitablly fall a sacrifice to JOB and PARTY'.[26]

At the Society's Meeting on the evening of the 18th, the Committee's motion on members in arrears was accepted in its essentials. The opinions expressed in the *Gazetteer* were clearly given weight, as no ballot was held for the candidates proposed for membership on the 11th October, and a motion was carried 'That any Member who joined in proposing any candidate at the last meeting may now have leave to withdraw the name of any such candidate if he thinks fit'.[27] Stewart's supporters were not prepared to accept this rebuff, and at the next meeting, held on 25th October, the 76 names proposed on the 11th came up for election. Before that, however, his case was also stated in the newspapers. The *Public Advertiser* for 24th October published a long and carefully worded letter of justification from 'A member of the Society of Arts', containing this appeal:

I would beg, Gentlemen, to point out: how [can] Danger . . . arise from an Acquisition of sixty to seventy Members, all men of character, most of them of Fashion and Rank, whose Situation in life put them in the way of giving great Encouragement and Support to the Society, besides the benefit of their Subscriptions?

NEW MEMBERS DISENFRANCHISED: TIMOTHY BRECKNOCK AND LEMUEL DOLE NELME INTERVENE

The Society's minutes show that at the commencement of the meeting held on 25th October 1769 a motion to postpone still further the ballot for the 76 new members proposed on 11th October was defeated. They then record the election as a member of one person only, William Pulteney, Esq., whose name had headed the list of those proposed on the 11th.[28] The riddle of the missing 75 is explained in an account of the meeting printed in the *Gazetteer* which gives arguments and details of procedure not to be found in the minutes.[29] The *Gazetteer* reported 'the fullest meeting of the Society for the encouragement of Arts, Manufactures etc., that has been known for these five years past'. It described the proposal to allow an 'extraordinary influx of new members' as 'calculated only to serve the particular purpose of voting for a new Secretary, in the room of the late Dr. Templeman' and as leading to a debate in which 'On one side it was argued, that the gentlemen proposed to be balloted for as new members, were either persons of great rank, great property, or great encouragers of arts and manufactures, and therefore they ought to be admitted. On the other, it was argued . . . that if these gentlemen were, in fact, such great promoters of arts and manufactures, it could not but seem a little problematical, why they did not offer to become members of the Society before this critical period.' After reporting 'much altercation', when insinuations of a 'Ministerial job' were made against Sir Charles Whitworth, the Vice President in the Chair, and Sir Thomas Robinson, an influential member who apparently supported the 'new-creation',[30] the *Gazetteer* went on to describe a first ballot for William Pulteney, which is not reported in the minutes.

Instead of the required two-thirds majority, only 59 members were said to have voted for Pulteney and 69 against him. He was, as the *Gazetteer* puts it, 'blackballed with a vengeance'—a most unusual proceeding for the Society. The newspaper described the effect:

> The sense of the Society having been fully expressed in this instance, the other candidates would not risk the hazard of a ballot, and their respective proposers had leave given them to *withdraw* their proposed friends, on condition that Mr. Pulteney might be balloted for a second time. This stipulation was agreed to, and on the second ballot Mr. Pulteney was declared a Member, *eighty-four* voting *for* him and only fourteen *against* him.

The minutes confirm the passing of a resolution allowing members to withdraw the names of any persons they had proposed for membership. The presentation by Samuel More and Timothy Brecknock of 'Petitions and Memorials' for the vacant Secretaryship is also recorded. The *Gazetteer* states that John Stewart 'having no written Memorial ready to present declared that he would present [it] . . . at the next meeting', the minutes of which show that he carried out his intention.

By delaying the presentation of his petition Stewart was breaking the regulations made by the Society when it had first heard of the death of Dr. Templeman. These provided for the receipt of applications from candidates on or before 25th October and for the election of a new Secretary on 14th November.[31] One of Stewart's enemies used this as an argument against him in the *Gazetteer*[32] and suggested that he was 'by such neglect precluded from offering himself as a candidate':

> I well know [continued the *Gazetteer's* correspondent] the resolution was ordered to be advertised in the public papers, and that it has been neglected, because, as is said, the resolution ought to have been confirmed.[33] But do we not know that orders to the Secretary for advertising any business of the Society, have never been supposed to want confirmation? And does it not appear that the public knew this, as one person[34] offered himself a Candidate last Wednesday who is not a Member of the Society? What plea then can be made for a Member[35] present at that Meeting who gave his assent to the resolution, and who ought to be well versed in the proceedings of the Society, being guilty of so great a neglect? In short to prevent the animosities and heats in the Society increasing, it is sincerely wished by many members that next Wednesday we may confirm the resolutions of the first meeting, and end the present contest as soon as possible.

In fact the meeting held on 1st November passed resolutions which were quite contrary in intention. The date for receiving applications from candidates was put forward to 3rd January 1770, and that of the election to the 23rd of the same month. But the triumph of what the *Gazetteer* called the 'North British Party' was short-lived, for on 8th November the Society decreed that 'no one elected a Member after the declaration of a Vacancy in any of the Offices of Secretary, Assistant Secretary, Register, or Collector . . . be entitled to vote at the election for such an office'. Thus Stewart's supporters had to abandon all thought of packing the Society. They had to face instead a protracted struggle with Samuel More's following to capture the esteem and goodwill of the Society at large. Each side may be said to have blundered in its initial campaign. Stewart was mistaken in allowing so many supporters to be proposed for membership on 11th October.

More's friends did him no service by their virulent display of anti-Scottish sentiments and their attempt to disqualify Stewart by technicalities.

Both Stewart and More had to face the public criticisms of Timothy Brecknock, a candidate who made a virtue of being an outsider. He had begun advertising on the 24th September, the day following Dr. Templeman's death, and his initial notices were straightforward appeals for the 'Patronage and Protection' of the members of the Society, resembling those put out by More and Stewart. On 20th October he changed their form to that of an open letter to the Society:

> My Lords and Gentlemen,
> The continued divisions and party feuds, which must unavoidably happen if you elect a MEMBER of your Society into one of its lucrative offices, were foreseen at the very institution of your Society. Very wisely it was ordained by one of your fundamental laws, 'that the Secretary SHALL NOT BE A MEMBER'. Conformant to this fundamental law, the late Dr. Peter Templeman, who was NOT A MEMBER of your Society, was elected Secretary, in opposition to two Gentlemen who were ACTUALLY MEMBERS of it. The present candidates for your favour are Mr. More, Mr. Stewart and myself. Messieurs More and Stewart are both of them members; I have not that honour; my only ambition is to be,
>
> > My Lords and Gentlemen,
> > Your diligent and most obedient
> > humble servant
> > T. BRECKNOCK[36]

Later in the month Brecknock suggested in his notices that More and Stewart were 'both immersed in trade' and could not therefore 'offer their whole time to the service of the Society'. As he had 'neither place, pension, nor employment under the Government' and was 'totally disengaged from all kinds of business' he considered that he had 'some advantage over my two competitors'.[37]

As a regular contributor to the *Gazetteer* on questions of legal history, Brecknock may have been given favoured treatment by the editors. His intended candidature was treated as a news item. The issue for Saturday 21st October 1769 reported: 'We hear that a gentleman of universally admitted literary abilities, and unexceptionable in every respect, will be proposed a candidate on Wednesday at the Society of Arts, for the Secretaryship.'

The use of the word 'literary' and the date makes it certain that the candidate referred to was Brecknock.[38] Of the correctness of the flattering epithets no corroboration seems possible. Reference has already been made to his satirical verse.[39] In one of his notices he stated that his 'life has been a life of literature'. He was the author of an enthusiastic exposition of the Regal power called *Droit Le Roy, Or a Digest of the Rights and Prerogatives of the Imperial Crown of Great Britain.*[40] This work had brought him under the censure of the House of Lords, and he had revenged himself by prosecuting Lord Chief Justice Camden for appearing in court wearing bands made of French cambric contrary to the Act of 1745.[41] In 1766 his love of recondite legal points had caused him to demand the arrest of the Tripoline Ambassador for being a professed infidel.[42] Twenty years later he was himself to answer a capital charge in the Irish courts, when his forensic skill could not save him from the scaffold.[43] In the election for the Secretaryship Brecknock mustered one vote.

The fourth contestant, Lemuel Dole Nelme, equalled Brecknock in the esoteric nature of his interests and had an even more curious approach to his candidature. Nelme combined his clerkship at the Board of Trade with a passionate interest in the study of English.[44] In his Memorial for the Secretaryship, which he presented on 20th December 1769, he informed the Society

> that he hath employed [a] great part of his life in the Study of the Old English Language which he firmly believes to have been the primitive Language of Europe. The radical Characters being only thirteen in number, he finds to be geographical and hieroglyphical, fully sufficient for all the purposes of communication, and easy to be understood by all Nations; because those Characters are derived from the two most simple and most perfect Figures in Nature, the Line and the Circle, the undoubted Radix of All Arts and Sciences; Therefore Your Memorialist apprehends his discovery becomes a proper Subject for the Consideration and Encouragement of Your Patriotic Society.

At this point it must have ceased to be clear to the Society whether Nelme addressed them as a candidate for the Secretaryship or as one for a prize in linguistics. His concluding paragraph suggests that he saw no contradiction in the dual rôle:

> That your Memorialist is by birth and affection a BRITON; who, unassisted by power, unattached to party, and influenced only by the general social Motive of a reciprocal communication of Benefits, doth humbly offer to Your consideration an Investigation of his said Discovery, and therewith (in conformity to Your Advertisement of the 8th of November) the most diligent and ardent exertion of all his Talents, as Your Secretary; which honour conferred on him without any Influence or Solicitation, except by this Memorial, will display the benevolent disposition of the Society towards the

humblest Merit; excite in Your Memorialist a double degree of Gratitude, and enable him to elucidate the excellency of the Language of Britain; which by its native power and simplicity, he apprehends, may be made instrumental in diffusing that Language, and Christianity, among all the Polite, and Savage Nations, who are connected with the British Empire by Sovereignty or by Commerce.[45]

A month before delivering his Memorial Nelme had almost certainly inspired a suggestion that the Secretaryship should be given to 'such a person as should, before a certain day, send to the Society the best essay on the English Language'. The suggestion appeared in an anonymous contribution to the *Gazetteer,* which included much of the matter subsequently used by Nelme in his Memorial, as well as a proposal that the Society's Secretary should be forbidden to correspond in any language other than English.[46]

In spite of his experience at the Board of Trade 'nearly allied to the Duty of a Secretary of your Society',[47] Nelme showed little understanding of the Society's constitution—it would seem doubtful if he had read the *Rules and Orders* concerning the duties of the Secretary—and no appreciation of the importance the Society attached to the exchange of letters with corresponding members overseas. It is not surprising that he polled no votes.

THE FINAL PHASE

Although persons who became members of the Society after 1st November 1769 were barred from voting in the forthcoming election for the Secretaryship, some supporters of John Stewart's candidature were elected after this date. Between 15th November 1769 and 17th January 1770 thirty-two of the names put forward in his interest on 11th October and subsequently withdrawn were proposed for membership.[48] On 15th November, Edmund Burke in company with Viscount Fortrose was proposed.[49] Stewart had written to Burke on 7th October: 'If you choose to be proposed yourself, for a member, you will be so kind as to let me know. You may believe I should be proud of the Occasion and you would be sure of being given in with very respectable names.'[50] The date of a reply by Burke is not known, but it may be assumed to have been prompt in view of his immediate response to Stewart's other suggestions.[51] Even had Stewart known that Burke would consent to have his name put forward on 11th October, which would have been the earliest opportunity, he would hardly have wished to include it in the numerous company then proposed. The subsequent meetings of the Society were inopportune because of the controversy already described. By proposing Burke's name on 15th November, Stewart's supporters were able to demonstrate that his influential friends had not abandoned him because of the reverses his cause had suffered by the disenfranchisement of new members. By reproposing names they had been forced to withdraw, they could prove that such persons wished to join the Society because they believed in the value of its work and not merely to give their vote to their nominee as Secretary.

Stewart's newspaper enemies called him 'an assiduous humble servant of the opposition',[52] but they also endeavoured to make out that his campaign for the Secretaryship was 'a ministerial job'.[53] His brother, Thomas Stewart, was alleged to have made 'the original canvass . . . dated from the Secretary of State's office; which it was presumed would influence the dependants of the Ministry'.[54] Thomas, who was an active member of the Society and a Committee Chairman, was supposed to be himself aiming at the Secretaryship, for John's friends would soon 'Come again into the Ministry' and give him a government appointment, upon which Thomas would 'relinquish the place he now holds in the Secretary of State's Office and . . . be, by the said interest saddled on the Society . . . It is not, therefore, to be wondered at that T.S., should be so officious as he appears to be, in promoting the election of his brother J.'

This absurd suggestion was made in a letter from 'Several Members' which appeared in the *Gazetteer* on 9th November. In it the public was informed for the first time of Burke's activity on behalf of John Stewart:

> but what indeed seems most surprising (we had almost said alarming) is, that circular letters have been sent to many members signed E—— B——e; several of which we have seen; and from the elegance and precision with which they are written, should have judged them the production of a gentleman justly celebrated as an orator in the cause of Liberty, in the most respectable assembly in the globe. But as modesty is the well known concomitant of merit, we are almost led to doubt of their being genuine; for however strong the private friendship of B—— to S—— may be, with what degree of propriety can any person (affluent in his fortune, conspicuous by his abilities, and of undoubted public virtue) endeavour to obtrude a principal officer on a Society founded on the most useful and disinterested principles of any yet established; of which he has never been a member, and consequently entirely unacquainted with the necessary qualifications and business of the Secretary.[55]

Burke was elected a member of the Society on 22nd November 1769, and his connection with it is perpetuated by Barry's painting. He shared its interests in scientific agriculture and was a friend of many of its members.[56] He certainly regarded Stewart as worthy of the office of Secretary. He had written to the Earl of Hardwicke on 20th October 1769:

My Lord,

The Secretaryship of the Society of Arts is vacant by the Death of doctor Templeman. I believe it will be your Lordship's wish to have it filled in the best manner. On that principle permit me to recommend Mr. John Stewart to your Lordship's favour and protection. He is a man of great and various knowledge, an excellent Linguist and of great personal worth. He is known to and valued by Lord Rockingham; I need not therefore add that he is much my friend and that it will greatly oblige me, if your Lordship will honour him with your Vote. I am with the greatest regard and Esteem

My Lord,

Your Lordship's most obedient
and faithful humble Servant
EDM. BURKE[57]

Nine days later, writing to the Marquess of Rockingham, he showed another face. Towards the end of a lengthy letter largely devoted to political matters, he wrote: 'Stewart will, I hope, succeed in his little pursuit—he has been a great attender on that Society—but if he had never set his foot within their doors he has but too much abilities for their paltry business.'[58]

The postponement of the election day from 14th November to 23rd January no doubt caused a slackening of public interest in the campaign, and the last letter published on the subject in the *Gazetteer* appeared on 16th November. The candidates continued to insert notices soliciting support, although these were also discontinued between 20th December and 20th January. Samuel More reopened the campaign by publishing a notice on 20th January. It reappeared on the 23rd, the day of the election, with a postscript urging 'the early appearance of Mr. More's friends'. In the same issue John Stewart published a plainly worded and restrained request to all members to attend and to vote, and Timothy Brecknock repeated his view that only non-members were eligible to stand as candidates. The Editors declined to publish a letter they had received from 'A constant reader' which they stated to be a reflection 'on the character of one of the candidates for the place of Secretary to the Society of Arts . . . neither safe for us, nor just to the candidate, to assert for truth'.[59]

The election meeting began at 11 a.m. and lasted for five hours. Lord Romney, the President, presided until 12.15 p.m., Vice President George Eckersall from then until 3 p.m., and Vice President Owen Salusbury Brereton for the last hour. Five scrutineers, including Thomas Stewart and

Lauchlin Macleane, were elected by show of hands at the start of the meeting. Counting took place between 4 p.m. and 8 p.m., at which hour Vice President Brereton resumed the chair. The scrutineers then announced

> That they had proceeded to open the Balloting Glass and found the lists to be 487 in number as follows:
>
> For Mr. S. More   292
>   Mr. J. Stewart   192
>   Mr. Brecknock   1
>   Irregular lists   2
>
> Whereupon the Vice-President in the Chair declared Mr. Samuel More to be duly Elected Secretary.[60]

Thus ended the contest which had distracted the Society ever since the death of Dr. Templeman four months before. So well and for so long did More discharge his office that several historians of the Society have given to his tenure the symmetrical dating 1769-99, forgetting the troubled interregnum, when his succession must have seemed far from certain.[61]

For the other candidates there remained divergent fates. Nelme retained his clerkship at the Board of Trade, gaining in seniority as the years passed. In 1772 he was appointed the Secretary of a newly founded charitable Society which shared its president (Lord Romney) with the Society of Arts—the Society for the Relief of Persons confined for Small Debts—and he was noted as a former holder of that worthy office by the *European Magazine* when it recorded his death in 1786.[62] Brecknock perished as a felon in Ireland in the same year.[63] In 1771 Stewart attained high office under the East India Company such as had been his original ambition.[64] Upon him and his friend Lauchlin Macleane rests the blame for introducing the ways of Westminster and India House into the Society. Yet it must not be supposed that 'cabal and corruption' came to and went from the Society in one year of the eighteenth century.[65] They were manifest in it both before and after 1769. But in that year they were especially virulent. Fortunately More's lengthy secretaryship minimized such scandal as a tolerant age might have attached to the Society. Soon after his triumph a correspondent wished him 'all the joy and happiness he can possibly expect in being elected Secretary to the most respectable Society in the world'.[66]

19

'MR. MORE OF THE ADELPHI': NOTES ON THE LIFE AND WORK OF SAMUEL MORE, SECRETARY OF THE SOCIETY, 1770-1799

G. E. Mercer

Thomas Mortimer, an early member of the Society, began his Valedictory Memoir of Samuel More (who is referred to as More hereafter to distinguish him from the other Samuel Mores in his family) in the *European Magazine* for December 1799, 'Few private individuals have attracted more notice, or for a long period of years deserved such commendation from numerous classes of his fellow subjects, as the Gentleman of whose meritorious conduct in a very respectable station we are now to give a satisfactory sketch'.

Education and Training

Mortimer says that More was educated by his father Thomas, 'a respectable schoolmaster in Channel [Cannon] Row'. This is wrong, for More in his will states that his father was Samuel.[1] His brother Thomas, however, may have taken over his father's school, and More may have been edu-

Originally appeared in *Jnl. RSA*, 127 (Jan., Feb., Mar., 1979), 96-103, 173-79, 237-44. Material defining More's family background has been eliminated here to allow for a full reprinting of information about his service to the Society.

Samuel More; from the engraving by William Sharp after the painting by
Benjamin West. Courtesy of the RSA.

cated there. It is clear that in addition to a sound classical education More
received instruction in arithmetic and accounts and was taught the 'good
round hand . . . legible, tidy and speedy' which was the glory of English
penmanship at the time. His education was sufficient for the Society of
Apothecaries, who on 3rd August 1742 accepted him as an apprentice to
Mr. John De Vall of Whitechapel for a consideration of £84.[2]

At the time More was apprenticed, Dr. William Lewis, who was elected

FRS in 1747, was giving highly esteemed courses of lectures on Chemistry and Pharmacy in a laboratory off Fetter Lane.[3] The circumstances suggest that More must have attended these as part of his professional training, and thus were laid the foundations of Lewis and More's later friendship. By 1750 More was qualified, but there is nothing in the Apothecaries' records to show whether he was accepted into the livery. Nor is there any information about what he then did. He may have continued to help De Vall; or set up as an apothecary on his own; or worked as an assistant to Lewis.

It is known, however, that by 1760 More was practising as an apothecary in Jermyn Street, for in December of that year a letter of his to Dr. Charles Morton, Secretary to the Royal Society, about a cure he had effected was important enough to be read to that body. More described how he had restored the crippled hands of a dyer's apprentice, which had defeated other apothecaries and the doctors at St. Thomas's Hospital where the patient had been treated for several months. He decided that the condition arose from constant immersion in strong acid and treated the hands with an alkali ointment which in time restored full use to them.[4] The case had been referred to More on the recommendation of the dyer's foreman, which suggests that he was already establishing a reputation for himself.

More was by then closely associated with Lewis, who had retired to Kingston in 1747 to give himself time for research and writing. There he had written two books, one of which, *Experimental History of Materia Medica,* was still regarded as a standard authority as late as 1810, when a new edition was published, edited by John Aikin, M.D., the father of Arthur Aikin, who became Secretary of the Society in 1817. He had also had time to develop the ideas about the benefits to commerce and industry of the systematic application of scientific knowledge and method which he had formed in London. In this work Lewis was closely associated with his friends Stephen Hales, who lived across the river at Teddington, Robert Dossie and Peter Shaw, all chemical authors of repute, and John Woulfe, Dr. Morris and Dr. Fordyce, who were practical industrial chemists. As they were all connected with the newly established Society for the Encouragement of Arts, Manufactures and Commerce, it must have been on their advice, bearing in mind his reputation as a skilled chemist, that from 1755 Lewis was used by the Society as a chemical consultant.

More was then helping Lewis. There are reports in More's writing in the Society's archives on cobalt and zaffer dated 8th February 1756 which may relate to an undated note by him on the same subject, probably written in March 1756.[5] In his major work *The Philosophical Commerce of the*

Arts (*Commercium Philosophico-Technicum*) which contained a considered statement of his views on the benefits of chemical research to industry,
supported by accounts of many experiments on materials, dyes and textiles, Lewis in Part I (pp. 628-30) describes experiments on gold coloured
glass by his 'ingenious friend Mr. More'.

Membership of the Society

By 1760 More, through the quality of his work and his friendship and
close collaboration with Lewis, had widened his own scientific experience
and knowledge and was becoming known as a research chemist of skill
and application, particularly to the important chemists in the Society. It
is clear too that he shared their convictions about the growing value of
chemistry to industry; and that through his friendship with industrialists
such as John Wilkinson, he was becoming deeply interested in the practical
problems of industry and commerce. It is not surprising therefore that on
13th May 1761 (fourteen months after his cousin Samuel) he was elected a
Member of the Society on the proposal of Henry Baker, a founding Member; or that on 6th June he was one of a small select group who observed
the Transit of Venus from the roof of the British Museum as guests of
James Ferguson the astronomer.[6]

More's sponsors had chosen wisely. From the start he gave to all the
Society's business, whether scientific or not, assiduous attention and zeal,
and undiminished energy. The record shows the wide-ranging versatility
of his mind and the high degree of administrative skill he brought to the
Society's affairs.

The first meeting he attended as a Member of the Society was of the
Chemistry Committee—on 29th October. A week later he was asked to
take the chair of that Committee, and he presided over many of its meetings until on 10th November 1762 he was formally elected Chairman with
Nicholas Crisp. He filled that office until 11th November 1767, when he
declined re-election. In his first Session he regularly attended meetings of
the Polite Arts and Mechanics Committees; and on 9th February 1762 was
appointed Chairman of an *ad hoc* Committee to consider the arrangements
for the 1762 Exhibition of Paintings. He took the chair at the Manufactures Committee on 15th February 1762. In all he attended 147 meetings of
the Society and its Committees in his first Session.

This pattern was maintained during the eight full Sessions of his membership. He served on all the main committees, often as Chairman. On
14th October 1768 he even presided at an Ordinary Meeting of the Soci-

ety. In addition he served on many *ad hoc* Committees to consider various aspects of the Society's administration. Altogether he attended some 650 Committee Meetings, mostly during his first six Sessions. If attendance at Society Meetings is added, his total attendances were about 950, even though his attendances at Committees dropped to 31 and 25 in the 1767-8 and 1768-9 sessions, respectively, when increasingly he acted as Secretary as Templeman's health declined.

As a Member More introduced 29 other Members and supported 32 others. His nominees came from various walks of life and included John Wilkinson (whom he proposed within a few months of becoming a Member himself), John Cockshutt, Jukes Coulson, Samuel Garbett, Peter Dollond, Edward Delaval, FRS, Dr. Alstromer, the Swedish botanist and a pupil of Linnaeus's, and Dr. Zeigler, a Swiss scientist and friend of Lewis's.

Templeman died on 23rd September 1769 and in his will left More five guineas for a mourning ring as a 'monument of our uninterrupted friendship'. More reported his death to the Society on 11th October and was thanked for his services during Templeman's ill health. He then announced his intention of standing for election as Secretary, thus opening 'The Contest for the Secretaryship' described by D. G. C. Allan, which was ended on 23rd January 1770, when More was elected by 292 votes from a total of 487 cast.[7]

HIS WORK FOR THE SOCIETY, 1761-99

The Move of the Society to the Adelphi

The decision to move to the Adelphi was a declaration of faith in the Society and its future when its financial prospects were by no means bright. The negotiations with the Adam brothers, described in Mr. Allan's work *The Houses of the Royal Society of Arts* were conducted by a committee of the most influential members, aided by two members with specialist qualifications: Matthew Duane, a lawyer expert in conveyancing, and John Phillips, a furniture-maker and master builder. They both received the Society's Gold Medal for their services.

The actual move from Denmark Court in June 1774 was planned in great detail by the House Committee, and the transfer of the Society's possessions to its new House in the Adelphi was the responsibility of Alexander Bailey, the Registrar. The records do not suggest that More's responsibility was great, although he must have been much involved in the many practical problems which arose from the move and during the settling-in period. The move is mentioned here because it was the most important single development for the future of the Society during More's period of office.

Chemistry

'I was bred a chymist and am aquainted with the Science of Chymistry. I have always made the Arts that depend on Chymistry my particular study.' Thus did More describe himself to the Select Committee of the House of Commons considering fossil alkali when he appeared before it on 21st June 1780.[8] When he was elected a Member, the Society, stimulated by men such as Dossie, Shaw, Morris and Fordyce, was already extending its interest in the application of chemistry to the industrial arts. Premiums were being offered for the manufacture of potash in North America; for the purification of train oil; for a native varnish to replace the imported French product; for the manufacture of sal ammoniac in England. With some of these Lewis and More were already concerned. The speed with which More was established as Chairman of the Chemistry Committee and became actively involved in its experimental work indicates that his election was intended to provide the Society with a young and practical research chemist with sufficient skill and enthusiasm to share responsibility for the development of this important part of its work. He was soon fully occupied.

At the request of the Chemistry Committee[9] he tested and reported on verdigris and varnish (1762-3), borax (with Fordyce) and cobalt (1763-4), sessamin seed, amato dye, sago and vermicelli for the committee of Colonies and Trade (1766-7). On 3rd August 1763 Crisp and he were requested by the Society to obtain 'a compleat apparatus for performing experiments', as described by Lewis in the *Commercium Philosophico-Technicum*, at a cost not exceeding 20 guineas. From 1763 he and Lewis were working together on Virginian nitre: an account of More's work is in the Chemistry Committee Minutes for 16th July 1764. On the 23rd July both he and Lewis were thanked by the Society for their 'obliging care and accuracy in making the experiments'. With Dossie continuing his task of publicizing North American potash, for which he received the Society's Gold Medal on 11th February 1767, Lewis and More continued their researches into the material itself, for which Lewis received a Gold Medal on 25th February 1767 while More, whose important contribution to the work was emphasized by Lewis, received the Society's thanks. A paper on this research was prepared by Lewis and published, as was Dossie's paper. They were considered to have made a valuable contribution to the development of the manufacture of potash in North America.

More's practical work did not cease when he became Secretary, and the minutes show many examples of his activity. Even as late as 1798 there are reports to the Chemistry Committee on experiments and tests made by him. The Gold Medal awarded to Messrs. Walker Ward and Co. of Derby in May 1795 for developing a method of manufacturing white lead, which reduced the health risk from the dangerous dust, was granted on the strength of a report by More after he had visited the works. In November 1797 he offered to experiment on cobalt from a mine on the Earl of Egremont's land in Cumberland.[10]

More's Journals reveal that he continued to practise as an apothecary on his travels and may have done so in London, although there is no evidence of this. Since he was both a chemist and an apothecary, it is permissible to assume that he influenced the Society's decision to concern itself with the health hazards from the dangerous chemical by-products of industrial processes such as the mercurial vapour released in water-gilding (1771), and the harmful dust in manufacturing white lead (1783).

The friendship between More and Lewis continued until the latter's death in 1781, when he bequeathed to More the Gold Medal he had received from the Society. The surviving fragments of their correspondence (Egerton MSS 1941 and Wedgwood MSS 38405-39) concern chiefly experiments on minerals. More's article on portable furnaces in the 1786 *Transactions* was based on work done by Lewis.

More was already friendly with John Wilkinson, the ironmaster, when he joined the Society, for on 20th February 1762 he was putting Wilkinson's proposal for a premium for using coke to make pig iron before the Chemistry Committee. It is not clear, however, when he and Wedgwood first met. It may have been through Lewis. The friendship really developed after Bentley came to London in 1770 as Wedgwood's partner. The two men had a common interest in the chemical and technical problems of pottery manufacture and exchanged the results of their research. Increasingly, through the Society and on his own, More was able to provide Wedgwood with samples of ores, especially cobalt, clays and sands. From 1772, after John Bradby Blake, More's friend and protégé, arrived in Canton as a supercargo in the East India Company, he was able to supply Wedgwood with samples of Chinese porcelains and clays.[11]

From his own knowledge and experience, and his wide acquaintance with other scientists and manufacturers, More was also able to offer Wedgwood much valuable advice and many useful suggestions on many relevant matters, including design. He provided many of the engravings and sketches used by Wedgwood for his portrait medallions.

Wedgwood had a high opinion of More's chemical and scientific skill and used him often as a chemical consultant. Wedgwood's letters to Bentley contain many requests for More's help in scientific matters and in obtaining materials.

The two men clearly had the highest personal regard for each other. 'Everyone knows him [More] to be a Conjuror', wrote Wedgwood to Bentley in 1775;[12] and he included a portrait medallion of More in his Class X, 'Heads of Illustrious Moderns from Chaucer to the Present Time', as indicated in the 1779 Wedgwood and Bentley catalogue. More in 1775 told Wedgwood, 'Nothing concerning Wedgwood do I consider unimportant'.[13]

Through Wedgwood and his many visits to Etruria, More was able to establish friendly relations with the important chemists in the Midlands—Keir, Watt, Black, Collinson—and others interested in chemistry such as Erasmus Darwin and Withering. He may have met Withering when he visited Lewis at Kingston in 1766. He was also friendly with Joseph Fry, the industrial chemist at Battersea, whose son Joseph Storrs Fry (the founder of the cocoa firm J. S. Fry and Son in Bristol) reminded More in a letter of 11th February 1792 about his visits to Fry senior and 'the intimacy which subsisted between my dear father and thyself'.[14] He often saw Joseph Priestley, Wilkinson's brother-in-law, in Birmingham and helped with his experiments.

More's work on dyes and textiles, and the Society's interest in them, also brought him into contact with the Manchester chemists such as Charles Taylor (who succeeded him as Secretary), Henry Wilson, Cooper and others.

By 1780, More's reputation as a chemist was high, and in June of that year he was called as an expert witness by the Select Committee of the Commons considering the duties levied on fossil alkali, to testify to the quality of the alkali made by Keir, Black, Watt and Peter Collinson. He was also asked to test and report on the alkali made by Joseph Fry.[15] As Secretary of the Society he gave evidence to other Select Committees of the House about the Society's work (some of which he had done) on verdigris and on Phillips' Insect Powder.[16]

The newly re-constituted Committee of the Privy Council for Trade at this time also began to consult the Society, as described by Mr. Allan in his study of the subject, and More appeared as the Society's spokesman on many matters.[17] He was used in his own right as an expert witness in one or two cases, for example Dr. Gordon's new method of dyeing blacks, when he attended several meetings, and in October 1787 he received an honorarium of £100 from the Committee 'as compensation for the calls made on him'.[18]

Mineralogy

The study of minerals and geology gave More an abiding interest in metals and the technology required for the machines and manufactures arising from their use. Lewis and he worked on them, and the Journal of his visit to Devon and Cornwall in 1763 contains accounts of several visits (some underground) to the Cornish tin mines. On his later excursions he took every opportunity to visit mines, when he took particular note of the machines (pumps, lifting gear, etc.) used and of working conditions underground. He studied the geology of areas he visited and took samples of rocks so that he had a large collection of stone and minerals. His friend George Berg, a Member of the Society who died in 1775, was a mineralogist and a chemist: he left More his collection of ores when he died. It has already been noted that More's knowledge of ores, sands and clays was of particular value to Wedgwood.

More's other great friend John Wilkinson, nicknamed 'Iron-mad' Wilkinson because he continually preached and demonstrated that iron was capable of many uses, was one of the most important ironmasters in the country. It was he who suggested that the Coalbrookdale Bridge should be made of cast iron; and he made an iron boat for use on the Severn. The stables and outhouses at his house at Castlehead were roofed with iron, and he was buried in an iron coffin. More spent much time with him and often stayed at his houses at Wrexham and Castlehead. Another of his friends was Richard Crawshay, the ironmaster who did so much to develop the Welsh iron industry near Cardiff and to construct a network of canals there. He was very friendly, too, with Thomas Williams, the Copper King, who was largely responsible for the growth of the Parys Copper Company, and who for a time monopolized the copper industry in the United Kingdom, at a time when it was the world's largest producer. More frequently visited the Parys mine at Anglesey, and his Journals contain many detailed descriptions of the processes used there, and at the Company's important works at Holywell in North Wales and Ravenhead (near the present St. Helens) in South Lancashire.

More was on good terms with Abraham Darby III and Richard Reynolds, both of whom became Members of the Society, and he visited Coalbrookdale when he could, attracted by the high quality of the engine work done there and the Company's willingness to experiment.

His interest in the theoretical side of geology was underlined by a letter he wrote to Sir Joseph Banks, FRS, in 1781 about the striking similarity between the scoriae (long filaments of vitrified matter like spun glass) reported in Sir William Hamilton's accounts of Vesuvius, and the thread-like scoriae found near blast furnaces.[19] In 1783 he wrote to Banks about a meteor he observed near Coalbrookdale on 18th August.[20] (This was in fact a fireball and was reported by many people from the Shetlands to Paris.) Again in August 1786 he wrote to Banks about an earthquake in the Lake District.[21]

Mechanics

More was convinced of the importance of mechanical innovation and deplored the difficulty of removing old and rooted prejudices. On his travels he paid great attention to the machines he saw, and he went out of his way to see new ones which he carefully described and whose improvements he noted. He was quick to visit Bloomfield Colliery to see Watt's new steam engine when it was installed in February 1776.

Although More insisted that he was only a theoretical mechanic, the Egerton MSS 1941 contain a sketch of a beamless engine operated by pulleys, which is ascribed to him, and a sketch[22] of 'Mr. More's famous plough to be operated by horses'.[23] There is no other evidence for either of these. More's invention of the dynamometer is well documented. It was a device consisting of a spring and index, designed for the Society in 1772 and made at its expense, to measure the force of draught used in ploughing. It is mentioned in Hudson and Luckhurst's History (p. 83) and is fully described in the *Annals of Agriculture* by Arthur Young, who considered that it did 'great Honour to More's talents'.[24] The minutes of the Mechanics Committee for 24th December 1791 record that the implement was then used to measure the force exerted by a special extractor to draw iron bolts from ship's timbers.

More's reputation as a mechanic was such that he was called as a witness for Arkwright in the three trials concerning his patent in 1781 and 1785. Although at the first trial in 1781 More had deposed that Arkwright's machine could not be made from the specification, he maintained in 1785 that from his knowledge of other machines and a careful adherence to the specification he could 'direct a skilful artificer to make the machine'.[25] He explained that at the first trial he had not realized that in giving his testimony he could use his knowledge of other machines and so had given his opinion strictly on the terms of the specification. In the third trial, More said, 'My situation in life is well known . . . I am not a practical mechanic'. Counsel replied, 'I know you to be a theoretical mechanic, very ingenious and a man of Science'. This view was endorsed by the judge, who described More as 'a very ingenious sensible man'. Of greater significance, in his summing up in this trial the judge made much use of More's evidence.

More was also called as a witness in the case involving Watt's patent for his steam engine, Boulton and Watt *vs* Bull, in 1792, but his evidence was limited to confirming the originality and genuine nature of Watt's patent for his condenser because More had been wrongly quoted as saying that it was not Watt's invention.[26]

Manufactures

More's scientific and mechanical knowledge, and his friendships with Wedgwood, Boulton, Garbett and other prominent manufacturers, gave him useful insight into the growing range of British manufactures and the practices and problems of British industry. His duties as Secretary of the Society obliged him to keep abreast of technological development and advances, and his belief in the need for improvement found full scope on his travels, when his enthusiasm and advice, and the stimulus his own ideas gave, encouraged many to try out new possibilities and to report them to the Society. Thomas Greaves, a paper-maker of Warrington who won a Silver Medal, wrote to More on 10th August 1787, 'When you were here last summer with Mr. Wilkinson you was desirous that I should attempt of making paper from the bark of withies'.[27] There are many similar letters in the Archives.

More was, of course, also responsible for testing new ideas for manufactures submitted to the Society. The housekeeper George Cockings and his wife wore boots sent to the Society to test whether they were waterproof. His own household was used to judge the value of substitutes for yeast and starch.

Agriculture

Until the establishment of the Board of Agriculture in 1793 and the appointment of More's friend Arthur Young (who had earlier been Chairman of the Society's Committee for Agriculture) as its Secretary, the Society had operated largely on its own to improve agricultural knowledge, practices and implements. Local societies such as the Norfolk Society for the Encouragement of Agriculture (1775) or the Bath Society (1777), which were modelled on the Society in London, were set up originally to complement the Society's efforts at the county or regional level. A good account of the Society's work at this time is given in Chapter 5 of Trueman Wood's History of the Society.

It is my impression that More's interest in agriculture developed after he joined the Society and met practical farmers determined to improve agricultural practice, such as John Arbuthnot and John Reynolds; and that this interest was stimulated and focused by his friendship with Arthur Young. As might be expected, he was chiefly concerned with machinery and tools, and in the scientific and chemical aspects of agriculture. His correspondence with Young discusses new implements or improvements on old ones, and Young clearly had a great respect for More's mechanical ingenuity and skill. More was quite ready to question Priestley's views, as for example on the chemical effect of water on the soil.[28]

More became a keen and knowledgeable observer of conditions and practices at first hand on his travels. He discussed crops and cultivation, manures and seeds with farmers and landowners, and even farm labourers. Letters to him mention agricultural matters that he had raised on tour and enclose reports for the Society's information. A paper dated 30th October 1798, on improvements to the King's Farm in the Great Park at Windsor, was sent by Nathaniel Kent, the Supervisor of the Farm and a Member of the Society, after More had asked him for an account of them 'to communicate to the public'.[29]

Colonies and Trade

Apart from a day's journey to Calais with John Wilkinson in 1783 to meet the latter's daughter, there is no evidence that More travelled outside the United Kingdom. In common with his generation, however, he realized that the development of new sources of materials and markets overseas were essential to the prosperity of the country. He had sufficient imagination to share his knowledge and experience with those who were seeking to introduce into the Colonies new cash crops or sources of food and modern methods, such as Thomas Dancer, who introduced cinnamon into Jamaica, and Dr. Alexander, who established a botanical garden at St. Vincent. In a letter of 21st October 1791 to Dancer in which he speaks of barilla, potash, pimento and cloves, More wrote: 'Excuse my having written so much on these points. They suit my disposition and situation in life, and when an opportunity presents itself I am led insensibly to talk about them'.[30] And, of course, Dossie, Lewis and he had done so much in the 1760s to help the manufacture of potash in North America.

More was not optimistic about Bligh's expedition to take breadfruit from the Pacific to the West Indies, however. In a prophetic letter to Abraham Osorio dated 4th November 1786 (just after Bligh had sailed) he wrote of the difficulties of keeping plants 'in a state of vegetation' on a long sea voyage through severe climatic changes.[31] He believed that it would be better to ship the plants, efficiently packed, to Panama and thence overland to Portobello for shipment to the West Indies. He ended the letter: 'At a future date I may perhaps trouble you with my thoughts on cutting a canal through the Isthmus of Darien'.

In more immediately practical terms More was also able to be of service to the Colonies by arranging for the testing of new products and plants by London merchants, and so to compare them with those already recognized and to provide useful advice on ways of improving them.

Polite Arts

More was regarded as 'a man of taste' and was appointed to the Polite Arts Committee soon after his election to the Society. In 1763 and 1764 he won two premiums of twenty guineas each for two sets of impressions in paste of antique cameos and intaglios. The first, containing eighty-two samples, was submitted under cover of a letter of 8th November 1762 in More's writing but signed with the somewhat transparent pseudonym SEROM.[32] Dossie said that the impressions, 'some of which were very fine in the original and well taken off in the impression', were 'of a mixt nature having some dependence both on the mechanical and chemical arts'.[33]

It was presumably from the best of these impressions that More in October 1779, as listed in paper 31 of the MS Transactions for 1779-80, presented to the Society two frames containing ten impressions each from antique gems in paste. Alas, they cannot now be found.

More was also concerned to stimulate good-quality engraving and the introduction of new methods and techniques, as was recognized by William Sharp, who engraved the West portrait of More.

More was a collector of coins and was interested in their design and manufacture. His will mentions a collection of prints of Hedlinger's medals engraved by Haid of Augsburg, also a collection of provincial coins and a zebra wood workbox containing many English and foreign coins.[34] In 1788, when Matthew Boulton, with Watt's steam engine adapted to operate coining presses, was urging the Mint to produce a new copper coinage, More designed a George III halfpenny.[35] A specimen is in the British Museum.

The commercial tokens then being used by manufacturers and others as currency, in the absence of an effective copper coinage, also attracted More's attention. He designed a token for Arkwright in 1790 and wanted Boulton to manufacture it,[36] and he may have had a hand in the design of the very successful Anglesey tokens produced by his friend Thomas Williams for the Parys Copper Company. Letters in the Boulton and Watt papers show that Boulton on several occasions not only sent More dies of medals and coins to be engraved in London, where the workmanship was better, but also sought his advice on questions of design.

Administration

I have described More's functional activities in some detail to indicate the enthusiasm with which he espoused the Society's whole cause and the originality and versatility of his mind as it engaged with the different parts of the mission. There was also the drudgery of keeping the administrative machine in working order. During each session except for Sundays there was seldom, if ever, a night free from meetings of the Society, or of its Committees, requiring More's attendance. To the many callers at Denmark Court or the Adelphi he had to show unwearying attention; and it was his duty to maintain a satisfactory network of advisers and helpers to assist with the Society's developing activities.

To all these affairs he brought administrative ability and experience of a high order. He expressed himself clearly and fluently in writing and in speech, as the Discourses he made in the 1790s at the Annual Distributions of Premiums and Awards show. He had enough knowledge of French and German to conduct correspondence and translate scientific papers therein.

On 19th December 1786 he was able to demonstrate his proficiency in Latin at the first academic examination arranged by the Society. Dr. Egan of Greenwich applied for the Society's Gold Medal, offered in 1783, at the suggestion of William Shipley, to the master of a school within thirty miles of London who could produce at least four boys able to converse in Latin. (Similar offers had been made for equal proficiency in German, Italian and French.)[37]

The examination was conducted by a committee of twenty-five 'learned and classical members' of the Society. The text of a piece of English extolling the virtues of the study of Latin, prepared by More, and of the answers of the five scholars who took part, are reported in full in the Polite Arts Committee Minutes. The recommendation that Dr. Egan should receive the Gold Medal, the best boy a Silver Gilt Medal, and the other four boys Silver Medals was approved by the Society on 20th December.

In a letter dated 11th March 1787 Egan thanked More on behalf of the boys for the way in which he had read their translations and taken down their answers to the questions.[38] When the Medals were presented at the Annual Distribution of Awards on 6th May 1787, Egan thanked the Society with an address in Latin.

One of More's chief administrative tasks after 1783 was the production of the annual volumes of the Society's *Transactions* referred to by Mr. Allan in his Inaugural Study of 'The Origin and Growth of the Society's Archives'.[39] The first volume produced in 1783 inevitably involved many meetings of the Papers and Correspondence Committee and a great deal of work for More, who was much occupied with many problems of printing, paper, format, etc. He was responsible for the selection of the material to be considered for publication and for the writing of the Preface and the linking passages, although these were usually accepted without much amendment by the Committee and the Society. As the pattern of publication became settled and the functional Committees took more part in indicating material for publication, however, the Papers and Correspondence Committee confined itself to the principles and policies to be followed, and the detailed preparation of the volumes was left to More. In 1799 only three meetings of the Committee were needed to approve the 17th volume.

In addition to the *Transactions*, More was called upon to prepare papers for publication. In the 1780s numerous entries were received for a premium offered for an international set of Standards and Measures, but no entry was thought worthy of an award. On 5th March 1794 More was asked to produce a paper on the subject, and this he submitted to the Mechanics Committee on 30th April 1794. The manuscript in More's hand, which is in two parts in the Society's Loose Archives (C/5/71 and C/6/58), shows only two slight amendments by the Committee, and the version at pp. 292-301 in Vol. 12 (1794) of the *Transactions* is virtually as More wrote it. Trueman Wood suggests that the Society was moved in this matter by the attempts of the French National Assembly to fix on a theoretical standard, i.e., a metre. More's paper deprecated such a reference for the construction of an invariable standard of weights and measures and proposed a system based on the accurate copying of the standard measures, as of the pound then preserved at the Exchequer. His system anticipated the later legislation on weights and measures which provided for the accurate copying of existing standards.

More's evidence at the Arkwright trials throws interesting light on two other aspects of his work. Asked if he would have any difficulty in drawing up a specification for Arkwright's machine, he replied, 'I think not. I am continually drawing up specifications to machines. There seldom is a day when machines don't come before me and I draw up a specification for them.'

The second concerns patents. More said, 'No man in the United Kingdom is so often consulted upon patents as I am who gets nothing by it'. The Society believed that any innovation it inspired should be freely available, and a successful candidate was required to agree that the invention should be lodged in the Society's Model Room with a description. Any suggestion that an innovation had been, or would be, patented, involved disqualification; and the Society was not prepared to advise the Government on matters for which patents had been sought.

More's industrial friends, such as Wedgwood, Boulton and Watt, regarded their innovations as valuable assets and guarded them closely: they therefore did not compete for the Society's awards. More's personal view may have been much the same, for in 1784 he advised his friend William Parker and Argand to take out a patent for the latter's lamp,[40] and in 1791 he advised the Commissioners of Victualling on a more efficient method of controlling the temperature of brewing beer for which the inventor, Long, had already taken out patents in 1790.[41]

More's benevolent attitude to the new Societies which were being set up is important, for it heralded the policy consistently followed since then. In his 1799 Discourse he said that they strengthened rather than weakened the Society of Arts; and that they 'were entitled to obtain every encouragement they may be found to deserve or that it is in the power of the Society to give'. He did much to foster cordial relations with them and particularly with such as the Norfolk Society and the Bath Society, which sought to supplement on a regional basis what the Society was doing nationally. Letters in the archives show how grateful the regional Societies were for his help.

Although More when helping Templeman in 1768 had brought to light a fraud in the claims for premiums for sowing carrots and lucerne between 1761 and 1764, which led to the expulsion from the Society of Dr. John Stephens of Lincoln's Inn,[42] the control of the Society's finances was primarily the concern of the Accounts Committee, which met monthly, and the Collector, who collected subscriptions and handled the money. The

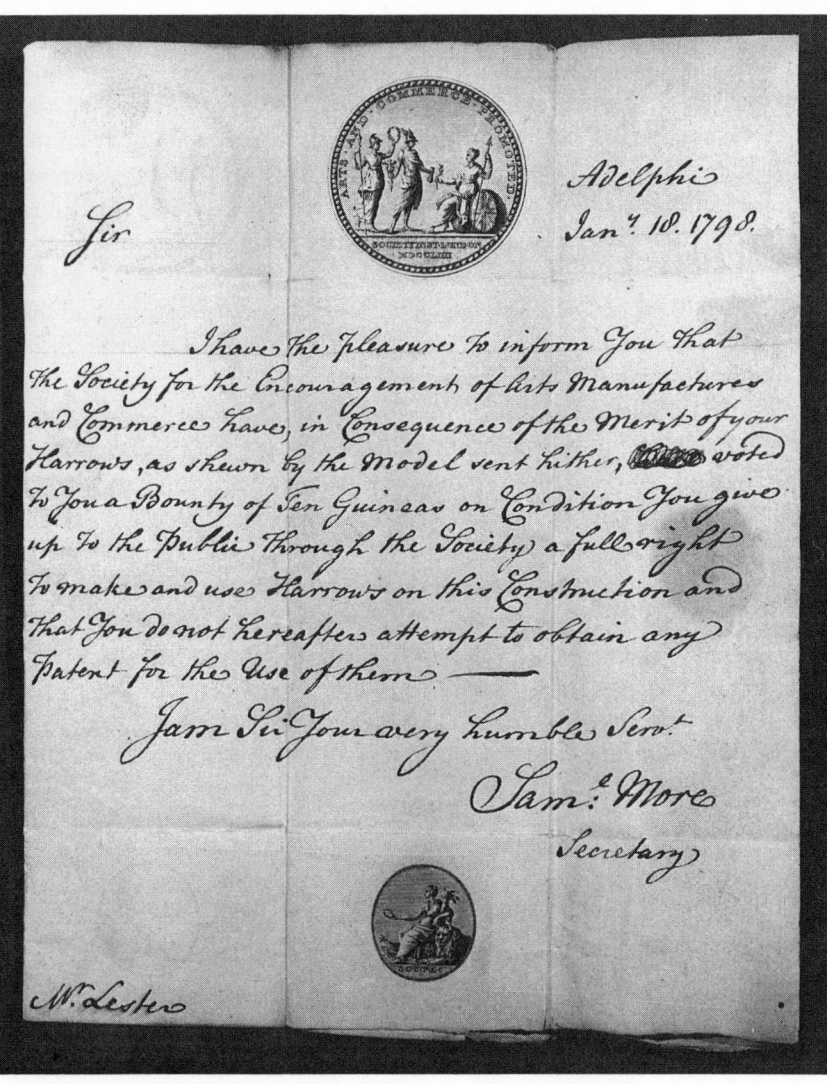

Letter from Samuel More to William Lester of Newport Pagnell; courtesy of the RSA. It is evidence of the Society's policy not to reward inventions that were to be patented.

post of Collector was never easy to fill, and after the death of Abraham Brooksbank in 1777, both Peter Duvall (1778-9) and John Heywood (1780-1) were obliged to resign because of their ways of handling the Society's money and their reluctance to provide satisfactory explanations of their dealings. Peter Duvall was suspended in 1779 following a special inquiry into the conduct of all the Society's officers, including the Secretary.[43] The Committee of Inquiry found that the Secretary had 'performed his duties with the utmost exactness and assiduity except in the article relative to the money accounts which the Committee of Accounts and the Collector have turned into another channel'.[44] This may have been a form of wording intended only to mean that Duvall's misconduct as Collector was being considered separately by the Accounts Committee. It may have been a criticism of More, in that he had not taken any action when Duvall failed to pay staff salaries promptly. If it was an adverse comment, it is the only one in the Society's records during More's Secretaryship and clearly made no difference to the regard in which More was held, for the Society, having approved the Special Committee's report on him, took no further action on it.[45]

The papers concerning Duvall were sealed by More on 2nd February 1780 on the Society's instruction. They remained sealed until recent times, when they were opened by Miss Clarke, then Librarian. They are now in the Archives as B/4/37-9.

SAMUEL MORE THE MAN: AN ASSESSMENT OF HIS ACHIEVEMENT

More's Travels

The statement of the Secretary's duties in Section 3 of the *Rules and Orders of the Society*, published in 1770, required that 'he shall visit manufacturers, or apply to manufacturers, for information when required to do so by the Society: and he shall, as much as possible, endeavour to make himself acquainted with the nature and circumstances of the several arts of this and other countries'.

Nothing could have been more in accord with More's own inclination, and he observed the direction closely. He had spent two months touring Devon and Cornwall on horseback with his friend John Newcombe in 1763, and he used most, and perhaps all, of the summer recesses from June to October in each year to make extended visits out of London. There is definite evidence (although scanty in some cases) of 14 tours after his appointment as Secretary, and there were almost certainly others. He usually visited Etruria and the Midlands, Anglesey, and John Wilkinson's homes at Wrexham and Castlehead in North Lancashire, and Coalbrookdale.

Six Journals in More's hand have recently come to light covering excursions to Devon and Cornwall (1763); the Midlands and Lancashire (1776, 1780 and 1783); North Wales, Anglesey and Lancashire (1784); and Northumberland (1785). I have only seen brief digests of these Journals, but it seems that they will throw much light on eighteenth-century industry and practices; and indeed on many other aspects of life. Furthermore, through his comments and the things he observed, much will be learned about More's own opinions and character. When the Journals finally become available, I shall be interested to see how far they confirm or correct the conclusions I have reached in the absence of firmer detailed evidence.

I was fortunate, however, to find a large extract from More's 1780 Journal, and a shorter one from 1776, in the Wedgwood MSS in the British Library.[46] These, with other letters and papers mentioned in this study, show how More's tough mind and body carried him through long and arduous days (often on horseback and in bad weather), and how nothing was too small or apparently irrelevant for his observant eye and inquiring spirit. He travelled far to see anything that caught his attention; fine scenery, geological formations, agricultural developments, new machines and industrial processes, improvements or changes since his last visit were all carefully recorded and described. As much notice was taken of an interesting casual road-side conversation as of a more formal visit.

He was particularly conscientious about the Society's business. In 1763 when the Society was financing Blake's experiment in bringing fresh fish to London, More kept a meticulous record of the prices of all kinds of fish at the markets and small ports he visited. His later Journals note the local prices of meat, provisions, etc. He called on Members of the Society in the localities he visited, and everywhere he explained what the Society was trying to do and encouraged people to communicate new ideas or practices. I have indicated how a conversation at Warrington in 1786 encouraged Thomas Greaves, a paper-maker, to manufacture paper from the bark of withies, which won him a Silver Medal, and there are other examples in the Society's Archives.

Most of More's excursions were based on long visits to his three close friends, who all became Members of the Society: Wedgwood at Etruria; Wilkinson at Wrexham and/or Castlehead; and Thomas Williams in North Wales and Anglesey. He regularly visited Warrington, where he was friendly with John Aikin, M.D., and Priestley, and Birmingham to see his other close friends Matthew Boulton and James Watt and to meet informally and occasionally dine with the Members of the Lunar Society, including Erasmus Darwin, William Withering, and John Whitehurst, and later Priestley when he moved there. More often called at Coalbrookdale and Ketley, attracted by the excellence of the work done there, and stayed with his friends Abraham Darby III and Richard and William Reynolds. He enjoyed their company and told Abraham Darby in 1787 that he 'was never more happy' than when with them. Mrs. More sometimes accompanied him on his travels and was a welcome guest. Occasionally she left him to make the more energetic local excursions on his own; the Journals often mention that she dined with their friends, for example, when More went underground at Ketley in July 1780 to see one of Reynolds's steam engines, and at Bersham in July 1783 to observe trials of new valves for a Watt engine.

Their visits, particularly those to the Wedgwoods at Etruria, were not all spent on serious matters, for the Journals refer to sight-seeing visits in which the ladies took part—excursions in Derbyshire, visiting the Wrekin, where More slid down to demonstrate the quickest way, and sailing in Anglesey. Occasionally More practised as an apothecary, usually in consultation with the local man, and the Journals record meetings between him and his erstwhile patients. In July 1780, with Mr. Hately, steward to Lord Dudley, he was a commissioner to arbitrate in a dispute concerning an engine between a Mr. Cole, its maker, and the proprietors of the Worcester Water Works.

Apart from the tours noted in the Journals, there is evidence of other journeys. In 1786, More visited the lead mines at Alston Moor (staying in a miner's house) to study the efforts of the Quaker owners through their Society of Miners to improve social, working and health conditions for their men.[47] He rode from there to Castlehead via Penrith, Ullswater and the Kirkstone Pass and Windermere; and on arriving at Castlehead had enough energy to write to Banks about an earthquake in the neighbourhood on 11th August.

He visited the Earl of Egremont, and the Earl's mistress Mrs. Wyndham, at Petworth on at least two occasions. He was there in July 1799 when the onset of his last illness compelled him to return to London. In November 1797 More, writing to the Earl, gave notice that he was contemplating a visit to Cumberland in 1798 and would be glad to visit the Egremont estate there.[48] Mr. George Butler, in a letter of 22nd November 1793, referring to a pump installed at Downe (in Kent) writes: 'You may possibly recollect my well at Downe'.[49] In 1785, when the Mechanics Committee was considering a pulverizing mill, More correctly recalled that he had seen a similar mill at Colchester.

More's Health

To have maintained such an arduous regime in eighteenth-century conditions demanded mental and physical toughness and stamina. More had the necessary strong constitution. Apart from gout, he seems to have suffered only from two short, sharp attacks of fever (possibly influenza) and from falling off his horse at Alnwick Castle in August 1785. Although the Society's records have only one reference to More's being ill during his service, his own letters show that he had severe attacks of gout and was confined to his rooms in 1789, 1795 and 1798. He reminded the Earl of Egremont in 1797 that they had first met several years earlier (1789?) in More's bedroom at the Adelphi, when he was suffering from gout and the Earl had brought a sample of cobalt for him.[50] As More lived in the building it seems that he still attended to business and went to meetings during these attacks unless absolutely incapacitated. The obituary notice in the *Transactions* observed that he died 'less a martyr to old age as to infirmity, being worn out with almost perpetual attacks of gout with which he had for many years been very heavily afflicted'.

Mortimer, in his Memoir, says that after More had returned from Petworth in July 1799 he resumed his duties but was weak and languid. He continued in the office until 7th October, when he took to his bed. He died on Thursday 11th October. He was buried privately in the family vault in the burial ground of St. Margaret's, Westminster, at the chapel in the Broadway, on 21st October, 'most honourably attended' by the Duke of Norfolk, President of the Society, Francis Stephens, a Vice President, and his executors.

More's Will

At his death More was not a rich man, and his estate was valued at under £2000.[51] He provided for his sister-in-law Elizabeth Vincent, and there were smaller legacies to the daughters of his friend Richard Crawshay, the South Wales ironmaster. He left his own Gold Medal to John Wilkinson; that bequeathed to him by Lewis to Thomas Williams; and the one left to him by George Berg to Richard Crawshay. Anne Law (later Lady Ellenborough), the daughter of his niece Elizabeth and George Towry, received a pearl snuff box and 'a fine liturgy of the Church of England bound in shagreen with silver clasps and ornamented in superb fashion by . . . prints collected with great attention and expense' by More's father. His executors were George Towry and William Newcombe.

Honours

More's value to the Society was recognized and honoured during his lifetime. During his service his salary was increased from £150 to £200 a year, including an allowance of £20 a year for coals and candles. At the Anniversary Dinner of the Society at the Crown and Anchor Tavern in the Strand on 22nd March 1785 his health was drunk with acclaim, and he replied in 'a manly, eloquent and modest speech'.[52] As a mark of the Society's regard it was decided that his portrait should be included in the panel representing 'the Society' in Barry's painting in the Great Room. In April 1794 he was awarded the Society's Gold Medal 'for eminent services'.

In June 1796 it was agreed by the Society that More's portrait should be painted as an acknowledgement of the esteem in which he was held and 'to perpetuate his memory and preserve his likeness'. More was asked to make the necessary arrangements, and he offered the commission to Benjamin West. The portrait now hangs in the Committee Room: it was considered by the Polite Arts Committee to be 'a strong likeness'. The demand for copies from Members was so great that the Society in 1797 agreed to underwrite an engraving by William Sharp (also chosen by More), and more than 250 copies were sold. I have not been able to find any evidence about the Drummond portrait of More painted in 1793 or the circumstances in which it was painted.

More's qualities were recognized by other Societies. He was honoured in 1785 by election to the Dublin Society for Improving Husbandry and Manufactures. In 1786 he was elected a Foreign Member of the American Philosophical Society in company with such men as Priestley, three years before Sir Joseph Banks received a similar honour.

The Man

More was descended from a hard-working and intelligent family of writing masters who had prospered in the difficult world of the seventeenth century. Orphaned as he was, he needed these qualities to succeed, and it is not to be wondered at if occasionally he seemed to be well satisfied with his achievements. The discipline of his thought and the high quality and suppleness of his mind served both him and the Society well, and he was held in high esteem by all who knew him.

His scientific training and practice had sharpened his essentially practical mind without impairing the qualities of imagination and speculation which he brought to the application of science and technology to industry. Several years after his death this approach was illustrated in the *Gentleman's Magazine* for 1804 (Part II, p. 1223). It is there reported that when he was asked about the best book on farming, he replied *Robinson Crusoe*. It was a book that 'has been translated into more languages and given more conduct to life than most books. It may be said with truth and justice that it has been the cause of making many seamen into good seamen, and of calling into activity all the powers and resources of mind and body. It will for ever be read with amusement and instruction'. Defoe had died when More was a boy, but it is interesting that his son-in-law Henry Baker had sponsored More's election to the Society.

The West portrait suggests a well-built man of perhaps 5 ft. 10 in. of good and sound physique. His face is strong but stern. Personally I think that the Drummond portrait may have been a truer likeness. The face depicted there bears the marks of pain and illness, but it suggests qualities of compassion and humour which I do not see in the West painting. Although only occasional touches of humour show through the formality of More's correspondence, his Journals indicate that he was capable of an almost school-boy sense of fun—as when at the age of 60 he climbed to the roof of a Folly at Alnwick Castle and stood cheering, or slid down the Wrekin on his seat.

The *Gentleman's Magazine* in reporting More's death deplored the loss of a valuable member of the Community, and the obituary notice in the *Transactions* called him 'a very excellent officer whose private worth was not inferior to his public virtues'. Members of the Society found him approachable and interested in them and what they had to say, and they appreciated the cheerful hospitality dispensed by More and his wife. In turn the Mores were welcome guests, and their friends found them sincere and helpful. More could on occasions be severe, and he was not in any way disposed to allow people to put upon him, as some of his answers to Counsel in the Arkwright trial clearly indicate. There is a delightful letter of 27th April 1775 from John Phillips to More apologizing for mis-spelling his name by including an extra 'o', which suggests that he was sensitive about the correct spelling.[53]

His gout suggests that he was fond of good living, for he was a gregarious man who mixed freely with people. His Journals contain much information about the social customs of the time. He enjoyed travel and open-air activities in general and recorded many interesting incidents and conversations. It is apparent, however, that he enjoyed most the company of men who could appreciate and match his own intelligence, such as the Members of the Lunar Society. He was very much at home with tough, and even unscrupulous, men such as Wilkinson, Williams and Crawshay, for he admired their drive and their determination first to stimulate, and then to use, innovation in technological and industrial processes.

His Friends

A list of More's close friends reads like a Roll of Honour of the Industrial Revolution, and needs no comment. William Lewis, Josiah Wedgwood, Thomas Bentley, Matthew Boulton, James Watt, Joseph Priestley, Arthur Young, John Wilkinson, Thomas Williams and Richard Crawshay were his familiars, and they all at different times gladly sought and received his help. Other important friends were Abraham Darby III, Richard and William Reynolds of Coalbrookdale and Ketley, Erasmus Darwin, John Whitehurst, William Withering and William Small of the Lunar Society. Manufacturers such as Samuel Garbett, Jukes Coulson, William Parker, the cut glass manufacturer, and Peter Dollond, the optician, all claimed, and in various ways benefited from, his friendship. We must remember, too, others such as James Auriol, who became Secretary of the Royal Institution and whose son Samuel was More's godson and received a small legacy at his death, and John Imison, the Manchester printer, who in 1781 dedicated his book *The School of Arts* to More in acknowledgement of his friendship and help.

He also had some close family friends: John Newcombe, Francis Vincent and George Towry. John Newcombe was a linen draper living at Cheapside who married Francis Vincent's sister Elizabeth at Lamb's Chapel on 22nd February 1750. He came from a Devon family living at Exeter, and when he and More made their two-month visit to Devon and Cornwall in 1763, More stayed with Newcombe's family. John Newcombe was the father of William (born in 1757) who became a successful banker. He married Francis Vincent's daughter Mary, who received a legacy of £200, the 'best set of Derby tea china' and other pieces under More's will.

Francis Vincent was cousin to More's wife Keturah. He was the same age as More and died three weeks after him. They had been friends for many years, probably from More's apprenticeship days. Francis's father, Giles, who had built up a prosperous trade as a Portugal packer, was ruined by the Lisbon earthquake in 1755 in which his second son, also named Giles, was killed, and Francis spent his life re-constructing the family business. It was he who paid for the education of his brother

William at Westminster School. This was the William who officiated at the marriage of More and Keturah, and who became successively Headmaster of Westminster School and Dean of the Abbey. Francis signed as a witness to More's marriage. In 1770 he became a Member of the Society.

George Phillips Towry had married More's niece Elizabeth in 1766. After she died in 1769, Towry helped his widowed mother-in-law, Eleanor, and her other daughter, Sydney, and they seem to have relied on him rather than on More. This reliance, however, may have been more apparent than real, for the friendship between More and Towry was close and continued until More died, when Towry became one of his executors.

The Society's Expert Advisers and Assistants

It is necessary in considering the effectiveness of More's work to remember that the successful operation of the Society's policy of encouraging innovation through the award of premiums depended upon a sensitive network of people (not necessarily Members of the Society) and businesses with expert knowledge and practical experience, able and willing usually without payment to advise and/or to give practical help in testing new materials and techniques. It was not a formal organization, but it covered most aspects of the commercial, industrial and scientific problems of the time. While it had developed because of the Society, it was available to others. The businessmen, scientists, farmers and others assisting the Society's work benefited by the early knowledge they received of new ideas, products, materials and processes.

On becoming Secretary More inherited a basic organization which as a Member he had helped to create, but it was greatly enlarged as the Society's work developed. More, with his own up-to-date knowledge and experience of the contemporary industrial and scientific scene and his valuable range of friendships, was well equipped to deal with this expansion and to operate the network to the best effect. He was able not only to obtain the best-available opinion and advice for the Society but also to help those Members who were experimenting on lines suggested by it. In a letter of thanks to More, dated 2nd November 1772, John Crow of Faversham, wanting to sell madder he had grown, wrote of 'the gentleman you recommended me to at Bankside whom I hope will be a customer'.[54]

Important manufacturers such as Wedgwood, Wilkinson and Boulton both helped and used the organization. Wedgwood was always ready to test new materials and frequently sought More's help in getting things done through its agency. Boulton sent the dies of medals and coins to More to be engraved in London because of the better workmanship there: in his turn More wanted Boulton to manufacture Arkwright's tokens, and he put other business in Boulton's way. The Government through its Select Committees and the Committee of the Privy Council for Trade made use of the organisation in various ways through the Society, and Lord Hawkesbury, President of the Committee, consulted More about an engraver.[55] In February 1782 More advised Towry on the way to persuade the Royal Academy to withdraw its opposition to a Spectaculum or Court Fair to be held in the Pantheon, in which Towry had a share; and when that approach was successful he gave very detailed advice and recommendations about the best designers and manufacturers in the country to be invited to exhibit.[56] This correspondence is specifically mentioned because it is an excellent example of how More was able to bring people together for their mutual benefit. In October 1783 he wrote to James Watt about 'a curious lathe, a most complete engine of its kind with a prodigious number of tools of curious workmanship' costing 200 guineas in all, and said he could get the first offer for Watt or Boulton or any of their friends if they wanted it.[57]

He acted as a consultant chemist for William Reynolds when Reynolds made trials of bitumen ('Native Tar') discovered at Coalport in 1787. More assembled the results and made suggestions for treating the bitumen to produce pitch (Asphaltum), which he thought might 'serve valuable purposes', in a letter of 6th December 1787 to Abraham Darby III. Reynolds in consequence developed the Coalport Tar Tunnel commercially. It produced 1000 barrels a day initially and sold mainly pitch, but production declined in the 1820s and was abandoned in 1843.[58]

By the 1780s, through the knowledge he had acquired in operating the network, his important friendships with the principal manufacturers, and the technical and commercial information about new developments which he sedulously collected on his travels, More had an unrivalled, perhaps uniquely wide, knowledge of the technical, scientific and industrial world in which he was living. His advice was frequently sought and readily given, and he was accepted as an impartial and wise counsellor. 'There is great reason to believe', said the obituary note in the Society's *Transactions*, 'that some of the first mechanicians and manufacturers of this country have at different times been indebted to him for useful hints and observations'. They were in fact often indebted for more than hints and observations, for More had a reassuring and enviable reputation, particularly among those living away from London, as a man who could get things done. William Pitt, the Prime Minister, had consulted him on points of material consequence to the commercial interests of the country. Wedgwood in 1775 had said to Bentley, 'Everyone knows him to be a Conjuror'.[59] Priestley writing to Wedgwood on 26th August 1787, was more precise: 'Mr. More, who is with you, and is a kind of necessary man for all philosophers, may perhaps be able to procure the specimens [of some special stone Priestley wanted] for me. If any one can come at them *he* can, and I have often experienced his readiness to oblige me.'[60]

The reputation that More had acquired was, I believe, the product of the three factors I have tried to bring out in this part of the study: his character and versatile talents and skills; the importance and variety of his friendships and his ability to get on with all kinds of people; and the network of people and firms ready to use new ideas. There was a fourth factor—the Society.

The Society and More

I have left the Society to the last because it is the most difficult element in the story to define and assess. It is, however, also the most important. It is difficult at any time to distinguish between the work of the Society and the work of its Secretary, for they act and react on each other. In More's day the Society laid down policies (although More undoubtedly influenced them), and much of the detailed work was done by the Committees. The records show that More was at all times loyal to the Society, acting only as its spokesman, and that he worked within the framework of and limits imposed by the Society.

Nevertheless the organization and procedures of the Society at that time inevitably left areas in which More had to use his own judgement; usually, as the many votes of thanks to him in the Minutes show, to the Society's satisfaction. This was particularly true in regard to the network of advisers. Members of Committees and the Society frequently suggested those who might help the Society in its activities, but the responsibility for obtaining advice and arranging tests rested with the Secretary. The result was that the helpers tended to think rather of More than of the Society.

Secondly, it seems that More pleased himself about his excursions, which he regarded as holidays. In his early days the Society formally agreed to a leave of absence during the summer recess, but later this is not recorded. Nor is there any evidence of his ever asking the Society's permission for any of his journeys or of his submitting a report on his return. There is certainly no record of his expenses being reimbursed. He decided where to go, what and whom to see, and when, although he no doubt paid strict attention to any suggestions that might have been made. The requirements of his work, and both his official and personal inclination, made it imperative that he should keep the friendships he had cultivated in good repair; and that he should keep himself well informed of all current developments. By so doing More was carrying out his instructions and properly serving the interest of the Society, which in turn, through its premiums and the stimulation of innovation which it encouraged, provided the conditions in which More's qualities and experience could operate most effectively. The benefit was mutual, and the linking of the man and the institution in the phrase 'Mr. More of the Adelphi' seemed natural.

More's Achievement

Two years before More died, the third edition of the *Encyclopaedia Britannica* (1797) described the Society as 'one of the most important in Britain. Much money has been expended by it and many are the valuable effects which it has produced. Among them we reckon not only the discoveries it has excited but the institution of other Societies on the same principles to which it has given birth; and we do not hesitate to conclude that future ages will consider the founding of this Society as one of the most remarkable epochs in the history of the Arts'.[61]

This encomium says much for More's energy and drive. He had handled the Society's business with skill and dignity. His qualities of mind and character and his enthusiastic support of the Society's objects, harnessed to an indefatigable attention to its affairs and a willingness to travel far and wide to further its interests, had made its work known nationally; Ministers, including the Prime Minister, sought his opinion. The leading manufacturers and agriculturists, such as Arthur Young, recognized the possibilities in the Society's stimulation of innovation, and most of them were either Members or consultants. The practical help which More gave to other young Societies enabled them to become established and to develop.

In a variety of ways, unobtrusively but effectively, More had influenced technological and industrial developments of great significance, and his advice and that of the Society was sought and frequently adopted. By 1797 the Society was stronger, better known and more firmly established than it had been in 1761.

More's influence on these developments was well recognized. The *Gentleman's Magazine* in 1799 spoke of him as 'a very able and faithful servant who had conducted the Society's business with great respect and prosperity'. The obituary in the *Transactions* remarked, 'his unwearied zeal in the execution of an office to which he had been enthusiastically de-

voted for 30 years and his extensive knowledge of every subject connected
with the Institution are well known and must be generally acknowledged',
and called him 'a very excellent officer'. At the Annual Dinner in March
1800, the Society's President, the Duke of Norfolk, in inviting the company to drink 'a silent glass' to More's memory, said that he had filled
for so long and ably a difficult post with propriety and judgement. He
feared that no other person could fill such an important office so well.[62]
(At the 1801 Dinner, however, the Duke acknowledged that his fear had
been mistaken and paid tribute to the work of Charles Taylor.)

'Mr. More of the Adelphi' was indeed a true man of parts in the full
eighteenth-century sense. My researches convince me that he ranks with
the best of the Society's Secretaries and that further information about
him, if it comes to light, may well prove that he was the greatest.

Postscript

Although it did not become apparent for some time, the death of More
marked the effective end of an era. The new Societies, which the Society and he had encouraged, and the professional associations which were
established early in the nineteenth century, gradually took over activities
which had been fostered by the Society. The idea of encouraging innovation by the award of premiums lost its force, and it became difficult to
find money for them. The Society's procedures, always cumbersome, led
to argument and frustration at meetings.

There had been important suggestions for reform in More's day. At a
Society meeting on 22nd February 1784, William Greene had proposed the
introduction of a course of lectures on Experimental Philosophy. Valentine
Green on 1st March 1797 had put forward a scheme to vest the govern-
ment of the Society and the control of its staff in a Council to consist of the
President, Vice Presidents, Committee Chairmen, and 35 elected Members.
(A similar proposal was contemplated by John Ellis, the naturalist, in 1758,
although it seems doubtful that it was presented to the Society.[63])

Trueman Wood reports that Aikin realized the need for change but
could not get his ideas accepted, although lectures as a regular part of the
Society's policy of publicizing new developments were accepted in 1829 on
Aikin's suggestion.[64] It was not until April 1843 that the main reform of
establishing a Council very much on the lines proposed by Valentine Green
and Ellis was approved, and then only after much trial and tribulation
which nearly wrecked the Society.

20

THE CHRONOLOGY OF JAMES BARRY'S
WORK FOR THE SOCIETY'S GREAT ROOM

D. G. C. Allan

Some twenty-eight years elapsed between the acceptance by the Society of Barry's offer to undertake single-handed what had been thought appropriate for ten artists to perform and the time, so near his own death, when he was requested to add the portrait of the lately slain Horatio Nelson to the cycle. Except in the first five years of the period he was not, of course, continuously engaged on the paintings; yet they were never far from his thoughts, and although he hoped to follow them with an even greater achievement and seemed to want in 1790 to say goodbye to them for ever, their 'increasing celebrity' and the intrinsic interest of their subject matter helped to counteract the painful recollections of disappointed hopes and manic jealousies and bind him to further periods of involvement in what he called his 'very extensive work in the Great Room'.[1] Barry's association with the work falls into six phases:

 I. Five years of hard and enthusiastic work on the project, 1777-82. This was a time of creativity and optimism for the artist when all six pictures were largely completed.

 II. Three years of anticipation and disappointment regarding the reception of the paintings, 1782-4.

Originally appeared in *Jnl. RSA*, 131 (Mar., Apr., 1983), 214-21, 283-89.

III. Two years of renewed hope and further despair, following the comple-
tion of the Prince of Wales's portrait in the fifth picture, 1789-90.
IV. Seven years of gradual reconciliation culminating in the additions of
1798 and the rewards of 1799.
V. The additions of 1801 when Barry's idiosyncrasies were given free rein.
VI. Two unrealized additions, November 1801 and November 1805.

THE FIRST PHASE: CREATIVITY AND OPTIMISM,
1772-82

On 27th March 1777 Barry received from the Secretary of the
Society, Samuel More, a copy of the resolution accepting his offer to decorate the Great Room with paintings 'analogous to the views of the Institution'.[2] By the 19th of the following month, as he told Sir George Savile
in a letter of that date, he had begun the work. Barry's letter to Savile
makes it clear that the artist had already worked out the subject of the first
painting: 'the story of Orpheus reclaiming mankind from a savage state,
as it is glanced at by Horace'. He had not, however, at this stage hit on
the *Grecian Harvest Home* as the subject of the second painting and was
thinking of following the first directly with what was to be the subject
of the third painting: 'that point of time at the Olympic games when the
Hellanodics are distributing the rewards'. This was to be followed by two
subjects which he did not in fact include in his scheme: 'the contest and
matching of the competitors' and 'Prodicus reading to the assembly his
performance of the choice of Hercules, Aetion the painter, and a number
of other ingenious men, producing their several performances'. After these
there would be three pictures dedicated 'to matters of more recent discovery, and more immediately relating to the abilities of our own people'.[3]
The *Orpheus* was to be where the *Grecian Harvest Home* is now, the
Olympic Victors would be in its existing position, 'the contest and matching' would be in the place of *The Triumph of the Thames,* and 'Prodicus
and Aetion' in that of *The Society*. The wall which now holds the *Elysium*
would be occupied by two of the 'modern' pictures, and the third would
end the series where it now begins, that is in the place at present occupied
by the *Orpheus*. At what stage Barry departed from this scheme by painting the *Harvest Home* we cannot say. Its links with Poussin's *Worship of
the Golden Calf,* then in the possession of Lord Radnor, a Vice President
of the Society, have long since been noted, and Dr. Pressly has recently
seen in it certain Christian symbols which suggest it as a natural sequel to
the St. John the Baptist–Orpheus.[4] Certainly Barry needed a stage inter-

mediate between mankind in a savage state and classical times to make sense of the story of the progress of human culture, and this he makes clear in his 1783 *Account*. Probably he had completed the work by the end of 1777 when his mind was definitely occupied with beginning the *Olympic Victors* painting. On 27th December he wrote to the Earl of Chatham expressing his 'earnest wish to avail myself of your Lordship's portrait, Lord Cambden's [*sic*] and Sir George Savile's as three of the Hellanodics or Judges', and soon after the Earl's death on 11th May 1778 Barry decided to introduce him into the *Olympic Victors* in the character of Pericles.[5] He did not include portraits of either Camden or Savile or, it would seem, of any other living personages apart from himself as Timanthes in this painting. Savile would appear in the fifth painting, *The Society*, and other portraits of what Barry called his 'contemporaries of worth', though not Camden's, would be placed there and in the fourth and sixth pictures.

For various reasons Barry flanked his assembly of athletes, spectators and judges with a pair of statues: Minerva to the right and Hercules to the left. Hercules is shown 'treading down envy' with Barry as Timanthes, the Greek painter, sitting near the base and under threat from the jealous serpent. This is our first hint of the artist's persecution mania which caused him so much unhappiness and stimulated him to so much richness of invention. Yet in general at this point in his work he was confident and optimistic, if we accept an unusually warm letter addressed to his friend Joseph Bonomi as having been composed in the early autumn of 1778, though written from a street he did not settle in until 1788:

> Castle Street
> Thursday morning
>
> Dear Bonomi,
>   The first two pictures for the Adelphi are nearly finished I mean the Crowning the Victors at Olympia and Harvest Home—As you expressed a wish to see them you can do so at the great Rooms—you know to what extent I value your opinion therefore I shall feel thankful to you to call between two and four—I am to tell you that I am in high favour with a *certain party*.
>   Believe me to be
>   Yours sincerely
>   James Barry[6]

Another letter written by Barry on the subject of his paintings for the Great Room is dated 28th October 1778 and is addressed to the Society. It shows that by then the artist had, as he put it, 'very considerably advanced' in his work and was now beginning to complete the fifth painting,

The Distribution of Premiums in the Society of Arts.[7] This would suggest
that the fourth painting, *Commerce, or the Triumph of the Thames,* was
already near completion, since we can well imagine that Barry would have
wanted to get this largely allegorical picture out of the way before starting
on the more time-consuming work of assembling a series of portraits of
contemporary personalities. The *Thames* was, however, destined to contain representations of two persons from modern times: Captain Cook,
whose portrait by Dance was used as a model by Barry, presumably
round about the time of the great navigator's death in February 1779, and
Dr. Burney, the epitome of British musical achievement, whose portrait
was presumably not inserted in the *Thames* until Reynolds had completed
the work upon which it was based in 1781.[8] Probably Barry took time
off from his major preoccupations with the fifth and sixth paintings to
introduce these two portraits in the *Thames.*

Barry called his fifth picture 'a limb necessary for the uniformity of my
subject. I mean the annual distributions of Rewards made by [the] Society'. 'There offers here', he continued in his letter to the Society of 28th
October 1778, 'a proper opportunity of introducing between forty and
fifty portraits of such of your members as it may be most agreeable to
the wishes of the Society to transmit to posterity in this work.' This letter
was at once referred by the Society to its Committee of Polite Arts, which
reached the rather general conclusion that the introduction of 'Portraits of
Members . . . is likely in its consequence to prove beneficial to the Society
and therefore proper to be carried into execution'. Although this resolution failed to satisfy the Society at its meeting on 11th November, the
Committee reached the same conclusion when it was asked to reconsider
the matter on the 13th. Eventually on 19th November, the Society accepted
two motions giving some general guidance to the Artist:

> that the Presidency of the Society are proper persons to have their portraits
> introduced into the painting now executing by Mr. Barry . . . that it be
> recommended to the Artist to introduce the portrait of Mr. Shipley as the
> founder of the Society.

This did not mean, however, that the artist could proceed with his final
selection of portraits. After postponing the question from 25th November
to 9th December, the Society defined 'the Presidency' as 'the original President, and Vice-Presidents and such of their successors in office, as far as
may be complied with, who continued therein during their lives or to the
present time' and resolved that 'Portraits of the Ladies who are members or
have continued so during their lives be also introduced into the painting'.[9]

Before this on 4th December Samuel More, the Secretary of the Society, seems to have begun approaching the Presidency. Letters have survived which show that on that day both Lord Radnor and the Duke of Richmond wrote saying they were 'always ready to obey the commands of the Society'. On 13th December Sir George Savile wrote to say that he would give a sitting 'after the holidays'. The next day Charles Marsham wrote from Weymouth promising to sit 'on his return to London', Lord Romney from Maidstone to say that he was 'always ready', and Earl Percy from Northumberland House to the same effect. On the 15th John Eckersall wrote to say that the only portrait of his late father available for copying was unsuitable, and on the 16th Lord Harcourt wrote saying where a portrait of his father could be found. These replies were all reported to a meeting of the Society held on 16th December, when, almost as an afterthought, a motion was carried 'that a copy of the Several Resolutions relative to the introducing Portraits into the Paintings carrying on for the decoration of the Great Room be delivered to Mr. Barry'.[10]

Thus seven weeks after his first approach to the Society the artist was informed of its views. His terms of reference left him with the possibility of including some 21 Presidents and Vice Presidents, 8 lady members and William Shipley—assuming of course that he could obtain either sittings or portraits to copy. Barry only managed to include Shipley, two lady members, and fourteen portraits from the Presidency. Of the twelve other portraits named by Barry as present in the painting, six were ordinary male members or ex-members of the Society, one was Samuel More the Secretary, and five were not members at all. In choosing this latter group Barry was clearly guided by his current preoccupation with fame and virtue and was by no means uninfluenced by personal predilections and current literary fashions. Idealism and eccentricity, needless to say, went hand in hand.

Of the six ordinary male members or ex-members Barry selected, Arthur Young was probably the most acceptable by virtue of his contribution to the Society's work, and Johnson for his general reputation. William Lock, though active as a patron of the arts, was not especially prominent in the Society's affairs. Unlike Johnson and Burke, however, he was a current subscriber. Burke and Hunter were famous for their work outside and not inside the Society. Though Hunter was a current subscriber, Soame Jenyns presented what Dr. Ronald Rompkey, his most recent biographer, calls 'a curious case of membership or non-membership'. Jenyns had first been elected in 1761 but never paid his subscription. Only after he had seen himself in Barry's painting did he rejoin the Society. Dr. Rompkey suggested that Barry had been impressed by Jenyns' *A View of the Internal Evidence*

James Barry, *The Distribution of Premiums in the Society of Arts*, c. 1778-1801; the fifth picture for the Society's Great Room. Courtesy of the RSA.

Outline and key to portraits in the fifth picture.

1. Arthur Young.* 2. Samuel More. 3. Charles Marsham.† 4. William Shipley.* 5. An unnamed 'farmer'. 6. Lord Romney.† 7. Owen Salusbury Brereton.† 8. Prince of Wales and hidden behind him, Joshua Steele.† 9. Duchess of Northumberland.§ 10. Earl Percy.† 11. Sir George Savile.† 12. Dr. Hurd, Bishop of Worcester. 13. Mrs. Montagu.§ 14. Unnamed head. 15. Soame Jenyns.* 16. Unnamed 'young female'. 17. James Harris. 18. Unnamed female head. 19. Unnamed girl holding a medal of the Society of Arts. 20. Duchess of Rutland. 21. Dr. Johnson.* 22. Duchess of Devonshire. 23. Unnamed female figure (possibly Lady Betty Germaine§). 24. Dejected boy. 25. William Lock.* 26. Premium-winning boy. 27. Duke of Northumberland.† 28. Dr. William Hunter.* 29. Edmund Burke.* 30. Duke of Richmond.† 31. 2nd Earl of Radnor.† 32. Edward Hooper.† 33. Keane Fitzgerald.† 34. Dr. Stephen Hales.† 35. Lord Folkestone.† 36. 1st Earl of Radnor.†

*Ordinary members (male) †Vice-Presidents and Presidents §Lady members

James Barry, *Elysium, or The State of Final Retribution*, c. 1779-1801; the sixth picture, right panel. Courtesy of the RSA.

Outline and key to portraits, etc., in the sixth picture, right panel.

Upper range, left to right: 1. Ghiberti. 2. Donatello. 3. Michelangelo. 4. Leonardo. 5. Raphael. 6. Parmigianino. 7. Titian. 8. Correggio. 9. Apelles. 10. One of a group of unnamed figures. *Middle range, left to right:* 11. Domenichino. 12. Annibale Carracci. 13. Phidias. 14. 'Two Greek Painters'. 15. Poussin. 16. The Sicyonian Maid 'with the shade of her lover'. 17. Callimachus. 18. Pamphilus. 19. Angelic guard (added in 1798). *Lower range, left to right:* 20. Francis I. 21. Lord Arundel. 22. Grotius. 23. Pope Adrian. 24. Unnamed figure, possibly Johan van Oldenbarnevelt. 25. Father Paul Sarpi. *Tartarus, upper range, left to right:* 26. A malicious whisperer (added 1783). 27. A miser. 28. Pride. *Tartarus, middle range, left to right:* 29. A warrior. 30. A spendthrift. 31. An anonymous detractor. 32. A woman dragged down by her hair. 33. A glutton. *The figures of an enraged King, a worldly Pope, and a Covenanter are shown at the bottom right of the panel.*

of the Christian Religion (1776), an *apologia* for Christianity on ethical grounds.[11] Next to Jenyns in the picture is James Harris, M.P. and classicist, but not a member of the Society, and above Mrs. Montagu, the best-known lady member, is another distinguished non-member, Dr. Richard Hurd, Bishop of Worcester and writer on Horace. As to what Barry called 'the two beautiful duchesses of Rutland and Devonshire', they were not members, and he probably included them to show he was the equal of Reynolds and Gainsborough in portraying feminine beauty. The figure shown standing behind the Duchess of Devonshire may conceivably be a portrait of Lady Betty Germaine. In the 1783 *Account* Barry complained that after being 'long delayed' by the Society's Secretary he could not obtain a picture to copy of this important deceased lady member and so omitted her from the composition. It is quite likely, however, that he subsequently decided to suggest her presence by this partially hidden figure in widow's weeds.[12] Highest in rank was of course the Prince of Wales, then a potential patron of the Society. He was unable to grant Barry a sitting until 1789, so only his body, clad magnificently in Garter Robes, would be painted before the first exhibition of 1783.

Although Barry complained that the fifth picture cost him 'more time than all the rest of the work', there is evidence to show that from as early as September 1779 his thoughts were turning towards the sixth picture, and it is probable that he spent at least three years on this, the final picture of the series. His intention was to illustrate 'Elysium, or the state of final retribution', containing the assembled portraits of 'great and good men of all ages'. By the time the first exhibition of his pictures began, the *Elysium* portrayed over one hundred personages. They are named in his lengthy account of the pictures which is full of literary and historical allusions, citing Thomson's *Seasons* and Milton's *Paradise Lost* to assist the reader/viewer in understanding the meaning of the composition. Every detail had for him some special significance, and although most of his ideas would have been commonplace to 'progressive' men of his time, his nationality and his religion gave it a personal slant. In a prominent position near Marcus Brutus he showed William Molyneux 'of the Kingdom of Ireland', 'with the case of his country in his hand'. Among the poets he placed Ossian with 'the Irish harp, and the lank black hair and open unreserved countenance, peculiar to his country'; an imaginary figure 'sent to Heaven' by Barry, as Walpole observed, 'after obliging him first to go and be born in Ireland'. By stressing the doctrine of religious toleration, he was able to give a generous representation to Catholic figures in the *Elysium*. Thus Pascal matches Bishop Butler, Pope Adrian and Father Paul

Sarpi accompany Grotius, Roger Bacon appears in the full habit of 'an English Franciscan' and Adrian wears a triple crown. In Tartarus, though a worldly Pope flounders in a fiery sea, Barry was far harsher in commenting 'on the wretch on his left [who] holds that execrable engine of hypocrisy, injustice and cruelty, *the Solemn League and Covenant*'. For in spite of his love of Greek republicanism, it was said that he 'invariably worshipped the character and memory of Charles I, and detested the selfishness and hypocrisy of the parties who planned and achieved his downfall'. Beneath the sceptre of the Archangel he painted the famous Vandyck profile, with Colbert and Francis I placed to echo the remainder of the triple portrait.

In the autumn of 1779 Barry had appealed for 'portraits of philosophers, lawgivers, poets, or other personages of any age or nation whose discoveries and abilities in useful arts or letters have been beneficial to mankind'. The Penn family supplied him with a medallion of William Penn to copy, Sir William Musgrave gave him the use of his extensive collection of engraved portraits and Timothy Hollis drew his attention 'to many of the excellent characters found in modern history, with whose portraits his portfolios were furnished'.[13] In January 1780 it was thought he might wish to borrow paintings from the Royal Society's collection to assist him in his work on the *Elysium*, and in the same month, orders were given to clear the wall over the Great Room door whenever he should be ready to have his picture hung. By November all the pictures would appear to have been fixed to the walls, since covers were ordered for them so that the Society could meet in the room. A year later frames were ordered, and by January 1782 the members of the Society eagerly awaited news of the completion of the project.[14]

THE SECOND PHASE: ANTICIPATION AND DISAPPOINTMENT, 1782-4

Barry responded to inquiries made by the Society early in February 1782 by stating 'that the pictures can be finished by April so far as to be exhibited', and sums of money were accordingly voted to meet the costs of an exhibition and the printing of a descriptive catalogue. Yet he told a deputation of two members from a Society meeting on 6th March that he had 'no intention of exhibiting this year his work not being sufficiently advanced'.[15]

He did not explain what circumstances had delayed the completion. Perhaps he still hoped to gain a sitting from the Prince of Wales? Whatever the reason or reasons, we can be certain that he was already in an emotionally charged mood in regard to his work for the Society. This is shown by passages in his lengthy *Account* of the pictures which he had hoped to publish in April 1782. He writes of an 'insult' he had received from the Secretary, Samuel More, 'early in the work' over the question of handling funds voted for the payment of the models which 'had well nigh tempted me to throw up the whole business in disgust'. He endeavoured to forestall criticism of the paintings by promising 'to go over the whole work, and lick it into such general effect, force of colour and light, and shade, as will be more reconcileable to my own ideas of the necessary mechanical conduct: several crudities will be removed by the general accord or harmony; many parts that are too forcible will be weakened; and many that are too weak will be strengthened, and brought forward upon the eye. All these subordinate considerations I wished to reserve for an agreeable entertainment, after so much labour of a more serious and essential kind, which required my whole undivided attention'. He admitted that his account lacked 'order and arrangment' because parts of it had been written 'to amuse myself during a state of very disagreeable suspense, in which it was impossible for me to paint, whilst it was so doubtful whether I should ever be able to obtain that exhibition of my work, which was to be my sole reward from those for whom I had undertaken it'.[16]

At the end of the year the unfortunate Samuel More was ordered to 'wait on Mr. Barry' and inform him that the Society having elected General Eliott a Vice President intended to obtain his portrait 'that it may be introduced into the Pictures Painting by him'. The wording of the resolution suggests that Barry might still have been at work, though no portrait of Eliott seems to have been undertaken. By April 1783 Barry was once again confident, probably as a result of the tactful behaviour of Valentine Green. A meeting of the Society held on 2nd April heard a letter from the artist:

> My Lords and Gentlemen
> The Pictures in the Great Room will (with God's blessing) be in the state I should wish to exhibit them by the 21st inst. It is not necessary for the Society to give themselves the trouble of adding any other Gentlemen to the Committee as there will be nothing to do which Mr. Green is not equal to or which he can now think a trouble after the Great pains he has so obligingly taken through the whole business.
> I have the honour to be
> Your most Obedt. humble servt. James Barry

On the 16th the Society decided to make 'a respectful application' to the King, inviting him 'to take a view of [the] Pictures before they be publicly Exhibited' and heard a further letter from Barry read aloud:

> Mr. Barry presents his respectful Compliments to the Right Honourable the President, Vice-Presidents and the rest of the members of the Society for the Encouragement of Arts, Manufactures and Commerce and would be happy they would do him the honour to see his work in the Society's Great Room the day before the Exhibition is opened to the Public of which day due notice will be given in the public Papers. Society's Great Room 16 April 1783.

Barry himself being present, 'by desire of the Society', thanks were returned to him from the Chair for the invitation.

The King could not come, but the Society was ready with its own honours for the artist. The minutes of an extraordinary meeting held at 11 a.m., Saturday 26th April record:

> It was proposed to view the Historical Paintings in the Great Room, executed by James Barry, Esq. RA and Professor of Painting to the Royal Academy, and after attentive inspection
>
> Resolved that the Series of Pictures illustrating in their design, the progress of Human Knowledge and the advancement of useful and elegant arts, from a very early period to the present Era, is a work of great Excellence of composition, masterly Execution and Classical information, and must be deemed a National Ornament as well as a Monument of the talents and Ingenuity of the Artist.
>
> The Society therefore desirous of giving most ample testimony of his eminent abilities unanimously voted him their thanks and ordered that this resolution be published in the News Papers.[17]

The first Exhibition gained the artist considerable critical acclaim. A total of 6541 tickets sold, though not spectacularly high, seemed to promise a growth of public interest which in the next year might yield a sum sufficient to satisfy Barry's financial needs. Yet the not unsurprising failure of the King to give countenance to the work was blamed by Barry on the machinations of Richard Dalton and his 'Myrmidons' of whom Samuel More was the 'foreman'. Throughout 1783 Barry seems to have felt himself under threat from that quarter, and he composed a public letter to Dalton and a further description of his perfidy to be printed in the 1784 edition of the *Account* of the paintings. During the same period Barry was seeking subscriptions for a set of engravings after the pictures. The catalogue of the Exhibition ended with a prospectus containing the following characteristic caveat:

> As to the Importance of this Work, and its Pretentions to public Patronage, the Author of it thinks that the Arts of Self-Commendation usually practised in soliciting Subscriptions would on this Occasion be unworthy of the Nation, of the Work, and of himself; and he hopes altogether unnecessary.[18]

When William Peters, one of Barry's fellow Academicians, told Barry five days after the 1783 Exhibition had opened that the Duke of Rutland wished to subscribe to the prints, he unwittingly set off an explosive train of suspicion in the artist's mind. By May Barry was hearing rumours that he had told Peters he 'would have no such paltry fellows as Dukes upon my list of subscribers', and in the heat of his anger at this slander he decided to add another figure to the far right corner of the 'Elysium', where various evils were already personified amidst the fiery torments of Tartarus. Visitors to the 1784 exhibition were able to see

> one of those people who from pride, laziness, or malevolence, give themselves up to the government of envious or other malicious whisperers, and proceed to dislikes and hostility from what they hear, without doing the justice either to themselves or others of taking the trouble to examine with the necessary attention whether what is reported to them be a calumny or not. The figure is represented blindfolded, as he lived, with a dagger in each hand, and vipers pulling him down by the ears. Noxious as this character is, and frequently as we meet it in life, yet I should have omitted and passed it by, as I have many others, were it not for an unlucky adventure which I did not seek, but which sought me during the exhibition.[19]

The attendance figures for the 1784 exhibition were disappointingly low. We cannot say how many attended in the first month since we only have the total—some 3511—for the whole six weeks from 25th April to 5th June. Presumably most who came did so in that month, since on the 26th May the Handel Festival opened at Westminster Abbey. This 'empty hubbub of hundreds of fiddles and drums', as Barry intemperately called it, attracted immense public interest. The *Gentleman's Magazine* summed up its impact:

> Habituated as we are to public exhibitions, and having had the opportunity of beholding whatever has engaged the notice of the metropolis for many years, we may be allowed to speak from comparison;—on experience, therefore, we say, that so grand and beautiful a spectacle, with at the same time a feast so rich and perfect, has not been presented to the public eye within our memory.[20]

The nobility and persons of quality flocked to this 'Jubilee of hackneyed German music'. Had they bestowed a tenth part of that interest on his paintings, Barry believed, 'matters would have gone very differently with the Exhibition in the Adelphi'.[21] For the succeeding five years he left his paintings untouched. As he later put it, 'I contented myself as well as I could and went to work on the engravings'.[22]

THE THIRD PHASE: RENEWED HOPE AND FURTHER
DESPAIR, 1789-90

In May 1789 Barry's first series of engravings from the Adelphi
pictures had reached proof stage, and he took the occasion to show them
to Lord Romney, President of the Society, and to remind him of the need
to obtain a sitting from the Prince of Wales, 'as neither the prints could be
published, nor the picture finished, until that was obtained'.[23] The Prince
granted a first sitting on 28th June, and soon afterwards Barry, taking
advantage of the Society's annual Recess, went to the Great Room and
painted a preliminary version of the portrait's head into the fifth painting
and retouched the other canvases. In November Barry obtained a second
sitting from the Prince, and when he received the Society's official notification that the Prince was willing to sit for the second time, he had the
satisfaction of informing More that this event had already taken place. On
23rd December he wrote to the Society requesting 'that an opportunity be
afforded him of finishing that portrait of the Prince which is in the fifth
picture of the series in their great room, and at the same time, he has the
happiness of informing the Society that, as there is not much to do, their
meetings need not be interrupted'. More replied in the Society's name, saying that the meetings would be adjourned until 13th January, and by the
last mentioned date Barry was able to state that 'on Thursday last'—that
is 7th January 1790—the series of pictures 'were finished'.[24]

Barry now waited for something more than the formal 'thanks' he received in reply to his letter. Since October in the previous year Valentine
Green and his other friends in the Society had been suggesting some tangible reward. The honorary pallet in Gold, perpetual membership and the
right to hold another exhibition at his own expense were first proposed.
In February it was suggested that he should receive £200 and perpetual
membership. Eventually, on 4th March, only the permission to hold an
exhibition 'for anytime not exceeding two months' at his own expense was
granted.[25] Hoping at least for some formal record of his friends' attempts
to secure for him a more suitable reward, Barry sought in vain for copies
of the Society's minutes relating to his affairs. He afterwards told in his
own words how strongly he felt this rebuff. He showed the Society's letters
to a friend 'of much skill and experience' in the world and asked him to
decide what was to be done. The unnamed friend agreed with Barry 'that
it was best to take no further notice of it' and be like Xanthippus who
speedily quitted Carthage after the service he had rendered it. He further

warned Barry that the Society might 'seek out some pretext for quarrel or dislike' to hide their lack of generosity. There was nothing 'further to do, but to give God thanks, and get back again as fast as you can to your own business of painting, after having been thus for ten years of the best part of your life, separated from it by the cursed delays which have intervened since the exhibition of your work in 1783'. Barry replied:

> Bravo . . . you have spoken like an oracle, but only do not charge any of this delay, procrastination, and listlessness to me: you know with what rapidity and silence I carried on the work, the public never having been once disturbed with the mention of it, until it was exhibited in 1783 and 1784, and although another work of similar extent and importance, might have been more than effected by the time which has been lost since, and would have been much more agreeable to my wishes; yet please to recollect that this time has been unavoidably employed in extricating myself from the difficulties in which the doing of that work left me. I thank God that it is now happily effected, you shall never have reason to accuse me of wasting any more attention upon that business, and whatever I shall do from henceforward, care shall be taken that all the circumstances belonging to it shall be out of the power of others, depending only on God and myself.[26]

THE FOURTH PHASE: GRADUAL RECONCILIATION BETWEEN THE ARTIST AND THE SOCIETY, 1792-99

On 16th May 1792 the Society again heard officially from the artist. Having completed the plates of the first series of engravings after the paintings in the Great Room, Barry himself saw a set through the press and presented it to the Society with what, it may be assumed, was a tactful accompanying letter. The thanks of the Society were ordered to be sent to him with notification of the 'peculiar pleasure' with which his prints had been received. Slightly mollified, Barry composed a lengthy letter to the Society which he published early in 1793. It contained a description of the engravings and an account of his dealings with the institution in the years down to 1790. Although it included the bitter sentiments previously quoted, the conclusion contained what Dr. Pressly has so aptly called a 'wedded sigh':

> Here my Lords and Gentlemen, I shall close this letter, with too much respect and value for the Head, and many of the members of your institution, to let any sourness and ill humour remain on my mind. It was, perhaps, impossible, in a miscellaneous society like yours, that matters should be other than they have been. My work, which remains in your great room, has allied

James Barry, *Elysium, or The State of Final Retribution*, c. 1779-1801; the sixth picture, left panel. Courtesy of the RSA.

Outline and key to the sixth picture, left panel.

Top range, left to right: 1. Francis Bacon. 2. Copernicus. 3. Galileo. 4. Newton. 5. Superior Angel (added 1798). 6. Superior Angel. 7. As 5. 8. 3rd Earl of Shaftesbury. 9. Locke. 10. Unnamed head. 11. Zeno. 12. Aristotle. 13. Pla⦁). 14. William Harvey. *Middle range, left to right:* 15. Unnamed head. 16. Thales. 17. Descartes. 18. Archimedes. 19. Inferior Angel. 20. Roger Bacon. 21. Columbus. 22. Epaminondas (the plan of the battle of Leuctra was added to his shield in 1801). 23. Socrates. 24. Lucius Junius Brutus. 25. Cato the Younger. 26. Sir Thomas More. 27. Marcus Junius Brutus. 28. William Molyneux. 29. Robert Boyle. *Upper right centre:* 30. Bishop Bartolomeo de las Casas and other Dominicans with a flock of native worshippers (added 1801). 31. Brahma. 32. Confucius. 33. Manco Capac.

us so nearly that we must, as is usual in such cases, take each other for better for worse, and bear with whatever frailties cannot be remedied. I shall send with this letter one of the prints of the new design, where the Legislator of Maryland takes the first place, instead of the Legislator of Pennsylvania; it may be either bound up, placed in the same portfolio, or put with frame and glass along with the other prints of the rest of the work, which I had last year the honour of presenting to the Society.

With great respect and value for the views of the Society, and the most sincere good-wishes for its furtherance and prosperity, I have, my Lords and Gentlemen, the honour of subscribing myself.

Your most obedient humble servant,

JAMES BARRY, P.P.R.A.*

Castle-street, Oxford-Market,
Feb. 25th 1793

At its meeting on 24th April 1793 the Society noted the gift of the pamphlet and ordered 'that the . . . Print be accepted and carefully preserved'.[27]

In spite of his promise not to waste 'any more attention on that business', Barry had continued to be much concerned with his paintings for the Society. The print of 'The Legislator of Maryland' showed a revision of the central portion of the *Elysium* and was the first of a new series of seven engravings related to that painting and to the *Olympic Victors*, three more of which were published in 1795. In 1796 his relations with the Society became extremely cordial, and he responded in surprisingly gracious terms to two requests: one to permit Thomas Philips to study the paintings in order to colour a set of the prints and another to lend his portrait of the late Edward Hooper so that an engraving could be made of it for the Society's *Transactions*. In the latter instance he dealt directly with the Secretary, Samuel More, and appears to have overcome his original antagonism towards that individual.[28]

In the controversial *Letter to the Dilettanti Society respecting the Obtention of certain matters essentially necessary for the Improvement of Public Taste and for accomplishing the original Views of the Royal Academy*, which he published in the following year, Barry paid public tribute to the 'cheerful politeness and punctuality' he had received from the 'heads and members' of the Society of Arts. The 'little temporary heats' resulting in part from his 'own infirmity of temper' had now subsided, and his heart overflowed with gratitude. What pleased him in particular was the total freedom he had been granted in the choice of subjects for

---

* Professor of Painting of the Royal Academy.

the paintings in the Great Room and the 'matter of which they were composed'. Had he not been so engrossed on his large prints from the *Elysium* he would have retouched the painting itself, giving it 'greater energy and effect'. Soon he would 'request this indulgence of the Society'.[29] On 2nd May 1798 Barry presented a copy of this pamphlet to the Society with a request to be allowed to 'retouch' his paintings in the Great Room and 'do away with the ill effects of the varnish with which [they] had been too undeservedly covered'. He was granted access to the Great Room during the Society's recess and in the course of the summer made several significant additions to the *Elysium*.

Back in the Great Room with brush and pallet for the first time for eight years, Barry could not resist doing more than 're-touching' the sixth painting. His additions to the angelic population—two figures of 'superior intellect' in the 'reserved knowledge' group, an angel strewing flowers above Lycurgus and extra recruits for the celestial warriors who guarded the cliff of heaven—could all be justified as giving 'greater energy and effect' to the picture. But the new portraits he introduced into his assembly of the 'Great and Good men of all ages' represented minor but definite extensions of the picture's message. Without consultation with the Society he proclaimed his enthusiasm for religious toleration by putting the figure of the German Jewish philosopher Moses Mendelssohn amongst the group of English poets and playwrights, his veneration for Christian achievement in the Dark Ages by inserting Cassiodorus and a Monk in place of Leo X amongst the patrons of art, and his new found admiration for Sir Joshua Reynolds by placing that recently deceased painter's portrait adjacent to Van Dyck and Rubens and pointing at Michelangelo.

When his time limit was up, he wrote to the Society reporting this extra work on the sixth painting and suggesting that he should also add the portraits of the Lord Mayor of London and of the Duke of Norfolk, then President of the Society, to the fifth painting. The Committee of Polite Arts reported to a meeting of the Society held on 7th November, 'that the Picture in the series of Pictures painted by Mr. Barry in the Society's Great Room is so complete that the Committee cannot recommend to the Society to agree with the proposal made by Mr. Barry in his Letter'. The Society approved this report and asked the Secretary to inform Barry of their decision. Before a new rift could develop, however, Barry's friends in the Society secured for him three substantial honours: on 9th January 1799 he was voted a gold medal and two hundred guineas, and on the 16th of the same month he was elected a life member 'without being subjected to any contribution'. His satisfaction was intense, and he even managed a word of sympathy for the dangerously ill Samuel More. In the letter to the

Society he asked More to read on 23rd January he promised 'to show [his] grateful sense of that honour, in any matters where the Society may think [his] opinion of the least use'.[30]

THE FIFTH PHASE: THE TRIUMPH OF IDIOSYNCRASY, 1801

In 1800 Barry obliged the Society with further presents of his engravings and by supervising the new Secretary's (Dr. Charles Taylor's) revised account of the paintings in the Great Room. On 31st March 1801 he wrote asking to be allowed to paint two extra paintings for the Great Room to replace the existing portraits of Lords Folkestone and Romney, and to varnish parts of his own work. The Society at first acceded to both requests, but when the President, the Duke of Norfolk, opposed the idea of moving the portraits of his two predecessors, Barry withdrew that proposal. His decision was reported at a meeting of the Society held on 20th May, and two weeks later on 3rd June it was 'Ordered that Mr. Barry be furnished with the moving Gallery ladders, Brushes, Colours and all such other necessary Articles as he may want and such assistance as he may stand in need of, to varnish and clean the Pictures in the Great Room'.[31]

The members must have known that Barry would again take the opportunity to modify his paintings, but we may imagine that none would have dared venture into the Great Room while he was at work. He seems first of all to have tackled the fourth painting, the *Thames,* which had suddenly reminded him of the design for a trophy commemorating British Naval victories which had first occurred to him when a national competition for such a monument had been advertised in 1799. Barry described what happened as a result of this conjunction of ideas:

> On his coming to work in the Great-Room after the recess of the Society, 'the Thames, or the Triumph of Navigation', was in such unison and so much of a piece with his naval trophy, that the idea of giving it existence in that picture, recurred back again upon him with accumulated and irresistible force; he could turn no where that it was not present to him, and thus haunted and persecuted, he felt himself obliged to go to Pall-Mall, where all the naval pillars and trophies were exhibited, and where he hoped to find something which would so answer the intended purpose, as to set his mind at rest, and thereby enable him to go on with his other work. In this he was disappointed and infinitely more eager than ever, he came back to the Great-Room, rolled on the scaffold to the picture of the Thames, and began such a trophy of a Mausoleum, observatory, and light-house, as is no where else in existence, and he believes never had existence before.[32]

James Barry, *Elysium, or The State of Final Retribution*, c. 1779-1801; the sixth picture, centre panel. Courtesy of the RSA.

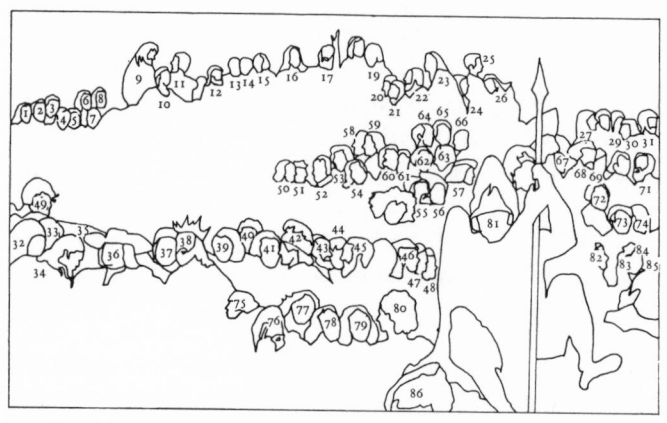

Outline and key to the sixth picture, centre panel.

Top range, left to right: 1. Congreve. 2. Ben Jonson. 3. Otway. 4. Terence. 5. Molière. 6. Racine. 7. Menander. 8. Corneille. 9. Ossian. 10. Sappho. 11. Alcaeus. 12. Chaucer. 13. Unnamed figure. 14. Spenser. 15. Shakespeare. 16. Milton. 17. Homer. 18. Virgil. 19. Fenelon. 20. Unnamed figure. 21. Tasso. 22. Ariosto. 23. Dante. 24. Petrarch. 25. Boccaccio. 26. Laura. 27. Cimabue. 28. Giotto. 29. Dürer. 30. Brunelleschi. 31. Masaccio. *Lower range, left to right:* 32. Solon. 33. Numa. 34. Lycurgus. 35. Zaleucus. 36. Penn. 37. Minos. 38. Alfred. 39. Trajan. 40. Antoninus. 41. Peter the Great. 42. The Black Prince. 43. Henry IV of France. 44. Unnamed one-eyed figure. 45. Andrea Doria. 46. Lorenzo de Medici. 47. Louis XIV. 48. Alexander the Great. 49. Angel strewing flowers (added 1798). *Middle range, left to right:* 50. Swift. 51. Erasmus. 52. Cervantes. 53. Sterne. 54. Pope. 55. Inigo Jones. 56. Wren. 57. Hogarth. *Upper middle range, left to right:* 58. William Mason. 59. Gray. 60. Dryden. 61. Addison. 62. Richardson. 63. Moses Mendelssohn (added 1798). 64. Goldsmith. 65. Thomson. 66. Fielding. 67. Van Dyck. 68. Rubens. 69. Le Brun. 70. Le Sueur. 71. Giulio Romano. 72. Reynolds (added 1798). 73. Giles Hussey. 74. Unnamed figure. *Lower range, left to right:* 75. Unnamed harp bearer. 76. Origen. 77. Bossuet (added 1801). 78. Pascal. 79. Bishop Butler. 80. Expounding Angel. 81. Archangel Gabriel, chief of the Angelic Guard. 82. Charles I. 83. Colbert. 84. A Monk. 85. Cassiodorus. 86. 'An Archangel weighing something which is not seen'.

The fifth painting was also used as a vehicle to illustrate Barry's current obsessions. His mind ran on coins and medals, the Privy Council having consulted the Royal Academy about the first matter and the Society of Arts having asked his own opinion in regard to the second. In a letter to the Earl of Liverpool dated 3rd July 1801 he described in a confused manner what occurred:

> As I am now during the recess of the Society of Arts, etc. doing something to the pictures in their Great Room, in consequence of the obliging injunctions of many members of the Society, and even from the chair, respecting a new die for their medal, the old one having been judged to be no longer fit for use, a happy opportunity has fairly offered for communicating in an entire and complete manner my idea respecting the improvement of medals and coins, and I have accordingly painted two large models for medals and coins in a very conspicuous part of the picture of the Society [33] . . . I have brought in one figure stooping immediately over them, looking very intensely on a medal, and holding in his other hand a letter or paper, on which is written, 'on the gusto of medals and coins, and the best mode of preserving them from injury by friction', which was the identical patriotic wish of his Majesty's Most Honourable Privy Council, so gracefully and exemplarily, though unsuccessfully, communicated to the Royal Academy. The section of such a coin as was required is also introduced on the same paper.[34]

Barry placed these curious additions in the left-hand corner of the picture and thus overpainted part of the figure of Shipley. He balanced them by placing in the right-hand corner a tea urn of his own invention whose simple and practical design suggested 'The primaeval egg of ancient Mother Night suspended between two mysterious serpents' and thus echoed the story of the creation of the world told by Orpheus in the first painting.[35] To the right of the tea urn he placed two scrolls with inscriptions 'stating that they contained drawings of antiquities in Peru and of pyramids in Mexico', and at its foot he placed another inscribed 'from Upper Canada to South Sea'. Only the initiated would have known that Barry was at that time much concerned with the history of South America, but most members of the Society would have recognised the reference to Alexander Mackenzie's premium-winning expedition across Canada to the Pacific.

Barry's interest in South America had been sparked off by his friendship with General Francisco de Miranda of Venezuela, and this in turn resulted in an addition to the sixth painting, the *Elysium*. Miranda impressed Barry with his 'manly arguments . . . in the justification of defensive and necessary war', so that the artist first engraved on a detailed print and then painted on to the actual canvas of the painting the plan of the tactics employed at the ancient victory of Leuctra. This detail was shown on the shield of Epaminondas, in the foreground of the left-hand panel. To the middle distance of this same panel Barry added the small figure of Bishop Las Casas with some of his flock of South American Indians and a Dominican missionary Friar. Following this religious and Catholic theme, his other recorded addition was the figure of Bishop Bossuet, whom he introduced between Origen and Pascal in the sitting group above the angel's wing in the middle of the central panel.[36]

THE SIXTH PHASE: TWO UNREALIZED ADDITIONS, 1801-6

Barry described most of his 1801 additions in a letter which was read to a Society meeting on 11th November of that year and for which, since he was himself present, he received the Society's thanks from the chair. Two weeks later he offered to paint another 'Medallion' in the fifth picture, and his offer was accepted by the Society. Dr. Pressly believes that this would have shown Barry's revised design for the Society's medal— two large heads of Minerva and Mercury which the artist was at that time proposing for adoption by the Society.[37] Thwarted in his high-handed attempts to get this design adopted by the Society, he seems rather uncharacteristically to have decided not to make use of this opportunity to score off his rivals. Paradoxically it was one of these, the despised 'decorator' Flaxman, who four years later was asked to make use of Barry's idea in a medal design for the Society.[38] For the next three years there was no talk of further additions to the paintings, though Barry continued to be associated with the Society in various ways. During 1802 he produced two large prints of details from the *Elysium;* in 1803 he advised on the production of an abridged account of the paintings, and in 1804 he was consulted about the skylight in the Great Room and asked to allow his portrait to be engraved as a frontispiece to Volume 20 of the *Transactions.*[39] The final projected amendment to the paintings came in 1805, the year before his death.

This time the Society took the initiative. At a meeting held on 13th November, some three weeks after the Battle of Trafalgar, the following resolution was adopted:

> That the Society participating in the General grief for the loss which Commerce one of the great objects of its support, and all the best interests of the British Nation have sustained by the death of the great Lord Nelson, is

James Barry, detail of the fourth picture showing the 'naval pillar' added in 1801. Courtesy of the RSA.

anxious to pay a speedy tribute to such a character, and to give a place to his Lordship's Portrait among those worthies whose final retribution in Elysium holds out from the walls of the Great Room a series of glorious examples for the emulation of posterity. That Mr. Barry be requested to make this addition to the Picture in any way he shall judge best, and that every possible facility be afforded to the undertaking which Mr. Barry may require provided he shall favour the Society by granting their request. Agreed to.

Barry undertook to do this work, but stipulated that 'the most proper and advantageous situation for this commemoration' was the fourth painting, the *Thames*. The Society agreed to this on 4th December, and Barry would probably have undertaken the work in the summer recess of 1806.[40] His death on 22nd February, resulting it is said from a chill contracted while participating in an election held in the Great Room on a cold day some three weeks before, brought to an end this saga of his work there. The moving funeral tributes paid by the Society have often been mentioned and were formally recorded in the preface to the Society's *Transactions*, Volume 23, dated 24th March 1806. One line from that preface summarized the Society's feelings: 'Mr. Barry's paintings, in the Great Room of the Society, will remain a monument to perpetuate his memory, honourable to himself, and valuable to the Society.'[41]

APPENDIX I

Officers and Committee Chairmen of the Society, 1755-1800

Presidents

Jacob, Viscount Folkestone, 1755-61
Robert, Lord Romney, 1761-93
Charles, Duke of Norfolk, 1794-1815

Vice Presidents

Robert, Lord Romney, 1755-61
(Sir) Charles Whitworth, 1755-77
James Theobald, 1755-69
Rev. Dr. Stephen Hales, 1755-61
George Henry, Earl of Litchfield,
  1758-72
Simon, Earl Harcourt, 1758-77
Hugh, Lord Willoughby of Parham,
  1758-64
Edward Hooper, 1758-95
George Eckersall, 1759-71
Charles, Duke of Richmond, 1761-
  1806
Sir George Savile, 1761-83
Richard Long, 1761-68
William Fitzherbert, 1761-71
Hugh, Earl, then Duke, of Northum-
  berland, 1765-86
Owen Salusbury Brereton, 1769-98

Charles Marsham (3rd Baron
  Romney), 1771-1811
Keane Fitzgerald, 1772-81
William, Earl of Radnor, 1773-76
Jacob, Earl of Radnor, 1778-1828
Hugh, Earl Percy (2nd Duke of
  Northumberland), 1778-1817
Joshua Steele, 1778-84
General Sir George Eliott (Lord
  Heathfield), 1782-90
Sir Herbert Mackworth, 1783-91
James Davison, 1783-93
Sir William Dolben, 1784-1814
Sir Watkin Lewes, 1786-1806
George, Duke of Montagu, 1787-89
Charles, Duke of Norfolk, 1791-94
Charles, Lord Hawkesbury (Earl of
  Liverpool), 1791-1808
Thomas Boothby Parkyns (Lord
  Rancliffe), 1792-1800
William Henry, Duke of Portland,
  1794-1806
Thomas Pitt, 1794-1825
Francis Stephens, 1796-1800
Hon. Robert Clifford, 1799-1817

Committee Chairmen

Roman figures in parentheses indicate the number of Committee Reports presented to the Society; arabic figures, the number of meetings chaired by the individual, as shown in Loose Minutes (RSA, L.A. A1/37-9) and in Bound Minutes (RSA, Min. Comm., 1758-60). Dates without parenthetical reference indicate election to a committee chairmanship from November 1760 onwards, or after 1783 in the case of the Committee of Miscellaneous Matters.

Committee of Accounts

(Sir) Charles Whitworth, M.P., 1756 (ii), 1757 (i)

Peter Wyche, 1757 (i), 1759 (1)

George Foster Tufnell, 1758 (i)

Henry Baker, 1759 (1), 1761, 1764-70

Thomas Manningham, M.D., 1759 (12), 1760 (8), 1761

John Alex Stainsby, 1759 (2)

Nicholas Crisp, 1762

Joseph Grove, 1762-63

John Fotherby, 1763-72

John Barnfather, 1771-74

Abraham Osorio, 1773-82

William Ashburner, 1776-79

James Hebert, 1780-1804

John Wingfield, 1783-86

Francis Stephens, 1788-90

Nathaniel Conant, 1791-99

Committee of Correspondence

John Spencer Colepeper, 1760 (1), 1761-62

John Paterson, 1760 (1)

Joshua Steele, 1760 (5)

John Alexander Stainsby, 1761-66

Richard Whishaw, 1763-67

Rev. Edward Darrell, 1767-69

Rev. John Bosworth, 1768-69

Benjamin Goodison, 1770-72, 1775-78

Abraham Osorio, 1770-74

Robert Bland, 1773-74

Valentine Green, 1775-76, 1778-79, 1787-97

Peter Chauvany, 1777, 1779-86

Charles Smith, 1780-82

Joseph Pourcin, 1784-86

Robert Dower, 1787-90

*Edward Bancroft, M.D., 1791-1804, 1809-13

Samuel Ferris, M.D., 1799

George Wilson, 1800

Committee of Polite Arts

Thomas Manningham, M.D., 1757 (i), 1758 (i)

Edward Hooper, 1758 (6), 1759 (2)

William Fitzherbert, 1758 (1), 1759 (2)

Samuel Bennet, 1759 (1)

Thomas Brand, 1759 (5), 1760 (13), 1761-62

Richard Howe Chester, 1759 (2), 1760 (1)

Thomas Hollis, 1759 (6)

John Lockman, 1759 (1)

Richard Long, 1759 (10)

Allan Ramsay, 1759 (1), 1760 (1)

Joshua Steele, 1759 (3)

Israel Wilkes, 1759 (3)

William Burch, 1761-62

John Barnard, 1763-64

Matthew Duane, 1763-84

Alexander Kellet, 1765-70

Thomas Butler, 1771-72

Alexander Johnson, M.D., 1773-76

Edward Bridgen, 1777-79

Valentine Green, 1780-86

Caleb Whitefoord, 1785-99

John Parrish, 1787-92

Matthew Michell, 1792-1804

John Griffin, 1800

Committee of Agriculture

Philip Carteret Webb, 1757 (i)

Isaac Maddox, Bishop of Worcester, 1757 (ii)

George Foster Tufnell, 1758 (2)

Henry Baker, 1759 (1)

William Burch, 1759 (3)

Nicholas Crisp, 1759 (2)

Edward Hooper, 1757 (1)

Richard Long, 1759 (5)

Thomas Manningham, M.D., 1759 (6)

Peter Wyche, 1759 (4), 1760 (5), 1761-62

William Watson, M.D., 1760 (1)

James Parsons, M.D., 1761-67

Henry Dodwell, 1763-71

John Arbuthnot, 1768-76

Arthur Young, 1773-76

(Sir) William Fordyce, M.D., 1777

Nathaniel Jarman, 1777-85

James Hebert, 1778-79

John Pratt, 1780-93

Alexander Small, 1785-87

James Cooke, 1788-93

George Butler, 1794

Rev. Stephen Eaton, 1794-1801

Samuel Dunn, 1795-98

Lannoy Richard Cousmaker, 1799

John Middleton, 1800-1801

Committee of Manufactures

(Sir) Charles Whitworth, M.P., 1756 (ii), 1757 (i)

Archibald Hume Campbell, 1756 (i)

Edward Wade, 1757 (i)

Edward Hooper, 1758 (3)

Peter Wyche, 1758 (1), 1759 (6), 1760 (5)

John Blake, 1759 (1)

Bourchier Cleeve, 1759 (1)

William Fitzherbert, M.P., 1759 (1)

Charles Lowth, 1759 (1), 1760 (2)

Israel Wilkes, 1759 (1)

William Watson, M.D., 1760 (3)

Jonas Hanway, 1761-66

Thomas Moore, 1760 (1), 1761

William Shirley, 1762

Richard Washington, 1763-66

Michael Lovell, 1767-83

John Jackson, 1768-78

Peter Chauvany, 1779

George Friend, 1780-83

Charles Smith, 1784-89

†John Baynes, 1784-92

Samuel Dunn, 1790

William Hewlett, 1791

John Baker, 1793-99

Samuel Maskall, 1793-1800

John Hinckley, 1800-1801

Committee of Mechanics

Samuel Burroughs, 1757 (i)

William Fitzherbert, M.P., 1758 (1)

James Theobald, 1758 (2)

John Chetwode, 1759 (1)

Richard Long, 1759 (1)

Sir George Savile, M.P., 1759 (1), 1760 (1)

Joshua Steele, 1759 (1), 1761

Francis Stratford, 1759 (3)

Admiral (Sir) Charles Knowles, 1760 (1)

Thomas, Viscount Parker (3rd Earl of Macclesfield), 1760 (2)

Joseph Gardiner, 1761-62

John Wyatt, 1762-64, 1769-77

Thomas Yeoman, 1763-77

James Parsons, M.D., 1760 (i)

John Barrow, 1765-68

Joseph Hodskinson, 1778-81

Joseph Hurlock, 1778-90

Joseph Nickalls, 1782

Samuel Ewer, 1783-89

Nathaniel Bishop, 1790-91

William Lumley, 1791-98

John Read, 1792-98

George Howe Browne, 1799-1803

Committee of Chemistry

Nicholas Crisp, 1756 (i), 1757 (i),
1759 (1), 1760 (1), 1761, 1762

(Sir) Charles Whitworth, M.P., 1756
(2, ii), 1757 (i)

Henry Strachey, 1757 (i)

George Eckersall, 1758 (1)

Richard Long, 1759 (2)

Michael Morris, M.D., 1759 (2), 1760
(1), 1761, 1770-74

William Watson, M.D., 1759 (7),
1760 (12)

William Cadogan, M.D., 1760 (1)

James Parsons, M.D., 1760 (1)

Samuel More, 1762-67

Alexander Small, 1762, 1765-66,
1769-74, 1780-83

George Fordyce, M.D., 1763-64,
1777

Thomas Denman, M.D., 1767-68

Charles Irwin, M.D., 1767-69, 1775

Robert Bland, 1775-76

John Wingfield, 1776-82

John Butts, 1778-79

Thomas Gibbes, 1783-84

Edward Kendrick, 1784-96

Henry Jackson, M.D., 1785-87

Sir John Ingilby, Bart., 1788-89

Granville Penn, 1790

George Wilson, 1791-99

Thomas Apreece Soley, 1797-99

Edward Howard, 1800

Henry Coxwell, 1800-25

Committee of Colonies and Trade

James Theobald, 1756 (i)

Thomas Manningham, M.D.,
1758 (2)

William Burch, 1759 (1)

George Eckersall, 1759 (1)

John Pownall, 1759 (2), 1760 (2),
1761-64

Peter Wyche, 1759 (1), 1760 (3)

Israel Wilkes, 1759 (3)

Benjamin Franklin, 1759 (1), 1760,
1761

Joshua Steele, 1759 (2)

William Watson, M.D., 1759 (5)

Edward Bridgen, 1762-66

Matthew Harrison, 1765-66

James Clark, 1767-72, 1774-79

John Stewart, 1767-68

Thomas Stewart, 1768-70

Alexander Johnson, 1771-73

John Millar, M.D., 1773-74

John Lind, 1775-78

Caleb Whitefoord, 1778-80, 1783-85

Richard Masefield, 1780-82

Vaughan Lindsell, 1780-85

John Samuel, 1785-87

Daniel Zurhorst, 1786

Edward Webster, 1787-89

Joseph Pourcin, 1788-1800

John Baker, 1790-1801

Committee of Miscellaneous Matters

Thomas Manningham, M.D., 1756
(i), 1757 (ii), 1758 (i), 1760 (2)

(Sir) Charles Whitworth, M.P., 1756
(iii), 1758 (2)

Nicholas Crisp, 1756 (i), 1760 (1),
1761 (1), 1762 (9)

Isaac Maddox, Bishop of Worcester,
1757 (i)

Henry Baker, 1757 (ii), 1760 (8), 1761
(1), 1762 (5), 1764 (1)

Henry Strachey, 1757 (i)

Thomas Hollis, 1757 (i)

Samuel Bennet, 1758 (1), 1759 (1),
1760 (5)

Thomas Brand, 1759 (1), 1761 (1)

John Gilbert Cooper, Jnr., 1759 (1)

George Eckersall, 1759 (2), 1760 (1)

Alexander Scott, 1759 (1)
Israel Wilkes, 1759 (7)
John Blake, 1760 (1), 1761 (1)
John Spencer Colepeper, 1769 (2),
    1761 (14), 1762 (6), 1766 (1)
Robert Dossie, 1760 (1), 1761 (1),
    1766 (2), 1768 (3)
James Parsons, M.D., 1760 (3), 1761
    (6), 1762 (4), 1763 (1)
Sir Thomas Robinson, Bart., 1760
    (8), 1761 (4), 1762 (4), 1764 (4),
    1765 (5)
Joshua Steele, 1760 (13), 1761 (14),
    1762 (3), 1778 (2), 1779 (6)
William Watson, M.D., 1760 (3)
Peter Wyche, 1760 (3), 1761 (6)
William Burch, 1761 (1)
Samuel Chandler, 1761 (2)
John Clayton, 1761 (1)
Henry Dodwell, 1761 (2), 1766 (1),
    1769 (2)
Jacob, Viscount Folkestone, 1761 (1)
Jonas Hanway, 1761 (2), 1762 (2)
Joseph Gardiner, 1761 (1), 1762 (10),
    1764 (2)
Thomas Lawrence, M.D., 1761 (3)
John Pindar, 1761 (1)
John Lockman, 1761 (2)
Michael Morris, M.D., 1761 (1)
William Shirley, 1761 (2), 1762 (1)
Francis Smart, 1761 (1)
George Foster Tufnell, 1761 (1)
Keane Fitzgerald, 1762 (1), 1768 (1)
Edward Hooper, 1762 (1)
Rev. Thomas Hollingsberry, 1762 (2),
    1763 (15)
John Hort, 1762 (2)
John, 11th Baron St. John and Bletso,
    1762 (1)
Samuel More, 1762 (29), 1766 (2, ii),
    1767 (1)
Christopher Pinchbeck, 1762 (1)
Richard Washington, 1762 (1), 1763

(3), 1764 (1), 1765 (1), 1766 (1),
    1767 (3), 1768 (1)
Thomas Butler, 1764 (1)
Matthew Harrison, 1764 (1)
Matthew Duane, 1764 (10)
John Barron, 1766 (1)
Alexander Kellet, 1766 (1), 1767 (1),
    1769 (2)
Alexander Small, 1766 (1), 1769 (2),
    1782 (3)
Thomas Yeoman, 1766 (1), 1767 (2),
    1768 (1), 1776 (1)
John Hannah, 1767 (2)
John Fotherby, 1767 (1), 1770 (1),
    1771 (1)
William Stephenson, 1767 (1),
    1768 (1)
Michael Lovell, 1768 (1), 1776 (1, i)
John Tinker, 1768 (1)
John Lewis, 1769 (3)
Abraham Osorio, 1769 (1), 1770 (3),
    1771 (2), 1772 (1), 1773 (1), 1774
    (1), 1775 (3), 1779 (5)
Thomas Stewart, 1771 (1)
Alexander Johnson, M.D., 1773 (2),
    1774 (6), 1775 (1), 1776 (1)
Robert Bland, 1775 (2)
William Ashburner, 1776 (1)
Arthur Young, 1777 (1)
Joseph Hodskinson, 1779 (1)
Valentine Green, 1780 (1), 1781 (1),
    1782 (1)
Nathaniel Jarman, 1782 (1)
Peter Chauvany, 1783
George Friend, 1783
James Hebert, 1784
Joseph Jacob, 1784-1809
Owen Williams, 1785
Abraham Hall, 1786-94
John Henderson, 1795-97
William Kirkby, 1798-1823

Financial and Salaried Officers

Treasurers and Collectors

John Goodchild, Snr. (Treasurer),
1755-56
John Goodchild, Jnr. (Treasurer),
1757-58
George Box (Collector), 1760-70
Thomas Dawson (Collector), 1771
Abraham Brooksbank (Collector),
1771-77
Peter Duvall (Collector), 1778-79
John Heywood (Collector), 1780-81
George Cockings (Acting Collector),
1781-96
Stephen Theodore Borman (Collector), 1797-1800

Secretaries

William Shipley, 1755-56
George Box, 1757-59

Dr. Peter Templeman, 1760-69
George Box (Acting), 1769-70
Samuel More, 1770-99

Registers

William Shipley, 1757-60
Edward Grant Tuckwell, 1761-66
William Bailey, 1767-73
Alexander Mabyn Bailey, 1773-79
George Cockings, 1779-99

Assistant Secretaries

George Box, 1756-57, 1760-78
Richard Samuel, 1779-87
John Samuel, 1787-97
Thomas Taylor, 1798-1806

*Only Bancroft's name appears in the published list of committee chairmen for 1792 (RSA, *Trans.*, Vol. 16 [1798], p. 379).
†Baynes is listed in RSA, *Trans.*, Vol. 10 (1792), p. 282.

APPENDIX 2

Membership and Subscriptions, 1755-1800

Year	Paying Members	Total Collected		New Members	Members in Arrears*
		£	s.		
1755	104	360.	19	99	—
1756	—	632.	2	109	—
1757	—	1,203.	3	262	—
1758	708	1,731.	9	—	—
1759	—	2,001.	6	—	—
1760	1,350	3,482.	17	—	—
1761	—	3,656.	4	—	—
1762	—	4,533.	18	—	—
1763	—	4,614.	15	—	—
1764	2,136	4,131.	15	—	—
1765	1,690	3,081.	15	121	—
1766	1,465	2,910.	19	119	—
1767	1,331	2,381.	11	92	—
1768	1,139	1,940.	6	52	—
1769	1,415	1,818.	10	66	—
1770	1,376	1,616.	12	64	—
1771	1,304	1,626.	4	97	—
1772	1,315	1,637.	14	101	—
1773	650	1,760.	17	65	1,151
1774	584	1,466.	17	80	1,119
1775	515	1,323.		39	1,175
1776	454	1,174.	18	24	1,181

APPENDIX 2 *Continued*

Year	Paying Members	Total Collected		New Members	Members in Arrears*
		£	s.		
1777	—	1,060.	10	—	—
1778	—	898.	17	—	—
1779	—	—		—	—
1780	—	—		—	—
1781	331	796.	18	31	19
1782	311	784.	7	33	26
1783	317	802.	4	77	32
1784	320	848.	8	45	31
1785	—	—		—	
1786	381	1,140.	6	96	
1787	487	1,340.	17	155	
1788	478	1,246.	7	103	
1789	513	1,329.	6	137	
1790	581	1,582.	16	122	
1791	588	1,451.	2	142	
1792	590	1,517.	5	78	
1793	—	—		—	
1794	584	1,418.	11	81	
1795	532	1,410.	3	77	
1796	510	1,471.	1	164	
1797	569	1,517.	15	82	
1798	632	1,635.	18	106	
1799	574	1,471.	3	—	
1800	625	1,802.	16	252	

Sources: Numbers of paying members, 1755, 1758, 1760, from printed membership lists; total subscriptions collected, 1755-65, given in RSA, MS Account Book, 1755-65; numbers of new members, 1755-57, calculated from RSA, Soc. Min., 1755-57; numbers of paying members, 1764-72, total subscriptions collected, 1766-72, and numbers of new members, 1765-72, estimated from RSA, MS Subscription Books, 1764-72; all figures from 1773 onwards taken from RSA, Min. Comm. (Accounts), 1773-1800. Figures for 1779, 1780, 1785 and 1793 are not available.
* No data available for the years 1786-1800

NOTES

GENERAL INTRODUCTION

1. See R. Rübberdt, *Die ökonomischen Sozietäten* (Würzburg, 1934), and H. Hubrig, *Die patriotischen Gesellschaften des 18. Jahrhunderts* (Weinheim, Berlin, 1957).

2. The official form of the Society's name in this period.

3. See for example, T. Smollett, *History of England from the Revolution to the death of George II* (London, 1763-5), Book 3, chap. 10, p. 55; *Encyclopaedia Britannica*, 3rd ed. (Dublin, 1786), Vol. 17, p. 587; C. Williams, trans., *Sophie in London* (1786; 1933), p. 161; P.N. Chantreau, *Voyage dans les trois royaumes d'Angleterre, d'Ecosse et d'Irelande* (Paris, 1792), pp. 174-9.

4. S.A.L., Minutes, 1 June 1758, quoted J. Evans, *A History of the Society of Antiquaries* (Oxford, 1956), p. 125.

5. T. Smollett, *History of England* (1758-65, 1806, 6 vols.), Vol. 5, pp. 448-9, quoted Trueman Wood, *History of the Royal Society of Arts* (London, 1913), p. 52,

and G.S. Rousseau, ' "No boasted Academy of Christendom": Smollett and the Society of Arts,' *Jnl. RSA*, 121 (1973), p. 469. Dr. Rousseau's article contains a detailed commentary on the passage.

6. T. Mortimer, *Concise Account* (1763), pp. i-iv, v, 63.

7. C. Powell to William Shipley, *c.* Apr. 1754 (G.B. 1: 34).

8. R. Bridgen, *Short Account* (1765), p. 16.

9. R. Dossie, *Memoirs of Agriculture and Other Oeconomical Arts*, 3 vols. (London, 1768-82), Vol. 2, p. vii.

10. For Rockingham's attitude, see his letter to Edmund Burke, 15 Oct. 1769, printed L.S. Sutherland (ed.), *The Correspondence of Edmund Burke*, Vol. 2 (Cambridge, 1960), p. 95.

11. D.G.C. Allan, *The Houses of the Royal Society of Arts* (London, 1974), p. 13.

12. J.G. Gazley, 'Arthur Young and the Society of Arts', *Journal of Economic History*, 1 (1941), pp. 132-3, 146-7.

13. Society of Arts, *Register of Premiums and Bounties* (1778), pp. 24, 56.

14. A. Young, *Annals of Agriculture*, Vol. 1 (1784), p. 64n.

15. In 1783 the Royal Society had 482 Home Fellows as compared with the Society of Arts' 317 Subscribing Members. In 1784 the Society of Antiquaries had 376 Subscribing Fellows and was 'beginning to be both large and fashionable'; in that year the Society of Arts had 320 Subscribing Members (Royal Society, *Lists of Fellows*; Evans, op. cit., p. 187).

16. See A. Ure, *The Cotton Manufacture of Great Britain*, Vol. 1 (1836), p. 219; C. Knight, *The Pictorial History of England, being a history of the people as well as a history of the Kingdom* (London, 1857), p. 681; G.J. French, *The Life and Times of Samuel Crompton* (1859), pp. 4-5.

17. S.T. Davenport, 'The Society of Arts, past and present' with 'Discussion', *Jnl. S. of A.*, 17 (1868), pp. 10, 127, 143, 160; reprinted from the *Journal* in book form by W. Trouncer, in 1869.

18. H.B. Wheatley, 'The Society of Arts', *Engineering*, 51 (1891), pp. 83, 134, 163, 173, 231, 278, 361, 451.

19. J. Newman, 'The Enigma of Joshua Steele', *Jnl. Barbados Museum and Historical Society*, 19, No. 1 (1951), p. 6.

20. B. Williams, *The Whig Supremacy*, 2nd ed. (Oxford, 1962), pp. 407-8; J. Steven Watson, *The Reign of George III* (Oxford, 1962), p. 28; L. Woodward, *The Age of Reform*, 2nd ed. (Oxford, 1962), p. 500; S. Pargellis and D.J. Medley, *Bibliography of British History, the Eighteenth Century, 1714-1789* (Oxford, 1951), p. 160.

21. Wood, op. cit., p. 18. In 1908 King Edward VII granted the Society permission to adopt the prefix 'Royal'. The abbreviated form 'RSA' came into use in 1988.

22. *Economic History Review*, 2nd Series, 8 (1956), p. 117.

23. T.S. Ashton, *The Industrial Revolution, 1760-1830* (1948), pp. 13, 21, 62, 128.

24. W. Bowden, *Industrial Society in England towards the End of the Eighteenth Century* (New York, 1925), pp. 40-44.

25. N. J. Smelser, *Social Change in the Industrial Revolution: An Application of Theory to the Lancashire Cotton Industry, 1779-1840* (1959), pp. 82-5, 144.

26. K. W. Luckhurst, 'Some Aspects of the History of the Society of Arts, London, 1754-1952', Ph.D. thesis, University of London, 1957, chaps. 2-6, 8.

27. D. C. Coleman, 'Premiums for Paper: The Society and The Early Paper Industry', *Jnl. RSA,* 107 (1959), p. 361.

28. R. E. Schofield, 'The Society of Arts and the Lunar Society of Birmingham', *Jnl. RSA,* 107 (1959), p. 513.

29. Marquess of Rockingham to Edmund Burke, 15th Oct. 1769.

1. DR. JOHNSON AND THE SOCIETY

1. *Engineering,* 52 (1891), p. 83.

2. *Jnl. RSA,* 48 (1900), pp. 829-31.

3. Sir H. T. Wood, *History of the Royal Society of Arts* (London, 1913), p. 40.

4. D. Hudson and K. W. Luckhurst, *The Royal Society of Arts, 1754-1954* (London, 1954), p. 29. Referred to hereafter as Hudson and Luckhurst.

5. *Boswell's Life of Johnson,* ed. G. Birkbeck Hill; revised L. F. Powell (Oxford, 1934-50), Vol. 2, p. 139. Referred to hereafter as *Life.*

6. *Life,* Vol. 2, p. 139.

7. *Biographia Britannica,* 2nd ed. (London, 1789), Vol. 4, p. 266.

8. A painter and architect, he was known as 'Athenian' Stuart from his studies in Greek architecture. He designed the Society's first medal.

9. *Life,* Vol. 4, p. 11.

10. For a thorough account of Dossie's life and activities in the Society, see F. W. Gibbs, 'Robert Dossie (1717-77) and the Society of Arts', *Annals of Science,* 7 (1951), pp. 149-72.

11. Robert Dossie, *Memoirs of Agriculture and Other Oeconomical Arts,* 3 vols. (London, 1768-82).

12. *Life,* Vol. 4, p. 11.

13. Ibid., pp. 11-12. It is possible that the candidacy was for one of the Society's awards.

14. Ibid., p. 97.

15. Ibid.

16. *Proceedings of the Committee . . . for Cloathing the French Prisoners of War* (London, 1760). The book, a small folio, is rare, but the British Library and the Bodleian have copies. For further details, see Allen Hazen, *Samuel Johnson's Prefaces & Dedications* (New Haven, 1937), pp. 189-93. Referred to hereafter as Hazen.

17. Hudson and Luckhurst, p. 36. For details of Johnson's involvement with the artists, see 'The Papers of the Society of Artists of Great Britain', *Walpole Society,*

Vol. 4 (Oxford, 1918), pp. 113-30. There are a number of references to Johnson in this article, and the letter and memorandum look unmistakably like his work. See also 'Art Exhibitions of the Society', *Jnl. RSA*, 43 (1895), pp. 857-61.

18. See *Life*, Vol. 1, p. 363 n. 2, and Hazen, pp. 200-205.

19. See James L. Clifford, 'Some Problems of Johnson's Obscure Middle Years', *Johnson, Boswell and Their Circle* (Oxford, 1965), pp. 99-110.

20. *Boswell's London Journal, 1762-63*, ed. Frederick A. Pottle (London, 1950), pp. 60-61.

21. Soc. Min., 1754-7, for 24th Nov. and 1st Dec. 1756.

22. Ibid., 1757-8.

23. Ibid.

24. Ibid., 1758-9.

25. Ibid.

26. Ibid., 1760.

27. Misc. Comm. Min., 1760-78 ('Making Great Room more Commodious').

28. See the Society's MS Sub. Bk.

29. Soc. Min., 1760-61.

30. Ibid. (Polite Arts).

31. Ibid. (Chemistry).

32. Ibid. (Mechanics). That Samuel Johnson's name should appear on such a committee as this, or any of the others, is no surprise. Indeed, the Society's records tend not only to amplify but also to complement what is known about Johnson's interest in things mechanical. See, for instance, the accounts of Johnson's involvement with Lewis Paul's roller-spinning invention in Alfred P. Wadsworth and Julia De Lucy Mann, *The Cotton Trade and Industrial Lancashire* (Manchester, 1931), and Ruth M. Cowhig, 'Dr. Samuel Johnson in Textile History', *Skinner's Silk and Rayon Record* (August 1955), pp. 854-6. Both the above sources recount Johnson's interest in Paul's process and his efforts to reconcile Paul, Dr. Richard James and Edward Cave over the financial disputes that arose from the latter's investments in Paul's invention. See also *The Letters of Samuel Johnson*, ed. R. W. Chapman (Oxford, 1952), for more details about the dispute. My special thanks to Mr. James Harrison, engineer, and Fellow of the Royal Society of Arts, for the useful information he gave me about this aspect of Johnson's life.

33. Min. Comm., 1761-2 (Mechanics).

34. Ibid. (Polite Arts).

35. Ibid. (Manufactures).

36. For the best clarification of this problem, see W. H. Bond, 'Thomas Hollis and Samuel Johnson', in *Johnson and His Age*, ed. James Engell (Cambridge, Mass., 1984), pp. 83-105.

37. Soc. Min., 1761-2.

38. Ibid.

39. Misc. Comm. Min., 1760-78 ('On Preserving Water Sweet').

40. Ibid.

41. Ibid.

42. Ibid.

43. Quoted from 'Premiums Offered By the Society Instituted At London For the Encouragement of Arts, Manufactures And Commerce, London, 1761', p. 57, in 'Premiums List of Members, &c.', 1756-62, in the Society's Library.

44. Soc. Min., 1761-62.

45. Misc. Comm. Min., 1760-78 ('On Treatise on the Arts of Peace').

46. Soc. Min., 1761-2. In the margin is the note 'Another Treatise on the Arts of Peace'.

47. Misc. Comm. Min., 1760-78 ('On Treatise on the Arts of Peace').

48. Ibid. Hawkesworth apparently did not write the work. See J. L. Abbott, 'John Hawkesworth and the "Treatise on the Arts of Peace" ', *Jnl. RSA* (1967), pp. 645-49.

49. Soc. Min., 1761-62.

50. Ibid.

51. Ibid.

52. J. Barry, *An Account of a Series of Pictures in the Great Room of the Society of Arts, Manufactures and Commerce, at the Adelphi* (London, 1783), p. 74. Johnson himself paid tribute to Barry's great work. Boswell writes: 'We talked of Mr. Barry's exhibition of his pictures. JOHNSON: "Whatever the hand may have done, the mind has done its part. There is a grasp of mind there which you find no where else." ' *Life*, Vol. 4, p. 224. See also D. G. C. Allan, 'Barry and Johnson', *Jnl. RSA*, 133 (1985), pp. 628-32.

2. 'COMPASSION AND HORROR IN EVERY HUMANE MIND'

1. For a succinct introduction to eighteenth-century prostitution, see Richard B. Schwartz, *Daily Life in Johnson's London* (Madison, Wis., 1983).

2. *Some Considerations* (London, n.d.), p. 2. This is attributed to Defoe in the British Library catalogue and confirmed by Defoe's biographer, Professor Paula Backscheider, in private correspondence. *Satan's Harvest Home* (London, 1749), p. 1. *A Picture of England,* translated from the French (Dublin, 1791), pp. 188-9, 193, 194-6. Hereafter cited as D'Archenholz.

3. D'Archenholz, p. 193.

4. See *Engravings by Hogarth,* ed. Sean Shesgreen (New York, 1973).

5. *Adventurer,* no. 86 (London, 1793), Vol. 3, p. 140.

6. *Boswell's London Journal, 1762-63,* ed. Frederick A. Pottle (New York, 1950), pp. 49, 54, 83-4, 332. Hereafter cited as *London Journal.*

7. *London Journal,* Appendix 1, pp. 335-7. *Boswell's Life of Johnson,* ed. G. Birkbeck Hill; revised L. F. Powell (Oxford, 1934-50), Vol. 1, pp. 104-5. Johnson took the figure from 'an Irish painter, whom he knew at Birmingham'. Hereafter cited as *Life.* D'Archenholz, p. 191.

8. *London Journal,* pp. 230-1, 237, 240, 255.

9. *A Modest Defence* (London, 1724), pp. 2, 9-10, 12-13, 66, 73. In his edition for the Augustan Reprint Society (William Andrews Clark Memorial Library Publication No. 162, 1973), Richard I. Cook argues that, like Swift in an even more famous 'modest' proposal, Mandeville speaks ironically, defending what he really means to attack. Ironic or not, Mandeville contributed fundamentally to the century's debate over prostitution. His regulated brothels resemble, in fact, later reformist, work-based centres advocated by Robert Dingley and others where Christian-mercantilist, not sexual, values were stressed.

10. One of the two copies in the British Library (BL, PC 30 h. 2) for 1788 has the names of the various ladies, ordinarily disguised by dashes, filled in.

11. *London Journal*, pp. 255-6, 259-62.

12. *Life*, Vol. 3, pp. 17-18.

13. *Life*, Vol. 4, pp. 395-6.

14. Watkins, *Perilous Balance: The Tragic Genius of Swift, Johnson and Sterne* (Princeton, N.J., 1939), p. 52. Balderston, 'Johnson's Vile Melancholy', in *The Age of Johnson: Essays Presented to Chauncey B. Tinker* (New Haven, Conn., 1949), pp. 3-14. Hereafter cited as Balderson. Meyer, 'Some Observations on the Rescue of Fallen Women', *Psychoanalytic Quarterly*, 53 (1984), pp. 211-12. Professor Donald Greene kindly called this and the following essay to the authors' attention.

15. For a useful assessment of Johnson's views on prostitution, see Sherry O'Donnell, ' "Tricked Out for Sale": Samuel Johnson's Attitude Toward Prostitution', *Transactions of the Samuel Johnson Society of the North West*, 9 (1978), pp. 119-35.

16. *Johnsonian Miscellanies*, ed. G. Birkbeck Hill (New York, 1970), Vol. 2, p. 326. Hereafter cited as *Johnsonian Miscellanies*.

17. See James L. Clifford, *Dictionary Johnson* (New York, 1979), chap. 6, and John L. Abbott, *John Hawkesworth: Eighteenth-Century Man of Letters* (Madison, Wis., 1982), chap. 2. James Gray, 'Arras/Helas!: A Fresh Look at Samuel Johnson's French', in *Johnson After Two Hundred Years*, ed. Paul J. Korshin (Philadelphia, Penn., 1986), pp. 84-6. While Balderston's provocative essay remains a necessary first address to Johnson's sexual life, some elements in it seem dated, especially her yoking of Johnson's tic to Freudian, Adlerian and Jungian explanations (p. 4 n. 9). With far more data it is difficult to differentiate Boswell's venereal attacks from more general urological complaints. See William B. Ober, M.D., *Boswell's Clap and Other Essays* (Carbondale and Edwardsville, Ill., 1979), pp. 1-42.

18. *Johnsonian Miscellanies*, Vol. 2, pp. 168-9.

19. *Life*, Vol. 1, p. 224.

20. *The Oxford Authors: Samuel Johnson*, ed. Donald Greene (Oxford, 1984), pp. 251-2. Hereafter cited as Greene.

21. Greene, pp. 252, 256.

22. See John L. Abbott, 'Dr Johnson and the Society', *Jnl. RSA* 115 (1967), pp. 395-400, 486-91, and 'Johnson's Membership of the Society Reconsidered', 133 (1985), pp. 618-22.

23. D. G. C. Allan, *The Houses of the Royal Society of Arts* (London, 1974), p. 3. 'The Move to the Adelphi in *1774*', *Jnl. RSA*, 122 (1974), pp. 383-8.

24. H. Phillips, *Mid Georgian London* (London, 1964), pp. 142-5; J. Hanway, *Thoughts on the plan for a Magdalen House* (London, 1758), p. 42; *London Chronicle*, Vol. 3, p. 386, 22-5 April 1758.

25. Thomas Dekker, *The Honest Whore, Part the second* (1630), Act 5, Scene 2; J. Nichols, *The Works of William Hogarth* (London, 1822), p. 2; A. Babbington, *A House in Bow Street: Crime and Magistracy, 1740-1881* (London, 1969), pp. 88-9; D. G. C. Allan and R. E. Schofield, *Stephen Hales: Scientist and Philanthropist* (London, 1979), p. 24; H. F. B. Compston, *The Magdalen Hospital: The Story of a Great Charity* (London, 1917), p. 17.

26. R. K. McClure, *Coram's Children: The London Foundling Hospital in the Eighteenth Century* (New Haven and London, 1981), pp. 37-75. The 'Register of Governors' is printed in R. H. Nichols and F. A. Wray, *The History of the Foundling Hospital* (London, 1935), pp. 360-9. The Society of Arts' printed membership list for 8 March 1758 contains the names of some forty governors of the Foundling Hospital. Isaac Maddox (1697-1759), Bishop of Worcester after 1743, became a governor of the Hospital in 1753 and was a foundation member of the Society in the following year.

27. J. Hanway, op. cit., p. 12.

28. Soc. Min., 22 March 1758. For Hanway's membership of the Society, see D. G. C. Allan, 'Jonas Hanway and the Society of Arts', *Jnl. RSA*, 124 (1986), pp. 650-2. This essay is part of the Jonas Hanway Symposium sponsored by the Society.

29. H. Baker to W. Arderon, 14 Dec. 1764, Victoria and Albert Museum, Arderon-Baker MSS, Vol. 4, p. 213; Robert Dodsley to the Society, 17 March 1756, G.B. 3: 62, quoted J. E. Tierney, 'Robert Dodsley: The First Printer and Stationer to the Society', *Jnl. RSA*, 131 (1983), p. 482; Society of Arts, *Notice 'to the Publick'* (1754); *Plan* (1756), p. 2.

30. B. Cleeve to the Society (1756) RSA, L.A. A1/22; *Commons Journals*, Vol. 26, p. 289.

31. William Bailey to the Society, 3 Feb. 1757, G.B. 1: 133; Society of Arts, *Premium List* (1758), p. 22; Society of Arts, *Rules and Orders* (1758), p. 2.

32. There is no record after 14 Dec. 1757.

33. Soc. Min., 22 Mar. 1758.

34. Ibid., 29 Mar., 5 Apr. 1758.

35. Ibid., 12 Apr. 1758; Society of Arts, *Premium List* (1758), pp. 30-1.

36. Soc. Min., 17 May 1758.

37. RSA, L.A. (M.) A2/58-9, 23 May 1758.

38. Ibid., 30 May 1758.

39. *Life*, Vol. 3, pp. 216, 514. E. L. McAdam, Jr., 'Dr Johnson and Saunders Welch's *Proposals*', *R.E.S.*, New Series, 4 (1953), p. 340. Hereafter cited as McAdam.

40. McAdam, pp. 344-5.

41. RSA, L.A. (M.) A2/58-9, 6 June 1758.

42. Soc. Min., 7 June 1758.

43. See J. S. Taylor, *Jonas Hanway: Founder of the Marine Society* (London and Berkeley, 1985), pp. 76, 92-9. RSA MS. Sub. Bk., 1754-63.

44. Johnson's hostile review, which also included an attack on the religious instruction in the Foundling Hospital, appeared in the *Literary Magazine* in the 15 Apr.–15 May 1757 issue. Hanway and other governors were deeply upset, and for a time Johnson was threatened with legal action. He was apparently never connected with the review, at least at this time. See Ruth K. McClure, 'Johnson's Criticism of The Foundling Hospital And Its Consequences', *R.E.S.*, New Series, 27 (1976), pp. 2-26. Hanway's most recent biographer, James Stephen Taylor, suggests the Hanway-'Wormwood' parody (op. cit., p. 54). For Johnson's comment to Boswell, see *Life*, Vol. 2, p. 122.

3. THOMAS HOLLIS AND THE SOCIETY, 1756-1774

1. D. Hudson and K. W. Luckhurst, *The Royal Society of Arts, 1754-1954* (London, 1954), p. 28. Hereafter cited as Hudson and Luckhurst.

2. I am indebted to Miss Carolyn Elizabeth Jakeman, Assistant Librarian for Reference in the Houghton Library of Harvard University, for kindly allowing me to consult the Hollis *Diary. Diary* entries are quoted by permission of Harvard College.

3. For studies of Hollis's life see Caroline Robbins, 'The Strenuous Whig, Thomas Hollis of Lincoln's Inn', *William & Mary Quarterly*, 3rd Series, 7 (1950), pp. 406-53. Hereafter cited as Robbins. See also *Memoirs of Thomas Hollis* (London, 1780); *Trans.*, Vol. 23 (1805), pp. iii-iv; W. H. Bond, 'Letters from Thomas Hollis of Lincoln's Inn to Andrew Eliot', *Proceedings of the Massachusetts Historical Society*, 99 (1987), pp. 76-167.

4. *Boswell's Life of Johnson*, ed. G. Birkbeck Hill; revised L. F. Powell (Oxford, 1934-50), Vol. 4, pp. 97-8.

5. John Nichols, *Illustrations of Literary History* (London, 1831), Vol. 4, p. 157.

6. Soc. Min., 1754-7, 1757-8.

7. Soc. Min., 1757-8.

8. Ibid.

9. Soc. Min., 1757-8, 1758-9.

10. Soc. Min., 1758-9.

11. Ibid.

12. Sir H. T. Wood, *History of the Royal Society of Arts* (London, 1913), pp. 219-20. Hereafter cited as Wood.

13. Soc. Min., 1758-9.

14. Robbins, pp. 408, 412.

15. Soc. Min., 1758-9.

16. Ibid.

17. Min. Comm., 1758-60 (Drawings); Soc. Min., 1758-9.

18. Hudson and Luckhurst write: 'G. M. Moser (1704-1803), the German-born chaser and enameller, and his daughter Mary Moser (d. 1819), the flower-painter, were both remarkable artists whose merit was recognized by the Society in its early years' (p. 44).

19. Soc. Min., 1759-60; Min. Comm., 1758-60 (untitled).

20. Soc. Min., 1759-60; Min. Comm., 1758-60 (untitled).

21. Soc. Min., 1759-60; Min. Comm., 1758-60 (Officers) for dates cited.

22. Soc. Min., 1759-60 and 1760. The artists' exhibition was one of the Society's most important undertakings at this time in the fine arts. The functions of some of the other committees mentioned may seem strange to a twentieth-century reader, but it is clear that care was taken to ensure, among other things, that proper elections took place.

23. Soc. Min., 1760-61.

24. Robbins, p. 431. Wood notes, 'The constitution of the Society, at first and for very many years, was on a purely democratic basis', but also cites Melford's letter to Sir Watkin Phillips in *Humphry Clinker*: 'My uncle is extremely fond of the Institution, which will certainly be productive of great advantages to the public, if from its democratical form, it does not degenerate into cabal and corruption' (p. 18).

25. Soc. Min., 1761-2.

26. Min. Comm., 1761-2 (Mechanics); Soc. Min., 1760-61, 1761-2, for dates cited.

27. Hudson and Luckhurst write: 'Probably the most sensational of all the Society's early trials took place on May 21, 1761, when a three-storey building which had been specially erected at the Society's expense near the end of Titchfield Street, Marlebone, was set on fire in order to test an extinguisher invented by Ambrose Godfrey, the well-known chemist, of Southampton Street, Covent Garden. This device, called a "Fire Watch", consisted of explosive balls, fired by a match and fuse, which were thrown into the blaze and, as they burst, scattered a fire-quenching or "suffocating" liquid over the flames' (pp. 108-9). The test was a success.

28. See Walter M. Stern, 'Fish Supplies for London in the 1760s: An Experiment in Overland Transport', *Jnl. RSA*, 118 (1970), pp. 360-5, 430-5.

29. Soc. Min., 1761-2, 1762-3. For Shipley's schemes, see D. G. C. Allan, *William Shipley* (London, 1968), pp. 90-2. I examine Hollis's, Johnson's and Hawkesworth's connections with a Society manuscript entitled 'The Treatise on the Arts of Peace' in 'John Hawkesworth and "The Treatise on the Arts of Peace"', *Jnl. RSA*, 115 (1967), pp. 645-49.

30. Soc. Min., 1762-3, 1763-4.

31. Wood writes that Mary Bruce Strange, daughter of Sir Robert Strange, the eminent engraver, won premiums in 1764 and 1765 for drawings (p. 205).

32. An able illumination of Hollis's somewhat cryptic remark can be found in D. G. C. Allan, 'The Contest for the Secretaryship, 1769-1770', (chapter 18).

33. Min. Comm., 1769-70 (Chemistry, Agriculture, Polite Arts).

4. NICHOLAS CRISP, FOUNDING MEMBER OF THE SOCIETY OF ARTS

1. Thomas Mortimer, *A Concise Account of the Rise, Progress and Present State of the Society* (London, 1763), p. 8.

2. The basis of our knowledge of Crisp is a paper by Aubrey Toppin, 'Contributions to the History of Porcelain-Making in London', *English Ceramic Circle Transactions*, No. 1 (London, 1933), pp. 30-43, henceforward referred to as 'Toppin, *Contributions*'.

3. Will dated 2nd Dec. 1708, proved 8th Feb. 1708/9. See Frederick A. Crisp, *Collections Relating to the Family of Crispe* (1882), pp. 60-61.

4. I am indebted to Commander W. R. Miller, Clerk of the Worshipful Company of Haberdashers, for details of these apprenticeships.

5. The earlier Trade Directories preserved at the Guildhall Library do not give Crisp's professions; the earliest to list him is the *Complete Guide* (1744), which gives him as 'Crips, Nicholas, Bow Churchyard'.

6. Miss Susan Hare of the Goldsmiths' Company has searched the surviving records of the Company without success, but tells the writer that the records for small-workers for the years 1739-58 are missing. I should also like to acknowledge here the help of Mr. Claude Blair and other members of the Department of Metalwork at the Victoria and Albert Museum. Mr. A. J. B. Kiddell kindly searched sale records at Messrs. Sotheby's in the hope of tracing watches by Crisp, but without avail.

7. Dr. Bernard Watney gave me the date of this wedding. The Register is Guildhall Library MS 4429/2.

8. Toppin, *Contributions*, p. 40.

9. E. Morton Nance, 'Soaprock Licences', *English Ceramic Circle Transactions,* Vol. 1, No. 3 (1935), pp. 78-9.

10. R. J. Charleston and J. V. G. Mallet, 'A Problematical Group of Eighteenth Century Porcelains', *English Ceramic Circle Transactions*, Vol. 8, part 1 (1971), p. 106.

11. Francis E. Burrell, 'Some Advertisements of Ceramic Interest', *English Ceramic Circle Transactions,* Vol. 5, part 3 (1962), p. 178.

12. See F. H. Garner and Michael Archer, *English Delftware* (London, 1972), p. 50.

13. Aubrey Toppin, 'Battersea: Ceramic and Kindred Associations', *Transactions of the English Ceramic Circle*, Vol. 2, No. 9 (1946), pp. 167-8. The name 'Territthouse' puzzled Toppin, but 'Turret House' was probably meant. A seventeenth-century house in Chelsea was known in 1744 as 'Turret House' apparently because it had a windowed cupola on its roof. The Battersea Rate books are preserved at Battersea Library, Lavender Hill.

14. Toppin, *Contributions,* pp. 30-1. The Kentish Town porcelain has not been identified, if indeed Bolton succeeded in making any before financial disaster overtook his backers.

15. See Ann Cox-Johnson, 'Patrons to a Sculptor: the Society and John Bacon, R.A.', *Jnl. RSA*, 110 (1961-2), pp. 705ff., and the same author's *John Bacon, R.A., 1740-1799*, London, St. Marylebone Society Publication No. 4 (1961). The Rev. Richard Cecil wrote an obituary of Bacon in the *Gentleman's Magazine*, 69 (1799), p. 108, and later enlarged it into *Memoirs of John Bacon* (London, 1801). A more fanciful account of Bacon's early life is given by Allan Cunningham, *Lives of the British Painters, Sculptors and Architects* (London, 1830).

16. *The British Magazine and Review; or, Universal Miscellany*, Oct. 1782, Vol. 1, p. 256, here quoted from Toppin, *Contributions*, p. 38.

17. See Charleston and Mallet, op. cit., pp. 80-121. (This tentative speculation as to the identity of Crisp's porcelain has since been disproved by excavations on the factory site. See n. 92.)

18. The full title of this work, of which a copy exists in the Guildhall Library, is *A Refutation of Sir Crisp Gascoyne's Address to the Liverymen of London by a clear State of the Case of Elizabeth Canning in a Narrative of Facts, Ranged in a Regular Series, and Supported by the Information and Affidavits of Near Eighty Witnesses of Good Credit*. The authors are given as Nicholas Crisp, J. Payne, James Harriott, Edward Rossiter, Thomas Cox and John Carter, in that order.

19. Soc. Min., 28th Apr. 1755. The book does not now survive in the Society's Library.

20. E.g. Samuel Chandler, John Ellicott and John Howard.

21. PRO B1 31-42, 220, pp. 60-62.

22. See Toppin, *Contributions*, p. 43, for Mrs. Esdaile's comments based on an unpublished life of John Bacon by his son.

23. Guildhall Library MS 5009. The first entry of his name is on 7th Feb. 1753, and the last is on 23rd Aug. 1763. After that there are no further Vestry Minutes until Feb. 1765.

24. See D. G. C. Allan, *The Houses of the Royal Society of Arts* (London, 1966), pp. 6-11.

25. Letter to the Rev. William Borlase, Rector of Ludgvan, the natural-historian of Cornwall. Morrab Library, Penzance, *Borlase Incoming Letter-Books*.

26. D. G. C. Allan, *William Shipley* (London, 1968), p. 55.

27. Dr. D. G. C. Allan has kindly provided me with the following list of members proposed by Crisp: Edward Athawes, Esq.; Mr. James Ayscough; Alex. Baxter, Esq.; Mr. John Bradney, Apoth; Sam. Burroughs, Esq.; George Buxton, M.D.; Sam. Chandler, D.D.; Rev. Mr. John Chayter; Mr. John Ellicott; Mr. Edward Ellicott; Mr. John Field, Seed Merchant; Mr. William Field, Cheesemonger; John Howard, Esq.; Mr. Francis Hurt, Gent.; Mr. James Johnson; Mr. John Kirke; Thos. Lucas, Esq.; Mr. John Man; Mr. Henry Proctor Major; Mr. James Pearson; Sam. Ruggles; Sam Shore, Jnr., Esq.; Mr. Nath. Sheffield, Attorney; Michael Henry Spang; Robt. Sumpton, Esq.; John Van Rixtell; William Whitaker; Jonathan Worrall, Esq.

28. For the Ellicotts, see R. K. Foulkes, 'The Ellicotts, A Family of Clockmakers', *Antiquarian Horology*, Vol. 3, No. 4 (Sept. 1960), pp. 102-10.

29. Frederick A. Crisp, *Collections Relating to the Family of Crispe* (London, 1882), p. 61.

30. Soc. Min., 15th Dec. 1756.

31. Soc. Min., 5th Sept. 1756.

32. Soc. Min., 24th Nov. 1756.

33. Soc. Min., 19th Jan. 1757.

34. G.B. 3: 76. Part of this document is quoted in Charleston and Mallet, op. cit., p. 111.

35. Soc. Min., 4th Feb. 1756.

36. G.B. 1: 84.

37. Min. Comm. (Chemistry), 10th Mar., 19th May 1764.

38. Soc. Min., 15th Nov. 1758.

39. Soc. Min., 13th Dec. 1758.

40. E.g., Soc. Min. 3rd, 17th and 24th Mar. 1756, when Grignion's proposal for a premium to any apprentice in the watch-trade for 'the best plain watch-movement' was considered and rejected; or Soc. Min., 2nd and 9th May 1759, and Min. Comm., 8th May 1759, when although Crisp and John Ellicott were appointed to a Committee on the Rev. Mr. Gainsborough's proposals for improvement of time-pieces, Crisp does not seem to have attended the Committee.

41. Soc. Min., 2nd, 9th and 16th Feb. 1757.

42. Soc. Min., 16th Apr. 1755.

43. G.B. 3: 59. Printed in full by Charleston and Mallet, op. cit., Appendix II, pp. 120-21.

44. Soc. Min., 12th Jan. 1757; 9th Feb. 1757.

45. Soc. Min., 2nd May 1759; 9th May 1759; Min. Comm. (Chemistry), 10th Feb. 1759.

46. Min. Comm. (Chemistry), 15th Feb. 1760.

47. Min. Comm. (Chemistry), 15th and 29th Jan. 1765.

48. Soc. Min., 7th and 14th Apr. 1756. See also Baker's Correspondence with William Arderon in the Forster Collection, Victoria and Albert Museum.

49. RSA, L.A. A1/9, N. Crisp, 26th Apr. 1756.

50. D. G. C. Allan, 'Notions of Economic Policy Expressed by the Society's Correspondents and in Its Publications', Studies in the Society's Archives No. 2, *Jnl. RSA,* 106 (1957-8), p. 800.

51. On 6th Apr. 1757, Crisp presented to the Society 'an impression of the Seal of the British Museum' (Soc. Min.).

52. Soc. Min., 7th and 14th Dec. 1757.

53. Soc. Min., 5th May 1756.

54. Soc. Min., 4th Jan. 1758.

55. Bernard Watney, *English Blue and White Porcelain of the 18th Century* (London, 1963), p. 7.

56. Soc. Min., 12th Mar., 28th, 30th Apr., 7th May 1755. See also Charleston and Mallet, op. cit., pp. 109-10.

57. G.B. 1: 20.

58. Soc. Min., 5th Sept. and 6th Oct. 1756.

59. Soc. Min., 4th Jan. 1758 and 21st Nov. 1759.

60. Soc. Min., 11th Jan. 1764; Min. Comm. (Chemistry), 28th Jan. 1764. I have assumed that the Mr. Williams whose opinion the Chemistry Committee sought was the 'Mr. Stephen Williams, Linen Draper, Poultry' proposed and elected to the Society soon afterwards (Soc. Min., 21st and 28th Mar.).

61. G.B. 8: 104.

62. Min. Comm. (Chemistry), 11th Feb. 1764.

63. Soc. Min., 15th Feb. 1764. Possibly the motions and counter-motions for expelling John Finlayson for having disturbed the peace of the Society, which troubled the Society's meetings that spring, may have arisen over the award of the premium to Crisp.

64. Min. Comm. (Chemistry), 21st Apr. 1764.

65. Soc. Min., 2nd May 1764.

66. PRO B1/41, 220, pp. 48-52, dated 24th Feb. 1764.

67. *London Gazette*, No. 10353, 1st-4th Oct. 1763.

68. PRO B1/41,220, pp. 48-52, 24th Feb. 1764.

69. *London Gazette*, No. 10367, 19th-22nd Nov. 1763; PRO IND. 22650, 220, p. 42. As already recorded by Toppin, *Contributions*, Edward, son of Thomas Crisp, had been apprenticed to Nicholas on 3rd July 1753, obtaining his freedom on 7th July 1761.

70. This account is attached to a document dated 24th March 1764, PRO C12/1008/1.

71. Document dated 24th March 1764 in PRO C12/1008/1.

72. Ibid.

73. Document of 25th Jan. 1764, in PRO C12/1008/1.

74. Documents dated 7th July 1762, in PRO C12/1005, and 24th Mar. 1764, in PRO C12/1008/1.

75. Document dated 19th Dec. 1763, in PRO C12/1008/1.

76. PRO B1/42, 220, pp. 60-62. I should like to correct the impression that Crisp misapplied this fund, given in Charleston and Mallet, op. cit., p. 108. For this error I alone was to blame.

77. Aubrey Toppin, 'Contributions to the History of Porcelain-making in London', *English Ceramic Circle Transactions*, Vol. 1, No. 1, p. 41. Ann Cox-Johnson, *Jnl. RSA*, 110 (1961-2), p. 706, followed Toppin into this error.

78. Cox-Johnson, *John Bacon*, p. 3.

79. Toppin, *Contributions*, p. 41.

80. Guildhall Library MSS 11316. I have not seen the advertisement of 1762 which the late Sir Ambrose Heal showed to Aubrey Toppin, and which, according to the latter, showed 'Crisp's Cornhill shop' as 'next door to Johnson's Coffee House' (Toppin, *Contributions*, p. 41), but this advertisement may refer to a Mary Crisp who appears in the Land Tax Register for the Second Precinct of the Ward

of Cornhill in 1764 and 1765, or to a Thomas Crisp bracketed with a John Taylor in the Third Precinct of Cornhill Ward in 1764.

81. Dr. D. G. C. Allan drew my attention to these lists, which are dated 6th June 1750; 23rd Jan. 1772; 12th Oct. 1774.

82. See Bernard Watney, 'The King, the Nun and Other Figures', *English Ceramic Circle Transactions*, Vol. 7, part 1 (London, 1968), p. 51; Charleston and Mallet, op. cit., p. 103. The announcement was carried both by *Felix Farley's Bristol Journal* for Dec. and by *The London Chronicle* for 25th-27th Dec.

83. Min. Comm. (Chemistry). In 1764 Crisp attended Chemistry Committees on 10th Mar.; 19th May; 25th July; 26th Sept.; 24th Oct.; 22nd Dec. In 1765 he attended meetings of the Committee of Chemistry on 5th, 10th, 15th, 26th and 29th Jan.; 2nd, 16th and 23rd Feb.; 1st June. After this time there appear to have been no Chemistry Committees between 15th June (when Crisp was absent) and 7th Dec., when Crisp was present.

84. For the Bovey Tracey pottery, see Llewellynn Jewitt, *The Ceramic Art of Great Britain* (London, 1878), Vol. 1, pp. 343-6; Charleston and Mallet, op. cit., pp. 101-3; Norman Stretton, 'The Indio Pottery at Bovey Tracey', *English Ceramic Circle Transactions*, Vol. 8, part 2 (1972), pp. 124-36.

85. 'Josiah Wedgwood's Journey into Cornwall', ed. Geoffrey Wills [Cyril Staal], *Proceedings of the Wedgwood Society*, No. 1 (London, 1956), pp. 47-8.

86. Mr. Cyril Staal, who has kindly checked the church registers at Bovey Tracey, tells me that Nicholas Crisp was buried there on 9th July 1774.

87. See E. A. Fry (ed.), *Devon Wills and Administrations* (Plymouth, 1908).

88. *Gentleman's Magazine*, 58 (1788), p. 1127.

89. Ibid., 58 (1788), p. 839.

90. Ibid., 64 (1794), p. 578.

91. Wedgwood Archives, Barlaston. I owe the transcription to the kindness of Mr. William Billington. Wedgwood could have questioned Samuel More about Crisp when the Secretary of the Society of Arts visited him at Etruria in Aug. 1774.

92. Important new information, mainly concerned with Crisp's porcelain-making, has come to light since the publication of the above paper. This does not much affect the biography of Crisp, but the reader is referred in particular to Geoffrey Wills, 'The Plymouth Porcelain Factory, Letters to Thomas Pitt, Parts 1 and 2', *Apollo* (December 1980, January 1981); Nancy Valpy, documents published in *Transactions of the English Ceramic Circle*, Vol. 11, part 2 (1982), pp. 124-25, and Vol. 13, part 1 (1987), pp. 86-88; Frank Britton, *London Delftware* (London, 1987), p. 61; Geoffrey Godden, *Encyclopaedia of British Porcelain Manufacturers* (London, 1988), pp. 268-71; Bernard Watney, 'The Vauxhall China Works, 1751-1764', *Transactions of the English Ceramic Circle*, Vol. 13, part 3 (1989), pp. 212-22, with appendices by Derek Seeley, Roy Stevenson and Mavis Bimson, pp. 223-27. The last-mentioned paper incorporates the results of Excavations by the Museum of London that made possible the identification of Crisp's Vauxhall porcelain.

5. CALEB WHITEFOORD, FRS, FSA, 1734-1810

1. W. A. S. Hewins, *The Whitefoord Papers*, (London, 1898), pp. xxvii, 260. For the careers of Caleb and his father see Hewins, and the two articles in the *Dictionary of National Biography*. The family papers are now in the Additional Manuscripts at the British Library. See also my article 'Caleb Whitefoord, 1734-1810', *The Connoisseur*, Nov. 1975, pp. 195-9, portions of which are incorporated in the present study by kind permission of Mr. William Allan, Editor of *The Connoisseur*.

2. Hewins, p. 143; Anon., 'Memoir of Caleb Whitefoord, Esq.', *European Magazine* (Mar., 1810), p. 164.

3. Hewins, p. xxiii; 'Memoir', pp. 164-5; J. T. Smith, *Nollekens and His Times* (London, 1949), p. 164.

4. W. T. Whitley, *Artists and Their Friends in England* (London, 1928), Vol. 1, p. 320; D. Hudson, *Sir Joshua Reynolds* (London, 1954), pp. 125, 159-60, 219; *Trans.*, Vol. 29 (1811), p. iv; BL, Add. MSS 36, 593; Sir H. T. Wood, *History of the Royal Society of Arts* (London, 1913), p. 518; 'Memoir', p. 165; C. C. Sellars, *Benjamin Franklin in Portraiture* (New Haven and London, 1962), pp. 408-9, 420; D. G. C. Allan, *William Shipley, Founder of the Royal Society of Arts* (London, 1968), p. 234; Hewins, pp. 248, 261-3.

5. Soc. Min., 6th Jan. 1766, 4th Nov. 1778, 3rd Nov. 1779, 1st Nov. 1780, 7th Nov. 1781, 5th Nov. 1783; Min. Comm. (Correspondence and Papers), 21st Jan., 4th Feb., 11th Mar., 6th June 1779, 26th Feb. 1780, 27th Feb. 1782, 11th Feb., 15th Nov. 1785; Min. Comm. (Miscellaneous), 22nd Feb., 18th Mar., 1st Apr. 1779; Min. Comm. (Accounts), 3rd Feb. 1784, 4th Mar. 1785.

6. Min. Comm. (Colonies and Trade), 1778-84, and 22nd Mar. 1785; Soc. Min., 2nd Nov. 1785.

7. RSA, Red Book no. 177 (Caleb Whitefoord to the Society, 14th Dec. 1785), partly printed in D. Hudson and K. W. Luckhurst, *The Royal Society of Arts, 1754-1954* (London, 1954), p. 26.

8. Soc. Min., 14th and 21st Dec. 1785. See also Wood, op. cit., p. 322; J. Richardson, *George IV, A Portrait* (London, 1966), pp. 49-50. D. G. C. Allan, 'The Society of Arts and Government, 1754-1800', *Eighteenth Century Studies*, 7 (1974), p. 443.

9. BL, Add. MSS 36, 595, f. 299.

10. Min. Comm. (Polite Arts), 1785-1800, and 2nd Dec. 1785, 5th Dec. 1786, 17th Apr. 1793, 18th Feb., 30th Apr. 1794, 20th Mar. 1795, 20th Apr. 1796, 19th Apr. 1797. Caleb's second chairman in the Polite Arts Committee was John Parrish until 1792 and then Matthew Michell. For the various artist prize-winners mentioned, see Wood, op. cit., pp. 177-203, and John Gage, 'Turner and the Society of Arts', *Jnl. RSA*, 111 (1963), p. 842.

11. Soc. Min., 25th Jan. 1797; Min. Comm. (Polite Arts), 6th Feb. 1797.

12. Soc. Min., 1800, under dates mentioned, and 1801-10. BL, Add. MSS 36,595, f. 299; Caleb Whitefoord to his wife, c. 1801 (BL Add. MSS 36,594, f. 27).

13. Soc. Min., 7th Feb. 1810. Whitefoord had been in the chair on 10th January (Soc. Min.); he was taken 'suddenly ill while at dinner' on 2nd Feb. and died at midnight on 4th Feb. (*Morning Post,* quoted J. Greig (ed.), *The Farrington Diary* (London, 1920), Vol. 6, p. 7. The Society published an obituary with an engraved Portrait in the *Transactions* for 1811 (Vol. 29, pp. iii-vii).

14. London County Council, *Survey of London: Vol. XVIII, The Strand* (London, 1937), pp. 83, 112, 132; J. Ogden, *Isaac Disraeli* (Oxford, 1969), p. 135; Smith, op. cit., pp. 163-6.

15. Smith, op. cit., pp. 163, 217; J. T. Smith, *Book for a Rainy Day* (1905 ed.), p. 114.

16. A. Cunningham, *Life of Wilkie* (London, 1845), pp. 384-6; Hewins, pp. 270-75; A. S. Marks, 'David Wilkie's "Letter of Introduction" ', *Burlington Magazine,* 110 (1968), p. 123; Christie, Sale Catalogue (15th June 1810).

17. *European Magazine* (Mar., 1810), p. 163.

6. ARTISTS AND THE SOCIETY IN THE EIGHTEENTH CENTURY

1. J. Nichols, *Literary Anecdotes of the Eighteenth Century,* Vol. 5 (London, 1812), pp. 275-6.

2. D. G. C. Allan, *William Shipley: Founder of the Royal Society of Arts,* 2nd ed. (London, 1979), pp. 46-54. Cited hereafter as *William Shipley.*

3. Henry Baker to William Borlase, 6th Aug. 1754, and William Borlase to Henry Baker, n.d. (Penzance, Morrab Library, Borlase MSS, Incoming Letter Book 4, 168, Outgoing Letter Book 14, 113).

4. RSA, Rough Minute Book, 22nd Mar. 1754, printed *William Shipley,* p. 189.

5. Ibid., pp. 16-17.

6. D. G. C. Allan and R. E. Schofield, *Stephen Hales: Scientist and Philanthropist* (London, 1980), pp. 100-107.

7. J. Gwynn, *An Essay on Design . . .* (London, 1749), pp. 22, 26, 30, 31.

8. Anon., 'A Plan for an Academy for Sculpture and Painting', RSA, Dr. Templeman's Transactions (MS) Vol. 1, pp. 32-48; Anon., *The Plan of an Academy for the better Cultivation, Improvement and Encouragement of Painting, Sculpture, Architecture, and the Arts of Design in general; the Abstract of a Royal Charter as proposed for Establishing the same; and a short introduction* (London, 1755), quoted J. Pye, *Patronage of British Art* (London, 1845), pp. 78-9. The extracts quoted by Pye vary only slightly from the Society's MS version. See also E. Edwards, *Anecdotes of Painting* (London, 1808), pp. xxii-xxiii.

9. Soc. Min., 19th Feb. 1755.

10. 'The Papers of the Society of Artists of Great Britain', *Walpole Society,* 6 (1917-18), pp. 113-30.

11. John Astley (1724-87), the portrait painter, had married a rich widow who bequeathed him estates in Cheshire in 1762. Christian Zincke (*c.* 1684-1767) was retired from a very lucrative practice as an enamel painter. Unless otherwise stated,

information regarding artists has been extracted from the standard biographical dictionaries, including R. Gunnis, *Dictionary of British Sculptors, 1660-1851* (London, 1953) and E. Waterhouse, *The Dictionary of British 18th Century Painters* (Woodbridge, 1981). The styles and occupations of the members are those given in MS Sub. Bk., 1755-64.

12. Henry Cheere (1703-81) played a distinguished part in the local government of Westminster and was knighted in 1760 when presenting a congratulatory address from the county of Middlesex to King George III on his accession. In 1766 he was created a baronet.

13. The constitution, or 'Plan', as it was called, was adopted on 19th Feb. 1755.

14. Soc. Min., 18th Dec. 1754.

15. 'He was not interested', writes Derek Hudson, 'in improving spinning wheels or machines for slicing turnips' (D. Hudson, *Sir Joshua Reynolds,* London, 1959, p. 88).

16. Thomas Hollis, MS Diary, 20th Dec. 1760, quoted J. L. Abbott, 'Thomas Hollis and the Society, 1756-74', *Jnl. RSA*, 119 (1971), p. 806; W. Hogarth, MS 'Apology for Painters' *c.* 1760-61, printed and edited by M. Kitson, *Walpole Society,* Vol. 41, 1968, pp. 68-87.

17. Horace Walpole, MS 'Book of Materials', pp. 152, 186 (Lewis Walpole Library, Farmington, Conn.). In the year following his election Ramsay served as a judge for the drawing premium, settled the regulations to be observed for candidates drawing at the St. Martin's Lane Academy and was nominated to *ad hoc* committees (see Soc. Min., 11th Jan., 1st Mar., 17th May 1758; RSA, L.A. M.A2/12; Min. Comm. Drawings, 3rd Feb. 1758). His interest in the Society would have sprung naturally from his early connection with the Edinburgh Society for encouraging arts, manufactures and agriculture in Scotland (see A. Smart, *The Life and Art of Allan Ramsay,* London, 1952, pp. 72-9).

18. Society of Arts, *Plan* (1755), p. 2; *Rules and Orders* (1758), pp. 14-15; (1760), pp. 18-19; Soc. Min., 26th Nov. 1755, 23rd Feb. 1757, and 9th and 16th Mar., 14th Dec. 1757; 4th Jan., 8th Nov. 1758; 27th May 1760.

19. Society of Arts, *Rules and Orders* (1758), pp. 13-14.

20. Soc. Min., 12th Nov. 1760, 11th Nov. 1761, 10th Nov. 1762.

21. Society of Arts, *Rules and Orders* (1758), p. 15; (1760), pp. 18-19; (1762), p. 20; RSA, Soc. Min., 2nd and 9th Dec. 1761.

22. The figures appear to be: 1762, 8 out of 39; 1763, 5 out of 36; 1764, 1 out of 29 (calculated, like all the records of attendances referred to in this study, from the appropriate minute books). Further identification of members named in these sources might modify the figures. The chairmen were Thomas Brand (1761-2), Thomas Hollis's friend and heir, William Birch (1761-6) and John Barnard (1763-4), who are called 'Esquires' in the MS Sub. Bk., and Matthew Duane (1763-84), who was a successful conveyancer and numismatist (see MS Sub. Bk. 1754-63; J. Disney, *Memoirs of Thomas Brand Hollis, Esq.,* London, 1808, p. 5; *DNB* under Duane).

23. See W. T. Whitley, *Artists and Their Friends in England, 1700-1799* (Lon-

don, 1928), pp. 185-6; Soc. Min., 22nd and 28th Feb., 7th and 12th Mar. 1764; 16th and 23rd Jan. 1765.

24. Figures calculated from Society of Arts, *Premiums* [offered], 1758- ; *Register of Premiums and Bounties given by the Society* (1778), pp. 31-50; R. Dossie, *Memoirs of Agriculture and other Oeconomical Arts*, Vol. 2 (London, 1782), pp. 391-443.

25. Sir H. T. Wood, *The History of the Royal Society of Arts* (London, 1913), pp. 152-3.

26. D. Hudson and K. W. Luckhurst, *The Royal Society of Arts, 1754-1954* (London, 1954), p. 47; W. T. Whitley, op. cit., Vol. 1, pp. 191-2; R. Dossie, op. cit., Vol. 2, p. 431.

27. J. L. Abbott, 'Thomas Hollis and the Society, 1756-1774', *Jnl. RSA,* 119 (1971), pp. 711, 803, 874; J. Sunderland, 'Mortimer, Pine and Some Political Aspects of English History Painting', *Burlington Magazine,* 116 (1974), p. 317.

28. See, for example, [H. Baker], 'Advantages arising from the Society for encouraging Arts', *Gentleman's Magazine,* 26 (1756), p. 62. The original MS 'written by Mr. H. Baker signed Wm. Shipley' is G.B. 1: 83.

29. Allan, *William Shipley,* pp. 91, 119.

30. Society of Arts, *List of the Society . . . 6th June 1770; . . . 12th October 1774* (1770, 1774); figures estimated from MS Sub. Bk., 1764-72; Min. Comm. (Accounts), 1773-4, 1777-8.

31. W. M. Stern, 'Fish Supplies for London in the 1760s', *Jnl. RSA,* 118 (1970), p. 433; D. G. C. Allan, *The Houses of the Royal Society of Arts* (London, 1974), p. 61.

32. Soc. Min., and Min. Comm. (Polite Arts), under dates.

33. Min. Comm. (Polite Arts), 29th Apr. 1768. For the John Stephens case, see Hudson and Luckhurst, op. cit., pp. 59-60.

34. Valentine Green (*b.* 1739; *d.* 1813). Born in Worcester, where he studied line engraving, he came to London in 1765 and had great success with his mezzotints. In 1775 he became an ARA and was appointed Mezzotint Engraver to the King (see A. Whitman, *Valentine Green,* London, 1902). Samuel Hieronymus Grimm (*b.* 1733; *d.* 1794). Born in Switzerland and came to London from Paris in 1768. He was celebrated for his topographical works (R. M. Clay, *Samuel Hieronymus Grimm,* London, 1939).

35. R. Dossie, *Memoirs of Agriculture and other Oeconomical Arts,* Vol. 3 (London, 1782), p. xxviii; *Trans.,* Vol. 1 (1783), p. iv; J. Barry, *An Account of a Series of Pictures in the Great Room of the Society of Arts . . .* (London, 1783), pp. 209-17.

36. Min. Comm. (Accounts), 1775-87, 1787-95, 1796-1803; MS Sub. Bks., 1773-92, 1793-1802.

37. For the comment on Godefroy's election, see J. H. de Magellan's letter to the Society, 22nd Feb. 1775 (RSA, L.A. E1/41). For Barry's attitude to other artists, see A. Huxley, ed., *The Autobiography and Memoirs of Benjamin Robert Haydon (1789-1864),* Vol. 2 (London, 1926), p. 714. A list of the artist members with

the dates of their election is given in Appendix I. Appendix II shows the attendances of artist members at the Committee of Polite Arts.

38. M. Betham Edwards, ed., *Autobiography of Arthur Young* (London, 1889), p. 59.

39. V. Green to S. More, 20th Mar. 1798 (RSA, L.A. C12/96). Green was re-elected a member on 27th Jan. 1802 and was often present at the Polite Arts Committee in subsequent years.

40. Soc. Min., 15th Feb. 1797; Misc. Comm. Min., 19th Dec. 1799; W. Hewins, ed., *The Whitefoord Papers* (Oxford, 1898), pp. 250-351; A. Whitman, *Valentine Green* (London, 1902), p. 23; D. G. C. Allan, 'Caleb Whitefoord, FRS, FSA, 1734-1810: Committee Chairman and Vice President of the Society', *Jnl. RSA*, 127 (1979), pp. 306, 371.

41. V. Green, copy of his letter to the President and Council of the Royal Academy, 1st Oct. 1783 (RSA, L.A. A10/33).

42. *Trans.*, Vol. 12 (1796), p. 276; Min. Comm. (Polite Arts) 16th May 1798.

43. *Trans.*, Vol. 1 (1783), p. 49; S. More, MS 'Discourse', 1799. The premium for designs for calicos was revived in 1801 (see *Trans.*, Vol. 19 (1801), pp. viii, 40-41).

44. J. Barry, *An Account of a Series of Pictures* . . . (London, 1783), p. 93.

45. This selection of names is based on Wood, op. cit., pp. 162-212, and is not intended to be comprehensive. Further detailed study of the Polite Arts premiums winners is required. See for example, A. Cox-Johnson, 'Patrons to a Sculptor: The Society and John Bacon, RA', *Jnl. RSA*, 110 (1962), p. 705; J. Gage, 'Turner and the Society of Arts', *Jnl. RSA*, 111 (1963), p. 842; J. Thomas, 'John Flaxman, RA, 1755-1826', *Jnl. RSA*, 104 (1956), p. 43.

46. S. More, MS 'Discourse', 1797.

47. K. M. Heleniak, 'William Mulready, RA, 1786-1863, and the Society of Arts', *Jnl. RSA*, 125 (1976), p. 468; Wood, op. & loc. cit.

48. C. Knight, *London*, Vol. 5 (London, 1843), pp. 353-68; *Jnl. S of A*, 28 (1880), p. 6; Sir H. T. Wood, *Directory of the Royal Society of Arts* (London, 1909), pp. 7, 55; RSA, MS Signature Book, *c.* 1754–*c.* 1764. Hogarth's signature, as True-man Wood noted, is crossed out (Wood, *History of the Royal Society of Arts*, pp. 39, 48).

7. 'A VERY ANCIENT, USEFUL AND CURIOUS ART'

1. Soc. Min., 24th Jan. 1759. For the development of the Society's committee system and the premiums for the 'Polite Arts', see D. G. C. Allan, 'Artists and the Society in the Eighteenth Century,' *Jnl. RSA*, 132 (1984), pp. 273-6.

2. Cf. the letters of Gavin Hamilton to the Earl of Shelburne, in *A Catalogue of Ancient Marbles at Lansdowne House*, ed. A. H. Smith (London, 1889).

3. H. Rollett, *Die drei Meister der Gemmoglyptik, Antonio, Giovanni und Luigi Pichler* (Wien, 1874).

4. His collection by 1791 numbered over 15,000. See *A Descriptive Catalogue of a General Collection of Ancient and Modern Engraved Gems . . . taken from the most celebrated Cabinets in Europe; and Cast in Coloured Pastes, White Enamel, and Sulphur,* by James Tassie, Modeller; Arranged and Described by R. E. Raspe, 2 vols. (London, 1791), and G. Seidmann, 'The Tassie Collection of Casts and Pastes after Engraved Gems at Edinburgh', in *The Society of Jewellery Historians' Newsletter* No. 11 (Feb. 1981). The Society's founder, William Shipley, supplied his friend Henry Baker with 100 impressions of the best gems in his collection in 1751; see D. G. C. Allan, *William Shipley* (London, 1969), p. 178.

5. See Francis Haskell and Nicholas Penny, *Taste and the Antique* (New Haven and London, 1981).

6. Cf. cameo portrait of Oliver Cromwell, attributed to Thomas Simon (1618-65), *The Hermitage, English Art Sixteenth to Nineteenth Century* (Leningrad and London, 1979), No. 26; Horace Walpole (ed. Dallaway), *Anecdotes of Painting in England* (London, 1862), Vol. 2, p. 697 ff., on Charles Christian Reisen (1680-1725), whose 'excellence lay in imitating the heroes and empresses of antiquity', p. 698. Neither Simon nor Reisen was of English ancestry.

7. Paste in private collection. His MS account book is in the collection of the Society of Antiquaries, London.

8. On Natter, see Elisabeth Nau, *Lorenz Natter* (Biberach, 1966). On Hollis's gem collection, see *Memoirs of Thomas Hollis, Esq.* (London, 1780), Vol. 1, pp. 80 f., 822 ff.

9. E.g., in Christian Dehn's, as described by Federico Dolce, *Descrizione istorica del Museo di Cristiano Dehn* (Rome, 1772), G. 108; a *Drunken Hercules*, the same stone reproduced by Ennio Quirinio Visconti in his Collection of Impressions made for Prince Agostino Chigi, *Opere Varie*, ed. Giovanni Labus (Milan, 1829), Vol. 2, p. 225, No. 230; two stones in James Tassie's collection, Raspe, op. cit., Nos. 4512, 5869; [John Disney], *Memoirs of Thomas Brand* (priv. pr. London, 1808), p. 21.

10. Min. Comm. (Polite Arts), 10th Mar. 1759.

11. Min. Comm. (Polite Arts), 7th June 1759. See Duane's Sale Catalogue, Gerard, 1785, 2nd Part, 13th, 14th June.

12. Min. Comm. (Polite Arts), 4th July 1759.

13. Haskell and Penny, p. 264.

14. Min. Comm. (Polite Arts), 1st Feb. 1760. Soc. Min., 30th Jan. 1760, 6th and 13th Feb. 1760.

15. Raspe, op. cit., Nos. 8828, 8829.

16. See Advertisement above, note 10.

17. List of premiums offered for 1760, Classes 76, 77, 78 and 43.

18. Most contemporary handbooks offer recipes for improving the colours of stones. See e.g., Giuseppe Antonio Guattani, *Memorie enciclopediche romane* (Rome, 1810), Vol. 5, p. 60. And this was of great concern even later in the nineteenth century. See Archibald Billing, *The Science of Gems, Jewels, Coins and Medals* (London, 1875), pp. 110-13.

19. Although the printed lists for 1760 give details (see note 17 above), there are no references in the MS books of Society or Committee Minutes to premiums for gem-engraving for that year.

20. Min. Comm. (Polite Arts), 18th Dec. 1761, 8th Jan. 1762.

21. Records of his baptism and his parents' marriage have not yet been discovered, but his family relationships have been established through his own will and those of his connections. A number of reference books, even recent publications, following *Naglers Künstlerlexikon,* assign his birth to Hamburg, 1755, of German parents (which would have made him a Society prize-winner at the age of five).

22. There are no entries in apprenticeship tax records, but seal-engraving, not being a guilded craft, may have been exempt. 'Hayward's Lists', for Rome, 1773, BM Print Room.

23. See Catalogues of the exhibitions of the Society of Artists for 1760, 1764-74.

24. Min. Comm. (Polite Arts), 19th Nov. 1762, 4th Feb. 1763. G. E. Mercer, 'Mr. More of the Adelphi', *Jnl. RSA,* 127 (1979), p. 173.

25. See note 4 above.

26. *A Register of the Premiums and Bounties given by the Society* (London, 1778), p. 53: 'Pastes, 1767, For Portraits in Ditto Mr Tassie, Bounty 10.10'.

27. See List of Premiums offered for Engraving on Gems, Cameos, Intaglios, 1759-66, 1768.

28. These figures, drawn from the Society's manuscript and contemporary printed records, are set out here in detail, as those given by Robert Dossie (*Memoirs of Agriculture and other Oeconomical Arts,* Vol. 1, 1768, p. 223, and Vol. 3, 1782, pp. 440f.), do not agree with the documents.

29. Min. Comm. (Polite Arts), 30th Dec. 1763, 6th Jan. 1764. As five candidates altogether were disqualified by the Extra Meeting of the Society on 14th July 1762, one wonders if the Society was gripped by a fear of conspiracy at the time.

30. On the brothers Brown, see Exhibition Catalogue, The Hermitage (Leningrad, 1976), *Reznye Kamni Uilyama i Tcharl'za Braunov,* by Yu O. Kagan.

31. MS letter, RA, SA/36/24, dated 15th Nov. 1769.

32. Sidney Hutchinson, 'The Royal Academy Schools', *Journal of the Walpole Society,* 38 (1962), p. 132. Burch joined as the 48th Student, 2nd Sept. 1769.

33. Printed list of premiums offered for 1763, Classes 199-206. Premiums awarded, 1764 (payments were made after the New Year), in *A Register of the Premiums and Bounties given by the Society* . . . (London, 1778).

34. Ibid., years 1759-78. See note 28 above.

35. Much of Wray's work consisted in cutting armorial seals, and Natter, also a medallist, travelled Europe to seek employment, eventually dying in Russia; see sources quoted in notes 7 and 8, above.

36. *The Universal Director* . . . by Mr. Mortimer (London, 1763).

37. See Society of Artists of Great Britain, exhibition catalogues for 1760, 1764-72. Burch was elected a Fellow (i.e. member) of the Society on 19th February 1765 (see MS Minute Book 1 of the Society of Artists of Great Britain, RA, MS Collection), and a Director in successor to the seal-cutter Christopher Seaton, *c.* 1768-9.

Marchant is first described as a Fellow in the exhibition catalogue for 1772, but is supposed to have been listed among the members in 1765; quoted in A. Graves, *The Society of Artists of Great Britain, 1761-1791* (London, 1907), p. 308.

38. *The Monthly Magazine* for March 1814, Vol. 1, p. 192.

39. *Proofs from Gems . . .* , by Edward Burch, RA (London, 1795), 9 f. Burch executed two medals of Hunter (see Colonel Grant's list in *Brit. Num. J.*, 1937 *et seq.*) in 1774 and 1786, and was the maker of a wax model for a bronze écorché figure for him: see Martin Kemp, *Dr. William Hunter at the Royal Academy of Arts* (Glasgow, 1975), p. 16 f. I am indebted to Thomas Stainton and J. Baldwin for drawing my attention to these references to Burch's medals and wax.

40. See *Proofs from Gems,* No. 54.

41. *The Exhibition of the Royal Academy MDCCLXX. The Second.* Nos. 20-22 (A. Graves, *The Royal Academy of Arts,* [London, 1905] omits Burch's exhibits for 1770); Sidney C. Hutchinson, *The History of the Royal Academy, 1768-1968* (London, 1968), 59; *Proofs from Gems,* Nos. 10, 14, 68, 19; Raspe, op. cit., No. 14779.

42. See *A Catalogue of the Pictures, Sculptures, Designs in Architecture, Models, Drawings, Prints &c. exhibited by the Society of Artists of Great-Britain . . .* (London, 1765), No. 16; and subsequent years, to 1774.

43. MS letter dated 1st Oct. 1768, RA, SA/34/14. For wax models exhibited by Burch, see e.g., Society of Artists 1766, No. 202; by Marchant, ibid., 1769, No. 204.

44. George C. Williamson, *John Russell, RA* (London, 1894), p. 47.

45. Society of Artists, 1771, No. 219; *The Memoirs of Thomas Jones,* Walpole Society, Vol. 32 (London, 1951), p. 21, diary for 8th June 1769.

46. *The Diary of Joseph Farington,* edited by K. Garlick, A. Macintyre and K. Cave, 16 vols. (New Haven, 1978-84).

47. On L'Advocaat, MS letter by Marchant dated 30th May 1781 to the 4th Duke of Marlborough, BM, Blenheim Papers, LM 6/18; Matthew Duane's Sale, Gerard, 3rd May–13th June 1785, marked-up copy, Bod., Douce C.590, 3, 96; *Bacchus and Ariadne,* No. 96. *Mr. Marchant's Impressions of Gems* (Advertisement to Subscribers) (London, *c.* 1792).

48. M. H. Nevil Story-Maskelyne, *The Marlborough Gems* (privately printed, 1870), No. 304.

49. On Marchant's life and subsequent career, see my *Nathaniel Marchant, Gem-Engraver, 1739-1816,* Walpole Society Vol. 53 (1987).

50. Copy of letter by Marchant to Ozias Humphry, in *Royal Academy Exhibition Catalogue* for 1809, oppos. p. 666, grangerized set by James Hughes Anderdon, BM Print Room.

51. This is a brief summary of the lengthy deliberations reported in Soc. Min., 19th and 26th May 1802, 21st Dec. 1803, 11th Jan. 1804, 3rd and 10th Apr. 1805; and Min. Comm. (Polite Arts), 9th Apr. 1801–27th Apr. 1805.

52. RA Exhibition catalogue for 1808, No. 697.

8. THE SOCIETY AND WOOD ENGRAVING
IN THE EIGHTEENTH CENTURY

1. William Shipley, *Scheme for Putting the Proposals in Execution* (1753). The full text is to be found in Thomas Mortimer's *Concise Account of the Rise, Progress and Present State of the Society of Arts* (London, 1763), pp. 13-18.

2. The terms wood *cut* and wood *engraving* have always been used synonymously—even Thomas Bewick referred to his own exemplary engravings on wood as 'cuts'. Unhappily, this habit has excluded two excellent technical terms that, used consistently, could have discretely and accurately identified the two distinct processes of producing printing surfaces in wood. As the two processes were practised side by side during the eighteenth century—even before Bewick's birth—it has been thought prudent by the author when referring generically to the activity to use such phrases as 'printing from the wood block' and 'the wood-block print' unless he is sufficiently confident of having identified the process, in which case the specific term is used. For a recent, and very helpful, technical description of the two processes, see Walter Chamberlain's *Manual of Wood Engraving* (London, 1978).

3. 'I have said . . . little of wooden cuts; that art never was executed in any perfection in England: engraving on metal was a signal improvement of the art, and supplied the defects of cuttings in wood', wrote Horace Walpole in a footnote to his *Catalogue of Engravers* (London, 1782), p. 4. The reputation for excellent line engraving in Britain during the eighteenth century rested in the hands of such engravers as William Woollett, Robert Strange and William Sharp. See Richard T. Godfrey, *Printmaking in Britain* (Oxford, 1978).

4. Only three days separate the initial suggestion of the premium (Soc. Min., 7th Mar. 1759) from the drafting of it (Min. Comm. [Polite Arts], 10th Mar. 1759).

5. For brief information on Major and Pine see the entries in the *Dictionary of National Biography* and *Bryan's Dictionary of Painters and Engravers*.

6. The contemporary wood-block print being regarded so marginally by collectors and engravers alike in the eighteenth century, it is likely that Major and Pine would have had little sympathy with the process.

7. Baker had, significantly, served an apprenticeship with a London bookseller and was to be connected with the publishing profession throughout his later life as an author, poet, editor and translator. In 1756 he presented a short paper to the Society, *Observations on the Present State of Printing in England* (G.B. 1: 106, dated 7th Apr. 1756) and wrote a memorandum to the committee considering a premium for the making of paper in which he drew their attention to an English-made paper 'in imitation of the French' reputed to be suitable for the printing of copper-plate engravings (MS Trans., Vol. 2, 1754-8, p. 181; the memorandum is dated 18th Feb. 1756).

8. Min. Comm. (Polite Arts), 10th Mar. 1759.

9. The importance the Society attached to 'drawing' as a discipline underpinning all the arts and arts related to commerce is attested by the awards for drawing

which were among the first premiums offered. William Shipley, of course, was a drawing-master.

10. See T. D. Barlow, *Woodcuts of Albrecht Dürer* (London, 1948) for a representative collection of work; and David Rosand and Michelangelo Muraro, *Titian and the Venetian Woodcut* (Washington, 1976) for a study of the monumental prints (and others) made after the painter's designs.

11. Min. Comm. (Polite Arts), 27th Dec. 1760.

12. Ibid., 3rd Dec. 1762.

13. The 1762 premium raised the age limit once more, from twenty-one to twenty-five, and further increased the value of the premium from twelve to fifteen guineas. Min. Comm. (Polite Arts), 3rd Dec. 1762.

14. The vote was taken on only three candidates. In the eighteenth century the premiums for wood engraving appeared never to have attracted many competitors—reflecting the numbers then practising the trade rather than lack of interest in the Society's awards.

15. Published by the Society in 1778.

16. Regrettably little is known about either of these interesting wood-cutters. There is a brief entry for Watts in *Bryan's Dictionary*, and it seems likely that Walpole was referring to James Deacon in his *Anecdotes of Painting in England* in the entry for one John Deacon.

17. Cambiaso's drawings were admired by connoisseurs, and there are also wood-cut prints attributed to him, although it is considered he did no more than draw the designs that were later cut by others. See *Bryan's Dictionary*.

18. See D. G. C. Allan, 'The Society for the Encouragement of Arts, Manufactures and Commerce: Organization, Membership and Objectives in the First Three Decades (1755-84): An Example of Voluntary Economic and Social Policy in the Eighteenth Century', Ph.D. thesis submitted to the University of London, 1979.

19. From the beginning of the eighteenth century the possibility of making cheap printing blocks out of the material used in the manufacture of the types themselves had been seen as an alternative to wood cuts or engravings. Nothing really substantial came of this particular form of printing in relief, although the seriousness with which it was considered is here demonstrated by the Society.

20. Min. Comm. (Polite Arts), 11th Apr. 1774.

21. Despite being a *relief* printing process—and therefore in theory identical in nature to the types used in the letterpress printing process itself—wood engraving in practice needed a great deal of care and patience in the preliminary make-ready and subsequent printing at the press if it was to print at all well; it was one thing to pull a discrete proof from a block—as Watts's and Deacon's prints were—and quite another to print it adequately and accurately when locked in the press with the type.

22. Allan, op. cit., pp. 143-4.

23. The printer was James Phillips. For brief information on him, see H. R.

Plomer *et al.*, *A Dictionary of the Printers and Booksellers Who Were at Work in England, Scotland & Ireland from 1726-1775* (Oxford, Bibliographical Society, 1932). The printer John Browne might also have been a member of the committee. The presence of the printer(s) is important. The condition that the wood engravings to be submitted for the premium should be 'united with the letter press' is an eminently practical one, providing as it does *evidence* of the process's applicability and commercial viability.

24. Coleman died in 1807 and was well enough known in printing and publishing circles for his death to have been noted by C. H. Timperley in his *Encyclopaedia of Literary and Typographical Anecdote* (2 vols., London, 1977), p. 831. (First published 1839; the above reprint taken from the 1842 edition.)

25. For brief information on Hodgson, see *A Memoir of Thomas Bewick Written by Himself,* edited by Iain Bain (Oxford, 1979), p. 70. *Bryan's Dictionary* incorrectly says he was employed by Bewick in 1776.

26. *A Memoir of Thomas Bewick,* pp. 41-2.

27. Hodgson's work in the following year appeared in Sir John Hawkins's *History of Music* (1776).

28. All three engravings illustrate literary subjects, and it is a fact that the Society was never able, in the eighteenth century, to encourage the application of engraving on wood to illustrations of technical or scientific treatises.

29. Min. Comm. (Polite Arts), 13th Mar. 1778. This decision may have been prompted by the fact that on the two occasions between 1774 and 1778 when the premium was offered, the successful candidate both times was none other than William Coleman.

30. This print was, significantly, by one of Thomas Bewick's ex-apprentices, Charlton Nesbit.

31. See, for example, Walpole, *Catalogue of Engravers*, p. 4.

32. It is true to say that the status of *commercial* engraving on wood throughout its history was never to be completely resolved. At the conclusion of a lecture given to the Printing Historical Society ('Commercial Engraving on Wood: The Period of Decline, 1880-1900', 11th Apr. 1978) the first question asked of the author was 'Was nineteenth-century commercial engraving on wood an art or a trade?'.

33. The Society did not see itself as a publishing house, and yet had it taken an entrepreneurial rôle in publishing, it could have most effectively promoted wood engraving through the dissemination of cheaply illustrated works on scientific and technical subjects. It would appear that not until the 1820s and 1830s—when the Society for the Diffusion of Useful Knowledge took advantage of the process to illustrate its treatises and articles in the *Penny Magazine*—was good engraving significantly employed to illustrate these subjects. A part of the author's current research programme is committed to a study of the SDUK's archives, together with those of other early nineteenth-century publishing houses, with a view to clarifying more accurately the use and status of commercial engraving on wood at

this time. For the present, interested readers could consult R. Altick, *The English Common Reader* (London, 1963), P. Hollis, *The Pauper Press* (London, 1970) and R. K. Webb, *The British Working-Class Reader* (London, 1955), for general and background knowledge.

34. *A Memoir of Thomas Bewick*, pp. 77-8.

9. THE SOCIETY AND THE SURVEYS OF ENGLISH COUNTIES, 1759-1809

1. For Borlase, see *DNB* and his *Observations on the Antiquities Historical and Monumental of the County of Cornwall* (Oxford, 1754) and *The Natural History of Cornwall* (Oxford, 1758). G. R. Crone, *Maps and Their Makers* (London, 1953), p. 142, describes Herman Moll (*c.* 1688-1732) as 'the best of a poor field' among British cartographers in the first decades of the eighteenth century. *Gentleman's Magazine*, 18 (1748), p. 1. The article also expressed the view that 'the nation ought to encourage general meridians thro' Britain . . . as has been done in France'. For Baker, see *DNB*.

2. Borlase was probably referring to the Survey of Cornwall by Thomas Martyn published in 1748. Rylands English MS 19, Vol. 6, pp. 178, 204.

3. G.B. 1: 85. Rylands English MS 19, Vol. 6, p. 298. For a description of the *Carte de Cassini* project, see Lloyd A. Brown, *The Story of Maps* (Boston, 1949), pp. 250-5.

4. Min. Comm. (Polite Arts), 10th Mar. 1759.

5. Min. Comm. (Polite Arts), 15th Mar. 1759, 24th Mar. 1759. See Sir John Fortesque (ed.), *The Correspondence of King George the Third*, Vol. 1, 1760-7 (London, 1927), 328-9, which shows that a similar idea was entertained contemporaneously by William (later General) Roy, who argued that county maps could be used to fill in the topographical details of a 'General Military Map of England'. The evidence is quoted by R. A. Skelton, 'The Origins of the Ordnance Survey of Great Britain', *The Geographical Journal*, 128 (1962), p. 419, to whom I am indebted for the reference. Robert Dossie, *Memoirs of Agriculture, and other Oeconomical Arts*, Vol. 1 (London, 1768), p. 309.

6. Min. Comm. (Polite Arts), 19th Nov. 1759, 3rd Dec. 1760, 10th Mar. 1760.

7. For example, John Hammond, *The Practical Surveyor*, 3rd ed. (London, 1750), has a section illustrating the applications of the 'New Theodolite' devised by Jonathan Sisson. R. A. Skelton, op. cit., p. 416. G.B. 5: 48. The letter is anonymous.

8. Min. Comm. (Polite Arts), 10th Mar. 1760. For a full list of county maps, see Elizabeth M. Rodger, *The Large Scale County Maps of the British Isles, 1596-1850* (Oxford, 1960).

9. *DNB* has an article on Donn. G.B. 4: 116; 5: 51, 58. The surveying instruments may have been obtained from George Adams, the London instrument-maker, who is listed as one of the collectors of subscriptions on the Prospectus which Donn issued for his map. Candidates had to inform the Society of their intention to map

a particular county to avoid unnecessary competition, or, as Robert Dossie puts it, 'the rivalship in sale of several maps of the same kind'.

10. *Proposals for Surveying and Making a New and Accurate Map of the County of Devon.* By Benjamin Donn. G.B. 9: 40. Although not incorporated in the published advertisement, the time stipulation was communicated to candidates in 1760. The date of publication is given in the imprint of the map.

11. G.B. 10: 31.

12. William Bemrose, *The Life and Work of Joseph Wright* (London, 1885), p. 9. Richard Gough, *British Topography* (London, 1780), Vol. 1, p. 518, states that Whyman, who surveyed John Prior's map of Leicestershire, was an assistant to Burdett on the Derbyshire survey. Some biographical details of Kitchin are given in Thomas Chubb, *The Printed Maps in the Atlases of Great Britain and Ireland* (London, 1927), p. 437.

13. Advertisement in *Derby Mercury*, 17th Apr. 1767. Min. Comm. (Polite Arts), 5th June 1767.

14. They are Peacock and Price, but the minutes give their surnames only. Their proposals were not acceptable to the Society in Soc. Min., 12th Mar. 1760.

15. Accounts of Rocque are given in Hugh Phillips, 'John Rocque's Career', *London Topographical Record*, 20, no. 85 (1953), pp. 9-25, and J. Varley, 'John Rocque, Engraver, Cartographer and Mapseller', *Imago Mundo*, 5 (1948), pp. 83-91. RSA, L.A. A/17/22. Soc. Min., 25th Nov. 1761. Proposals for printing the map of the three counties with a specimen area had been published in 1751. BL Maps 187.1.2.

16. Isaac Taylor, the county surveyor, has been wrongly identified but is correctly identified on the cover of the facsimile of his map of Hampshire published in 1933 by the Hampshire Field Club and Archaeological Society. I am grateful to Mr. Richard Newton of Henley-in-Arden for bringing this to my notice. Over one hundred of Taylor's estate maps have survived. I am grateful to Mr. F. W. Steer for this information. Min. Comm. (Polite Arts), 19th Nov. 1762, 29th Nov. 1765. Gough, op. cit., Vol. 1, p. 328.

17. *DNB* has an article on Jefferys. See also Thomas Chubb, *A Descriptive Catalogue of the Printed Maps of Gloucestershire, 1577-1911* (Britson, 1912), pp. 435-6. For a full list of maps see Rodger, op. cit. In the Library of the Royal Geographical Society there is a MS 'Catalogue of Drawings and Engraved Maps, Charts and Plans; the Property of Mr. Thomas Jefferys (1775)'. This throws light on his methods of county surveying, insofar as reference is made to items such as 'A Drawing of the Triangles relating to the Survey of Bedfordshire', 'Plane table Sheets, relating to the Survey of Buckinghamshire', etc. Gough, op. cit., p. 478.

18. Soc. Min., 20th Nov. 1765, 24th Mar. 1769.

19. W. W. Rouse Ball and J. A. Venn (eds.), *Admissions to Trinity College, Cambridge,* Vol. III (London, 1911), p. 62. RSA, L.A. A/17/23. Bodleian, Gough, Gen. Topog., p. 207. G.B. 4: 105. Thompson had published a plan of Newcastle in 1746, and surveyed the estates; his activities are given in R. Welford, 'Early Newcastle

Typography', *Archaeologia Aeliana*, 3rd Series, III (1907), pp. 27-30. Soc. Min., 5th Mar. 1760 (Thompson's survey). Charles Wilkinson, who may have undertaken some estate surveys in the Nottingham area, can tentatively be identified as the founder of the 'Nottingham Academy' in 1777, where he taught mathematics. He died in 1786. Min. Comm. (Polite Arts), 30th Nov. 1764 (Wilkinson's proposal). Gough, op. cit., p. 78 (Jefferys' commission).

20. They are so described in *Trans.*, Vol. 2 (1784), p. 240.

21. Dossie, *Memoirs*, Vol. I (1768), p. 311. Min. Comm. (Polite Arts), 1st Feb. 1771. Soc. Min., 20th Feb. 1771.

22. See Rodger, *County Maps*. In 1769 Benjamin Donn submitted his 'Map of the County II miles round the city of Bristol' to the Society—Min. Comm. (Polite Arts), 24th Nov. 1769—and his 'Map or Chart of the whole World'—Soc. Min., 20th Feb. 1771. In 1771 proposals for a map of Essex, possibly that published by John Chapman and Peter André in 1777, were submitted—Soc. Min., 23rd Jan. 1771.

23. G.B. A: 83. In the previous year Armstrong had completed a one-inch county map of Durham engraved and published by Thomas Jefferys. The imprint of the map shows it was surveyed by Lieut. Andrew Armstrong and Son, and engraved by Thomas Kitchin (the engraver of Burdett's Derbyshire). G.B. A: 84 (for second letter). Harold Whitaker, *A Descriptive List of the Maps of Northumberland* (Newcastle-upon-Tyne, 1949), p. 80, points out that Armstrong's seems to be the first map to bear the name 'Roman Wall' and to show it terminating at Wallsend. It was not previously shown to extend beyond Newcastle. For other details, see G.B. A: 84. Statement of costs is attached to G.B. A: 83.

24. Min. Comm. (Polite Arts), 27th Oct. 1769, 24th Nov. 1769, 10th Dec. 1779. Soc. Min., 6th Feb. 1782. Armstrong produced maps of Berwickshire (1771), the Lothians (1773) and Ayrshire (1775), all with the assistance of his son.

25. Some biographical details of Prior are given in Basil L. Gimson and Percy Russell, *Leicestershire Maps, A Brief Survey* (Leicester, 1947), pp. 17-19. Min. Comm. (Polite Arts), 20th Feb. 1778. Soc. Min., 25th Mar. 1778.

26. Min. Comm. (Polite Arts), 20th Dec. 1782, 7th Feb. 1783. *Trans.*, Vol. 2 (1784), p. 240. RSA, MS Trans., 1782-3, p. 10.

27. Hodskinson served as engraver to Bedfordshire and Cumberland, and as surveyor (with John Ainslie and Thomas Donald) to his Yorkshire. Faden was appointed Geographer to King George III by a Warrant, 19th June 1783 (PRO LC 3/67, p. 154). RSA, MS Trans., 1783-4, p. 14 (Young's comment). The reference is to John Kirby's map of Suffolk (1736), more primitive in style than the other maps under discussion in this essay.

28. *Trans.*, Vol. 5 (1787), pp. 321-2. Unsuccessful applications were made by William Pitt (who cannot be satisfactorily identified) for a survey of Rutland undertaken by his son and presumably by Joseph Lindley and William Crosley (1790) for a map of Surrey. See Min. Comm. (Polite Arts), 15th Feb. 1793, 20th Feb. 1795. There is also a letter of inquiry from Joseph Lindley (RSA, L.A. C1/96, dated Jan. 1797).

29. In Bodleian, Gough, Gen. Topog., Richard Gough notes the sale of a number of copper-plates to Faden. Min. Comm. (Polite Arts), 27th Mar. 1793. The words 'pecuniary reward' are Faden's in a letter to the Society referred to in Soc. Min., 1st May 1793.

30. For an account of Yeakell, Gardner, and Gream, see Skelton, op. cit., pp. 416-19. Min. Comm. (Polite Arts), 27th Apr. 1796. RSA, L.A. 6/21. The maps were then returned to Faden's workshops for mounting at the Society's expense.

31. Armstrong had proposed a map of Norfolk, whose prospectus appeared in the *Norfolk Chronicle* of May 1779. On 19th May 1787, however, the same newspaper announced that 'in consequence of the engagement with Mr. Armstrong being dissolved the Committee had accepted the offer of Mr. Faden, to carry out the survey'. In *Norfolk Chronicle*, 26th May 1787, Armstrong attacked Faden, whom he described as 'a Retailer of Geography in London', and repeated his 'determination to pursue the work to its final completion'. Faden, however, proceeded with his survey. Min. Comm. (Polite Arts), 3rd May, 7th Apr. 1798. PRO WO 78/323, is a one-inch-to-one-mile map of Norfolk, 1793. I owe this reference to Mr. R. A. Skelton. The question is posed: did Faden make use of these materials in his Norfolk? For John Cary, see Herbert George Fordham, *John Cary, Engraver, Map, Chart and Print-seller and Globe-maker, 1754-1835* (Cambridge, 1925), p. xvi.

32. Min. Comm. (Polite Arts), 25th Feb. 1802, 6th May 1806. *Bryan's Dictionary of Painters and Engravers*, new ed. revised under G. C. Williamson, Vol. 4 (1904), p. 10, has an article on Neele. Although completely based on Ordnance Survey data, the 1801 map was in fact privately published by William Faden.

33. In 1798 Sherriff had completed 'A Map of Upwards 25 miles Round the Town of Birmingham', which was published by Faden, and in 1823 a map of the Liverpool District. Min. Comm. (Polite Arts), 6th May 1806. William Larkin published maps of a number of Irish counties, including Galway, Leitrim, Meath, Sligo and Waterford.

34. Horwood had sought the Society's support intermittently since 1791. See Min. Comm. (Polite Arts), 16th Mar. 1791, 20th Feb. 1795, 12th Dec. 1800, 13th May 1801, 30th Apr. 1803. For Evans, see Soc. Min., 10th May 1797, 31st Mar. 1802. Min. Comm. (Polite Arts), 13th May 1800, 5th May 1801, 25th Mar. 1802. John Cary published the map which had been surveyed by Joseph Singer. Min. Comm. (Polite Arts), 5th May 1804, shows that 18 'Certificates' testifying to the accuracy of the survey were read before an award of the gold medal was recommended. Robert Baugh engraved John Evans' map of North Wales, but he both surveyed and engraved the Shropshire map.

35. Sir H. T. Wood, *History of the Royal Society of Arts* (London, 1913), p. 298. Edward Lynam, 'The development of symbols, lettering, ornament, and colour on English maps'. *Proceedings of the British Records Association*, No. 4 (1939), p. 29.

36. RSA, MS Trans., 1782-3, p. 10. John Cary's *New English Atlas* (1804) and Charles Smith's *New English Atlas* (1804) resemble each other closely, and both seem to have incorporated data from the new eighteenth-century county maps. See, for example, P. D. A. Harvey and H. Thorpe, *The Printed Maps of Warwickshire,*

1576-1900 (Warwick, 1959), pp. 42-3, and Gimson and Russell, *Leicestershire Maps*, pp. 25-7.

37. William Mudge and Isaac Dalby, *An Account of the operations carried on for accomplishing a trigonometrical survey of England*, 3 vols. (London, 1799-1811), Vol. 1, p. xi. Gough, *British Topography*, p. 108.

38. *Trans.*, Vol. 6 (1788), p. 154. G.B. 10: 33. Much material on the Armstrongs is given in John Strawhorn, 'An Introduction to Armstrongs' Map', in John Straw-horn (ed.), *Ayrshire at the time of Burns*, Ayrshire Archaeological and Natural History Society (Ayr, 1959), pp. 232-55.

39. Gough, op. cit., pp. 2, 297-8. *Report from the Select Committee on the Survey and Valuation of Ireland*, Parliamentary Papers, 1824, Vol. 8, p. 8.

40. *DNB*. The statement about Donn refers to subscribers to a course of lectures which Donn gave on experimental philosophy in Bristol, but presumably he displayed comparable energy in promoting his own topographical maps. Bodleian, Gough, Gen. Topog., contains a prospectus of the map giving a list of subscribers on the day of publication. A list of subscribers was printed as a special sheet of the map. Yates's demand is found in *The General Advertiser* (Liverpool), 7th Dec. 1786.

10. THE SOCIETY AND THE IMPROVEMENT OF WHALING

1. William Scoresby, *An Account of the Arctic Regions*. Vol. 2, *The Whale Fishery* (1820, reprinted 1969). Scoresby was captain of a Whitby whaling vessel, as had been his father. For the early history, he relied mainly on S. B. J. Noel, *Mémoire sur l'Antiquité de la Pèche de la Baleine par les Nations Européennes* (Paris, 1795). Whales are mammals. To apply the term 'fishing' to them is therefore inappropriate. It is generally used, however, because their habitat is the sea, and it will be employed hereafter. Gordon Jackson, *The British Whaling Trade* (1978), appeared after this paper had been completed.

2. Scoresby, op. cit., pp. 3-4, 10-14; J. T. Jenkins, *A History of the Whale Fisheries* (1921), pp. 26-7, 59-67.

3. Henry Elking, *A View of the Greenland Trade and Whale Fishery. With the National and Private Advantages thereof* (1722), printed in J. R. McCulloch (ed.), *A Select Collection of Scarce and Valuable Economic Tracts*, pp. 85-6; Jenkins, op. cit., pp. 65-74; Scoresby, op. cit., pp. 5, 16-19.

4. Jenkins, op. cit., pp. 78-9, 82-3, 93-108, 113-15, 132.

5. For the Great Fishery, cf. W. M. Stern, 'The Stimulus given by the Society of Arts to Herring Curing in Britain', *Jnl. RSA* 122 (July, 1974), pp. 533-4.

6. Scoresby, op. cit., pp. 41-2, 55-9, 148-9; Jenkins, op. cit., pp. 132, 136, 140; Elking, op. cit., p. 88.

7. Gordon Jackson, 'Government Bounties and the Establishment of the Scottish Whaling Trade, 1750-1800', in John Butt and J. T. Ward (eds.), *Scottish Themes: Essays in honour of Professor S. G. E. Lythe* (1976), p. 47.

8. Jenkins, op. cit., pp. 162-3; Elking, op. cit., p. 90. The company was consti-

tuted by 4 & 5 Will. & Mary, cap. 17 and its increase in capital authorized by 7 & 8 Will. & Mary, cap. 33.

9. Elking, op. cit.; Scoresby, op. cit., p. 104; Jenkins, op. cit., pp. 180-3. The Act granting freedom from import duties was 10 Geo. I, cap. 16; the exemption was extended to whales caught in Davis Straits by 12 Geo. I, cap. 26.

10. Jenkins, op. cit., p. 52; K. W. Luckhurst, 'Some Aspects of the History of the Society of Arts, London, 1754-1952', Unpubl. Ph.D. thesis, London University, 1957, p. i.

11. Scoresby, op. cit., pp. 177, 418-19, 436; Jenkins, op. cit., pp. 40-41, 45.

12. Jenkins, op. cit., p. 42; Scoresby, op. cit., pp. 434-5.

13. Jenkins, op. cit., pp. 39-40; Scoresby, op. cit., pp. 392, 420-21, 434; Jackson, loc. cit., p. 49; George Francis Dow, *Whale ships and Whaling* (1925), pp. 8-9; Soc. Min., Vol. 5, fo. 74.

14. Jenkins, op. cit., pp. 39-40, 43-5; Scoresby, op. cit., pp. 90, 403-4, 408, 414; Dow, op. cit., p. 17.

15. Elking, op. cit., pp. 78, 87; Scoresby, op. cit., pp. 175-7, 292-308, 401; Jenkins, op. cit., pp. 42-4.

16. Robert Dossie, *Memoirs of Agriculture and other Oeconomical Arts*, Vol. 1 (1768), pp. 187-8; F. W. Gibbs, 'Robert Dossie (1717-1777) and the Society of Arts', *Annals of Science*, 7, No. 2 (June, 1951), pp. 154-6, 162; *idem*, 'Peter Shaw and the Revival of Chemistry', loc. cit., 7, No. 3 (Sept., 1951), p. 234.

17. *Gentleman's Magazine*, 26 (1756), pp. 130-31; Dossie, op. cit., pp. 188-9; Soc. Min., Vol. 4, fo. 121-2; Vol. 5, fo. 61, 74, Vol. 6, fo. 90, 94, 196; Min. Comm. (Chemistry) 1760-61, fo. 8.

18. Min. Comm. (Chem.), 1760-61, fo. 40-49, 51-3; Soc. Min., Vol. 6, fo. 196-8, 234, 284; Sir Henry Trueman Wood, *History of the Royal Society of Arts* (1913), pp. 282-3, 331; Gibbs, 'Robert Dossie . . .', pp. 158, 162-3, 168.

19. Min. Comm. (Chem.), 1760-61, fo. 41-9, 51-4; Soc. Min., Vol. 6, fo. 280-81, 284; Vol. 7, fo. 2-5.

20. When publishing his methods in the *Gentleman's Magazine*, 31 (1761), pp. 495-6, and the *Annual Register*, 4 (1761), pp. 142-5, Dossie described process No. 1 as applying to any kind of fish oil and included in process No. 2 instructions specifically relating to cod oil. From process No. 3 he particularly excluded seal oil as unsuitable for purification by heat.

21. Min. Comm. (Chem.), 1760-61, fo. 46-49, 58, 60-63, 1761/62, fo. 1-18; Soc. Min., Vol. 7, fo. 32.

22. Min. Comm. (Chem.), 1760-61, fo. 47, 51-2; *Annual Register*, 4 (1761), pp. 142-5; *Gentleman's Magazine*, 31 (1761), pp. 495-6.

23. Soc. Min., Vol. 7, fo. 25, 32, 37-8, 40; Min. Comm. (Chem.) 1761-62, fo. 18-20, 23-4, 26-7, 29, 37-8.

24. Soc. Min., Vol. 7, fo. 38, 71, 177-9; Min. Comm. (Chem.) 1761/62, fo. 24-6, 28-31, 34-5, 37-40, 42-6; Gibbs, 'Robert Dossie . . .', pp. 163-4; *Annual Register*, 4 (1761), pp. 142-5. *Gentleman's Magazine*, 31 (1761), pp. 495-6; 32 (1762), p. 225.

25. *Trans.*, Vol. 20 (1802), pp. 209-39.

26. This account relies on Scoresby, op. cit., pp. 187-210, 233-45; Jenkins, op. cit., pp. 216-17.

27. 25 Chas. II, cap. 7, secs. 1, 2; 2 Will. & Mary, cap. 4, sec. ii.

28. 9 Will. III, cap. 23.

29. 9 Will. III, cap. 45, sec. ii, 4 & 5 Anne, cap. 23, sec. vi, 6 Anne, cap. 27, sec. x, 6 Anne, cap. 73, sec. ix.

30. 1 Anne, cap. 16, secs. 1, 2.

31. 10 Geo. I, cap. 16, 12 Geo. I, cap. 26, sec. 7, 5 Geo. II, cap. 28, sec. 1.

32. 6 Geo. II, cap. 33, secs. 1, 2, continued by 22 Geo. II, cap. 45, 27 Geo. II, cap. 18, sec. 7, 28 Geo II, cap. 20, 4 Geo. III, cap. 22, 8 Geo. III, cap. 27, 58 Geo. III, cap. 15.

33. 13 Geo. II, cap. 28, 22 Geo. II, cap. 45.

34. Scoresby, op. cit., pp. 73-86, 111; Jenkins, op. cit., pp. 184-5, 306.

35. Scoresby, op. cit., pp. 70, 79-80, 227-8; Wood, op. cit., pp. 4-5.

36. Soc. Min., Vol. 20 (1774-75), fo. 75-80; Vol. 22 (1776-77), fo. 58, 61; Vol. 27 (1781-82), fo. 78-9; Min. Comm. (Mechanics).

37. Min. Comm. (Mechanics).

38. Scoresby, op. cit., pp. 173-4, 224-5.

39. Soc. Min., Vol. 16 (1770-71), fo. 32, 39, 41; Min. Comm. (Mechanics), 1770-71, fo. 7-8.

40. Alexander Mabyn Bailey, *One Hundred and Six Copper Plates of Mechanical Machines, and Implements of Husbandry, approved and adopted by the Society for the Encouragement of Arts, Manufacture and Commerce* (1782), Vol. 2, chap. 9, p. 61.

41. Soc. Min., Vol. 17 (1771-72), fo. 4, 80-81, 83; Vol. 18 (1772-73), fo. 27, 31; Min. Comm. (Mechanics), 1771-72, fo. 4, 7-8, 12-13, 17, 20-24, 1772-73, fo. 8-15.

42. Min. Comm. (Mechanics), 1772-73, fo. 23-6, 32-3, 1774-75, fo. 1-2, 25; *Trans.* 1773-74 (Mechanics), fo. 79-82.

43. Min. Comm. (Mechanics), 1775-76, fo. 21-2, 47, 1776-77, fo. 10-14, 19; Soc. Min., Vol. 21 (1775-76), fo. 79.

44. Min. Comm. (Mechanics), 1776-77, fo. 19-21, 24, 40-41, 45-8, 52-5, 1777-78, fo. 137-9, 157-8.

45. Soc. Min., Vol. 28 (1782-83), fo. 76; Min. Comm. (Mechanics), 1782-83, fo. 179-83, 1785-86, fo. 159-60.

46. Min. Comm. (Mechanics), 1782-83, fo. 185, 1783-84, fo. 194, 1784-85, fo. 161, 1785-86, fo. 159.

47. Min. Comm. (Mechanics), 1785-86, fo. 206, 208-9, 1786-87, fo. 184-5, 221, 227-8, 1787-88, fo. 183-4, 1788-89, fo. 176, 1791-92, fo. 207-8, 236-7, 239-41.

48. Min. Comm. (Mechanics), 1792-93, fo. 192, 200-203.

49. Bailey, op. cit., p. 61; *Trans.*, 1774-75 (Mechanics), fo. 101-3, Vol. 1 (1783), p. 321, Vol. 2 (1784), p. 181; Min. Comm. (Mechanics), 1771-72, fo. 8, 1774-75, fo. 47, 1775-76, fo. 6-7, 9, 15, 29, 47.

50. Min. Comm. (Mechanics), 1775-76, fo. 21, 1776-77, fo. 10-14, 24, 1781-82, fo. 168-9.

51. Min. Comm. (Mechanics), 1785-86, fo. 183-4, 193, 1789-90, fo. 193-5, 222, 1790-91, fo. 164, 1791-92, fo. 183-4; Soc. Min., Vol. 37 (1791-92), fo. 35.

52. Min. Comm. (Mechanics), 1791-92, fo. 208-9, 235-6, 1792-93, fo. 200-203.

11. SAMUEL JOHNSON AND HISTORY PAINTING

1. Subsequent to the present study, Morris Brownell's definitive study appeared —*Samuel Johnson's Attitude to the Arts* (Oxford, 1989).

2. W. T. Whitley, *Artists and Their Friends in England, 1700-1799,* Vol. 2 (London, 1928), p. 14.

3. 'The Papers of the Society of Artists of Great Britain,' *Walpole Society,* 6 (1918), pp. 113-30.

4. William Sandby, *The History of the Royal Academy of Arts . . . ,* Vol. 1 (London, 1862), p. 36.

5. *Boswell's Life of Johnson,* ed. G. Birkbeck Hill, revised L. F. Powell (Oxford, 1934-50), Vol. 2, pp. 364-5.

6. Min. Comm. (Premiums), 29th Nov. 1758, 19th Jan., 2nd Feb. 1759.

7. Soc. Min., Vol. 3, 1758-9, pp. 154-5.

8. Ibid., Vol. 6, 1760-61, p. 193.

9. *Premiums Offered by the Society Instituted at London for the Encouragement of Arts, Manufactures and Commerce,* volume including 1763, p. 44 no. 217. This note allows me to correct a confusing footnote in my article, 'Mortimer, Pine and some Political Aspects of English History Painting', *Burlington Magazine,* 116 (1974), pp. 317-26. In footnote 34, I confused the volumes.

10. Soc. Min., Vol. 3, 1758-9, pp. 154-5.

11. In 1760, Casali won the 2nd premium of 50 gns with the *Assassination of Edward the Martyr;* in 1761 he won the 1st premium of 100 gns with *King Stephen, Brought Prisoner to Empress Matilda;* and in 1762 he again won the 1st premium of 100 gns with *Gonhilda's Honour Vindicated.* See Robert Dossie, *Memoirs of Agriculture, and other Oeconomical Arts,* Vol. 3 (London, 1782), p. 431. The paintings of *Edward the Martyr* and *Gunhilda* are now at Burton Constable Hall, Yorkshire. The *King Stephen* is untraced.

12. A 'Samuel Johnson Symposium', held at the Royal Society of Arts on 18th Jan. 1985, covered various aspects of Johnson's connection with the Society. This article is an expanded version of a paper given at this symposium. See also James L. Clifford, *Dictionary Johnson: The Middle Years of Samuel Johnson* (New York, 1979); John L. Abbott, 'Dr. Johnson and the Society', *Jnl. RSA,* 115 (Apr.-May, 1967), pp. 395-400, 486-91.

13. Quotations from the *Idler,* no. 45, are taken from *The Yale Edition of the Works of Samuel Johnson,* Vol. 2, *The Idler and the Adventurer* (New Haven, 1963), edited by John M. Bullitt and L. F. Powell, pp. 139-42.

14. For example: Anthony Ashley Cooper, 3rd Earl of Shaftesbury, *Letter Concerning the Art or Science of Design,* 1712; Jonathan Richardson, *The Theory of Painting,* 1715; idem, *Essay on the Art of Criticism,* 1719; idem, *The Science*

of a Connoisseur, 1719; *idem, An Account of Some of the Statues, Bas-reliefs, Drawings and Pictures in Italy*, 1722. See also: Rensselaer W. Lee, *Ut Pictura Poesis: The Humanistic Theory of Painting* (New York, 1967); Johannes Dobai, *Die Kunstliteratur des Klassizismus und der Romantik in England*, Vol. 1, *1700-1750* (Bern, 1974); L. Lipking, *The Ordering of the Arts in 18th Century England* (Princeton, 1970).

15. For an early 18th century series of paintings illustrating episodes from the life of Charles I, see: Kenneth Sharpe and Robert Raines, 'The Story of Charles I', part 1, *Connoisseur*, 184 (Sept., 1973), pp. 38-46; part 2, *Connoisseur* (July, 1974), pp. 192-5.

16. See Lee, op. cit., for a detailed discussion of *ut pictura poesis*.

17. Benjamin West's painting, signed and dated 1782, is now in the Montclair Art Museum, Montclair, N.J. For full details, see: Helmut von Erffa and Allen Staley, *The Paintings of Benjamin West* (New Haven, 1986), pp. 204-6, cat. no. 83. Professor Richard Schwartz kindly pointed out that the inspiration for Johnson's envisioning the moment of Cromwell's dismissal of Parliament was likely his own piece *A Debate Between the Committee of the House of Commons and Oliver Cromwell*. The latter was an abridgement Johnson did for the *Gentleman's Magazine* of a 1660 pamphlet entitled 'Monarchy Asserted' (Feb.-Mar., 1741).

18. Quoted from Roy Strong, *Re-creating the Past: British History and The Victorian Painter* (The Pierpont Morgan Library, 1978), p. 148.

19. Yeames's painting is in the Walker Art Gallery, Liverpool.

20. For more information, see Strong, op. cit.

21. According to John Galt, *The Life, Studies and Works of Benjamin West, Esq. . . .*, Vol. 2 (London, 1820), p. 7.

22. Von Erffa and Staley, op. cit., pp. 165-6, cat. no. 5.

23. Ibid., p. 203, cat. no. 77.

24. Ibid., pp. 211-14, cat. nos. 93, 94.

25. Galt, op. cit., Vol. 2, p. 48. For a full discussion of West's painting in relation to the then current ideas about 'History' painting, see: Charles Mitchell, 'Benjamin West's "Death of General Wolfe" and the Popular History Piece', *Journal of the Warburg and Courtauld Institutes*, 7 (Jan.-June, 1944), pp. 20-33.

26. References to these premiums can be found in the relevant volumes of *Premiums Offered by the Society . . .* But I quote here from Robert Dossie, *Memoirs of Agriculture, and other Oeconomical Arts*, Vol. 3, 1782, p. 422. Premiums were bestowed from 1764-76 for 'HISTORICAL DRAWINGS, the Subject from the Greek or Roman History; *Original Compositions*, of five or more Human Figures, the principal not less than eight inches high; made under the Age of 25 Years; to divide 30 Guineas.' Also, Dossie, op. cit., p. 432; premiums were bestowed from 1764 to 1766 for 'In CHIARO-OSCURO, *Original Historical Pictures*, the Subject from the Greek or Roman History; with five or more Figures; the principal not less than 15 inches: Candidates Age under 28 Years: Premium 25 and 15 Guineas.' In 1766 the size of the figures in this category was enlarged to 30 inches and the

premium doubled in value. In 1766 the first premium of 50 guineas was won by Andrea Casali with *Lucretia Relating Tarquin's Violence*. References in the *Premiums Offered by the Society* . . . volumes give the preceding year to that given in Dossie, showing that the premiums were offered in the year preceding that in which they were bestowed.

27. Jules David Prown, *John Singleton Copley* (Washington, D.C., 1966), Vol. 2, pp. 302-10.

28. Paul de Rapin-Thoyras, *Histoire d'Angleterre—depuis l'invasion de Jules César . . . jusqu 'à l'avénement de George II à la Couronne* (The Hague, 1724-36). The first English edition, *The History of England . . . Done into English with additional notes . . . by N. Tindall*, 1725-31.

29. For further information about the depiction of English history by artists in the 18th century and early 19th century, see T. S. R. Boase, 'Macklin and Bowyer', *Journal of the Warburg and Courtauld Institutes*, 26 (1963), pp. 148-77.

30. References to the premiums bestowed are in Dossie, op. cit., pp. 431-2. Dossie lists the premiums given for British History between 1760 and 1773, except for the years 1766-7 and 1771-2, when no premiums were given. Robert Edge Pine's *Surrender of Calais to Edward III* is now only known through an engraving after the picture by F. Aliamet. John Hamilton Mortimer's *St. Paul Preaching to the Ancient Britons* is now in the Guildhall, High Wycombe.

31. These references to *Boadicea* are taken from the useful index of paintings in Strong, op. cit.

32. Angelica Kauffmann's painting of *Queen Eleanora* . . . was exhibited at the Royal Academy in 1776 (catalogue no. 155). This picture, or a version of it, was sold at Sotheby's, London, 22nd March 1972. An engraving after the picture was published 1st March 1780 (British Museum, Department of Prints and Drawings). William Blake's line engraving of *Queen Eleanora* . . . was published 18th Aug. 1793 (British Museum, Department of Prints and Drawings).

33. Von Erffa and Staley, op. cit., p. 168, cat. no. 10; Galt, op. cit., Vol. 2, p. 25, states that George III proposed the subject to West.

34. David's *Death of Socrates* is in the Metropolitan Museum, New York.

35. James Barry, *An Account of a Series of Pictures in the Great Room of the Society of Arts, Manufactures and Commerce, at the Adelphi*, 1783.

12. A CAMPAIGN TO PROMOTE THE PROSPERITY OF COLONIAL VIRGINIA

1. William Waller Henning, ed., *The Statutes at Large* . . . (Richmond, New York, Philadelphia, 1809-23), Vol. 7, pp. 288-90.

2. H. R. McIlwaine (ed.), *Journal of the House of Burgesses of Virginia, 1758-61* (Richmond, 1908), pp. 88, 109, 120, 124, 128; *Legislative Journals of the Council of Colonial Virginia* (Richmond, 1918-19), Vol. 3, p. 1215.

3. G.B. 4: 141. F. Fauquier, 22nd Apr. 1760.

4. [William G. Stanard], 'Virginia Council Journals', *The Virginia Magazine of History and Biography* (hereafter *V.M.H.B.*), 32 (1924), p. 20.

5. Fairfax Harrison, 'The Will of Charles Carter of Cleve', *V.M.H.B.*, 31 (1923), pp. 39-42.

6. Ibid., pp. 64-5; W. G. Stanard, 'Harrison of James River', *V.M.H.B.*, 32 (1924), p. 98.

7. *Museum Rusticum et Commerciale*, Vol. 1 (London, 1764), p. 197.

8. G.B. 6: 47, C. Carter, received 6th May 1761.

9. R. L. Hilldrup, 'The Salt Supply of North Carolina during the American Revolution', *The North Carolina Historical Review*, 22 (Oct., 1945), p. 394; William L. Saunders, ed., *Colonial Records of North Carolina*, Vol. 5 (Raleigh, 1887), pp. 322-4.

10. Lucian J. Fosdick, *The French Blood in America* (New York, 1906), pp. 15, 345.

11. H. R. McIlwaine (ed.), *Journals of the House of Burgesses of Virginia, 1619-1658/9* (Richmond, 1915), p. 10; Charles E. Hatch, 'Mulberry Trees and Silkworms: Sericulture in Early Virginia', *V.M.H.B.*, 65 (1957), pp. 3-61.

12. William Stith, *The History of the First Discovery and Settlement of Virginia* (New York, 1865), p. 177.

13. [John Mitchell?], *American Husbandry*, ed. Harry J. Carmen (New York, 1939), p. 192.

14. G.B. 2: 52, C. Carter, 28th May 1762. This letter was received by the Society on 28th Sept. 1762.

15. University of Virginia Library, Sabine Hall Papers. Extract of a letter from Peter Wyche to Charles Carter, Aug. 1763.

16. Herbert Thatcher, 'Dr. Mitchell, M.D., F.R.S., of Virginia', *V.M.H.B.*, 39 (1931), p. 129.

17. Charles K. Hallowell, 'Timothy Grass', *Collier's Encyclopedia* (New York, 1950-51), Vol. 18, p. 577.

18. G.B., loc. cit.

19. Min. Comm. (Colonies and Trade), 22nd Nov. 1763. Quoted D. Hudson and K. W. Luckhurst, *The Royal Society of Arts, 1754-1954*, p. 160.

20. G.B. 2: 51, 10th Apr. 1762.

21. Carter's spelling is 'Tolor'.

22. O. E. Jennings and Audrey Avinoff, *Wild Flowers of Western Pennsylvania and the Upper Ohio Basin* (Pittsburgh, 1953), plate 81.

23. St. Julien Ravennel Childs, *Malaria and Colonization in the Carolina Low Country* (John Hopkins Studies in Historical and Political Science 58, Baltimore, 1940), pp. 12-15.

24. *Webster's New International Dictionary of the English Language*, 2nd ed. (Springfield, Mass., 1939), p. 1334.

25. William Byrd, 'Letters of William Byrd II, and Sir Hans Sloane Relative to Plants and Minerals of Virginia', *William and Mary Quarterly*, 2nd Series, 1 (1921), pp. 190, 192.

26. Wyndham B. Blanton, *Medicine in Virginia in the Eighteenth Century* (Richmond, 1931), pp. 168, 197.

27. G.B. 6: 45, C. Carter, n.d.

28. 'Papers of Archibald Stuart', *William and Mary Quarterly*, 2nd Series, 5 (1925), pp. 291-2.

29. *The Virginia Gazette* (Purdie and Dixon), 12th Feb. 1767, pp. 2-3.

30. G.B., loc. cit.

31. See George MacLaren Brydon, *Virginia's Mother Church and the Political Conditions under which it Grew*, Vol. 2 (Philadelphia, 1952), pp. 288-320.

32. G.B. 6: 49, P. Wyche, 30th May 1761. Wyche's figures were an exaggeration. The Society had less than 1,500 members in 1761 (see Hudson and Luckhurst, op. cit., p. 364). Its income from subscriptions was £3,656 4s. (MS Ledger, 1755-66).

33. Donald C. Peattie, 'Alexander Garden', *Dictionary of American Biography*, Vol. 7 (New York, 1931), pp. 132-3.

34. G.B. 7: 116, C. Carter, 21st Aug. 1762.

35. Conway Zirkle, 'John Clayton and Our Colonial Botany', *V.M.H.B.*, 67 (1959), p. 288.

36. University of Virginia Library, Sabine Hall Papers. Extract of Peter Wyche's letter to Colonel Charles Carter, Aug. 1763; Fred Coleman Sears, *Productive Small Fruit Culture* (Philadelphia, 1920), pp. 279-90.

37. Sheffield Central Library, Wentworth-Woodhouse Muniments, No. R61-6.

38. G.B. 6: 49, P. Wyche, 30th May 1761.

39. Wentworth-Woodhouse Muniments, loc. cit.

40. Ibid.

41. G.B. 6: 49.

42. G.B. 7: 116.

43. G.B. 7: 110, W. Lewis, 8th July 1763; for William Lewis, see *Dictionary of National Biography*.

44. G.B. 3, S. More, n.d.

45. Ibid., 6: 49, C. Carter, 30th May 1761; for Ambrose Godfrey, see *DNB*.

46. G.B. 7: 15, C. Dick, 22nd June 1762.

47. Ibid., 16, C. Dick (enclosure with letter of 22nd June 1762).

48. Soc. Min., 20th Oct. 1762; quoted Hudson and Luckhurst, op. cit., p. 154.

49. University of Virginia Library, Sabine Hall Papers. Charles Carter, Sr., to Landon Carter, Cleve, 3rd June 1763.

50. Wentworth-Woodhouse Muniments, loc. cit.

51. *The Virginia Gazette* (Purdie and Dixon), 19th Nov. 1772, p. 2; 11th Nov. 1773, p. 2.

52. Meyer Jacobstein, *The Tobacco Industry in the United States* (Studies in History, Economics and Public Law of Columbia University 26, New York, 1907), p. 28.

13. 'THE PRESENT UNHAPPY DISPUTES'

1. Reference to these events in the Society's domestic history will be found in the MS Minutes under the dates given.

2. Min. Comm. (Colonies and Trade), 27th Feb. 1778. See also D. G. C. Allan, 'The Society of Arts and the Committee of the Privy Council for Trade, 1786-1815', *Jnl. RSA*, 109 (1961), pp. 389, 629, 807, 979.

3. See Society of Arts, *Premiums . . . [offered]*, 1755-; *Register of the Premiums and Bounties given by the Society* (London, 1778), pp. 16-19; *Trans.*, Vol. 2 (1783), p. 229.

4. W. Shipley to B. Franklin, 1st Sept. 1756, American Philosophical Society, Franklin MSS, printed in *The Papers of Benjamin Franklin*, Vol. 6 (New Haven, 1963), pp. 499-50.

5. S. Madden to W. Shipley, 26th Nov. 1759, G.B. 3: 119.

6. Quoted J. Nichols, *Illustrations of Literary History*, Vol. 6 (London, 1831), p. 157, and J. L. Abbott, 'Thomas Hollis and the Society, 1756-1774', *Jnl. RSA*, 119 (1971), p. 713.

7. R. Pringle to the Society, 7th Apr. 1758, G.B. 2: 25 (printed W. B. Edgar, 'A Letter from South Carolina', *Jnl. RSA*, 122 [1974], p. 96); A. Garden to John Ellis, 17th Feb. 1759, G.B. 4: 37; E. Antill to the Society, 28th Feb. 1769, G.B. A: 69; B. Gale to B. Franklin, 10th Dec. 1770, Am. Phil. Soc., Franklin MSS, printed in *The Papers of Benjamin Franklin*, Vol. 17 (New Haven, 1973), p. 297.

8. J. P. Greene, 'The Alienation of Benjamin Franklin—British American', *Jnl. RSA*, 124 (1976), pp. 52-70.

9. B. Franklin to Samuel Cooper, 8th June 1770, printed in W. B. Willcox (ed.), *The Papers of Benjamin Franklin*, Vol. 17 (New Haven, 1973), pp. 163-4.

10. Willcox, op. cit., Vol. 17, pp. 365-66.

11. Min. Comm. (Mechanics), 5th Feb. 1767, 18th Mar. 1773; (Agriculture), 31st May 1769; J. P. Greene, op. cit.; K. M. Kenyon, *Benjamin Franklin at Twyford* (Winchester, n.d.).

12. *Gentleman's Magazine*, 45 (1775), pp. 331, 358, 405.

13. Ibid., 46 (1776), pp. 187, 344, 345, 346, 348, 352, 353, 355, 361. The headache cure involved putting a tin dish on 'the bare head filled with water' and adding up to 2 ounces 'of melten lead therein, whyle he hath it upon the head'. A. Valentine, *The British Establishment, 1760-1784: An Eighteenth-Century Biographical Dictionary* (Norman, Ok., 1970), Vol. 1, p. 177, commented on the Duchess of Kingston's trial that it 'occasioned greater popular interest and larger aristocratic crowds than any debates on the American war or other less interesting issues!'

14. Society of Arts, *Plan*, 19th Feb. 1755.

15. Figures calculated from the Society's minutes and printed membership lists. No lists seem to have been preserved for the years 1778-83.

16. See D. G. C. Allan (ed.), *The American Correspondence and Transactions of the Royal Society of Arts, 1755-1840* (Microfilm publication, East Ardsley, 1963). The post-1770 correspondent was Aaron Loocock (see below, note 27).

17. Sir H. T. Wood, *The History of the Royal Society of Arts* (London, 1913), p. 38, mentions only Franklin. D. Hudson and K. W. Luckhurst, *The Royal Society of Arts, 1754-1954* (London, 1954), pp. 153-4, refer to Franklin, Garden, and Charles Carter of Virginia. See also E. N. Da C. Andrade, 'Benjamin Franklin in London', *Jnl. RSA*, 104 (1956), p. 216.

18. The list was published on 1st Aug. 1777 (see Appendix), and Fisher was elected on 19th Nov. 1777. For Waln, see *Pennsylvania Archives*, 1st Series, Vol. 8, 1953, pp. 100-107.

19. Unless otherwise stated, biographical details have been extracted from one or other of the following works: *The Dictionary of American Biography,* and L. Sabine, *Biographical Sketches of Loyalists of the American Rebellion* (Boston, 1864).

20. *Memoirs of the American Academy of Arts and Sciences,* Vol. 1 (1785), p. xx.

21. J. R. Alden, *A History of the American Revolution: Britain and the Loss of the Thirteen Colonies* (London, 1969), pp. 198-9.

22. R. P. McCormick, 'The Society, the Grape and New Jersey', *Jnl. RSA*, 110 (1962), pp. 120-21.

23. B. Hindle, *The Pursuit of Science in Revolutionary America, 1735-1789* (Chapel Hill, N.C., 1956), pp. 220, 234.

24. See L. L. Knight, *Georgia's Roster of the Revolution* (Baltimore, 1920), under Farley.

25. Benjamin Smith died in 1770 (see W. B. Edgar and N. L. Bailey, *The Biographical Directory of the South Carolina House of Representatives. Vol. 2, The Common House of Assembly, 1692-1775* [Columbia, S.C., 1977] under name). Thomas Shirley, merchant residing at Charleston *c.* 1759-65 'in very genteel fashion', may also have died before the conflict (see *The Papers of Henry Laurens* [Columbia, S.C., 1974], Vol. 4, p. 96n). Louis du Menil de St. Pierre had returned to England in 1772 to collect more settlers for the township he had established in 1762 and had failed to obtain financial support (A. H. Hirsch, *The Huguenots of Colonial South Carolina* [Durham, N.C., 1928], pp. 42-4, 206-10). The Reverend Charles Woodmason had moved to Maryland in 1773 and at the end of 1774, being considered 'an enemy to American Liberty', had fled to England (see C. Woodmason, *The Carolina Backcountry on the Eve of Revolution: The Journal and Writings of Charles Woodmason, Anglican Itinerant* [Chapel Hill, N.C., 1953], p. XXXII).

26. E. Berkeley and D. S. Berkeley, *Dr. Alexander Garden of Charles Town* (Chapel Hill, 1969), pp. 263-9.

27. Edgar and Bailey, op. cit., under Loocock; A. Loocock to the Society, 16th Jan. 1775, RSA, L.A. A7/45.

28. Edgar and Bailey, op. cit., under name.

29. *Pennsylvania Magazine of History and Biography,* 1937, p. 67.

30. For Kearney, see E. A. Jones, 'The Loyalists of New Jersey', *New Jersey Hist. Soc. Coll.,* Vol. 10, 1927. The description of West's painting is quoted in Sabine, op. cit., Vol. 1, p. 442.

31. W. Brown, *The King's Friends* (Providence, R.I., 1965), p. 281.

32. Elihu's mother's maiden name was Lyman (see F. B. Dexter, *Biographical Sketches of the Graduates of Yale College, October 1701–May 1745* [New York, 1885], Vol. 1, p. 427).

33. Letter dated 9th May 1776, quoted M. Beth Norton, *The British Americans* (London, 1974), p. 132.

34. Unless otherwise stated, the sources for the political stand of persons mentioned are the *Dictionary of National Biography* and A. Valentine, *The British Establishment, 1760-1784: An Eighteenth-Century Biographical Dictionary* (Norman, Ok., 1970).

35. *Gentleman's Magazine,* 46 (1776), p. 129.

36. American Philosophical Society MSS, Franklin Papers, Vol. 12, 53, cited M. H. Combe Martin, 'Joshua Steele', *Jnl. RSA,* 117 (1969), p. 133.

37. C. Whitefoord to J. Hutchinson and J. Vaughan, 25th Feb. 1791, printed W. A. S. Hewins (ed.), *The Whitefoord Papers* (Oxford, 1898), p. 211.

38. B. Franklin to A. Small, 5th Nov. 1789, printed W. T. Franklin, ed., *The Private Correspondence of Benjamin Franklin,* Vol. 1 (London, 1817), pp. 263-4.

39. Quoted J. G. Gazley, *The Life of Arthur Young, 1741-1820* (Philadelphia, 1973), pp. 120-1.

40. S. More to American Philosophical Society, 7th Dec. 1786, Am. Phil. Soc. MSS; B. Franklin to S. More, 5th Nov. 1789, printed W. T. Franklin, op. cit., p. 262.

41. G. Cockings, *Arts, Manufactures and Commerce: A Poem* (London, 1766), p. 3.

42. Quoted in W. B. Pemberton, *Lord North* (London, 1938), p. 241.

43. J. Barry, *An Account of a Series of Pictures in the Great Room of the Society of Arts . . .* (London, 1783), p. 71n. (quoting *La Nouvelle de la Republique des Lettres et des Arts, 1st July 1781*); D. G. C. Allan, 'The Society of Arts and Government, 1754-1800', *Eighteenth-Century Studies,* 7, no. 4, 1974; W. L. Pressly, *The Life and Art of James Barry* (New Haven and London, 1981), pp. 77-82.

44. Society of Arts, *Register of Premiums and Bounties given by the Society* (1778), p. 19.

45. Min. Comm. (Correspondence and Papers), under date.

46. Min. Comm. (Colonies and Trade), 14th Jan. 1777; Soc. Min., 22nd Jan. 1777; Society of Arts, *Premiums offered . . .,* 1780, p. 40; *Trans.,* Vol. 1 (1783), p. 250.

47. For the Society's interest in Canadian hemp, see D. G. C. Allan, 'Colonel William Tatham, an Anglo-American Member of the Society, 1801-1804', *Jnl. RSA,* 108 (1960), pp. 229-33; and for U.S. premiums, see Alexander Hamilton, 'Report on Manufactures, 1791', printed R. Birley (ed.), *Speeches and Documents in American History,* Vol. 1, *1776-1815* (London, 1944), pp. 208-14. Hamilton was elected on 12th Mar. 1788 (Soc. Min., under date).

14. SOME NOTES ON THE GERMANIC ASSOCIATIONS OF THE SOCIETY IN THE EIGHTEENTH CENTURY

1. Another example of an economic society which was modelled on the Society of Arts was 'The Russian Free Economic Society'. See Prof. J. A. Prescott's article 'The Russian Free (Imperial) Economic Society (1765-1917)', *Jnl. RSA*, 114 (1965-6), pp. 33-7.

2. E.g., in J. J. Volkmann, *Neueste Reisen durch England, vorzüglich in Absicht auf die Kunstsammlungen, Naturgeschichte, Oekonomie, Manufakturen und Landsitze der Grafen.* 4 Vols. (Leipzig, 1781-2).

3. Mrs. Sophie von La Roche wrote her diary for her daughters in Germany. Her visit to England was from 29th Aug. to 12th Oct. 1786. The Diary, written in German, was translated by Clare Williams.

4. C. G. Rössig, 'Betrachtungen über englisches und sächsisches Manufakturwesen', *Journal für Fabrik, Manufaktur, Handlung und Mode,* 20, (Jan.-July, 1801), pp. 353 ff.

5. W. H. G. Armytage, 'The "Common Market" of Science', in Alfred Cobban (ed.), *The Eighteenth Century, Europe in the Age of Enlightenment* (London, 1969), pp. 95-122.

6. J. Sutherland, *A Preface to Eighteenth-Century Poetry* (London, 1966), p. 55.

7. D. C. Coleman, 'Premiums for Paper: The Society and the Early Paper Industry', *Jnl. RSA,* 107 (1958-9), pp. 361-5.

8. D. Hudson and K. W. Luckhurst, *The Royal Society of Arts, 1754-1954* (London, 1954), p. 9.

9. G. Fester, *Die Entwicklung der chemischen Technik bis zu den Anfängen der Grossindustrie, ein technologisch-historischer Versuch* (Wiesbaden, 1969), p. 205.

10. In the 'Staats- und Gelehrtenzeitung des Hamburgischen Correspondenten' (Hamburg, 1752), his colours are called 'ponceau sans pareil'.

11. G.B. 3: 31.

12. *Premiums offered by the Society . . . ,* 1760.

13. A. Wolf, *A History of Science, Technology and Philosophy in the 18th Century* (London, 1952), p. 514.

14. G.B. 8: 119.

15. Min. Comm. (Chemistry), 7th Dec. 1765.

16. Ibid., 14th Dec. 1765.

17. Hudson and Luckhurst, op. cit., p. 96.

18. L. Trengove, 'Chemistry at the Royal Society of London in the Eighteenth Century—Metals', *Annals of Science,* 21 (1965), pp. 175-201, 177 ff.

19. *Premiums offered . . . ,* 1756.

20. G.B. 3: 74.

21. Trengove, op. cit., pp. 200 f.

22. *Trans.* Vol. 1 (1783), pp. 16-17.

23. G.B. 3: 74.

24. R. Dossie, *Memoirs of Agriculture* . . . 3 Vols. (London, 1768-82), Vol. 1, p. 23.

25. G.B. 7: 10.

26. Dossie, op. cit., Vol. 3, p. 457.

27. G.B. 2: 68.

28. Ibid.

29. G.B. B: 146.

30. D. Hunter, *Papermaking* (London, 1947), p. 332.

31. A. R. Beddows, review article, 'The Provision of Year-Round succulent Feed for Livestock in Great Britain, 1557-1963', *Herbage Abstracts,* 35, No. 3 (Sept., 1965), pp. 151-7, 152.

32. Ibid., p. 153.

33. G.B. 5: 40.

34. *Physikalisch-ökonomische Auszüge,* 7 (1765), p. 276.

35. R. Rübberdt, *Die ökonomischen Sozietäten* (Würzburg, 1934), p. 10.

36. H. Hubrig, *Die patriotischen Gesellschaften des 18. Jahrhunderts* (Weinheim, Berlin, 1957), p. 36 f.

37. G.B. 2: 113.

38. *6. Anzeige der Leipziger Sozietät,* 13th Jan. 1766.

39. R. Forberger, *Die Manufaktur in Sachsen von Ende des 16. bis zum Anfang des 19. Jahrhunderts* (Berlin, 1958), p. 90.

40. G.B. 2: 66.

41. Min. Comm. (Manufactures), 14th Oct. 1766.

42. Ibid., 13th Jan. 1767.

43. Ibid.

44. G.B. 2: 112.

45. Ibid.

46. *Vierter Auszug aus dem Protokoll der Leipziger Sozietät über die Verhandlungen der zweiten Klasse* (Leipzig, 1769).

47. Ibid.

48. G.B. A: 37.

49. G.B. 8: 102.

50. G.B. A: 37.

51. *Annalen der Niedersächsischen Landwirtschaft,* Vol. 3 (Celle, 1801), p. 236.

52. *Leipziger Intelligenzblatt,* 1765, p. 125.

53. *Akten und Protokolle der Ökonomischen Gesellschaft,* 1764-5.

54. G.B. 10: 2.

55. Shipley was aware of the importance of the example of English societies to 'the watchful inhabitants of the neighbouring nations'. See his 'Plan to Extend the Maidstone Society', 1786, printed D. G. C. Allan, *William Shipley, Founder of the Royal Society of Arts* (London, 1968), p. 202.

56. *Trans.* Vol. 10 (1792), p. 275.

57. *Verhandlungen und Schriften der Hamburgischen Gesellschaft zur Beforderung der Kunste und nutzlichen Wissenschaften,* Vol. 3 (1795), p. 366.

58. L. Berchthold, *Essay to direct and extend the inquiries of Patriotic Travellers*, Vol. 1 (London, 1789), p. 372; cited Allan, op. cit., p. 18. (Significantly, Berchthold links Howard the prison reformer and Hawes the life-saver with Shipley.)

15. COUNT FRANCESCO ALGAROTTI AND THE SOCIETY

1. Soc. Min., 22 Dec. 1762-3. Edward Hooper was a member of the Society from 1755 and served as Vice President from 1758 to his death in 1795. He listed Hern Court, Dorset, as his country address.

2. See *Il neutonianismo per le dame, ovvero dialoghi sopra le luce e i colori* (Naples, 1737; English translation by Elizabeth Carter, proofs revised by Dr. Johnson, London, 1739); *Saggio sopra l'opera in musica* (Venice, 1755; revised edition Livorno, 1763; English translation anonymous, London, 1767, and Glasgow, 1768).

3. Soc. Min., 29 Dec. 1762-3.

4. Ibid., p. 63.

5. Algarotti had visited London several times in the 1730s. He was elected a Fellow of the Royal Society in 1736 'on account of his great knowledge in all parts of philosophical and mathematical learning'. On 27th May of the same year he along with Andreas Celsius of Uppsala and Marquis Scipio Maffei of Verona were elected Honorary Members of the Society of Antiquaries as 'Foreigners of Eminent Note and Learning'. See Richard Northcott, *Francesco Algarotti: A reprint of his essay on opera and a sketch of his life* (London, 1917), p. 8, and Joan Evans, *A History of the Society of Antiquaries* (Oxford, 1956), p. 87.

6. See John Abbott, 'Thomas Hollis and the Society, 1756-1774', *Jnl. RSA*, 119 (1971), pp. 711-15, 803-7, 874-8.

7. Archdeacon Francis Blackburne, compiler of the *Memoirs of Thomas Hollis, Esq. F.R. and A.S.S.* (2 vols., London, 1780), states: 'While Mr. Hollis was abroad, he made many valuable friendships with men of learning and eminence, favourers and promoters of polite arts and useful sciences. Among these were . . . Count Algarotti, a Bolognese; a learned, polite, accomplished nobleman, well known in the learned world by his many ingenious works' (Vol. 1, p. 59). Blackburne writes further that Algarotti 'became (upon Mr. Hollis's recommendation, it is believed) fellow of the . . . society for promoting arts and commerce' (Ibid., p. 199). A copy of the *Memoirs of Thomas Hollis* is in the Society's library. Hereafter referred to as *Memoirs*.

8. Fifteen letters from Hollis to Howe are preserved in a collection of 'Letters to William Taylor How. 1760-1768' in BL, Add. MSS 26889. The two became acquainted in September 1760. The diary of Thomas Hollis, 6 vols., now in the Houghton Library, Harvard University, records the beginning of their relationship and accounts for the undated 'Memorandum' in the British Library.

9. For information on other of Hollis's private projects see Caroline Robbins, 'The Strenuous Whig, Thomas Hollis of Lincoln's Inn', *William & Mary Quarterly*, 3rd Series, 7 (1950), pp. 406-53, and her 'Library of Liberty—Assembled for Harvard College by Thomas Hollis of Lincoln's Inn', *Harvard Library Bulletin*, 5

(1951), pp. 5-23, 181-96; also Hans Utz, 'Die Hollis-Sammlung in Bern', *Schriften der Literarischen Gesellschaft Bern,* Vol. 8 (Bern, 1959).

10. BL, Add. MSS 26889.

11. Confirmed by Soc. Min., 12th, 19th Jan. 1762-63.

12. BL, Add. MSS 26889.

13. Thomas Hollis's correspondence with William Pitt concerning the dedication of Algarotti's essay on opera to Pitt is preserved in the Chatham Papers in the Public Record Office, 30/8/40. Nine letters by Pitt, Howe and Hollis concerning that dedication were printed in the *Gentleman's Magazine,* 75 (Feb., 1805), pp. 106-9, as 'Original Letters to and from the Right Hon. William Pitt; afterwards Earl of Chatham'.

14. English translation [by 'Mr. Lockman'?] from *An essay on painting written in Italian by Count Algarotti F.R.S., F.S.A.* (London, 1764), pp. iii-vii. For the original Italian text, see Francesco Algarotti, *Saggio sopra la pittura* (Livorno, 1763), copy in the Society's library.

15. The original letter in Italian is in G.B. 7: 87. It is also printed in *Opere del Conte Algarotti* (Venice, 1791), Vol. 10, pp. 154-6. Two other letters from Algarotti preserved in the Guard Book are dated 'Bologna 7 Giugno 1763' (No. 138) and 'Bologna 6 Sept. 1763' (No. 117).

16. *Memoirs,* Vol. 2, p. 710. In his diary (6 vols., now in the Houghton Library, Harvard University; hereafter referred to as Diary) entry for 6th May 1763, Hollis writes: 'Finished several letters for the foreign post. Dined at home alone. Just afterwards received a letter from Mr. How at Pisa, in which were some circumstances, in answer to a letter of mine to him which gave me great uneasiness. Acknowledged it directly, & will reply to it fully the tenth. . . . Went to bed & slept brokenly from the aflictions arising from Mr. How's letter.'

17. Hollis's life 'plan' is explained in several extant letters and also clearly in his Diary entry for 12th November 1760.

18. BL, Add. MSS 26889.

19. The Society's copies of the essays in Italian are still in the Society's library. Peter Templeman, M.D., was Secretary of the Society from 1760 to 1769.

20. The Diary entries at this time record Hollis's preoccupation with the parcels from Algarotti.

21. BL, Add. MSS 26889.

22. Ibid. In the letter he continues to protest the dedication of the *Saggio sopra l'Accademia di Franchia che è in Roma* to him: 'But, Sir, what can I write concerning the Dedication? You have heaped honors on a man without mark & without Likelyhood; from the biased representations of his friends, and a too hasty opinion formed of him from a few plain transactions which had, somehow fallen within your knowledge.'

23. *Saggio sopra la pittura*, Livorno, Presso Mareo Coltellini, 1763 (cm. 10 × 16.2, 148 pp.). This is actually the fourth edition, revised. Initially it was included in Algarotti's *Discorsi sopra differenti soggetti* (Venice, Presso Giambattista Pas-

quali, 1755) with a dedication to 'Signor Marchese XXX', signed '20 maggio 1755'. It appeared as a separate print of 44 pages the following year, the text having been reworked, the publisher not indicated. In 1757 the essay appears in *Opere varie del Conte Francesco Algarotti* (Venice, Pasquali), Vol. 2, pp. 225-75, with a new dedication to 'Signore Giuseppe Smith / Console della Nazione Inglese / in Venezia.' Again the text has been reworked. The 1763 edition, dedicated to the Society on 17th March 1762, is the final and greatly expanded version of the *Saggio sopra la pittura*.

24. Also quoted in *Memoirs,* Vol. 1, p. 199.

25. BL, Add. MSS 26889.

26. G.B. 7: 121. Valtravers was Thomas Hollis's intermediary in Switzerland for his anonymous donations of books to the public library of Bern.

27. *The Monthly Review,* 30 (1764), p. 351.

28. Ibid., p. 354.

29. According to *A List of the Society for the Encouragement of Arts, Manufactures and Commerce* (London, 1765), p. 40, Mr. John Lockman, Gent., of Brownlow Street was a Society member.

30. *Essai sur la Peinture et sur l'Académie de France établie à Rome . . . traduit de l'italien par M. Pingeron* (Paris, 1769).

31. *Versuch über die Architectur, Mahlerey und musicalischer Oper, aus dem Italienischer des Grafen Algarotti, übersetzt von R. E. Raspe* (Cassel, 1769).

32. G.B. 7: 117.

33. *Memoirs,* Vol. 1, p. 201.

34. Algarotti refers to the Society as the 'illustre Accademia' in his last letter to the Society. (See G.B. 7: 117.) The last phrase is from a letter written by Thomas Hollis to the *London Chronicle,* 5th July 1764, concerning Algarotti. (See *Memoirs,* Vol. 1, p. 201.)

35. *Memoirs,* Vol. 1, p. 199.

36. Ibid., p. 200. Blackburne does not indicate to whom the letter was written. Possibly it was Thomas Brand, Hollis's good friend and heir, who commissioned Blackburne to compile the *Memoirs* after Hollis's death in 1774.

37. *Opere del conte Algarotti* (17 vols., Venice, 1791), Vol. 10, p. 178. 'In consequenza di tutto questo, la supplico volermi riguardare d'ora innanzi come suo ministro commissario ed agent in Italia. . . . e me felicissimo in mio particolare, se potrò mai darle alcun segno di quella profonda gratitudine e stima, con cui ho l'onore di sottoscrivermi!'

38. See John Abbott, 'John Hawkesworth and The Treatise on the Arts of Peace', *Jnl. RSA,* 115 (July, 1967), pp. 645-9.

39. Soc. Min., 16 Dec. 1761-2: 'The Treatise on the Arts of Peace was referred to the Consideration of a committee, and the following Noblemen and Gentlemen were named to be of the Committee viz.

'All the Vice presidents. Mr. Stan. Baker, Mr. Thos. Hollis, Mr. Brand, Mr. Hoole, Mr. Colepepper, Mr. Dodevoll, Mr. Gardiner, Dr. Franklin, Dr. Parsons, Mr. S. Johnson, Mr. J. Gibbon, Mr. Shirley, Mr. Wyche, Mr. Thos. Wood, Mr. Blake, Mr. Smith, Mr. Robt. Woll, Mr. Grignion, Mr. Hert, Mr. Dossie.'

40. Diary of Thomas Hollis, 6 vols., the Houghton Library, Harvard University.

41. *Memoirs,* Vol. 1, p. 209.

42. BL, Add. MSS 26889.

43. Ibid.

44. See Diary entries for 15th Oct. 1763; 6th, 13th, 18th, 19th, 20th, 22nd, and 25th Nov. 1763; and 14th, 15th, and 16th Jan. 1764, regarding gifts to Algarotti.

45. BL, Add. MSS 26889.

46. Thomas Jenkins was a Corresponding Member of the Society as well as a member of the Society of Antiquaries from 1757. See Evans, op. cit., p. 118, for additional information on Jenkins and other artists whom Hollis patronized.

47. Quoted in *Memoirs,* Vol. 1, p. 234.

48. BL, Add. MSS 26889.

16. EARLY CONTACTS OF THE SOCIETY WITH RUSSIA

1. *Trans.,* Vol. 17 (1798), pp. 339-60, 434.

2. Soc. Min., 30th Apr. 1755.

3. G.B. 2: 27.

4. R. Dossie, *Memoirs of Agriculture,* Vol. 1 (1768), pp. 258-91. For a full discussion of the Society's concern with rhubarb, see C. M. Foust, 'The Society of Arts and Rhubarb', *Jnl. RSA,* 136 (1988), pp. 275-6, 350-2, 434-7.

5. Cf. *Philosophical Transactions,* Vol. 55 (1765), 290-3; *Letters and Papers on Agriculture,* Vol. 1 (1780), 185-223.

6. H. T. Wood, *History of the Royal Society of Arts* (London, 1913), pp. 283-4; D. Hudson and K. W. Luckhurst, *The Royal Society of Arts, 1754-1954* (London, 1954), pp. 94-5.

7. Soc. Min., 25th June 1766. See also 18th June 1766.

8. On Rogerson, see my 'John Rogerson: Physician to Catherine the Great', *Canadian Slavic Studies,* 4, No. 3 (1970), pp. 594-601.

9. *Trans.,* Vol. 10 (1792), p. 436.

10. Sir John Carr, *A Northern Summer* (London, 1805), p. 327.

11. On Guthrie, see my 'Arcticus and *The Bee* (1790-4): An Episode in Anglo-Russian Cultural Relations', *Oxford Slavonic Papers,* New Series, 2 (1969), pp. 62-76; Jessie M. Sweet, 'Matthew Guthrie (1743-1807): An Eighteenth-Century Gemmologist', *Annals of Science,* 20, No. 4 (1964), pp. 245-302; K. A. Papmehl, 'Matthew Guthrie—The Forgotten Student of 18th Century Russia', *Canadian Slavonic Papers,* 11, No. 2 (1969), pp. 167-81.

12. *Trans.,* Vol. 17 (1799), pp. 307-24, 432.

13. On the Hynam family in Russia, see Herbert Swan, *Home on the Neva* (London, 1968), pp. 47-59.

14. *Trans.,* Vol. 10 (1972), p. 436.

15. Ibid., Vol. 22 (1804), p. 500.

16. Soc. Min., 24th May 1769.

17. Chevalier de Corberon, *Journal intime,* Vol. 2 (Paris, 1901), p. 183.

18. MS Sub. Bk. (1773-92). Among those members present at the meeting of the Society's Committee for Polite Arts on 10th Dec. 1782 is 'Mr. Smirnove'. The meeting gave its approval to Shipley's 'improved plan of Education' (see D. G. C. Allan, *William Shipley, Founder of the Royal Society of Arts* (London, 1968), p. 115, and *Jnl. RSA,* 114 (1966), p. 1029. It is easy to imagine that Smirnov would have been interested in Shipley's proposals.

19. Pushkin House, Leningrad, Manuscript Department, Fond 620, A. A. Samborskii, Unit 61, No. 29, f. 29v. In 1770 Princess Ekaterina Dashkova visited the Society's premises in the Strand and was impressed by the collection of machines and implements.

20. Ibid., No. 51, f. 68v.

21. William Coxe, *Travels in Poland, Russia, Sweden, and Denmark,* Vol. 2 (London, 1784), p. 154.

22. *Sbornik Imperatorskogo Russiiskogo istoricheskogo obshchestva* ('Documents of the Imperial Russian Historical Society'), Vol. 44 (Spb., 1885), pp. 606-7.

23. *Autobiography of Arthur Young with Selections from His Correspondence,* edited by M. Betham-Edwards (London, 1898), p. 387.

24. BL, Add. MSS 35128, f. 469.

25. For a study of Smirnov, see my 'Yakov Smirnov—A Russian Priest of Many Parts', *Oxford Slavonic Papers,* New Series, 8 (1975), pp. 37-52. The rôle played by Smirnov and Samborskii in popularizing English agricultural methods in Russia is examined in detail in chapter 3, 'To Speed the Plough', of my book *'By the Banks of the Thames': Russians in Eighteenth-Century Britain.* Newtonville, Mass., 1980.

26. 'Zhurnal Ivana Sudakova v bytnosti evo v Anglii, dlia primechaniia ekonomicheskikh i protchikh, do Zemledeliia kasaiushchikhsia Nadobnostei' ('The Journal of Ivan Sudakov during His Stay in England for the Observation of Economic and All Other Matters Pertaining to Agriculture'), 4 vols., Lenin Library, Moscow, Manuscript Department, Fond 313, Fedorov, No. 25, Vol. 1, f. 3. The translated excerpts which follow are from vol. 4, ff. 38v-41v.

27. Soc. Min., 20th Apr. 1785.

28. Ibid.

29. *Trans.,* Vol. 1, p. 313. The Russians were generally very interested in plans and designs of English machines and implements, and in this connection the appearance of six Russian names (including those of Chernyshev and Samborskii) among the subscribers to William Bailey's *The Advancement of Arts, Manufactures and Commerce; or, descriptions of the useful machines and models contained in the Repository of the Society . . . of Arts* (London, 1772) is revealing.

30. Wood, op. cit., p. 69.

17. ROBERT DODSLEY

1. Jenour's shop was opposite St. Dunstan's, Fleet Street, and Richardson's new printing house (1755), in White Lyon Court off Fleet Street. Richardson had been elected to the Society on 17th September 1755. While Richardson and Jenour were located in London's hub of printing and bookselling, Dodsley's shop in Pall Mall stood on the other side of town, in the fashionable St. James's area and not far from the Houses of Parliament.

2. For much of the biographical detail, I am indebted to Ralph Straus, *Robert Dodsley, Poet, Publisher and Playwright* (London, 1910). See also *The Correspondence of Robert Dodsley, 1733-1764*, ed. James E. Tierney (Cambridge, 1988).

3. *The Toy-Shop* passed through seven editions in two years.

4. Boswell, *The Life*, ed. G. B. Hill (Oxford, 1934), Vol. 1, pp. 182, 326.

5. *The Toy-Shop* (1735), *The King and the Miller of Mansfield* (1737), *Sir John Cockle at Court* (1738).

6. The unique character and utility of these two collections continues. Modern reprints have been issued by Benjamin Blom, Inc., and Scholarly Press, respectively.

7. Powell's letter proposing the separate societies had been first read at the meeting of 20th Aug. 1755. For a full account of this affair, see D. G. C. Allan, *William Shipley, Founder of the Royal Society of Arts* (London, 1968), pp. 58-67.

8. G.B. 3: 26.

9. *Gentleman's Magazine*, 25 (1755), pp. 505-6.

10. G.B. 3: 62. Although the manuscript is not in Dodsley's hand, it does carry his signature.

11. On pp. 17-18 of *History of the Royal Society of Arts* (London, 1913), Sir Henry Trueman Wood says that the name 'The Society for the Encouragement of Arts, Manufactures, and Commerce', 'soon proved too long and cumbrous, and very soon after its foundation the shorter name, "Society of Arts", was adopted.' He notes, for instance, that the *Gentleman's Magazine* on July 1755 referred to it as such. If we can judge from the lengthy titles Dodsley proposed as late as December 1756, however, discovering a more appropriate title concerned (at least a part of) the membership as much as abbreviating their existing one. It will be remembered that, although referred to by the populace—and indeed by the membership itself— by the handier titles 'Society of Arts' and 'Premium Society', the original full title was the one adopted in the Society's charter in 1847.

12. Robert Dodsley, Letter Book, Birmingham Public Libraries, ff. 11-13.

13. G.B. 3: 63. Although pseudonymous, the manuscript is clearly in Dodsley's hand.

14. To avoid the proliferation of notes, it is understood that all dates of Dodsley's Society activities mentioned in the text correspond to entry dates in the Society's Minutes.

15. John Abbott, 'John Hawkesworth and "The Treatise on the Arts of Peace." ' *Jnl. RSA*, 115 (1967), pp. 645-9.

16. Houghton Library, Harvard University, fMS Thr 12. Although undated, the letter was most likely written in October, possibly November.

17. Robert Dodsley Letter Book, Birmingham Public Libraries, ff. 63-65.

18. Finally the frustrated Dodsley, with Lord Chesterfield's intercession, offered *Cleone* to John Rich for the Covent Garden theatre. There it was acted on 2nd December 1758 with much acclaim, and much to the dismay of Garrick.

19. See his letters to William Shenstone for this period: BL, Add. MSS 28, 959.

20. Ibid.

21. Min. Comm., 1758-9. Dodsley's attendance at this meeting accorded with Society policy: 'Notwithstanding particular Gentlemen are named for each Committee, every Member that shall please to attend is of every Committee' (*Rules and Orders of the Society of Arts*, 1758, pp. 14-15).

22. For instance, although Dodsley's bills for 1758 (£114 10s. 7d.) amounted to only approximately 6½ per cent of the Society's income for that year (£1,731), they represented more than three times what it paid for its rental of quarters in the same year. (See Wood, p. 21, and Allan, p. 79.)

23. Two matters probably contributed to this delay. In 1759, when its Treasurer, John Goodchild II, fell into debt and had to settle with his creditors, the Society suffered some loss and removed him from office. Its dispensing of funds, consequently, was briefly interrupted and from that time came under closer scrutiny. (See Wood, p. 21.) Secondly, the Society's activities were probably encumbered by its removal from Castle Court to new quarters in Denmark Court during late June. (See Soc. Min., 1759-60.)

24. James Dodsley was proposed at the 2nd May 1759 meeting by Henry Baker and elected on 9th May.

18. THE CONTEST FOR THE SECRETARYSHIP, 1769-1770

1. Sir H. T. Wood, *History of the Royal Society of Arts* (London, 1913), pp. 24, 334.

2. L. S. Sutherland (ed.), *The Correspondence of Edmund Burke*, Vol. 2, *July 1768–June 1774* (Cambridge, 1960), p. 35, n. 2; J. N. M. Maclean, *Reward is Secondary* (London, 1963), Chap. 8, pt. 2. The assistance given by Dr. Sutherland and Mr. Maclean in the preparation of this study is gratefully acknowledged.

3. Wood, op. cit., pp. 326-7. More had been a member since 1761.

4. Timothy Brecknock, eldest son of Timothy Brecknock of Eye, Northampton, attended Pembroke College, Oxford; he was admitted to Lincoln's Inn on 19th May 1738. A MS note on the title page of the British Library copy credits him with the authorship of a satirical poem *The Important Triflers* (London, 1748).

5. Lemuel Dole Nelme 'was admitted to the seat of the eighth clerk' at the Board of Trade on 24th Nov. 1764. *Journal for the Commissioners for Trade and Plantations from January, 1764, to December, 1767*, p. 117.

6. W. Campbell Smith, 'Dr. Peter Templeman and his appointment as Secretary of the Society in 1760', *Jnl. RSA*, 108 (1960), p. 771.

7. Soc. Min., 11th Oct. 1769.

8. See below, n. 9.

9. Sheffield City Libraries, Fitzwilliam MSS (hereafter Sheffield), Bk. 139. John Stewart to Edmund Burke, 24th Sept. 1769. These MSS are quoted by kind permission of the Earl Fitzwilliam.

10. Sutherland, op. cit., p. 89. Edmund Burke to the Marquess of Rockingham, 9th Oct. 1769. ('Mr. Burke will have informed you of my present views and of the Assistance I presumed to expect from your Friendship.' John Stewart to Edmund Burke, 7th Oct. 1769. Sheffield, Bk. 140.)

11. Sutherland, op. cit., p. 95. The Marquess of Rockingham to Edmund Burke, 15th Oct. 1769. 'I have spoken to Quarme . . . also . . . to some others.' George and Robert Quarme were old Yorkshire friends of Rockingham's. Burke told him they were members, which was in fact the case. Sutherland, op. cit., p. 89, n. 2.

12. Lord Edmond Fitzmaurice, *Life of William, Earl of Shelburne*, Vol. 1 (London, 1912), p. 364.

13. RSA, L.A. A6/72. John Stewart's Memorial for the Secretaryship.

14. BL, Add. MSS, 29, 138, ff. 83-4.

15. Sheffield, Bk. 139.

16. Campbell Smith, op. cit.

17. Sir L. Namier, *England in the Age of the American Revolution*, 2nd ed. (London, 1961), p. 272 n.1.; L. S. Sutherland, *The East India Company in Eighteenth-Century Politics* (Oxford, 1952), pp. 143, 192; Maclean, op. cit.

18. Sutherland, *East India Company*.

19. Soc. Min., 11th Oct. 1769. Thomas Stewart had been a member of the Society since 1766. John Stewart and Archibald Stewart, of York Buildings, the cousins of the candidate, had also been members of the Society.

20. Soc. Min., 11th Oct. 1769.

21. Min. Comm. (Miscellaneous), 14th Oct. 1769.

22. MS Sub. Bk., 1764-72.

23. Sir Robert Fletcher, whom Stewart had proposed as a member and who had East India Company associations which might have linked him with Lauchlin Macleane; John Johnstone, Thomas Lane and John Woodhouse, who had similar associations (see Sutherland, *East India Company*, pp. 180n., 116, 102, 207); Charles Stuart, who had been proposed by Thomas Stewart, the candidate's brother; Maurice Morgan, Thomas Stewart's colleague at the Secretary of State's Office; Dr. John Blair, William Franks, Charles Maxwell, and John Maddocks, who were connected with Lauchlin Macleane, and Henry Macleane, Lauchlin's youngest brother. (Information supplied through the courtesy of Mr. J. N. M. Maclean.)

24. *Public Advertiser*, 27th, 28th, 29th, 30th Sept., 4th, 6th, 11th, 21st Oct.

1769; *Gazetteer and New Daily Advertiser*, 26th, 27th, 28th Sept; 2nd, 9th, 12th, 16th, 17th, 18th, 19th, 20th, 21st, 23rd, 25th, 28th, 30th, 31st Oct. 1769.

25. William Johnstone changed his name to Pulteney when he married an heiress to the Earl of Bath's fortune. His was the first of the 76 names proposed by Stewart's friends as members of the Society on 11th Oct. 1769.

26. *Gazetteer and New Daily Advertiser*, 18th Oct. 1769.

27. Soc. Min., 18th Oct. 1769.

28. Soc. Min., 25th Oct. 1769; see note 25 above. William Pulteney's great fortune would have assured him of special treatment.

29. *Gazetteer and New Daily Advertiser*, 28th Oct. 1769. The proprietor of the *Gazetteer* at this date was Charles Green Say, who had been a member of the Society since 1764. His newspaper steered a middle course between Government and Opposition. See R. L. Haig, *The Gazetteer, 1735-1797* (Carbondale, 1960).

30. Wood, op. cit., pp. 43, 45.

31. Soc. Min., 11th Oct. 1769.

32. *Gazetteer and New Daily Advertiser*, 2nd Nov. 1769. Letter signed 'A Member', dated 30th Oct. 1769.

33. Soc. Min., 11th Oct. 1769. The minutes confirm this order, but no advertisements seem to have appeared.

34. Timothy Brecknock.

35. John Stewart.

36. *Gazetteer and New Daily Advertiser*, 20th Oct. 1769. In 1760 Templeman had defeated Robert Dossie and Matthew Maty, both members. The Rules and Orders since 1760 had stated that the Secretary could not be a member; presumably this did not disqualify members from competing for the office.

37. Ibid., 28th Oct. 1769. More was an apothecary.

38. He presented his petition on Wednesday, 25th Oct.

39. See note 4 above.

40. Published 1764. See *Journals of the House of Lords*, Vol. 30, pp. 480-1.

41. Lord John Russell (ed.), *Correspondence of John 4th Duke of Bedford* (London, 1846), Vol. 3, p. 339.

42. *Calendar of Home Office Papers of The Reign of George III, 1766-1769*, pp. 62-3.

43. He was hanged for conspiring and procuring the death of two Irishmen: *Gentleman's Magazine*, 56 (1786), pp. 434, 520. For more details of the case and some other examples of Brecknock's legal sophistries, see W. R. Wilde, *The Life and Times of George Robert Fitzgerald commonly called Fighting Fitzgerald* (Dublin, 1852), pp. 76-84, 88-99.

44. See note 5 above.

45. RSA, L.A. A6/73; Soc. Min., 20th Dec. 1769.

46. *Gazetteer and Daily Advertiser*, 16th Nov. 1769.

47. Nelme's Memorial (RSA, L.A., loc. cit.).

48. Eleven of the names were reproposed on 15th Nov., sixteen on 22nd Nov., two on 29th Nov., two on 6th Dec. 1769 and one on 17th Jan. 1770. See Soc. Min., under these dates.

49. Kenneth Mackenzie, Viscount Fortrose and afterwards Earl of Seaforth, 1744-81.

50. Sheffield, Bk. 140.

51. See Burke's letter to Rockingham, 9th Oct. 1769 (printed in Sutherland [ed.], *Correspondence of Edmund Burke*, Vol. 2, p. 89).

52. *Gazetteer and New Daily Advertiser*, 3rd Nov. 1769.

53. Ibid., 28th Oct. 1769.

54. Ibid., 3rd Nov. 1769.

55. Ibid., 9th Nov. 1769.

56. In his letter to Burke on 7th Oct., John Stewart gave him information about 'a new invented Hand Mill' which he had found in the Society's Repository and an improved straw-cutting machine (Sheffield, Bk. 140).

57. Sutherland (ed.), *Correspondence of Edmund Burke*, Vol. 2, pp. 95-6.

58. Ibid., p. 103.

59. Possibly a reference to Stewart's disreputable private life, for which see the memoirs of his mistress, Mrs. James Eastick (neé Anne Bailey), published in 1771. She wrote of the election: 'Mr. Stewart put up for a place at the Society for the Encouragement of Arts and Sciences, which he lost and I have heard it hinted that some think I was the occasion of it'. Quoted Maclean, op. cit., p. 506; see also pp. 189, 289.

60. Soc. Min., 23rd Jan. 1770.

61. See 'Lists of Officers of the Society of Arts', *Jnl. RSA*, 28 (1880), pp. 381-2; and subsequent published lists.

62. *European Magazine*, 9 (1786); Reports of the Society for the Relief of Persons confined for Small Debts, 1772-87.

63. See note 43 above.

64. He became Secretary and Judge Advocate at Bengal, though not for long. Dismissed in 1775, he returned to England to plead his cause with the Company, and was successful in obtaining the nomination to another post in Bengal, but died within a few weeks of his arrival there in 1778. (See Maclean, op. cit., pp. 284, 437.)

65. Smollett's phrase, quoted Wood, op. cit., p. 18 n.2.

66. G.B.A: 135. John Reynolds to Samuel More, 18th Mar. 1770. An abridged version of this article appeared under the title 'Electioneering and Jobbery in an Eighteenth Century Scientific Society: The Dispute for the Secretaryship of the Society of Arts, 1769-70,' in *History Studies*, No. 2 (1968), pp. 21-34.

19. 'MR. MORE OF THE ADELPHI'

1. PCC, Prob. 11/1333, f. 792.

2. Minutes, Private Court, Society of Apothecaries, Guildhall MSS, 6200, Vol. 6, p. 181.

3. F. W. Gibbs, 'W. M. Lewis, MB, FRS', *Annals of Science*, 8 (1952), No. 2.

4. Royal Society, *Trans.*, Vol. 51, pt. ii (1760), pp. 936-7.

5. G.B. 1: 13, 15, 98.

6. BL, Add. MSS 4440. f. 218.

7. *Jnl. RSA*, 112 (1963-4), pp. 715 ff., 865 ff.; 113 (1964-5), pp. 33 ff., 199 ff.

8. House of Commons Journal, Vol. 37, pp. 913-15.

9. Detailed references to Society archives are not given, except in a few cases, as the text is sufficiently explicit.

10. More to Egremont, 23rd Nov. 1797. Petworth Archives, 70. West Sussex Record Office.

11. See Memorial on J. B. Blake in *Annual Register*, 1775, Part 2, pp. 30-31.

12. Wedgwood MSS 18581-25.

13. Wedgwood MSS 4253/6; *Jnl. RSA*, 84 (1936), p. 810. The complete letter contains a suggested modification of a Wedgwood 'cream vessel' with a sketch.

14. RSA Red Book of Letters before 1850, p. 53.

15. H. of C. Journal, Vol. 37, pp. 913-15, 929-30.

16. H. of C. Journal, Vol. 38, pp. 311, 467-72.

17. *Jnl. RSA*, 109 (1961), pp. 389-94, 629-32, 807-10, 979-80.

18. Committee Minutes, PRO BT/5/4.

19. *Phil. Trans.*, Vol. 72, pt. 1, pp. 50-52.

20. *Royal Society Letters and Papers*, Vol. 1, p. 37.

21. *Phil. Trans.*, Vol. 77, p. 35. Manuscript Letters and Papers, Vol. 9, p. 14.

22. BL, Egerton MS 1941, H 33/34.

23. Ibid., f. 26 (sketch and note).

24. *Annals of Agriculture*, 1785, Vol. 1, pp. 113-14.

25. Arkwright *vs* Peter Nightingale. Court of Common Pleas, 17th February 1785: Trial of a Cause by Writ of Scire Facias in King's Bench, 25th June 1785, printed for Hughes and Walsh. London, 1785.

26. *Biographical Dictionary of Eminent Scotsmen* (Chambers, Blackie & Son, 1856), Vol. 4, p. 427.

27. *Trans.*, Vol. 4, p. 162.

28. E.g., More to Young, 18th Feb. 1783 (BL, Add. MSS 35126, f. 227). More after challenging Priestley's idea says, 'I am not philosopher enough to argue the point against Dr. P. and Mr. Y.'

29. *Trans.*, Vol. 17, 1.4, p. 119.

30. RSA, Letters sent by Order, 1770-1816, pp. 144-5.

31. RSA, L.A. A/13/30.

32. G.B. 7: 39.

33. R. Dossie, *Memoirs of Agriculture*, Vol. 1, pp. 34-5.

34. PCC, Prob. 11/1333, f. 792.

35. *English Copper, Tin and Bronze Coins in the British Museum, 1558-1958*, Section B, pp. 237-8, Plate 75, No. 929.

36. Birmingham Central Libraries (Assay Office MSS), Boulton and Watt papers, Box 2, p. 93.

37. *Trans.*, Vol. 1, p. 194.

38. *Trans.*, Vol. 5, p. 111.

39. *Jnl. RSA*, 106 (1954), pp. 623-9.

40. Boulton and Watt Papers, Box M.2, More to Boulton, 24th Jan. 1784.

41. Peter Mathias, *The Brewing Industry in England, 1700-1830* (Cambridge, 1959), pp. 74-5. Patents No. 1754 of 4th June and No. 1769 of 27th July 1790.

42. Soc. Min., 30th Mar. and 20th Apr. 1768.

43. Soc. Min., 27th Oct. 1779.

44. Min. Comm., 1st Nov. 1779.

45. Soc. Min., 3rd Nov. 1779.

46. Collection of Ms. Anne Turner, London. See also Wedgwood Abstracts, BL, Add. MSS 28316, pp. 47-8 (1776) and 147-56 (1780).

47. *Phil Trans.*, Vol. 77, p. 35.

48. Petworth Archive 70.

49. *Trans.*, Vol. 12, p. 286.

50. Petworth Archive 70.

51. PCC, Prob 11/1333, f. 792. Administration PRC 1R 26.

52. Mortimer, *European Magazine*, Dec. 1799, p. 365.

53. RSA, MS Trans., 1774-5, p. 128.

54. RSA, Letters, 1770-1806, p. 274.

55. BL, Add. MSS 38224, f. 315, More to Hawkesbury.

56. Ellenborough Papers (Towry), PRO 30/12/2/3, ff. 67-70.

57. Birmingham Central Library: Birmingham Assay Office, Boulton & Watt papers, Box 2M.

58. Shropshire Record Office, 1987, Box 20; B. Trinder, *History of the Industrial Revolution in Shropshire* (London, 1973), p. 220.

59. Wedgwood MSS E. 18581-25.

60. Scientific Correspondence of Joseph Priestley, BL 010920. 1. 2, pp. 84-8.

61. *Encyclopaedia Britannica*, 3rd ed. (1797), Vol. 17, p. 587.

62. R. Ackerman, *The Microcosm of London* (1904 ed.), Vol. 3, p. 64.

63. R. A. Rauschenberg, 'John Ellis, Naturalist: An Early Member of the Society', *Jnl. RSA*, 126 (1977-8), pp. 578 and 581 nn. 18 and 19.

64. Sir Henry Trueman Wood, *History of the Royal Society of Arts* (London, 1913), p. 343. Arthur Aikin was secretary of the Society from 1817 to 1839.

20. THE CHRONOLOGY OF JAMES BARRY'S WORK FOR THE SOCIETY'S GREAT ROOM

1. 'Increasing celebrity' occurs in B's letter to Cooper Penrose, 13th July 1803, printed in E. Fryer (ed.), *The Works of James Barry,* London, 1809 (cited hereafter as *Works*) Vol. 2, p. 663, and 'very extensive work' in B's letter to the Society, 6th Jan. 1803 (RSA, Barry Letter Books, Vol. 2, p. 101. The Letter Books will be cited hereafter as LB). 'B' is used for Barry throughout these references.

2. Soc. Min., under date.

3. B to Sir George Savile, 19th Apr. 1777 (printed *Works* Vol. 1, p. 254). In his *Account of a Series of Pictures in the Great Room of the Society of Arts . . .* (London, 1783), p. 25 (cited hereafter as *Account*), B said he began in July, which is presumably when he would first have had unrestricted access to the Great Room, as the Society would by then have been in recess.

4. F. Saxl and R. Wittkower, *British Art and the Mediterranean* (London, 1948), p. 64; D. G. C. Allan, 'The Progress of Human Culture and Knowledge', *Connoisseur,* 186 (1974), pp. 100-109; W. L. Pressly, *The Life and Art of James Barry* (New Haven and London, 1981), p. 100.

5. B to the Earl of Chatham, 27th Dec. 1777, PRO 30/8/18, pt. 2, quoted Pressly, op. cit., p. 98; *Account,* p. 54.

6. B to J. Bonomi, n.d., RSA, L.A., Add. MSS 3/11.

7. B to the Society, 28th Oct. 1778, RSA, LB, Vol. 1, pp. 18-21.

8. Pressly, op. cit., p. 103.

9. Soc. Min., 28th Oct. 1778, and under dates mentioned; Min. Comm. (Polite Arts), under dates mentioned.

10. RSA, LB, Vol. 1, pp. 30-46; Soc. Min., under date.

11. MS Sub. Bks., 1754-63, 1764-72, 1773-92; Sir H. T. Wood, *History of the Royal Society of Arts* (London, 1913), pp. 28-46; R. Rompkey, 'Soame Jenyns, MP: A Curious Case of Membership', *Jnl. RSA,* 120 (1973), pp. 536-42.

12. National Library of Ireland, Barry MSS 5672, f. p. 11 (which is an undated list in B's handwriting of all the persons named in the 1783 *Account* of the fifth picture plus 'Lady B. Germaine . . . Lady Radnor . . . [and] Dr. Louth [Bishop of London]'). (Reference kindly supplied by Dr. David H. Solkin, author of the study 'Some Preparatory Drawings by James Barry for the "Progress of Human Culture and Knowledge" ', *Jnl. RSA,* 124 [1976], pp. 684-87.) See also *Account,* p. 74.

13. *Account,* p. 90; RSA, LB, Vol. 1, p. 22; *Works,* Vol. 1, p. 272. For Musgrave, see F. Lugt, *Les Marques de Collections de Dessins et D'Estampes* (Amsterdam, 1921), p. 328; for Hollis, see *Gentleman's Magazine,* 69 (1791), p. 306; Allan, op. cit., pt. 2.

14. Soc. Min., 5th, 12th, 26th Jan., 1st Nov. 1780, 14th Nov. 1781, 30th Jan. 1782.

15. Soc. Min., under date, and 30th Jan., 6th Feb. 1782.

16. *Account,* p. 218.

17. The texts of the resolutions and letters are those given in the Soc. Min. under the dates mentioned.

18. B, *Catalogue of a Series of Pictures upon the Subject of Human Culture, Painted for the Society . . . of Arts . . .* (London, 1783), p. 4.

19. *Account* (1784 edition with 'Addenda'), pp. 226-44.

20. *Gentleman's Magazine,* 55 (1784), p. 391.

21. B to the Society, 26th Oct. 1784, RSA, LB, Vol. 1, pp. 66-8.

22. B to the Society, 23rd Feb. 1793, printed in *Works,* Vol. 2, p. 464. (In this letter B gives the attendance figures at the two exhibitions.)

23. B to the Society, 23rd Feb. 1793, printed in *Works,* Vol. 2, pp. 419-74.

24. Soc. Min. under dates mentioned, B to the Society, 23rd Dec. 1789 and 13th Jan. 1790 (LB, Vol. 1, pp. 118-20).

25. Soc. Min., 28th Oct. 1789, 10th Feb. 1790, and under dates mentioned.

26. As note 23 above.

27. As note 23 above. See also Pressly, op. cit., p. 121, and Soc. Min., under dates.

28. Soc. Min., 24th Feb., 2nd Mar., 4th May, 1st June 1796.

29. B, *Letter to the Dilettanti Society* (London, 1797), pp. 53-4; Soc. Min., under dates.

30. B to the Society, 1st Oct. 1798, 23rd Jan. 1799 (LB, Vol. 2, nos. 2 and 3); B to S. More, 23rd Jan. 1799 (LB, Vol. 1, loose letter); Soc. Min., under dates.

31. Soc. Min., 9th Apr., 21st and 28th May 1800, 9th Apr. 1801, and under dates mentioned; B to the Society, 31st Mar. and 6th May 1801 (LB, Vol. 2, nos. 4 and 5). See also W. L. Pressly, 'James Barry's Proposed Extensions to his Adelphi Series', *Jnl. RSA,* 126 (1978), pp. 233-7, 296-301.

32. B to the Society, 25th Oct. 1801 (see *Works,* Vol. 2, p. 655).

33. B described the designs on the two models for medals or coins as 'the head of Alfred the Great, improver and founder' and 'a female head, with the imperial shield of the United Kingdom of Great Britain and Ireland'. These corresponded with his first suggestions for a new medal for the Society except that the head of George III would have been used instead of King Alfred's (B to the Society, 25th Oct. 1801, LB, Vol. 2, no. 6, printed in edited form in *Works,* Vol. 2, pp. 647-61. See also *Trans.,* Vol. 19, 1801, pp. xlix-l). The naval pillar is described in this letter.

34. B to the Earl of Liverpool, 3rd July 1801, quoted in his letter to the Society of 25th Oct. (see *Works,* Vol. 2, p. 649).

35. B to the Society, 25th Oct. 1801 (*Works,* Vol. 2, p. 660); *Trans.,* Vol. 19, (1801), p. lxi.

36. B to the Society, 6th Jan. 1803 (LB, Vol. 2, no. 10, with loose MS inserts); C. Taylor, MS note, n.d. (LB, Vol. 2, no. 14). I am indebted to Dr. Pressly for locating B's reference to the inscribed scrolls (see Pressly, *Life and Art of James Barry,* p. 292). For Alexander Mackenzie's premiums, see Wood, op. cit., pp. 108-9.

37. Soc. Min., 25th Nov. 1801 and under dates mentioned; Pressly, op. cit., p. 294.

38. Soc. Min., 4th Dec. 1805.

39. Ibid., 12th Jan. 1803, 30th May, 12th Dec. 1804. For his engravings, see Pressly, op. cit., p. 279.

40. Soc. Min., under dates.

41. *Trans.*, Vol. 23 (1805), pp. xviii-xix; *Works*, Vol. 1, pp. 300-3; Pressly, op. cit., p. 189 and p. 225 ref. 32; *James Barry, The Artist as Hero* (London, 1983), pp. 18-20. The outline and keys to Barry's fifth and sixth paintings for the Society were first published in *Connoisseur*, 188 (1975), and have been here modified to take account of the suggestions made by Dr. W. L. Pressly in Appendix I of his *Life and Art of James Barry*. The compilation of the key to *Elysium* was undertaken with the help of Miss Rita Comerford in 1970-74, and with warm encouragement from Mr. J. S. Skidmore. Barry's membership of the Society and his interest in British history is explored in my articles 'James Barry as a Member of the Society', *Jnl. RSA*, 135 (1987), pp. 330-3; and 'James Barry and British History', *Jnl. RSA*, 136 (1988), pp. 727-30.

CONTRIBUTORS

JOHN LAWRENCE ABBOTT teaches at the University of Connecticut and is the author of *John Hawkesworth: Eighteenth-Century Man of Letters* (1982).

DAVID GUY CHARLES ALLAN is Historical Adviser to the Royal Society of Arts in London and is the author of *William Shipley: Founder of the Royal Society of Arts* (1968, 1979) and, with R. E. Schofield, *Stephen Hales: Scientist and Philanthropist* (1980).

HANS-JOACHIM BRAUN teaches at the University of the Ruhr, Bochum, Germany, and is the author of *Technologische Beziehungen zwischen Deutschland und England von der Mitte des 17. bis zum Ausgang des 18. Jahrhunderts* (1974).

A. G. CROSS teaches at Cambridge University and has written *'By the Banks of the Thames': Russians in Eighteenth-Century Britain* (1980).

LEO J. DE FREITAS taught at the Royal College of Art in London and is the author of *John Tenniel's Wood-Engraved Illustrations to the Alice Stories* (1988).

JOHN BRIAN HARLEY teaches at the University of Wisconsin–Milwaukee and is the author of *Mapping the American Revolutionary War* (1978).

ROBERT LEROY HILLDRUP taught at Mary Washington College, University of Virginia, until his death. He contributed to *North Carolina Historical Review* and *Virginia Magazine of History and Biography*.

GEORGE TRUETT HOLLIS taught at East Los Angeles College.

JOHN VALENTINE GRANVILLE MALLET was Keeper of the Department of Ceramics at the Victoria and Albert Museum, London, from 1976 to 1989 and has contributed to *Apollo, Burlington Magazine* and *Transactions of the English Ceramic Circle.*

GEORGE EDWARD MERCER, O.B.E., was Secretary to the Royal Society of Arts from 1961 to 1973 and is the author of *The Cole Papers* (1985).

GERTRUD SEIDMANN taught at the universities of Southampton and Oxford and is the author of *Nathaniel Marchant, Gem-Engraver, 1739-1816*, Walpole Society Vol. 53 (1989).

WALTER MARCEL STERN taught at the London School of Economics and is the author of *Britain Yesterday and Today* (1962, 1971).

JOHN SUNDERLAND is Librarian of the Witt Library at the Courtauld Institute of Art in London and is the author of *Painting in Britain, 1525-1975* (1976).

JAMES E. TIERNEY teaches at the University of Missouri–St. Louis and is the editor of *The Correspondence of Robert Dodsley, 1733-1764* (1988).

INDEX

Lenin State Library, 198, 273
Leonidas (Glover), 282
Leo X, 352
Leske, N. G., 244
Lester, William, 323
Letter to the Clergy of Virginia (Bland), 207
Letter of Introduction (Wilkie), 84
Letter from a Merchant (Tucker), 218–19
Letter to the Right Reverend Father in God, the Lord Bishop of London (Carter), 207
Lewes, Sir Watkin, 359
Lewis, John, 363
Lewis, William, 67, 210–11, 308–9, 310, 312–13, 315, 319, 327, 330
Lewis, Wilmarth, 284
Lichtenstein, Johann Franz von, 252
Lieberich, Jacob, 242
Life of Nollekens (Smith), 84
Linck, J. H., 241
Lind, John, 229, 362
Lindsell, Vaughan, 362
Linnaeus, Carl von, 311
Litchfield, George Henry, Earl of, 359
Literary Magazine, 37, 374 (n. 44)
Liverpool, Earl of (Charles, Lord Hawkesbury), 332, 355, 359
Livingston, Philip, 223, 224, 235
Lloyd, Evan, 52, 130
Lochée, J. C., 113
Lock, William, 340
Locke, John, 13, 232
Lockman, John, 360, 363
Lockman (translator), 254, 260
Logan (harpoon maker), 180
Lohmann, John Gottlob, 67
London (Johnson), 282, 283
London Chronicle, 29, 37, 283
London Company, 203
London Evening Post, 283
London Gazette, 69
London Journal, 11

Long, Richard, 44, 359, 360, 361, 362
Long (inventor), 322
Loocock, Aaron, 225, 235
Louis XIV (king of France), 92
Louis XV (king of France), 143
Lovell, James, 226
Lovell, Michael, 361, 363
Lowth, Charles, 361
Ludlow, Edmund, 187
Lumley, William, 361
Lunar Society, xxi–xxii, 325–26, 329–30
Lund, Benjamin, 58
Lyman, Phineas, 227
Lynam, Edward, 154

McArdel, James, 117
McDougall, Stephen, 148
Mackenzie, Alexander, 355
Mackworth, Sir Herbert, 359
Macleane, Lauchlin, 295, 305–6
Maclise, Daniel, 114
Macquer (silk maker), 239, 241
Madden, Samuel, 93, 216
Maddox, Isaac (bishop of Worcester), 29, 361, 362, 373 (n. 26)
Madison, James, 224, 236
Madison, Rev. James, 224
Maffei, Marquis Scipio, 409 (n. 5)
Magalhaens, Jean, 270
Magdalen Hospital, 36
Main (proposer of Johnson), 11
Major, Thomas, 40–41, 117, 133, 134, 389 (n. 6)
Malone (author), 27
Malyn (Committee member), 181
Mandeville, Bernard, 23–24, 27–28, 372 (n. 9)
Mandeville, George, 70
Manini, Gaetano, 100, 117
Manningham, Richard, 284
Manningham, Thomas, 42, 47, 51, 360, 361, 362